BECOMING PROPERTY: ART, THEORY AND LAW IN EARLY MODERN FRANCE

KATIE SCOTT

Yale University Press, New Haven and London

First published by Yale University Press 2018

302 Temple Street, P. O. Box 209040,
New Haven, CT 06520-9040
47 Bedford Square, London WC1B 3DP

yalebooks.com | yalebooks.co.uk

ISBN 978-0-300-222791 HB
Library of Congress Control Number: 2018939153

10 9 8 7 6 5 4 3 2 1
2022 2021 2020 2019 2018

Cover image: Altered composite image of Jacob Christoph Le Blon, portrait of Cardinal André-Hercule de Fleury, 1738, mezzotint (612 × 459 mm), various colour proofs, British Museum, London.

Designed by Joana Pestana
Typeset by M Rules

Printed in China

For Stephen

CONTENTS

ACKNOWLEDGEMENTS

This book depends for its historical evidence on the extraordinary scholarship of print historians, especially those at the Bibliothèque nationale in Paris and the British Museum in London. Citation of the books, catalogues and articles by Pierre Casselle, Corinne Le Bitouzé, Maxime Préaud and Antony Griffiths in the notes and bibliography does not do adequate justice to the debt I owe them, and the same is true of the specialist scholars Peter Fuhring, Marianne Grivel, Véronique Meyer and Christian Michel. I do not pretend to the expertise in print history that comes with the sustained study of prints as physical objects, nor do I have the breadth and depth of knowledge of those who have made the study of prints in museums, libraries and archives their life's work. Rather, I have been pleased to follow in their footsteps.

I thank the Courtauld Institute of Art, its directors, its heads of research and my colleagues who, over many years, have encouraged and supported the research presented between these covers. Specifically I thank those friends and fellow researchers who have read chapters of the book and provided essential criticism and suggestions. They are Stephen Bann, Steve Edwards, Matthew Hunter, Marcia Pointon, Julian Stallabrass, Joanna Woodall and Richard Wrigley. I also thank Caroline Arscott, Emma Barker, Mechthild Fend, Colin Jones, Satish Padiyar, David Solkin, Richard Taws and Hannah Williams, who have made the University of London an exciting playground in which to research and teach. And I owe an incalculable amount also to the international community of *dixhuitièmistes*, present and sadly past, with whom I have been happy to work and exchange ideas over many years: René Démoris and Mary Sheriff, also Colin Bailey, Philippe Bordes, Juliet Carey, Charlotte Guichard, Liliane Hilaire-Pérez, Melissa Hyde, Mia Jackson, Étienne Jollet, Anne Lafont, Ewa Lajer-Burcharth, Andrew McClellan, Lesley Miller, Susan Siegfried, Kristel Smentek, Michael Sonenscher and Kate Tunstall. I thank Thisbe Granger and above all Rosemary Roberts for their careful preparation of the text for publication, and Karin Kyburz for essential picture research and photographic ordering. Finally, I thank Gillian Malpass of Yale University Press very warmly for commissioning this book and Mark Eastment and Lydia Cooper for taking on the project and overseeing its publication.

The book's research was enabled by the generous financial support of the Leverhulme Trust and the British Academy for which I thank them. Parts of some of the chapters have already seen publication in the *Oxford Art Journal*, 21/1 (1998) (chapter 2); *Les Chemins de la nouveauté: Innover, inventer au regard de l'histoire*, Liliane Hilaire-Pérez and Anne-François Garçon (eds) (Paris, 2003) (chapter 4); and the *Journal of Design History*, 13/1 (2000) (chapter 5). Thanks are therefore also due for permission to reproduce these essays here.

For his brisk injunctions to get the book done and his affectionate indulgence of my many repeated failures to do so, I thank Stephen Deuchar, to whom this book is dedicated with all my love. For their faith, encouragement and liberating indifference to the outcome of this project, I thank Hannah, Seth, Grace and Faith.

ABBREVIATIONS

AAF	*Archives de l'art français*
AN	Archives nationales, Paris
ANMC	Archives nationales, Minutier central des notaires de Paris
Annales ESC	*Annales: Économies, sociétés, civilisations*
BM	*Burlington Magazine*
BnF	Bibliothèque nationale de France, Paris
BnF Arsenal	Bibliothèque nationale de France, Bibliothèque de l'Arsenal, Paris
BnF Gallica	Bibliothèque nationale de France, Bibliothèque numérique <www.bnf.fr/fr/collections_et_services.html>
BSHAF	*Bulletin de la Société de l'histoire de l'art français*
CDR	*Correspondance des directeurs de l'Académie de France à Rome avec les surintendants des bâtiments*, ed. Anatole de Montaiglon, 18 vols (Paris, 1887–1912)
ENSBA	Ecole nationale supérieure des beaux-arts, Paris
Falconnet	Ambroise Falconnet, *Le Barreau français, partie moderne*, 2 vols (Paris, 1806–7)
GBA	*Gazette des beaux-arts*
HEF	Rogier Chartier and Henri-Jean Martin (eds), *L'Histoire de l'édition française*, 4 vols (Paris, 1983–7)
IFF	Jean Lara, *Inventaire du fond français après 1800*, 15 vols (Paris, 1930–)
INHA	Institut national d'histoire de l'art, Paris
JMH	*Journal of Modern History*
LM*Con*	*Les Conférences de l'Académie royale de peinture et de sculpture, 1648–1792*, ed. Jacqueline Lichtenstein and Christian Michel, 6 vols (Paris, 2007–15)
MdF	*Mercure de France*
NAAF	*Nouvelles archives de l'art français*
NE	*Nouvelles de l'estampe*
OAJ	*Oxford Art Journal*
PQ	*Print Quarterly*
Préaud, *DEE*	Maxime Préaud et al., *Dictionnaire des éditeurs d'estampes à Paris sous l'ancien régime* (Paris, 1987)
PSC	*Primary Sources on Copyright (1450–1900)*, ed. L. Bently and M. Kretschmer, <www.copyrighthistory.org> [references include the country and the date of the document]
P-V	*Procès-verbaux de l'Académie royale de peinture et de sculpture, 1648–1792*, ed. Anatole de Montaiglon, 10 vols (Paris, 1875–92)
RDE	*Recherches sur Diderot et sur l'Encyclopédie*
RHMC	*Revue d'histoire moderne et contemporaine*
SVEC	*Studies on Voltaire and the Eighteenth Century*
YFS	*Yale French Studies*

KEY DATES
Table of privileges, statutes and regulations

Dates in bold type indicate the most important entries.

1507	Eloy d'Amerval's privilege for *Le Livre de la déablerie*	*PSC*, France
1530	Francesco Pellegrino's privilege for *La Fleur de la science de pourtraicture*	BnF Arsenal; BnF Gallica
1586	Simon Marion's plea on privileges: *Plaidoyez second sur l'impression des Œuvres de Sénèque, reveues et annotées par feu Marc Antoine de Muret*	*PSC*, France
1618	Founding statutes and regulations of the Paris book trade: *Lettres patentes du roy pour le règlement des libraires, imprimeurs et relieurs de cette ville de Paris*	*PSC*, France
1637	Abraham Bosse and Charles de La Font's privilege for colour printing	BnF, Mss. f.f. 21732, fols 138–40
1649	Regulations of the Paris book trade: *Lettres obtenuës par aucuns des imprimeurs et libraires de Paris en l'année 1649*	*PSC*, France
1656	Charles Le Brun's privilege	BnF, Imprimées F5001/171
1660	Edict of Saint Jean-de-Luz on engraving: *Arrêt du Conseil d'état qui maintient et garde l'Art de la Gravûre de Taille-douce, au burein et à l'eau forte*	*PSC*, France
1665	*Arrest et règlement du Conseil touchant les privilèges et continuations d'iceux, pour l'impression et réimpression des livres tant anciens que nouveaux*	*PSC*, France
1667	Decree on works from the Cabinet du roi: *Arrest du Conseil d'état*, 22 Dec. 1667	BnF, Mss. f.f. 21732, fols 150–51
1675	Nicolas de Poilly's privilege	BnF, Mss. f.f. 22119/33
1676	Decree on academic sculpture: *Arrest du Conseil portant deffenses de copier et mouler les ouvrages des sculpteurs de l'Académie*	*PSC*, France
1687	Regulations of the Paris book trade: *Statuts et règlemens des imprimeurs et libraires de Paris* (1687)	*PSC*, France

1704	Trade regulations for maps: *Arrêt du Conseil d'état*, 17 Oct. 1704	BnF, Mss. f.f. 22119/48
1714	Decree on the fine arts: *Arrest du Conseil d'état du roy, portant privilège à l'Académie royale de peinture & de sculpture, et aux Académiciens, de faire imprimer et graver leurs ouvrages*	PSC, France
1725	Regulations of the Paris book trade: *Arrêt du conseil portant réglement sur le fait de la librairie et imprimerie*	PSC, France; BnF Gallica
1725-6	Pierre-Jacques Blondel's memorandum on the book trade: *Mémoire sur les vexations qu'exercent les libraires et imprimeurs de Paris* (n.d.)	PSC, France
1725-6	Louis d'Héricourt's memorandum on the book trade: *Mémoire de Louis d'Héricourt à Monseigneur le Garde des sceaux* (n.d.)	PSC, France
1730-34	Statutes and regulations of the Paris Corporation des maîtres peintres et sculpteurs: *Confirmation des statuts pour la Communauté et Académie de Saint-Luc*	AN, K 1032/1
1737	Jacob Christoph Le Blon's privilege for colour printing	AN, E 2159
1741	Jacques Gautier's privilege for colour printing	AN, E 1184A
1744	National booksellers' and printers' regulations: *Code de la librairie et imprimerie de Paris, ou Conférence du règlement arrêté au Conseil d'état du roy, le 28 février 1723 et rendu commun pour tout le royaume, par arrêt du Conseil d'état du 24 mars 1744*	PSC, France
1745	Jacques Gautier's privilege	BnF, Mss. f.f. 21958
1745	Étienne Charpentier's privilege	BnF, Mss. f.f. 21958
1757	Pierre-François Basan, *Exposé du sieur Basan et autres ses confrères graveurs en taille-douce contre la communauté des libraires, Septembre 1757*	BnF, Mss. f.f. 22076/73
1759	Jean-Louis Regnard de Montenault's privilege for La Fontaine's *Fables*	BnF, Mss. f.f. 21961
1759	André-François Le Breton's privilege for the *Encyclopédie*	BnF, Mss. f.f. 21962
1761	*Arrest du Conseil d'état privé du roi, qui déclare nulle l'opposition faite par les libraires de Paris au privilège accordé par Sa Majesté aux demoiselles de La Fontaine*	PSC, France
1762	Royal declaration on privileges granted to inventors: *Déclaration du roy concernant les privilèges en fait de commerce*	PSC, France
1763	Denis Diderot, *Lettre ... sur le commerce de la librairie*	PSC, France

1764	Paris booksellers' memorandum: *Représentations et observations en forme de mémoire sur l'état ancien et actuel de la librairie, ses règlements, ses privilèges et autres objets relatifs à son commerce et aux gens de lettres*	*PSC*, France
1764	Gabriel Huquier's memorandum on privileges and their renewal: *Projet en forme de mémoire pour l'assurance et le renouvellement des privilèges accordés à l'art de la gravure en taille-douce, et pour l'établissement d'une commission à l'effet d'empêcher aucune copie ou contrefaçon des ouvrages de gravure en taille-douce quelconque dans toute l'étendue du royaume*, Jan. 1764	BnF, Mss. f.f. 22120/60
1764	Charles-Nicolas Cochin *fils*'s draft decree for engravers: *Project d'arrest du Conseil pour les graveurs*	BnF, Mss. f.f. 22120/68
1765	Veuve Calas's privilege	BnF, Mss. f.f. 21963
1766	Decree for the bronze-casters for the protection of models	AN, AD XI/18
1767	Jean-Baptiste Greuze's privilege	BnF, Mss. f.f. 21964
1776	Jean-François Gaultier de Biauzat's memorandum for the provincial booksellers: *Mémoire à consulter pour les libraires et imprimeurs de Lyon, Rouen, Toulouse, Marseille et Nîmes*	*PSC*, France
1776	Étienne Gaucher's privilege	BnF, Mss. f.f. 21967
1776	François-Denis Née's privilege	BnF, Mss. f.f. 21967
1777	Royal declaration on painting and sculpture: *Déclaration en faveur de l'Académie royale de peinture et de sculpture*	*PSC*, France
1777	Decree on the duration of privileges: *Arrest du Conseil d'état du roi, portant règlement sur la durée des priviléges en librairie, du 30 août 1777*	*PSC*, France
1777	Simon-Nicolas-Henri Linguet's memorandum on privilege: *Opinion de Linguet touchant l'arrêt sur les privilèges*	*PSC*, France
1778	Jacques-Charles Bar's privilege for *Recueil de tous les costume des ordres religieux et militaires*	BnF, Mss. f.f. 21967
1778	Jacques Esnault and Michel Rapilly's privilege for *Gallerie des modes et costumes français*	BnF, Mss. f.f. 21967
1778	Abbé Pluquet's letters on the book trade: *Lettres à un ami sur les arrêts du Conseil du 30 août 1777 concernant la librairie et l'imprimerie* (1778)	*PSC*, France
1778	Regulation for the wallpaper makers: *Règlement concernant la contrefaçon des papiers peints et tontisses, dans la Communauté des relieurs [et] papetiers-colleurs en meubles*, 11 Sept. 1778	BnF, F-21198/56 (Gallica)

1789	Philibert-Louis Debucourt's privilege	BnF, Mss. f.f. 21971
1790	Abbé Sieyès's report on censorship: *Rapport de M. l'abbé Sieyès sur la liberté de la presse, et projet de loi contre les délits qui peuvent se commettre par la voie de l'impression, et par la publication des écrits et des gravures*	*PSC*, France
1790	Stanislas-Jean de Boufflers's report on inventions: *Rapport de M. de Boufflers, au nom du Comité d'agriculture et de commerce, relatif aux encouragements et aux privilèges à accorder aux inventeurs de machines et de découvertes industrielles*	*PSC*, France
1790-91	Pierre-François Basan, Charles-Étienne Gaucher and Nicolas Ponce's petition to the Assemblée nationale: *Adresse à l'Assemblée nationale, par les graveurs et propriétaires de planches gravées* (1791)	BnF Gallica
1791	Isaac Le Chapelier's report on the dramatic arts: *Rapport fait par M. Le Chapelier au nom du Comité de constitution, sur la pétition des auteurs dramatiques*	*PSC*, France
1791	François Hell's report to the Assemblée nationale: *Rapport fait à l'Assemblée nationale par M. Hell sur la propriété des productions scientifiques ou littéraires*	*PSC*, France
1793	Literary and Artistic Property Act: *Décret de la Convention nationale du dix-neuf juillet 1793 relatif aux droits de propriété des auteurs d'écrits en tout genre, des compositeurs de musique, des peintres et des dessinateurs*	*PSC*, France
1794	Petition of the citizen plaster-casters	AN, F^{17} 1304
1814	Judgment of the Cour de cassation on sculpture: *Robin c. Romagnesi, Cour de cassation, du 17 novembre 1814*	*PSC*, France

Table of copy disputes (formal and informal)

1706	Guillaume Delisle *c.* Jean-Baptiste I Nolin (maps)	BnF, Mss f.f. 22119/51–52; f.f. 21733/61–68
1731	Nicolas Lancret *c.* Antoine-François Radigues (portrait prints)	AN, Y13742
1742	Jean-Louis Daudet and Robert-Menge Pariset *c.* Étienne Charpentier (ornament prints)	BnF, Mss f.f. 22120/13–18
1759-60	*Affaire* La Fontaine (book illustrations)	BnF, Mss n.a.f. 3345/381–6, 403–8, 420–24, 462
1759-61	*Affaire l'Encyclopédie* (plates)	*Année littéraire*, 7 (1759); 8 (1760)
1776	Charles-Étienne Gaucher *c.* Jacques Esnault and Michel Rapilly (portrait prints)	AN, AD XI/18
1776	François-Denis Née and Louis-Joseph Masquelier *c.* Jacques Esnault and Michel Rapilly (genre scenes)	BnF, printed memoranda
1779	Jacques Esnault and Michel Rapilly *c.* André Basset (fashion plates)	AN, Y576 (30 Apr 1779)
1800-01	Jean-Daniel Auber *c.* Pierre Jean (Napoleon's campaigns)	BL, printed memoranda, F.37*(14), F.39*(6)
1802-03	Jacques-Louis Bance *c.* Pierre Simon (wallpaper)	Printed memoranda, Falconnet, vol. 2
1828	Henri Grèvedon *c.* Joseph Planat and Jérôme Châtillon	*Journal des tribunaux* (1 Jan 1829)
1834	Francesco Antommarchi *c.* Massino (Napoleon's death mask)	*Journal des tribunaux* (11 Dec 1834)

INTRODUCTION: ARTISTS, AUTHORSHIP AND PROPERTY

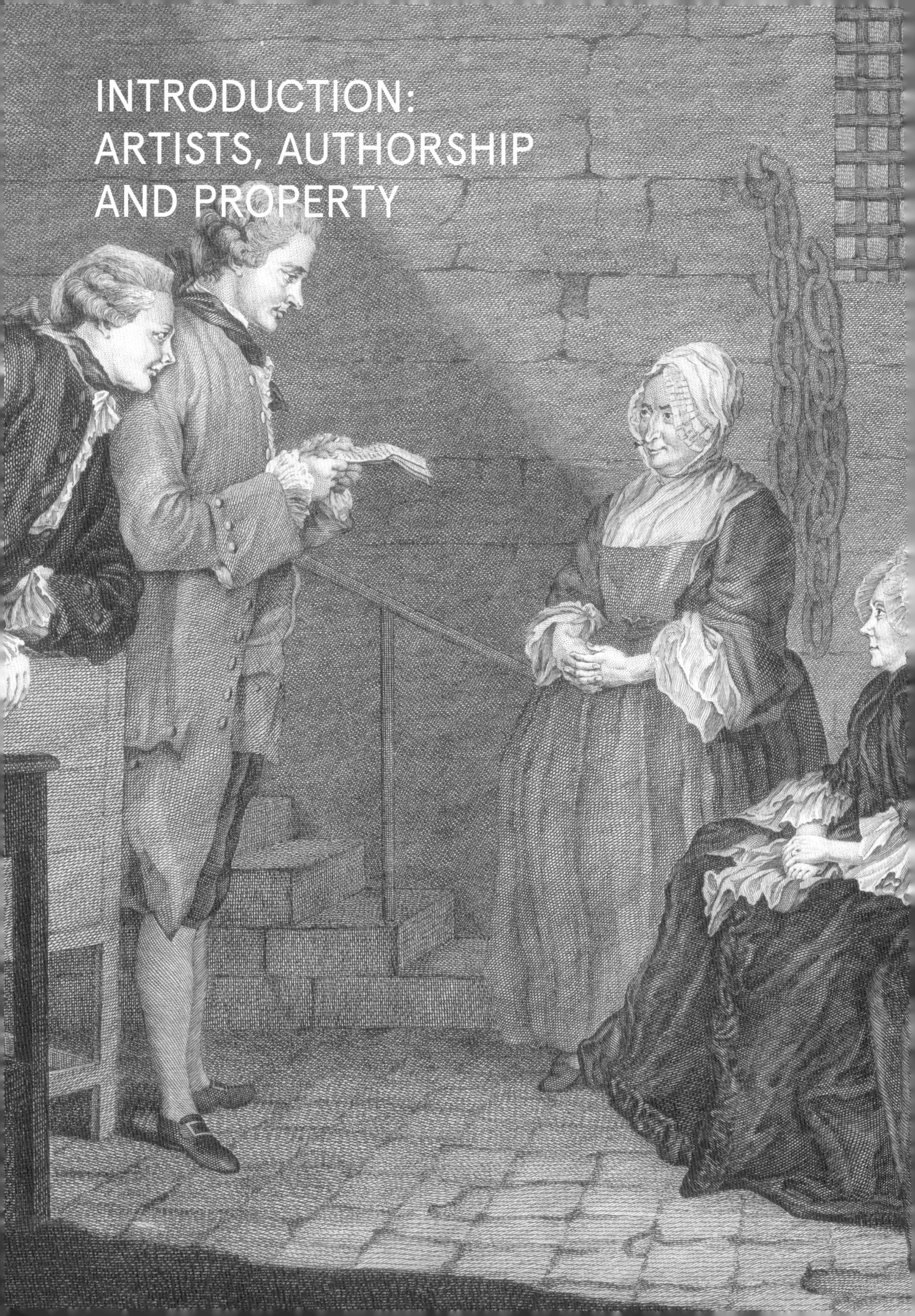

ISSUES

This book is about the relationship between the visual arts and the law concerning their reproduction in France from the beginning of the sixteenth century to the French Revolution. In it I examine how and why art came to assume a distinct legal form, becoming intellectual property. Today the notion that art is in essence intellectual and that artists have property rights in their works is so seemingly self-evident that we sometimes forget that in pre-capitalist economies art assumed other definitions, other identities: in the icon, for example, that of divine matter, in the faithful representation of nature, that of skilled performance and enchanted technology. Becoming intellectual property was not achieved without struggle and fundamental shifts in the conceptualisation of art and in art theory. This introduction outlines some of the issues at stake and provides tools for the study of art's intersection with law.

The history of intellectual property is also a history of authorship. To assign intellectual property to a work of art is to presuppose the existence of an author who, in one creative act, transforms matter and fixes it in a unique and distinct ideational form, to which a claim of property in its artistic expression can be made. In the eighteenth century, this author was one – more specifically – whose creations had been reproduced; the rights of copy were in those reproductions. But, as scholars have observed, the notion of authorship is no more obvious, timeless and stable than that of intellectual property. Roland Barthes's dramatic announcement of 'the death of the author' in 1967 made startlingly clear its historical contingency. Michael Foucault, responding to Barthes a year later, proposed a more complete theoretical and historical reconstruction of the now absent author in a lecture published in 1969.[1] The concept of the author, he contended, is a tool for the organisation of knowledge and power. Not only is it historically determined, but it is also ideologically charged and often contested. To answer his own question 'What is an author?' Foucault connected the emergence of this discursive figure with the appearance at the end of the eighteenth century of a bourgeois subject and bourgeois forms of property. Historians have since questioned the accuracy of his periodisation, arguing that his genealogy of authorship was too short. Evidence to support the presumption of a fully-fledged bourgeois economy undergirding copyright and other intellectual property regimes, is, others insist, wanting in the case of France.[2] Moreover, the 'author function' was present in European literary discourse as early as the fourteenth century. Indeed, Renaissance princes granted the first prerogatives to 'authors' in their inventions and literary works at a time when feudal forms of land tenure were very much the norm. It was nevertheless not until the eighteenth century that control of copying in the visual arts was assigned by right to the author, and to all others (printers, publishers, bronze- and plaster-casters, printmakers and wallpaper makers) only by cession of the author's right. And it was only in the eighteenth century that questions about the nature of intangible property in art works and about the extent, purpose and desirability of such property were formulated and debated at length for the first time. This book's centre of gravity is, therefore, the long eighteenth century, the historical moment whose significance Foucault first intuited.[3]

That said, in contrast to literary historians and historians of science, art historians have not been especially concerned with authorship, legally speaking;[4] their focus is more often the artist as an historical entity. The reasons are several. To start with, the primary art market was, and overwhelmingly remains, the market for paintings, sculpture and other unique works. Prints, cast sculpture and other multiples, original and reproductive, which are the objects of copyright, constitute at most a secondary, or supplementary art market. The material trace of the artist's signature, not copyright, is the prime index of artistic authorship, the mark of the artist's presence in the work. Consequently, the history of collecting and the so-called science of connoisseurship provide the main contexts within which the artist as author is discussed.[5]

If the singular, or non-multiple nature of art's primary media has limited the interest in authorship as a legal concept, so too has the technology of print before photography. In the eighteenth century, the majority of prints were reproductive, which is to say that printmakers engraved and etched the paintings, drawings and sculptures of others more often than they produced their own original works. In the reproductive print, both the artist whose work is reproduced and the printmaker responsible for the reproduction have equal claim to being *the* author. (I do not mean to suggest by this that printmaking was an inherently more collective and collaborative enterprise than the production of printed texts, for example, but simply to note that, in the case of prints, collaboration was publicly acknowledged by conventions of signature not found in books.)[6] Reproduction by engraving or etching was a secondary artistic event: production repeated. The equivocation provoked by this duality of function remains to this day: some museums catalogue and keep their print collections by the artists whose works are reproduced, some by printmaker; still others do both. To the accumulation of signatures arising from the collaborative nature of print production, which confounds easy answers to the question 'Who was the author?', add the fact that only some artists, and not necessarily those judged the most historically and art-historically significant, chose to have their works engraved. Of them, a smaller number still sought copy-protection for their works. The history of art that can be told from the study of copyright is therefore limited – you could even say distorted – in a way that it is not in the case of literature, whose history since the invention of the printing press is very largely the story of printed books, where the combined legal form of permission to publish and copyright was, in *ancien-régime* France, mandatory for all but a small minority of texts. The history of copyright does not reproduce the history of art as it is traditionally told, nor does it affirm the canon. In the eighteenth century, Watteau, Chardin, Boucher, Fragonard and David did not obtain copyrights for their works. But Charles-Antoine Coypel, Nicolas Lancret, Jean-Baptiste Oudry and Jean-Baptiste Greuze did.[7] Which is not to say that the 'Watteau', 'Chardin', 'Boucher', etc., prints that circulated in the market did so unprotected. Jean de Jullienne, as 'owner of several Paintings' by Antoine Watteau, obtained a *privilège* (the word for copyright before 1793), to protect the engravings made after them, in part realisation of his broader programme to reproduce Watteau's oeuvre.[8] The Academician printmaker Charles-Nicolas Cochin *père* on several occasions secured privileges for his etchings after Jean Siméon Chardin.[9] And the successful publisher and printseller Gabriel Huquier petitioned and was granted copy-protection for a miscellany of unspecified works in the late 1730s, at the time when he was publishing prints after François Boucher and presumably with them in mind.[10] Copyright represents not an alternative history of art exactly, but one that imperfectly registers developments in the art world and only confusedly signals historical claims to genius.

In a ground-breaking and brilliant essay, Molly Nesbit identifies where the interest in copyright primarily lies for art historians: with the art object.[11] She makes a point of noting the levelling, almost iconoclastic, effect of copyright law, the way it deals with art and artists even-handedly, recognising hierarchies neither of talent nor of genre. In law, culture is flat, as she puts it. Its blindness to distinctions within the field is balanced, however, by its sharp determination of the edges of the field: copyright is concerned only with cultural forms of labour. Industry is beyond the pale. However, industry discovers new materials and creates new media that are potentially the stuff of the cultural forms of the future. In the nineteenth and early twentieth centuries, the period that concerns Nesbit, the newcomers were photography, sound recording and film. By presenting themselves as candidates for copyright, these 'uninvited guests' tested both the definition of art and the limits of the law. For art history, copyright is not just, nor perhaps even first, a question of authors, it is a question of art. Were Eugène Atget's photographs, which he termed 'documents', legally art? What of Marcel Duchamp's ready-mades? In picking Atget and Duchamp as instances of 'What was an author?', Nesbit chooses not the ideal figure of the Romantic author, the poster-boy for literary copyright and its histories, but artists who deliberately and openly confronted and manipulated law in order to force it to accommodate their work, work that ran the gamut from infra-ordinary commercial culture to the extraordinary exploits of high modernism.

Since 1987, the year of Nesbit's essay, questions of copyright's scope have continued to preoccupy scholars and to challenge courts. The important volume *Dear Images: Art, Copyright and Culture* (2002), edited by Daniel McClean and Karsten Schubert, asks whether the protection of copyright can be extended to cover artistic forms provocatively devoid of originality and creativity ('appropriation art'), or without material form as such and consisting only of content or idea ('conceptual art'). It also asks 'What are the social and political consequences of the incorporation of new digital media into existing copyright law?'[12] Certainly not the last, photography was also not the first of copyright's uninvited guests. Looking back rather than forwards from 1793, the date of the first Literary and Artistic Property Act in France, we see the printed image, the humble woodcut, leading the works to which copy-protection in books was first 'extended' in the sixteenth century.[13] In 1515 Jacques Signot was granted a privilege for *La Totale et Vraie Description de tous les passaiges... par lesquels on peut passer et entrer des Gaules es Ytalies* (1517), specifically for its illustrative map, a fold-out of the Alps of northern Italy, which also circulated independently of the book.[14] The social and historical circumstances in which law and the image came together in the early 1500s, and in the late 1800s, or early 1900s, or early 2000s (the later periods that concern Nesbit, and McClean and Schubert) were, however, manifestly different. When, in the nineteenth century, photography 'seized' the law, taking it by surprise, to use Bernard Edelman's telling phrase, it challenged copyright as an established institution.[15] At the time of the woodcut, by contrast, copy-protection was emergent. The claims made on behalf of the image were not addressed to a clearly defined and stable body of privilege law.[16] Rather, the image participated in the formation of those prerogatives; it helped to give them contour and content. I argue for the legal agency of the image and suggest how it may have contributed to the becoming property of intellectual works by force of its opticality.

This book, then, is about the history of copy-protection in France from the time when the first monopolies for woodcuts were issued up to the early 1800s: until 1834, to be exact, the date of the case of Napoleon's death mask, tried not directly under the 1793 Act, which regulated copying only in 'two-dimensional art', but following the interpretation of the Act by the Cour de cassation in a ruling of 1814, which extended copyright law to three-dimensional art objects. The first chapter tells the longer half of this often fraught commercial story, in the course of which the legal basis and rationale for monopolies in print shifted from the command of royal prerogative to a right arising from authorship. I analyse that transformation in the early modern debates over the terms, conditions and purposes of copy regulation, specifically in relation to the illustrated book, a self-selecting example as an art object in which privilege in text and image literally come together. In the broadest sense, the chapter asks what difference the similarities and differences between image and text make to the definition, application and uptake of privilege in the early modern period. Art's candidacy for copyright was dependent on its supposed immateriality – that is, on a conceptualisation of art (like text) as ontologically distinct from the materials and techniques of its realisation. The case I make for art's contribution to intellectual property law lies, paradoxically, in its visualisation, and consequent reconceptualisation of property as a tangible thing (not as the aggregate of social relations over a thing), via its technologies of illusion. The questions raised in the chapter about when the expression of an intangible artistic idea became an exclusive property in law, about how that property was embodied specifically in the author, about what economic conditions gave rise to copy-protection and what kinds of legal and political authority it presupposed are not, however, fully answered there; they are referred to throughout the book and are directly addressed again in the final chapter, which, returning to the picture book among other printed objects, deals with the second and shorter half of the story: copyright during and immediately after the French Revolution.

Between the first and last chapters, this history of privilege slows, and copyright is addressed thematically. Such a change of tempo and tack was prompted partly by the contingency of history. Before the Revolution, intellectual property laws were local to trades, professions and city jurisdictions: to printing and printmaking, casting, designing and inventing, to Paris, Lyon and Rouen, etc. Regulations were drawn up and implemented by a host of competing royal agencies and corporate bodies with semi-governmental authority, which were culturally as well as bureaucratically distinct but whose jurisdictions often overlapped: the Chancellerie (Royal Chancery) for books and prints, academies and trade guilds for sculpture and engraving, and the Bureau du commerce (Board of Trade) for machines, designs and inventions. One of the points of the book, manifest in its organisation, is that the new laws of the 1790s imposed clarity of purpose and bureaucratic simplicity on the enmeshed particularities of *ancien-régime* legislation. What are treated separately in chapters 1, 2 and 4 – the Chancellerie's regulation of printed books, the Académie royale de peinture et de sculpture's copy-protection for sculpture and engraving, and the Bureau du commerce's privileges for inventions, known today as patents – are considered together as a national code in chapter 5.

More significantly, the middle chapters directly address relations between aesthetic and legal concepts. Nesbit assumes that art and law constitute parallel worlds. According to her, the 1793 Act was neither the cause nor the effect of changes in late eighteenth- and nineteenth-century French art, such as the invention of the Romantic artist, the collapse of the hierarchy of genres, the decline of the official Salon and the rise of the avant-garde. Anne Barron has similarly rejected a causal connection between copyright and art theory, Romantic or Modernist. For Barron, a legal rationalist in this, law progresses according to its own internal logic. Similarities in the definition of the art work in law and in art theory when they occur – in Modernism, for instance – are, she says, simple 'convergences'.[17] Thus the history of copyright law, as formulated by her, is tangential to the history of art. In Nesbit's work, by contrast, law is not superstructural, like art; rather, copyright is part and parcel of the economy. The market produced copyrights and they in turn reproduced market relations. By this reasoning, copyrights in woodcuts and intaglio prints could be seen as a means of safeguarding the surplus value extracted from the labour of reproduction.

In 1639 the print publisher François Langlois recruited François Collignon to etch for the Paris art market copies of eight marine views by the Italian printmaker Stefano della Bella, which had first been published in Florence. A condition of Collignon's contract was that he should make no further copies of the prints for other Paris dealers.[18] Hypocrisy in business is not the point here. Nor are the ethics of authorial right, a right at that time not recognised in law. The prohibition on copying in Collignon's contract simply served to maximise Langlois's control over those, like Collignon, whom he had working for him.[19] Copyright law arguably obscures those relations of production by diverting attention from the power relations *within* workshops to relations of trade *between* workshops – that is, to the surface dynamics of competitive markets. This book does not primarily explore the material and social practice of print production that copyright tends to occlude, in part for lack of adequate data. Contracts like the one between Langlois and Collignon are rare, though Langlois's importance as a publisher suggests that its terms were standard.[20] I analyse, instead, how art theory was instrumentalised by the market and acquired material purchase through law: art theory as a practice, you could say. *Ut pictura poesis*, the title of the first chapter, is therefore more than a conceit to denote law poetically that became common to both word and image. It signals the argument of the book: that art-theoretical concepts were, in fact, constitutive of property law and its cultural forms in early modern France. Moreover, those concepts were not inspiration, expression and imagination, characteristic of Romanticism, but rather emulation, imitation and invention, central to the humanistic theory of art.

By the beginning of the eighteenth century, the analogy of painting with poetry was utterly conventional, virtually a cliché. Its original purpose of securing a liberal status for art by making prominent painting's intelligence had been achieved by the theorisation of *pictura* in the sixteenth and seventeenth centuries as an art of imaginative composition, an art, that is, in which the idea was visualised in the mind of the artist prior to execution.[21] Comparative analysis of text and image to reveal structural homologies in verbal and visual signs had been superseded in the early eighteenth century by general, and theoretically looser, considerations of the similarities between the two. The art theorist Roger de Piles used the maxim *ut pictura poesis* prosaically, not metaphorically, to observe that poetry and painting 'start from the same place, follow the same path, arrive at the same destination and draw their reputation from the earliest times'.[22] He was not compelled by defensiveness to stress the nobility and intellectual talent of the artist–performer; he confidently directed his reader's attention, instead, at art's works, its painterly products. He reserved particular praise, moreover, for those pictures that in resembling poetry also resembled books – that is, commodities able freely and publicly to circulate.[23] The abbé Du Bos similarly described reproductive prints as 'poème(s) en prose' because they broadcast the 'poetry' of the painted originals, and in so doing put them within humanity's reach.[24] Liberation of art and artist was construed by de Piles and Du Bos not in terms of a transcendence of craft and guild but in relation to the emancipation of works of art from private collections for public enlightenment.[25] Insofar as metaphorical language transports the meaning of a word or phrase from one context to another,[26] lending its signification to the new domain by comparison, we can perhaps say that de Piles and Du Bos removed Horace's axiom *ut pictura poesis* from its place of exalted origin in classical rhetoric to the flat planes of commerce and bourgeois aesthetics, where it came to serve the interests of entrepreneurs through copyright. In de Piles and Du Bos, commoditisation is not, we can also note, in conflict with the concept of public domain; through the mediation of print it helped to produce it. Chapter 1 outlines print's transformation of painting, and traces the development of the law's first acts to control and enclose the market for its reproductions.

The second chapter, 'Emulation', examines the sculpture and print privileges enjoyed by the Académie from the late seventeenth century and asks why Academicians were slow, possibly even reluctant, to take advantage of their own prerogatives, which were free and unlimited. It asks, moreover, why Academicians sometimes even opted for book privileges to protect printed reproductions of their work, privileges issued by the Chancellerie, which rarely exceeded 20 years' duration and were expensive to buy. Part of the answer lies in the economics of the print trade: Academicians generally sold their compositions outright to engravers and publishers for reproduction and were not financially interested in the exploitation of the prints. Moreover, insofar as they shared de Piles's view of the moral superiority of works made public by publication, they accepted reputation as their reward, not profit. But another part of the answer lies in the collective culture of the Académie. Emulation signifies the ethical commitment of members to work within an artistic tradition and perpetuate its artistic values, a commitment fulfilled by the practice of copying that was sometimes lifelong.[27] The attentive, patient and sustained copying of exempla that characterised academic emulation is, in this sense, the antithesis of the alienated social relations of marketplace culture in which the works of others exist for the commercial copyist in a calculated means–ends rapport of profit. Academicians were able to negotiate the contrary demands to repeat and also to innovate seemingly without crisis until the eighteenth century because the Académie reserved for itself the right informally to impose norms of practice, and to judge the point at which respectful imitation tipped into servile and illegitimate copying. However, expansion of the art market, growth in the print trade and, from mid-century, regularly staged public exhibitions undermined the authority of the Académie's self-regulation. Accusations of plagiarism proliferated in the 1750s and 1760s and suggest that the unprecedented levels of public scrutiny at the Salon and via prints engendered an anxiety of influence. The discourses of privilege and of crime provided, as we shall see, some of the terms in which to articulate a response.

The requests for privilege and the charges of plagiarism at the Académie mostly concerned either history painting or narrative sculpture, genres in which the role of the imagination was undisputed and the selective working of tradition its ideal objective. But how did the law interpolate art defined rather as imitation, as an exact copy, or impression, of nature? Can you copyright a copy? These questions formed the crux of an important court case about piracy in the 1770s involving a print after a pencil portrait by the Academician Charles-Nicolas Cochin *fils*, which is explored at some length in chapter 3. Portraiture was itself a test case for privilege because it incorporated, at one end of likeness, wax portraits, mechanically reproduced directly from the body, and, at the other end, *portraits de fantaisie*, or portrait fictions. Untangling the crossed lines dividing original and copy, model and image was at the heart of the Cochin case.[28] Its resolution later informed the revision of the Académie's privilege in the royal *Déclaration* on painting and sculpture in 1777, and it prompted a shift in the meaning of expression in academic theory. Thereafter, 'expression' referred not to the depiction of the passions in history painting and figurative sculpture; rather it denoted the artist's manner and the more or less overt signs of his or her subjectivity. This case of infringement and related others were, you could say, the origin of the epistemological and judicial divide between content and form, and idea and expression, dichotomies upon which modern regimes of copyright and Modernist art theory depend.

Copyright protected *disegno*. It had no jurisdiction over colour that was not first articulated into form by line. This is not to say that hue, printed on paper or cloth, was denied privilege, but rather that privilege in books and patterns did not protect colour and colour combinations in prints and stuffs as such. Colour became private property only when invention was located in the chemistry of the colourant, or in the technology by which colour was delivered to an object. Law protected such inventions with patents, confusingly also called privileges in the eighteenth century. Colour printing was one such invention, and the vexed question of its attribution and ownership is the subject of chapter 4. Patents were concerned with the materiality of the image in a way that copyright, by definition, was not. Over time, as Peter Kelly has observed, technologies acquire independence from the materiality that engenders them to the point of becoming invisible, seemingly immaterial; but at the moment of their invention, they draw particular attention to the physical link between the maker and the art object, and they index the inventor's subjective endeavours to master the matter of art.[29] In chapter 4 I therefore argue, *contra* Foucault's claim that the author was bracketed out in science at the very time he or she emerged in literature,[30] that modern notions of possessive artistic genius were formed perhaps more effectively in conflicts for credit in such tangible scientific processes and ways of making than in the expression of intangible ideas notionally conjured from the imagination.

All three chapters examine questions about ownership of the image that arose within art discourse and concerned early modern art's highest calling: the depiction of the human figure. The minor genres of landscape and still life were scarcely mentioned in the debates on copy regulation in the arts. The last chapter, which picks up the legal tale of copyright at the end of the eighteenth century, combines the historical and thematic insofar as the 1793 *Décret de la Convention nationale* (Literary and Artistic Property Act), or so-called 'Act of the Rights of Genius', is examined in the context of that which it excludes as well as that which it encompasses: industry. The flower occupied a place in textile design that the body held in art, but the parallels between art and design in privilege end there. In the *ancien régime*, guild regulations on copying in, for example, the silk industry always recognised the artificiality, the inventiveness of flower motifs, even those praised for exceptional naturalism. Arguments to refute charges of infringement, therefore, did not (like portraiture) cite truth to nature but rather the inescapably collaborative character of design. They questioned, too, design's intrinsic artistry, arguing that smallness and simplicity put some patterns below the threshold of privilege. After the Revolution, however, and after the passage into law of the 1793 Act under the Terror, determination of what constituted a work of genius, and thus a subject of the Act, was discussed in terms less of art than of utility. The Revolution raised questions about equality and fraternity in the relations between art and industry. The so-called 'dependency' of the design trades on art, which in the *ancien régime* had enforced their subordination, required after 1789 that art actively support its brother industry in order that the nation should prosper. Fittingly, chapter 5 brings discussion to a close on the ideological matter of relations between copyright and the public domain.

A final point, to explain my preponderantly thematic approach to intellectual property, is that the advent of copyright in France in 1793 was not, from a cultural point of view, and possibly even a legal point of view, a before-and-after event. Questions of definition in relation to kinds of property, kinds of author, kinds of copy and modes of dissemination had still to be settled, and tensions in the Revolution's laws arose in part from the submerged residue of unresolved debate from the preceding privilege regime with which it appears to break decisively. While marking the point where the fistful of modern copyright concepts – notably originality, idea/expression and property – first thrust into view, chapter 5 also circles back to point to the theoretical ideas analysed in the central chapters of the book. The gap of almost a decade between the passage of the Act and the first significant cases to be tried under it during the Consulat suggests continuing uncertainty about the status of the copy in art.

FORMALITIES

In what remains of the introduction I shall give an account of the formalities of early modern copy protection and an explanation of some of its key terms, aware that it is in this very red tape and jargon that law seems most alien and unattractive, most other from art. And not just from art, since it is in their language, procedures and paperwork that *ancien-régime* privileges differ most conspicuously from modern intellectual property laws. Those familiar with the protocols of *ancien-régime* privilege from the important scholarship of Marianne Grivel, Peter Fuhring and Antony Griffiths may choose at this point to move on to the first chapter.[31] Those unfamiliar with it should find this historical induction helpful.

Formalities – those of registration, notification and deposit – are not requirements of copyright today because the property-like nature of that right is said to arise directly from the author's act of creation.[32] The constitutive role of such formalities in establishing monopolies in early modern copy regimes marks, therefore, one of the principal differences between modern and early modern forms of intellectual property. Of many legal terms, the two I introduce at this preliminary stage are *privilège* and *contrefaçon*, each for slightly different reasons: *privilège* because, though its meaning seems and is, at one level, obvious, it articulates also a legal distinction between prerogatives and rights that is fundamental to the conceptualisation of intellectual property; and *contrefaçon* (for which there is no equivalent English word, but which means an 'infringing copy') because it refers to a crime that caused particular difficulties of definition and detection for art and therefore draws attention to the challenges faced by the law when confronting the image. Moreover, insofar as *privilège* and *contrefaçon* are respectively connected with obtaining and defending copyrights, these terms allow me to introduce the institutions principally involved in granting and prosecuting privilege law in early modern France:[33] the Chancellerie and the Châtelet.

Formalities were, in one sense, the steps that those seeking to protect a book, or other intellectual work, from copying had to take in order to secure privilege, and which enabled prosecution in the event of infringement. In the seventeenth and eighteenth centuries, the Chancellerie issued most of the copyrights for books, prints and maps. Among the papers of the Bureau de la librairie[34] – a special division of Chancellerie formed at the beginning of the eighteenth century to deal with the rapidly expanding administrative responsibility of regulating the book trade – is a short memorandum outlining those steps.[35] They were as follows. The person wishing to obtain a privilege – artist, printmaker, publisher or investor – addressed his or her request, with a copy of the work for which protection was sought, to the king directly, or indirectly via his Chancellor (Chancelier).[36] Books, which were subject to pre-publication censorship, were at this point delegated for scrutiny to one of the Chancellerie's royal censors.[37] Prints, however, were not subject to censorship, so applications for privilege in prints were considered without further ado at the Conseil du roi, at which the Chancellor presided.[38] In a copy of Jean Baudouin's French edition of Cesare Ripa's *Iconologie* (1636), dedicated to Chancelier Séguier, the eighteenth-century architect and designer Gilles-Marie Oppenord sketched a scene (fig. **1**) that conflates these moments of request and judgment.[39] Oppenord depicted the engraver, Jacques de Bie, presenting Séguier with a copy of the book and the Chancellor offering privilege in return, invoked by the attributes of his office: the mace and the casket of seals by his throne.[40] The Bureau de la librairie's memorandum does not make clear whether, privilege having been granted, it was at this point that the *lettres patentes* were sent to the Parlement for registration, or whether registration followed the attachment of seals. Both steps were essential. In theory, the Parlement could object to the issuance of letters in any particular instance; in practice, it rarely did so. At the office of the Grand sceau the parchment letters patent were sealed with a yellow seal appended *sur deux queues*.[41] It was the seal that gave the letters the force of law. The final step was to enter the letters into the public record at the bureau of the Paris book guild, the Corporation des libraires et maîtres imprimeurs, within three months of issuance.[42] The memorandum is terse and practical. However, Oppenord's elaborate marginal decoration indicates that ceremony and ritual attended the legal and bureaucratic process. It is a measure of both the symbolic and the economic importance attached to the embodiment of these acts in parchment and sealing wax that the documents are listed in the after-death inventories of artists, alongside marriage contracts, wills and deeds of property.[43] The oeuvre of the printmaker

Pierre-Philippe Choffard, compiled in the early nineteenth century and acquired by the Bibliothèque nationale, has, moreover, incorporated into its front matter for display, a parchment fragment of letters patent obtained by him – manifestation of the union in *c.*1800 of artistic and legal notions of authorship.

Some trade guilds did more than record royal privileges; they imposed their own copy regulations. These were, of course, local to the jurisdiction of the particular city guild. Articles 69 and 70 of the 1730 statutes of the Paris Corporation des maîtres peintres et sculpteurs forbad its members to copy and to reproduce one another's works without the written consent of the author.[44] In 1766 the capital's bronze-casters (*fondeurs*) obtained a decree from the Parlement to protect their models from 'theft' by *marchands-merciers*, jewellers, gilders and furniture makers, a protection that they also made available to non-guild members: to goldsmiths and sculptors, specifically.[45] The Lyon silk merchants' and weavers' guild introduced copy-protection for silk designs in 1737; in 1786 their local proscription was extended to the silk industry nationally and became the basis for design patents, equivalent to privileges in print, to which they were, indeed, often compared.[46]

Meanwhile, from the end of the seventeenth century, Academicians were able to obtain privileges for sculpture and engravings from the Académie royale de peinture et de sculpture by presenting either casts or impressions of their works at one of the Académie's bi-monthly general meetings. Following collective scrutiny, the privileges that were granted were noted in the Académie's minutes. Separate registers, or running lists, were also kept of statues and prints awarded protection, but formal letters under the Académie's seal, equivalent to those issued by the Chancellerie, were not apparently a condition of protection.[47]

Inventors, whether master artisans or Academicians, enjoyed the freedom to go over the heads of guilds and apply for an exclusive privilege to work and exploit an invention via a number of royal institutions. In 1699, the Académie royale des sciences was formally charged with the inspection and evaluation of inventions for which royal protection was sought. In 1722, the Bureau du commerce was founded as an advisory committee to the Conseil du roi, and Academicians were co-opted as consultants to work directly for the government under the authority of the Contrôleur général des finances, whose role with regard to patent-privileges was roughly equivalent to the Chancellor's in relation to copy-privileges. The process of obtaining an inventor's privilege was more time-consuming and risky than that of securing an author's privilege. It required disclosure of the invention and verification of its viability and commercial benefit by a committee of experts that often took months, not weeks, during which the chances of secret leaking were high. Unlike modern patents secured on grounds of novelty, inventions in the *ancien régime* could hope for protection only if they were in accord with royal policy and advanced state objectives in trade and industry.[48] In view of these complexities, it is highly likely that artists and artisans who produced paper instruments (maps) or manufactured figured products (textiles, wallpaper) sought print privilege or copyright, rather than patent-privilege, wherever possible.[49]

The operative nature of *ancien-régime* copyright is clearly evident in instances where the 'author' failed to obtain and register a privilege. In the 1740s, the Lyon print dealers Jean-Louis Daudet and Robert-Menge Pariset became embroiled in a dispute with the Paris printmaker Étienne Charpentier over sets of ornament prints that Alexis Peyrotte had designed for them. In 1745, Charpentier obtained a privilege for his own copies of Peyrotte's *découpures*.[50] Notwithstanding Daudet and Pariset's undisputed status as the instigators and originators of the designs, even, indeed, as the self-proclaimed 'inventors' of this entirely new genre of large-scale cut-out Rococo pattern for the decoration of screens and other domestic furnishings, their failure to obtain a privilege themselves in 1742, when they first published the prints, put Charpentier's privilege legally beyond challenge. There was no case to answer. Privilege had turned Charpentier's copies into originals and Daudet and Pariset's originals potentially into *contrefaçons*.[51]

Daudet and Pariset's case against Charpentier, had they obtained a privilege, would have depended on proof that the latter knew from where the designs originated, and could not claim to have copied them innocently from foreign imports. Not until the nineteenth century did nations enter into international copyright agreements. In the *ancien régime*, the difference between legal and illegal appropriation was sometimes a question also of national borders.[52] Daudet and Pariset, proceeding as if privileged, provided the necessary proof in the form of business letters that demonstrated that they had themselves supplied Charpentier with the originals.[53] They could also have cited the inscription of their *executit* on the works themselves. Attaching notice was another formality of privilege – precisely the formality that generally prevented pirates from disclaiming knowledge of a prohibition to copy. Although the globally recognised symbol of copyright, ©, is today widely attached to all manner of designs and reproductions, the international Berne Convention for the Protection of Literary and Artistic Works (1886) rendered such notification obsolete; copyright today is the presumption of all intellectual works.

'Avec Privilège du Roy', 'Cum Privilegio Regis', and the corresponding abbreviations 'A.P.R.' and 'C.P.R.', were the *ancien régime*'s copyright symbol. Only printmakers were allowed this very short form of notice; by 1704, cartographers were required to expand the notice by the addition of the date of issue.[54] In books, the formality of notification was yet more exacting: it was conditional on reproduction of the letters in full or in extract, at the front or back of the book.[55] Not unaware of these legal conditions, poets sometimes had fun with law: Isaac de Benserade famously set his privilege for the *Métamorphoses en rondeaux* (1676) 'en rondeau'. Artists were not often inspired to such wit. Oppenord's drawing in the lower margin of Baudouin's 'Extraict du Privilege du Roy' in his copy of Ripa depicts the rape of Leda by a swan (fig. **2**). Nothing obviously connects Oppenord's retelling of Jovian shape-shifting with the transformation of copy-free work into private property notionally accomplished by Louis's notice of privilege. The focus is on Leda. However, Oppenord's handling of ornamental form, like Benserade's treatment of rhyme, may perhaps be viewed as evidence of his understanding of privilege's agency. The scene is boldly and forcefully framed; moreover, that frame is shaped as a clasp. The capped upward swing of the volutes grips the scene and marks it out as a discrete entity and personal thing. The phrase 'Avec Privilège du Roy' worked, with or without actual frames, to enclose, demarcate and give notice of intellectual property[56] – with one remarkable exception: the prints published by the Cabinet du roi, the king's printworks, were not at first inscribed with his privilege. Probably, this was because his prints were nominally gifts, not (officially) for sale.

The third and last privilege formality was the requirement to deposit. Litigation necessitated a reliable reference copy to determine whether infringement had occurred. The obligation to deposit was not, however, coincident with that of registration. Not until the mid-seventeenth century, more than a century after the privilege system began, did it become mandatory for prints. Marianne Grivel speculates that, until then, the Crown had not been sufficiently interested in prints to make it a legal condition to cede copies when privilege was granted, in the manner of books, deposits of which François I had made mandatory by the ordinance of Montpellier in 1537.[57] If printmakers and publishers fulfilled to the letter the condition of attaching notice – indeed, many were only too ready to inscribe their works 'Avec Privilège du Roy' whether legally entitled to do so or not – the condition of deposit was a source of considerable tension and was widely resisted in the print trade. Conditions of deposit for Chancellerie privilege were much the most onerous: from 1704 privilege entailed the deposit of eight impressions of the print granted protection.[58]

The copy regulations of the Académie royale de peinture et de sculpture, by contrast, demanded a single cast of a sculpture and two impressions of a print.[59] The difference is explained by the fact that deposit, in the case of Chancellerie privilege, fulfilled more than the internal, legal demands placed upon it by the possibility of litigation; it also fulfilled objectives external to copyright. It was an instrument for building the royal collections: three of every eight deposits were destined for the Bibliothèque du roi, the Cabinet du roi and the Louvre. Two copies were assigned to the Chancellor and the Chancellerie. The three remaining copies fell to the Paris booksellers' guild. One of these may have been the prime copy, the 'object-in-law', but the two others constituted compensation in kind for the labour of processing privilege carried out by the capital's *libraires*. Engravers and printsellers, as already noted, strongly objected, and the incidence of non-compliance was high.[60] Since the Berne Convention, the copyright requirement to deposit, like the requirement to register and to attach notice, has fallen out of use, although in most European countries, including France and Britain, deposit in the country's premier libraries continues to be mandatory for all new publications, and these libraries are still conventionally called 'copyright libraries', though nothing any longer connects copyright and legal deposit.

No such extra-privilege requirements attached to the privileges of trades other than the trade in books. The Paris master painters and sculptors did not, in fact, require deposit of any kind. Neither did the so-called Grande fabrique – the merchant weavers' guild of Lyon. Those in the silk industry were of the view that a centralised deposit of patterns, far from protecting design, would constitute a more readily accessible resource of new patterns for design pirates. The Paris bronze-casters, by contrast, viewed deposit as essential to enforcement of their regulations: members were required to submit one finished, detailed scale drawing of their models, or what is today called a 'blueprint'. These blueprints were signed, dated, numbered and entered into registers for reference. One such register survives.[61]

The formalities themselves, and the particulars of their variations according to trade and institution, characterised *ancien-régime* copy regulation as an artefact of legal invention and royal authority. Claude-Marin Saugrain thought it necessary in 1744 to collate the proliferating array of regulations regarding the publishing, printing and selling of books and prints, including those relating to privilege, and organise them into a code, and to publish that code in a cheap, handy duodecimo format that all in the trade might keep beside them in order to learn the legal protocols and written rules that were self-evidently neither natural nor instinctive.[62]

TERMS

To this point I have been using the word *privilège* (and its English equivalent, 'privilege') interchangeably with 'copyright' (and 'patent'), as if the difference were no more than linguistic and easily overcome by translation. Seventeenth- and eighteenth-century dictionaries indicate that the difference between them was, in fact, substantive. This book is, in a sense, the history of the shifts in the legal and cultural meanings of *privilège* over the three centuries from the 1490s to 1793. In 1793, the Literary and Artistic Property Act redefined privileges as rights (*droits*); accordingly, having preferred to use the word 'privilege' in the bulk of the book, I switch to modern terminology in the last chapter, which is about both copyright and design patents during and immediately after the Revolution.

The definition of *privilège* given in the *Dictionnaire de l'Académie françoise* (1694) was much broader than its meaning in law. What we learn from this wider semantic field is that privilege was a profoundly social concept; it was defined by agency, or the power to give or refuse, to demand and obtain, to use or abuse an entitlement to do something to the exclusion of others. The instances of linguistic use cited indicate that privilege was, moreover, associated conventionally with social distinction: 'many fine privileges are attached to the office of Secrétaire du roi. It is a privilege of rank, [...] of the Nobility.'[63] In short, it was marked in everyday use by distinctions of class and, implicitly, of gender. As a principle of exception, privilege denoted value; the Académie française selected the superlatives 'fair', 'exclusive' and 'extensive' to qualify it. Jacques Savary des Bruslons's *Dictionnaire universel de commerce* (1723), a dictionary of things not words, inasmuch as it defined the things denoted by words and not the grammatical and lexical meaning of the words themselves, gave the specialist and legal meaning of privilege: 'exclusiveness', nothing more. It denoted permission from the king to those of his choosing, 'to make and to sell a kind of merchandise, either to the exclusion of all others or in competition with them'.[64] The contexts were very different – in this second instance, that of the law, the state and the bourgeois world of commerce and industry. Here, privilege was inclusive, admitting *petit*-traders *and* ennobled artists, women *and* men.[65] The question of whether the polite and legal definitions of privilege were related or merely homonymous, whether – that is to say – the symbolic value of privilege inhered in or, on the contrary, was unconnected to its legal and instrumental function is further explored in chapter 1.

Of the two kinds of privilege to which Savary referred, the first (to make to the exclusion of all others) was termed *privilège exclusif*, the second (to make in competition with them) *privilège simple*. Exclusive privileges were subdivided further into those that were general, conferring the prerogative to distribute and sell books and inventions throughout the kingdom, and those that were local to a particular town. Privileges of all kinds were recognised as implements of trade and could be obtained by anyone, no matter what the nature of their involvement in the enterprise. Privilege was not therefore, the prerogative of the author as it is in copyright. In the seventeenth and eighteenth centuries, publishers and distributors, who in the case of prints might also be the engraver of the work, usually applied for privilege. In fact, privilege was not predicated on making at all. In 1765, an exclusive privilege to protect Jean-Baptiste Delafosse's print after Louis Carrogis de Carmontelle's pencil portrait of the *Malheureuse Famille Calas* was obtained in the name of Mme Calas, the widow of the Protestant martyr tortured and wrongly executed for murder in 1762, whose cause was taken up by the *philosophes*. A benevolent few, led by Baron Grimm, had commissioned the print to commemorate Calas's complete post-mortem exoneration, and to help raise money for the family left destitute by legal costs and the collapse of the family business.[66] Mme Calas was to benefit not only from the print subscription but also from any fines and damages that might arise from successful prosecutions for infringement; pirate copies were rightly anticipated of so topical and controversial a subject.[67] The terms of this privilege were exceptional. The non-executive privilege applicant was more usually an investor or underwriter. And so closely was privilege connected with the business end of literary pursuit that many thought it tainted the writer. If Antoine Furetière's *Dictionnaire universel* (1690) identifies the author as the intended beneficiary of book privileges, those he had in mind were not the *illustres* of the Académie française but hacks and literary entrepreneurs who lived by their pens, making a trade of writing.[68]

In contrast, the 1793 Literary and Artistic Property Act legally invoked and recognised the rights of authors. In the 1798 (5th) edition of the *Dictionnaire de l'Académie françoise*, the word *droit* is identified as a moral concept both in its legal setting where it is an attribute of justice, and in everyday use: 'straight', meaning upright and honest.[69] Rights, unlike privileges, are pre-contractual – that is to say, pre-social; we come into the world with them as 'rights of man' and of woman. Although the Académie's dictionary does not define rights in this way explicitly, it implies, by reference to natural rights, that they are inherent, equal and universal. Unlike the crafted, even bespoke nature of the privileges conferred by written statute, rights are uniform: not 'exclusive' or 'simple', not general or local. They are also not temporal, and so not like privileges arbitrarily fixed at X or Y years' duration. They are perpetual. We can neither be joined to, nor separated from, our rights, unlike privileges that were granted as a favour, or in exchange for loyalty, or out of national utility, or for money. There is no imagining, no depicting of rights along the lines of Oppenord's doodled vignette (fig. **1**) because there is no personal story of getting them, either glorious or banal.

The liberty of the individual seized by the Revolution had, however, to be tempered by equality and fraternity, or the needs of others. A term was set on copyright to instate a public domain for everyone to exploit. The logic of the limit was nevertheless natural and not arbitrary: the author's death, plus ten years, or, to put it another way, the lifetime of two generations.[70] By so enshrining in law a relation of identity between the maker and his or her work, any damage to the one was logically construed as an injury to the other. The property right of the Republic's authors was in this sense as much moral as economic and it gave rise from the early nineteenth century to actions where financial gain was negligible. For example, in January 1829 the caricaturist Jean-Jacques Grandville took legal action against piracy of his witty lithographic satires the *Métamorphoses du jour* (1829), which had been copied and printed on sweet wrappers for New Year.[71] For Grandville the case was about control of the context in which his work circulated and was viewed. It concerned his reputation and was only secondarily about money.

What brought about the shift from privileges to rights? Briefly, to anticipate explanations to follow, from the 1630s privilege holders began to renew privileges before they expired. Statute made granting such renewals conditional on the augmentation of the original by one quarter, a condition not easily met by images, given the near impossibility of expanding a compositional work with supplementary figures, a larger landscape, more still-life props, etc., in the way it was possible to add a new introduction, further chapters, extra tables and appendices, etc., to a book.[72] However, by the end of the seventeenth century, print publishers, like booksellers, were obtaining extensions without augmentation.[73] As renewals became unconditional and virtually automatic, privileges turned green, so to speak. They became perpetual; in law, such judicial orders were sealed with green wax not yellow. And they gave rise to what Peter Baldwin has recently called the copyright wars.[74] Provincial book and print publishers with few privileges pitted themselves against those in the capital who had many more, were better able to perpetuate them and who thus dominated the market for books, music and maps. The lawyers, hired to defend the self-interested and initially ad hoc renewal initiatives of the Paris publishers and booksellers, found in property a serviceable discursive weapon. Property was, you could say, a hypothetical for describing and understanding the phenomenon that privilege had de facto become. Working back from the fact of perpetual privilege, they argued for its reconceptualisation as a kind of thing. So arguing made sense of the reality on the ground. Moreover, anchoring privilege in the work of the author strengthened the case that could be made by the publisher for perpetual privilege by aligning authorial labour with the legal principle of property right.

To propose such a pragmatic and narrowly instrumental view of the law falls significantly short of explaining how privileges and rights also became manifest in artistic culture. In order for the property analogy to take hold outside the legal mind, and away from the lawyer's office and the law courts, and for it to become current, it had to be rehearsed, debated, critiqued and, finally, accepted in the workshop and the studio, at the Académie and the Salon, and in public discourse. This was no simple matter. De Piles's praise of the *tableau* notwithstanding, the view of art as a commodity in which artists had property-like prerogatives was not easily reconciled with the high moral purpose that the Académie attributed to art and the value it gave to reputation. Lynn Hunt argues that inventing rights involves hearts as well as minds, emotion as well as reason.[75] She points out that, in order for rights to become self-evident and universal truths, people have first to identify with one another and to recognise themselves as sharing a common humanity. Empathy is thus the key to rights. Men and women in the *ancien régime* were led to think of others as fundamentally like themselves, says Hunt, by cases such as that of Calas *père*, when crimes were reframed in political terms.

Jean Calas was a Protestant whose son committed suicide. The father was accused of his son's murder, a murder he had allegedly committed to prevent his son from converting to Catholicism. Jean Calas was arrested, imprisoned, tortured and executed on the wheel. He maintained his innocence throughout his ordeal. The *philosophes*' critique of torture and religious intolerance re-presented this case of murder as a case about the right to a fair trial. Carmontelle and Delafosse's group portrait print (fig. **3**) evokes Calas's unjust fate by his absence. Chains that once detained him hang inert and empty on the back wall. His mourning family fills the cell he once occupied. A table casts a long, crepusculine shadow across the foreground. In the stark black and white world of print, the black bodies of the mourners index by inversion the purity of his soul.[76] In focusing on the emotional and material consequences of the guilty verdict for Calas's family, servant and friends, which news of its overturning cannot fully repair, the image raises sympathy from the level of the individual and personal to that of the social. The widow's Christian virtues of temperance and fortitude, expressed in the continence of her profile and the resignation of her hands, arguably provoked sympathy for her in the viewer, and a political feeling for rights and toleration. The scene has, of course, nothing directly to say about property rights; the poverty of the setting and the modesty of the sitters' dress merely allude to the family's unjustly reduced circumstances.

Intellectual property rights are more distant still from its discourse. And yet the straight and simple rhetoric of Carmontelle's portrayal characterises also the print's honest and empathetic inducement to benevolence, supported 'Avec Privilège du Roy'. By sale of the print, the outrage done to Mme Calas by one legal process was to be mitigated by another, thanks to the transfer of the print's 'privilege' complete and intact to her by gift.[77] Intellectual property is, here, not only a legal 'fabulation', or discursive abstraction; it is en route to becoming an embodied right, security in which promotes, in this case, charity.[78]

In 1694 the *Dictionnaire de l'Académie françoise* listed both 'prerogative' and 'right' along with 'advantages' and 'gifts' among the hybrid forms that privilege could assume. The gifts that were simultaneously rights were not things, but properties of the body, like beauty, and those of the mind, like reason and law.[79] The aim in what follows will be to understand how these legal, affective and aesthetic meanings intersected or collided and served as contexts for one another.

The noun *contrefaçon* denoted a copy, specifically one that infringed a work protected by privilege. It is a more straightforward word than *privilège* because uniquely a term of criminal law; it is not often found in dictionaries other than legal ones in the eighteenth century, though the verb *contrefaire*, to copy, imitate, or render similar, was in everyday use, as was the adjective *contrefait*: copied.[80] By the eighteenth century the artistic sense of *contrefait* to denote realism, tracked by Peter Parshall in Northern Renaissance picturing, had been lost.[81] So muddled, indeed, was artistic opinion on the meaning of *contrefaçon* by 1800 that the engraver and printseller François-Étienne Joubert was compelled to write a short tract on the subject to enlighten those who regarded it as inherently equivocal and beyond explanation.[82] In neither Joubert's text, nor legal discourse, do the verb and noun specifically designate a subject. Unlike the author indexed by copyright, the pirate is something of an abstraction, a spectral figure lacking the shape and substance assigned the author by virtue of *œuvre*, manner and signature.[83] The early modern print pirate had no recuperable *œuvre* for the simple reason that the penalty for infringement included the complete destruction of the offending copper plates, and all known impressions.[84] The pirate had no manner either, because the essence of piracy was to pass as another, and to that end he or she often created under cover of anonymity.[85]

What the pirate lacked in identity and character, his or her production momentarily made up for in specificity. The definition of *contrefaçon* was produced, as Joseph-Nicolas Guyot noted in his *Répertoire universel et raisonné de jurisprudence* (1775–83), by the ruling of the judge after inquisition into the facts, interrogation of the witnesses and careful scrutiny of the work.[86] As Joubert put it, 'only the word [*contrefaçon*] makes the thing'.[87] *Contrefaçon* was, in this sense, a 'speech act', in contrast to *privilège*, which describes a prerogative. Letters patent prohibited copies in whole and in part, reduced or enlarged, but were unable to give a definition of infringement as such. Only a judgment established for certain whether a copy was also a *contrefaçon*. Originals and copies were closely compared, coloured inks were sometimes used to mark points and lines of criminal coincidence in designs, and the language of court memoranda became specific, that is, forensic.[88]

Allegations of infringement were heard at the Châtelet, Paris's main criminal and civil court.[89] Lawsuits were prepared and managed by officers of the court, or *procureurs* (prosecutors). As agents of the plaintiff or the defendant, the *procureurs* filed the necessary court documents, and prepared the evidence.[90] Oral pleading in court on relevant principles of law was the responsibility of *avocats* (barristers), who likewise represented the interested parties. Their pleas were often written up in the form of *mémoires judiciaires* and printed, and in the later eighteenth century they were distributed to a readership that extended significantly beyond the law courts.[91] Sarah Maza has shown how, in some instances, legal issues in private lives became, thanks to such publicity, 'public affairs'.[92] Although it would be over-ambitious to argue that cases of privilege in art became *causes célèbres* on a par with the Rose-Girl of Salency or the Diamond Necklace affairs, the published memoranda in the Fréron portrait case and in the case of the *Tableaux* of Napoleon's Italian campaigns did ensure that questions of copyright became topics of conversation and debate in the art world. These briefs are important sources in what follows.

Typically the memoranda began with the 'facts'. In cases of infringement, the onus was on the plaintiff to prove that the accused had had opportunity to make the offending copy and therefore that the similarity in *disegno* was not the result of a coincidence of ideas. Publication of a print generally sufficed to establish opportunity, but the accounts to the police of alleged offences often included details about how the original came into the hands of the defendant. Copying having been established, and offending items having been seized, the next step was to determine in court whether the copy was sufficiently comprehensive and sufficiently close to constitute a crime. Lawyers and judges often relied on the testimony of experts to establish that copying had occurred. Only those with first-hand knowledge in the arts could, it was felt, say whether similarities between works arose from a common model or idea, and whether differences were genuine, and not superficial falsifications of the original made in order to disguise infringement. Sometimes such professional opinion led to legal errors. For example, in 1706, the cartographer Guillaume Delisle brought a case against the mapseller Jean-Baptiste I Nolin for copying his map of North America and incorporating it into a *mappa mundi*.[93] Delisle's original had not been engraved, however, and the author had not thought to petition for a privilege for it either.[94] Nolin, meanwhile, had obtained a privilege for his map of the world.[95] As in the case of Peyrotte's *découpures*, technically there was no case to answer. However, such was the weight of opinion of the appointed experts from the Académie royale des sciences, who unanimously found that the coincidences between the two maps could be explained only by blind copying, and so convinced were they of the injustice of such copying, that Nolin was found guilty and punished.[96]

The ruling is revealing on two counts. First, it suggests that value had played a part. Unlike Daudet and Pariset's printed ornaments, dismissed by the Chancellor as too 'miserable' to have warranted protection, Delisle's advances in the mapping of California and the Gulf of Mexico were judged so important and so personal that absence of privilege was no barrier to successful prosecution.[97] In law, culture was not always flat, *pace* Nesbit: value sometimes inflected judgments on privilege infringement. Second, although privilege formally protected reproductions (prints and casts), in practice a broader understanding of infringement was sometimes in play: here it included the original, a drawing. The statutes of the Paris Corporation des maîtres peintres et sculpteurs and the Académie royale de peinture et de sculpture both contained articles that prohibited the copying of their members' works, regardless of medium (that is, in paint and in bronze, in plaster and in print) and of their members' names.[98] There was, in the *ancien régime*, a lack of clarity about the legal remit of *contrefaçon*: it could refer to copies, reproductions and fakes, to both infringement and to fraud.

Our historical knowledge of *contrefaçon* is thin by comparison to our understanding of *privilège*. Connoisseurship has militated against the survival of copies in both public and private collections.[99] We know, however, that the legitimate and black markets in art were not as opposed and distinct as the negative discursive construction of the pirate implies. The throng of impossible social types depicted in a satire on fake news in 1760 (fig. 4) includes – along with the dancer who never misses a step at the centre – the taverner who never dilutes his drink, the honest merchant, the truth-telling trickster, etc., *and* the printmaker who never illegally copies. Artists and printmakers moved back and forth between the two economies, and print publishers often operated in both. Prints suggest, moreover, that a market for cheap copies could coexist with a market for connoisseurs so long as the piracies (prints or casts) did not threaten demand for the high-end originals. The relatively untroubled coexistence of print privilege and print piracy is partly explained by the intellectual property's double history: in law and in implementation. Prohibition was only as good as its enforcement, and enforcement did not follow automatically from the issuance of a privilege. The number of infringements that led to litigation in the *ancien régime* was low. *Bleak House* may have had no equivalent in French literature, but stories of fortunes lost and lives wasted in litigation were commonplace in the eighteenth century and may have served as a deterrent.[100] Only in exceptional circumstances, when matters of either reputation or exceptional gain were at stake, did artists overcome their caution and go to law.

In June 1731 the Academician Nicolas Lancret pursued a case of *contrefaçon* against a printmaker and three printsellers for copies of Laurent Cars's engraving after his portrait of the celebrated dancer Marie-Anne Cupis de Camargo, fulsomely advertised in the *Mercure de France* six months earlier.[101] The ill-fated pirate, Antoine-François Radigues, had unwittingly attempted to sell impressions of his counterfeit to Lancret himself.[102] Outrage is probably not sufficient to explain Lancret's suit. That he wanted fully and immediately to benefit from the sale of Cars's print is obvious, but it is also likely that, by enforcing his print monopoly and thereby ensuring that his studio on the quai de la Mégisserie was the only outlet for the likeness, he was also attempting to safeguard the market for the painted copies and variants produced by his workshop.[103] There was much at stake. Lancret won. However the judge reduced the penalty and damages for infringement set by the terms of Lancret's privilege from 6,000 *livres* to 20 *livres* in the case of Radigues and to just 2 *livres* in the cases of each of the sellers.[104] Jules Guiffrey, who first studied this lawsuit, interpreted the sentence as evidence that the judge regarded the crime as trivial.[105] More likely the judge took account of the defendants' ability to pay. Whatever the case, the outcome confirms the limits of privilege to secure reparation even when successful. Artists therefore often resorted to other means:[106] in 1735 Cochin *père* put a notice in the *Mercure de France* to warn collectors of a glut of copies after the prints of Sébastien Le Clerc, and to advertise his shop as the only source of authentic and copyrighted impressions of Le Clerc's works.[107] Philibert-Louis Debucourt, who obtained the last privilege for an image before the Revolution, adopted as a safer measure a practice common in the case of books: he signed and numbered impressions – in this case, his colour print *Annette et Lubin* – on the back, in order to reassure purchasers that these were the 'real thing'.[108]

Contrefaçons, like the various Carmagos, confront us with the historical realities of the market that law and the discourse on privilege translated and articulated into its own largely abstract terms. This book is, in the broadest sense, about the commoditisation of art in the early modern period and about the legal instruments that helped to transform painters, sculptors and printmakers from court artists, patronised and pensioned by the great, into bourgeois entrepreneurs.

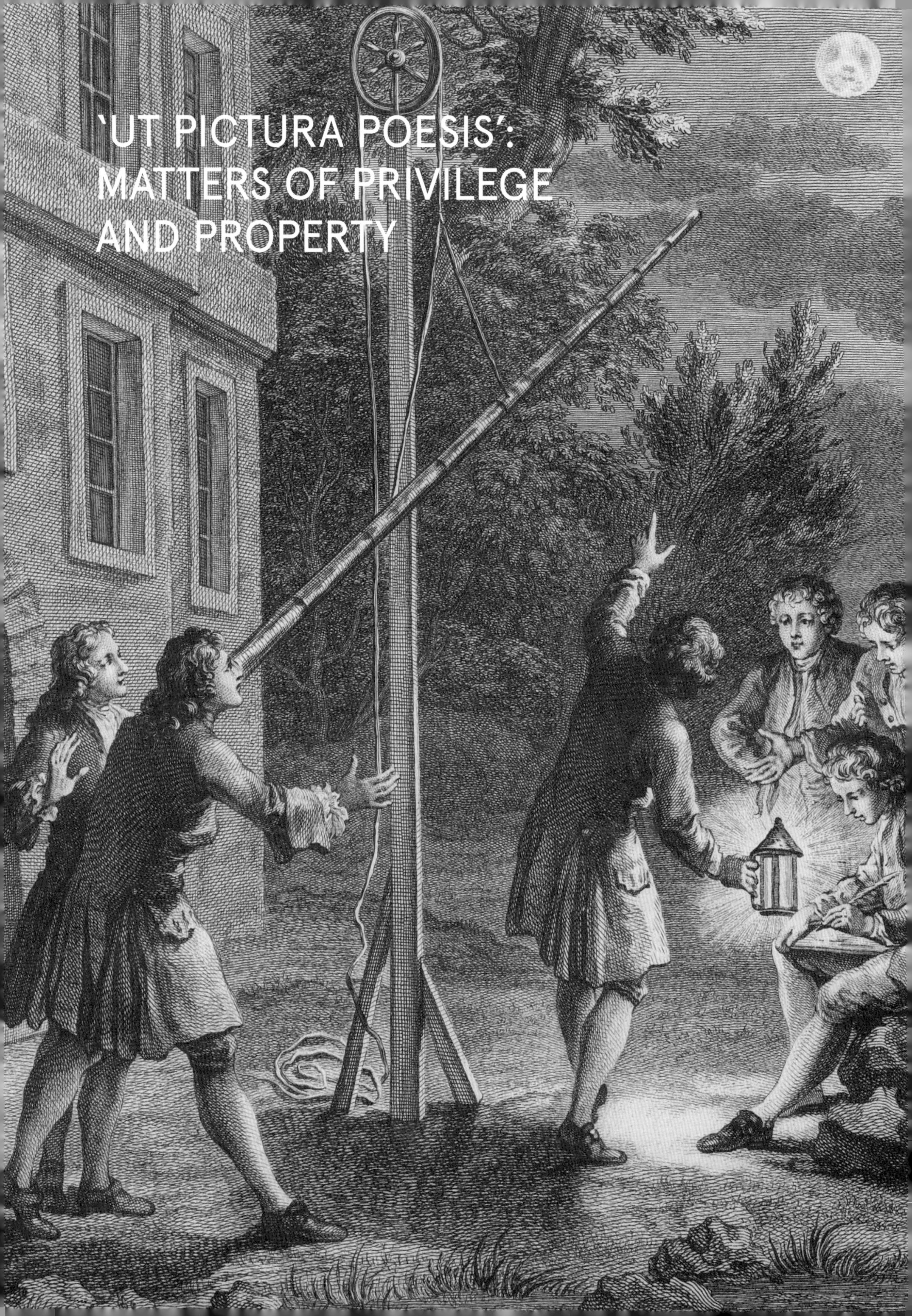

‘UT PICTURA POESIS’: MATTERS OF PRIVILEGE AND PROPERTY

Copyright was unknown before the printing press, and in France it was slow to develop thereafter. Termed *privilège*, copyright in the *ancien régime* was 'personal', a *privi-legium*, or private law.[1] Granted to the individual and not to the order, office, title or place to which he or she belonged,[2] it was issued by the king or other authority in the form of an open letter of instruction, called a 'letter patent'.[3] In time, and not without opposition, a rule of copy-privilege emerged from this extempore practice and was formalised and integrated into the regulations of the printing trades. In this first chapter, I retrace the long history of privilege legislation from the sixteenth to the eighteenth centuries, analysing its evolution from the point of view of the king and his government, on the one hand, and, on the other, from that of writers, artists and their publishers – the beneficiaries. I ask, how did it work and in whose interests? And what meaning attached to it, what did it signify? Charles Le Brun, Louis XIV's Premier peintre from 1664, and Jean-Baptiste Greuze, the darling of the critics and the public in the 1760s, emerge as important figures for understanding the ways in which artists identified with the notion of authorship articulated by privilege and employed law to protect their work, and also how the meanings and uses of privilege changed in the course of the century that separates them.

The forward direction of this historical account is interrupted in the middle by two cases of disputed monopoly. They are not cases in the legal sense – that is, instances of law created by judges in the process of resolving disputes. France's legal system is generally cited as a model of civil law, in which only legislation counts as a source for legal decision-making, and where judgments on particular cases generally have little precedential value. Neither of these 'cases' in fact went to court. However, from the petitions of the plaintiffs, the reports of the accused and the visual forms of the disputed works there emerges a different, a more vivid and complex picture of the particular ways in which art was conceptualised by privilege at a crucial moment in the legal debate. The first case concerned a new illustrated edition of a celebrated text – Jean de La Fontaine's *Fables choisies* (1668–79) – for which the publisher had requested a privilege in contravention of an existing monopoly. In the second, the issue was not the privilege but the originality that was supposedly its legal basis: the plates for Diderot and d'Alembert's *Encyclopédie* (1762–72) were said to have originated in the work, and therefore the property, of others. Related in many ways,[4] the two publications are, as instances of copy-privilege, nevertheless reversals of each other: no privilege in law in the first but a categorical authorial claim; undeniable legal right in the other, but a highly disputable assertion of authorship. They illustrated arguments for the private profits and the public costs of finding property in intellectual works, and they did so at the historical moment of transition from feudalism to capitalism.

To either side of this diptych, two sections recount the changes and developments in 'copyright' law, from the earliest privileges issued in the reign of Charles VIII (1483–98), to the last significant decree regulating bookselling and the printing trades promulgated under Louis XVI (r. 1774–92): the *arrêt* of 1777. The landmark dates and events along the way are briefly these: the 1566 Ordinance of Moulins by which earlier censorship acts were linked to privilege; the chartering in 1618 of the Corporation des libraires et maîtres imprimeurs de Paris, and the incorporation of privilege in its statutes; the extension of pre-publication censorship and privilege from new books to all books in 1649; the regulations arising from a ruling of the Conseil du roi in 1665, which upheld unlimited renewals of privilege's term, rendering it de facto perpetual; the decades of the 1720s and 1760s, when battles between the Paris and the provincial booksellers over renewal were at a height; and the *arrêt* of 1777, by force of which an article of commercial law for merchant booksellers, publishers and printers was seemingly transformed by the Conseil du roi into a principle of civil law for authors by tacit recognition of their claim to property in their work. (See Key dates, pp. 9–12.) Not all of these customs, rules and decisions were also relevant to printed pictures but, by determining the legal discourse on privilege, they established the terms in which copy-protection for images was articulated and regulated, and in relation to which it was theorised and debated.[5]

Both the simple, chronological history of the legislation and the more convoluted and composite account of artistic practices in the La Fontaine and *Encyclopédie* cases engage with the question of authorship first raised by Michel Foucault. Foucault readily confessed to a singular concern with the what, or constructed nature, of the author; he left to others the how, when and why of the writer's individuation.[6] The historian Carla Hesse has taken up that inquiry for books in France, demonstrating in the process the very equivocal response of the Enlightenment to the legal and economic gains made by the book trade and its authors from the sixteenth century, and especially under Absolutism.[7] This chapter attempts a parallel inquiry in relation to artists and prints.[8]

I have used Horace's famous phrase *ut pictura, poesis* ('in painting, as in poetry'), for this chapter's title to draw attention to the way in which similarity in text–image relations has generally underpinned historical accounts of copyright's extension from literature to art. In so doing, I want to question the exact fit of that relation of supposed identity between the printed image and the printed word in the context of law. Having explored their material and technological differences, we shall then ask, what influence did these differences have on the conceptualisation of privilege and the formulation of its terms? Nowhere were the conjunctions and disjunctions between word and image more apparent, perhaps, than in the illustrated book. In books, word and image cohabit. The text–image relation in books was more than a material, formal and technological one. It was embedded in social and economic relations: in the skills, workshops, supply chains and marketplaces of the early modern printing trades. In the illustrations for La Fontaine's *Fables* and in the plates for Diderot and d'Alembert's *Encyclopédie*, we shall see how conflicting conceptualisations of authorship and ownership were materialised in the illustrations and also how legal arguments in disputes over market share were variously shaped by the operations of such images. Horace's static simile of poetry and painting, was, I shall argue, transformed by its contact with the laws of the market into a dynamic modern analogy, by means of which both were yoked to a third term, 'property', the better to achieve the mixed end of honour and profit.

FROM TEXT TO IMAGE: THE EARLY HISTORY OF PRIVILEGE

· *Privilèges exclusifs* and Renaissance monarchy ·

Eighteenth-century accounts of the beginning of privilege represented it as the coordinated response of the monarchy and book trade to the progress of printing. The lawyer Louis d'Héricourt and the *philosophe* Denis Diderot, writing on behalf of the Paris booksellers and printers, respectively in 1725 and 1763, invoked an innocent state before privileges, characterised on the one hand by 'liberty', or the freedom of everyone to print 'that which seemed good to him',[9] and on the other by 'reasonable profits' realised in non-competitive markets, where reprinting was, they alleged, unknown.[10] In the reign of Henri II (1547–59), however, liberty turned into licence: peace was threatened by the publication of opinion contrary to religion, law and order, and the balance of trade was violated by 'greedy and mediocre men' who undercut quality and honest profit with 'malicious' reprints.[11] These transgressions, d'Héricourt and Diderot agreed, gave rise to privilege.

If d'Héricourt and Diderot were, in fact, mistaken in the coincidence they supposed between the introduction of compulsory licensing and privilege, they were not in suggesting that privilege was a response to the expanding and competitive market for books, brought about by the introduction of printing. In 1469, Johann Speyer had been given a privilege by the Collegio of Venice, the first of its kind in Europe, to protect the new technology that he had brought with him to the Republic from Mainz.[12] The first recorded privilege in France, granted in 1498, was not a similar inducement directed at foreign printers; it offered protection to an already established industry, the first printing press in France having been set up in Paris in 1470.[13] In the fifteenth century, France was the third largest producer of books after Germany and Italy, and it doubled its output in the first 20 years of the following century.[14] The cost of press, type and especially paper was not trivial.[15] Moreover, significant resources of capital were needed to finance an edition and keep printing presses active during the interval before returns from sales came in. For these reasons, Lucien Febvre and Henri-Jean Martin characterise the new industry, concentrated in Paris, Lyon and Rouen, as commodity production from the beginning.[16] A small-scale transition in the economy, from *scriptorium* to printing shop, was, they imply, aligned with transformations apparently occurring on a much larger scale, in the economy as a whole.

Privilege, by this account, is a reflection of that change. According to Elizabeth Armstrong, it rapidly established itself as the norm for new books, though it was not available for old. Her study of the early years of the privilege system charts the issuance of more than four hundred privileges between 1498 and 1526.[17] Of these titles, 50 per cent was made up of theological and law books in more or less equal measure.[18] Were we to relate the conditions of producing books to their contents, specifically to legal humanism, it might be tempting to follow d'Héricourt and Diderot and see in Renaissance privilege the origin of intellectual property – property defined, that is, according to Roman law, and entailing absolute rights of possession and alienation.[19] The language and the terms of the first privileges suggest otherwise.

Sixteenth-century letters patent emphasise the relationship between the petitioner and the figure of legal authority more than they do the thing in hand. That relationship is represented as personal: the petitioner is reported to have made his or her request for privilege to the king directly, and the king enunciates his reply in person.[20] Routinely called 'supplicant' or 'servant', the petitioner is always known, and always named. Moreover, she, or more often he, is addressed in the terms of courtesy, as 'our dear' and 'our best-beloved'. Love implies a bond that pre-dates the moment of application and that will endure beyond the instant of gratification. In terms of the opposition between gift and commodity, classically used to model the differences between so-called traditional societies and modern capitalist economies, early privileges in France would seem to belong more to the personal and durable relations characteristic of the first than to the impersonal and transient relations that define the second, notwithstanding the fact that they served the interests of commodity producers.[21] Liberality was a princely virtue of the first importance in pre-modernity, and was explicitly invoked in the first fully recorded book privilege in France, issued to Eloy d'Amerval: in January 1507 Louis XII had 'pleasure' in showing the poet his 'grace' and 'magnanimity', looked 'favourably upon his petition' and granted it.[22] Privileges were, in this sense, similar to appointments, pensions, lodgings, exemptions, gratifications and other *dons* that kings gave in return for the talents of the gifted.[23] Indeed, one gift might entail another: in 1539 the printer and humanist scholar Robert Estienne was appointed the Imprimeur du roi pour le latin et l'hébreu, to which office was newly attached an entitlement to a five-year royal privilege on any work of which he should choose to print the first edition.[24]

Gifts are defined not only by the continued presence of persons (giver and receiver) in them – that is, by their inalienability; they are also marked by reciprocity. Something must be returned.[25] A petition for privilege was sometimes preceded and sometimes followed by a gift of the book itself.[26] In Estienne's edition of Luigi Alamanni's *La coltivatione*, for which he was granted a ten-year privilege on 28 August 1546, such exchanges are registered in the book: the text of the privilege was printed in full, facing the dedication to François I, the two leaves inseparable, forming an independent gathering, in most cases bound into copies of the poem at the back.[27] But counter-gifts need not be thought of solely in directly relevant and tangibly expressed forms. They were also offered in labour and loyalty. D'Amerval was granted a privilege in 1507 because, like others 'of our particular *servants*', his 'labours' served the king.[28] More directly, between 1537 and 1547 Estienne was given exceptional six-year privileges for printing and publishing a number of books and pamphlets on François I's wars in Italy, on his alliance with the Ottoman Empire and on the inaugural events of reigns.[29] Moreover, the title-pages of the official accounts of François I's funeral and Henri II's coronation, which Estienne was responsible for printing, are each inscribed 'By order and privilege of the said Lord [king]', and thus bring patronage and privilege into direct typographical and discursive relation.

When, in 1552, Estienne wrote about his years of royal service, he acknowledged François's 'great liberality' and his unstinting protection against the envious and malicious attacks of others, and he sought to reconcile his flight from France with his 'duty' to so magnanimous a king and to his public.[30] The assaults he spoke of were those of the Faculty of Theology at the Sorbonne; in celebrating the king's protection, he approved the precedence of secular over religious authority in matters of censorship. The king's permission to publish is presented as facilitative not repressive; it is, so to speak, his 'order', or patronage in legal form, and is thus protection under another name.[31] In Estienne's case it proved insufficient; he therefore believed himself relieved of his royal obligation. Estienne was, of course, a special case and not representative of publishers, printers and writers as a whole. But that is also the point. Privilege and permission in the sixteenth century were singular acts aimed at particular people in particular circumstances. Only after repeated acts of legislation, which culminated in the royal Ordinance of Moulins (1566), were privilege and permission formulated into something resembling a general rule.[32] By article 77 of the ordinance, all were prohibited from writing, printing and publishing libellous and defamatory works likely to disturb the peace; by article 78 none was allowed to print and publish new works without pre-publication permission and a privilege issued under the Grand sceau (great seal) of the Chancellerie. To this was added the requirement that the printer print his name, address and the privilege in the book in question.[33]

To emphasise the formalities of the early letters patent, and the relation between the petitioner and the figure of legal authority paraded in them, is to argue that in the sixteenth century privilege was not only, and perhaps not even primarily, a legal instrument for the construction and protection of monopolies in books. It is to suggest that when printers, publishers and writers printed 'Cum Privilegio Regis' or 'Avec Privilège du Roy' prominently on the title-pages of books, some even incorporating the title of protection into their makers' marks, they did so rather for the symbolic value the inscription entailed, for the prestige.[34] Of course, notification of privilege in books and later in prints by such inscriptions, or by reproduction of the letters patent, gave due warning to potential re-printers that legal monopoly had been secured. But at a time when litigation was long and expensive and its outcome uncertain,[35] the credit of royal attention converted the time and money invested in producing a book and acquiring a privilege into symbolic capital that could later be reconverted into material capital accumulated from higher sales. This in turn eased access to finance for the next publishing enterprise.[36] The instrumentality of privilege was, that is to say, positive and honorific as well as defensive; in short, privilege was articulated in the dominant ideology of patron–client relations.

Prestige also accrued to the king, through his support and protection for letters, arts and sciences. It is probably for this reason, as well as in order to strengthen the force of privilege, and of the state through privilege, that Henri II sought to monopolise responsibility for its issuance, curtailing the power to grant privilege, which before 1566 was enjoyed also by the University of Paris, the Prévôté de la ville de Paris (town hall) and, most importantly, the Parlements in Paris (France's highest sovereign court) and in the provinces.[37] He manoeuvred to engross the symbolic power and social capital that attach to the one able to outstrip all others in the performance of liberality, and to centralise rule of the book trade in his hands. The monarchy's eventual success in establishing mandatory pre-publication permissions and in virtually eliminating the privilege-conferring rights of all other authorities in the realm was a victory, that is, not only in the exercise, but also in the symbolic expression of the power of patronage.

· Privileges and prints in the sixteenth century ·

In a political culture where privilege was a resource of patronage, were writers, and by extension artists, authors? And were their writings and designs works? Foucault ties the emergence of the author to the market and to the instruments of its control: copyright and censorship.[38] In fact, the legal system is the first 'characteristic' he identifies with author-function, followed by the discursive practices of attribution and of the separation of the category 'author' from the historical person of the writer or artist. Copyright sets the historical scene around 1800 for his argument that authorship is an interpretative construct that arises from the way texts are dealt with in politics, law and literature. Although they are listed first and prioritised, institutional systems such as the law are nevertheless superstructural in Foucault's account. They are not the foundation upon which author-function rests, but a sphere of its operations, determined by history and culture. Armstrong's history of privilege *c.*1500 provides slim pickings to support the connections Foucault draws between discourses: in the first 25 years of the sixteenth century no more than 25 per cent of petitioners for Chancellerie privilege were writers. Meanwhile, artists and illustrators were virtually absent from the historical record, though 20 per cent or more of incunabula and early sixteenth-century books were illustrated.[39] The majority of those petitioning for privilege consisted of publishers and printers, very occasionally of patrons. Moreover, justification for monopoly, whether the writer's or the publisher's, was invariably expressed in economic terms: return on the 'pains and labours' performed by the applicant in producing the book – the physical thing. The relevance of the author and the work to the concept of privilege is thus open to question. And, given the priority seemingly attributed to money in the anticipated consequences of privilege, another question arises: was there a conflict at the heart of privilege between the culture and ideology of patronage, with its courtesies, duties and loyalties, and newer, proto-capitalist arguments about work and property?

Artists were doubly anonymous in privilege in the sixteenth century. Not only were they mostly absent as petitioners, even when others made mention of illustrations in their applications for protection, but also the designers and printmakers responsible were not generally named. For example, the privilege obtained by the poet and playwright Pierre Gringore in 1515 for *Les Fantasies de mère Sotte*, one the earliest of its kind for an illustrated book, made particular mention of the 28 figurative scenes (*histoires*) but identified neither the designer nor the printmaker.[40] The supplementary nature and secondary standing of illustration is, of course, the obvious explanation. But even in the case of those books excluded from privilege, such as bibles, prayer books and other liturgical manuals, and where protection could be solicited only on grounds of additions, notably ornaments, artists are rarely indicated. The figurative scenes and ornamental borders (*vignettes*), some *à Lantique*, others *à la Moderne*, for which the publisher Geoffroy Tory successfully petitioned for monopoly in 1524 to decorate his Latin Book of Hours (1525) are today widely attributed to him on grounds of style; he is not identified in the letters patent as the author.[41] Uncertainty continues to plague this instance of attribution, in part because the evidence of re-use of the woodblocks in the 1530s reveals that the *vignettes* – in some of which, *plaquettes* inscribed with Tory's name are suspended in the scrollwork – were further exploited by Simon de Colines, Tory's printer and collaborator on the Book of Hours; only the 'histories' belonged to Tory's stock.[42] Not until 1530, when the Italian artist Francesco Pellegrino petitioned for a privilege for a collection of 62 printed embroidery patterns, 'in the Arabian and Italian manner', entitled *La Fleur de la science de pourtraicture*, can we say unequivocally that an artist was granted a monopoly on the same basis as a writer, publisher, printer or cartographer.[43]

Tory and de Colines's Hours introduces another condition specific to image production in its relation to matters of privilege and authorship. Printmakers sold their woodblocks to publishers, just as writers sold their manuscripts. De Colines came to own the ornamental borders not because he was the designer but because they represented part of his share of the assets relating to the publication. But woodblocks were exploited commercially in different ways from manuscripts. While images were often commissioned for particular texts, those texts did not determine their trade life. Publishers in the fifteenth and early sixteenth centuries recycled illustrations, often including them in publications seemingly for no other purpose than to provide ornamental relief to the eye.[44] Eloy d'Amerval's *Le Livre de la déablerie* (1507), for example, is decorated on its title-page with a scene in which the writer is depicted, his name inscribed on the scroll that unfolds across his knees; elsewhere the poem sports an extra and superfluous recycled portrait of a writer in his study, made generic by arbitrary re-use.[45] Not only were images open to re-purposing, they were also materially indeterminate: woodblocks were often altered and re-cut for new ventures. The blocks of many of the 65 full-page, full-figure illustrations for Charles Estienne's *De dissectione partium corporis humani*, printed and published by de Colines in 1545, include insertions made of separately cut plugs representing dissected portions of anatomy that are nested into pre-existing blocks depicting the human figure.[46] Publication of the text had been delayed for six years because of a legal dispute about credit for the anatomies, but this was not between the writer Charles Estienne, holder of the privilege, and any one of the many draughtsmen and woodcutters involved directly and indirectly in producing the blocks, but between the writer and the surgeon, Estienne de La Rivière, responsible for the anatomical preparations.[47] It is impossible to talk about illustrators as authors in the sixteenth century, not only because they were both largely absent from and anonymous in privilege, but also because they were not the point of reference for the integrity and authenticity of their creations.

Armstrong speaks of an 'extension' of privilege from texts to images, but, as the discussion above indicates, there were historically determined and innate differences between the printed word and the printed picture.[48] Just as the status and role of the writer and artist were different, so too was the nature of their respective work. The immateriality of the text is a presumption of copyright; was the same true of privilege, and specifically of pictorial representations in law? A positive answer assumes a clear distinction between manuscripts and illuminations on the one hand and printed books and illustrations on the other. Many books of the period were hybrid: part printed, part painted.[49] Individual copies of Tory's and de Colines's 1525 Book of Hours are, for instance, variously hand-coloured.[50] It is not unreasonable, therefore, to suppose that a text was apprehended in the sixteenth century as a tangible thing and not necessarily as an abstract, intellectual composition.

Laurent Pfister has proposed a connection between the early discourse on privilege and the late medieval commentaries on the legal problem of *tabula picta* in Roman law: that is, on the question of to whom a manuscript belongs in cases where the owner of the parchment is not also the source of the writing or painting.[51] The answer depended on the nature of the union between pigments and support.[52] When colourants merely covered the wall, panel, canvas or paper, the status of the pigments and inks was that of 'accessory', and the owner of the support retained possession. However, painting a *picture* on a wall, panel, canvas or page resulted in a new 'specification' because the picture was neither of the support nor of the pigments but was *in* the conjunction or mixing of the two, which produced a new 'species'.[53] In the case of writing, a consensus was reached by the fifteenth century that writing was not ever an accessory, and that the writer necessarily enjoyed superior claim. With regard to painting, however, the greater entitlement of the artist was not completely settled by representation; it was also a matter of *dignitas* and was judged contingent on the value of the pigments used and the nobility of the subject matter.[54] In privilege we see divergence in the treatment of text and image occurring along similar lines. Reprinting 'the said book' was prohibited purely and simply. The prohibition of the reprinting of images required, by contrast, qualification of the ban's scope. Tory's privilege for his Book of Hours, for instance, forbad rival publishers and printers to copy the 'histories and *vignettes*'; additionally, it specified that such prohibition obtained 'whether all on a white, grey or red ground' – that is, irrespective of the colour of the support, and notwithstanding differences of size and scale.[55] The letters patent thereby drew attention to the image's materiality and implied that conditions could exist in which copying might be legitimate. In the absence of titles, words denoting the work of illustration were not sufficient absolutely to define it.[56] While privilege implicitly denied that the object of the requested monopoly was identical with the physical properties of the edition in question, case narratives of individual letters patent for illustrated books simultaneously constituted illustrations as surfaces to be looked at (not looked through or read) precisely by calling attention to their sensible properties: their colour and size.

The print scholar Charles Talbot has argued that this difference between text and image is inherent, and arises from the fact that the word (not the writing) is, as he put it, 'the reality of the printer'. With the invention of printing with movable type, that reality 'became available with every impression.'[57] By contrast, the printed image is a 'translation' of three dimensions into two and of painting into print. It is thus doubly removed from the real represented. This philosophical argument denies the printed word a sensible dimension, and overlooks the historical case for the role of form in the metaphysical construal of the text. In France, the dematerialisation of the printed word owed not a little to a later publication of Geoffroy Tory, his *Champfleury, au quel est contenu l'art et science de la... vrai proportion des lettres attiques... autrement lettres romaines... selon le corps et visage humain* (1529). This writing manual helped successfully to steer French publishing towards a level of typographical harmonisation – by the use of Roman letters of the same font, pitch and thickness – that produced an effacement of type in the process of reading.[58] Thereafter, the text, not the type, the writer not the printer emerged progressively as the reader's only acknowledged interlocutors.[59] In contrast, dematerialisation as an effect of the image was the product not only of techniques and technology, but also of genre and discourse. With regard to so-called 'portraits' of nerves, veins and arteries, Charles Estienne acknowledged in 1546 that he had no case against copyists, because the illustrations of his *De dissectione* (1545), which had been extensively pirated in between the pulling of first proofs in 1539 and the date of publication, were so many mirrors of nature, and (unlike 'histories', therefore) contained nothing of him in them.[60] Looking through, in the case of *ad vivum* depictions of nature or 'portraits' belonged to the practices and the self-effacing discourses of imitation particular to painting and to science.[61] The concern, such as it was, that Estienne did express about unauthorised copies in the preface of his book related to the danger to public information arising from the dissemination of inaccurate and potentially deceptive counterfeits, rather than to the personal injustice and injury he suffered from commercially aggressive copies.

To summarise: artists, unlike some writers, were not privilege-conscious in the sixteenth century.[62] Privilege was not an integral part of their artistic enterprise. Nor did artists make use of other self-promotional strategies to make known their authorship in law or in their work. Few woodcuts are signed or monogrammed.[63] The prints themselves, especially religious prints, belonged to a medieval workshop tradition of craft, in which the corporeal value of the image – the quality of the printing, the added value of the hand-colouring – prevailed. Dematerialisation of the image occurred with the emergence of genres of representation determined rather by discourses of imitation and informed by an optical experience of the world. But intangibility did not go hand in hand with subjectification – that is, with the inward indexing of the 'author'; discursively it was an effect of reference to objects out in the world.

One issue remains: the purpose of privilege. Whose interests did it serve? Armstrong notes that 'so persistent throughout the period are the references made by authors to the expectation of profit, if duly protected by privilege, that the question must be asked how they hoped to make this profit'.[64] Cynthia Brown's work on sixteenth-century vernacular writers reveals that poets and playwrights like Gringore were directly involved in the commercial exploitation of their work, overseeing its publication and managing its distribution.[65] It is unlikely, however, that Francesco Pellegrino, the one artist to obtain a privilege for his own work in the early sixteenth century, did the same. His pattern book was printed by Jacques Nyverd, a mid-range, mid-ranking printer in Paris, who in the 1520s and 1530s obtained privileges for a miscellany of leaflets and books in French, and whose resources to print, publish and distribute the embroidery patterns were significantly better than Pellegrino's, a recent arrival from Italy.[66] Even among writers, Gringore was exceptional. One is therefore led to ask whether the phrase 'great pain and efforts' (*grande peine et labeurs*), used by petitioners to justify their applications for privilege was, in fact, a figure of legal speech.

It has the ring of a commonplace. In the sixteenth century, 'pain' and 'efforts' belonged to ethics as well as to the discourse on commerce. Their origin was Hesiod's binary opposites *ponos* and *ergon*, or manual and cerebral labour. In this moral context, 'pain' and 'efforts' referred, therefore, to the quality of production, and not to the quantity of labour power used to estimate whether and for how long legal monopoly should be granted in order for business to profit. High *labeur*, or art, elevated objects of privilege above other forms of unalloyed toil and marked them out as worthy of protection.[67] Low *peine*, meanwhile, is more than a simple negative. Pierre Bourdieu enriches its historical meaning by relating it to proverbial lore, and by interpreting it in the context of a pre-capitalist peasant economy, which was, he argues, ideologically obedient to the logic of gift-exchange: 'Give to the earth and the earth will give to you.'[68] The rhetoric of courts, both law courts and royal courts, is, of course, another matter. But there is a good case for interpreting references to 'pains' in sixteenth-century privilege applications according to the same rules of reciprocity – that is (to paraphrase

Bourdieu), as justifying royal largesse by the care and attention brought to the task and offered to the king as tribute. As someone in the entourage of Rosso Fiorentino, a painter invited to France to lend his superior talent to the decoration of François I's new palace at Fontainebleau, Pellegrino was not only asking for market protection for his designs; like Rosso, he was honouring the king with a new style (*façon italique*) equal to His Majesty's cultural ambitions. Significantly, the page immediately following the transcription of the letters patent on page 2 of *La Fleur* is a knot pattern *semé de lis* – that is to say, a variant on the royal coat of arms, known to heraldry as *France ancien*; it is the only such French pattern in the book.

Both the formalities and the content of early privilege were articulated in the language and terms of feudal custom and ideology. Pellegrino was distinguished in his letters patent as a 'nobleman' (*noble homme*); copying of his 'inventions' and 'compositions' was prohibited for six years in reward for his service in fulfilling the king's ambition to 'comprehend in our kingdom all the proper and polite arts'. The lawyer Simon Marion, esteemed for his eloquence, and professionally active in more than one case of privilege infringement, called privilege, in fact, a 'right of patronage' (*droit de patronage*).[69] Insofar as it may also have been informed by Roman law, Ian Maclean proposes a connection with *ius prohibendi*, not *possidendi*: law relating to use, not ownership.[70] The context for *ius prohibendi* in Justinian's Institutes was resolution of disputes over land use, crucially when landed property is held in common. Privilege, though not about land but rather about a movable thing created by new technology and commercial capital, construed petitioners nevertheless as tenants, not freeholders. Moreover, ambiguity prevailed in this legal system over the nature of the art and the writing (material or intellectual) for which protection was sought. Finally, writers and artists were, in contrast to publishers, mostly 'peripheral' to its rule, to use Laurent Pfister's word.

· Privileges and the early modern state ·

The history of copy-privilege in the seventeenth century is often said to trace, on a smaller scale, grander developments occurring in the formation of the early modern state. Royal officialdom, Roland Mousnier calculated, increased more than tenfold between the beginning of the sixteenth century and the mid-seventeenth century; its purpose and effect were the centralisation and consolidation of royal power by means of bureaucracy.[71] Sixteenth-century royal ordinances, such as the Ordinance of Moulins (1566), had initiated the process of legal unification by putting laws into force throughout the kingdom. These reform ordinances were, however, very wide-ranging; the 86 articles of the 1566 ordinance, which included those on censorship and privilege mentioned above, covered almost all aspects of government. In the seventeenth century, legislation became more focused; so-called 'ordinances of codification' were directed at specific spheres of law, with the aim of bringing uniformity and coherence to its regulation.[72] The Chancellerie, responsible for the issuance of letters patent arising from legislation on privilege, enjoyed, after a brief period of inactivity during the reign of Henri IV, a heyday under the protection of Richelieu and the direction of Pierre Séguier, appointed Garde des sceaux (keeper of the seals) by Louis XIII in 1633 and Chancellor two years later. Séguier remained in office on and off until his death in 1672.[73] An expanded staff of censors and *secrétaires du roi* was recruited, many from the Sorbonne and the ranks of the recently founded Académie française, to whom Séguier entrusted the tasks of reading the submitted manuscripts, drafting the letters of privilege and recording the judgments made at the Chancellor's *séances*.[74] By the 1660s, book and print privileges had become sufficiently standard for Du Sault, a Chancellerie court usher, to devise and publish model letters for use by publishers, writers and printmakers.[75] This form of administrative governance seems to break with earlier *droits de patronage*, the power of which depended on presence.[76] Instead, the *embourgeoisement* of the state by the class of its officers led to an expanding body of commercial regulation that included privilege. By means of it the Absolutist monarchs of the seventeenth century took the art of government to the marketplace in order to ameliorate conditions there by meticulous, attentive and judicious control.[77] Understanding privilege in this new formation requires taking note both of the ways in which it was mediated by the bureaucracies charged with its administration and of the modes of authority that secured the privileged their benefits.

The Chancellerie was not the only body responsible for privilege. In the sixteenth century, the publishing industry in Paris had had no legal status other than as an accessory to the university.[78] Publishers, printers and booksellers had been hostile to any change in their organisation that might jeopardise the privileges that accrued to them as members of a 'liberal' profession. However, in 1618, shortly after the accession of Louis XIII, and owing to widespread disorder in the industry, the trade requested letters patent to establish a legal framework of association and of good professional practice for its members.[79] Privileges granted by the Chancellerie now required registration by the guild. The formation of the *libraires* into a guild (called a 'corporation') did more, however, than add a layer of bureaucracy to the process. Analysis of the statutes suggests that privilege was deeply embedded by them into the *libraires*' corporate habitus, and while it remained formally a royal prerogative, it was thereby en route to becoming a distinction of the corporation. Thus, rather than arguing for the increasing autonomy of the legal field, as the historical context of bureaucratisation might seem to invite, what I want to suggest is that the incorporation of privilege into guild governance brought it from the court and Conseil du roi to the door of the printshop, and led publishers and printers to conceive of themselves as legal subjects entering into special kinds of commercial contract as incorporated members.

To illustrate: the first article of the *libraires*' statutes, by confirming members in the enjoyment of their 'rights, privileges, franchises and prerogatives', bundled jurisdictional claims together; it implied both that copy-privilege constituted a concession among others, which guild membership had the power to bestow, and that, by acceding to one such right, privilege, franchise or prerogative, members necessarily acceded to them all.[80] More directly, by article 33, the Corporation des libraires et maîtres imprimeurs encompassed the king's privilege, translating it into its own prohibition from counterfeiting and trading in forged and reprinted editions. By article 12, meanwhile, the requirement to reproduce letters of privilege at the beginning or end of books was made mandatory; so too, by the same article, was the use of 'elegant type' and 'good-quality paper', and 'accurate proofreading',[81] leading to a conflation of the legal and the material that subsumed privilege further under the guild's manifest of corporate customs and everyday quality controls. Indeed, positioned between those articles that define conditions for membership on the one hand, and those that prohibit encroachment by non-members on the other, article 12 appears to be that upon which the distinction of master *libraire* and *imprimeur* actually turns: apprentices and journeymen might aspire, like masters, to publish privileged texts; writers were forbidden by article 14 to involve themselves directly in the publication and sale of their work.[82]

The most significant of the new measures introduced by the 1618 regulations was, arguably, the exclusion of writers from the manufacture of literary texts. While it did not prevent them petitioning for protection, when successfully obtained privilege was nevertheless rendered inactive in their hands. Careers like those of the playwright Gringore and the poet Clément Marot, who published and distributed their own works, were no longer possible under the new regime. Only by ceding material production to a printer or publisher – that is, to a member of the Corporation – could they make their works public. Thus, in the context of writing at least, from 1618 the Corporation represented (directly or indirectly) the interests of all privilege holders. In Joseph-Nicolas Guyot's typology of privileges, book privilege assumed, you could say, the appearance of a *privilège réel*, or privilege belonging to a place or order – for instance, a guild – in contradistinction to those attributed to individuals personally.[83] Moreover, by force of the Corporation's statutes the patrimonial ideology of privilege came to function increasingly in the economic foundation of the book industry. During the course of the seventeenth century the Paris Corporation acted to accumulate the legal authority and expand the scope of its appropriated right, maximising the economic advantages thereby accruing to its members. I do not want to suggest by this a division between the ideologies of the Crown and the commercial interests and objectives of the trade. On the contrary, consequent upon Chancelier Séguier's interventions in the elections of the guild's wardens in the 1640s, the Corporation was to all intents and purposes co-opted, transformed into an oligarchy loyal to the king.[84] However, it is also to recognise that in matters of privilege the Corporation was a mediator, not an intermediary.[85] Which is to say that in registering and communicating information about privilege it translated it into its own bourgeois terms and worked to extend the powers of its regulation to corporate and individual members' advantage.

In the 1630s and 1640s the capital's master *libraires* and *imprimeurs* began to enclose what is referred to today as the public domain and what in the sixteenth century was called 'la liberté de l'imprimerie', or the freedom of printing. Informally, the Chancellerie started to grant privileges in second editions – that is, in old texts formerly excluded from the regulations – and also to renew privileges on first editions.[86] These gains and this new trading position, secured by extra-legal favour, was in time consolidated in law. In 1649, new letters patent, issued after the first Fronde (1648–9) on behalf of the Paris *libraires*, added to the corpus of modern writers already indexed by privilege all works by 'the Church Fathers, Greek or Latin' and 'by [the] good Authors of antiquity', thereby hugely increasing the number of works potentially under monopoly and, incidentally, vastly expanding the canvas on which the king's role in the emergent fields of art, science and literature could be represented.[87] In 1665 (and following a dispute between the booksellers of Paris and Rouen), the informal custom of renewing privileges became statutory for both ancient and modern works, though in the case of the former only in circumstances where the work had been expanded or corrected 'considerably'.[88]

Together, the new regulations of 1649 and 1665 altered publishing practices profoundly and transformed perceptions of the literary field. In 1586, when Simon Marion expressed, perhaps for the first time in law, the 'sovereignty' that an 'author' may be said to have over his or her own work, he did so, as Pfister has noted, in order to defend not privilege but the world of print beyond its limits.[89] Marion contended that, in the absence of privilege having been obtained, a book once published could not be returned to the privacy of ownership. His choice of terms for the status of text pre- and post-publication is especially forceful and leaves little doubt where merit lies: in the hands of the author the manuscript is 'enslaved'; in print it is 'liberated' to circulate for the public.[90] Privilege, by this account, was slavery artificially extended beyond publication. The profit known to be made in real slavery served to demystify the motivation for privilege by analogy. Some 70 years later the publisher Antoine Vitré presented matters very differently. In the context of the long economic crisis that followed the Fronde (1648–53), the liberty of printing was, he insisted in his memorandum on privilege, no better than licence and chaos.[91] He mounted his defence of absolute protection (for all books and potentially for all time) on corporate grounds: restoring peace to the trade and securing quality products for consumers. Privilege was necessary to mitigate risk; only indirectly did he acknowledge that renewal also increased significantly the monetary value of literary assets.

In addition to the extension of power in particular privileges, in the 1640s the Chancellerie also devised a category of so-called 'general' privilege that it issued to favoured individuals for a genre or corpus of publications.[92] This and the measures put in place by the regulations of 1618, 1649 and 1665 had the collective effect of drawing lines of economic conflict between the Crown and its favoured circle of publishers in Paris on one hand, and the capital's more modest publishers, provincial booksellers and professional writers on the other.[93] Resistance was widespread, and ministerial and judicial attention in the second half of the seventeenth century, especially under Colbert, turned from legislating to the enforcement of privilege law.[94] The 1687 *Statuts et règlemens des imprimeurs et libraires de Paris*, the last to be promulgated in the seventeenth century, thus did little more than reiterate the rulings established in 1618, 1649 and 1665.[95] However, by arranging them in logical sequence under three consecutive clauses – prohibition (art. 65), privilege (art. 66), exemption (art. 67) – it assigned to privilege an autonomy and rationale newly powerful and persuasive. It implied, in other words, that privilege was not so much a royal gift as a given of the guild.[96]

The evidence of seventeenth-century letters patent seems, at first, to contradict this assertion. Their language and format appear unchanged, especially in instances of royal commission. In the letters for *Les Triomphes de Louis le juste, XIII* (1649), produced at the king's 'express command', the petitioner and engraver Jean Valdor is twice recognised and twice favoured: conventionally as 'Our dear and best-beloved', and in practical service as 'Our engraver'. In the book's preface, Valdor acknowledges the 'honour' of the charge, and expresses confidence in the 'liberality' of the 'Great'.[97] The king's privilege is reproduced, moreover, opposite an engraved monument to Louis XIII, an architectural metaphor for the text, for whose conservation and endurance the notice of the law, by its juxtaposition, is registered as the essential warranty.[98] Specific reference to gift-giving may have disappeared from the exact wording of letters of privilege but it was still, in this example, its explicit context. In the case of commercial publications also, such as Abel Langelier and Matthieu Guillemot's illustrated 1614 edition of Philostratus' *Imagines*, privilege was granted, the letters asserted, for 'the pleasing services' – specifically, publication of the 'various books' printed 'in honour of our kingdom' – that the publishers had 'performed on several and similar occasions' for Henri IV and some of his predecessors.[99]

The discrepancy between the economic functions of privilege, enacted by repeated revisions of the legislation concerning it, and its normative content, expressed in particular letters granted – norms of honour and service – may in part be explained by the endurance of law as a discursive institution.[100] But that institution did also evolve. There is a subtle but steady shift of focus in seventeenth-century letters patent from the subject to the object of privilege – that is, from the writer, printer or publisher in his or her relation to the sovereign to the book or print. The decision to illustrate Philostratus' *Imagines*, arguably the most important antique source of visual imagery after Ovid's *Metamorphoses*, was, according to the text of the privilege, prompted by a desire to promote the 'perfect understanding' of the text by supplying the 'corporeal eye' of the reader with those pictures that text alone could no more than suggest to the 'spiritual eye'.[101] Appreciation of the added value of the 68 full-page illustrations was thus as much the reason for the renewal of privilege as the obligation to return a service for those received. Indeed, note of the illustrations, commentaries, annotations and amplifications, 'never before seen', precedes reference in the letters to the sundry services of the publishers. Moreover, and perhaps as a direct consequence, the meaning of labour in privilege discourse also appears altered. Reference to 'pains' disappears, and labour is coupled instead with costs (*dépenses*). Langelier and Guillemot described their fear of being cheated of 'the fruit of their labour' and, if not that, of suffering 'a slow-down in sales', and thus 'loss of over 4,000 *écus* already spent on having plates engraved' were their application denied.[102] Not only did seventeenth-century privileges register and count costs in labour and capital, they also balanced them against the duration of privileges granted. In 1656, Pierre Corneille successfully petitioned for a renewal of privilege for, arguably, the publishing sensation of the century, his verse translation of Thomas à Kempis's *Imitation of Christ*, on the grounds that the duration of the five-year privilege granted for the first edition had not been long enough to recoup the cost of illustration.[103] The discrepancy between legislation and letters was, it seems, one in appearance only. The prioritisation of books, and of the work and costs necessary to their production in seventeenth-century petitions, registered the transformation in the organisation and economy of the book trade accomplished by the Corporation from 1618, and changes too in the discourse on exchange. Work and want, as Alain Guéry has argued, introduced a different understanding of exchange, one in which the good – that is, the commodity transacted – took precedence over the social relation that the exchange of the good created.[104]

Analysis to this point has focused on the part of the Paris Corporation des libraires et maîtres imprimeurs and its members in the evolution of copy-privilege; it has been much less concerned with the role of the king. The increasing importance of the objects of privilege and of conditions of trade could suggest a corresponding decline in the king's prestige. His signature was, after all, no longer the only one to sanction privilege; his Chancellor, and his Chancellor's *secrétaires*, might authorise them with their own names. At the same time, the reproduction of letters patent in books, made compulsory by article 12 of the 1618 regulations, established a space for representation of the king in every book. Claire Lévy-Lelouch notes that the king was thrust conspicuously and uniquely into view by it.[105] Or, to put it another way, by reproduction of letters patent, privilege was led to play a role in the reception of the books it protected. It assumed symbolic meaning: the ideological and economic supremacy of the state apparatus was asserted, and the king's role in constituting a public sphere of literature was fully displayed.[106] As a *discours d'escorte* in books, privilege transformed the king into an intercessory figure between the writer and the reader. For instance, Louis XIV acknowledged that Corneille's works were 'desired by the whole of our kingdom', and also by 'foreign Countries'; in granting the writer's request Louis appeared to enable the satisfaction of that desire. Utility, both commercial and educational, became the end that justified the monopolies in the king's gift.

The enhancement and extension of the terms of privilege legislation in the first half of the seventeenth century and its better enforcement, coupled in the second half with Colbert's systematic reduction of the number of printshops in France, significantly improved trading conditions for the capital's elite publishers and booksellers.[107] In so doing, arguably, it also created the trading environment for writers to become 'authors', living by their 'works'.[108] What of artists? The *libraires*' register of privileges awarded indicates, on the one hand, that in the seventeenth century many more artists, both designers and printmakers, joined the roll of petitioners, and that some even made privilege part of their regular practice.[109] On the other hand, the evidence of legislation reveals that privilege, as an issue, was a sideshow for the print trade when compared to the central struggle to preserve the profession's freedom, which dominated printmaking in the reigns of Louis XIII and Louis XIV. Though not about privilege directly, the freedom of printmakers was not without effect in relation to it: it preserved for them, and for artists more generally, the right directly to exploit their own creations commercially through print that writers had lost with the foundation of the Corporation des libraires et maîtres imprimeurs in 1618. In principle, at least, they were therefore better placed to cut the bonds of patronage, and to pursue profit individually in the market and become authors in the legal sense. Significant also to the emergence of the artist–author in the seventeenth century were disputes with the booksellers in the immediate aftermath of their incorporation. These, as we shall see, forced printmakers to define their position as creators not mechanics, a definition that was informed by changes in illustration technology. The introduction of intaglio print processes altered the organisation of book production and also both the layout of the printed page and the visuality of the image. It led, I shall suggest, on the one hand to the image's dematerialisation and on the other to its envisioning as a form of property like the depictions of property that it made possible. The emergence of property as a metaphor for intellectual works was linked, that is to say, to the rise in techniques for the representation and reproduction of the material world, which in turn provided a foundation for new ways of thinking about property.

By 1600 intaglio processes and copper-plate printing had largely replaced woodcut in book illustration. Intaglio prints, in which the lines of the design are incised onto a copper plate, either directly with a burin or indirectly by the action of acid, first began to appear in French books in the 1580s. The plates in André Thevet's *Les Vrais Pourtraits et vies des hommes illustres* (1584) were, according to the writer, a novelty, the work of the best engravers he had been able to attract from Flanders.[110] He therefore claimed credit for having first created a vogue for such illustrations in the capital.[111] Copper plates demanded different ink and better-quality paper than woodcuts, and to print them a rolling press, not a hand press, was needed.[112] Illustrations from such plates could not therefore be printed alongside letterpress in a single action, as could those from woodblocks – the text below Thevet's bust portraits is engraved not printed. Intaglio printing transformed the production of illustrated books. It separated the engraving shop from the printing house.[113] Separation, in turn, increased competition; significantly, in the period of transition from the 1580s to the 1630s pirate copying spiked.[114] The liberty of engravers, etchers and printsellers to practise their trades threatened the booksellers' monopoly on publishing books. In 1619, the intaglio printmakers legally challenged the booksellers' right to publish books with engraved illustrations.[115]

At the same time – that is, within months of the Paris Parlement's registration of the 1618 regulations – the Corporation's wardens raided the workshop of Melchior Tavernier the elder, a Flemish engraver and printseller, who, by the second decade of the seventeenth century, was running one of the largest and most important print enterprises in the capital.[116] A miscellany of books was seized, some illustrated, some almost certainly not, some allegedly printed and published by him, others merely on sale.[117] The Corporation's case relied on its statutes and on a series of court rulings (*arrêts*) that from 1577 had expressly forbidden all makers of woodcuts to have types in their shops and to print text.[118] Tavernier's case rested on royal letters patent that had granted him, and his father before him, permission 'to engrave prints' with accompanying 'explanatory and informative text'.[119] The Corporation's initial victory in the case was pyrrhic; in 1620 the Parlement also sanctioned replevin of Tavernier's stock, and while it forbad printmakers to print letterpress it made no mention of publishing illustrated books. The overlap between the book and print industries remained, and, predictably, within a couple of years, Tavernier and the Corporation were back before the Parlement. A single brief survives from each of these disputes, one for each side. They are so closely connected, the one from the second dispute, for Tavernier, responding point by point to the brief from the first for the Corporation, that the disputes may be treated as one. It was a measure of the issue's importance that the guild employed Louis Servin for their defence, one of the foremost barristers of the turn of the century and a *conseiller d'état*. His pleas, including that for the 1619 case, were published in his collected works and remained models of defence on the subject into the eighteenth century.[120]

This dispute, in attempting to establish definitions for the businesses of printers and printmakers in law, marshalled arguments that were of consequence for privilege, and articulated an author-function for the printmaker perhaps for the first time. Before proceeding we should first note that the aims of the parties were different: the booksellers wanted to establish a clear and rigid legal boundary between books and prints in order to draw under their control all printed objects that incorporated letterpress; Tavernier's aim was to preserve the blended nature of the early modern marketplace for printed goods and thereby license intaglio printmakers to publish illustrated books.[121] In his brief, Servin argued for difference, first by a technical enumeration of the instruments and processes respectively of printing and printmaking, and second by mobilising an embodied notion of the divine word after the Fall as simultaneously both written and printed, thereby establishing by order of priority the greater honour and superior right of printers and publishers of words over makers of graven images. He dismissed Tavernier as a vulgar 'Dominotier', or woodblock-cutter, and discredited the image as originally the work of 'the Serpent', though salvaged (he acknowledged) by the Catholic church for the sacred.[122] Printmakers were unsafe and not to be trusted with letters, and should not, he concluded, have access to the printing and publishing of text.

Technologies of print were also an issue addressed by Tavernier's barrister, Labbé. In Labbé's conspicuously secular and historical account, intaglio represents progress: an improvement on woodcut from which it is technologically distinct.[123] *Contra* Servin, Labbé argued that, as inventions, letterpress and intaglio were in fact alike in their modernity; that movable type was not a form of record among others of original divine utterance, but the recent reproduction of the written word. Moreover, he pointed out that for the Corporation des libraires to lay claim to superior qualities of intellect, skill and industry, and thus, by analogy, to the status of writers, its members would have to have been not merely typesetters and printers but the inventors of the die from which particular type was cast.[124] Such was not the case. In his brief, Labbé redrew the lines of distinction between the 'work of the mind' and that of 'the hand' invoked by Servin by matching them, respectively, not with word and image but with invention and reproduction: those responsible for drawing and engraving illustrations he categorised with the first, those involved in setting text with the second.[125] This realignment of engravers and writers, we may note, sometimes received visual expression in title-pages and frontispieces: sixteenth-century woodcuts had incorporated letterpress for titles, etc. In the seventeenth century, and in the context of poetry and fiction, the word was naturalised as cursive writing, the image voicing the author's word not the printer's reproduction of it.[126] More significantly, Labbé attributed qualities of intellect, skill and industry to specific individuals – to Abraham Ortelius and Gerardus Mercator, Jean Errard, Basilius Besler, Jacques Androuet du Cerceau, Pierre Le Muet and so on. Thus, if the plates of their respective books were by convention unsigned, their names served in the brief to index major developments in cartography, fortification, botany and architecture.[127] They functioned, that is to say, authorially.

Although justified by art, Tavernier's case rested in law on letters of privilege, 'privilege' meaning here permission to publish, not protection of monopoly. Labbé narrated the circumstances of their issuance in the familiar and conventional language of royal favour.[128] However, he justified Tavernier's request in terms of the freedom that man necessarily has to support himself and his family by putting his talents to work.[129] This quality of self-possessiveness was that which in later arguments about copyrights secured for the author his or her property in the work. Without getting ahead of history, we can note, however, that arguments about rights to work and entitlements to privilege came together in some letters patent in the 1630s and 1640s: for instance, the printmaker Melchior Tavernier the younger (the elder's nephew), petitioned for transfer of a privilege granted to the writer Pierre d'Hozier for a book on the Order of the Knights of the Holy Ghost, for which Tavernier and Abraham Bosse had provided the illustrations, in order to protect his work and investment, and also to defend him against those 'who want to prevent him from selling his work'.[130] The dual function proposed for the privilege – simultaneously to protect the engraver's skill to produce, publish and sell books, and to establish for him a temporary monopoly over the distribution and sale of the book in question – thus imputed an important relation between freedom of occupational choice and privilege over its products.

At around the same time that intaglio printmakers were starting to assert their authorial claims through litigation, by petitioning for privilege in their own names and by signing their work – Bosse's signature appears on all three plates depicting the 1633 ceremony of the Knights of the Holy Ghost at Fontainebleau in d'Hozier's book – a specifically authorial form of privilege was, according to Nicolas Schapira, in the process of formulation. It too was determined by the new conditions imposed by the 1618 booksellers' regulations, specifically by the exclusion of writers from the business of literature and by the requirement to print letters patent, or extracts from them, in their books.[131] Schapira argues that writers, with the help of Chancellerie personnel, appropriated letters patent as a form of peritext (comparable to a dedication, foreword or colophon), and used them both to promote themselves as authors and to render *honnête* the discourse on commercial monopolies.[132] The painter Charles Le Brun's privilege, granted in 1656, stands comparison in these regards with those of René Descartes, Georges de Scudéry and Jean Chapelain analysed by Schapira. The document was typeset, printed on a folio sheet and decorated with a band of printers' flowers, almost certainly for public display and the widest general notice.[133] In the text of the privilege, Le Brun is named and also identified by all his titles: at that early date in his distinguished career, he was already an *officier* of the Académie royale de peinture et de sculpture (founded in 1648), and a *peintre ordinaire du roi*. Moreover, Louis acknowledged in the letters that Le Brun 'performs daily to Our satisfaction and that of the public'.[134] Eulogy and portrayal were the definitive marks of the seventeenth-century author privilege. Eulogy extended, in Le Brun's letters, beyond his self to the celebration of his works: his paintings sacred and profane, which 'inspire devotion in Churches' and ornament 'our Palaces', are praised uniformly as 'excellent'.

What further distinguished author privilege from publisher privilege was its disavowal of labour and bourgeois trade. The terms of its discourse, that is to say, remained those of honour. The only acknowledgement of work in Le Brun's privilege was that 'painful' but elevated 'experience' of practical education necessary to win acclaim. The model letters produced in 1666 by Du Sault, a Chancellerie court usher, clarify that such 'work' was defined by expenditure not investment – that is, by spending that did not bear directly on production of the commodity: the artist pays to travel abroad in order to develop his or her talents and gain a reputation.[135] And since, to return to Le Brun, 'he has a very marked interest in retaining this esteem, which has spread as far as foreign Provinces', and which would be severely compromised or lost by the proliferation of 'bad copies', the letters granted the painter exclusive choice of printmakers for the reproduction of his work, and forbad all others 'to copy or engrave … or offer for sale' the painter's works.

In the case of writers, one might say that author privilege made a noble virtue out of commercial necessity; the loss of control of book production that authors suffered in 1618 was disguised as voluntary cession of an ignoble and debased task. Le Brun's disinterestedness was not similarly forced: he was free to publish and sell his own work. And if before the 1656 privilege his participation in print had amounted to no more than the occasional supply of designs for frontispieces and illustrations,[136] after its issuance he began to commit important resources of capital and organisation to the reproduction of his oeuvre.[137] At his death in 1690 his stock of copper plates numbered nearly 100 and was valued, with impressions, at 12,500 *livres*, which indicates revenue of consequence.[138] The prints, like the privilege, make no mention of Le Brun's control of the means of their production: his *executit*. Below each image, and to the left, his name is inscribed as author, specifically as the painter (*pinxit*), designer (*delineavit*) or inventor (*invenit*) of the image. It was the address of his printmakers (*sculpsit*), whose names were given to the right, that indicated shops and other outlets. Arguably, Le Brun's contradictory relation to print – display of privilege, omission of address – is best understood as a *féodalisation* of entrepreneurship. It was a stance perpetuated in the legal condition of his bequest of the plates to his heirs: entailed. Exchange value was, it seems, to remain subordinate to the purpose of honouring the memory of the artist's work.[139]

The occasion of the artist's death reveals his authorial privileges to have been actually more circumscribed than the letters proclaimed. The king requisitioned the vast bulk of Le Brun's artistic estate, even though the painter had felt at liberty to will parts of it to his wife and nephew,[140] and notwithstanding the fact that law had assigned him unlimited interests in all present and future works in print. The petition of his widow, Suzanne Butay, against that alienation – specifically against the loss of the drawings Le Brun had made to illustrate his treatise on the passions, unpublished at his death – exposes the non-coincidence of identification and possession in the early modern discourse on artistic authorship.[141] Le Brun's identification with his work was such that Butay begged the favour of a Flagellation and a Nativity that she might have some relic to remember him by; nevertheless, she bowed to the superior claims of the king to all her husband's creative output during the time of his appointment as Premier peintre (1661–90) when he was, she acknowledges, His Majesty's 'possession'.[142] The language of ownership in both petition and privilege related primarily to persons, not things: Le Brun belonged in person to the king and in representation – that is, in dignity – to himself. The two states of belonging were not in conflict. Belonging to the king was, in a society of honour, the necessary precondition of coming into oneself, of establishing a reputation. The ideology of artist privilege was not therefore a corollary of the penetration of the art world by commodity relations; rather, it was underpinned by the very relations of patronage, the absence of which summons rights, justice says, in order to protect authors from the sins of the market.

There were differences in force and not just of form and ideology between the commercial privileges of Tavernier the elder and the reputational one of Le Brun. Author privileges attracted preferential terms: they were generally longer – Le Brun's was in effect perpetual, for lack of a prescribed limit – and higher fines were set for infringements.[143] If better terms and high praise made author privilege more desirable, it did not lead in the second half of the seventeenth century to a noticeable rise in applications within the trade as a whole. Over the course of the century, artist and print privileges never exceeded five per annum.[144] There is no obvious explanation for the modest uptake. Rubens's successful lawsuit against the Paris engraver and publisher Jacob Honervogt for copying works protected by the privileges that the painter had obtained in 1619 and renewed in 1632 raised awareness of privilege and demonstrated the compelling force of French law: by a Parlement ruling in April 1635 all impressions of Honervogt's piracies were destroyed, he was fined, and hefty costs were awarded against him.[145] The reason was thus not lack of knowledge; Marianne Grivel claims that leading artists took note of Rubens's success.[146] It may have been lack of the necessary connections at the Chancellerie, and it may also have been economic. From the outset applicants had to pay to have their letters sealed with the Chancellerie's great seal.[147] Information about this expense in the sixteenth and seventeenth centuries is scant, but we know that by the early eighteenth century the charges were no longer indexed to cost but constituted a tariff of fees levied according to different types of privilege (local or national; of three, six or ten years' duration).[148] Moreover, the successful applicant was required to deposit impressions of the work, in number significantly in excess of the reference copy required in case of litigation, and representing therefore a further outlay to add to the reckoning when calculating whether or not to apply for legal protection.[149] However, more important in limiting recourse to privilege than either social ties or money was the alienation that artists, printmakers and print publishers almost certainly felt from a legal regime perceived as being in the control of, if not exclusively belonging to, the Corporation des libraires et maîtres imprimeurs de Paris.

The boundary between the two trades of bookselling and printmaking had been left unresolved by the Tavernier affair. In 1640, very possibly in order better to resist the continuing interference of the booksellers, a group of 23 predominantly Flemish printmakers and publishers drew up statutes and regulations for the formation of a printmakers' guild. The regulations were primarily directed at the internal organisation and management of the trade but, significantly, the last two of the 16 articles abrogated the right to obtain and register privileges for prints (art. 16) and to judge and penalise infringements (art. 15).[150] Those clauses indicate a desire to bring privilege within the compass of the profession and domesticate it; they suggest an intention to use it when administered by members. Nothing came of the plan, and the *libraires'* power of supervision over privilege in prints continued to rankle: half a century later, when the Paris booksellers and printers were in dispute with those of Lyon and Rouen over privilege renewals, they were in bitter conflict too with the capital's printmakers over deposits.[151] In 1703 the Corporation increased the number it required arbitrarily to three, an increase that infuriated engravers because booksellers 'know neither the value nor the beauty' of prints; they only wanted the additional copies for re-sale.[152]

The 1640 attempt to form a guild was not the only one.[153] In February 1660 another application was made, in the name of Jacques Setton, sieur de Lavenage, and this time it was momentarily successful. Less is known about it, or rather, what is known arises indirectly from opposition to it, opposition that was silent about the professional motives and commercial interests of the some 200 mostly unidentified printmakers and printsellers represented by Lavenage.[154] Lavenage's motive was almost certainly financial prospecting of some kind; the printmakers, publishers and sellers, among them Michel Lasne, in whose name he purported to speak, may nevertheless have expected real trade benefits to arise from this act of incorporation. Whether those anticipated benefits would have included in-house control of privilege, it is impossible to say. It may be significant, however, that among the points made to secure immediate repeal of the guild's foundation, the pastellist and engraver Robert Nanteuil listed the powerlessness of writers and publishers now 'to decorate their books with the works of this profession, because of the expense and tyranny of those who call themselves masters'.[155] By 1660 the *libraires* had managed to stop engravers and print publishers from publishing illustrated books by establishing a legal definition of print as an image with text of no more than six lines above or below, and not running over onto the verso;[156] in 1660 they appear to have supported Nanteuil in order also to overturn the engravers' power to control the price of work and, possibly, their independent regulation of privilege. In the *Abrégé de quelques raisons contre l'établissement d'une maîtrise en l'art de la gravure en taille-douce*, Nanteuil spoke successfully for the interests of those with royal warrants, or under royal protection – in short, for court artists – and seemingly against those from the commercial trade in Paris. I do not want to overstate the place of privilege in the struggle between the various class factions of the print trade at mid-century because the differences between so-called author privilege and commercial privilege were very largely discursive, not substantive, and cannot be neatly mapped onto court and corporation; but I do want to suggest that court artists were by social and cultural advantage better disposed and positioned to use privilege. Within eighteen months of the passage of the Edict of Saint Jean-de-Luz (May 1660), which reversed the decision on Lavenage and enshrined the freedom of printmaking in law, Nanteuil petitioned for and was granted a 21-year privilege on the model of Le Brun's. It listed the artist's accomplishments – his portrait of Louis 'fait d'après ma personne' conspicuous among them – and ambitions, and it desired that under this royal protection Nanteuil 'will work with ever greater concentration, care and application.'[157]

The institutional struggles between and within sectors of the printing trades were less important, however, in the history of privilege than the discourse on printmaking that those conflicts helped to shape. The objections of Nanteuil and elite printmakers to incorporation can be summarised by the word 'genius'. Printmaking was a liberal art, he claimed, and was therefore subject to no other law than genius. Genius in the context of the Edict of Saint Jean-de-Luz had little to do with its everyday, seventeenth-century meaning.[158] In the preamble of the *arrêt* it denoted a particular, not a universal human faculty, and referred to a specific class of professional person. It was not a talent or learned skill, and thus required neither apprenticeship, nor journeymanship, nor entry by ordeal into the profession.[159] Springing from the 'imagination', and not from knowledge, genius in the discourse of the *arrêt* denoted a private possession, fundamentally different from the corporate construction of skill as transferable and thus collective and public in nature.[160] Moreover, the *arrêt* recognised the individuality of genius by acknowledging that 'the manner of each Author of a Print is different from that of every other, there being diversity [of manner] as extensive and various as there are intentions'.[161] Not inherited, learned or made, genius was, according to the edict, an abstract quality. In the context of privilege, it broke absolutely with the discursive tradition that had formerly appeared to assign protection by honour of social status, by office or by role: Le Brun the king's painter, Nanteuil his engraver, and both Academicians. The printmaker and publisher Nicolas de Poilly's privilege, granted in June 1675 for a range of works, including 'several ideas of his Genius' and those he might 'invent' in the future, dispenses with courtly formalities.[162] Justification is exclusively a matter of 'vigils and labours', and commercial risk. The self-possession of genius – Poilly's, in this case – implied ownership in the products of genius and thus in exclusive rights to the financial returns generated by those products. Although property is not mentioned as such, envisaging talent as naturally occurring and freely and uniquely at the disposal of the person endowed – that is, as privately owned – entailed its becoming property in the reproduction of works of art.

The transition from woodcut to engraving also, arguably, played a part in the reconceptualisation of the printed image in law as intangible property. Intaglio stabilised the engraver's contribution and thereby sharpened its legal contour. While the practice of recycling woodcut ornaments such as headpieces and tailpieces continued, intaglio illustrations became text specific.[163] The cost and difficulty of reworking copper plates ensured that in the book industry the practice virtually disappeared.[164] Letters patent specifically prohibited not just the reprinting of a book, but the 'extraction' of its 'figures' for publication in others.[165] These changes together resulted in an illustrative image that was legally more distinct and singular, attributable to the work of one or at most two authors.[166] However, stabilisation does not alone account for the change in the image as the expression of genius's idea, though it was a necessary condition for it. When, at the turn of the seventeenth century, both woodcut and intaglio were in use, letters patent sometimes forbad the copying of designs both in the medium of the original and in its alternative.[167] Where note of the support in sixteenth-century privileges had drawn attention to the materiality of the image, reference in seventeenth-century letters patent to the lines of the illustration's *disegno*, and to the equivalence in law of relief and intaglio processes, deflected attention from matter and defined the privileged image instead as non-medium specific. Endorsement of that reconceptualisation was supplied in the conventional inscription *invenit* after the designer's name; it denied the significance of the medium of the original (painting or drawing), and attributed the image to the maker as invention.[168] In trade, by contrast, the materiality of the printed image remained significant because often consumer choice was determined more by the condition of the copper plate and the standard of printing than by the genius of the composition. In privilege law, the distinction between tangible and intangible, print and image, was also not always clear: Le Brun's privilege did not distinguish between painted, printed or other kinds of copies; it treated them as legally identical and proscribed them all.

To recapitulate: in the fifteenth and sixteenth centuries, privilege assumed the appearance of a gift. Its discourse bound Renaissance kings and their petitioners in reciprocal obligation, loyalty prompting and procuring largesse in an ongoing exchange. This articulation of privilege, though no longer dominant from the seventeenth century, nevertheless survived alongside new legal forms of that relation.[169] With the expansion of the privilege regime in the wake of the 1566 ordinance, which made privilege mandatory for all new publications, parts of its administration were devolved to the newly founded Corporation des libraires et maîtres imprimeurs. The privilege relation became more complex as petitioners began to understand and to promote their collective and individual interests in it. Consequently, the discourse on privilege ramified. The *peines*, *labeur* and *dépenses* that qualified petitioners' appeals, serving to define them as the especially worthy objects of the king's affectionate generosity, assumed new purposes. Redeployed in circumstances of renewable and thus seemingly perpetual privilege, 'effort', 'cost' and particularly 'labour' came to describe and eventually to define the particular relation of the petitioner to the work in question. Meanwhile, writers and artists, with the support of the Chancellerie's personnel, fashioned an author privilege for themselves, which promoted their dignity and assigned them, ideally, a lifetime's interest in their work. By the eighteenth century the two arguments were occasionally advanced together. In 1711, for instance, Veuve Cousinet petitioned for a privilege to protect her investment of capital and labour in the engraved works of the late François Chauveau, and she reinforced her claim to monopoly by reference to the 'excellence and rarity' of Chauveau's 'handsome genius'.[170] I have suggested, moreover, that it was precisely because printmakers like Chauveau were at liberty to realise their work independently that they as authors were able to advance a strong claim of exclusivity over its exploitation. The appeal to the author as genius had been made possible through the realignment of the analogy between poetry and painting, text and image, by reference not to matter and printing but by way of imagination and invention.

Beyond the account of this repositioning little has yet been said about the role visual art may have played in the changing conceptualisations of privilege. At around the same time that lawyers were beginning to advance the property-like nature of texts, artists were mastering and perfecting rules of perspective, and art theorists like Roger de Piles were proclaiming the peculiar power of images vividly to conjure things up in space, to make them present and palpable.[171] Important as perspective was to the practice of illusion in art, it was, William Ivins argues, even more important as a tool of general thought, because the two-way metrical relationship it rigorously establishes between the position and shape of things in pictorial representation and the forms and locations of those things in space enabled subjects to understand and control the reality that perspective objectified.[172] By means of perspective, property is grasped as a thing. What the discourses on privilege and art had in common by the end of the seventeenth century was their potential, you could say, for assigning the illusion of tangibility – property – to works of intellect.

CASES

Typically, case studies start with the observation of something unique – indeed, so exceptional in its singularity that it demands explanation.[173] Recent critical reviews of the case have emphasised its ubiquity in academic writing. However, study by case appears especially closely allied to Michel Foucault's 'practices': his examination of the way in which prisoners, or the insane or, in this case, publishers, writers and artists, came respectively to be imprisoned, or incarcerated or privileged. Practice shifts the target of analysis, removing it from institutions, theories and ideology, and redirects it towards tactics – in this instance, applications of privilege; to put it in Foucault's terms, it wrests attention from questions of what and raises instead the question of how. How did the practices of restricting and opening access to images, and of legally protecting or freely abandoning authors and others in the print market actually 'operate'?[174] The point is to grasp the conditions that made such distinctions not only legal but performable and generally acceptable and meaningful.

Why change the approach to privilege from what to how at this point? Because in terms of law, bureaucracy and the print trade, the history of privilege in the eighteenth century was, until 1777, broadly one of continuity. Booksellers, print publishers, printmakers, painters and also architects and designers carried on petitioning for privilege.[175] They appealed for protection for the same genres of imagery, adding to illustrations and sheet prints of architecture, fortification, natural history, portraiture and mythology, established in the seventeenth century, genre subjects, fashion plates and topographical views, especially those of royal palaces and monuments – Versailles, Marly and the Invalides especially.[176] Meanwhile the number of printsellers, publishers and printmakers had risen considerably in the second half of the seventeenth century.[177] By 1700, Paris was the undisputed capital of the European print trade, a position it maintained until the last decade of the *ancien régime*.[178] Applications for privilege continued to fluctuate between one and five per year until the late 1770s. Duration of privilege ranged, as in the seventeenth century, from three to 20 years, and the scope of images from cheap topical and devotional prints at one end of the spectrum to Jacques Fagnani's reprints after Jacques Callot and Jacques Gautier d'Agoty's coloured anatomical prints at the other.[179] However, if the number of those applying for privilege remained very much the same, the inscription 'Avec privilège du roi' on prints became virtually standard, whether protection had been obtained or not.[180]

At the Chancellerie in 1700, Chancelier Pontchartrain created a special department for the printing trades, the Bureau de la librairie.[181] In the same year its first head, the abbé Jean-Paul Bignon, organised a national survey of the book trade in order to understand better the industry under his control.[182] Questions arising in its wake about the continuing efficacy of Colbert's policies of closely controlling printers, capping the numbers of presses and prolonging the duration of privilege at a time of rapid growth and international competition did not result, however, in revision of the trade's regulations. The *Règlement* of 1723, which had been in preparation since 1710, was little more than a digest of the statutes promulgated over the course of the seventeenth century, topically arranged into a code.[183] The controversial clauses relating to privilege in old books and prints, and to prolongations of privilege, were deliberately rendered harmless in appearance by the concision of the code's phrasing, as Frédéric Rideau has noted,[184] though not sufficiently to blind everyone. In 1725, the abbot, tutor and man of letters Pierre-Jacques Blondel wrote an explosive memorandum on the 'vexations' of the Paris *libraires*. It was addressed to the public directly because, Blondel alleged, the guild had the Conseil du roi and the capital's magistrates in its pocket.[185] In describing the capital's *libraires* as 'corsairs' and accusing them of building huge fortunes by the abuse of privilege, the legitimate legal purpose of which was rather to prevent ruin, Blondel was saying nothing new.[186] With greater originality he described the impact of corruption and abuse on writers and journeymen printers.[187] He argued that the booksellers' monopoly to print and publish texts reversed the natural order in relations between authors and publishers, such that the author was manufactured in the interest of the publisher, rather than the publisher serving the interests of the writer. The fortune that the Mariette publishing house built on Louis Moréri's *Grand dictionnaire historique* (1674) by regular renewal of the privilege obtained by transfer in 1699, and the loss that Amédée-François Frézier, engineer and intrepid explorer, suffered at the hands of publishers who tricked him into ceding privilege and publication of his illustrated voyage to the South Seas were just two of Blondel's examples of publishers and writers stereotyped respectively as villains and heroes.[188] Such was the impact of his memorandum, which the guild had tried but failed to suppress, that two years later a ruling of the Conseil du roi ordered a review of all privileges and prolongations since 1718.[189]

The wardens of the Paris Corporation, among whom was one of Blondel's 'corsairs', Jean Mariette, also an art publisher and father of the better-known connoisseur Pierre-Jean, responded by lobbying the Garde des sceaux, Fleuriau d'Armenonville. To represent their case, they recruited Louis d'Héricourt, barrister of the late regent, Philippe d'Orléans, an authority on canon law and reputed for his powerful oratorical style.[190] In absolute contrast to Blondel, d'Héricourt issued a memorandum that focused not on facts but on principles, not on commerce but on law.[191] He mounted his defence of the booksellers' prerogatives on arguments from natural law. Natural law differs from positive or manmade law, in being unwritten, instinctive and innate: inscribed in every human heart. It functions as a first premise, assumed to be true, and serves as the guarantee of the conclusion it advances. It was generally invoked in appeals against the alleged injustice of positive laws. However, d'Héricourt used it to assert the justice of existing statutes, because, although they were written, he argued that natural law was contained or inscribed within them. D'Héricourt's memorandum caused considerable offence by its unprecedented marginalisation of the king's justice, eclipsed by natural law.[192] However, the critical review of privileges ordered by the Conseil du roi never took place, and the 1723 code, originally established for the Paris trade, was extended in 1744 to the kingdom as a whole.[193] If the eighteenth century, and more narrowly the Enlightenment, has a claim to playing a part in the fashioning of privilege in the *ancien régime*, it was not immediately manifest in legislation decreed by the Conseil du roi. By focusing on disputed cases *c.*1750–60, at a historical moment where underscoring the continuity of law might seem more appropriate, I shall show that it was neither obvious nor inevitable that the status of property, a hallmark of modern copyright, was assigned to works of poetry and painting in reproduction.

LA FONTAINE'S *FABLES*

In May 1752 Louis-Jean Regnard de Montenault, a nobleman, entrepreneur and amateur of letters and arts, obtained from the successors of La Fontaine's original publishers, Claude Barbin and Denys Thierry, permission to produce a new illustrated edition of the *Fables choisies* (1668–79).[194] The previous year he had acquired from Jean-Baptiste Oudry chalk drawings for the illustrations in question, six engravings after which were exhibited at the Salon in 1753.[195] Although the Salon *livret* announced that the first volume would be published that very year, the first volumes did not appear until 1755.[196] By then puffs had also appeared in the press. Notices in the *Mémoires de Trévoux*, the *Année littéraire* and the *Mercure de France* in 1754 predicted the book's perfection: 'typeface, paper, printing, printers' flowers, tailpieces. Nothing has been spared, neither in care, nor expense. The publishers, motivated only by their taste for the Arts and for Letters, and content with recouping their investment, have the glory of the nation as their [only] objective.'[197]

The same notices committed the publishers – the amateur de Montenault and the professionals Desaint and Saillant and Durand – to deliver the remaining two volumes by Easter 1756.[198] In the event, the third did not appear until 1757, while in 1759 production of the fourth was stalled for lack of funds.[199] Although the work was a critical success in the main, sales for the first three volumes disappointed. In the worsening economic situation of the Seven Years' War (1757–1763), trade looked unlikely to recover sufficiently for the publishers to salvage the enterprise.[200] In crisis, de Montenault wrote a number of memoranda to Guillaume-Chrétien de Lamoignon de Malesherbes, the head of the book trade since 1750, to solicit a government rescue, outlining a range of options.[201] One of these involved obtaining a privilege for the book, against the legal title of La Fontaine's publishers; the permission they had ceded to de Montenault, while making the new edition legal, had left it prey to piracy at home as well as abroad.[202]

De Montenault's case was addressed to the king, via his representative Malesherbes, as legislator rather than as dispenser of privileges. De Montenault argued that the condition of privilege in La Fontaine originally granted by Louis XIV required moderation in the name of equity. He was, that is to say, appealing to a higher authority: to justice itself. He demanded in its name the momentary suspension of the existing statutory rule of privilege sufficiently to allow its revision or even reinvention by reassertion of its supposed natural principle.[203] For persuasiveness, his case rested on his representation of image as both independent from and equal to text, and thus as entitled to equivalent treatment in law.

• *Fable III* 'The frog who wanted to be as big as an ox', or On equity •

To take the second point first: his *Fables*, de Montenault argued in his first memorandum, offered the public not a new setting of La Fontaine's words but; 'engravings, prints, drawings, which give new life to this celebrated text, and which, by the *tout ensemble*, constitute an entirely distinct and new book, such that the typography of the work is no more than an accessory to the main object, which demands works and knowledge of a different kind.'[204] The attached prospectus enumerated the novelties: a new typeface designed by Charles-Antoine Jombert and cast by Nicolas Gando the younger,[205] 119 tailpieces and *fleurons* cut by Jean-Michel Papillon and Nicolas Le Sueur after designs by Jean-Jacques Bachelier (fig. **5**)[206] and 276 full-page intaglio plates or *tableaux* (fig. **6**), in place of the 134 headpieces engraved by François Chauveau for the first edition.[207]

In the context of printmaking, this assertion of the bulk and artistic importance of the new visual components resurrected an argument made by Tavernier the elder about the legal definition of a work as a book or a print – namely, that it hinges not on the nature but on the relative value of the two things. In the context of privilege, 'new life' and the sheer number of novelties point to de Montenault's awareness of the specific clauses of the privilege regime governing the terms of its renewal. Booksellers and publishers were legally forbidden by the regulations of 1618 and 1665 to obtain extensions of privilege unless the content of the book was augmented by one quarter.[208] Only then could publishers like de Montenault be said to be offering the public 'an entirely distinct and new book'. Fables belonged to that category of early modern literature whose openness of form to revision and augmentation made them especially suited to the legalities of the marketplace.[209] And in fact La Fontaine had on two separate occasions – in 1677 and 1692 – provided Barbin and Thierry with additional fables to facilitate the renewal of their copy-privilege.

Although the 1723 code glossed over the terms of renewal, de Montenault was convinced, evidently, that his case would be more persuasive were it informed by them. On top of describing the material additions his edition made to the original text, he also argued the case for privilege in terms of authorship. He deliberately elided Oudry's drawing with La Fontaine's writing. Thus, notwithstanding the studied artifice, indeed the conscious game of illusion in the illustration of the first fable (fig. **6**) and the knowing and clever play in many of those that follow with the pictorial tradition inaugurated by Chauveau[210] (figs **7**, **8**), Oudry is said to have composed his illustrations after nature (not following Chauveau or La Fontaine), just as La Fontaine's verse is characterised not by emulation (of Aesop or Phaedrus) but by the 'light, playful and naive expressions with which it faithfully copied ideal nature...'[211] The parallels between the poet and the painter were so striking that, in conclusion, de Montenault noted that Oudry 'knew how to appropriate the ideas of the Poet in his drawings so well that one could say that the same Muse directed [his] pencil in order to trace them [the fables] in a manner as poetic, as clever and as natural. One can therefore rightly call him the La Fontaine of painting.'[212]

The illustrations, in short, were an extension of the text, not an accessory. De Montenault was not alone in inflating the conceit. In a significant number of illustrations, Oudry wittily incorporates the poet by visualising his name: magnificent fountains serve as lively counterpoints to his foxes, stalks, crows, ants and flies (figs **9**, **10**), which become by a reciprocal act of identification so many ciphers to celebrate the great animal-painter's name.[213]

In the competition for privilege, de Montenault was, however, silent about the salience of visuality to his case. He was content simply to legitimise his request for parity-in-privilege in Oudry's alleged ambition for equality-in-genius. Having invoked the illustrations, he left them to speak for themselves. Of course, neither their purpose nor their meaning addresses privilege directly. Answering W. J. T. Mitchell's provocative question 'what do pictures want?' may, however, suggest how they operated indirectly within privilege.[214] The illustrations, unlike their author, do not want to be equivalent, nor even equal to poetry; what they want is to be real.

In contrast to Chauveau's emblem-like *vignettes*, in which animals are foregrounded like actors on a stage against a painted backdrop, Oudry's animals are so integrated with their settings that they seem unaware of or indifferent to the reader: the ox in his 'Frog who wanted to be as big as an ox' (fig. **8**) lifts its muzzle and looks into, not out of, the picture. The illusion of spatial depth is created by the subtle gradation from darker, heavier foreground engraving to lighter, springier background etching. Atmosphere is suggested by serene patches of hatching interrupted by denser movements of cross-hatching, and matter is described tangibly in, for instance, the contrast at the pond's edge between flatter, striated paper water and felted whorls of inky ground, between the cracked, knobbly bark of the willows' trunks and the light, feathered lines of their whipped-back branches. In eighteenth-century terms, Oudry's depictions are *naïf* – that is, artlessly real.[215]

Such indeed is the quality of their truth that fable is all but undermined. 'The frog who wanted to be as big as an ox' does not resonate with the brisk exchange of alternately pleading and scornful animal talk that ultimately proved fatal to the ambitious frog.[216] Rather, it promotes a material communication with the viewer in stuff and things – closer you could say to the mute dialogue between the young slave Aesop and his master, narrated in the poet's 'Life' at the beginning of the de Montenault *Fables*. There, identification of the culprit in the famous mystery of the stolen figs was solved by vomit: material, not verbal evidence of the content of the thief's stomach.[217] By means of illusion Oudry similarly makes the manifestly fabulous (talking animals) real, the intangible idea seemingly tangible.

To return to Mitchell's question: convinced that the power of images has been fetishistically overrated, he asks it as a better alternative to the more conventional 'what do pictures do?' Desire, he notes, is usually reserved for 'objects of discrimination' (slaves like Aesop, women, people of colour). When using its language, we replace a model of domination with one of weakness, in which the power of the subaltern consists merely in being invited to speak.[218] Oudry's picture fables, under-privileged by convention of accessorial status and by terms of legal cession, spoke to the law of their desire for equal rights with poetry, not by turning into language but rather by resistance to it.

If, in summary, arguments about the relation of text and image, poetry and painting – a leitmotif in litigation since Tavernier's dispute with the booksellers over a century earlier[219] – continued to structure quarrels about privilege, they did so in significantly revised ways. La Fontaine had given an ironic twist to his retelling of the pretensions of Aesop's fabular frog: he confessed that the consequences of ambition were no longer fatal, and that self-love and self-promotion were everywhere to be seen.[220] Emulation was, he quipped, a universal law of nature. In a parallel move, de Montenault asked for a privilege not in the normative sense of the word[221] but rather for his 'rights' – that is, for the proper regard of his relation to others arising from his nature as man. He alleged that he had been tricked by the booksellers into accepting a cession in lieu of a title 'more capable of protecting his rights', and that for lack of being able to pursue piracies directly he was, in fact, grievously, if not unlawfully, separated from them.[222] In short, de Montenault broached privilege regulations not as the sum total of decrees and letters patent enacted by positive law, but as an ordering order or definite spirit that preceded the foundation of those sovereign institutions that granted and enforced them.[223] He separated in the memoranda his requests for various benefits, which the king had the power to bestow, from his claims for justice by the apriority of natural law.[224]

• *Fable LVI* 'The lion become old', or On the revision of privilege •

In his pursuit of his rights, could de Montenault be said to have assumed the role of the horse, wolf or bull in La Fontaine's fifty-sixth fable (fig. **11**), in which the three each contribute a blow and collectively kill the once terrible lion, weakened by age? According to Walter Benjamin, when consciousness of the latent presence of violence in a legal institution fades, the institution itself falls into ruin.[225] Had the king's power in privilege been forgotten in the routine renewal of privilege? Did justification for legal monopoly consequently reach for a different set of arguments in its own defence? The status of de Montenault's particular case as one of artistic privilege in general depends on the answers to these questions.

Although, in the memoranda, de Montenault mocked the *libraires* as philistine mechanics of the text, his target was not, in truth, the publishers and printers, either personally or corporately, but the authority upon which their assumption of monopoly relied. Or, to put it differently, in order to render moot the Barbin and Thierry monopoly, de Montenault challenged not the legal concession in question but the juridical nature that privilege had assumed, at odds with its original purpose of promoting emulation and progress in the arts.[226] In the letters patent that he drafted for his own monopoly, de Montenault lists, as convention dictated, 'cares', 'preparations' and 'expenses' among the justifying 'causes' for privilege, but he also asserted his entitlement, or right in justice, to 'free and complete possession'.[227] If property is not claimed explicitly in the memoranda, it is everywhere implied; moreover, it is at the heart of the argument for the edition's novelty and value, articulated in the editor's preface.

Unlike Le Brun, whose creative genius and artistic estate were, as noted above, deemed inseparable from his royal patron's activating will, Oudry the illustrator is represented as absolutely independent.[228] The La Fontaine drawings were, the foreword affirms, his recreation: 'he invented them for his own satisfaction, and in those chosen moments of fantasy when the Artist energetically grasps the idea of his subject and gives free play to his genius'.[229] In this, too, Oudry followed La Fontaine. The poet had, according to the prefatory 'Life', similarly composed his fables at leisure: that is, without bending to the command of another – patron or publisher.[230] The duchesse de Bouillon dubbed him a 'Fabulist', or bestiary incarnate, in order to say that 'the *Fables* were the natural product of the ideas that were all arranged in his head.'[231] Ideas were not put to him in the stately form of a commission but lodged within him to be drawn out at will: at his will.[232] That such ideas were believed to remain interior, private, though on occasion laboured into particular public expression, is indicated by de Montenault's observation that Oudry's 'fabulous' ideas were by no means exhausted by the drawings in question but had furnished material for countless paintings exhibited at the Salons and hanging in *cabinets* at Versailles and in the capital.[233]

The relationship between author and ideas proposed by de Montenault is thus fundamentally proprietary. As such, the terms of his plea to Malesherbes were probably informed by John Locke's labour theory of property, which had been mobilised in the defence of the prerogatives of the Paris Corporation des libraires et maîtres imprimeurs in disputes in the 1720s. According to Locke, man exercises a proprietary right over some part of God's common store when he has 'mixed his labour with [a thing] and joined to it something that is his own'.[234] The legal doctrine of mixture, according to which the merging of two or more things together to produce a new third, thereby effecting a change of specification or property, is familiar from the debate on *tabula picta* in the Middle Ages, but with this difference: the labour of representation is itself proposed as one of the tangible possessions in play.[235] For, according to Locke, labour is 'the unquestionable Property of the Labourer, no Man but he can have a right to what that is once joined to'.[236]

D'Héricourt had used this claim in the Mariette memorandum as the foundation of his defence of the inalienability of privilege. He argued that a manuscript 'is so much the property of its Author that it is no more possible to deprive him of it than it is to deprive him of his money, goods or even land'.[237] Privileges were thus only seemingly, or superficially, 'marks of the King's benevolence and Protection' – that is, of his power of patronage – because, actually, 'it is not the privileges granted to the booksellers by the King that makes them owners of the works they print but only the purchase of the manuscript'.[238] Through purchase, he argued, they entered absolutely into the proprietary rights that the author had earned through his labour in creation.

D'Héricourt's memorandum thus enacted a fundamental revision of the discourse on privilege: reason, or a philosophical conceptualisation of the property in authored things, replaced the attributive power of kings.[239] To persuade, d'Héricourt prefaced his assertion with the story of the origins of property: it comes into existence because man is destined by nature for society and turns to labour to materialise this bond dynamically through exchange.[240] Labour is, you could say, a natural *datum*, and private property its necessary, and therefore just, outcome. A manuscript, or rather the text of a manuscript, is compared to a 'good' or a 'fruit': 'it is the fruit of a labour that is personal to him [the author], over which he must have the freedom to dispose as he pleases in order to procure, in addition to honour ... a profit to supply his needs'.[241] The primitive author is to himself his own capital,[242] which when worked turns him a profit in the form of fruit. 'Fruit' thus denotes whatever was produced by property without the integrity of that property being compromised.

The privilege sought by de Montenault for the *Fables* was, following this principle, to cover not only the edition in question but extracts made from it in the form of sheet prints: single items and sets.[243] In 1760 the *Année littéraire* announced, along with the publication of volume 4 of the *Fables*, the separate availability of the illustrations,[244] and in November of the same year the *Mercure de France* advertised the first suite of a 'collection' of the tailpieces and printers' flowers after the Bachelier woodcuts, but etched expressly for this new purpose by Pierre-Philippe Choffard (figs **5**, **12**).[245] Oudry's illustrations, described by de Montenault as the 'fruit' of the studies he made from nature, are thus by d'Héricourt's 'proposition' legally as well as figuratively so.[246]

The analogy of 'text' (in the broad sense of any artistic expression) and fruit is not built, like *ut pictura poesis* in humanist theory, on a set of more or less strained resemblances; it is, rather, an injunction to regard the text and proceed *as if* it were fruit, a strategic use of analogy that accelerates the argument for ownership by riding roughshod over the awkward linkage between material property rights and conventions of intellectual property protection.[247] In the specific context of visual art, it promotes the transfer of concern from meaning to illusion. To proceed 'as if' is not only to regard the depicted scene as real, but to act like the dog in *Fable CXX* (fig. **13**) and chase after 'shadows', as if the illusion conjured up were true: to listen, that is, to the fictional exchange between frog and ox (*Fable III*; fig. **8**), to taste the revenge taken by the animal populace against their king (*Fable LVI*; fig. **11**), to touch the tapestry world in which cicada and ant meet (*Fable I*; fig. **6**) etc., by extension to lay hold of the expression of Oudry's ideas.[248] Alain-Marie Bassy notes the paradox of the *merveilleux* in Oudry's case: it arises not from the manifestly fictional and blatantly artificial, but rather from an excess of the real, from the magic of *trompe l'œil*. The illustrations are, we may note, given architectural frames as if integral with a wall, as if part of the fixed furniture of a house. They not only conjure up the illusion of things in the world, they announce themselves private property on the page: ring-fenced.[249]

If de Montenault was influenced in his case-making by d'Héricourt, there is irony in the fact that he turned back onto specific bookseller arguments first advanced to defend the privileges they enjoyed corporately. Natural law, unlike positive law, makes no allowance for honour and hierarchy. It is uniform, undivided, equal; precisely open to all.[250] The Paris booksellers could not monopolise its discourse, even as they fought to preserve their monopolies by its logic. In fact, the priority assigned to the natural body and the individual in the discourse on rights sits uneasily with the corporate language and collective solidarity of early modern guilds. In his memorandum, d'Héricourt first defined privileges as rights in relation to writing, then later he described them as 'barricades' (*barrières*) or defences in the context of printing, publishing and bookselling.[251] However, de Montenault was not a bookseller, nor did he belong to the corporatist culture of the artisanal class. His arguments did not, therefore, rely for extra ethical purchase on the high claims of the supposed collective good. Rather, his case depended totally on the rights he acquired with the purchase of the drawings.[252]

D'Héricourt maintained that once a manuscript passed from the author–vendor to the buyer–publisher the new owner assumed full and outright possession, as of a house or a piece of land.[253] The purchaser of a manuscript entered into the identity of its author precisely to the extent that he entered contractually into the latter's right. The interrelatedness of a labour theory of property and the theory of commercial contracts takes on particular interest and significance here because of the determination to confuse them for the sake of greater theoretical persuasiveness. Thus, while de Montenault gives only summary detail of his financial dealings with Oudry, he eloquently represents his role as entrepreneur, using pseudo-authorial and artistic terms and categories in order to distinguish his *Fables* from those of ordinary – that is, merchant – booksellers. So much so that he asserts without hesitation that La Fontaine's publishers would have been incapable of carrying it out. They had, he said, recognised this edition as beyond their strength.[254]

In the memoranda it is the edition itself that is represented as the compositional 'idea' – one that demanded of de Montenault not simply investment but research, organisation and judgment. He had had to seek out and select the best materials, artists and creative work in the fields of papermaking, typesetting and printmaking.[255] He had chosen woodcut for the book ornaments not to cut cost but in order to resurrect an art shamefully fallen into decline.[256] He had secured excellence, too, in the illustrations by engaging Charles-Nicolas Cochin *fils* 'to translate' Oudry's sketches into exact and detailed drawings for better replication by engraving (figs **14–16**).[257] He had distributed the task of reproduction to some 20 of the best printmakers, and had overseen the printing on presses especially installed at his house in the rue Sainte-Anne.[258] And finally, in a manner quite unprecedented, de Montenault had also accomplished the perfect integration of woodcut and intaglio, ornament and illustration visually by imposing a single coherent scale of proportions across all the pictorial elements in the book.[259] In effect, de Montenault assumes the form of a collective subject in the memoranda, one who combines intellectual, mechanical and financial skills, a subjectivity both sufficiently coherent to appear singularly possessive and sufficiently loose to incorporate the division of labour necessary to successful commercial enterprise.

That economic direction was to a certain degree dressed up as artistic direction suggests that privilege, as right, not only transformed authors into commodities – identities circulating in the marketplace – but also encouraged capital to assume the appearance of art. The more so, no doubt, after the Paris booksellers suffered a second reverse: in addition to de Montenault's ultimately successful bid for a privilege, granted in 1760, an *arrêt* of the Conseil du roi in September 1761 confirmed the poet's destitute granddaughters in their 'natural right' as direct heirs also to publish an edition of the text of the *Fables*.[260] Rights belong to subjects by moral as well as by economic imperative.

DIDEROT AND D'ALEMBERT'S *ENCYCLOPÉDIE*

If de Montenault's case for privilege rested on a claim of authorship – Oudry's and his own – it was justified by reference to another recurrent theme of emergent copyright discourse: public utility. A trope of privilege since the 1630s, it was appropriated by de Montenault to argue that, by granting him a privilege, the Crown would encourage emulation. Others would see, as he had, an incentive in bold and financially risky publishing ventures.[261] Moreover, the text of the privilege finally issued for the *Fables* in 1760 cites, in vindication of the monopoly, a desire not only to endorse de Montenault's zeal, but also 'to excite, by his example, other amateurs and men of letters who have always prospered in our realm, [...] and to animate a new emulation in printing which has been cultivated with as much success as reputation'.[262] Adopting a rhetoric more commonly mobilised for works of erudition, it proposed monopolies as instruments to stimulate progress in the arts, against the view that, by privatising the circulation of knowledge, privilege actually limited the dissemination and thus the further exploitation of ideas.[263] To be sure, in the introduction to the *Fables*, de Montenault argued that reproduction alone ensured publicity: by force of print, works of art were brought out of the amateur's *cabinet* and circulated abroad.[264] But the protection sought was nevertheless designed to exclude competition, to impede the production of cheaper formats, and thereby to restrict the material pleasures and moral benefits of the *Fables* to an elite market.

In the sixteenth century the market in unprotected works had been vast. Over the course of the seventeenth century it had gradually been enclosed, in spite of concerted opposition from provincial booksellers and the Parlements.[265] The number of works never privileged declined, the number reverting to the public domain dwindled and the temporal scope of privilege in books lengthened. As a matter of example, Aesop's *Fables*, the urtext upon which the *Fables* of La Fontaine and many others were based, was taken into privilege in 1649.[266] Malesherbes's unforeseen refusal in 1761 to renew Barbin and Thierry's original privilege for the text of La Fontaine's *Fables* was met with disbelief, renewals having become a formality.[267] And de Montenault's privilege was secured for 30 years, significantly longer than Barbin's inaugural monopoly of 12 years' duration.

At the same time the Baconian notion that the advancement of knowledge and progress of reason was a collective labour, achieved by the creative reworking of the cultural commons, continued to gain ground.[268] Privilege, as Carla Hesse has observed, thus brought into conflict two equally powerful strands of Enlightenment ideology: recognition of the individual as a rights-bearing subject and the election and defence of an autonomous sphere of public knowledge.[269] De Montenault's *Fables* have provided an instance of the first; the 17 text volumes of the *Encyclopédie, ou Dictionnaire raisonné des sciences, des arts et des métiers*, jointly edited by Denis Diderot and Jean Le Rond d'Alembert, and the nine volumes of 2,885 plates, together arguably *the* defining document of the Enlightenment,[270] will serve to explore the second.

• PRIVILÈGE d'impression s[ingulier] m[asculin] (*Librairie*) (vol. 13, p. 391) •

In the same year that de Montenault was lobbying for a privilege, Malesherbes was overseeing the cancellation of the *Encyclopédie*'s publication licence, the first seven volumes of which had appeared in the years since 1751.[271] There could have been no clearer reminder that privilege was not, as the chevalier de Jaucourt later defined it, a grant '*alone* to have permission to publish this or that book', but authorisation to publish at all.[272] Withdrawal of the licence had potentially serious commercial consequences. The first edition of the *Encyclopédie* was, like de Montenault's *Fables*, a luxury object, ornamented with headbands, tailpieces and decorated letters by Jean-Michel Papillon (fig. **17**).[273] It had been financed by subscription.[274] A ruling of the Conseil du roi in July 1759 ordered the publishers to reimburse its two thousand plus subscribers for the outstanding volumes of text whose future it now definitively proscribed.[275] Rather than accept the certain bankruptcy that would result from such a course of action, Diderot and the publishers decided to offer their subscribers and the public 'a thousand images', in lieu of the remaining text. Illustrative plates had been promised by the prospectus and had been in preparation since the late 1740s. André-François Le Breton, in the name of his associates and partners, obtained a privilege for them on 9 November 1759.[276]

• CONTREFAIRE v[erbe] act[if] (*terme de Librairie*) (vol. 4, p. 133) •

Before printing of the first volume of the *Recueil de planches, sur les sciences, les arts libéraux, et les arts méchaniques* (1762) had finished, the *Année littéraire* for 1759 had published the first of two letters from the architect and printmaker Pierre Patte to its editor, Élie-Catherine Fréron, alleging that the *Recueil*'s plates were plagiarised.[277] Patte's outburst arose from disillusionment. His privileged position as a subeditor and engraver on the *Recueil* had made him acutely aware of the contradiction between the promises made in the prospectus and 'Discours préliminaire' and what was actually being prepared for subscribers and the wider interested public.[278] 'The exposé that I am going to give you', Patte promised, 'will prove to you, Monsieur, that this dimension of the mechanical Arts, promoted as an encyclopaedic marvel, is [in fact] the grandest and most adroit plagiarism ever perhaps recorded in the annals of literature.'[279] The stated objective of depicting the trades by direct observation of machines and operations in the workshops of France was being met by the cheaper and more practical expedient of copying the illustrations produced at the direction of the Académie royale des sciences for the *Description des arts et métiers* fifty years earlier but left unpublished by the editor René-Antoine de Réaumur.[280]

Patte's denunciation was not simply of the many and particular instances of shop-floor copying by lazy or inadequate draughtsmen and printmakers. It was an accusation levelled rather at the editor, Diderot, that he encouraged copying as a covert strategy and intrinsic function of the *Encyclopédie*'s design process, and had pursued it cynically as a financial expedient.[281] 'Hence, no more trips, no more payments for Drawings; it was nothing more than a workshop matter; the *Encyclopédie* was supplied to the Public without delay.'[282]

In Patte's exposé, drawings are to prints what manuscripts were to books. Only drawings constituted evidence of original practice. When reporting in his second letter to Fréron on the outcome of the Académie's inspection of the allegedly offending images *chez* Antoine-Claude Briasson, one of the *Encyclopédie*'s publishers,[283] he regarded it as damning that for the mechanical arts there were none to be found, only prints. By contrast the inspectors saw many drawings for the liberal arts and sciences, 'most of them old, original and after nature, and almost all executed with colour wash and larger than the template to which they had to be adjusted'.[284] No drawings, therefore no right to copy or reproduce, and logically no privilege to prevent others from doing the same.

Of the prints, Briasson admitted to having at his disposal only 40 of the Réaumur corpus, a modest fraction of those listed by Patte as ones for which 'the *Encyclopédistes* have no drawings, but only the impressions of Mr Réaumur's Plates as models'.[285] While the publishers freely admitted that 'they had profited from these prints by imitating their format' (the *Encyclopédie*'s trademark division of the plates into an upper-register scene or *tableau* and a lower-register chart of tools and equipment (figs **18**–**22**)), of the 40, in fact, 'only two or three ... by a few points of similarity, appear to have served as models for those of the booksellers on the same subjects'.[286]

Baffled by the Académie's reluctance publicly to corroborate Patte's accusations – indeed, by its willingness to be blinded by affirmations of proper conduct – modern scholars have conducted their own investigations of the charges.[287] The close correspondence between many of the *Encyclopédie*'s articles and the illustrations of the *Description*, even after the reworking and replacement of some plates following Patte's exposé,[288] has led to the general conclusion that Patte was right.

In the case of charcoal production, which Patte particularly singled out, a proof impression of Claude Lucas's print (fig. **19**) after Jean Chaufourier's drawing (fig. **18**), with Diderot's annotations, survives.[289] It clearly formed the basis of two of Louis-Jacques Goussier's three plates for the *Encyclopédie*, even though the four-stage sequence of stacking logs against a 'chimney', covering it with turfs, setting it alight and raking out, described as a smoothly articulated progress from foreground to background by Chaufourier, was roughly divided in two by Goussier, the building and the burning, or preparation and execution, allocated to separate plates and *vignettes* (figs **20**, **21**), beneath which Goussier introduced line drawings of clamp formations in place of Chaufourier's depictions of tools. The tools Goussier assigned to a completely separate illustration (fig. **22**).[290] That, at an earlier stage, the *Encyclopédie*'s illustration had, in fact, followed Chaufourier's original almost exactly was borne out (as Patte noted) by the figure references in Diderot's article 'Charcoal', which correspond not to the numbers and letters on Goussier's plates but to those on Lucas's engraving.

Such examples could be multiplied, and Patte, of course, unhesitatingly drew attention to other instances in his reviews of individual volumes of the *Description des arts et métiers* as they were published from 1761.[291] What makes the issue of malicious copying interesting in the present context is not so much the fact of it as the justifications, and even the flat denials of its having taken place, that it occasioned in some quarters.

• RECUEIL s[ingulier] m[asculin] (*Belles-Lettres*) (vol. 13, p. 868) •

The notice in reply to Patte's first letter, placed in the newspapers in order to contain the scandal, invited readers to present themselves at the publishers to review the evidence.[292] Short and to the point, it did not directly acknowledge Patte's accusation. Instead, by dividing the public into those 'for and against' the *Encyclopédie*, it implied that the question of plagiarism was answered by the kind of thing an encyclopaedia is. 'The aim of an Encyclopaedia', according to Diderot, 'is to assemble knowledge scattered across the earth's surface and to reveal its general system to those with whom we live and to those who will follow us.'[293] Questions of possessive authorship were thus at odds with the conception and purpose of the project. Land did not provide a metaphor for the private property in ideas. It was, in a literal sense, the vast, common and unbounded place across which was found scattered rational perception of often anonymous fact.

Those who cultivated learning did so, according to Diderot, in one of two ways: by augmentation of the scope of human knowledge through discovery and invention, or by the abridgement, collation and arrangement of those same discoveries in order that 'more people are enlightened and that each person participates in the enlightenment of their century according to his or her ability'.[294] If the status of authorship attached to the first, or invention, it was not to the inventor's superior credit, for his or her specialist knowledge was 'particular'.[295] Only, writes Diderot, to those who select, order, abridge and articulate by cross-reference belongs the 'genius' of general knowledge.[296]

Thus when the *philosophe* introduced analogy it was to make vivid that difference. Facts were like pieces of coal: only when they were properly gathered together did they catch fire.[297] 'Recueil', the collective noun used in the title to describe the *Encyclopédie*'s conflagration 'of plates', has much in common with 'Encyclopédie': it too denotes 'a reasoned collection of all things worthy of note', '[a] kind of storehouse in which [are] disposed the best and the most beautiful passages from authors in order always to have them ready for use'.[298] The purpose of both text and image was to make general knowledge public and useful by the rationalisation and dissemination of the facts already known.

To that end, the role of the artist and the meaning of artistic labour in the *Encyclopédie* were significantly different from those found in the case of the *Fables*.[299] While there can be no doubt of Diderot's commitment to the plates,[300] the prospectus names no authors, neither draughtsmen nor engravers. Madeleine Pinault Sørensen has fleshed out the identities of many of those who, in the event, signed the plates, and confirms their modest reputations and often mediocre talent;[301] tellingly, Diderot referred to them in his correspondence as *travailleurs*.

Few drawings by Goussier, Jacques-Raymond Lucotte and Philippe Petit-Radel, three of the most prolific draughtsmen, survive, unlike Oudry's *esquisses* for the *Fables*, every one of which was, by the time of de Montenault's petition, meticulously preserved and all bound into two dark-blue leather volumes with gold tooling and marble endpapers.[302] Loss of such a large body of graphic work speaks of more than accident, rather of systematic neglect, arguably precisely because the related questions of authorship and ownership were impossible to determine. Two annotated drawings (figs **23**, **24**), rejected proposals by Desgerantins, of the art of the featherman (*plumassier*) provide detail on the division of responsibility for design content. Rejected, according to Desgerantins, because he 'had multiplied the plates inappropriately', the commissioning editors had agreed '[t]o Use some of the figures' if he was 'willing to Edit them',[303] specifically by moving certain items in plate I from the tool section to the *vignette* (yet to be drawn) and filling the resulting gaps with tools and equipment culled from plate II, excepting the cauldron, to be integrated into the descriptive scene.

The many more surviving drawings for Réaumur's *Description des arts et métiers* suggest this was standard practice and, moreover, that such editorial intervention transformed the designs, often damaging the original drawings by excisions or additions of detail (figs **25**, **26**), to the point that some plates were entirely assembled from dispersed elements. Design, here, is neither internal nor private but the outcome of distributed cognition – that is, the collective and negotiated decision-making between artists, the drafters of accompanying and related texts and of course the editor.[304] Patte's outrage was stirred, note, not by injury done to Jean Chaufourier, Louis Simonneau, Louis Bretez and others, the draughtsmen employed on the *Description*, but to Réaumur, 'author', like Diderot, though not a line was drawn by either one.[305]

• DESCRIPTION s[ingulier] f[éminin] (*Hist[oire] nat[urelle]*) (*Belles-Lettres*) (vol. 4, pp. 878–9) •

The author was thus not the point of reference in the introduction to the plates; focus settled instead on explaining the visual template and on promoting the value of immediate publication.[306] The discourse of the plates was descriptive. And description enjoyed mixed fortunes in the eighteenth century.[307]

'Description' was a fallen term in *Belles-Lettres*, the field of knowledge to which the *Encyclopédie* also assigns 'Recueil'. The abbé Mallet gave its literary definition as itself an 'imperfect and imprecise definition' of the means by which 'one tries to make a thing known' by reference 'to the properties and circumstances particular to it, so as to give an idea of it, distinguishing it from other things, but not so as to draw out its nature and essence'.[308] 'Accident' was, according to Mallet, the synonym of 'description' because descriptions are little more than lists of accidental properties.[309] In virtual contradiction, but sharing Mallet's visual emphasis, the naturalist Louis Daubenton argued that in the sciences 'definition' in fact constitutes description – that is, good description, description regulated by fitness to purpose, proportionality, systematicity and openness to comparison.[310] In short, description is assigned an important epistemological function.

In the *Encyclopédie*'s 'Discours préliminaire', d'Alembert briefly elaborated the principles informing visual description or illustration in the trades: it proceeded from the simple to the complex, and from the general to the particular,[311] which when translated onto the page generated the layout in which general scenes or *vignettes* preceded depictions of particular tools, and simple hand tools came before complex and specialised equipment. Systematically applied and fitting, such formalised conventions of description would not only be individually definitive but, by implication, also enable comparison between arts, in the manner of comparative anatomy, for example.[312]

If d'Alembert first made the case for description's utility in the history of the mechanical arts, Diderot, in the article 'Encyclopédie', registered the constant need for its rigorous regulation by principle in order to fulfil that case. A request to Papillon for text and image on wallpaper manufacture had elicited two thick notebooks of close-lined manuscript and a dozen anecdotal drawings (fig. **27**) crowded with figures and arranged in multiple strips: all *vignette* and few tools.[313] A proper understanding of the relative importance of wallpaper would, according to Diderot – indeed, should – have dictated a half-plate and a single page of text. Papillon's contribution was rejected. Diderot substituted for it his own measured description of the art of making marbled paper.[314]

According to d'Alembert and Diderot, the *Encyclopédie*'s plates are consciously and energetically engaged in the production of knowledge via a kind of description proper not to poetry but to natural history. But in order to understand how, as descriptive images, the plates themselves resisted accusations of plagiarism, it may be better to think of these definitions of description as not so much distinct and opposed as dialectically related. That is to say, just as we can conjecture that in the text of the *Encyclopédie* the new, scientific notion (*Hist. nat.*) of description performed a critique by juxtaposition with the classic, poetical idea (*Belles-Lettres*), so we can propose that its plates existed in active, critical dialogue with their sources.

The plates for 'Diamond-cutting', for instance (figs **28–30**), appear to copy almost exactly those after Louis Bretez (figs **31**, **32**) for Réaumur. Such differences as there are between them seem trivial: the elimination of roof beams and floor tiles from the workshop in Bretez's first *vignette* (fig. **31**), along with one of the figures, and the repositioning of the donkey lathe at right-angles to the picture plane (fig. **28**); the re-siting of the windows from side to back in the second vignette (figs **32**, **29**), in addition to the elimination of one of the wheels, the occlusion of the lathe beyond, of which Bretez offers a mini-section, and the introduction of a figure operating the machine.

These seemingly minor and pointless changes amount in fact to a consistent and sustained strategy of clarification and definition. Most significantly, Goussier divides the donkey-drive from the lathe. Bretez had depicted input and output as a dynamic and integrated unity: he arranged the lathe diagonally to the donkey (fig. **31**) so that the transmission of force from one to the other is manifest. Likewise, he exhibits the lathe by mini-section (fig. **33**) in order that the reader may not lose sight of the purpose of the machine when it is viewed from behind. By contrast, Goussier presents drive and lathe as simple and separate components. Thus while the drive is visible in plate I (fig. **28**), the manner by which the energy it produces is relayed to the lathe, is not;[315] meanwhile plate II (fig. **29**) depicts a drive that could, in principle, be connected to any machine.

In short, one can argue that the revisions Goussier brought to his plates served to replace Bretez's 'poetic' descriptions of complex particularities by general definitions in terms of simple, almost standard formal units that could be variously added together. In the process, Goussier stripped his designs of the picturesque or *naïf* accidents that make Bretez's drawings so arresting: notably, of the diagonal lines of shadow in fig. **31** that cut across the tiles, segmenting the floor asymmetrically into corners of light and dark and casting intricate patterns beneath the lathe, and of the pools of shadow that gather beneath the wheels in figs **32** and **33**, and also of the lines of wood grain in the posts of the frame, one of which is not only obtrusive but dramatically placed *en repoussoir*. Finally, with regard to the tools and lathe, he generally substitutes plans and sections (figs **28–30**) for Bretez's views in the round, and separates by a dividing line (fig. **28**), differently scaled drawings of tools and machines, images that Bretez had allowed to cohabit irrationally on the page (fig. **31**).

Illustration in the *Recueil* may have appeared formally indistinguishable from plagiarism to those 'against' the whole philosophic enterprise, but to those 'for' the *Encyclopédie* it performed eclecticism in a critical mode, its borrowings producing knowledge genealogically – that is, by revision in time.[316] Revision was, however, not only a matter of the further rationalisation of the *Description*'s visual format and systematisation of its descriptive discourse, it was also a question of primary, first-hand, observation. Although Diderot cautioned that in disciplines one has yet to master it is always better to start with the known rather than to correct and risk error by wanting to correct everything, like *faux* amateurs or *demi*-connoisseurs, it was no less important thereafter to subject the established written record to trial, by active engagement with the material world.[317] The universalising, atemporal objectives of the *Recueil*'s visual discourse, discernible in Goussier's systematic excisions of the contingent and accidental in depictions of the trades, thus came into conflict with the equally urgent ambition to represent the latest objects, processes and machines.

As Daniel Rosenberg has noted, Diderot repeatedly made clear that the question of the status of knowledge *in* time was crucial to the successful realisation of the encyclopaedic project as he envisaged it.[318] In the article 'Encyclopédie', Diderot roundly critiqued research initiatives whose slow progress or interrupted development robbed them of both accuracy and utility. Within 20 years, he says, plates require substantial reworking, having become obsolete in detail: mere 'portraits of lost originals', or of 'superseded technologies'.[319]

In the *Recueil* he promised that '[t]he prodigious number of figures included notwithstanding, we have been careful hardly to admit any that do not represent extant machines at work in the world ... There is nothing here that is superfluous, or outdated, or idealised; everything is alive and in action.'[320] Animation is not the resurrection of tradition that Oudry apparently accomplished by force of imagination. Rather, liveliness belongs to the thing depicted, to the machine, and confirms its continuing utility and purpose. Thus if the plates of the *Encyclopédie* were not always created *ex nihilo*, the *materia* or engravings from which they were made was, Diderot implied, subjected to empirical verification and thus veridification: where possible, the image was corrected, where not, cancelled. In this discourse of making and matching, visual signs are not 'realistic' or 'illusionistic' – that is, self-consciously verisimilar – but are assumed to be transparent – that is, devoid of marks of artistic agency. The work is consequently not good or bad, original or copy, so much as true or false. In sum, the image is a privileged form of representation for technology because it is veridical and timely. In the *Encyclopédie*, it is not the signature but the date that gives value, the value of currency, and thus authority to the plates.

• PLAGIARISME, ou selon d'autres PLAGIAT s[ingulier] m[asculin] (*Littérat[ure]*) (vol. 12, p. 679) •

This discussion of the grounds upon which the *Encyclopédie*'s plates resisted Patte's charge of *contrefaçon* is justified by the perspective it affords of the philosophic context that allowed a charge of plagiarism, if not of breach of privilege, to be made. According to the *Encyclopédie*, plagiarism's specific field of operation is literature, which belonged to the domain of *Imagination*, according to the *Encyclopédie*'s 'Système figuré des connoissances humaines' ('Figurative table of human knowledge').[321] In *Histoire*, the sphere of learning, to which the same table assigned the mechanical arts, ideas are not innate but derive from the senses. Authorial claims to them are consequently weaker. The 'plagiarist' is the agent who steals intellectual property from 'other authors', a malign author; but in a world without authors, only facts, there are, arguably, no plagiarists either. In such a world, the foundation of ethics and law rests on utility not right.

In a review of the Salon of 1767 Diderot offered the following justification for the systematic borrowings of the *Encyclopédie*. Having remarked of the rather pitiful pair of drawings by Jacques-François Amand depicting interiors respectively of a gilder's and a joiner's workshop that they could have served as *vignettes* for the plates,[322] he added bitterly that the *Recueil* was a project 'that we undertook in the midst of every obstacle, that the Académie [des sciences] had started 60 years ago, which it did not pursue, even with all the resources of the government imaginable, & which it has restarted out of shame & jealousy and which it will abandon [again] from aversion and apathy.'[323] He was repeating more pointedly criticism earlier levelled generally in the *Encyclopédie* at major state-sponsored projects under Louis XIV.[324] In the Republic of Letters, failure to publish knowledge out of 'sordid self-interest' or for lack of commitment and energy, was, according to Diderot, no less criminal than withholding information for commercial advantage in manufacture or trade. Secrecy and apathy, sins of corporate privilege committed respectively by guilds and academies, were two faces of the same coin.

By appropriating the knowledge of the trades embedded in the stalled designs of the *Description*, in order to disclose and disseminate it immediately, Diderot was pursuing at a pictorial register a duty already performed at a textual one: that of broadcasting established conventions, and outing discoveries and inventions for the greater progress of mankind.[325] Indeed, in the article 'Plagiarisme' Diderot made copying not only a defensible strategy of encyclopaedias but a positive obligation: 'Lexicographers, those at least who concern themselves with the arts and sciences, need, it seems, to be excused from the common laws of mine and thine. They pretend neither to build on their own resources, nor to draw from these the materials necessary to the production of their own work. The character of a good dictionary, of the kind we hope to produce here, in fact consists in large part in making use of the best discoveries of others. What we borrow from others we borrow openly, in broad daylight, citing the sources from which we have drawn ... If we appropriate, it is only in the manner of bees, which gather [pollen] only for the public good. One could not say that we loot other authors exactly, but [rather] that we draw from them contributions to the benefit of letters.'[326]

Crucially, of course, borrowings from the *Description* had not been made in broad daylight, nor, in the case of the arts and trades, had there seemingly been any intention to cite sources, though in science the existence and the high symbolic value of a tradition of visual representation was to ensure that scientific depiction in the *Recueil*, of anatomy especially, openly acknowledged, indeed positively flaunted, its derivations: from Vesalius, Bidloo, Albinus, etc.[327] Turning a distinction made by d'Alembert in relation to synonyms against him, and against his former co-editor, Patte might have said that the *Recueil* misrepresented itself as a 'suite' to the *Encyclopédie* and not as the 'continuation' of the *Description* that it was: 'one writes a continuation of the work of another and a suite of one's own [work]'.[328]

The article 'Plagiarisme' and the textual acknowledgements in the volumes of plates both post-dated the *Recueil contra Description* affair and very likely registered the greater editorial caution in its wake. However, with respect to technology and the trades, at least, intellectual property rights remained mostly subordinated to the public good. The public good set a term to privilege, after which it was handed over to the commons. In the case of the *Recueil*, the privilege was for 15 years, the duration that from 1762 became legally binding on all patent-privileges – privileges, that is, in science and technology; copy-privileges remained open potentially to a longer term.[329] Public benefit was additionally ensured by the deposit of copies of the works in question, not just as evidence in case of future litigation but also as resources of reference in publicly accessible places: at the Bibliothèque du roi and at the Cabinet du roi. Diderot is known to have borrowed extensively from both to compose and edit articles and illustrations for the *Encyclopédie*;[330] the *Recueil*, in turn, would expand those same collections, furnishing visual and textual sources from which the next generation of bees might borrow and gather.[331]

· DROIT DE COPIE s[ingulier] m[asculin] (*terme de Librairie*) (vol. 5, pp. 146–7) ·

In the context of the privilege debate, Diderot is, of course, better remembered as a champion of authorship, and thus of privilege, than of the public domain. In the so-called *Lettre sur le commerce de la librairie*, written in 1763, that is to say within months of the controversy over the *Encyclopédie*'s plates having subsided, Diderot eloquently articulates the perpetual property claims of authors, and by cession, those of the publishers and booksellers to whom they sold their manuscripts.[332]

The *Lettre* is strewn with property-like figures of speech, land, fields, houses and vines conjuring up a pastoral legal setting for privilege not unrelated to the fictional landscape of La Fontaine's *Fables*, the case that Diderot cites more than any other as having first made the argument for copy*right* unanswerable.[333] He points out that the gesture of restoring the right to publish the *Fables* to La Fontaine's grandchildren was an empty one if such a right is not absolute and perpetual.[334] Following d'Héricourt, his argument has its foundation in a labour theory of property, which, ironically, is utterly at odds with the urban world of work graphically recorded in the *Encyclopédie*, and at odds too with the labour-saving rather than labour-expending means by which the illustrations were in fact realised.

The tracing, cutting, arranging, adapting and pasting by which piracy is accomplished resembles rather the strategies of 'first occupancy', defined by Michel-Antoine David, publisher, with Le Breton, Briasson and Durand, of the *Encyclopédie*, in the article 'Droit de copie'. He describes it as the proprietary mode by which some fugitive resource – *foreign* books and prints in the main – were legitimately – that is, without breach of the law of privilege – hunted down, captured, copied, published, reduced in fact to property, for the first time in France.[335] 'Right to copy' here is not a right derived from work but one based on violence, the violence freely at one's disposal in circumstances beyond the statute of positive law. As Walter Benjamin explains, because natural law is a discourse on just ends, not just means, appropriation by force where violence has not been contractually surrendered to the state is both legitimate and naturally lawful.[336] First occupancy arguments are an older, feudal story about the institution of property, one that had served the early modern state well on the international stage to justify the monopolies it offered as incentives to import foreign inventions for the national benefit; but on the domestic stage it was a notion in the process of being eroded by the bourgeois claims of labour.[337]

The trials of publication experienced respectively by de Montenault and Diderot gave rise to the articulation of contradictory meanings of property, but meanings nevertheless united by a common view that by reducing ideas to property of some kind, private or public, a positive action would ensue. Society would prosper either by the aggregated profit of individuals or by the general enrichment of the commons.

SISTER ARTS

Cases disrupt. As exceptions, not examples, they can put categories in doubt: privilege, the author, the work. Neither of the two disputes analysed was, admittedly, a case strictly speaking. Neither went to court. The affair of the *Encyclopédie*'s plates did become a public controversy, it was tried in the press and left a trace in the debate, but Regnard de Montenault's campaign for privilege was conducted privately.[338] While certainly exceptional, the case of the *Fables* was not, therefore, exemplary at the time. However, de Montenault's challenge is a 'case' for our research because it directly broaches the question of the authorial autonomy of the visual in the illustrated book, and because, by calling attention to the phenomenology of perception, it provides evidence of the way images served to reconceptualise the privileged work as rightfully so, by virtue of the optical illusion as well as the legal logic of private property. Similarly, in the case of the *Recueil* the charge of plagiarism draws attention to the visual arguments of the plates, arguments that disarmed accusations of servile imitation, re-purposing copying as a critical intervention. Further, it raised questions about the utility of privilege, given the restrictions it imposed on the circulation of knowledge.

These particular case studies were carefully chosen, despite their equivocal status in law. They are useful because simultaneously they fit – anchored as they are in law – and they misfire – being not quite substantive enough for litigation but using the words 'author' and 'work' to secure economic and ideological advantages in excess of the conventional meaning of those words. In both instances, commercial competition prompted philosophical questions about what kind of legal thing an image is. The claim to autonomy, though not made in so many words, relates to and possibly helped to bring about the reconfiguration of the arts in the mid-eighteenth century by which, according to Paul Oskar Kristeller, a flat 'system' of arts, regrouped around imitation, took the place of the vertical structure of dependency of painting on poetry, image on text, dominant in the Renaissance.[339] Moreover, the self-conscious illusionism of the *Fables* has suggested that the route to such autonomy for image was prepared not by reason alone but also by the senses. If imitation was a necessary condition for privilege in art, it was not sufficient; the case of the *Encyclopédie* has suggested that not all representations were categorically amenable to privilege.

To return now to the larger narrative of the chapter, we pick up the thread of the state's utilisation and administration of privilege and the art world's response where we left it after the Régence. The legal arguments of those for and against privilege in the book trade may appear little changed between the 1720s and the 1760s, but the government's understanding of its regulatory role had shifted significantly. Printmakers and print publishers, meanwhile, were becoming both individually and collectively more engaged in debates on privilege. The experience of working on such major capital ventures as the *Fables* and the *Encyclopédie* may have had something to do with this: as we shall have occasion to see, Cochin and Jombert took a stand on the *arrêt* of 1777.

· Privilege and Enlightenment governance ·

In March 1764, in the immediate aftermath of the de Montenault and Diderot cases, the wardens of the Paris Corporation des libraires et maîtres imprimeurs, led by Le Breton, sent the new Directeur de la librairie, Antoine de Sartine, *Représentations et observations en forme de mémoire sur l'état ancien et actuel de la librairie*.[340] A year earlier Sartine had asked his friend Diderot for 'information' and 'ideas' on the capital's book industry, and it was Diderot's draft *Lettre* that formed the basis of Le Breton's memorandum.[341] But the circumstances that prompted the guild to write to Sartine were not the *directeur*'s desire for knowledge; rather, it was the decision still pending on the *affaire* La Fontaine.[342] The Paris booksellers had appealed against the transfer of the privilege to the poet's heirs. That Aumont et Cie, the holders of Barbin and Thierry's original 1668 privilege, should be dispossessed of their literary property was, they claimed, without precedent in rulings on matters of the sovereign's 'grace', the purpose of which never was 'to oppress one of his subjects in order to favour another'.[343] Le Breton's aim was, however, both short- and long-term. In the short term, he hoped by this historical account of privilege also to provide Sartine with an 'unassailable obstacle' with which immediately to block the demands of the granddaughters of La Fontaine, and in the longer run he sought to render Sartine permanently proof against both present and future claims that threatened the rights and prerogatives of the Paris Corporation.[344]

Représentations et observations substantially recapitulates the arguments advanced by d'Héricourt in the Mariette memorandum, and Diderot admitted as much in his draft *Lettre*.[345] Aware, no doubt, of the government's angry reaction in 1726, Le Breton excised all reference to d'Héricourt's document in the Corporation's redrafted text of the memorandum. The actions of the Corporation and the Crown were aligned wherever possible. The Conseil du roi and the wardens were portrayed as having acted together.[346] The concepts of property and proprietor recur throughout the text and are no less crucial to the argument for perpetual privilege than they had been in 1725, but *Représentations et observations* styled its case, instead, by repeated and conspicuous references to commerce and merchants.[347] It thereby shifted attention from questions of the legal nature of privilege to economic questions about the distribution of books. The hero is the innovative and entrepreneurial merchant who risks his fortune to bring exceptional books to the market.[348] Adventurously, he commits huge sums on an edition and hopes to sell sufficiently fast to meet his obligations by the time loans are due. The longer, the better, the more erudite and the more elaborate the book, the greater the capital advances and, ordinarily, the slower the return.[349] To handle such risk and finance future ventures, the publisher needed to secure capital assets (manuscripts with privileges), either to sell, or against which to borrow.[350] 'Labour', once paired with 'pains' and then with 'expenses' in justifications for privilege, was now coupled to 'advances'. Threat to the automatic renewal of privilege would, the Corporation argued, destroy the delicate balance of outgoings and income, and destabilise the Paris book industry as a whole.

The Paris *libraires* opened up a second line of defence to offset the obviously self-serving arguments of its elite; the memorandum spoke also of the benefit privilege brought to the consumer. This was an argument about standards. To counter the case made for deregulation, and the consequent fall in prices resulting from competition, Le Breton forecast, instead, a race to the bottom. Poor-quality paper, types, typesetting, printing and proofing, which characterised reprinting, would, he said, become the norm. And rather than increase gross sales, cheap shoddiness would revolt the customer and kill demand.[351] Failure legally to protect the exchange value of intellectual property would, paradoxically, result in the erosion of standards in the medium of its reproduction. 'Quality' books, such as Bernard de Montfaucon's *Antiquité expliquée* (1719), would no longer find publishers, and the unhappy schoolboy would prefer ignorance to difficult and ugly books.[352] Privilege was, Le Breton implied, on the side of the consumer and the Enlightenment. The temptation to extract exploitative levels of profit from privilege was sufficiently contained, the memorandum argued, by the competition from foreign reprints.[353] The wardens thus concluded that only the rigorous enforcement of the 1723 code would secure justice for legitimate booksellers and protect the standards in the industry that consumers expected. The wardens urged Sartine to that end, insisting that in article 1 of the code and those that followed privileges were 'safety measures' pure and simple, and that the purchase of a work engendered an 'unassailable property' whose 'continuous printing and reprinting' belonged exclusively to the owner.[354]

We do not know how Sartine responded.[355] Not like Fleuriau d'Armenonville in 1726: he instigated neither a review of renewals nor a reform of privilege. Instead, he ordered a national survey of the book trade, the broadest, most systematic and thorough of its kind in the eighteenth century. Using specially devised printed forms to standardise answers and facilitate collation of the data, the survey sought to measure, among other things, the impact of the 1723 code.[356] According to Roger Chartier, who mapped the results of a later survey of 1776 and compared them to those of the very first, carried out in 1701, the knowledge gathered at regular intervals by the state made absolutely clear the economic failure of the system of privileges and the legacy of Colbert's policy of controlling printers and restricting the number of presses.[357] In the increasingly diverse urban economy of the eighteenth century, towns and their merchant guilds no longer functioned to stabilise and harmonise production, if they ever had; instead, trades competed openly. The flip side of Paris's history of success in the book industry was a provincial tale of short-term recessions on top of long-term decline.

The fact of Sartine's 1764 survey, and the greater importance it accorded to information than to legal precedent, point to a change in governmental rationality.[358] Foucault's account of the epistemic shift in how government thought, from a mercantilist paradigm, anchored in a concept of national wealth and articulated in a juridical discourse on trades and markets, to what he calls a 'veridical' discourse, focused on population, usefully draws attention to the way commerce was reconceptualised at the mid-century as an economic function in its own right, known and understood according to its own criteria and data.[359] Foucault attributed the change of priorities in state governance from a static model of production to a circulatory model of commerce to the writings of the Physiocrats. An essay on the guilds by the Inspecteur général des manufactures et du commerce, Simon Clicquot-Blervache, disciple of Vincent de Gournay, influential reformer and *intendant* of the Bureau du commerce in the 1750s, had observed that laws and regulations served the private interests of masters, not those of government,[360] a view endorsed by Malesherbes in the case of the book industry, specifically with regard to privilege.[361] Clicquot-Blervache's essay made a point of acknowledging the beginnings of a breakdown of the coalition between guilds and government that Le Breton's memorandum had repeatedly sought to obstruct. The government's responsibility, according to Clicquot-Blervache, was not to enable particular, local guilds to extract disproportionate rents from privilege at the expense of the national economy but to create conditions for growth and to manage circulation by directing free trade.[362] Its success in doing so was a measure of its strength and legitimacy, equal to, if not surpassing, war.[363]

Among those conditions, Physiocrats believed, were the deregulation of the labour market to enable more to become, in this case, publishers, printers and booksellers, and a repeal of quality controls. Clicquot-Blervache argued 'although it is useful to make good things, it is no less advantageous to make ordinary things, or even bad things, providing that the low price invites and secures consumption'.[364] Goods in the context of *laissez-faire* economic policy were commodities – that is, good or bad only in relation to market forces. Under the new *savoir*, price became the measure of the correctness or otherwise of the government's performance.[365] Opponents of the Paris *libraires* had regularly pointed to the artificially high, or 'false' price of new books on account of privilege.[366] The act of balancing in a quantitative sense (volumes of imports and exports, levels of trade in Paris and the provinces) and the ideal of equilibrium were to dominate the government's discourse on commerce after 1750.[367] Memoranda submitted in 1763–4 by the provinces acknowledged that Malesherbes's practice had in effect been to 'equalise' the benefits of Paris and elsewhere by tactical non-intervention and by removal of barriers to circulation: by turning a blind eye, that is, to reprinting.[368] Booksellers in Lyon, Rouen, Toulouse, Avignon and elsewhere hoped that in the spirit of reform Sartine would do the same. By contrast, the rhetoric of the Paris Corporation was resolutely mercantilist. In *Représentations et observations*, the verb 'to balance' retains its traditional meaning and denotes judgment – Le Breton's, Sartine's. It invoked Justice by allusion to her scales.[369]

In 1777, in the slipstream of the ultimately abortive attempt by Anne-Robert-Jacques Turgot, Contrôleur général des finances, to liberate urban trade by dissolving the guilds, the Paris publishers, printers and booksellers suffered the long-expected reform to their statutes, at the legal initiative of Louis XVI's new Garde des sceaux, Armand Thomas Hue de Miromesnil.[370] Between 1773 and 1775, a further dispute had arisen between Paris and the provinces, during which the lawyer Jean-François Gaultier de Biauzat vigorously denounced as specious the Paris booksellers' claim to property by analogy with natural law.[371] The preamble of the decree of 30 August 1777 concurred. It asserted that 'His Majesty has recognised that privilege in bookselling is a favour [*grâce*] which is founded in Justice', that is, in positive law.[372] Sartine had repeatedly been warned that the least willingness to admit the analogy between property and privilege was to risk 'destroying the minister's authority', reducing his power to 'une puissance passive', or weakness, while raising the holders of so-called *droits de privilège* to the status of 'a small republic independent of all authority'.[373] Gaultier de Biauzat was not himself concerned with the sovereignty of royal justice, but in calling the Paris Corporation's regime a tyranny and in recounting how the booksellers had 'surprised' the king's justice and taken it hostage he unintentionally suggested that the fears expressed in the 1777 decree had been realised. The decree insisted on the king's power to act, and to act (in fact) by refraining from action – by not renewing privileges automatically, or indeed at all in the case of 'old' books, and by returning to the public domain all books whose privileges had expired.[374] It belongs, in that sense – and paradoxically since it represented an instance of law – to 'la raison du moindre gouvernement', an ideological transformation within the state apparatus that imposed curtailment on direct intervention in the economy by government and promoted an open policy of *laissez-faire*.[375] It sided, seemingly, with lesser booksellers and publishers, with writers and with the provinces against the Paris-based merchant elite. The question of the right-like nature of the king's 'favour' did not, however, disappear completely. While the privileges secured by publishers were limited to the author's life (art. 4) or ten years, whichever should prove the longer, and could not be renewed except when the work really had been extended by one quarter (art. 2), article 5 recognised in authors for the first time a fundamental right or copyright in their own work, but only when they published and distributed that work themselves.[376]

· Authors and publishers ·

The disputes over the *Fables* and the *Encyclopédie* have less directly to say about authorship than about image in the debate on privilege law, because in neither case was an artist – painter, draughtsman or printmaker – either the plaintiff or the defendant. The legislation of 1777, on the other hand, prioritised the author, making him or her a unique and distinct agent in book and print privilege for the first time. It consigned publishers, printers and booksellers to second place, rendering the duration of their privileges merely conditional. As early as Blondel's memorandum of 1725, critics of privilege had supported their arguments for reform by representing authors and publishers as antagonists, and writing and trading as diametrically opposed. Publishers were stereotyped as avaricious, tyrannical and ignorant; the hapless writer was their exploited victim.[377] Even Diderot, writing in defence of privilege, had underlined the difficulties and hardships faced by writers in the marketplace – he implied at the hand of publishers.[378] Chartier has reminded us that until the nineteenth century the business and practices of writing and publishing more usually overlapped.[379] In the art world, printmaking and publishing were virtually indistinguishable; publishers were, or were formerly, printmakers, and both were potentially authors.[380] Separation of author and merchant was an effect not a cause of discourse and regulation. Was privilege in the later eighteenth century the occasion for the invention of a different kind of author-function?

In 1764 the printmakers Gabriel Huquier and Charles-Nicolas Cochin *fils* each wrote a proposal on privilege, copies of which are to be found among the papers of the Bureau de la librairie.[381] The fact that they were written and submitted at exactly the same time as the *libraires' Représentations et observations* cannot be coincidental, though whether Sartine again solicited the memoranda it is impossible to say. Both Huquier and Cochin were important figures. At that date Cochin was designing the *Encyclopédie*'s allegorical frontispiece and had, from the mid-1750s, been secretary of the Académie royale de peinture et de sculpture and officially responsible for the *détail des arts*, or the king's arts administration.[382] Huquier, having been a major publisher of new prints from the early 1730s, was on the point of enjoying the rewards of his business in semi-retirement. The opinion of both was informed. Huquier's memorandum, much the more substantive of the two, took as its point of departure not privilege but print piracy. 'Every day', Huquier alleged, 'copies of prints are openly sold on stalls in the streets and boulevards' of Paris.[383] He drew a picture of conflict, in which 'genius' was pitted against the 'merchant' and 'imagination' against greed. The professional identity of his merchant – printseller or bookseller – is deliberately left unclear. However, his portrayal fits the characterisation of the latter in earlier instances of disputed infraction: in 1757, the wardens of the Corporation des libraires et maîtres imprimeurs had seized from the engraver François Ledoux a print of the Battle of Hastenbeck on the grounds that it lacked a licence.[384] Not content with asserting their liberty to publish without permission, Paris's printmakers vilified the guild as 'sordidly' mercantile, savvy about trade and utterly ignorant of art.[385] The resemblance of Huquier's merchant to this stereotype had the effect of removing matters of commerce from the discussion of privilege as if they belonged to another professional domain. For Huquier and Cochin, privilege was officially a matter of reputation not of property and trade. Huquier noted, only as an afterthought seemingly, that *contrefaçons*, which were 'destructive of an artist's reputation', were 'also, I dare say, [destructive] of sales of their work'.[386] The artist's fortune, in takings and privileges, was entirely absent from Cochin's consideration. This is not to say that questions of sharp practice were not raised, debated and resolved among printmakers, but rather to acknowledge that they were not obviously so in discussions about privilege.[387]

'At the Chancellor's office there are privileges to be got', was the answer Huquier anticipated in response to the problems he identified in his state of the print trade report, an option he immediately dismissed on the grounds that privilege did not work as a deterrent to copying. For commercially minded printsellers and Grub Street artists, the temptation illegally to copy was simply too strong. In the decade preceding the printmakers' memoranda, which largely coincided with the Seven Years' War, privilege registration was, as Huquier's indifference could have predicted, at an all time low.[388] Neither Huquier nor Cochin had petitioned for one.[389] In fact, no artist, engraver or print publisher made a single successful application between 1761 and 1764. Of the two privileges registered in 1764 neither was for sheet prints, singly or in sets; both were for illustrated non-fiction books.[390] In the same decade there was just one print renewal.[391] With respect to duration, twice as many general privileges purchased were cheaper ones, of six to ten years, rather than the more expensive 20- or 30-year ones. Cost, not legal inadequacy was the most likely cause of low levels of petition. In 1757, the engraver and publisher Pierre-François Basan had objected strongly that privileges were prohibitively expensive. He explained to Malesherbes that they more than doubled the cost of the materials and labour (20–24 *livres*).[392] Peter Fuhring has calculated that the price of privileges increased almost fourfold over the course of the century from 31 *livres* 10 *sous* in 1704 to 101 *livres* 28 *sous* 70 years later.[393] The *libraire* Claude-François Simon, against whose proposal to make a form of privilege mandatory for all prints Basan's objections were primarily directed, complained rancorously that printmakers and publishers freely inscribed 'Avec Privilège du Roy' on their prints when none had been paid for.[394] If the figure of the disinterested author posited by anti-privilege campaigners as the alternative to the author–owner[395] was in the field of literature a writer with alternative sources of income such as a royal pension, in the print world it was an artist with few other options, and the trade-off between cost and protection often determined this author against petitioning for privilege.

There were notable exceptions. In 1767, the successful genre-painter Jean-Baptiste Greuze applied for and was granted a privilege for reproductive prints after five of his works. Like Le Brun's a century earlier, Greuze's privilege was extra-ordinary, not in his case by virtue of rhetoric (by eulogy of authorship), letters patent having become generic formalities by that date,[396] but rather insofar as an artist, a painter, had petitioned for one at all.[397] In 1759 Greuze had married the daughter of the *libraire* François Babuty, a specialist in devotional works, who occasionally had a hand in more ambitious illustrated publications such as de Montenault's *Fables*, apparently.[398] A respected and senior member of the Paris Corporation (warden in 1768), Babuty may have been the one who encouraged Greuze to publish his own works and to obtain privileges for them. Unlike Le Brun, Greuze did not hide his commercial interests. He alone took charge of the distribution and sale of his prints: it is his address that appears on the prints themselves,[399] and that is given in advertisements for them.[400] In the case of *Le Paralytique*, engraved by Jean-Jacques Flipart, the first of the five works listed in the privilege, the three-page advertisement in the *Mercure de France* concludes by giving, in addition to the painter's address, the price of the print: 16 *livres*.[401] The sum was huge.[402] Pierre-Jean Mariette remarked at the time that prints were making Greuze's fortune.[403] Twenty-five years later Greuze put a total figure on it: 300,000 *livres*.[404] The symbolic value and *honnête* social capital that formerly attached to author privilege did so no longer. Although Greuze was later to claim otherwise, in the 1760s and 1770s his studio was manifestly a commercial space and his prices spoke of a determination to profit.[405] Greuze's ideal of authorship was, moreover, one of independence and self-determination, aesthetically as well as economically. An anonymous critic noted that all prints after Greuze looked the same because the painter regarded engraving as literally reproductive.[406] He demanded exact copies in every detail. In other words, he ignored the materiality of the medium, rejected pictorial conventions for 'translating' paint into print and refused to share authorial control with his printmakers, instead imposing his signature, his intangible manner, on the way they copied his works.[407] The result was, in the eyes of some beholders, a hard, dry, black and white authorial monotony of characters and things.[408]

Are we in danger of overstating the roles played by privilege in the formation of Greuze's artistic identity and in his commercial success? He did not, after all, renew the six-year privilege for *Le Paralytique* and its companions, nor did he make any further applications for protection for prints he subsequently published after his works. To return to the comparison with Le Brun, the terms of whose 1656 letters patent were in law so much more possessive and protective than Greuze's, the foundation of Le Brun's fortune was nevertheless the patronage of the king and the court; his letters interpellated him as Louis' 'best-beloved' painter, and only secondarily acknowledged him as an author of prints. By contrast, Greuze's painting practice appeared modelled on the print trade. *Le Paralytique* was painted not on commission but as a speculation. It was unsold when it was exhibited at the Salon in 1763, where Diderot admired it for its intelligence, feeling and enthusiasm, hallmarks of genius run free.[409] In the same Salon review, the critic reproached Claude-Joseph Vernet for failings in *La Bergère des alpes* (1763), which he attributed entirely to the fact of the commission. 'One should give no instructions to an artist,' he observed. 'When one wants something by him, one should say "Make me a picture and choose your own subject...". Better yet would be to buy something already done.'[410] 'Already done': in such cases there can be no dispute over origin and ownership, which in 1690 had cost Suzanne Butay (Mme Le Brun) her legacy. Greuze may have allowed himself to be cheated by his wife, Gabrielle Babuty, but his entitlement as author was never in doubt. The notion of the author's property right formulated by privilege discourse informed Greuze's sense of artistic identity more profoundly than it did Le Brun's, notwithstanding the relative weakness of his 1767 letters and his subsequent indifference to the legal protection of his work. You could even say that it was Greuze who best exemplified the idea of the author-as-owner articulated and defended by Diderot for the Paris booksellers.

Huquier's and Cochin's conception of privilege as expressed in their 1764 proposals appears to have had more in common with Le Brun's than with Greuze's. Both Huquier and Cochin invoked the grace of royal protection. Moreover, Huquier prefaced his proposal by reference to the age of François I, the first in which engraving 'enjoyed the most beautiful privileges granted to the Liberal Arts', and promoted it as exemplary of the kind of regime in which the arts prosper by the *bienfaits* – privilege among them – of such a prince. However, recognition of privilege as positive law did not lead Huquier and Cochin to argue for repeal of privilege in old works nor for an end to renewals. On the contrary, both solicited the reinforcement of privilege for prints. Specifically, Huquier proposed that notification of publication be made mandatory for all prints (art. 1) except in instances where the work was the author's own (art. 3), that the guild be notified in writing of all intentions to copy (art. 4), that all new prints be deposited and registered at the Bureau de la librairie in three copies (art. 5) and, finally, that all prints be dated (art. 9) as well as signed for ease of verification.[411] Only such comprehensive measures would, he argued, arm authors to pursue *contrefacteurs* successfully. Reiteration of the freedom of the print trade (art. 2) was, it seems, no barrier to revision of protection from an opt-in to an opt-out regime. On closer inspection, however, Huquier's regulations required no more than notification. He argues for lists not letters patent and he reverses the onus for legality from the author to the copyist, who must now give notice of his or her desire to imitate. Thus, in its presumptions that to reprint is unlawful whether privilege has been obtained or not and that to copy is criminal unless permission has first been obtained, Huquier's proposal implicitly advanced a strong definition of the author's claim, one close, in fact, to the 'right' articulated by the Paris *libraires*.

Printmakers and publishers were, however, no more successful than the booksellers in moving Sartine to defensive action in 1764, nor is there evidence to suggest that, directly or indirectly, they played a part in the formulation of the *arrêt* of 1777. However, it was the print trade that provided evidence of the benefits to flow from allowing authors to assume responsibility for publishing and marketing their own works. In the period between Sartine's inquiry and de Miromesnil's decree, the booksellers' registers show that, as the economy recovered after the war, architects and *ornemanistes*, especially, sought and obtained privileges for works of scope and ambition that must have required significant capital advances – works that they published, or had published by print publishers, and which they sold at their own addresses. Between 1757 and 1768 Jean-François Neufforge published his eight-volume *Recueil élémentaire d'architecture*, and in 1772 Lucotte, who had worked on the plates of the *Encyclopédie*, entrusted the publication of his *Le Vignole moderne* to the print publishers Le Père and Avaulez. Jean-François Forty and Jean Lamour had meanwhile published *recueils* of their designs for metalwork, respectively in 1765 and 1767, and in 1768 Jean-Charles Delafosse obtained a privilege for the 108 plates that constituted his *Nouvelle iconologie*, published and sold 'chez l'auteur'.[412] More significant, perhaps, were the arguments about reputation. Cochin, in justification of his proposed decree, reported that several members of the Académie royale d'architecture had seen their reputations put at risk by 'incorrect', 'disfigured' and 'travestied' reproductions of their designs.[413] Huquier also spoke of 'infidelitées criminelles'.[414] This is not to say that notions of misrepresentation had not informed arguments about privilege in the past – Le Brun's letters patent had alluded to the threat of 'bad copies' – but it is to observe a subtle and significant shift in the discourse on privilege from inaccurate copies to disfigured authors – that is, from the object to the subject of privilege. Huquier's and Cochin's memoranda assume that the author is not subsidiary or incidental, not merely indexed by privilege but fully present in it; to put it differently, that in privilege law 'author' is not so much a function as a likeness.

The *arrêt* of 1777 entailed changes to the wording of the letters patent granting privilege: changes not to the four-part order of the writ (salutation, supplication, authorisation, prohibition) but to the manner in which the author was represented. To take as an example Jacques-Charles Bar's six-volume *Recueil de tous les costumes des ordres religieux et militaires* (1778–89), the first print publication to be granted a privilege under the new legislation, the author, though qualified conventionally as the king's beloved, is no longer passive, a mere referent in the text. The new law not only desires that he and his heirs 'should enjoy the effect of the present Privilege ... in perpetuity', but if he cede it to another, the duration of that other's privilege is calculated in relation to him: it is, 'as a consequence of the transfer, reduced to the life of the author'.[415] The author is thus the measure of the right and displaces all others as significant in relation to the work. Where the cessionary is reduced to the silhouette of a subordinate clause and to the bare facts of the dative to whom privilege sometimes devolves through exchange, the author is nominated by the letters and acts out his subjectivity as originator of both works and heirs. In short, as Jean-Luc Nancy notes of portraiture, everything in the privilege now bears upon the subject.[416] Paradoxically, given the ideology of grace, his 'portrait' replaces that of the king as the foundation of the new regime of privilege. By happy coincidence, the title-page of Bar's *Recueil* depicts its author deep in study, his palette and brushes on his right and books, portfolio, quill and the manuscript of the forthcoming volume on his left. If, arguably, pictorial illusion lent a measure of persuasiveness to the analogy of private property used by the Paris *libraires* to defend perpetual privilege in debates from the 1720s, portraiture, the art of exteriorising the subject (what Nancy calls the 'exposé-sujet'), served the Crown in 1777 to embody claims to that intellectual property in the legal figure of the author – painter, engraver and writer – and, by that authorial limitation, to free the book trade.

Can we conclude, then, that artists were broadly in favour of the *arrêt*? Book historians judge approval by effect and have noted that the legislation had little in the realm of letters. In the world of print, by contrast, the number of applications for privileges by painters, draughtsmen and printmakers rose appreciably after 1777, reaching double figures by the mid-1780s. Among the applicants were such big names as Jean-Michel Moreau *le jeune*, Nicolas de Launay, Noël Le Mire, Nicolas Ponce, Jean-François Janinet and Philibert-Louis Debucourt.[417] Predictably, applications proliferated for portraits and topographical views, but engravers of sheet prints after ancient and modern histories also requested privileges.[418] Moreover, among the many illustrated and picture books for which privileges were sought in the last decades of the eighteenth century, we can note that it was the author and engineer Claude-François Berthelot who in 1781 obtained a privilege for *La Mécanique appliquée aux arts et manufactures* in the genre of illustrated encyclopaedia formerly published by the *libraire* Le Breton, and that it was the engraver Jean-Pierre Simon who secured the privilege for a new edition of La Fontaine's *Fables* in 1784 for the plates 'avec texte'.[419] We can note, finally, that for commercial printmakers like François-Anne David privilege became a regular and no longer an exceptional instrument of trade.[420] The *arrêt* did, it seems, here unleash productive forces within the economy, as the reform movement had predicted it would. And yet, such developments notwithstanding, the domination of the print trade by a few prosperous publishers with large stocks of copper plates continued, according to Cochin.[421] The *arrêt* of 1777 hit them no less hard than it did the *libraires*, and painters and printmakers were not unsympathetic.

Jombert, the printer and co-publisher of de Montenault's edition of the *Fables*, had feared the anticipated loss of the capital's prerogatives in the early 1770s.[422] The same Jombert served Cochin as exemplary victim of the injustice of the new law. In a letter to the Rouennais painter Jean-Baptiste Descamps, Cochin broached the question of the reformed terms of privilege via news of their mutual friend[423] (Jombert had published both Cochin and Descamps).[424] Jombert's move into comfortable retirement after a lifetime of business and scholarship had been foiled, apparently, by the *arrêt*. The sale of his valuable stock of plates and privileges to his son Louis-Alexandre and his son-in-law the *libraire* Louis Cellot for 300,000 *livres*, agreed on 28 September 1775, which was to have financed the construction of a modest mansion in the rue de Pontoise, was in jeopardy. Curtailment of privilege to the life of the author or ten years had stripped the stock of value and the sons were now reluctant to honour the patrimonial contract. Cochin added himself to the list of the hundreds of ordinary others who found themselves in the same predicament: the winding up of his partnership with Pierre-André Jacqmin for reproduction of twelve marine views by Vernet after Jacqmin's death involved selling the plates to a printseller – Basan – in order to realise and divide the capital between himself and Jacqmin's heirs.[425] Cochin sought to secure Descamps's compassion for Basan, who, having acquired the paintings, plates and relevant privileges at some considerable expense, discovered that they were virtually worthless because the original privilege had almost run its course and, thanks to the *arrêt*, was no longer renewable. With these examples vividly in mind, Cochin asked Descamps to put himself in Jombert's shoes. Imagine that in order to enjoy the product of your work in peace and quiet you decide to sell your work and privilege. Impossible, by the legislative terms of 1777, except at a trivial and humiliating price because a second edition – of, in Descamps's case, *La Vie des peintres flamands, allemands et hollandois* – necessarily sells slower than the first and the privilege, meanwhile, is good for no more than a decade.

Cochin's examples group together not 'authors' (of which there is scarcely any mention here, unlike in his 1764 petition) but privilege holders: the miscellany of publishers, engravers, artistic directors, investors and artists. He established no hierarchy among them; indeed, he mocked the hierarchy that the new legislation attempted: 'Recognition of the author's property to the nth generation is loudly proclaimed, but what benefit is there to be had from a property that one can cede to no one?'[426] In this confidential and candid exchange between artists no mention is made of reputation, of piracy's disfiguring assaults upon the person of the author.

Rather, attention turns and returns almost obsessively throughout the long letter to property. Towards the end Cochin asks:

> by what right does the Garde des sceaux tell us that those things that have been regarded as property for over two hundred years, and as such have passed through a thousand hands, have figured in the division of the property of all estates, [and] in marriage contracts by which dowries are transferred &c. &c., by what right, I say, does he presume to allege that on his whim they will cease to be property?[427]

Outside the lawyer's cabinet, the analogy 'intellectual property' had become a matter of fact and feeling. It was passionately known. Diderot had described in another context the effect of usage and vulgarisation on context-specific language; he noted that 'most of the technical terms that we use today were originally neologisms; it is only the use of ages that strips them of their veneer of equivocation'.[428] In Cochin's hands not only was the literal sense of privilege, 'by grace of the king', lost, but so too the metaphorical origin of its translation into a form of property; the subtle, flowingly persuasive 'as if' of its becoming was forgotten and replaced retrospectively ('for over two hundred years') by a material entity, solidly present in all those contracts by which a bourgeois human life was privately weighed, measured and experienced: marriage, inheritance, contracts, exchange, etc. Absent too is any reference to creative labour, imagination, to drawings as the expression of art. Instead, pictures, drawings and plates were goods, precisely like all others. Indeed, it was the making singular and unique of *intellectual* property by the 1777 act, as a property that could not be traded intact without substantial loss of substance, to which Cochin, in the name of the printing trades, objected.

So defined, intellectual property is wielded like a blunt instrument against the government: 'by what right . . .?' Earlier in the letter he had conceded that privilege involved an exchange, and was not, therefore, strictly speaking a right. He answered his own rhetorical question 'What is a *Privilège du Roy*?' by describing the submission of the petitioner to the royal censor, in exchange for which the king 'on receiving my monetary tribute gives me his seal of approval and prohibits others from copying my Plates'. He added, in summary: 'on his part, it is an approbation, an authorisation to publish them, and for me, it is an exclusive privilege which assures me the enjoyment and the use of them'.[429] Only for the petitioner was privilege a matter of property, according to Cochin; for the king and his ministers it was, or should have been, purely a matter of policy. Taking advantage, perhaps, of the reticence of the *arrêt*'s preamble, its failure to elaborate upon the principles and the anticipated socio-economic consequences of the new legislation – that is, upon its utility – Cochin interpreted article 5 as giving rise to a very personal struggle, a tussle between author and king, one in which the king represented not the public interest but his own. 'Can you imagine', he asked Descamps indignantly, 'that the King can say to me, the property is yours for as long as you keep it, but the moment you cede it, it is mine?'[430]

By substituting 'mine' for 'the public's', the touted beneficiary in petitions for the limitation of privileges, Cochin effectively argued that in the *arrêt* we witness the actions of the body natural and its desires and pleasures, not the body politic: the king's justice was rather His Sovereign pleasure arbitrarily to withdraw as well as to bestow his favour, or to act tyrannically. Moreover, Cochin's examples served to show that in satisfying his own desires the king struck at the foundations of society. His cameo *drame bourgeois* depicts a society discomposed, divided by a law that, in retrospectively rendering the property in literary and artistic work ephemeral, set fathers against sons, partners against partners, and buyers against vendors. Indeed, in a letter of June 1778, and in a scene worthy of Greuze, whose *Malédiction paternelle* and *Le Fils ingrat* had, coincidentally, been engraved and published that very year, Cochin described Mme Jombert's death, the death of a most beloved friend, and laid responsibility for it squarely at the doors of de Miromesnil and his Directeur de la librairie, Le Camus de Neville, on account of the acute, nay fatal, anxiety their 'iniquitous' and 'greedy' support of the 1777 act had engendered.[431]

In between letters, Cochin had sent Descamps a copy of the abbé François-André-Adrien Pluquet's 1778 *Lettres à un ami sur les arrêts du Conseil du 30 août 1777*, which he recommended. He also reported on the letters and memoranda he had addressed to Le Camus de Neville and gave account of the meeting he had eventually had with the Garde des sceaux.[432] Pluquet's was not the only pamphlet to defend the cause of the Paris booksellers, but it was perhaps the one that offered the most straightforward and succinct recapitulation of d'Héricourt's description of literary work as property, and it exposed most clearly the contradictions of the legislation: the definition of the literary oeuvre as simultaneously more than conventional property, an extra-belonging – because fundamentally inalienable – and less than ordinary property – because non-transmittable in its entirety, that is, in perpetuity.[433] Moreover, Pluquet argued against the view that privilege had originated in favour and positive law, that the natural law of property, intellectual property, had, history showed, been abused and artificially manipulated as a fiscal instrument by modern governments to multiply by renewal the opportunities for raising revenue.[434] The fundamental error of the legislation was therefore to mistake the king's privilege for a right; *his* royal right over the works *he* privileged.

Pluquet attributed the move to reform the book trade to the *esprit philosophique* that was infecting the royal administration and influencing even the most judicious and zealous ministers. But de Miromesnil was no Malesherbes. Rather, he was a chancellor with nearly 20 years of first-hand experience of the book trade in the provinces, having been appointed first president of the Parlement of Normandy in 1757. He therefore needed little persuading of the devastating effect the Paris stranglehold on book privileges was continuing to have on publishing at Rouen, Lyon, Toulouse and elsewhere.[435] Not surprisingly, Cochin found de Miromesnil deaf to his arguments and unswerving in his championship of the new *arrêt*.[436] Cochin played for time. He argued the case for honouring all current privileges for up to 30 years, thus submitting only future generations to the new, more hazardous market conditions, by which time, as he confided to Descamps, 'd'icy là l'âne ou moy nous mourons', which was to say with La Fontaine that, since he had no intention of dying, in the interval his hopes were high for a change of regime.[437] Meanwhile, in order fully to register his displeasure, in the name of hundreds of other printmakers like himself he resigned his position as royal censor, a post he had held for more than 20 years.[438]

* * *

Cochin could not, obviously, have foreseen the revolution required in order that his wish for new copyright legislation be fulfilled. Nor did he live long enough to applaud the partial restitution of cessionary rights to authors by the 1793 Copyright Act.[439] To talk further about the circumstances that led to that change of heart, and about the disputes to which it inevitably gave rise would be to anticipate the work of the last chapter of this book. Suffice it at present to say that the conflict of rights between the author and the public remained the unresolved, possibly irresolvable, contradiction of intellectual property debate, a contradiction that was to become increasingly politicised in the 1790s. Although, as we shall have reason to see, the question of the scope of the 1793 Act, and of the identity of the arts that fell properly under its protective umbrella, was sometimes vexed, artists had by that date found their voice and no longer depended on the sisterhood of poetry to articulate their proprietary claims. Of course, the visual had always had a part to play in privilege, though not one fully acknowledged or fully embraced. It raised the spectre of the work of art's tangibility or materiality, and yet the discourse on intellectual property was predicated on the very opposite, on the intangibility of works of genius. The substance of the seen was required not as such, but as if. Visuality was thus both a repressed and an imperfectly resurrected property of art, which contributed significantly to the articulation of the first intellectual property rights. The chapters that here mediate the passage from dependency to autonomy, from a courtly sisterhood of the arts to a legally armed and bourgeois fraternity, address the various ways in which concepts central to the theory of *ut pictura poesis* – namely, emulation, imitation and invention – were worked and worked upon by their engagement in arguments about privilege respectively at the Académie, in court at the Châtelet and in the press.

EMULATION: PRIVILEGE AND PLAGIARISM

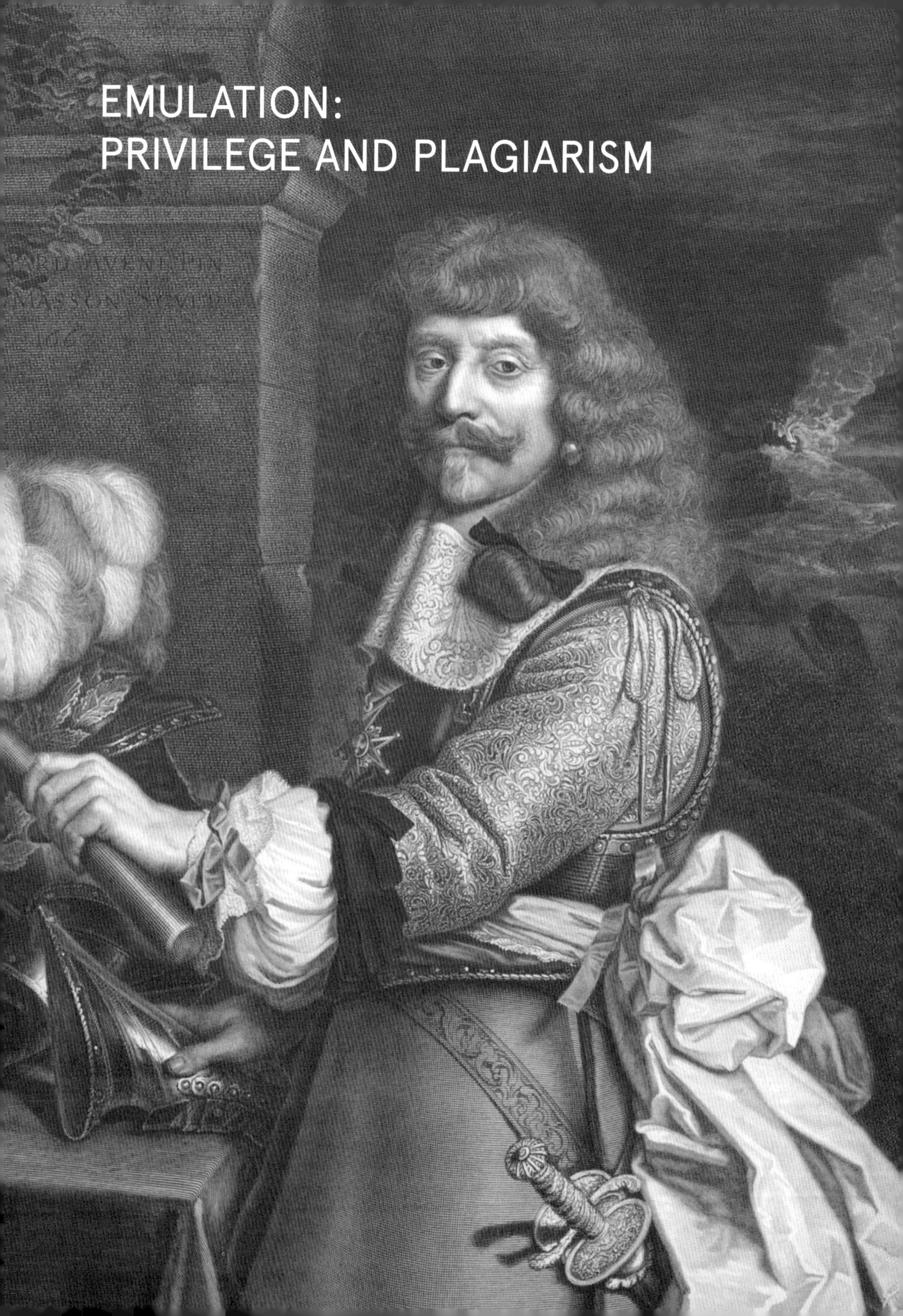

In March 1777, the Académie royale de peinture et de sculpture obtained new statutes, the first revision of its regulations in over a century. Article 8 of the royal *Déclaration en faveur de l'Académie royale de peinture et de sculpture*, which precedes the statutes proper, reads as follows:

> The principal goal that artists of our Académie royale set themselves is the reputation and honour that excellent works confer. In order to prevent the injury [*tort*] they would suffer were works to appear and be [falsely] attributed to their name, or were their own works to be badly copied without their permission, we renew the prohibitions made on this subject, to all Printmakers and the like, to publish any print [*estampe*] under the name of any member of the said Académie without his or her consent, or that of the Académie. Likewise, all Printmakers are forbidden to copy [*contrefaire*] or pirate the works of the Engravers of the Académie, or to sell pirated copies of any kind and on any pretext ... We also very expressly prohibit and forbid all sculptors of any kind or status, and in any possible circumstances, to cast, put on sale, or give to the public any one of the works of the sculptors of our Académie royale de peinture et de sculpture, or copies of them, without the permission of the author, or the permission of the Académie.[1]

Such forceful articulation of artists' prerogatives is unexpected in the light of the history of Chancellerie privilege outlined in chapter 1, in which artists were found to participate only exceptionally. Was there low uptake of Chancellerie privileges by artists before 1777 perhaps precisely because an alternative privilege regime was open to painters, sculptors and engravers through membership of the Académie? It is tempting to think so, not least because the 1777 *Déclaration* renewed and reinforced legislation introduced more than a century earlier. And yet artists appear to have been no more committed to registering for Académie privilege than they were enthusiastic about petitioning for Chancellerie letters patent. Moreover, research to date suggests that litigation under the Académie's copy regulations was almost non-existent.

Daniel McClean has argued that indifference to copyright is, in fact, intrinsic to the art world simply because Western artists produce originals in the double sense of unprecedented *and* singular art works, and intellectual property regimes are concerned with multiples and reproductions.[2] The particular historical circumstances that produced the 1777 *Déclaration* were not those relating to print piracy per se but concerned the status of the Académie in relation to the guilds; the Académie was determined that reinstatement of the Paris Corporation des maîtres peintres et sculpteurs, abolished by Turgot's Edicts of August 1776, should not lead to its revival as an institution to compete with the Académie. The minor part that article 8 appears on the surface to play in this objective confirms McClean's view that copyright is not an object of primary concern for artists, but it leaves unexplained the fact that the Académie on other occasions actively sought copy-privilege for its members. The aim of this chapter is to propose a more comprehensive account of this apparently inconsistent, even contradictory, relation to privilege law: simultaneously desired and neglected. Attention shifts from the legal history of privilege law – our concern in chapter 1 – to questions of salience: what value, what meanings did privilege have for the Académie and Academicians? In our pursuit of answers, we shall be concerned, therefore, not so much with the materialist or economic dimension of the academic concept of privilege, as with its social and ethical dimensions. Thus, we shall consider privilege's relation to the institutional interests of the Académie, notably those of belonging and distinction. The historical record of the Académie's routine administration sheds, as we shall see, important light on how and why privilege was incorporated into the social, professional and ethical concerns of Academicians and informed their artistic practices. More broadly, this chapter explores the relationship between Académie privilege and the informal, customary protocols developed by Academicians to control professional practice: positively by encouraging emulation and negatively by condemning plagiarism.

Briefly to review the eighteenth-century meanings of emulation and plagiarism: in chapter 1 we encountered emulation as a justification for privilege in letters patent. Emulation so defined was the spirit of commercial and mercantile ambition, excited and rewarded by legal monopolies, monopolies that lowered financial risk and supposedly inspired large, long and expensive ventures such as de Montenault's *Fables* and Le Breton's *Encyclopédie*. In polite discourse, by contrast, emulation was more usually associated with noble virtues, especially glory.[3] It was defined as the aristocratic passion that drives men of virtue or learning to pursue distinction, inspired by the model of great men. The Académie and its artists understood emulation in this sense as a noble vocation and an exercise in moral improvement. This chapter therefore asks not only if the introduction of privileges changed the conduct of artistic business, but also if it transformed the meaning of artistic emulation. The answer is not simple and straightforward because the context of artistic emulation was primarily the school, not the marketplace, and it therefore concerned the work of students, not authors. Turning to plagiarism: plagiarism was not about authorship in the legal sense; or rather, infringement of privilege was a special case of it – a copy liable to prosecution by grant of legal protection. However, it *was* about authorship in the artistic sense, and about authors of unique works as well as authors of multiples and reproductions. A suit for breach of privilege could, as noted in chapter 1, be brought against a printer, a publisher, an entrepreneur, in fact anyone involved in the production and sale of piracies, including, obviously, the printmaker. Accusations of plagiarism, by contrast, were levelled only at the plagiarist, the artist responsible for making and making away with the copy.[4] In constituting an authorial category that was at once narrower and broader than *contrefaçon* in law, plagiarism raised questions about personhood, about the relationship between persons defined by their status, gender and personal characteristics, as well as by their profession, and between persons and their works; that is, specifically, between Academicians and others, and between artists and their artistic progeny.[5]

Plagiarism was defined in eighteenth-century France less as a practice than as a charge; an accusation levelled at a person (*plagiaire*) who takes the works of others and attributes them and their virtues to themselves.[6] It was, so to speak, a blot in the eye of the beholder, and discussion of plagiarism must therefore consider the beholder's share.[7] Accusations could come from any quarter, without as well as within the profession and the Académie. But for such indictments to be articulated at all, arguably certain conditions are required: an art world of collectors, connoisseurs, exhibition goers, critics must have developed. Moreover, this public, visually educated at the Salons and by exposure to the vast and increasing number of relatively inexpensive reproductive prints, and therefore alert to and able to recognise instances of repetition as copying, must also feel compelled to interpret such acts in moral terms: as offensive and culpable. To bring the question of plagiarism back to matters of copyright, can we assume that, as rules regulating illegitimate and illegal reproduction in print were established and became entrenched, artists became self-conscious about their own copying practices and newly sensitive to the borrowings of others? A quantitative answer, positive or negative and based on a rise or fall in copying is clearly both impractical and absurdly reductive. The literary critic Harold Bloom has broached the question diagnostically, identifying symptoms of a qualitative intensification of the melancholy fear of plagiarism, or what he calls the 'anxiety of influence', which, he argues, derived from the Enlightenment's scepticism and spirit of critical inquiry. Unselfconscious imitation became impossible with the historicisation of its 'double inheritance' from the past: from antiquity and the Renaissance. In the arts, the neo- of Neoclassicism made artist and viewer more, not less, sensitive to repetition. The emergence of copyright and the rising offensiveness of plagiarism, by this account, predate and contribute to the emergence of Romanticism.[8]

The recurrent point of reference throughout this chapter, linking privilege, emulation and plagiarism, is print (and to a lesser extent casts). Objects of privilege, prints (and casts), were also the first pedagogic objects proposed to Académie students as examples for emulation and copying. They were, likewise, both the mundane instruments of plagiarism and also potentially victims of it. This chapter is thus broadly about the penetration of the fine arts by prints and print culture: its artistic properties, its use and exchange values and its laws. Engraving was valued above all for the clarity (*netteté*) and flow of its lines, for its capacity to reproduce the noble contours of the human figure and the force of painting's composition.[9] Only engravers were admitted to the Académie. The first members were François Chauveau, illustrator of La Fontaine's *Fables*, and Gilles Rousselet, engraver of Charles Le Brun, both admitted on 14 April 1663.[10] In the seventeenth and early eighteenth centuries many of them were also publishers and printsellers, with shops in the rue Saint-Jacques, the publishing and bookselling district of Paris.[11] By their presence in the Académie, the hard line that it tried to draw between the noble profession of art and the bourgeois business of trade remained for a long time blurred, and through them knowledge of Chancellerie privilege, and debates about it, will have been communicated to the membership from first-hand experience. Discussion of reproduction starts with Walter Benjamin's classic essay 'The Work of Art in the Age of Mechanical Reproduction' (1939) and often focuses on the destructive effect on art's cultic 'aura' that Benjamin assigns to it.[12] Our concern here is rather the creative role that reproduction may have played in the construction of the idea of intellectual property, the prime condition, ironically, of art's aura in our age of reproducibility.

ACADÉMIE PRIVILEGE

The two inaugural acts that granted the Académie privileges to protect the works by its members against unauthorised copies were issued by the Conseil du roi in 1676 and 1714. The first granted the Académie's sculptors an exclusive legal prerogative to reproduce their work, prohibiting anyone other than those expressly designated by the author from taking plaster casts of their works on pain of a fine of 1,000 *livres* plus damages and costs.[13] The *arrêt* required Academicians to mark their work with 'la marque de l'Académie' and to register and deposit casts of such works at the Académie's offices.[14] There was no fee, nor, crucially, was duration of the privilege limited. By the second *arrêt*, the Académie acquired a privilege for two-dimensional works, including 'Lectures, Addresses and Descriptions' and the 'Prints or Impressions' produced by its members.[15] Although the terms of the 1676 and 1714 regulations are broadly similar – the only conspicuous difference being an inflation in the later *arrêt* of the penalty for infringement in the case of print to 3,000 *livres* – the circumstances that respectively occasioned them were quite different.

The 1676 *arrêt* was the outcome of a campaign by the Académie's sculptors against the master sculptors of the Paris guild.[16] Two years earlier, François Girardon and Thomas Regnaudin had been deputed by the Académie to seek advice on what general measures could be taken in order to end widespread and unauthorised copying of works by Academicians; more than one sculptor was, it seems, pursuing a private suit at the Parlement.[17] The guild masters had defended their licence to copy on the grounds of their prerogative to mould and cast in plaster, a monopoly that the Académie did not challenge. Rather, the Academicians argued for an exemption in their case. Damage to the beauty of their work by unauthorised copying and disfigurement even of its composition (*ordonnance*) was, they said, a threat to their reputation. Although the sculptors did not articulate their claims specifically in terms of privilege, the right that they demanded to exclusive control over the reproduction of their works on the basis of authorship was broadly consistent with it. That said, the legitimacy of their case rested on their status as Academicians. The king's *arrêt* granted the request not to them as individuals but in the context of 'confirming the privileges that [His Majesty] has formerly accorded to the said Académie'.[18] Moreover, the Crown's reasons for doing so were not necessarily the same as the sculptors' reasons for asking.

The ceremonial presentation of the *arrêt* to the Académie by Le Brun, its Chancellor, in July 1676, and acknowledgement in the Académie minutes of the essential role played by Jean-Baptiste Colbert, the Surintendant des bâtiments du roi, in securing it,[19] suggest a connection between this *arrêt* and another, passed less than a decade earlier in 1667, which forbad printmakers to reproduce works from the Cabinet du roi unless authorised by Colbert to do so.[20] The purpose of this earlier *arrêt* was not to protect the intellectual property of artists, but rather to safeguard the lustre of the king's image, a purpose that the poet Nicolas Boileau endorsed in a satire addressed to Louis XIV:

Et j'approuve les soins du monarque guerrier
Qui ne pouvoit souffrir qu'un artisan grossier
Entreprit de tracer d'une main criminelle
Un portrait résérvé pour le pinceau d'Apelle...[21]

Both *arrêts* were thus part and parcel of Jean-Baptiste Colbert's programme to advertise Louis's *gloire*, nationally and internationally, via public monuments and prints.[22] Censorship, not trade, motivated their enactment: it was essential that the king's glory was manifest in the quality, as much as the content, of the works he commissioned. The engravings of the Cabinet du roi were not for sale before 1683; authors therefore had nothing personally to gain from the protection of the 1667 *arrêt*. While difficult to determine exactly because the record of applications for privilege is so thin, the sculptors' case appears to have been more complex. Antoine Coysevox made the sculptors' first and only formal and recorded request for protection.[23] It was for a bust of the young Louis XV (fig. **34**). In subject matter, the object of his request therefore fitted completely with the kind of works whose protection was met by the 1667 *arrêt*. But Coysevox must have hoped that the privilege, applied for in 1716, when demand for images of the new monarch was especially high, would also protect his work and his workshop's monopoly of its reproduction from outside competition.[24] Private and public interests coincided. Arguably privilege also responded to the customs and concerns of the Académie. Following note of the *arrêt*'s reception at the Académie, the minutes of the meeting record that painters and engravers must comply with article 9 of its statutes of 1651 and likewise present impressions of their work to the Académie for its scrutiny and authorisation before publication.[25] No prerogative derived from the presentation, inspection, deposit and registration of prints at this time. The nature of the procedures indicates that the Académie, like the Crown, also sought to control the quality of the work published in its name. The new privilege for sculpture was assimilated, we can assume, without friction into the older regulations for prints and was translated into the reputational terms of the Académie.

If the 1676 *arrêt* was reactive, prompted by instances of *contrefaçon*, or foul copying, the *arrêt* of 1714 was, by contrast, proactive. The Académie wanted to make itself and its works better known. Other royal academies had been granted general privileges for such purposes: the Académie royale des sciences, in 1699, to give one example.[26] What seems to have prompted the king's painters, sculptors and engravers to action was the Académie's move into new premises, at the Louvre.[27] To celebrate the forthcoming event, the secretary of the Académie, Nicolas Guérin, was commissioned to write a description of the new, handsome and prestigious six-room apartment; it was to be fully illustrated with plans and elevations, decorated with printers' ornaments, including a headpiece by Antoine Coypel and Benoît I Audran, and it was to be printed in quarto – that is, in a format to match the grandeur of the place.[28] In March 1714 the manuscript was complete and was given to Jacques Collombat, the Académie's printer, to print. Page proofs were circulated to the Académie the following April for inspection and for final decisions about format and font.[29] For the privilege required to publish the book, the Académie approached the abbé Bignon, appointed by Chancelier Pontchartrain in 1699 to oversee the royal academies, responsible also for the book trade from 1700, and (most importantly here) elected *conseiller-amateur* at the Académie royale in 1709.[30] The privilege granted was reproduced in its entirety in Guérin's book, and filled no fewer than five consecutive pages at the front, between the dedication to the duc d'Antin, the Directeur des bâtiments du roi, to whom the Académie owed its good fortune in the matter of accommodation, and the text proper of the *Description*.

The privilege does not, of course, form part of the narrative of the book, and to that extent looks alien to Guérin's portrait of the place – the bulky intrusion of law into the sphere of art. First impressions are misleading. The text is unusually long precisely because it contains a synoptic description or portrait of the Académie, which served to justify the king's latest favour:

> from the time it has pleased His Majesty to bestow on the Académie marks of his affection, the Académie has applied itself increasingly and with care to the cultivation of the Fine Arts, which have always been the domain of its expertise. And since the end His Majesty had in mind when establishing the said Académie, composed of the Kingdom's greatest talents, was not only that *the young should profit* from the instruction given daily at the Life School, in Geometry, Perspective and Anatomy, and by looking at the Masterpieces that are set them as Examples, but also that the *Public should be informed* of the progress made there in the Arts of Drawing, Painting and Sculpture, by making it party to the Lectures, Addresses and Descriptions by which [such] progress is made known, principally *by multiplying by engraving and printing the said Académie's most beautiful works, in order to keep them for posterity, the only means of perfecting the Arts and exciting emulation more and more.* TO THESE ENDS...[31] (my emphasis)

The terms of the privilege then follow. Privilege thus arose to meet the central public functions of the Académie – to teach and to enlighten – not the several private interests of its members. Moreover, the prints whose production was supported and encouraged by privilege generated in turn the keeping, perfecting and emulation of art, which led to collective, rather than individual, progress. The king's moral portrait of the Académie, inserted into the *arrêt*, mirrored in historical and ideological terms Guérin's physical 'description' of the place, the apartment at the Louvre, the first reception room of which was dominated by Henri Testelin's larger-than-life portrait of Louis XIV (1666–8), in which the depicted king performed justice on his *lit* and, as Guillet de Saint-Georges, a former secretary to the Académie, put it, established the conditions, legal and other, for art to emerge.[32] The origin of privilege thus appeared if not interior to then at least in some sense internalised by art. Rather than legal instruments, privileges from this vantage point assumed the substance of norms – that is, values whose meaning was intrinsic to the field of art and whose benefit exceeded that of private property and calculated gain.

So, what were these norms and values that took possession of privilege and made it, so to speak, academic? The terms of the Académie's contract with its printer obliged him to give the Académie 150 free copies of Guérin's book. The first 100 were distributed gratis to the Academicians at the March meeting in 1715, and the remaining 50 were offered to Guérin's daughter in recognition for the care and trouble her father had taken in writing the *Description*.[33] It was a tribute to the institution. Further publications directly linked to the Académie's institutional identity followed in 1721. The statements of approbation printed above privilege at the front of Jacques-Philippe Ferrand's *L'Art du feu ou de peindre en émail* and Antoine Coypel's *Discours prononcez dans les conférences de l'Académie royale* listed communication of the works as *conférences* or Académie lectures and the utility of the texts to its students as justifications for privilege.[34] Ownership at the Académie was a matter of recognition and acknowledgement. It was collective, and it encouraged a feeling of corporate belonging.[35] The *Procès-verbaux*, which recorded the discussions and decisions about privilege at the Académie's meetings, reinforce this impression.[36] Works of art brought before the Académie by members were described as *présents*. 'Present' occurs in the form of a noun, '[he] made a present of', and as a verb – ambiguously in the phrase '[he] presented', explicitly in '[he] gave'. The Académie responded that it had 'received' or 'accepted' the 'present', variously with 'satisfaction', 'gratitude' and 'thanks'.[37] The binding role of these presents is especially evident in the repeat pattern of gifts made by and on behalf of the Academician and sculptor Jean Thierry, much of whose career unfolded under the patronage of Philip V of Spain.[38] They are worth describing in order to show more clearly the web of social relations in which privilege was enmeshed.

Présent referred to gifts of different kinds, and distinguishing those that were also privileges is sometimes difficult, which is part of my point. In July 1734, Thierry charged the engraver Henri-Simon Thomassin with giving the Académie two impressions of the prints the engraver had made after two of the sculptor's fountain projects for La Granja de San Ildefonso, north of Madrid.[39] The following month Thomassin 'gave' the Académie 'the portrait of M. Thierry' (fig. **35**) that he had engraved after Nicolas de Largillière's painting; and at the Académie meeting in October the first item of business was the distribution among those present of impressions of the portrait of

Thierry, who had just come back from Lyon.[40] Finally, in April the following year the sculptor himself presented the Académie with the copper plate of the portrait and two framed impressions of the fountain prints.[41] On each occasion prints were 'given'; on separate occasions impressions of the same print were 'given' twice over, by both parties; and the portrait served first as substitute for, and then to announce the return of the sculptor, whose company his fellow Academicians were thus able to enjoy in proxy and then in person. Whereas Thierry's gifts were either single, framed impressions or multiple copies for distribution, Thomassin's presentations took the exact form of double copies, which suggests that, though given as *présents*, they were in fact (also) deposits, either in compliance with the statutes of 1651 or in relation to the *arrêt* of 1714. Whether gifts or deposits, or rather gifts-as-deposits, the concern of the Académie, drily minuted, was the intersubjective relations made and sustained by the exchange of the prints, not the things themselves. The prints were significant, that is to say, because they were prints by and after members, and because they contributed – explicitly through portraiture – to the constitution and commemoration of the Académie as a body.[42]

In that sense, print-presents at the Académie, in the immediate aftermath of the 1714 *arrêt*, appear to resemble the sixteenth- and seventeenth-century letters patent discussed in chapter 1. However, there are some notable differences of expression and meaning. To start with, the language register of the minutes is everyday and not the high rhetoric of law and patronage. Secondly, the marked asymmetries of power between correspondents in the *lettres patentes* was replaced at the Académie, the minutes imply, by parity among the assembled membership. This is not to say that the Académie was non-hierarchical. On the contrary, it was subdivided into officers, members, associate members and students. Moreover, engravers were formally subordinate to painters and sculptors and were excluded from the rank of officer.[43] It is, however, important to recognise that in the case of privilege, distinction between members was repressed. So while the Académie's graciousness echoes the king's, it does not appear to condescend. Finally, the *présents* of Academicians were not bargains, or disguised sales, as the king's gifts of Chancellerie privilege had become by the early eighteenth century. They were vivid expressions of belonging.

The symbolic capital of Académie privilege was evident also in the Académie's rituals. At the first assembly of every new year the Académie's founding statutes, to which the *arrêt* was added in 1714, were brought in state before the membership, carried into the Académie's meeting room in a ceremonial casket; the vellum deeds, with their heavy green wax seals, were taken out, presented and read out loud to the assembled company by the Académie's secretary.[44] Reading of the *arrêt* was also incorporated into the swearing-in of engravers as full members on presentation of their *morceaux de récéption*.[45] In February 1729, at the double reception of Charles-Nicolas Cochin *fils* and Laurent Cars, not only was the *arrêt* read out to all by Dubois de Saint-Gelais, the Académie's secretary, but the director, Louis de Boullogne, also made a particular point of repeating it to each of the two new members as a provision of their incorporation.[46] Moreover, not only did privilege mark the moment of entry into the Académie, it was also a principle for expulsion. In July 1719, in a dispute between the engraver Jean-Baptiste de Poilly and other Academicians over Poilly's alleged piracy of their works, the Académie threatened him not with a fine and confiscation of offending materials and tools but with loss of membership if he did not stop making illegitimate copies.[47] Privilege was an honour and part of an Academician's identity. In underlining the importance of the social relations in Académie privilege, I am arguing not only for its distinctiveness, by comparison to book privileges, but also for its particularity as a pre-capitalist social formation, in which status is primary and construed as a constituent part of the ego. Chancellerie privileges were, by the eighteenth century, arguably en route to legislating relations between commodities; Académie privilege, by contrast, fetishised social relations – between Academicians and between them and the commercial artists of the guilds.[48]

Clearly, privilege's utility was not confined to the social, to promoting sociability. It was also semiotic, a means of articulating and communicating claims. What then were the claims made by Académie privilege? What was the character of its effect of belonging? First, the Académie's privilege was overwhelmingly about authorship. Only exceptionally was the applicant the publisher of the print: Gaspard Duchange, for example, in 1738 requested a privilege to publish a breviary illustrated by members of the Académie, and in 1739 applied for another to bring out a second edition of the *Peintures de l'hôtel Lambert*, containing reproductions of Charles Le Brun's and Eustache Le Sueur's celebrated decorations for Louis Le Vau's Paris mansion.[49] Applications for privileges for sheet-prints were made by painters (the authors of the compositions) and by engravers of reproductions – four times as many by engravers as painters.[50] As regards the compositions engraved, the number of applications for the reproduction of works by non-members, mostly Old Masters, exceeded, though not by much, the total for designs by members. However, in terms of the artists reproduced, three times as many modern Academicians were represented in privilege applications between 1714 and 1789 as painters of the Italian and Northern schools.[51] Académie privilege was about authorship not in the abstract but very precisely in the context of belonging: it served first and foremost to promote by reproduction and dissemination the work of its living members.

Privilege was also about art. The 1714 *arrêt* was first invoked in November 1731, by Nicolas-Henri Tardieu. Having engraved Pierre Dulin's Carlo Borromeo altarpiece, he deposited two copies 'in accordance with the Privilege granted by the King to the Académie'.[52] The following year Cochin *père* presented two copies of his print after François Le Moyne's small easel painting *Jacob arrive en Mésopotamie, aperçoit Rachel et se fait connoître à elle* (fig. **36**), the print in which, according to the *Mercure de France*, the printmaker first endeavoured to realise the human figure on a grand scale.[53] Both were prints after history paintings, both were large; Cochin's was dedicated to Cardinal de Polignac and both prints were intended for connoisseurs like him. Quantitative analysis by subject matter of the applications for privilege over the course of the eighteenth century (see p. 305) suggests that history (to which portraiture can be added, since five of the seven portrait applications were for portraits of members of the royal family and the other two for portraits of artists of public note) continued to characterise, not to say define, Académie privilege, especially when the exceptional and distorting case of Jean Moyreau, engraver of Philips Wouwermans' complete oeuvre, is stripped out of the figures. As such, Académie privilege stood out from its everyday Chancellerie equivalent, not because the latter excluded history painting, but because book privilege was qualitatively neutral, and favoured designs for embroidery, fans, penmanship, wallpaper, indeed all forms of commercial art, as readily as art works of the very highest academic order and public consequence.[54]

Académie privilege made claims about the nature of this liberal art and about the relationship the artist has with his or her work. The *arrêts* of 1676 and 1714 make no mention of time, and minuted instances of privilege are also silent about duration. At one level this was because privilege was vested in the institution, itself founded in perpetuity.[55] However, that did not preclude it from setting a limit to the grants of protection it issued to individual members. Its choosing not to do so suggests that the Académie assumed that artists, as Academicians, enjoyed inalienable rights in their work. The claim of inalienability was established in law by a case that dealt not with reproduction, but with production, which was brought before the Paris Parlement, the highest court in the realm, in 1667. In that year, the Flemish sculptor and Academician Gérard Van Opstal sued Mme Duchemin, widow of the duchesse de Montpensier's former *intendant* (d. 1665), for payment for eight bas-reliefs, executed eight years earlier at their country estate at Bisseaux in Brie.[56] A statute of limitation applied in customary law to the work of craftsmen during the *ancien régime*: after a legally fixed period of time, debts were no longer redeemable against a person's estate.[57] Van Opstal was represented in court by Nicolas de Lamoignon, marquis de Bâville, the son of the first president of the Paris Parlement, whose 'glorious defence of the principles of art' confirmed its liberal status and established in law that the artist's right, as author, to payment should be no more limited than the immortality he conferred on his subjects by his portrayal.[58]

> Would you [he asked the bench] suffer that this art, which ennobles its materials, should itself be stripped of its own nobility, that time, which increases the value of [the artist's] works should rob him of his reward, and finally that those who confer immortality on others should themselves be limited to twelve months for payment and subjected to other degrading tasks?[59]

He answered for them, 'no', and they agreed with him: lapse of time cannot void a contract for a work that endures and whose exchange value and artistic value, or prestige, increase over time. This case about sculpture rehearsed a position on the rights of the author that was later crucial to

Académie privilege, and founded it not in the theory of natural rights – that is, on Lockean arguments about property in labour – but in a right of exception due to the extraordinary beauty and power of art. So important was the case to the Académie that it had the original copy of the brief that Henri Bessé de La Chapelle had drafted for de Bâville bound for safekeeping in its library, and published and disseminated it widely at its own expense.[60] The *plaidoirie* (speech for the defence) established the legal context within which to frame further legislation on the conditions of trade in art, and rehearsed arguments about perpetual rights that were transferable to the regulation on copying. A remarkable point about the Poilly affair, half a century later, is that no mention was made of privilege as such, either by the Académie or the plaintiffs, or indeed by the defendant, who could have argued that, in the absence of privileges actually having been obtained, there was no case to answer: perpetual and exclusive right of attribution was understood by one and all to exist by the moral right in art, prior to statute. Norms of proper behaviour with respect to the re-use of works by other Academicians were, it seems, so embedded that the dispute was resolved without law, and out of court.

De Bâville was able to establish a hierarchy of entitlement in Van Opstal's case by persuading the judges that the bas-reliefs were not just any kind of property but a personal kind, closely bound up with the artist's identity, from which they could not be entirely separated even when sold.[61] That identity was partly a matter of academic status, but de Bâville, having acknowledged the role of the Académie in making distinct the difference between the fine and mechanical arts, went on to identify a hierarchy of talent within the Académie itself, ranking Van Opstal highly for the particular character of his works.[62] It was these personal properties that provided the ground for the legal judgment, and secured exceptional prerogatives for art and artists. Van Opstal's works embodied not labour in the abstract, to which universal rights attached (Locke's model), but a particular and personal combination of 'learning' and 'deftness of skill'.[63] Nor did de Bâville represent Van Opstal as an abstract, rational agent: though Dutch (and therefore expected to attend carefully to his commercial interests, as his countrymen were reputed to do), he had neglected business and forgotten to chase up what he was owed.[64] In addition to providing one explanation for the perpetuity of privilege under the Académie's regime, the Van Opstal case also enables us to understand better why disputes involving Academicians over copies and copying in any medium often concerned questions about the work's autonomy and integrity and were only indirectly related to trade.

The Académie minutes record that in August 1691 it expelled a student for daring to retouch and finish a picture by Charles Le Brun.[65] The trouble and expense the Académie incurred to have posters announcing its sentence printed and posted indicates that there was more at stake than mere insubordination. Reiteration of the alleged invasions made by the student's hand, denoted by 'to retouch' and 'to finish', was intended by the authors of the Académie's verdict to convey the outrageous scope of his defacing: not only material, it had extended (the phrasing implies) to altering and resolving the unfinished in Le Brun's compositional idea. The student's 'graffiti' were experienced as an assault on Le Brun's identity, and the Académie reacted in shock to the violation on the painter's behalf. More than 60 years later, in March 1755, another distinguished Academician and history painter, François Boucher, advised the readers of the *Mercure de France* that a set of reproductions published by Claude Duflos (fig. **37**), and purporting to represent his work,

> has... been engraved after deformed copies, furtively drawn by the least able and least advanced pupils of this Painter. They later gave them to a Printmaker who, in turn, has finished them and put them on the market without the participation of the author. Boucher can neither recognise nor acknowledge his work in such unfaithful copies.[66]

Students are again the culprits but the circumstances are different: at issue in this case are printed copies, not the painted original. Nevertheless, it is Boucher's sense of self that has been injured, and the reader is witness to his humiliation; reproduction was, after all, what primarily shaped public perception of artistic identity in the era before photography.[67] For Boucher, the issue was not copies per se but their infidelity and lack of authenticity; the damage he was seeking to mitigate was to his person and reputation, not apparently his pocket. In both these disputes, authorship was embodied not in a nominal way but very particularly, in the persons of Le Brun and Boucher as artists and Academicians. Boucher's complaint suggests a further significant point. 'Recognition' and 'acknowledgement' were tropes in the discourse on biological legitimacy. In the *ancien régime*, questions of paternity were resolved in civil law by the father's formal recognition of his progeny before witnesses at the *hôtel de ville*.[68] Boucher's refusal to admit Duflos's copies and to see himself in them suggests that he regarded his creative work as offspring not property, as 'children' – literally, here, the so-called *enfants de Boucher* – to be claimed or disavowed but not owned.[69]

The privilege regime inaugurated at the Académie royale de peinture et de sculpture in the 1670s for sculpture and extended at the beginning of the next century to engraving, though identical in name and similar in some of its terms with privileges in texts, was, by this account, different from the Chancellerie regime in significant respects. That difference arose not from the challenge presented by the particular demands of vision and visual media to the provision already formulated for texts; rather, it was prompted by the liberal status of the artist, secured, ironically, by the poet in him.[70] Académie privilege was thus interpreted through, and deployed in the defence of the values of high art and public utility that justified its institution. It was at first blind to (or at least reserved in the articulation of) the private economic interest that individual members had in their works, and which privilege in the law of the book trade aimed to defend. Incorporated into the rituals of foundation and membership, privilege primarily mediated academic belonging.[71]

Why this academic reserve? The institutional explanation is surely inadequate. After all, other academies, such as the Académie royale des sciences, had also obtained privilege-conferring rights, and their members were not slow to take advantage of them.[72] Uniquely, the Académie royale de peinture et de sculpture was also a school. It was, therefore, a mixed body of members and others, artists and students. In copyright, the 'author' is categorically the only agent; agency at the Académie and in artistic discourse was more comprehensive. The Académie's purpose was to school the agency of those aspiring to authorship by initiating them into the conventions of art through both the artistic and the social practices of emulation. Belonging was not only an event, it was also a formation. It was therefore at the school and in the execution of what we might call the common law of the copy that the Académie's privilege assumed its distinctive moral meaning.

If the résumé of the school's functions in the *arrêt* of 1714 assigned priority to copying nature in the life class, supported by lessons in perspective and anatomy, reference is nevertheless also made to study 'in the presence of Works that are assigned as examples'.[73] At the Paris Académie such study took place informally, and often *extra muros*, facilitated by reproductive prints dedicated to the purpose, such as those in Élisabeth-Sophie Chéron's *Livre à déssiner composé de testes tirées des plus beaux ouvrages de Raphaël* (fig. **38**), for which she obtained a book privilege in 1706 and a copy of which she gave to the Académie.[74] It was rather at the Académie de France in Rome, established by Colbert in 1666, that the best students from the Académie royale were confronted with the finest models of art, ancient and modern, for sustained and systematic study.[75] That pupils learned better by example than by precept, allowing that the arts of painting and sculpture were, in fact, reducible to a set of abstract rules,[76] was never seriously questioned. This is not to say that the *pensionnaires* only copied – the inaugurating statutes prescribed a comprehensive curriculum of classes in history, mathematics, geometry and perspective (art. 8), anatomy (art. 9) and life drawing (art. 14)[77] – but it is to explain the overwhelming priority assigned to the regimen of copying (art. 11) and to matters relating to it in the letters between successive *surintendants*, *intendants* or *directeurs des bâtiments du roi* and the corresponding directors of the school in Rome. They discussed the general, banal and often vexed questions of access and working conditions in relation to copies, they debated the exemplarity of specific antique, Renaissance and Baroque models, and they assessed the success or failure of the students' emulative efforts.[78] From their letters a typology of copies emerges: copies were the work either of professionals or of students;[79] student copies were subdivided into those ordered and executed for the king and those undertaken for personal study.[80] In the first 30 years or more of the school's existence, so great was the king's desire for his own copies of the works of Raphael and other great Italian masters that Emmanuel Coquery described the Académie de France as little more than an extension of the Gobelins, where the copies were manufactured into tapestries and other decorative objects.[81]

By the eighteenth century the pressure to provide decoration for the royal palaces and gardens had abated, but the demand for copies was undiminished.[82] Copies of all kinds were present at the Palazzo Mancini, to which the duc d'Antin had the Académie de France removed in 1725: a professional copy of the king's portrait, sent from the copy workshop at Versailles, dominated the formal apartment on the first floor,[83] and student copies after Raphael and the Bolognese school and casts and copies after the antique decorated the salon and adjacent spaces.[84] Upstairs, on the third floor, the *pensionnaires* kept their own, mostly drawn copies, which, according to Nicolas Vleughels, the then director, provided 'un agréable ornement' for their own rooms.[85] The letters exchanged between Paris and Rome make virtually no mention of speculative or commercial copies, and the risk run by collectors of being duped by a copy was not a matter for extended comment.[86] But if 'copy' in this place and at this time was largely untroubled by questions of ontology and by concerns about authenticity, its double purpose did present theory with a paradox. As the reproductions must be fit for the king, the king's bureaucracy placed a premium on the perfect accuracy of such copies; at the same time, the Académie royale, notably in the person of its director, Antoine Coypel, warned students of the dangers of pedantic imitation, declaring the 'slavish copy' worthless, even absurd.[87]

The contradiction is one in appearance only. The 'slavish' copy was not so by some absolute measure of accuracy and in opposition to the 'free' copy (*belle infidèle*); rather it was slavish because executed after a single model. That is to say, the adjective 'slavish' indexed not a property of the work so much as a social relation: the coercive condition of execution that produced the exact copy. In the artisanal workshop, art academies alleged, the master imposed his manner on his apprentices in order to reproduce himself in them and thereby increase the productivity and profit of his enterprise.[88] By contrast, the good master, or Academician, put before his students 'Masterpieces by the great Masters'; he promoted progress in art for the benefit of all, and at the expense of maximising his own commercial advantage.[89] The Académie in Rome acted as the good master at an institutional level. By article 11 of its foundation statutes, copies born of a passion for self-improvement were substituted for work once done allegedly on demand and for money.[90] The directors' correspondence confirms copying as the performance of the good artistic life. Matthieu La Teulière, director of the Académie de France between 1684 and 1699, challenged Édouard Colbert de Villacerf's use of the word 'meuble' to denote students in Rome, or so much copying 'furniture' to be deployed at the *surintendant*'s will; 'disciple' was the directors' choice of word, which recognised moral and spiritual qualities in copying, and construed copyists as followers not mere things.[91] The exemplary artistic life was described in terms of love and duty, commonplaces not only in scripture but in classical ethics, in Aristotle and Cicero, in which the heads of the *bâtiments*, if not the directors of the school, were themselves thoroughly schooled. Colbert, having commissioned in 1679 copies of the

Borghese and Medici vases from the best sculptors in Rome, repeatedly requested the school's first director, Charles Errard, to ensure that the copies were executed not just with due diligence and care – qualities that money could procure – but lovingly.[92]

Love is the antithesis of the market, and artists are 'good' according to Colbert's definition, by virtue of the love they have for the intrinsic, not the exchange value of their art.[93] Such love assumed both a narrow form – *devoirs*,[94] or the materialisation of duty in copies – and a broader sense – moral comportment or emulation.[95] Emulation in the correspondence is agonistic. It is the pain that arises from knowing oneself lacking in merit. Charles-François Poerson, director of the school between 1704 and 1724, observed the agony of three students: Blanchard *fils*, whom Minerva had not favoured; Goupil, whom nature – that is, genius – had shunned; and Gaultier, whose love of art was unrequited.[96] In the *Nicomachean Ethics*, Aristotle contrasts emulation with envy. Envy, too, is pain, but its source is in that which belongs to another, not in what is lacking in the self. Emulation prompts action to recover the deficit, not by taking but by yielding to the model of that better other.[97] La Teulière remarked of *pensionnaire* Sarabat's response to Raphael, as Quintilian said of Cicero, that a man has had his reward when he has but loved his works.[98] Emulation in ethical discourse thus denoted identification with, and desire for, the exemplary other in the name of art and the king. In its presumption of hierarchy and self-justifying elitism, and with glory as its goal, the Aristotelian tradition of emulation propagated by Jesuit pedagogy was appropriated, notably by noble, moral and political discourse. Not surprisingly, it is everywhere recurrent in the duc d'Antin's letters to Rome, in place of Colbertian 'love', which owed perhaps more to the republican tradition of civic humanism.[99] Emulation demanded willing subordination to the rule of both precedence and precedent; in Vleughels's replies to d'Antin he communicated cause for gratification when students attracted compliments for their goodness (*sagesse*), conscientiousness (*assiduité*) and humility (*modestie*).[100]

What did this mean in terms of the copies actually executed? Art historians have generally been interested in the choice of works selected as models by the successive directors, and in the different responses of the *pensionnaires*.[101] However, the question here is not one of difference but the contrary: what did student copies have in common as 'good' copies? Edme Bouchardon, Jacques Dumont le Romain and Charles-Joseph Natoire, *pensionnaires* together in the mid-1720s, each made a copy of roughly the same dimensions and in red chalk of Benedetto Luti's *La comunione della Maddalena* (*c*.1715) (figs **39–41**).[102] All three started with a frame – that is, with the material boundaries of duty acknowledged and embraced; all three filled the space of that obligation, carefully and diligently covering the whole surface of the paper to the point of manifest completion. Although there are some minor discrepancies in the record of details, so balanced is each of the copies that nothing appears to have been either added or subtracted; the rhetoric is one of faithful and perfect imitation. Three decades later, on returning to Rome as director of the Académie de France, Natoire was to remember his generation's copying as vocational – that is, self-motivated not forced, moved, in fact, by love of beauty.[103] When student copies of the same model do differ – as, for instance, in the case of Bouchardon's and Natoire's copies after Angelo de Rossi's bas-relief for the tomb of Alexander VIII (*c.*1702) at Saint Peter's basilica (figs **42, 43**) – they do so conventionally, along the lines of medium, rather than idiosyncratically: the sculptor's copy acknowledges the original as an object lit from outside, the light falling unevenly on the cambered surface and accentuating the relief of different planes. By contrast, the painter's study focuses in on the figure of the pope and enters into the fiction of the depicted light within the sculpted frame.[104]

The prioritisation of line in all these copies confirms, were confirmation needed, the importance of line and composition to the academic concept of imitation and the definition of the good copy; it also invites comparison with print. Dumont le Romain's carefully controlled copy of Luti, with its unbroken, swelling contours and its parallel lines of hatching, replicates conventions of engraving, possibly even anticipates its translation into print. Tellingly, it was in the discourse on engraving that imitation was most explicitly articulated as an affective, inter-subjective relation, in which the copyist realises himself by sacrificing his identity to his model.[105] Perrin Stein has shown that, notwithstanding the general belief that printmaking was better studied in France than in Italy,[106] many students were in fact introduced to printmaking in Rome. She makes a case for etching as a playground of youthful experimentation and creativity.[107] An equally strong argument can, however, be made for printmaking as part and parcel of the school's ethics of the copy, whether or not its purpose was, in individual instances, exactly reproductive. The painter Pierre-Charles Trémolières, in Rome with Bouchardon in the early 1730s, produced more and less faithfully drawn, painted and etched copies after Giuseppe Maria Crespi's *I sette sacramenti* (1712), and while it is true that the paintings were privately commissioned, the prints were realised gratuitously – that is, neither by rule of the Académie, nor, apparently, with an immediate reward in mind.[108] In the following decade, *pensionnaires* under the directorship of Jean-François de Troy were invited to reproduce the director's own work: in 1742, for example, Louis-Joseph Le Lorrain etched as pendants de Troy's depictions of the deaths of Cleopatra and Lucretia.[109] No efforts appear to have been made to publish these prints; instead, impressions were pulled for private use, and as required, probably on the Académie's own printing press.[110] Like drawings and counterproofs, prints in Rome were exchanged between those – students, professionals and amateurs– in the circle of the Académie de France and, insofar as they were not for sale, they constituted a form of virtuous exchange in which morality and economy exactly coincided.

Copying became appropriative and competitive – 'envious', to use Aristotle's terminology – only when articulated at the level of Bourbon cultural policy. In the wake of the *bando* that in 1686 ended the legal export of works of ancient art from the Papal States, the letters between Paris and Rome indicate that successive directors worked hard to get access to important originals in order that their copyists might 'capture' their essence for

France.[111] Possession was here on a scale and at a level to preclude expression in the terms of a labour theory of property, even supposing that the king's *directeurs* and *surintendants* were disposed to think about copying in that way. The metaphors of war and hunting suggest that the policy of capture by reproduction owes more to the theory of first occupancy, or the freedom that a person – here a state – has to claim what it holds in its possession as its own.[112] The *pensionnaire* sculptor Pierre Lepautre gave visual expression to this strategy of *translatio studii et imperii* in his mighty figural group *Énée et Anchise*, begun in 1696 (fig. **44**).[113] *Translatio* is personified by the Trojan hero who carries or transmits the culture of, in this case, Rome – symbolised by the statuette of Minerva that Anchises holds in the niche of his arm – to France, or more precisely, in Villacerf's original plan, to the seat of the Bourbon government at Versailles.[114] In the event and after protracted delays, Lepautre's group, in which the sculptor sought to infuse classical narrative and diligently studied antique costume with the drama and modern sweep of Giambologna's *Il ratto delle Sabine*, was finally installed in Paris at the order of d'Antin, for whom works sent back from Rome were above all for the enrichment of the 'patrie'.[115] It stood in the Tuileries gardens where it became, in turn, an exemplum for later generations of artists.[116]

Whether in the context of learning or of cultural imperialism, the correspondence invariably discussed copies in terms of community: not just the reproduction of community through the efficient transfer of skill, but also belonging. Imitation and emulation are relational concepts, after all. It is impossible to know whether Bouchardon, Dumont le Romain and Natoire worked together at the church of Santa Caterina da Siena to copy Luti's altarpiece,[117] but the epistolary record tells of frequent other occasions during which *pensionnaires* developed those close temporal and physical as well as intellectual and artistic links both with one another and with the exemplary 'masterpiece', a culture of imitation that Deanna Petherbridge has termed 'copy as affiliation'.[118] Moreover, while students rarely signed their copies, being neither institutionally nor morally ready yet to claim ownership of their talent,[119] they did often inscribe their names in the vicinity of the exempla they copied. The chimney mantle in the Stanza di Eliodoro at the Vatican is covered in seventeenth- and eighteenth-century artists' graffiti clustered around the name of Poussin, apparently the first to sign his name, in 1627.[120] Moreover, they exchanged and treasured their drawn copies as 'souvenirs' of Rome; the drawings were, that is, more than a corpus of potentially useful sources.[121] In summary, a homology existed between discursive and social practices in Rome, rooted in the concept of emulation. If its paradigmatic discursive form was the academic commonplace that copies *produce* talent, its paradigmatic social form was discipleship, by collective practice of which the ideal model – Luti, Raphael – was perpetuated by the following embodied in the practices of *pensionnaires*. Copies were of and for the common good; 'works of genius', though equal in importance, were the opposite, because they advanced merely the individual.[122]

Emulation in pedagogical discourse signified the 'zeal' – the word is Poerson's, the language unmistakably Aristotelian – with which the students shouldered their artistic obligations.[123] Lepautre and later Bouchardon were notably exemplary, and their extreme dedication reproduced, in turn, emulation in others.[124] Where privilege is, in statute, crude – a binary system of lawful originals and criminal copies – emulation is subtle and belongs to a triadic schema of proportional values in things and persons. Emulation's objects are good only because they are, by definition, exemplary. In relation to them, emulation's subject stands not at one pole (good, or bad) but at the mid-point between the slavish copy and the absolute original. To rephrase this in ethical terms, the emulative subject acts in that space between the lack of ambition that had some settle for iteration and the over-ambition that prompted others to break with the Académie's norms in pursuit of extra – that is, personal – gain.[125] Emulation is copy *and* difference. And because, as Aristotle observes, the intermediate lacks an independent identity, the extremes dispute for its place, as if it were vacant.[126] Emulation was therefore put at risk by privilege. If the *arrêt* of 1714 was at first able, seemingly without contradiction, to prohibit unauthorised copying in order to promote emulation, it was only because privilege at the Académie was subsumed under a distributive rather than a commutative notion of justice. Or, to repeat the point in more familiar terms, the signification of Académie privilege exceeded its simple purpose of guaranteeing fairness in matters of exchange, so that in cases of infringement corrective compensation was made to those holding privileges. Académie privilege was informed by a notion of imitation that took account of the worth of executants and the value of models, as well as the exactness of copies. Not only did good models make good students, but good artists made good copies: the perfect or undetectable copy remained a trope of mastery and legitimacy in the biography of the early modern artist, the painter and the printmaker perhaps most especially.[127]

In September 1728 Vleughels entertained d'Antin with a 'petite historiette' about the *pensionnaires*, which he thought captured the *mœurs* of the school in Rome to advantage. Bouchardon, by then fêted and admired, believed himself superior in draughtsmanship on account of the life drawings he had made, which were so perfect that they had the appearance of relief. To dent his conceit, his fellow *pensionnaires* tricked him into mistaking a portrait drawn by another student directly onto a wall for a picture portrait, and mocked him when he tried to move the picture nearer to the light for a better look.[128] The dupe in such anecdotes is a person of supposed distinction – artist or connoisseur – who is exposed as lacking that degree of virtue to which he or she lays claim; in Bouchardon's case, the unique talent of *trompe l'œil* illusionism. The trick redistributes the just proportion of reward to merit by humiliating those whose apparent rank exceeds their actual entitlement to it.[129] Vleughels's account of the student prank is less than clear about the status of Bouchardon's drawings (after nature or the antique) and of the wall-painting (portrait from the life or copy). However, read in parallel with similar anecdotes that are, without doubt, about copies it suggests that, figuratively speaking, the perfect copy is to imitation what *trompe l'œil* is to the real. To illustrate: in Paris in 1728, Chardin was on the point of seeking entry to the Académie. Modesty prevented him from addressing the company directly. Instead, he left a selection of still lifes in the anteroom, where the director, the Flemish-trained Nicolas de Largillière, mistook them for masterpieces of the Dutch School. On learning his mistake, Largillière experienced no shame. On the contrary, his admiration for the works only increased and he recommended Chardin for immediate membership of the Académie. Of course Chardin's aim was not to deceive but to make himself known. The anecdote nevertheless served to redress apparent inequalities by raising Chardin, whose humble genre might seem to have precluded him from membership, to the very dignity of Academician by affirming that he was no simple imitator of low, everyday nature but the successful follower of great Northern masters. Although both anecdotes were about the nature of value in an economy of honour, about its proportionality in exchange, they also indirectly served to show that property is a relation of persons over things and not, as it appears under capitalism, one between persons and things.

Both anecdotes described the actions of a community determined by restricted entry[130] – school, Académie – and both communicated a sense of togetherness promoted by the just – that is, the proportionate distribution of honours in relation to good imitations: by depression of misplaced *gloire*, and by elevation of modesty. 'Bad', as opposed to merely incompetent, copies were, by implication, those executed by non-members, some of which were also made unlawful by privilege. Privilege at the Académie, whether exercised or not, symbolised its status. More than a legal resource at the service of Academicians individually, it was, you could say, totemic, a badge of honour in which a commons of value and meaning in ideal models was simultaneously shared by members and more or less jealously guarded from outsiders as an exclusive estate.[131] Emulation, insofar as it construed art as property, did so, by this account, not in terms of exclusive rights of possession but by denomination of the kinds of people through and among whom it could, or could not, legitimately circulate. To propose totem as an appropriate analogy is to draw on W. J. T. Mitchell's typology of object relations, and to differentiate the possessive relation in Académie privilege from both the 'being possessed' of idolatry and the 'having private possession in' of fetishism.[132] As totems of the academic mind, emulation and privilege self-consciously articulated collective belonging to an ongoing artistic tradition. For a copy to be classified as illegitimate in law as well as in art, for it to assume the guise of piracy and plagiarism, required a different conceptualisation of the good copy and a different moral language, in which the copy assumed less equivocal definition – in which 'good' is reduced to 'legal' and in which justice is a matter of rights.

PLAGIARISM

We might expect only trivial levels of alleged plagiarism in a culture where art is grounded in principles of emulation and imitation, and where privilege is embodied as a sign of status and belonging, as it was in France during the *ancien régime*. But scholars have identified two such cases, one of sculpture, the other of painting, both dating from the mid-eighteenth century, when successive *directeurs des bâtiments du roi* were embarked on reforming the arts in order to restore them to the glory days of Louis XIV under Colbert. Louis Réau, in his 1922 monograph on Étienne-Maurice Falconet, analyses the sculptor's attempts to gain full membership of the Académie, attempts that Réau alleges were frustrated and delayed by concerns that Falconet's *morceau de réception*, the diploma piece on which entry depended, was plagiarised.[133] In 1955 Jean Seznec published an article on Denis Diderot's accusations of intellectual property theft made against the history painter Jean-Baptiste Marie Pierre, Falconet's exact contemporary, with regard to pictures Pierre had sent to the Salon exhibitions.[134] Réau, Seznec and most later scholars have generally focused on the visual and documentary evidence in order to determine the status of the accusations – apocryphal or not – and to judge their validity.[135] There has been rather less interest in the charges as such, in the circumstances that enabled their enunciation, and in the significance of such scandals for a historical understanding of the formation of ideas of intellectual property in art and law. Plagiarism seems to imply a violation of property, and is therefore often aligned with matters of copyright, even though legal action rarely followed. It is also connected to impersonation, because, as Susan Stewart notes, 'the plagiarist poses as the originator of a discourse, making claims that the discourse bears a productive relation to his or her person'.[136] Questions of property and personhood, theft and imposture were, from the beginning, mixed up together in plagiarism: etymologically the word derived from the Latin *plagium*, meaning 'theft of a slave'.[137] As such, plagiarism was not just about owners; the status, age, gender, class and other attributes of personhood also shaped judgments about who could be a legitimate follower and heir of Michelangelo or Raphael, or, in the particular cases referred to here, of Pierre Puget and Annibale Carracci, and who could not.

The answer was not simple. Julie Hayes has described the Republic of Letters in the eighteenth century as structured by contradiction: by the decriminalisation of plagiarism in theory on the one hand, and by charges of it levelled violently against perceived miscreants in practice on the other. She suggests that, instead of approaching plagiarism as the wound inflicted by kidnapping or theft, we look to the meaning of the related word *plaga*, 'an open expanse', and think of plagiarism as a playing field, on which the 'author's rights, the market for originality, the authority of the past, and the sheer seduction of the beautiful other, all confusedly jostle one another'.[138] It is with the jostle in this network of conceptual categories – the original, the copy, privilege and plagiarism – and with the friction generated by it in the performance of practice that I am concerned in the rest of this chapter. The cases of Falconet and Pierre are reviewed, paying particular attention to where, when and how the allegation 'plagiarist' was made. Diderot's first attack occurred in his 1761 Salon review; that allegedly made against Falconet was published in a life of the artist in 1791. If the first was uttered outside the Académie by a man of letters and *philosophe*, not an artist, and was communicated discreetly in manuscript to an international elite, the second is harder to place. Concerning a period in the history of the Académie when the institution was consciously reflecting on its purpose and its founding principles and when the virtue of emulation was energetically upheld, the allegation was reported at a time when the same institution was in crisis, its membership bitterly divided and its practices openly attacked by some as despotic.[139] Its author, Jean-Baptiste-Claude Robin, a former student of the history painter Gabriel-François Doyen and a friend of Falconet, was one of the Académie's opponents and was eager to play his part in its suppression by publishing exposés of its failings. As Tomas Macsotay has observed, Robin was both an insider and an outsider, someone with privileged knowledge and a radical political agenda.[140]

• Falconet •

Ten years elapsed between Falconet's *agrément* in July 1744 on presentation of a selection of works to the Académie and his admission to full membership on delivery of the finished marble of his *Milon de Crotone* (fig. **45**) in August 1754.[141] At first, as Robin writes, the Milo had seemed 'superior', but then '[Falconet] was told that it bore [too close] a relation to the Puget at Versailles [fig. **47**]... As a consequence of this ridiculous allegation, he was required, against common practice, to make a new model representing the genius of sculpture, a model that was then to have been executed in marble as his *morceau de réception*. He was required to fulfil the task at the Académie, in one of its rooms, in accordance with an article in the 1751 regulation, which, sensibly, had often been ignored.'[142]

Robin goes on to say that, like the ancient Greek sculptor Polykleitos, Falconet had also been subjected to the inconsistent and contradictory advice of senior Academicians, and that although the resulting *Le Génie de la sculpture* (fig. **46**) was certainly not despised, it was predictably and ultimately found inferior to the Milo.[143] In the end, it was agreed that he should execute in marble the plaster model of the Milo, which had remained since his *agrément* in one of the Académie rooms. Réau, George Levitine and Alexander Schenker repeat this account, merely omitting to mention Polykleitos.[144] But many have doubted the truth of the story and so we need briefly to review the few alternative facts. The Académie's *Procès-verbaux* do not identify the works Falconet originally submitted; it is therefore a matter for conjecture that the sculptor proposed the Milo as his *morceau de réception* in the first place. The minutes, in fact, record an instruction to Falconet to present himself before the director, Pierre-Jacques Cazes, to determine the topic for his reception piece.[145] Given that *agréés* sculptors routinely proposed their own themes, there is some room to doubt the implication of the record that Falconet had advanced no such ideas himself.[146] Christian Michel is sceptical that vacillation on the question of subject matter in the summer and autumn of 1744 was ever the Académie's. He attributes indecision to Falconet instead, and discounts plagiarism as having been the issue.[147] Macsotay, by contrast, finds confirmation of the Académie's alleged anxiety of influence in its stipulation that Falconet realise both sketch and model of *Le Génie de la sculpture* at the Académie (to avoid any recurrence of contamination), and in the sculptor's subsequent revision of his first idea for the Milo in a second preparatory model (to distance himself from Puget). He dates return to the subject of the Milo to *c.*1753.[148]

An alternative approach is to look at the works and reconsider the alleged controversy in the light of Harold Bloom's typology of intrapoetic relations between 'strong' poets and their precursors.[149] Bloom's aim is to demystify the humanist view of influence as the unruffled productive integration of individual talent into tradition, and to expose the anxiety beneath.

When models of *Le Génie de la sculpture* and the Milo were exhibited in 1745, the Salon *livret* offered no explanation of the plaster Milo beyond 'man devoured by a lion'; for the terracotta *Génie de la sculpture*, however, it provided much more. The meaning of this second group made sense only when its source was identified. The *livret* identifies the antique fragment as the Belvedere Torso. It calls it a 'Monument', the 'principal objet' or exemplum of the art of sculpture.[150] By faithful representation of the Torso's incomplete condition – ruin not sketch – Falconet's group incorporated the exemplary work of another as 'other'. The interpretative component that, according to Bloom, is always present in every act of repetition, every instance of influence, produces an undoing here of the antique's limitless authority by substitution of part (Torso) for whole (the ideal), and by isolation of that part in quotation marks, so to speak. The formal arrangement of the marble group (fig. **46**) emphasises the separateness of the ancient fragment from the modern figure of Sculpture – identified in the *livret* as both Minerva and Invention. They face in opposite directions, seemingly unconscious of each other. Read like a bas-relief from left to right, time appears to flow through the figures: genius Minerva faces left, her eyes trained on the new – the not yet invented, sculpted or seen. The antique fragment turns the other way, back, greeting the past as its inevitable future. Oppositions of temporal direction are also acknowledged at the level of form: the figure of *Le Génie* is no less classical than the Torso, but whereas Falconet recollects the antique in the copy, repeating it backwards, in the Grecian profile of *Le Génie*, in the elegant folds of her drapery and the contrapposto of her pose, he repeats antiquity, recollecting it forwards in a new classicism.[151] The simultaneous conjunction and disjunction of the figures, represented in the reversed repetition of 'C' shapes, installs a fraught edge within the work, a front line along which the forces of inventive recollection and faithful repetition muster. Only Sculpture's chisel briefly punctures the smoothly tense, serpentine sweep of torso and drapery, the contest over the position of figure and attendant, framed and enframing, as yet imperfectly resolved.[152]

Falconet's Milo (fig. **45**) does not exhibit its model in the way *Le Génie de la sculpture* does; rather it reworks or oversculpts it on the surface, while not entirely effacing the generating original beneath.[153] Superficially, differences in format and scale set the compositions of Puget and Falconet clearly apart, but the very symmetry of the antitheses vertical/horizontal, large/small, left-facing/right-facing, etc., binds the works closely together at another level. Based on a classical source but itself without sculptural precedent, Puget's Milo was, in the eighteenth century, generally acknowledged a model of expression – to be specific, an *exemplum doloris*. Louis Petit de Bachaumont, connoisseur and man of letters, in an essay on painting, sculpture and architecture first published in 1751, described and praised the agony of the head and the stiffening resistance of the body's muscles, sinews and nerves at the lion's first, unexpected strike, down to the very last detail: he noted the tension in the athlete's toes.[154] Falconet's choice of moment, when tethered Milo is brought down by a second hit, and the lion moves round for the kill, sets the stage for an amplification of horror: the screams of pain that, according to Bachaumont, the viewer was merely prompted to imagine by Puget are distinctly represented by Falconet in the athlete's gaping mouth, his agonised profile sharply offset against the smooth stretch of his raised arm and shoulder. In this work, Falconet seems to have staked his claim to reception at the Académie on going a step beyond Puget's famous figuration of Ovid's narrative in a literal sense – that is, in creatively correcting the choice of temporal moment, while at the same time remaining faithful to its formal language, constraints of size notwithstanding:[155] he repeats the sublime quality of Puget's visualisation, exaggerates it even, by increasing the size and strength of the lion relative to Milo, thus making the tragic outcome inevitable, and by playing off the grand scale of the struggle and the dark enormity of Milo's pain against the smallness (66 × 64 cm) and whiteness of his marble piece. (Puget had simply aligned epic tale and gigantic figure – 2.7 × 1.4 metres.) Hyperbole – in both the dramatisation and description of the scene – characterises Falconet's response to Puget, a response that (and this is Bloom's principal argument about influence) is at once a repetition and a misreading of the precedent.[156] Falconet, like Milo, put his hand in a trap. Like him, also, he trusted and took pride in his own strength, his own art: by developing the narrative and playing with Puget's forms, Falconet presumed, in that split-second swerve of belatedness, to have found his distance from precedent and to have made a master of himself.

Was Falconet's pride, like Milo's, misplaced? How should we now interpret the Académie's alleged hostility to the modelled Milo at first, and its later unequivocal acknowledgement of the finished marble as the appropriate and therefore the better reception piece? Did the story of a reception like Chardin's in the 1720s, on the grounds of mistaken identity, no longer in the 1740s celebrate exceptional talent and meet the moral conditions of becoming an Academician? And did privilege play any part in transforming expectations of *morceaux de réception* as works of art?

The function of the *morceau de réception* was to mark the artist's official transition from student–apprentice to master and from copying to creative imitation. It materialised this turning point.[157] To that extent it would seem a perfect candidate for the Bloomian moment of switchback in the relation weak-modern/strong-ancient – a reversal, that is to say, of the patriarchal roles of father and son. This is to assume, however, that artists saw execution of the *morceau* as an opportunity to manifest their personal genius, rather than to demonstrate their title to be heirs to an artistic tradition by submission to the principles and values of the Académie.[158] Art theorist the abbé Du Bos represented the artist's coming of age not in terms of violent Oedipal struggle but rather in those of tolerance and fellowship: in acceding to his new estate, on equal terms with his father, the son learns to forgive his father's faults, as the father had formerly excused the errors of his son.[159] The emphasis is on continuity and incorporation. A link is maintained with the past, due homage paid to tradition, and simultaneously the precursor is safely set into history: influence is no longer inevitable but is now a matter of choice, or taste.[160] *Le Génie* staged that choice, by citing the Torso, and in so doing transformed the practice of emulation into a meta-discourse: the representation of the 'monument' is – that is to say – self-aware. Moreover, Minerva allegorised Falconet's act of imitation, renaming it Invention. In this, she was assisted by History and Mathematics, attributes identified by the Salon *livret* in the books near which she reclined in the 1745 model.[161]

In circumstances where authorship was the matter in hand, which it obviously was in the case of *morceaux de réception*, *Le Génie de la sculpture* thus seemingly offered a clearer statement of artistic autonomy than did the Milo, in which emulation was performed rather than narrated, and where Falconet followed Puget even in his deviation from the classical text by his signature substitution of a noble lion for Ovid's vulgar wolves.[162] And yet the Milo, not *Le Génie*, was ultimately preferred by Falconet and by the Académie. Moreover, Falconet's preparatory models suggest that the sculptor worked the idea for his Milo towards rather than away from Puget's masterpiece: he replaced his own first recumbent and virtually inert figure (fig. **48**) by a second (fig. **49**), supine still but Pugetesquely braced against assault.[163]

Falconet's undaunted, decade-long meditation on Puget begs another question: was his choice of model in the Milo not only deliberate but also as self-conscious as that in *Le Génie*? Puget's reputation as France's Michelangelo rested on the scope and quality of his talent;[164] importantly, it arose also from his audacity and independence. In the 1740s and 1750s, he was remembered at the Académie as the sculptor who, unlike François Girardon, would not yield and work to Charles Le Brun's designs.[165] This glorious self-possession extended to the manner of his work, for which, according to anecdote, nature alone served him as inspiration. When making the Milo, Puget allegedly searched unsuccessfully for a source for the athlete's legs; he discovered it at last in himself. Frustrated, he instinctively made the required gesture with his own leg, for lack of an ideal one, had it cast in plaster and then recycled it in the finished marble.[166]

Insofar as Falconet's ideal viewers – the officers of the Académie – could be relied upon to recognise his source, and to know something of Puget's 'life', Falconet's choice of referent in the Milo was, very possibly, no less a choice of invention in the academic sense than it was in *Le Génie de la sculpture*: invention embodied and invoked, instead of allegorising and representing.[167] If the mode and meaning of emulation in the two works was, by this analysis, less different than it first appears, it was nevertheless differently felt. Du Bos, when discussing the nature and causes of artistic genius in *Réflexions critiques sur la poésie et la peinture* (1719), identified among the attractions that masterpieces hold for the young person of genius their appearance of having anticipated him in his own creations.[168] The author of such masterworks represented, we could say, the ego ideal in which the latecomer, the student, sees himself reflected.[169] Emulation in the Milo takes the form of just such an impassioned act of self-recognition and identification. Viewed only obliquely in the charged composition and scale of Falconet's Milo, Puget surfaces directly in its play of textures (flesh, hide, cloth, bark and stone): in the skin of the piece. Puget was especially admired in the eighteenth century for his handling of flesh, for filling it with life, fire, force, energy – synonyms, all, of artistic genius.[170] The ecstasy of Falconet's influence by Puget, the genius sculptor, contrasts sharply with his relation to the antique instanced in *Le Génie de la sculpture*. If, to draw on Minerva's rational attributes, History enabled Sculpture to take her distance and measure from the past, to articulate the desire for likeness in terms of discontinuity, it did so at Mathematics' expense: by getting the Torso out of proportion. Its sublime, Herculean, monstrosity, its seductive otherness, is no more.[171] It is reduced by Falconet almost to the scale of a woman, transformed into virtual furniture: the back of a 'chaise à la grecque'. The result is not travesty; but in emptying the antique of some of its divinity, Falconet diminishes the mood of *Le Génie* to melancholy.[172] Moreover, while Falconet's deflationary strategy lessened the threat of such antique masterpieces to overwhelm disciples like him, it also limited, proportionally, the value of his own achievement.

Falconet's pride in the Milo was justified, ultimately, not because of its differences from Puget's prototype but because the earlier sculptor is duly acknowledged. Indeed, Puget's artistic identity was intrinsic to the meaning of Falconet's later version and to the terms in which he laid claim to Académie membership: *sono scultore, anch'io*. Cochin's story about Chardin underscored the painter's modesty, modesty the more brilliant because such was his talent that he could be mistaken for an Old Master. Falconet was ambitious, not modest. On the evidence of the Milo, he wanted legitimately to succeed, even surpass Puget, not be confused with him.[173] And if Robin's record of events is correct, in the 1740s and 1750s the Académie was becoming sensitive to the difference. Privilege, however, cannot have been strictly and directly responsible for such heightened awareness of issues of authorship, because Puget had not been an Academician and his works were therefore legally unprotected. We lack, moreover, record of the discussion, if discussion there was, on the manner in which the alleged plagiarism was accomplished, by means of casts or prints, the common tools of piracy, reference to which was virtually obligatory in demonstrations of copy crime.[174] But, indirectly, privilege may have had a bearing. From the mid-1730s to the mid-1750s application for Académie privilege was at an all-time high. Matters of authorship and reputation were therefore under regular review. Indeed, in the same *séance* in which Falconet was finally *reçu*, Jean Moyreau presented for approbation and privilege two impressions of *Le Quartier des vivandiers* after Wouwermans, thus, circumstantially, relating privilege in objects and the privilege of Académie subjects.[175]

· Plagiarism's playing field ·

Our review of the Falconet case has thus far involved little of the promised expansion of plagiarism's 'playing field'; the question of the past's authority has monopolised attention and the point of view has remained resolutely that of the Académie and its members. However, the exhibition of successive models and versions of *Le Génie de la sculpture* and the Milo in 1745, 1746 and 1755, offered the works for consideration to a general public of amateurs, connoisseurs, critics, collectors and spectators, whose response was not limited by attention to rules of admission or concern for tradition, nor exclusively informed by theories of art. The critic Étienne La Font de Saint-Yenne politely took note of *Le Génie de la sculpture*, remarking in passing that viewers had not found the allegorical idea realised in the finished composition.[176] Sculptural genius was identified, rather, in the small, rough sketch-models also submitted in 1746 by Jean-Baptiste Le Moyne and Jean-Joseph Vinache.[177] Genius was a sign of praise, too, a decade later in reviews of the Milo: one anonymous critic 'dared to call it an *effect of genius*'; only Genius, he argued, was inspired to choose such a heroic and terrifying subject.[178] Neither imitation nor Puget was mentioned anywhere;[179] the immediate thrill of the work was the sole vector of judgment. This is not to say that the concept of emulation was foreign to the Salon. On the contrary: when in 1737 the exhibition was first established on a regular basis as an annual and then a biennial event,[180] the *Mercure de France* identified it as an ideal context for 'noble emulation', or 'the natural impulse we have to succeed and make ourselves known'.[181] That view was anticipated in the exhibition catalogue of 1737, which the paper quoted: according to the *livret*, exhibition makes publicly evident the formation of each new generation's talent by the art of the last.[182] The shared vocabulary momentarily obscures differences of meaning. Noble emulation, prominent in pedagogical discourse, was being eroded in political discourse under pressure from the financial and commercial realities of Absolutism, and in cultural discourse it was under challenge from sensualist psychology, according to which all human action was motivated by desire (not virtue) and prompted by unease (not love).[183] For the *Mercure*'s reviewer, emulation was a drive, not a virtue. It was competitive rather than simply imitative and, insofar as it could be said to lead to the good, it was 'good' conceived narrowly, in terms of individual self-interest.

The differences are reinforced and in part explained when we take account of the context of the newspaper. In newspapers, news of the Salon and its exhibits share the crowded page with reports of other kinds of artistic event, predominantly notices of sale. In 1755, the year of the Milo, Falconet's fellow sculptor and Academician Lambert-Sigisbert Adam advertised the sale of his collection of antique and modern sculpture.[184] In April the collection was commended for its 'rarity', 'singularity' and 'variety'. A second notice, in June, added 'piquant' to the attractions already invoked.[185] In relation to the antique, such adjectives are remarkable. They belong to a vocabulary more readily associated with the Rococo and with the *Mercure*'s advertisements in the 1730s and 1740s for *pittoresque* ornament prints – in fact, with a style that in 1755 was the subject of a satire by Cochin published by the same paper.[186] The wit of Cochin's 'Lettre à M. l'abbé R***' lies in the ironic representation of the revival of the antique as the new modern. The Old Masters of the Rococo, on whose behalf Cochin allegedly wrote, admit that this recent 'revolution in taste' has forced them into antique imitations 'pour faire passer la marchandise'.[187] The 'seduction' of the antique other was manifest, too, in the resurrection of the ancient art of encaustic, or wax painting, of which the *Mercure* reported, in passing and without irony, that the 'impatience' with which painters were blindly experimenting with the technique was also known as 'noble emulation'.[188] In the context of the market for the new and the newsworthy, emulation was stripped of its association with tradition and virtue; it no longer denoted patient submission to the authority of the past, but rather the impatient exploitation of it now as the new.

It would be crudely reductive to explain shifts of meaning in the use of emulation by the change of context alone: from Académie to art market mediated by newsprint. Cochin was, moreover, an Academician, appointed in 1755 to the important office of *secrétaire* and *historiographe* of the Académie. However, his occasional writing took him out of the established world of the Académie's public authority and into a public sphere coalescing in areas of social life where informal practices of sociability – conversation, discussion in person and in print – enabled enlightened debate and the formation and circulation of public opinion. The abbé R*** to whom his letter was addressed was almost certainly Guillaume-Thomas Raynal, his friend and the editor of the *Mercure* from 1750 to 1755, a man of letters linked, if only by opposition, to philosophic circles.[189] From the time of his editorship, the *Mercure* adopted a more serious and critical approach to the arts, as sceptical of the alleged superiority of ancient wax over modern oil painting because described by Pliny, as it was of the advantage of Rococo decoration over the style of the *grand siècle* on grounds of comfort. The Enlightenment's desacralisation of the past brought with it an increasing specificity to terms such as 'imitation'. Positively connoted, 'imitation' referred, in the *Mercure*, either to the imitation of nature, or to the re-presentation of works of art in print. In 1755, the *Mercure*'s review of the Salon picked out the genre painter Jean-Baptiste Greuze for his imitation of nature, and it published Claude-Joseph Vernet's endorsement of Jean-Joseph Balechou's engraving of the marine view *Le Calme* (fig. **50**) as 'bien entendue', or a thoughtful translation.[190] Vernet's letter of avowal, published in September 1755, provided a positive contrast to Boucher's earlier letter of complaint in March about Duflos's travesties (fig. **37**), which a reply in mitigation of Duflos, published in May, had done little to assuage.[191] Anxiety about the authenticity and legality of imitations had increased with the Salon and the additional opportunities it provided for copying. The *arrêt* of 1714 was reproduced at the back of Salon *livrets*. Its immediate purpose was to prevent pirate editions of the catalogue, but it also served as a warning to visitors not to make free with the designs of the Académie's works on display: the prints by virtue of privilege law, the paintings and sculpture by extension. Of the three prints for which Académie privilege was requested in 1755, which included Jacques-Nicolas Tardieu's engraving after Jean-Marc Nattier's recent portrait of Marie Leszczinska, all were exhibits at the Salon and were also advertised in the *Mercure*.[192]

• Pierre •

If, as a consequence of the jostle of meanings of emulation and imitation in the eighteenth-century newspaper, the Salon emerged as a place of competition where artists hoped to shine, potentially to outshine (their rivals), it was at the same time a site for the public accounting of the results of this redefined emulation. The *Mercure*'s policy of impartiality, first articulated in 1737, forbad it to make judgments: it claimed only to report them.[193] But thirty years later Denis Diderot, writing for the *Correspondance littéraire*, argued that one of the critic's primary duties was to recognise and denounce as plagiarism 'borrowed' compositions, motifs, characters and expressions.[194] His exposure of Jean-Baptiste Marie Pierre occurred at the Salon of 1761, at which the painter had shown four history paintings, of which the most important if not the largest was a Deposition (1761) (fig. **51**), commissioned by the marquis de Marigny for the cathedral church of Saint-Louis at Versailles.[195] It was not much noticed by other critics; the abbé Le Blanc described it in the *Mercure* merely as big, and 'in the grand manner of the Carracci'.[196] Diderot, by contrast, thought it not so much 'in the manner of', as actually copied from Annibale Carracci's *Lamentation* (c.1604) (fig. **52**).

Jean Seznec's study of the affair has served to reinforce Diderot's claim. Seznec identifies further instances of 'plagiarism' in Pierre's Salon pictures, ones that escaped the eighteenth-century critic's notice, and he multiplies the sources on which the painter relied in any particular work.[197] His article, by showing that Pierre's *Descente de la croix* is in fact a combination of Correggio and Carracci, unintentionally identifies both the academic concept of invention as an art of combination and Diderot's rejection of genius defined metaphorically by allusion to the blending operations of the bee.[198] For Diderot, genius was not simply exceptional talent. It was something one was, rather than something one did or had.[199] If the plagiarist is, in one sense, genius's opposite, for lack of his or her defining spark, in another sense he or she is genius's difference, because plagiarism, not being innate, was open to explanation by external factors.[200] Diderot prefaced his charge against Pierre by noting: 'He is rich; he has had an education; he has made the trip to Rome; I am told he has a mind (*esprit*); he is under no pressure to finish his work.' The *philosophe* thereby set at a distance legitimate *causes morales* – youth, ignorance, stupidity, poverty – to excuse Pierre's 'mediocrity'.[201] Age and wealth were perceived as interdependent. Du Bos's plea for mercy on behalf of the young *émule*, whose own genius was improperly known to him, and who, hungry for recognition and a name, anticipated himself in others, misreading himself in their style and in their thoughts,[202] was also implicitly a plea for the artist whose fortune was yet to be made. Falconet's background was extremely modest; his family circumstances were such that he could not be spared to go to Rome.[203] By contrast, Pierre's official education had been thorough and was, in 1761, long since completed. He was an officer of the Académie and his wealth was legendary: the *Mercure* reported in January 1760 that he was among the 'citoyens riches' who had taken their silver to the Monnaie in order to support the war effort.[204] A mercenary crime in the mature, plagiarism was not only condemned by Du Bos as the brigandry of those who frequent Parnassus only to rob, it was mocked in explicitly monetary terms. He compared the plagiarist to a tax collector who extracts one arm, two heads or a whole group from Old Masters, each according to its particular worth.[205] Diderot drew attention to Pierre's wealth and status in order to deny him cover, and against this great weight of privilege the alleged pettiness of the painter's work will, we anticipate, appear unreasonable and unjust.

Introduction over, Diderot proceeded to an account of the altarpiece. Passing rapidly over Pierre's depiction of Christ – the head 'discoloured', 'putrid', and the body 'ignoble' and 'base'[206] – Diderot discovered, with feigned surprise, some beauty in the work: in the disposition of the figures, the character and expression of the women, and the harmonious palette of colours. The praise was calculated: a device to prelude prosecution of the artist by rhetorical questioning. 'But put your hand on your conscience and pay homage to the truth. Your *Descente de la croix*, is it not an imitation of Carracci's which is at the Palais Royal and which you know well?' There follows a detailed comparison: 'In the Carracci there is a mother of Christ seated, and in yours also. In Carracci, that mother is dying of pain, and in yours also. In Carracci, that pain links the actions of the other figures, and yours. In the Carracci, the son's head rests on her knees, and also in our friend Pierre's. Carracci's women are made afraid by the danger of this fainting mother, and yours also.'[207]

In view of his own recent experience as the accused in the case of the alleged plagiarism of the *Encyclopédie*'s plates, it is perhaps not surprising that Diderot, while inviting Pierre to confess to his copying, stopped short of using the word 'plagiarist' to condemn him.[208] However, his tone is forensic: the painter was accused of imitation, as if of a crime. A scene of wrongdoing was identified (the Palais Royal), opportunity established (as Premier peintre du duc d'Orléans, Pierre had easy access), and method and motive implied. Of the seven classic questions of investigation, it was in answer to 'how?' rather more, perhaps, than in reply to 'what?', 'why?' and 'when?' that anxiety about plagiarism surfaced. Although 'where?' established that paintings were at issue, Diderot invoked and described the coincident elements in Carracci and Pierre in such conspicuously linear terms – the seated silhouette of the mother, the lines of her suffering, the outline of Christ's head in the bed of her lap, the chain of grief linking the mourning women, and the network of their fear – that he brought printmaking more readily to mind.[209]

Print, as reproduction's primary medium, indexes in turn the mode of Pierre's appropriation – by an act of mental decoupage: an excision actually more selective and subtle than cutting up prints or shearing canvas, but seemingly no less tangible.[210] Scissors were not, I should say, one of the copyist's tools; tracing, pouncing, squaring, etc., or soft techniques of transfer are the ones described in contemporary drawing manuals.[211] All used a mediating *surface* (tracing paper, pounce paper, glass, a muslin veil). For Diderot, on the other hand, scissors were a defining mark of the trades and trade technologies described in the *Encyclopédie*, and it was also a metaphor for his own critical discernment.[212] The sharp efficiency of their force is highlighted, by contrast, later in the Salon *livret*, when Diderot was prompted by Joseph-François Parrocel's *Adoration des rois mages* (1761; Amiens Cathedral) to reflect upon the difficulties arising from the strong precursor: 'It seems to me that the precursor is more troublesome to his successors in painting than in letters. The imagination, it seems to me, is more tenacious than memory. I have paintings by Raphael more present in my mind than verse by Corneille or the most beautiful passages in Racine. There are figures that never leave me. I see them; they follow and obsess me. For example, Saint Barnabas who rends the clothes on his breast… [fig. **53**] how will I separate myself from spectres such as this? How do painters do it?'[213]

Diderot approached the problem differently here. He drew now on his own experience, describing influence from within. The direction of the action thus appears reversed: not Pierre's extraction of figures from Carracci, but how, putatively, to exorcise Rubens's magi and Raphael's Saint Barnabas respectively from Parrocel and Diderot. Moreover, the figures are agents, fetishes, not motifs. Diderot's response was emotional, his struggle internal. The distinction between memory and imagination that helps to clarify this articulation of influence as passionate and inspired draws on the *Encyclopédie*'s taxonomic table, according to which memory is the domain of the mechanical arts; the liberal arts belong to imagination. Pierre's mining of motifs in the *Lamentation* by copy, or from memory was accordingly mechanical, his altarpiece en route to commoditisation. In contrast, and to take one further example, such was the imaginative power of the 'great figures' in Jean-Baptiste-Henri Deshays's *Le Martyre de Saint André* (1761, Musée des beaux-arts, Rouen) and his *Saint Victor devant le tribunal préteur* (1761, lost) that whether borrowed or the artist's own, mattered not to Diderot, because so inspired was the appropriation that looking at Deshays he was '*not* tempted to accuse *him* of plagiarism'.[214] Pierre had made a trade of painting: he had adopted, Diderot implied, a mechanical approach to a liberal project.

To return to the text of Diderot's critique of Pierre, the conspicuous parallelism, or folding of his sentences so that the same – 'the mother of Christ', 'the head of her son', etc., in Carracci – is seen repeated in Pierre to the refrain 'in yours also', not only insisted on the synonymy of the two works, it also outlined the incisive manner in which repetition was supposedly carried out, implying that the figures in Carracci's altarpiece were so much property, tangibly and shabbily, if not actually illegally, trafficked from one work to the other.[215] Diderot did not recognise Carracci as having himself belonged to the same tradition of imitative emulation that later inspired Pierre; nor did he concede that Carracci's *Lamentation* was arguably as dependent on Raphael as Pierre's *Descente* was on Carracci. That is to say, he did not envisage Carracci and Pierre as persons intersubjectively related to others, including each other. Unlike Du Bos, he reduced their relationship to a relation between works – things. For Diderot the *Lamentation* was *the* original, not Carracci-the-model.

Diderot's concept of authorship, upon which he based his theory of artistic exchange, thus assumed that the painter was the absolute master of his or her work. In his review of Pierre's *Descente*, he anticipated in this regard a critique based on the metaphor of the bee that he launched later in *Lettre sur le commerce de la librairie* (1763): 'It is well known that the bee does not make honey for itself. But does man have the right to transact with his fellow man the way he does with the insect who makes the honey? The author is, I repeat, the master of his work, or none is master of his own property.'[216] Of course *this* bee is not the metaphor of imitation's eclectic gathering, of the artist as collector, or of free production, all of which it negates. It is an insect rather of the socio-economic discourse on natural law.

It concludes the famous paragraph that opens with Diderot's rhetorical question: 'What belongs to a man if not a work of the mind, the product of his education, his studies, his late nights, his time, his research, his observations, the best hours and moments of his life, if not his own thoughts, his heartfelt feelings, that most precious part of him, the part that does not die and that immortalises him?'[217] But if the issue is not, therefore, directly the ethical matter of art as a combinatory practice, Diderot's assertion of property rights, naturally inhering in the author's 'honey', made emulation logically impossible and morally illegitimate. The booksellers' privilege he was defending was at odds with privilege as a mark of academic following and belonging. Reputational privilege could be enhanced by acts of emulation; copy-privilege, on the other hand, registered every infraction as a deficit and as deceit.

Three questions arise from the events surrounding the reception of Falconet's Milo and the exhibition of Pierre's *Descente*. First, were they instances of a larger phenomenon? Second, how should we account for them? And third, what impact, if any, did they have? Although the short answer to the first is probably 'no' – *morceaux de réception* were often derivative and recognised as such without complaint up to the 1790s;[218] likewise Salon critics routinely noted the artistic debts painters and sculptors owed to one another and did not condemn them for it – this should not preclude consideration of the other two. The 1750s and 1760s are decades generally characterised as ones of reform in the arts, and emulation was the rallying call for the renaissance of the Académie.[219] Diderot's humiliation of one of its most esteemed officers, one publicly celebrated as both a French genius and the rightful heir to the Italian schools, does not, however, belong to the swell of reactionary criticism levelled by *parlementaire* circles at the monarchy for the failure of the Académie royale to live up to its mandate.[220] Anne Fastrup argues, in fact, that Diderot's Salon criticism marks his conscious withdrawal from the public sphere and from philosophical debate in the wake of the fraught reception of the *Encyclopédie*, and his exploration, instead, of the private realm of subjective experience.[221] While avoiding so sharp a distinction between social domains, I do want to suggest that Diderot's critique of Pierre was perhaps a response to the technologies and economies of print.

· Diderot's thoughts on plagiarism and on prints ·

That Diderot finally delivered his 'thoughts on plagiarism' in the same Salon review in which he also wrote an essay on printmaking is not, I think, a coincidence.[222] Print is the modus operandi of plagiarism in the 1765 'thoughts on plagiarism'; meanwhile, expertise in graphology, the forensic science of forgery and signature, introduces the discussion of printmaking. Although separated by folios of ekphrasis and critique, the concerns of the two digressions thus overlap. On their own, the 'thoughts' are disappointing. They no more than generalise and make explicit what Diderot had earlier implied in his analysis of Pierre's work. Prompted to return to plagiarism by another altarpiece, he now epitomised it by the genre of landscape. Diderot described once again the process by which a bit of turf here, a slice of pasture there, a cottage from this one and a mountain from that other one were appropriated by the plagiarist from a portfolio of prints to make a monstrous *fabrique*, and in so doing he slyly substituted a simile (land) for the metaphor of art as landed property.[223] More interesting is the essay on engraving. Diderot compares the science of engraving to that of writing by reference to graphology, a heuristic device that allows him to challenge received wisdom according to which engraving is a conventional language like writing, and not a natural language like painting, one that belongs, moreover, to the hand not to the mind.[224] And yet the careful analysis that follows of the regular, systematised and conventional web of lines and marks used by engravers to 'translate' painting into print rather confirmed this 'net of rationality' (as William Ivins puts it) in its function as a practical tool for the standard purpose of reproducing paintings efficiently and economically, at the cost of conveying the personal characteristics of the originals.[225] Diderot argued that, in the hand of the intelligent engraver, Raphael is not engraved like Guercino, or Guercino like Domenichino, or Domenichino like Michelangelo. At the same time, he reluctantly acknowledged that the routine printmaker worked according to habit and that his prints all looked alike.[226]

Benjamin's 1939 essay is the classic statement on the changes to the ontological status of the work of art wrought by mechanical reproduction. Like Diderot's conception of plagiarism, Benjaminian reproduction robs the original of its 'aura', detaching the image from the ritualistic and social relationships embodied by the work in its original time and place.[227] Through reproduction, the work becomes an autonomous image and a commodity. The growth of the reproductive print market in the eighteenth century was not without consequences. In a very direct way, it put serial production of paintings at risk. Reproductive print identified and fixed the painted work as the one and only original. Boucher was apparently hostile to unauthorised prints after his paintings, such as Duflos's *enfants*, precisely because it forced him to curtail his painting enterprise.[228] Indirectly, reproduction also reorganised human perception. Benjamin touches on this point only briefly because he is more concerned with the social changes expressed by these altered ways of seeing than with the visuality of mechanical reproduction per se.[229] Diderot, on the other hand, discussed the technologies and optical effects of engraving at some length.

Loss of colour and of the tact or touch of brushwork in reproduction made all painting linear: compositions of variously combined and arranged lines of figures, actions and passions.[230] This was especially true of the French manner of engraving, which by removal of bur from copper plates prior to printing produced characteristically sharp and bright impressions.[231] Diderot marvelled while listing the different things to be seen in Antoine Masson's engraving after Nicolas Mignard's portrait of Henri de Lorraine, comte d'Harcourt (fig. **54**): feathers, skin, hair, silk, lace, linen. More importantly, he analysed how we see: not by converting black-ink lines, dashes and dots on white paper back into the colours and textures of paint translated from canvas, but by reading the tight or loose 'weave' of the engraved text in terms of contours and planes, or figure and ground.[232] The haunting power of the apostle Barnabas (fig. **53**) arose, perhaps, from the fact that the burin detached him, in a certain sense, from the narrative unfolding around and below him, isolating him for the viewer. Without the original's hue, touch and dimensions, this monochrome, rational web imparted a strong family resemblance to academic history painting when reproduced, accentuating the conventional aspects of its tradition of *disegno*. Falconet observed a parallel heightening of contour and sharpening of idea in the case of casts.[233] For both Diderot and Falconet the reduced means of reproduction stripped art of its sensual properties, leaving truth. Moreover, such were its de-particularising consequences that styles, or what André Malraux called 'imaginary super-artists', commanded attention at the expense of individual hands.[234] In effect, the common reproductive print conditioned non-connoisseur viewers like Diderot to see similarity. At the same time, it created anxiety about identity: Raphael or Guercino? Guercino or Domenichino? Domenichino or Michelangelo? Which?

At the Salon of 1761, which Diderot hailed as a triumph of colour, he remarked, oddly, that he had initially thought two altarpieces hanging together, *Saint Benoît mourant reçoit le viatique* (1761; Musée des beaux-arts, Orléans) and *Saint Germain donne une médaille à Sainte Geneviève* (1760; lost), were the work of the same painter, a follower of Le Sueur. Later he discovered that the first was by Deshays, and its 'pair' by Joseph-Marie Vien.[235] The mistake is the more remarkable because Deshays and Vien exemplified the French School's divergent traditions of colour and line almost to the point of cliché. If, instead of dismissing Diderot's error as no more than that, we consider it instead in relation to print and the engravings he owned, we get a rather different picture. Diderot often treats the medium of print as transparent, as when he wrote of François de Poilly's engraving of *L'Évanouissement d'Esther*, 'In Poussin's *painting*, which I have before me…' (my emphasis). At other times he assigned print its own particular 'air équivoque', which made distinguishing between its portrayal of stone and flesh, statues and beings difficult and sometimes uncertain.[236] Reading painted canvas as printed paper extends the ambiguity of reproduction to authorship and the conflation Deshays–Vien. And, contrary to the eighteenth century's own belief that reproduction was an indispensable tool for the reputation of the painter, providing evidence of the truth of the painted original to set against its misrepresentation in malicious reviews,[237] reproduction was, for perhaps the majority who lacked everyday access to painting, the unconsciously accepted black and white 'weave' or veil that both ordered perception of the originals and helped to forge key critical terms used to evaluate them – whether original or copy.

To argue that reproduction, by its visuality, and by the scale of its market, the reach of its impact and the nature of its laws, reorganised perception in such a way that viewers were sensitised to similarity and attentive to repetition is to suggest that mediation of painting by print played a significant part in the reconceptualisation of art, from an elite form of social and professional practice based on following to a form of intellectual property materialised in the commodity. This is the kind of determinist argument sometimes advanced to connect the invention of the printing press directly to the emergence of early forms of copyright. However, there is a difference here. The Pierre affair was not one in which the painter was himself an interested party, and the transformation in the visual culture of the mid-century proposed here is in the eye of the beholder. As such, it was part and parcel of a much broader cultural transformation, which has been analysed by Thomas Crow, in which the regular staging of public exhibitions and the publication of art criticism worked to shift cultural and political power from the institutions of the state to the public and public opinion. Crow describes at length the role that the Salons played in the radicalisation of art politics in the 1770s and 1780s.[238] From 1773 censorship of art criticism was relaxed,[239] and in the newspaper reviews and pamphlets that proliferated in the wake of liberalisation, plagiarism became a stick with which to beat the Académie. Falconet's trials over his *morceau de réception* had concerned the sculptor's presumption to the rank of Academician; none of the evidence suggests that, in this case, the Académie and its hierarchy were themselves in question. Diderot's attack on Pierre similarly fell short of challenging the Académie's legitimacy and authority. Beginning with the anonymous *Dialogue sur la peinture*, a savage review of the 1773 Salon, the situation began to change. The author of the *Dialogue* accused Gabriel-François Doyen not simply of plagiarism but of being a plagiarist. His *morceau d'agrément* was a confection of two of Domenichino's masterpieces, his 1761 *morceau de réception* owed its merit to Pietro da Cortona, his famous 1767 altarpiece of *Le Miracle des ardents* for the Paris church of Saint-Roch was a pastiche of Rubens, Domenichino and Bourdon, and *La Dernière Communion de Saint Louis*, exhibited in 1773 and commissioned by the Crown for the high altar of the École militaire was a slavish repetition of Domenichino's *L'ultima comunione di San Girolamo* (1614): boy and man, student and Academician, Doyen's strategy of copying was unchanging.[240] His borrowings, said the critic in summing up, were systematic, calculated and mechanical: '[he] helps himself to the Old Masters in proportion to the size of the job'.[241]

So to attack Doyen, arguably the head of the French School of history painting in the 1770s, was to level a charge at the Académie and the academic system as a whole, to expose the principles of academic art as no more that the wholesale, monotonous and profit-seeking repetition of hackneyed conventions.[242] The accusation Diderot privately levelled at Pierre is, in the *Dialogue*, endemic to the modern French School.[243] A decade later, *Sur la peinture*, another anonymous radical Salon pamphlet, critiqued all followers as 'courtly' (not noble) and as 'tame' conformists who bowed to the Académie's 'corporate style' and 'ruling system' out of vanity and self-interest. 'We must count for something,' the critic has them say; 'after all, the Académie says so, and on questions of merit it decides.'[244] The difference between emulation and plagiarism was the difference between insiders and outsiders. The ideal of the learned artist that Doyen did so much to cultivate, by his copies in Rome and his large collection of reproductive prints, was being forced into retreat and making way for notions of individual and inventive genius.[245] *Émule* ('disciple'), retained its positive connotations only by reversal of its original meaning: not 'follower' but 'opponent, competitor'.[246] In 1762, the year when the Académie française redefined the word, it no longer signified a connecting agent, or the totem of belonging.

Emulation and plagiarism provide a framework for the *arrêt* of 1777, both an historical context and a set of normative values that gave it its particular, local salience. Requesting legal protection for the Académie as a body and the failure of its members to use that protection, as was largely the case in 1777, is only seemingly contradictory. Copying and piracy among members of the Académie was contained by shared values concerning their proper function as a means by which the membership reproduced itself and its artistic traditions. The correspondence of the Directeur des bâtiments du roi, the comte d'Angiviller, with the Académie over the new regulations indicates that he was largely responsible for the drafting of the *Déclaration*. The prominence he assigned to privilege in that document was possibly influenced by his indirect involvement in 1776 in a case of privilege at the Châtelet, which combined matters of forgery, piracy and counterfeit.[247] It had been instigated by the engravers François-Denis Née and Louis-Joseph Masquelier against the print publishers Jacques Esnault and Michel Rapilly over two genre portraits depicting the daily life of Voltaire and titled *Le Déjeuné de Ferney* (fig. **55**) and *Le Lever du philosophe de Ferney* (fig. **56**) but only the first of which had been copied after an original engraved by Née and Masquelier.[248] Née and Masquelier had no privilege for their print, and to give themselves a better chance of winning their suit had joined forces with Charles-Étienne Gaucher and Charles-Nicolas Cochin *fils*, who were pursuing the same dealers for piracy of their portrait of Élie-Catherine Fréron, for which the engraver Gaucher had obtained a Chancellerie privilege, the force of which was redoubled by that of the Académie, because Cochin (the portrait's author) was an Academician. Gaucher's portrait will be discussed in the next chapter; the print by Née and Masquelier is worth considering here because, although the Académie was not directly implicated, the terms used in the litigation and Cochin's role as an expert witness suggest that the Académie's conception of privilege inflected the articulation of the dispute.[249]

The legal briefs for Esnault and Rapilly do not survive, so our knowledge of their arguments is secondhand, via the replies of the prosecution. We know, however, that they mounted their defence against Née and Masquelier on the absence of privilege and on an interpretation of the Edict of Saint Jean-de-Luz (1660) that construed the engravers' liberty to work free of guild control as denoting, instead, the freedom of printmakers, publishers and printsellers to pirate prints unless expressly prohibited by privilege.[250] Liberty was, in short, the public's domain. It was no doubt in order to muddy the legal waters and obscure the key question of whether there was a privilege to defend that Née and Masquelier focused attention on authorship by way of signature. They addressed in their briefs not copying per se (its exactness, its scope) but the forging of their signatures and the poor quality of the copies, which, they said, taken together, damaged their reputation.[251] This was injured still more, they further claimed, by the *Lever du philosophe de Ferney*, 'sujet obscène', because although unsigned, the identical frame and the plagiarised format made 'tacit attribution' to them virtually inevitable.[252] Née and Masquelier's lawyer stressed the dangers of forgery and the legal responsibility of letter engravers to verify the attribution of names before inscribing them on copper plates.[253] Cochin, in his capacity as witness, reinforced the disavowal of copying and misattribution, ironically by countering Esnault and Rapilly's claim that copying was a generally licensed practice and the means by which the arts perfect themselves, proposing instead a legal definition of the copy: copy counts as infringement, he said, when the intention and objective is exchange, even when students are responsible.[254] The judge was convinced and ruled in Née and Masquelier's favour.[255] He accepted their claim to artistic status, even though they were not Academicians, and felt their pain. Esnault and Rapilly were fined and the plates and impressions were confiscated.

In January 1777, d'Angiviller wrote to Jean-Charles-Pierre Lenoir, the *lieutenant de police* and magistrate in the case, to thank him for the favourable outcome.[256] Not only had it rekindled concern for the Académie's own privilege, which had remained more or less neglected from mid-century, but the terms of the debate had also brought into sharp focus the distinction between art and trade, which was the basis of the Académie's foundation. The Née and Masquelier case helps to explain why article 8 of the *Déclaration* is preceded and given context by articles that prohibit Academicians as artists from trading in art and having shops (art. 2), and that direct all those in the art trade to join the reinstated Corporation des maîtres peintres et sculpteurs (art. 3).[257] Just as significant, however, is the fact that the case demonstrates that the reputational argument for privilege, as a right of exception, could be effectively deployed in court, even in the absence of a formal privilege in law. Reputational arguments could become commercial and legal instruments.

The migration of conceptual categories used in privilege debate was not unidirectional. In 1780, a dispute between Claude-Joseph Vernet and the engraver and print dealer François-Anne David broke out in the newspapers over David's publication of *Première et seconde vues des environs de Dunkerque* (fig. **57**), engraved by Auder and attributed to Vernet.[258] Not content with voicing Vernet's refutation of the prints as, in fact, not reproductions of paintings by him, Antoine Renou, the *secrétaire* of the Académie, quoted article 8 of the 1777 *Déclaration* in full.[259] Only the author, or the Académie, could authorise reproduction of an Academician's work. Renou, like Née and Masquelier, affirmed the reputational right of the artist and the Académie, but whereas the engravers of the Voltairiana had had to argue tactically, making a virtue of necessity, Renou proceeded in secure possession of the Académie's right. But the unofficial gloss that Renou gave the statute, following quotation of article 8, led it towards a new meaning, as if reputation alone was not enough:

> In selling this or that Painting or Sculpture, Painters and Sculptors do not sell their glory and their reputation. In order to part with those, one would have to substitute in place of their signatures – the seal of their claim in

matters of *gloire* – the name of the purchaser. Artists would be careful not to consent to such a thing and Collectors not to require it of them. The reputation of Artists is thus an inalienable possession which belongs to them exclusively, even when they no longer own their works; this is why the Sovereign has granted them the right to prevent assaults upon it.[260]

Renou's commentary focuses on individuals and their inalienable rights rather than on the images and their royal and Académie warrants. Moreover, the discourse on owning as belonging had made way, in his articulation of privilege, for a property form of ownership, one with absolute rights of possession and alienation. Renou may have been influenced in this by Née and Masquelier's suit, in the course of which they argued that their property as well as their persons had been attacked.[261] Or, like Cochin, he may have been abreast of the debates taking place in the field of letters.[262] Whatever the case, while Renou acknowledged the role of the royal 'Legislator' in the attribution of privilege, close reading of his text indicates rather that he felt privilege as a natural right, which the king 'wisely' confirmed.[263] Finally, the artistic and legal self that Renou imagined in Vernet was one defined not by academic status alone but also by his pictures, in which he was embodied. This is to suggest a shift in artistic subjectivity from an emphasis at the beginning of the century on properties of the self (Académie status) to an emphasis at the end on things owned by the self: intellectual property.

The causes of the shift are not hard to identify. A perceived intensification of print piracy during and after the Seven Years' War was identified by Cochin when he drafted a new privilege statute for the Académie in 1764, and it is implicit in Renou's later critique of David and his like.[264] Art criticism, as we have seen, also played its part; accusations of plagiarism had rendered artistic emulation self-conscious and anxious. Finally, the mediation of art by printed reproduction expanded the audiences for art and encouraged modes of viewing that were sensitive to similarity in composition and form. The discourse on Académie privilege was by these events nudged closer to the book trade's reconceptualisation of privilege as a natural right of property. In the last decades of the *ancien régime*, privilege at the Académie was becoming hybrid: a mix of alienable private property rights and inalienable personal and reputational claims to those characteristics of the artist embodied in the work (in Vernet's case, his eye for realistic detail, his taste for atmospheric effects, his choice of viewpoint, his flair for figures) – characteristics that made reputations. To that degree, Académie privilege could be said to resemble, perhaps even anticipate, nineteenth-century *droit moral*, or the legal recognition, in the continental tradition of intellectual property law, of the enlarged 'surface of vulnerability' of the artist by virtue of the extension of the artistic personality into the art work.[265]

PLATES

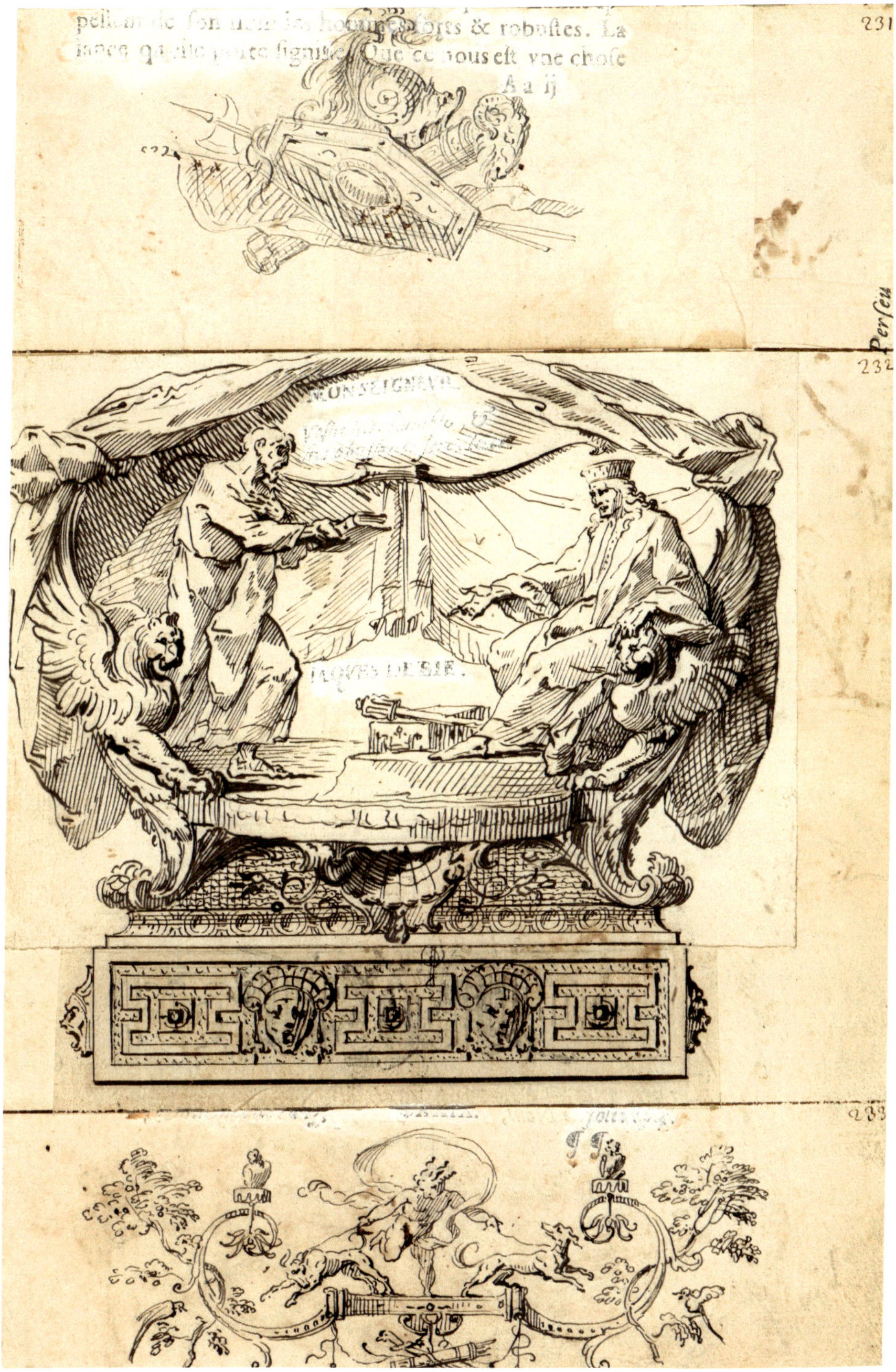

1 ↑ Jacques de Bie and Jean Baudouin, *Iconologie, ou Explication nouvelle de plusieurs images, emblèmes et autres figures* (1636), p. 232; Gilles-Marie Oppenord, sketch depicting de Bie presenting the book to Chancelier Séguier in return for a privilege, *c.*1713, pen and brown ink (325 × 219 mm), Canadian Centre for Architecture, Montreal.

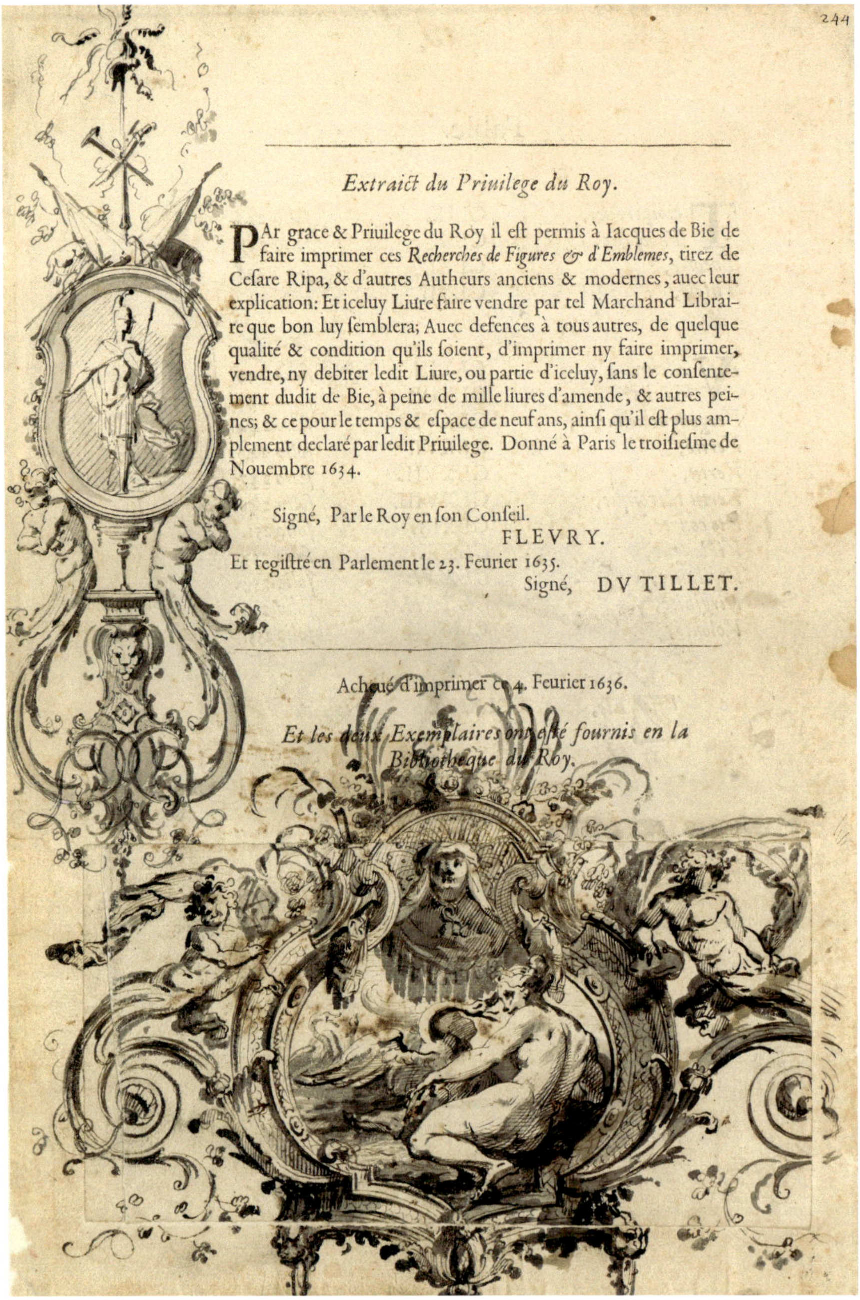

244

Extraict du Priuilege du Roy.

PAr grace & Priuilege du Roy il est permis à Iacques de Bie de faire imprimer ces *Recherches de Figures & d'Emblemes*, tirez de Cesare Ripa, & d'autres Autheurs anciens & modernes, auec leur explication: Et iceluy Liure faire vendre par tel Marchand Libraire que bon luy semblera; Auec defences à tous autres, de quelque qualité & condition qu'ils soient, d'imprimer ny faire imprimer, vendre, ny debiter ledit Liure, ou partie d'iceluy, sans le consentement dudit de Bie, à peine de mille liures d'amende, & autres peines; & ce pour le temps & espace de neuf ans, ainsi qu'il est plus amplement declaré par ledit Priuilege. Donné à Paris le troisiesme de Nouembre 1634.

Signé, Par le Roy en son Conseil.
FLEVRY.
Et registré en Parlement le 23. Feurier 1635.
Signé, DV TILLET.

Acheué d'imprimer ce 4. Feurier 1636.

Et les deux Exemplaires ont esté fournis en la Bibliotheque du Roy.

2 ↑ Jacques de Bie and Jean Baudouin, *Iconologie, ou Explication nouvelle de plusieurs images, emblèmes et autres figures* (1636); Gilles-Marie Oppenord, drawing depicting Leda and the swan, c.1713, pen and brown ink (322 × 219 mm), Canadian Centre for Architecture, Montreal.

3 ↗ Jean-Baptiste Delafosse after Louis Carrogis de Carmontelle, *La Malheureuse famille Calas*, etching and engraving, 1765 (355 × 432 mm), Bibliothèque nationale de France, Paris.

4 → Anon., *L'Arbre de Cracovie*, etching and engraving, 1760 (263 × 423 mm), Bibliothèque nationale de France, Paris, no. 17, 'Un graveur sans contrefaction'.

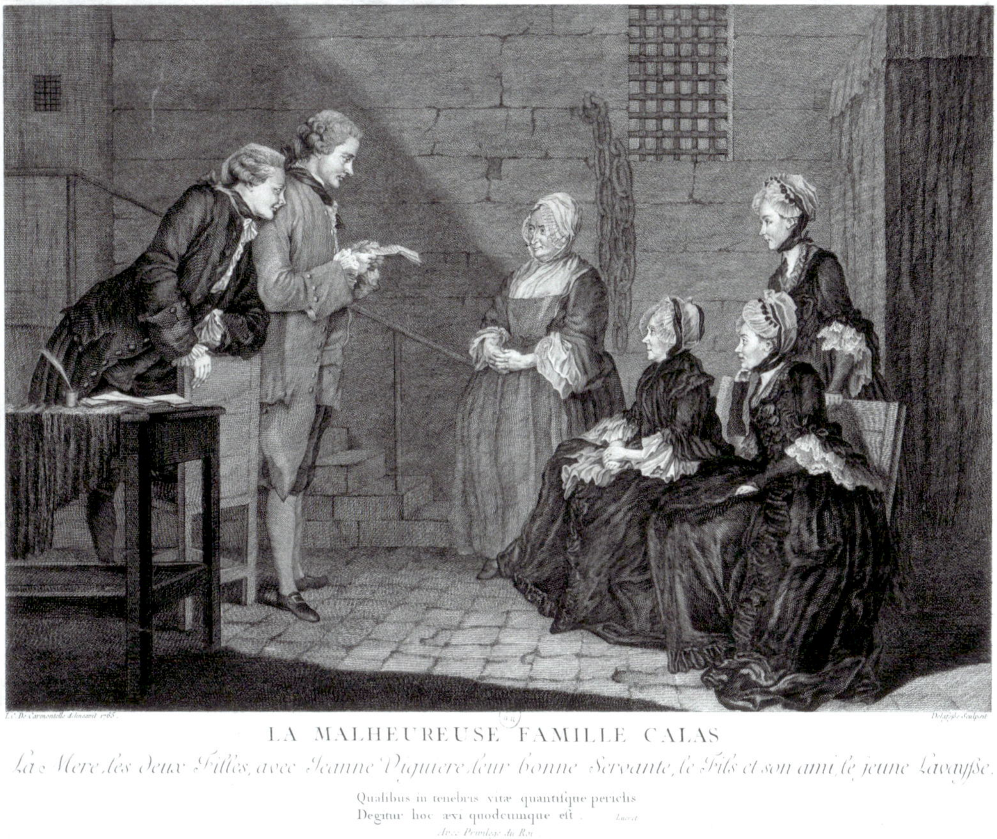
LA MALHEUREUSE FAMILLE CALAS
La Mere, les deux Filles, avec Jeanne Viguiere leur bonne Servante, le Fils et son ami le jeune Lavaysse.
Qualibus in tenebris vitæ quantisque periclis
Degitur hoc ævi quodcumque est.

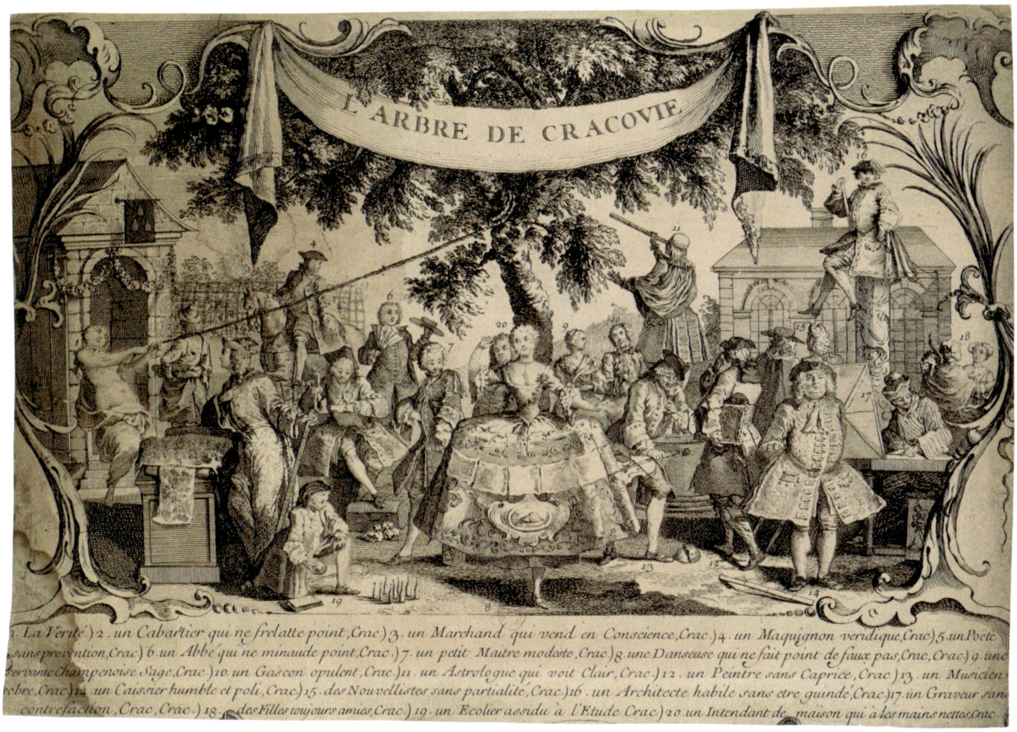
L'ARBRE DE CRACOVIE
1. La Verité) 2. un Cabartier qui ne frelatte point, Crac) 3. un Marchand qui vend en Conscience, Crac) 4. un Maquignon veridique, Crac) 5. un Poëte sans prevention, Crac) 6. un Abbé qui ne minaude point, Crac) 7. un petit Maitre modeste, Crac) 8. une Danseuse qui ne fait point de faux pas, Crac, Crac) 9. une Servante Champenoise Sage, Crac) 10. un Gascon opulent, Crac) 11. un Astrologue qui voit Clair, Crac) 12. un Peintre sans Caprice, Crac) 13. un Musicien sobre, Crac) 14. un Caissier humble et poli, Crac) 15. des Nouvellistes sans partialité, Crac) 16. un Architecte habile sans etre guindé, Crac) 17. un Graveur sans contrefaction, Crac, Crac) 18. des Filles toujours amies, Crac) 19. un Ecolier assidu à l'Etude Crac) 20. un Intendant de maison qui à les mains nettes, Crac.

FABLES

CHOISIES,

MISES EN VERS

PAR J. DE LA FONTAINE.

TOME PREMIER.

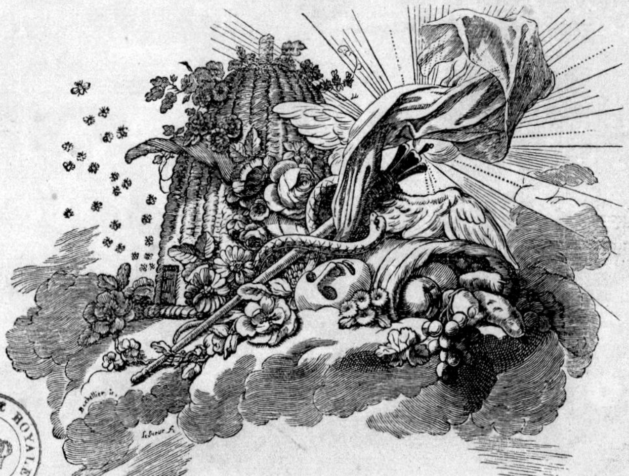

A PARIS,

Chez { DESAINT & SAILLANT, rue Saint Jean de Beauvais.
DURAND, rue du Foin, en entrant par la rue S. Jacques.

M. DCC. LV.

De l'Imprimerie de *CHARLES-ANTOINE JOMBERT.*

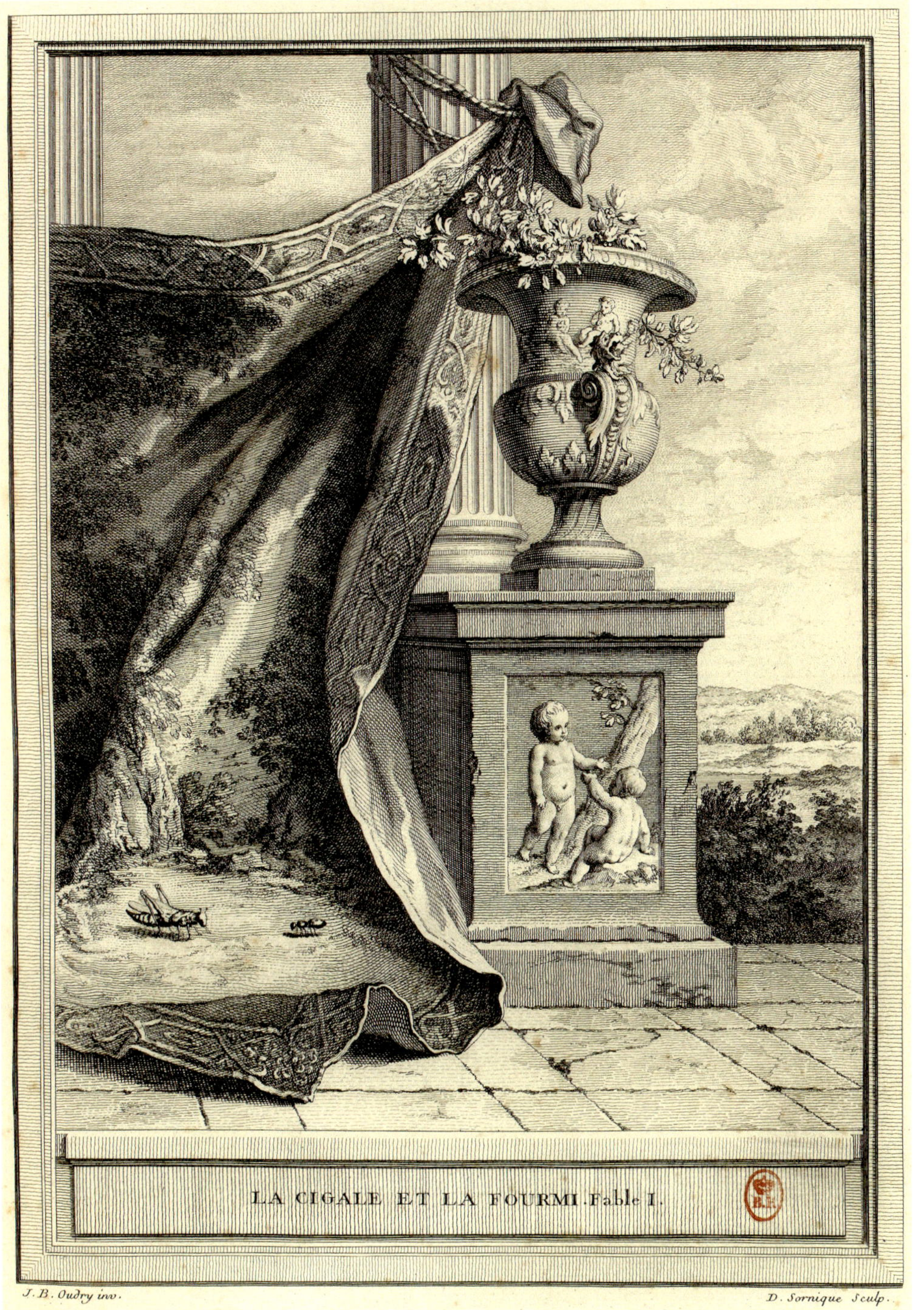

5 ← *Fables choisies, mises en vers par J. de La Fontaine*, vol. 1 (1755), title-page with a *fleuron* in woodcut by Nicolas Le Sueur after Jean-Jacques Bachelier.

6 ↑ Dominique Sornique after Jean-Baptiste Oudry, *La Cigale et la fourmi*, Fable I, etching and engraving (282 × 212 mm), for *Fables choisies, mises en vers par J. de La Fontaine*, vol. 1 (1755).

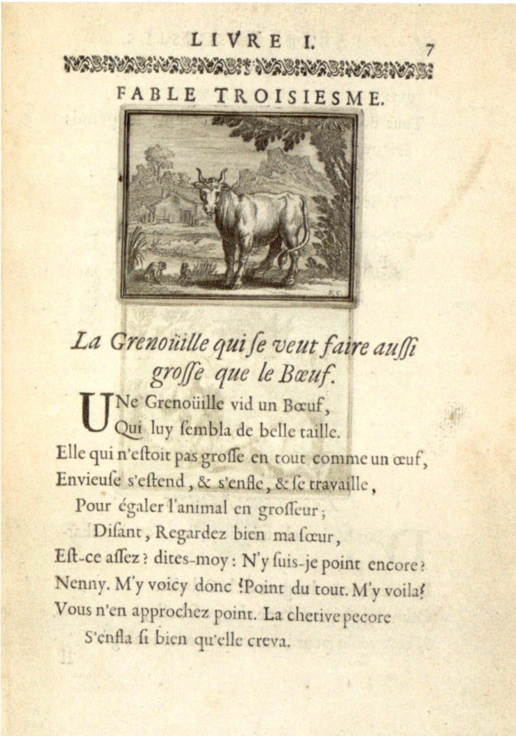

LIVRE I. 7

FABLE TROISIESME.

La Grenoüille qui se veut faire aussi grosse que le Bœuf.

UNe Grenoüille vid un Bœuf,
Qui luy sembla de belle taille.
Elle qui n'estoit pas grosse en tout comme un œuf,
Envieuse s'estend, & s'enfle, & se travaille,
Pour égaler l'animal en grosseur;
Disant, Regardez bien ma sœur,
Est-ce assez? dites-moy: N'y suis-je point encore?
Nenny. M'y voicy donc? Point du tout. M'y voila?
Vous n'en approchez point. La chetive pecore
S'enfla si bien qu'elle creva.

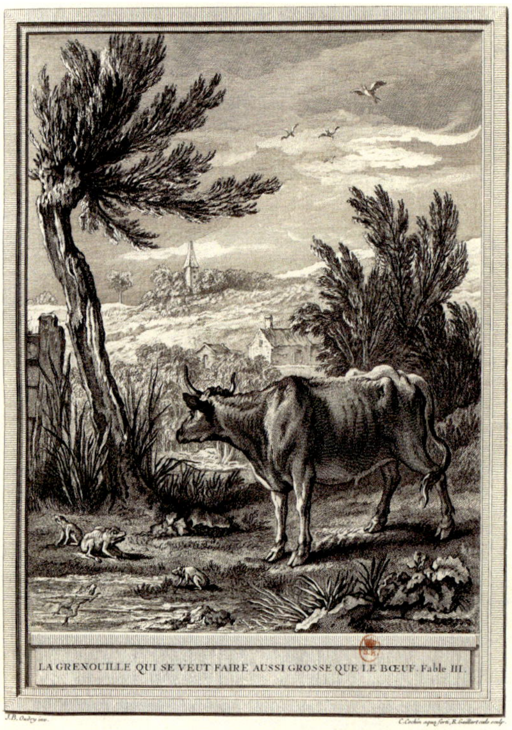

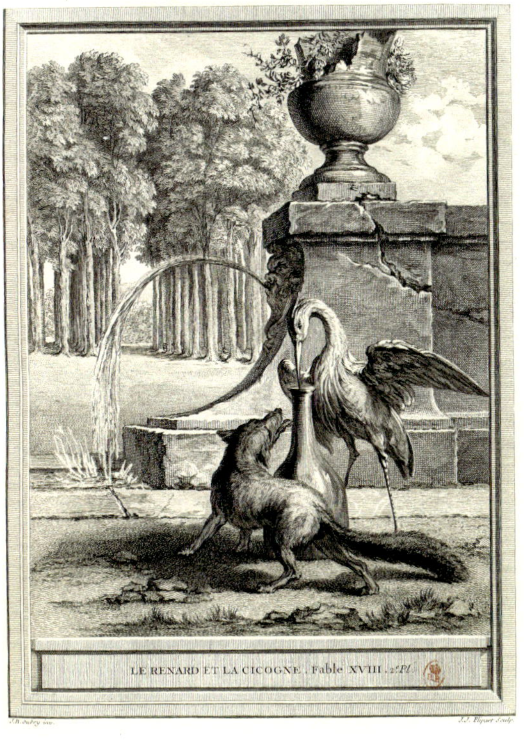

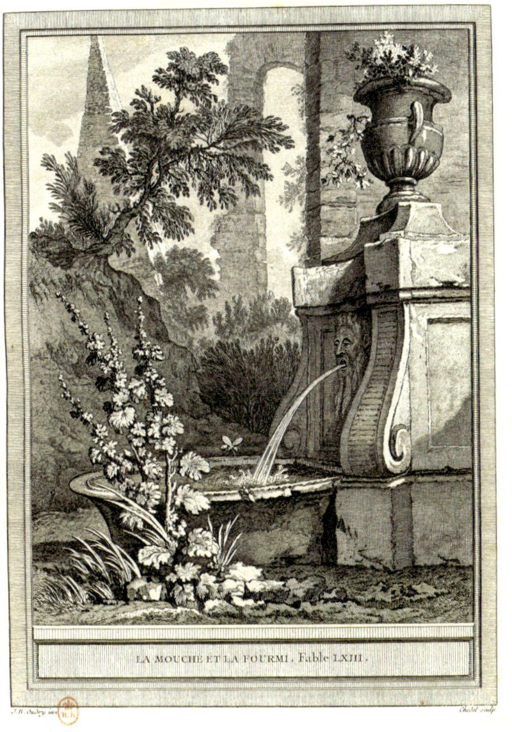

7 ↖ François Chauveau, *La Grenouille qui se veut faire aussi grosse que le bœuf*, Fable III, wood engraving (55 × 70 mm), for *Fables choisies, mises en vers par M. de La Fontaine* (1668), p. 7.

8 ← Charles-Nicolas Cochin *fils* and René Gaillard after Jean-Baptiste Oudry, *La Grenouille qui se veut faire aussi grosse que le bœuf*, Fable III, etching and engraving (282 × 212 mm), for *Fables choisies, mises en vers par J. de La Fontaine*, vol. 1 (1755).

9 ↖ Jean-Jacques Flipart after Jean-Baptiste Oudry, *Le Renard et la cigogne*, Fable XVIII, etching and engraving (282 × 212 mm), for *Fables choisies, mises en vers par J. de La Fontaine*, vol. 1 (1755).

10 ↑ Pierre Quentin Chedel after Jean-Baptiste Oudry, *La Mouche et la fourmi*, Fable LXIII, etching and engraving (282 × 212 mm), for *Fables choisies, mises en vers par J. de La Fontaine*, vol. 1 (1755).

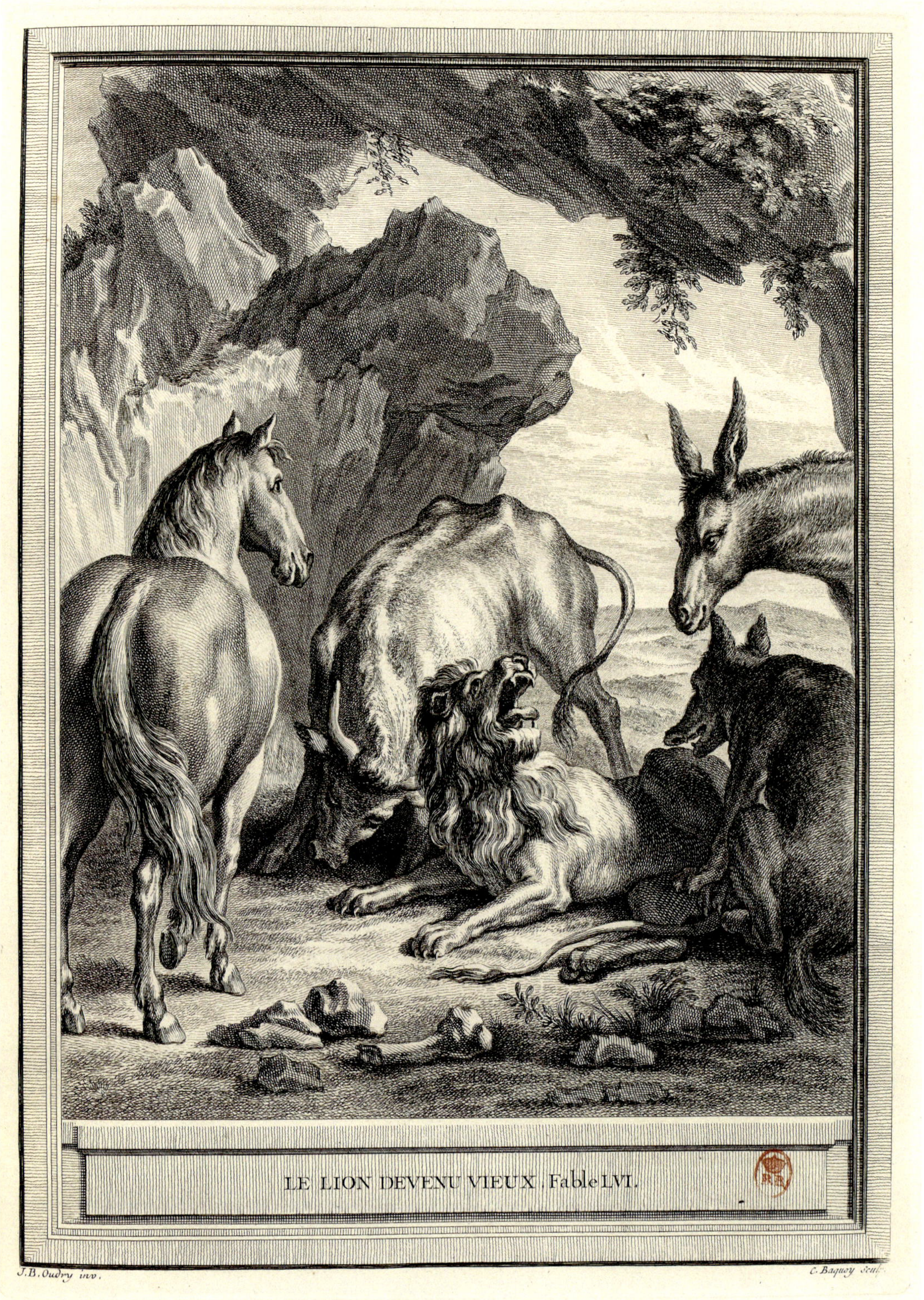
LE LION DEVENU VIEUX. Fable LVI.
J.B. Oudry inv.
C. Baquoy Sculp.

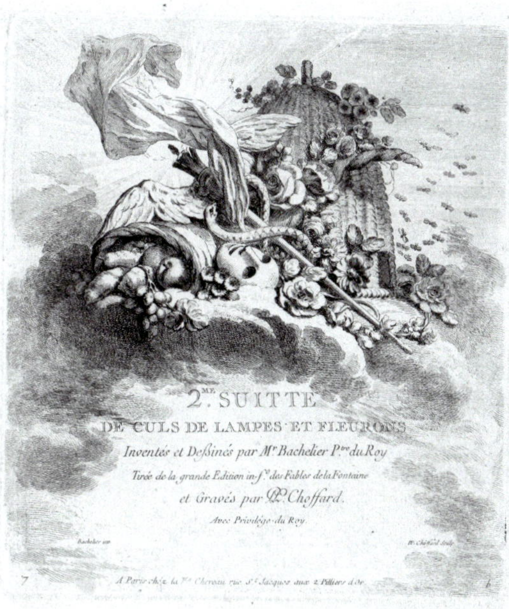

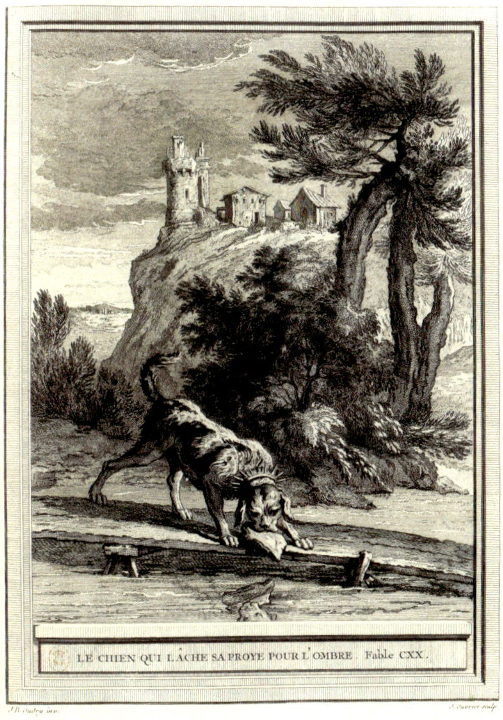

11 ← Jean-Charles Baquoy after Jean-Baptiste Oudry, *Le Lion devenu vieux*, Fable LVI, etching and engraving (282 × 212 mm), for *Fables choisies, mises en vers par J. de La Fontaine*, vol. 1 (1755).

12 ↑ Pierre-Philippe Choffard after Jean-Jacques Bachelier, *2me Suitte de culs de lampes et fleurons. . . tirée de la grande édition. . . des Fables de La Fontaine* (1760), title-page, etching (150 × 120 mm); Victoria and Albert Museum, London, inv. no. E.347-1952.

13 ↑ Jean Ouvrier after Jean-Baptiste Oudry, *Le Chien qui lâche sa proye pour l'ombre*, Fable CXX, etching and engraving (282 × 212 mm), for *Fables choisies, mises en vers par J. de La Fontaine*, vol. 2 (1755).

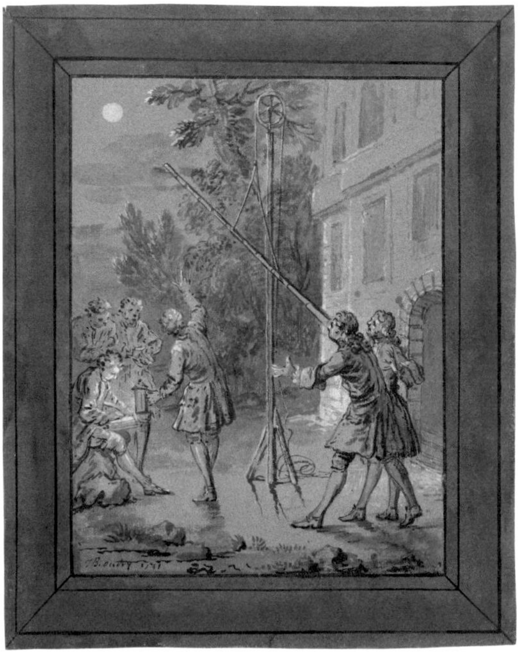

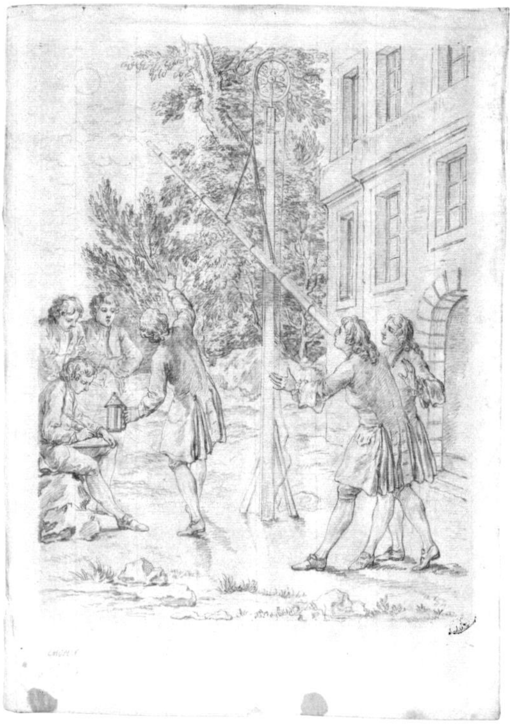

14 ↑ Jean-Baptiste Oudry, *Un Animal dans la lune*, 1731, pen, brush and black ink, with grey wash and white gouache highlights (311 × 257 mm), Rijksmuseum, Amsterdam.

15 ↑ Charles Nicolas Cochin *fils* after Jean-Baptiste Oudry, *Un Animal dans la lune*, black lead, squared for transfer, rubbed with red chalk on the verso, 1755? (248 × 195 mm), Musée Jean de La Fontaine, Château-Thierry.

16 → Jean Ouvrier after Jean-Baptiste Oudry, *Un Animal dans la lune*, Fable CXLII, etching and engraving (282 × 212 mm), for *Fables choisies, mises en vers par J. de La Fontaine*, vol. 3 (1755).

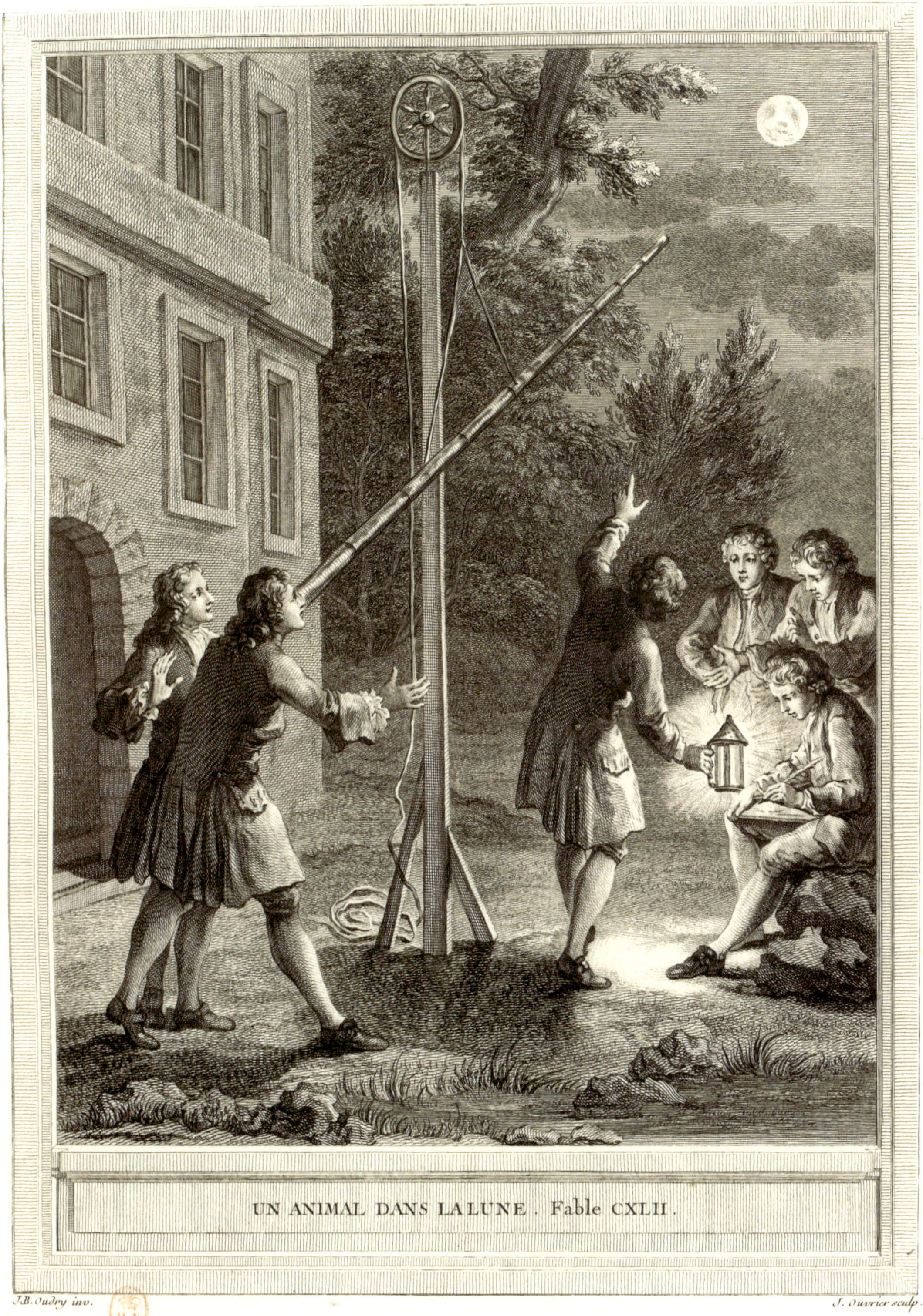

UN ANIMAL DANS LALUNE. Fable CXLII.

J.B. Oudry inv. J. Ouvrier sculp.

ENCYCLOPÉDIE,

OU

DICTIONNAIRE RAISONNÉ DES SCIENCES, DES ARTS ET DES MÉTIERS,

PAR UNE SOCIÉTÉ DE GENS DE LETTRES.

Mis en ordre & publié par M. *DIDEROT*, de l'Académie Royale des Sciences & des Belles-Lettres de Prusse ; & quant à la PARTIE MATHÉMATIQUE, par M. *D'ALEMBERT*, de l'Académie Royale des Sciences de Paris, de celle de Prusse, & de la Société Royale de Londres.

Tantùm series juncturaque pollet,
Tantùm de medio sumptis accedit honoris ! HORAT.

TOME PREMIER.

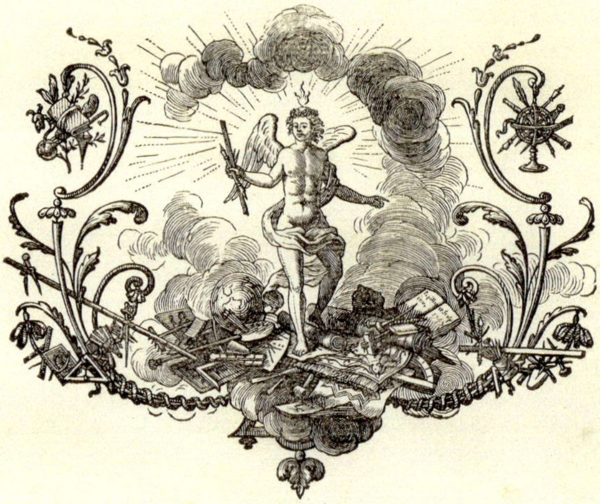

A PARIS,

Chez
BRIASSON, *rue Saint Jacques, à la Science.*
DAVID l'aîné, *rue Saint Jacques, à la Plume d'or.*
LE BRETON, Imprimeur ordinaire du Roy, *rue de la Harpe.*
DURAND, *rue Saint Jacques, à Saint Landry, & au Griffon.*

M. DCC. LI.

AVEC APPROBATION ET PRIVILEGE DU ROY.

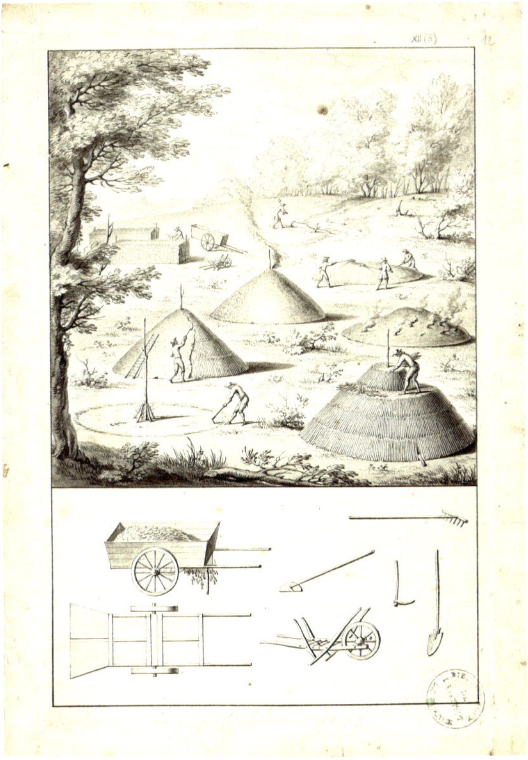

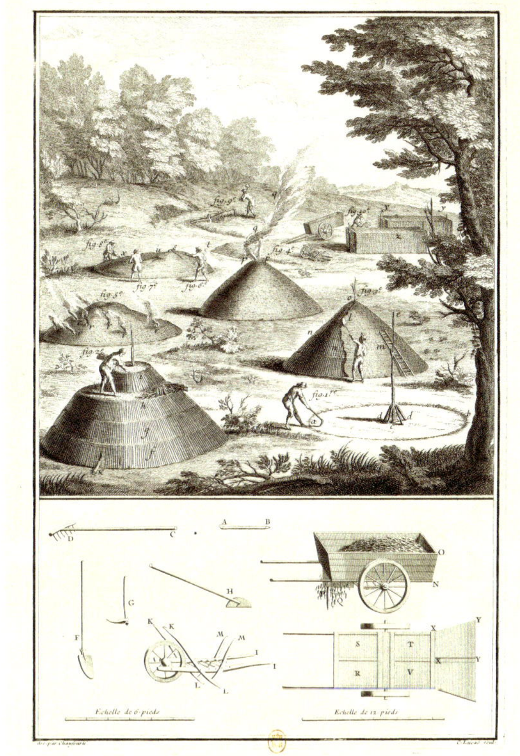

17 ← Denis Diderot and Jean Le Rond d'Alembert, *Encyclopédie, ou Dictionnaire raisonné des sciences, des arts et des métiers*, vol. 1 (1751), title-page with a *fleuron* in woodcut by Jean-Michel Papillon.

18 ↑ Jean Chaufourier, *Charbon de bois*, *c*.1690, pen, ink and wash (325 × 215 mm), for *Description des arts et métiers* (unpublished), Bibliothèque de l'Institut de France, Paris.

19 ↑ Claude Lucas after Jean Chaufourier, *Œconomie rustique, Charbon de bois*, *c*.1690, engraving (340 × 225 mm), for *Description des arts et métiers* (unpublished), Bibliothèque nationale de France, Paris.

Pl. I.

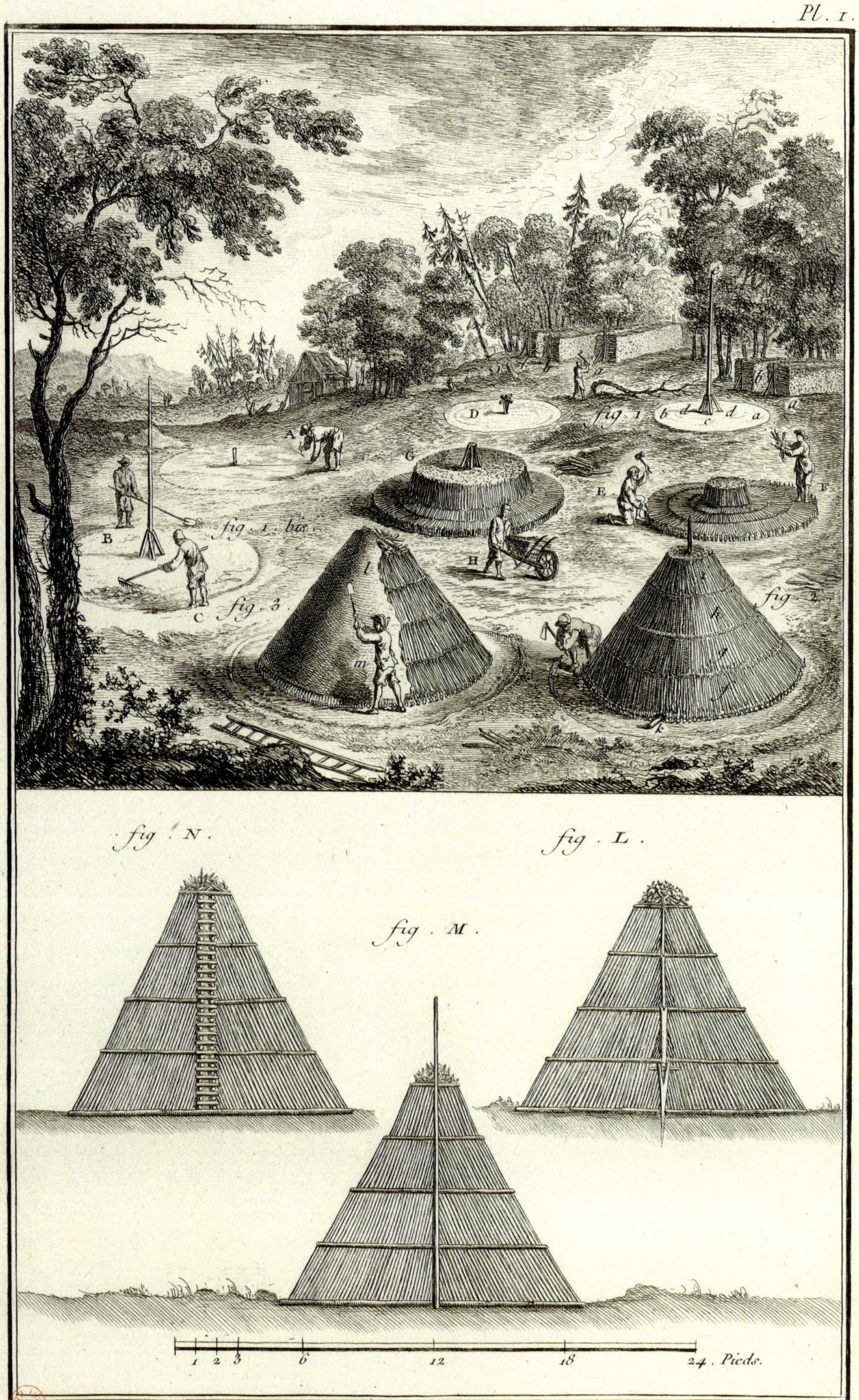

Œconomie Rustique, Charbon de Bois.

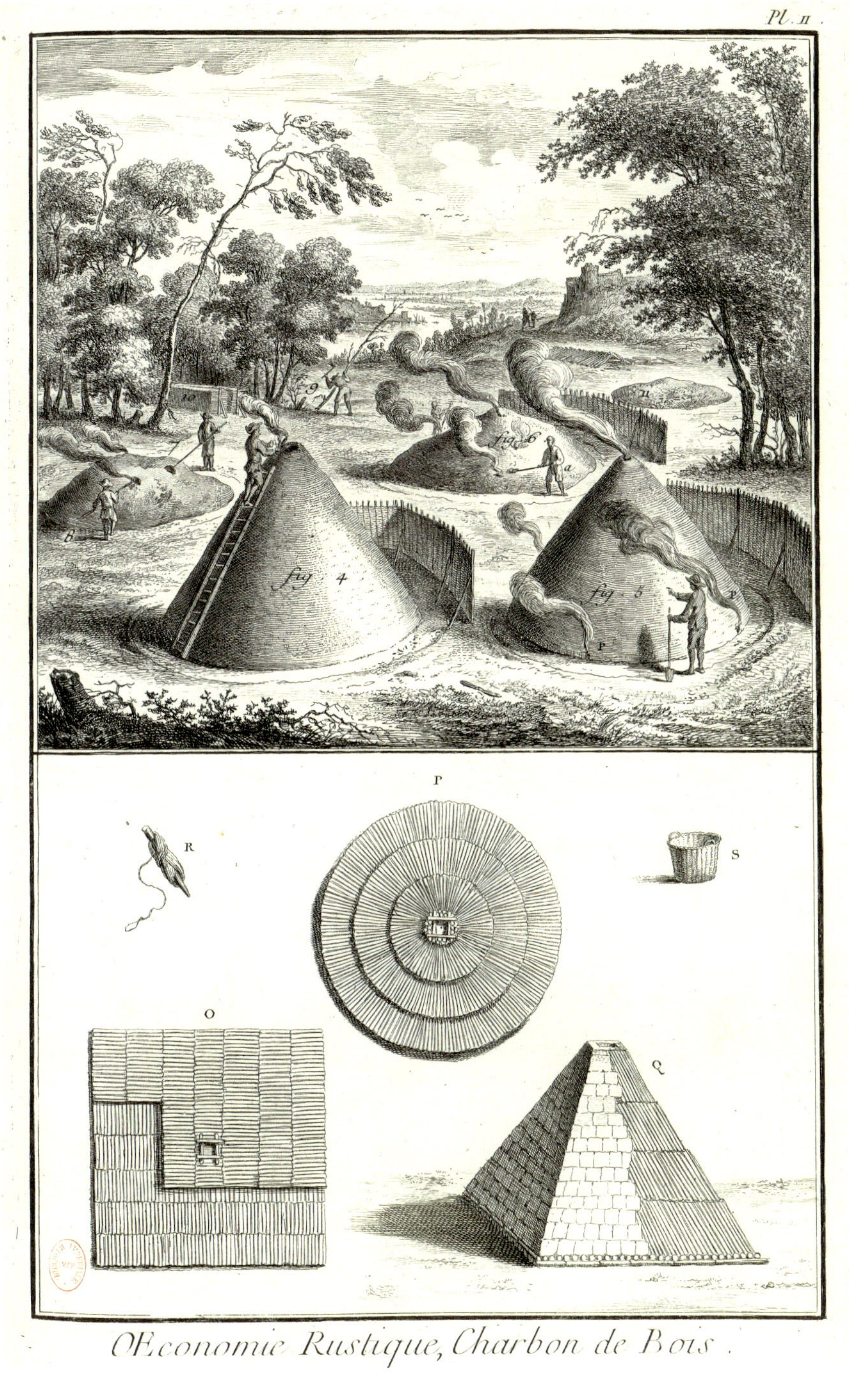

20 ← Robert Bernard after Louis-Jacques Goussier, *Œconomie rustique, Charbon de bois*, pl. I, engraving (358 × 225 mm), for Diderot and d'Alembert, *Encyclopédie, Recueil de planches*, vol. 1 (1762), Bibliothèque nationale de France, Paris.

21 ↑ Robert Bernard after Louis-Jacques Goussier, *Œconomie rustique, Charbon de bois*, pl. II, engraving (358 × 225 mm), for Diderot and d'Alembert, *Encyclopédie, Recueil de planches*, vol. 1 (1762), Bibliothèque nationale de France, Paris.

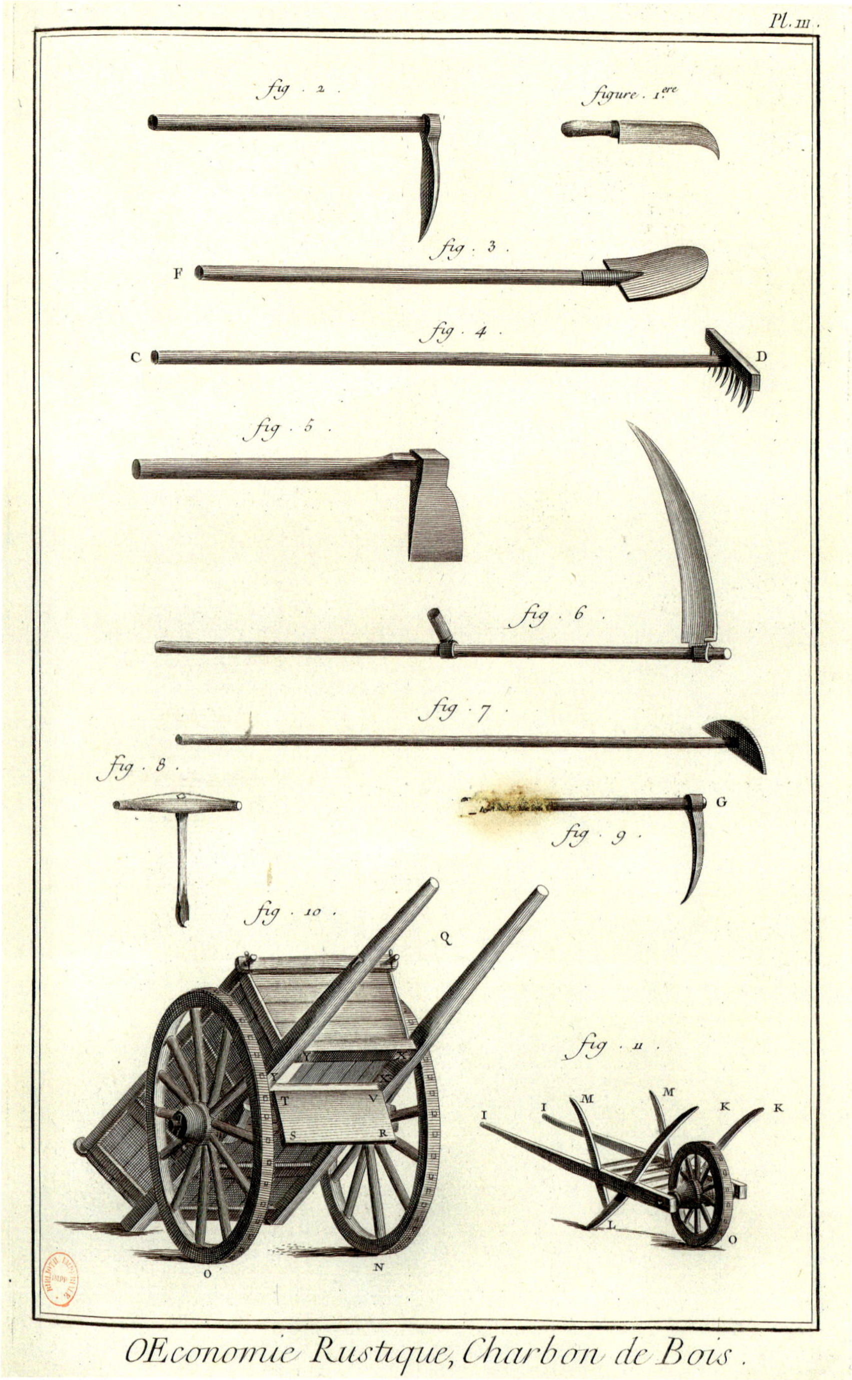

22 ↑ Robert Bernard after Louis-Jacques Goussier, *Œconomie rustique, Charbon de bois*, pl. III, engraving (358 × 225 mm), for Diderot and d'Alembert, *Encyclopédie, Recueil de planches*, vol. 1 (1762), Bibliothèque nationale de France, Paris.

23 ↗ Desgerantins, design for a plate illustrating the art of the featherman, *c.*1770, pen, ink and wash with annotations, formerly Musée des arts et traditions populaires, Paris.

24 → Desgerantins, design for a plate illustrating the art of the featherman, *c.*1770, pen, ink and wash with annotations, formerly Musée des arts et traditions populaires, Paris.

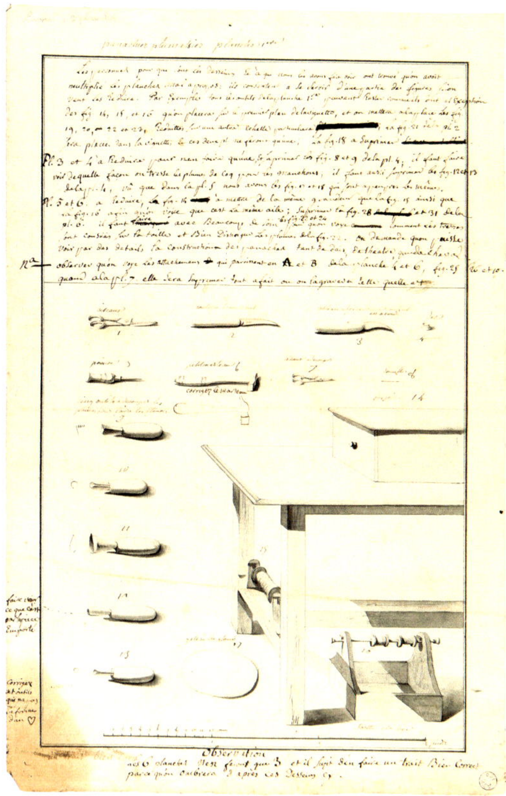

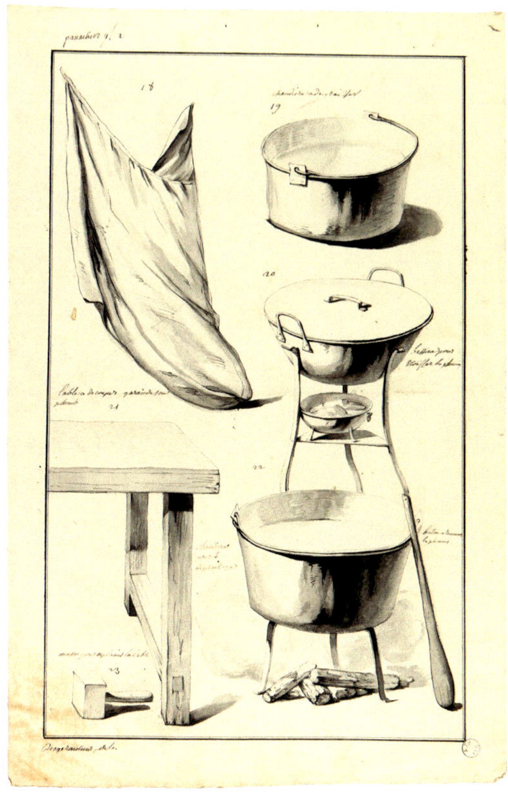

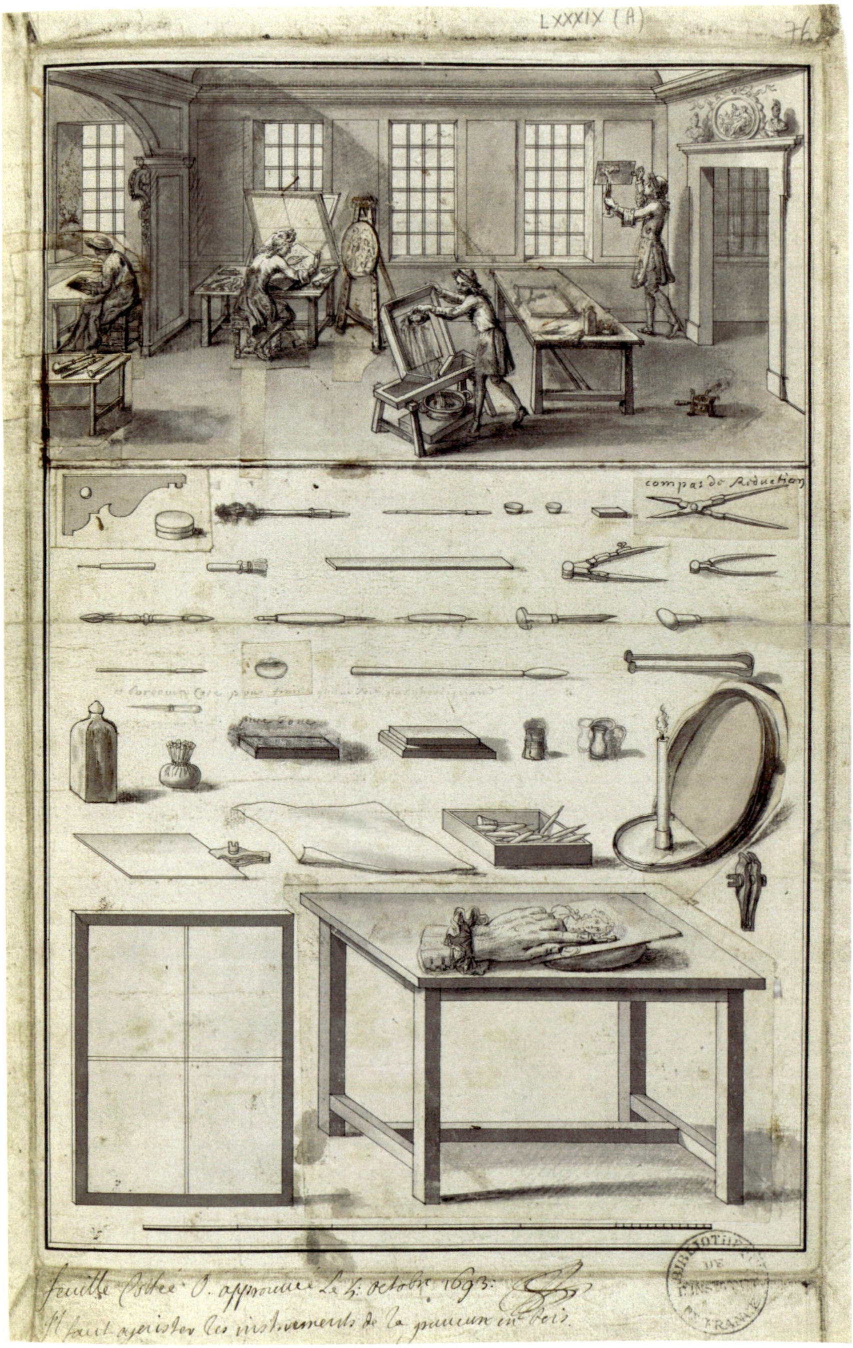

25 ↑ Anon., *La Gravure*, c.1690, pen and ink over graphite with reworkings and annotations (325 × 215 mm), for *Description des arts et métiers* (unpublished), Bibliothèque de l'Institut de France, Paris.

26 ↗ Verso of *La Gravure* (fig. 25), *c*.1690, showing elements cut from other drawings and pasted into place, signed off ('Bon'), the whole rubbed with red chalk for transfer, Bibliothèque de l'Institut de France, Paris.

27 → Jean-Michel Papillon, rejected design for a plate illustrating wallpaper manufacture, *c*.1759, pl. 5 of 7 for Diderot and d'Alembert, *Encyclopédie, Recueil de planches*, pen, ink and wash (365 × 275 mm), private collection.

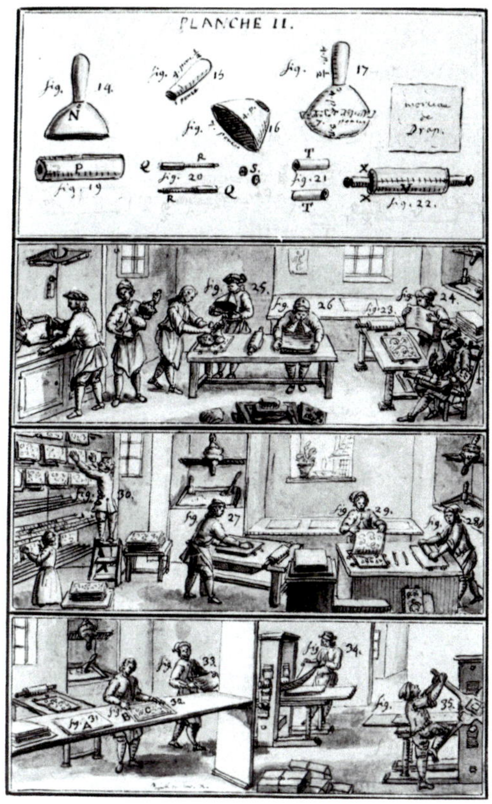
PLANCHE II.
fig. 14
fig. 15
fig. 16
fig. 17
fig. 19
fig. 20
fig. 21
fig. 22
fig. 23
fig. 24
fig. 25
fig. 26
fig. 27
fig. 28
fig. 29
fig. 30
fig. 31
fig. 32
fig. 33
fig. 34
fig. 35

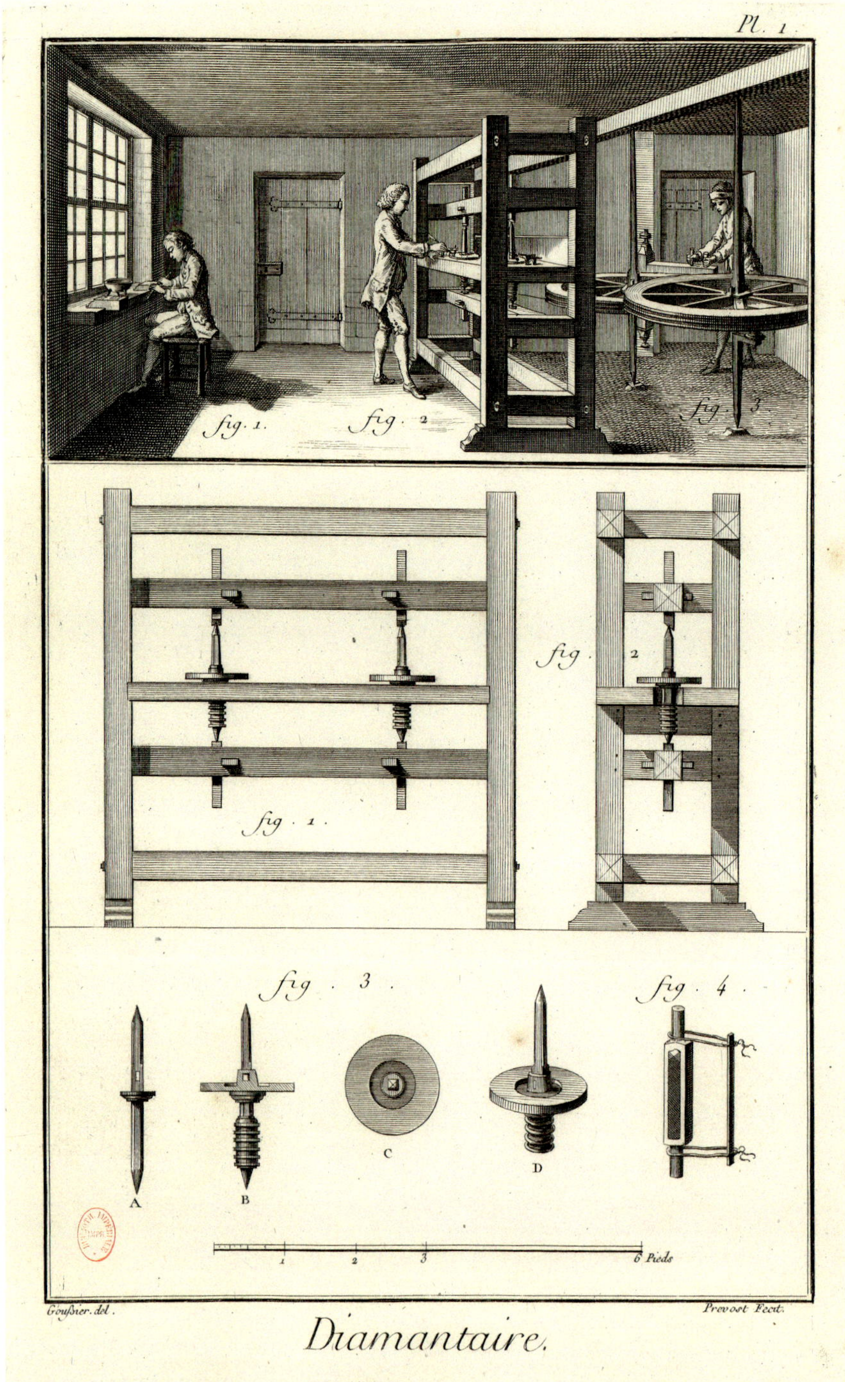

28 ↑ Robert Bernard after Louis-Jacques Goussier, *Diamantaire*, pl. I, engraving (356 × 230 mm), for Diderot and d'Alembert, *Encyclopédie, Recueil de planches*, vol. 2, bound as 3 (1763).

29 → Robert Bernard after Louis-Jacques Goussier, *Diamantaire*, pl. II, engraving (356 × 230 mm), for Diderot and d'Alembert, *Encyclopédie, Recueil de planches*, vol. 2, bound as 3 (1763).

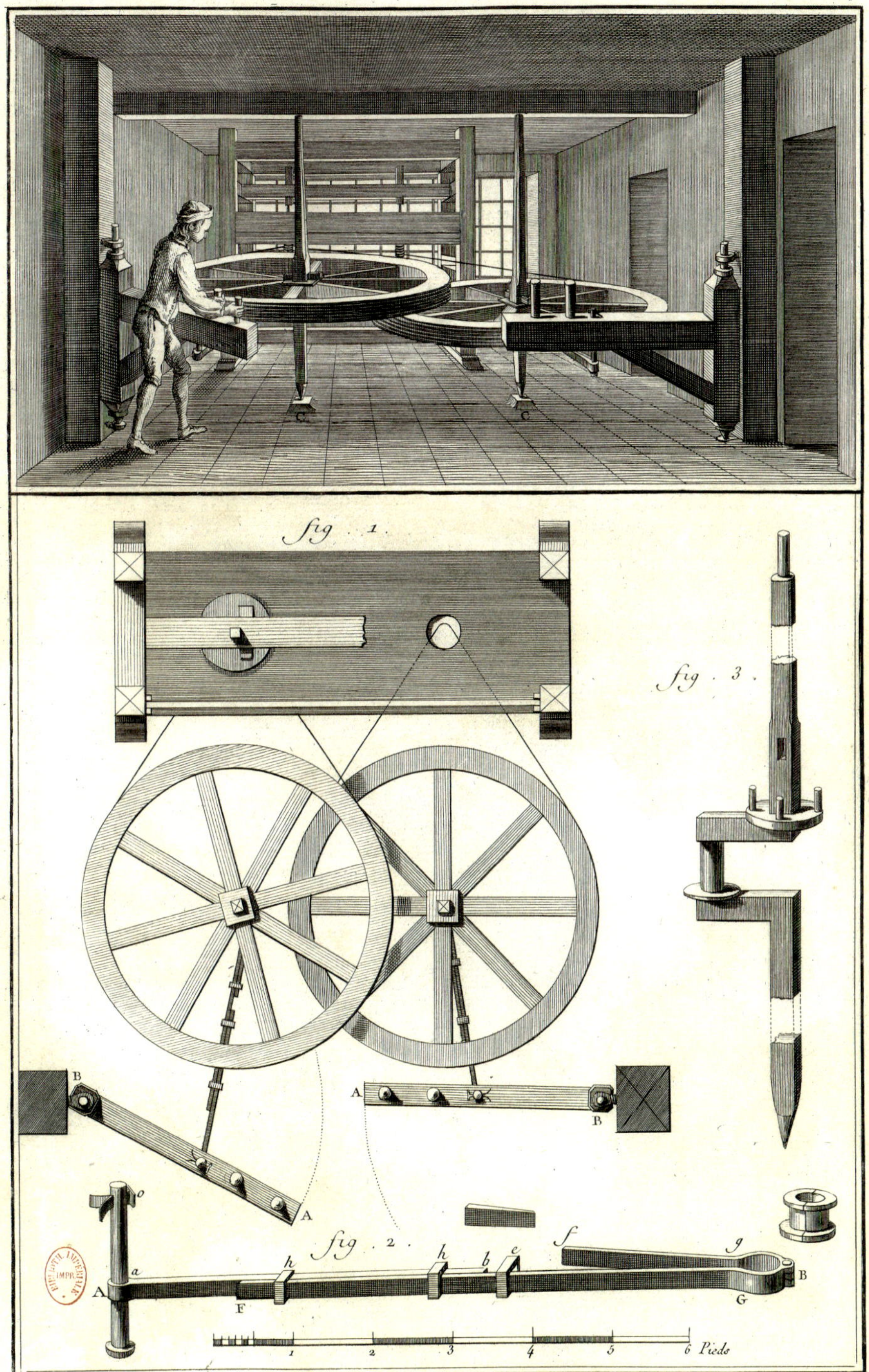

Goussier. del. Defhert Fecit.

Diamantaire.

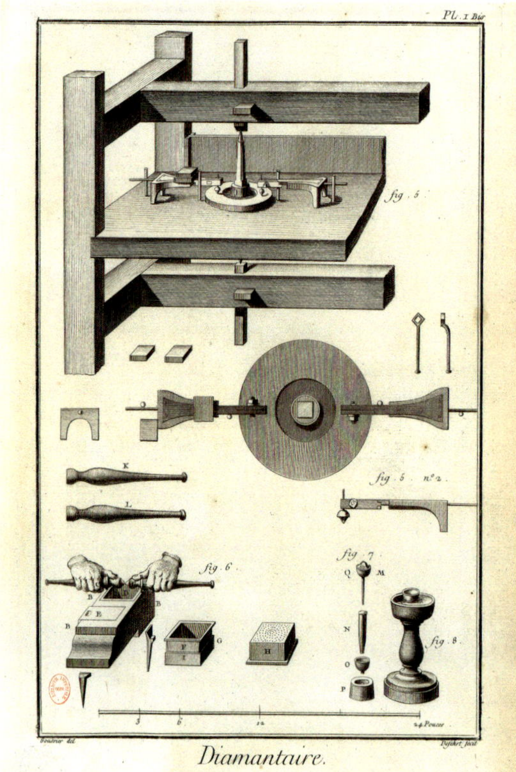

30 ↑ Robert Bernard after Louis-Jacques Goussier, *Diamantaire*, pl. I bis, engraving (356 × 230 mm), for Diderot and d'Alembert, *Encyclopédie, Recueil de planches*, vol. 2, bound as 3 (1763).

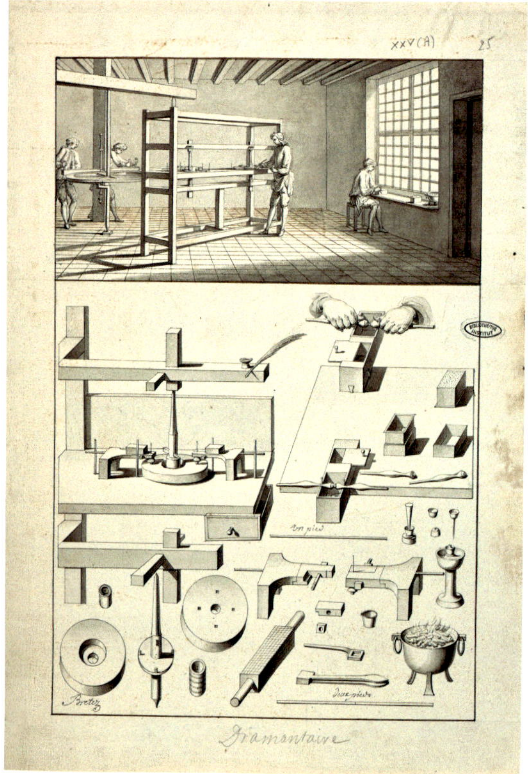

31 ↑ Louis Bretez, *Diamantaire*, c.1690, pen, ink and grey wash (325 × 215 mm), for *Description des arts et métiers* (unpublished), Bibliothèque de l'Institut de France, Paris.

32 → Louis Bretez and Jean Chaufourier, *Diamantaire*, c.1690, pen, ink and grey wash (325 × 215 mm), for *Description des arts et métiers* (unpublished), Bibliothèque de l'Institut de France, Paris.

XXVI(A) 26

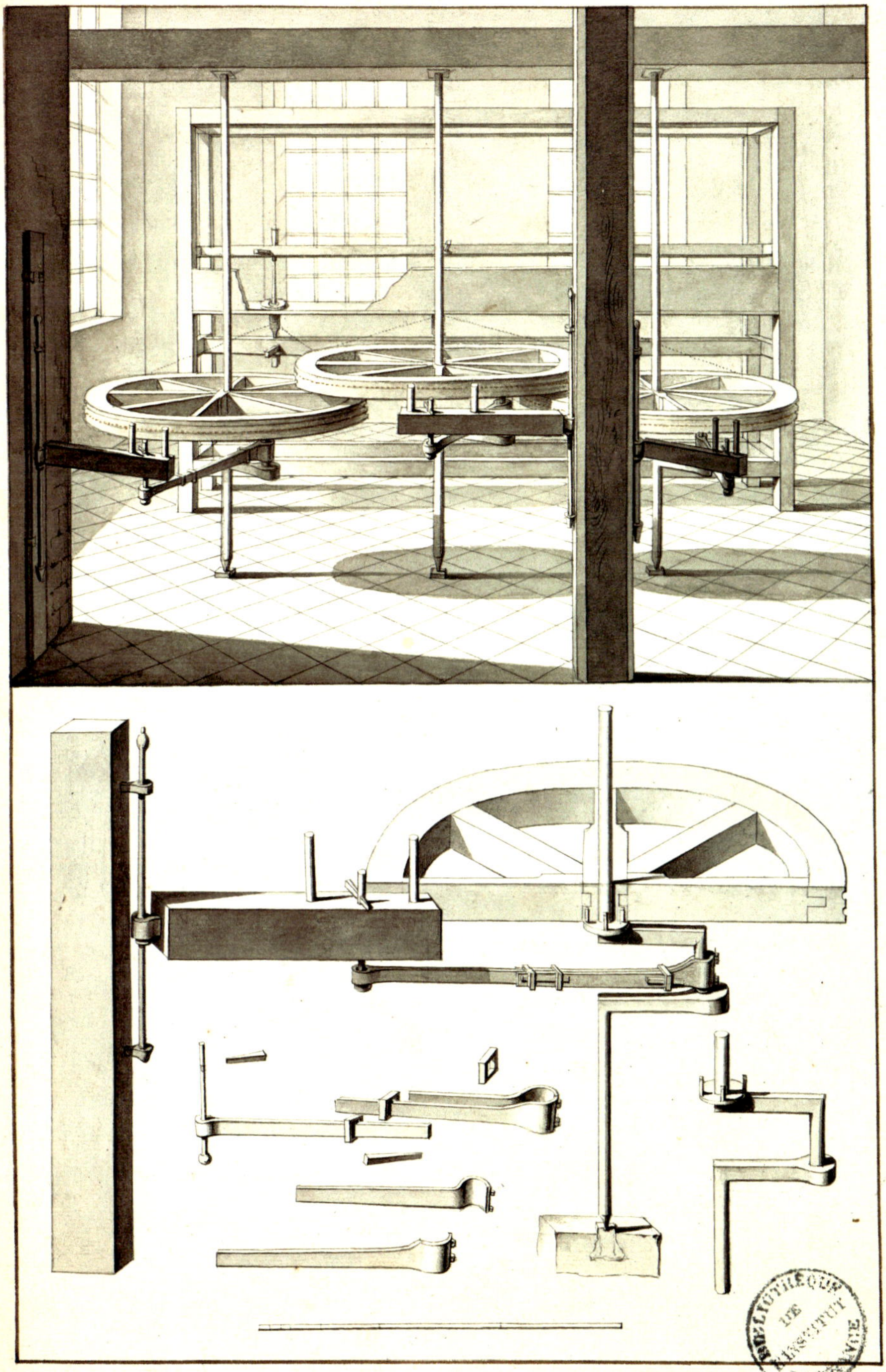

Diamantaire

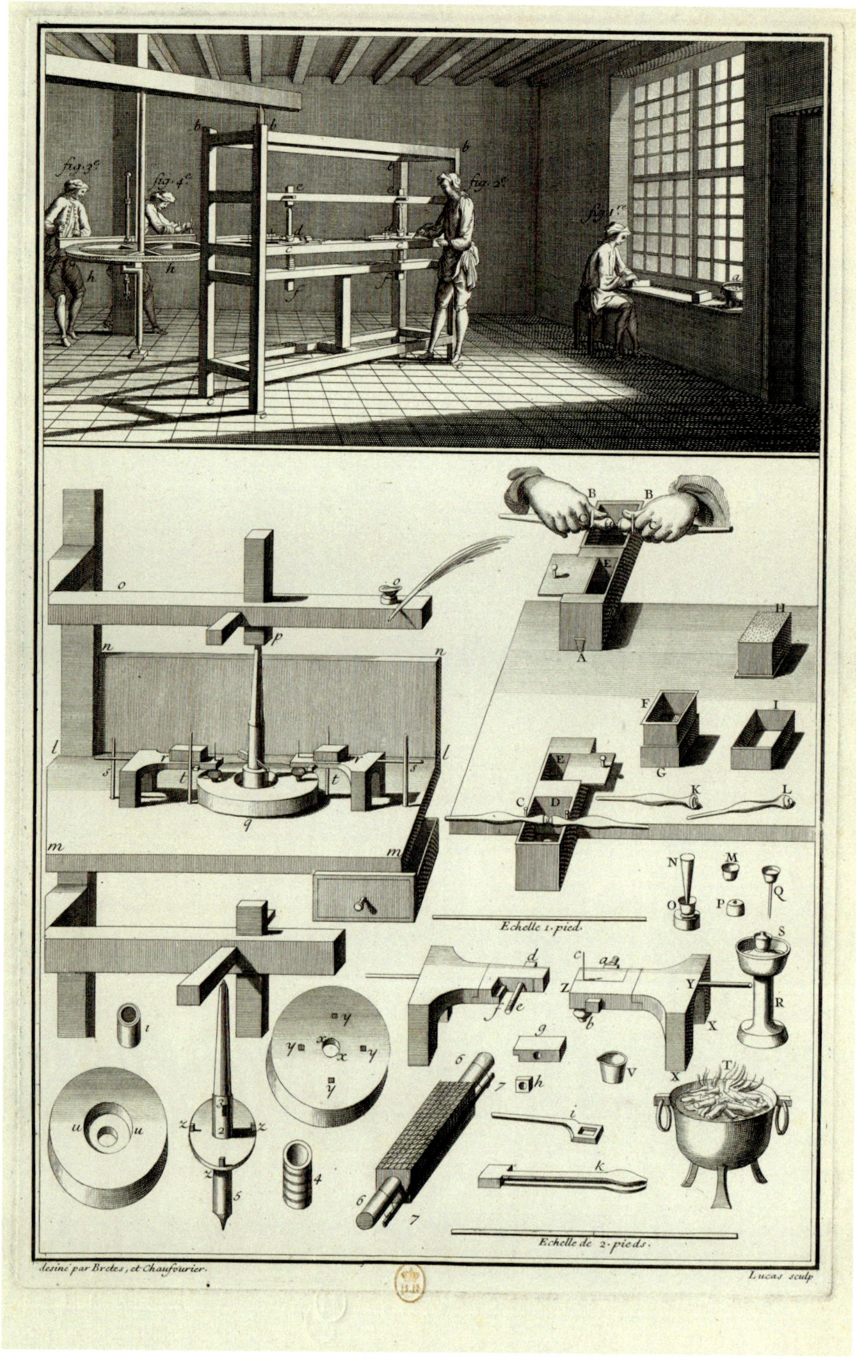

33 ↑ Claude Lucas after Louis Bretez and Jean Chaufourier, *Diamantaire*, *c*.1690, engraving (340 × 225 mm), for *Description des arts et métiers* (unpublished), Bibliothèque nationale de France, Paris, corpus Diderot, Réserve Ma-39-Boîte Fol.

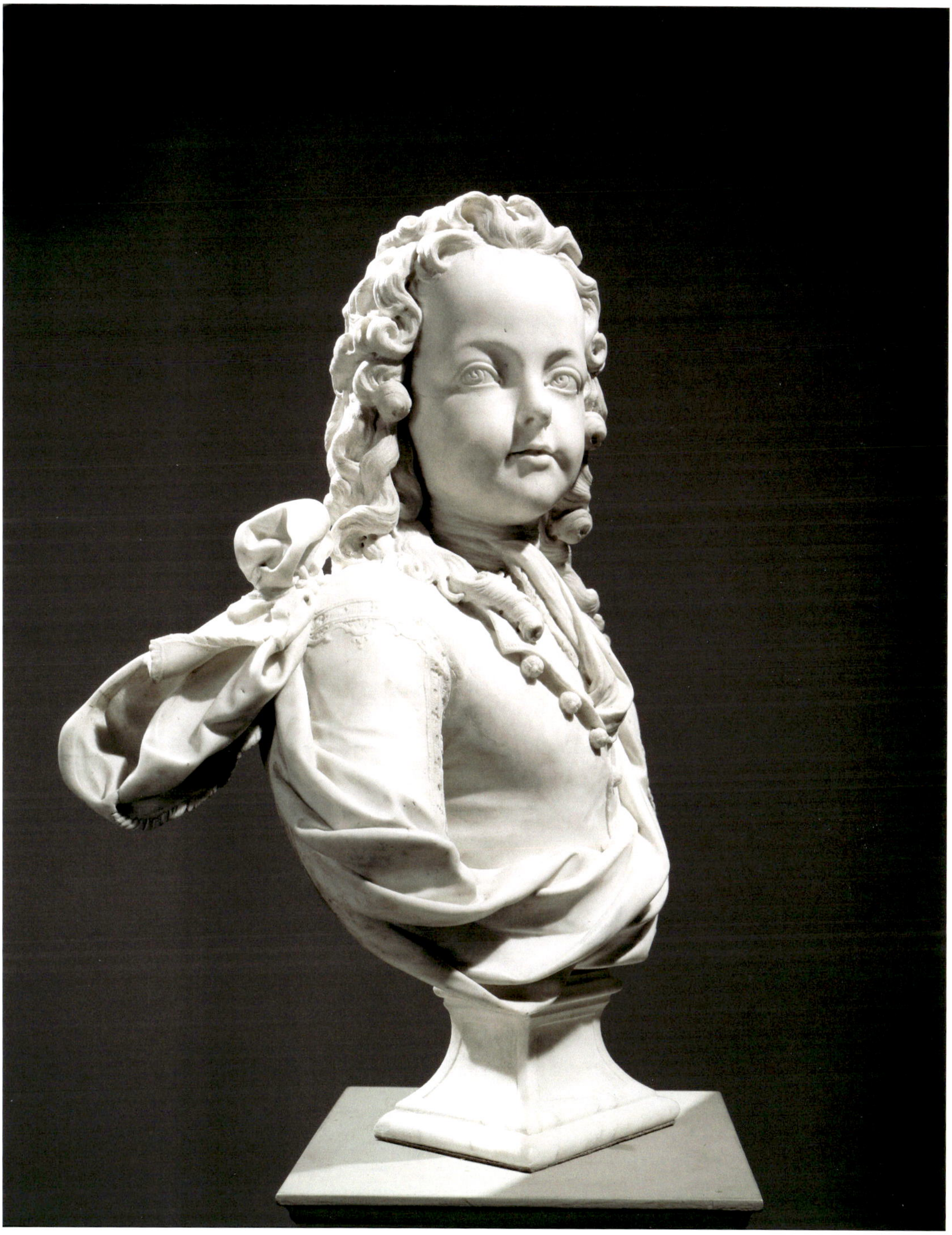

34 ↑ Antoine Coysevox, bust of Louis XV, aged 6, *c.*1716, marble
(h. 0.59 metres), Frick Collection, New York.

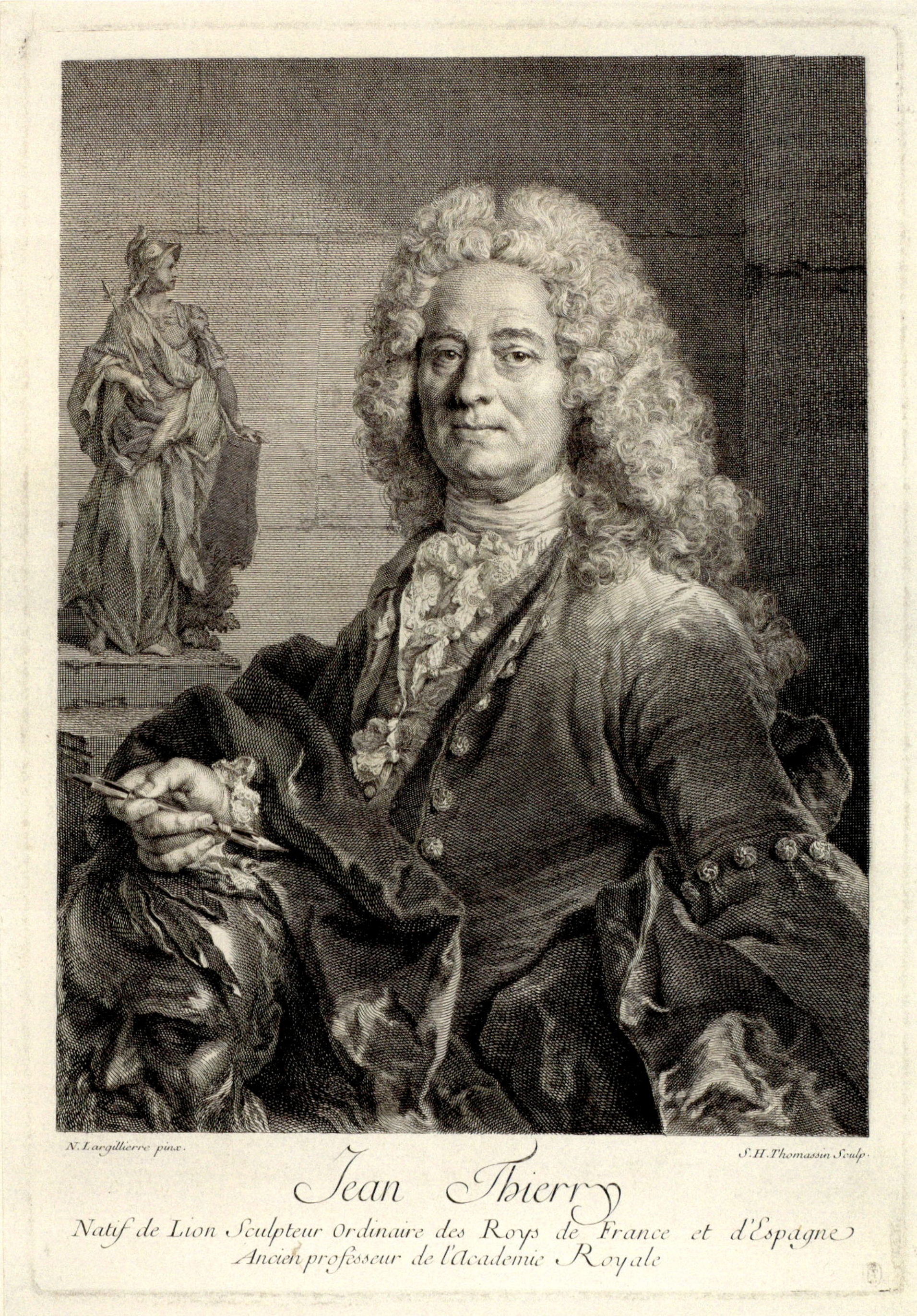

35 ↑ Henri-Simon Thomassin after Nicolas de Largillière, portrait of Jean Thierry, engraving, 1734 (298 × 253 mm), Fitzwilliam Museum, Cambridge.

36 ↗ Charles-Nicolas Cochin *père* after François Le Moyne, *Jacob arrive en Mésopotamie, aperçoit Rachel et se fait connoître à elle*, etching and engraving, 1732 (477 × 374 mm), British Museum, London.

37 → Claude-Augustin Duflos after François Boucher, *Le Pêcheur*, etching and engraving, 1753 (202 × 247 mm), British Museum, London.

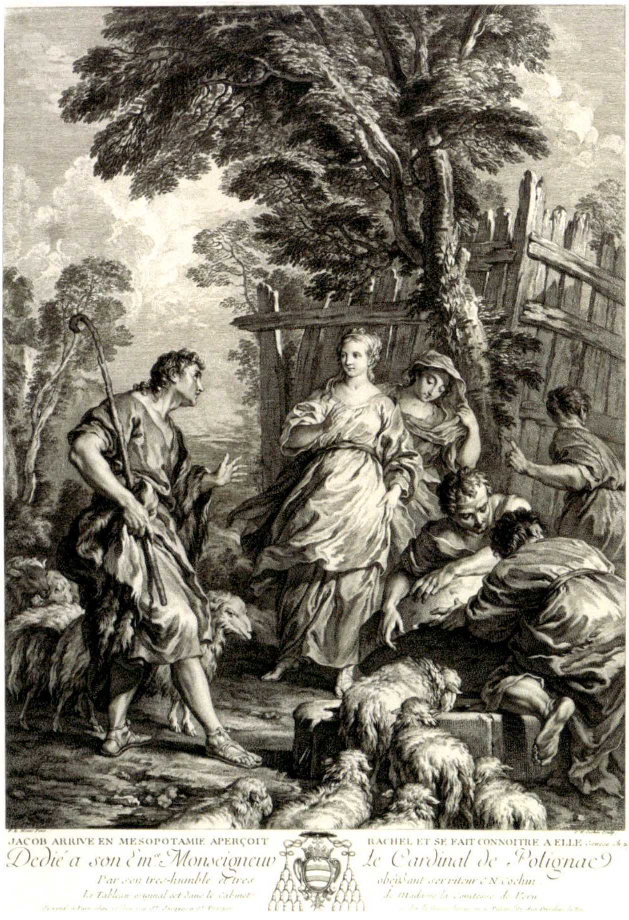
JACOB ARRIVE EN MESOPOTAMIE APERÇOIT RACHEL ET SE FAIT CONNOITRE A ELLE
Dedié a son Em.ce Monseigneur le Cardinal de Polignac
Par son tres-humble et tres obéissant serviteur C.N. Cochin
Le Tableau original est dans le Cabinet de Madame la Comtesse de Verrue

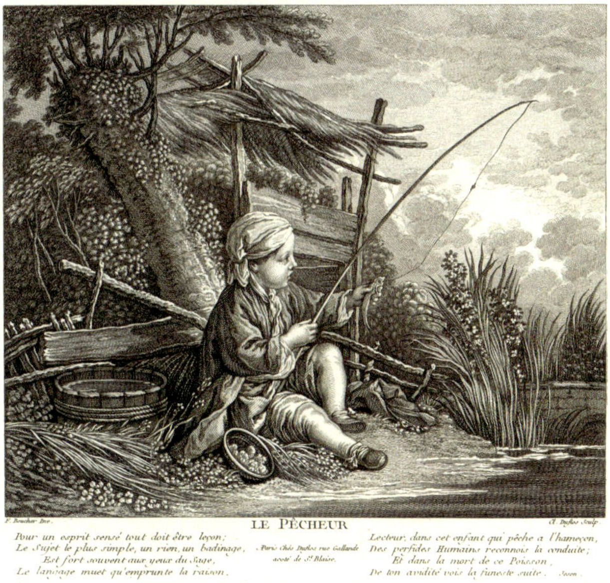
F. Boucher Inv.
Cl. Duflos Sculp.
LE PÊCHEUR
Pour un esprit sensé tout doit être leçon;
Le Sujet le plus simple, un rien, un badinage,
Est fort souvent aux yeux du Sage,
Le langage muet qu'emprunte la raison.
A Paris Chés Duflos rue Gallande
acoté de St. Blaise.
Lecteur, dans cet enfant qui pêche a l'hameçon,
Des perfides Humains reconnois la conduite;
Et dans la mort de ce Poisson,
De ton avidité vois la funeste suite.

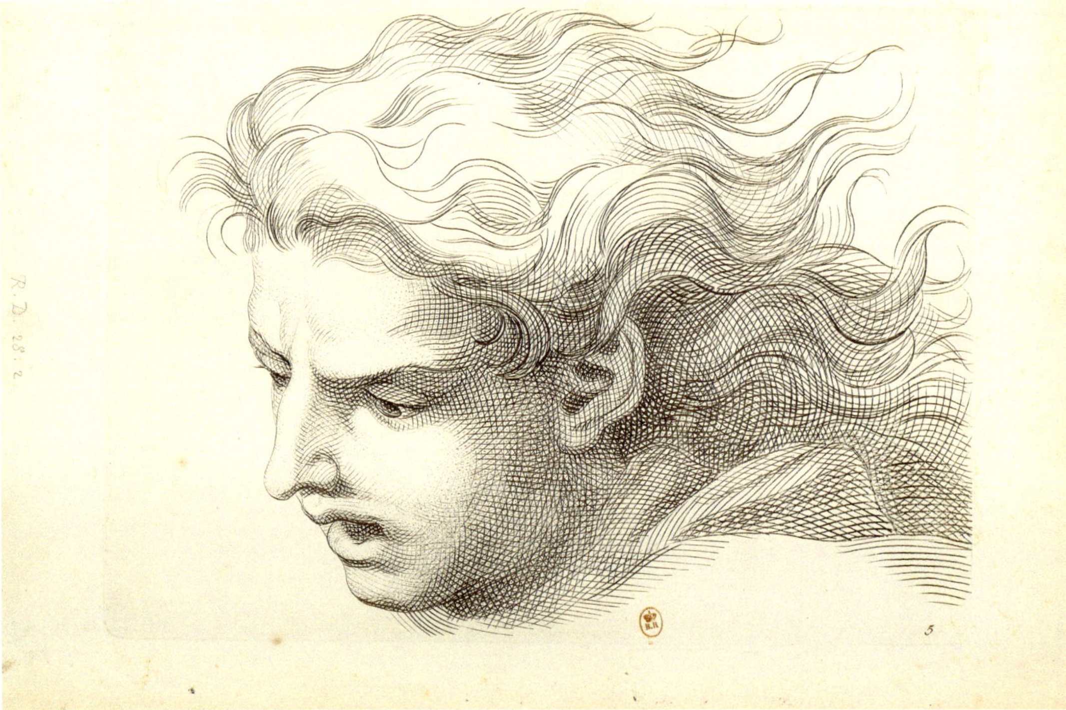

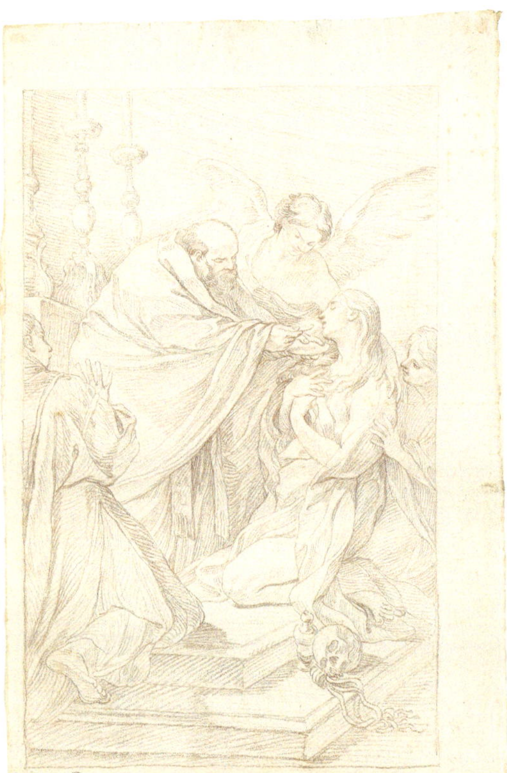

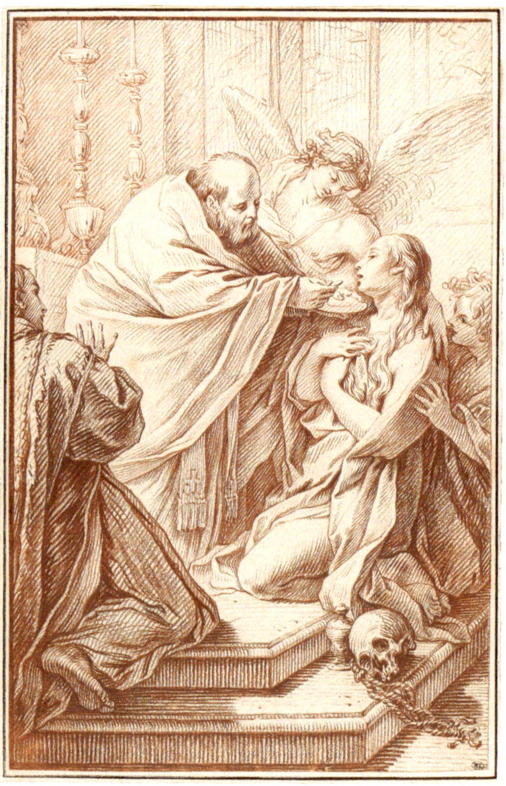

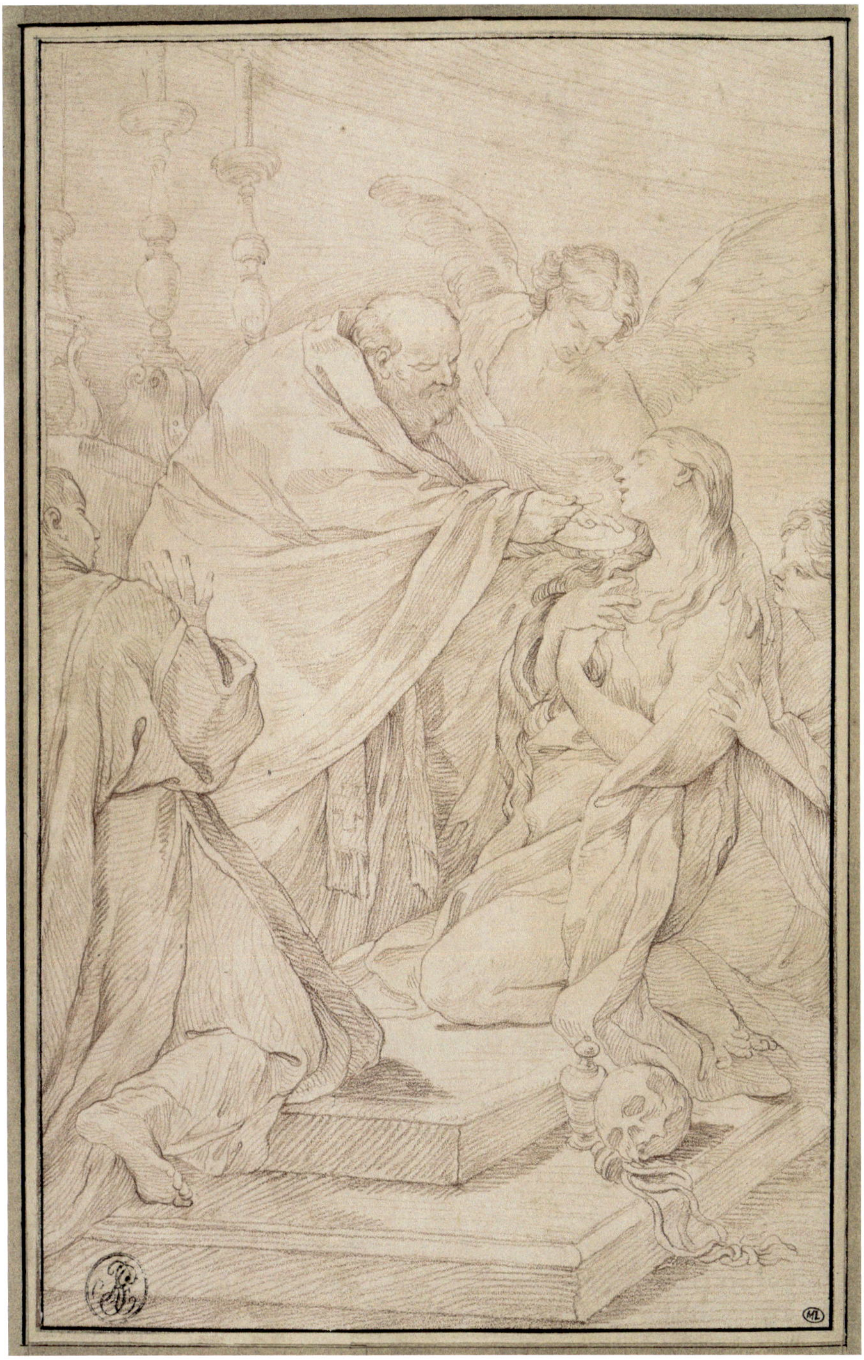

38 ↖ Élisabeth-Sophie Chéron de La Haye and Charles Simonneau, *Livre à déssiner composé de testes tirées des plus beaux ouvrages de Raphaël*, 1706, engraving (350 × 170 mm), Bibliothèque nationale de France, Paris.

39 ← Edme Bouchardon, copy after Benedetto Luti, *La comunione della Maddalena*, red chalk, *c*.1725 (365 × 249 mm), Département des arts graphiques, Musée du Louvre, Paris.

40 ← Jacques Dumont le Romain, copy after Benedetto Luti, *La comunione della Maddalena*, red chalk, *c*.1725 (330 × 239 mm), Département des arts graphiques, Musée du Louvre, Paris.

41 ↑ Charles-Joseph Natoire, copy after Benedetto Luti, *La comunione della Maddalena*, red chalk, *c*.1725 (330 × 209 mm), Département des arts graphiques, Musée du Louvre, Paris.

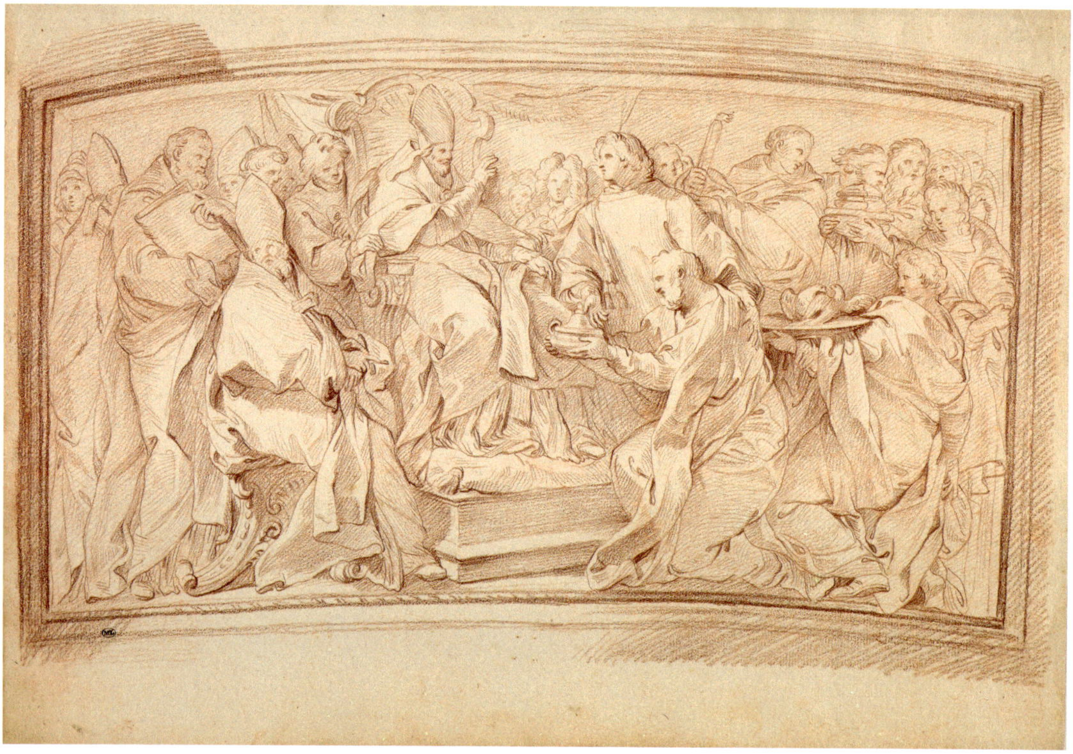

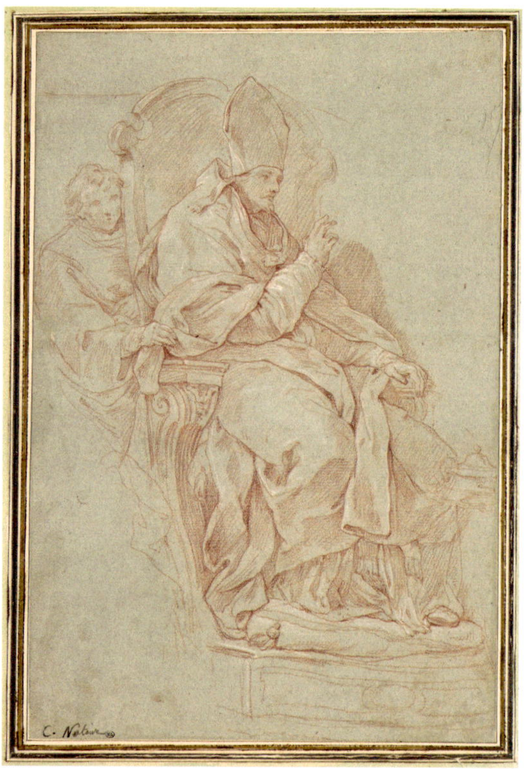

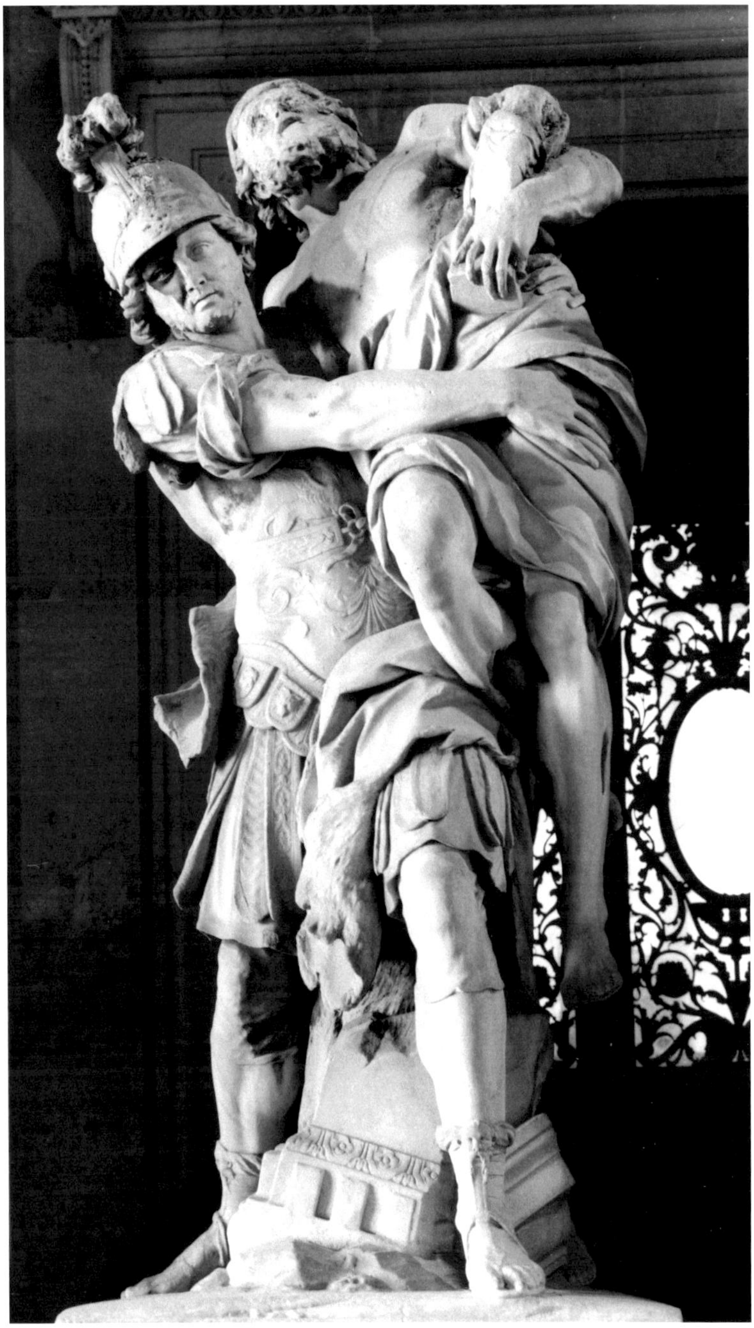

42 ↖ Edme Bouchardon, copy after Angelo de Rossi's bas-relief representing the canonisation of five saints, on the tomb of Pope Alexander VIII in Saint Peter's, Rome, red chalk, *c.*1725 (256 × 370 mm), Département des arts graphiques, Musée du Louvre, Paris.

43 ← Charles-Joseph Natoire, copy after Angelo de Rossi's bas-relief representing the canonisation of five saints, on the tomb of Pope Alexander VIII in Saint Peter's, Rome, red chalk, *c.*1725 (360 × 249 mm), Département des arts graphiques, Musée du Louvre, Paris.

44 ↑ Pierre Lepautre, *Énée et Anchise*, 1696–1717, marble (2.64 × 1.14 metres), Musée du Louvre, Paris.

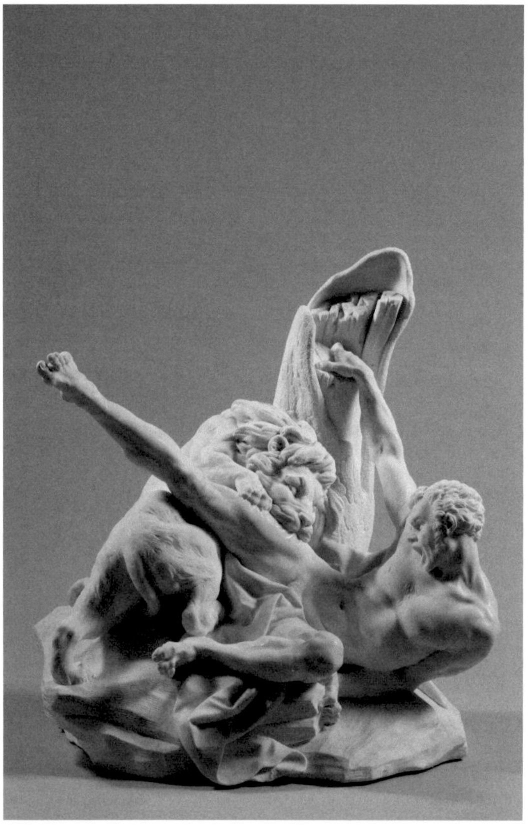

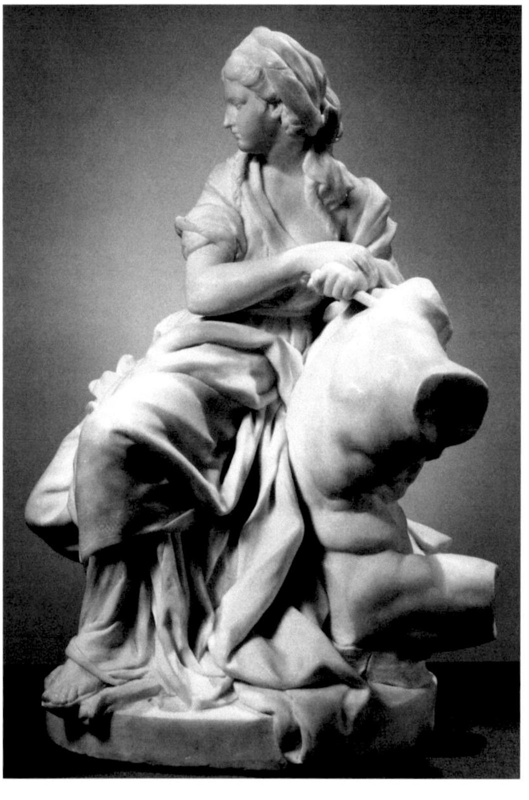

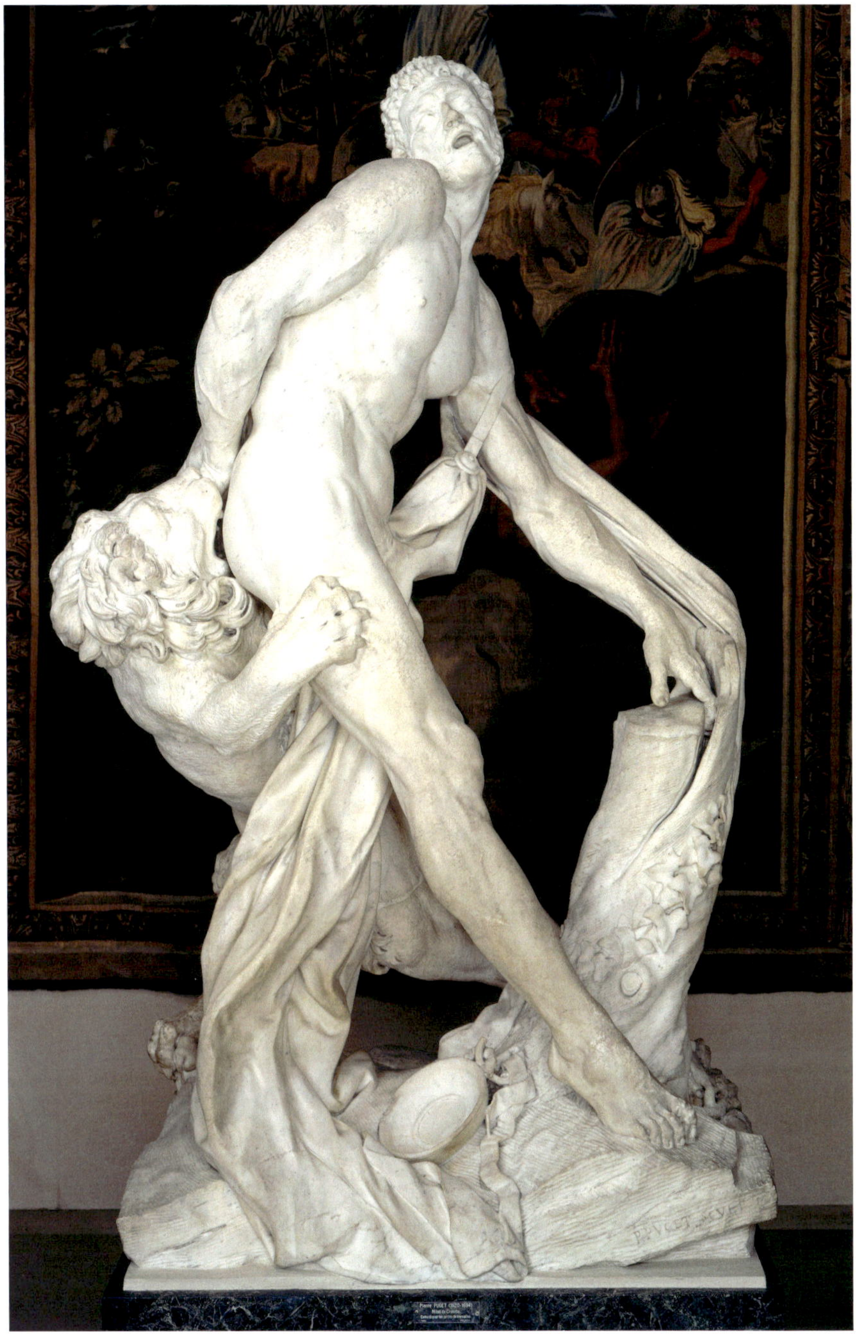

45 ↖ Étienne-Maurice Falconet, *Milon de Crotone*, 1754, marble (0.66 × 0.64 metres), Musée du Louvre, Paris.

46 ← Étienne-Maurice Falconet, *Le Génie de la sculpture*, 1746, marble (0.65 × 0.46 metres), Victoria and Albert Museum, London.

47 ↑ Pierre Puget, *Milon de Crotone*, 1682, marble (2.7 × 1.4 metres), Musée du Louvre, Paris.

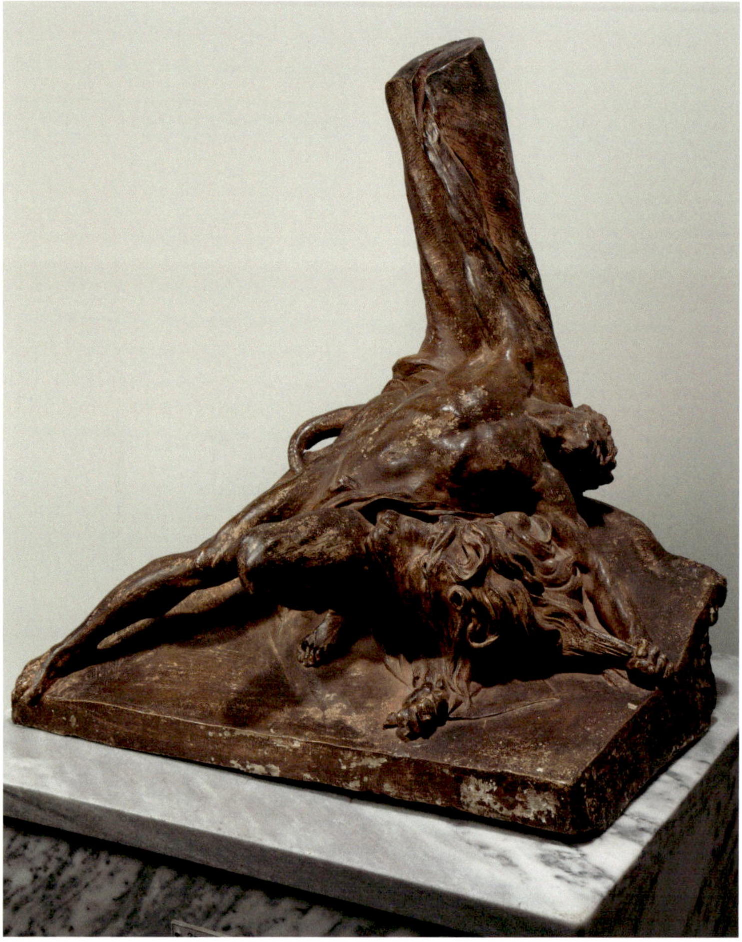

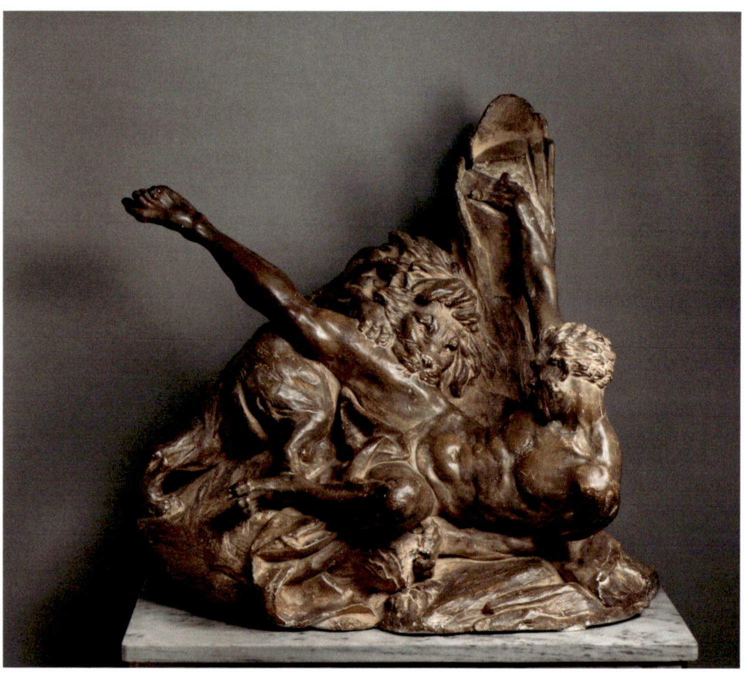

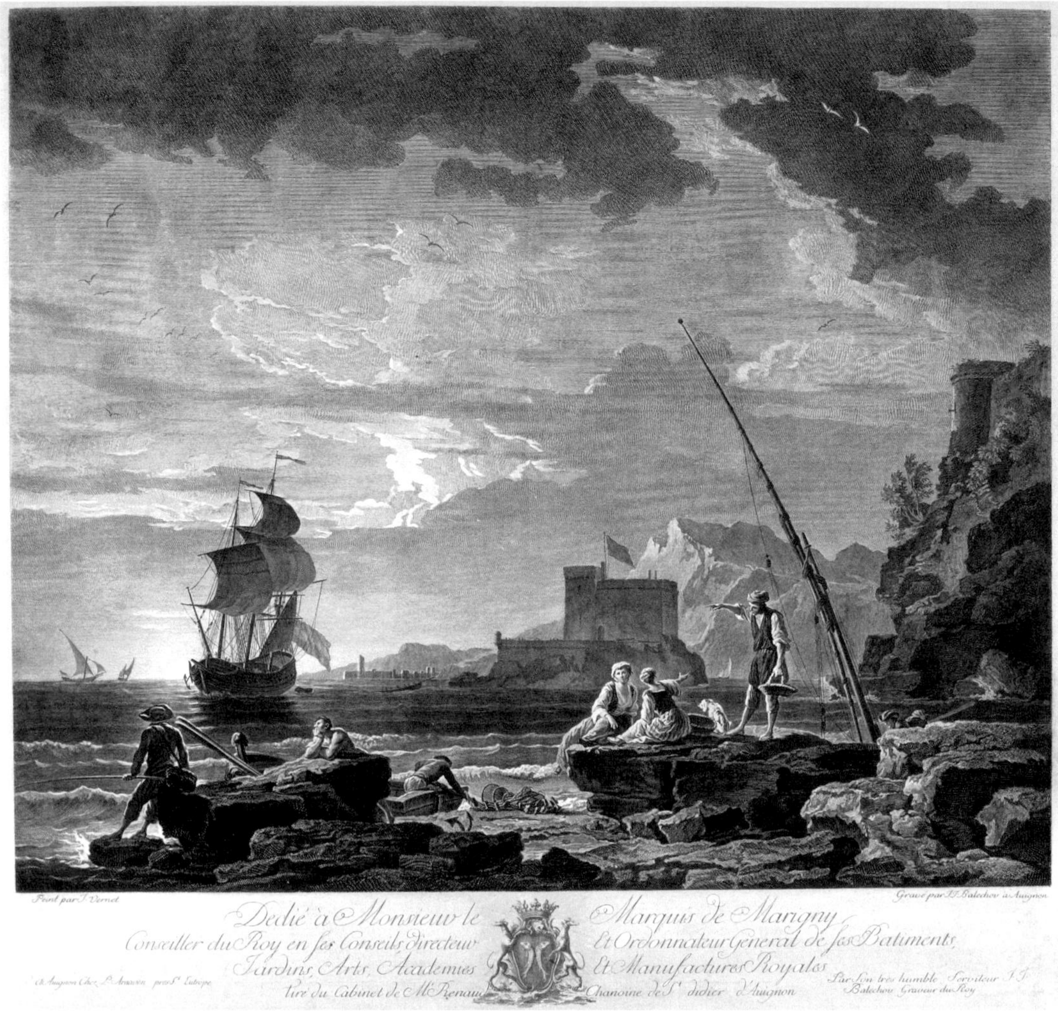

48 ↖ Étienne-Maurice Falconet, first model for *Milon de Crotone*, 1744, plaster (h. 0.57 metres), State Hermitage Museum, St Petersburg.

49 ← Étienne-Maurice Falconet, second model for *Milon de Crotone*, 1745, terracotta (h. 0.57 metres), State Hermitage Museum, St Petersburg.

50 ↑ Jean-Joseph Balechou after Claude-Joseph Vernet, *Le Calme*, engraving, 1755 (433 × 544 mm), Fogg Museum, Harvard Art Museums, Cambridge, MA.

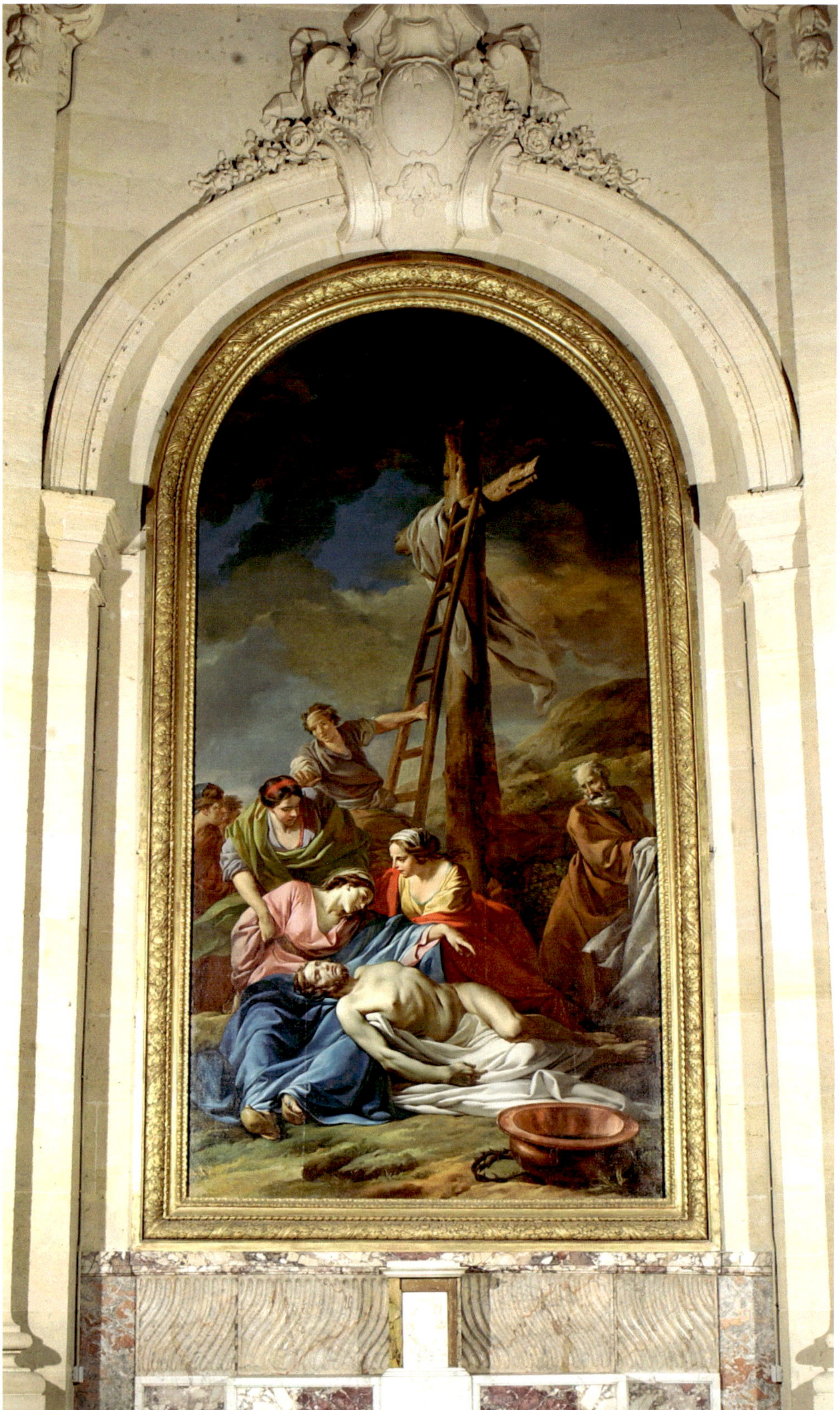

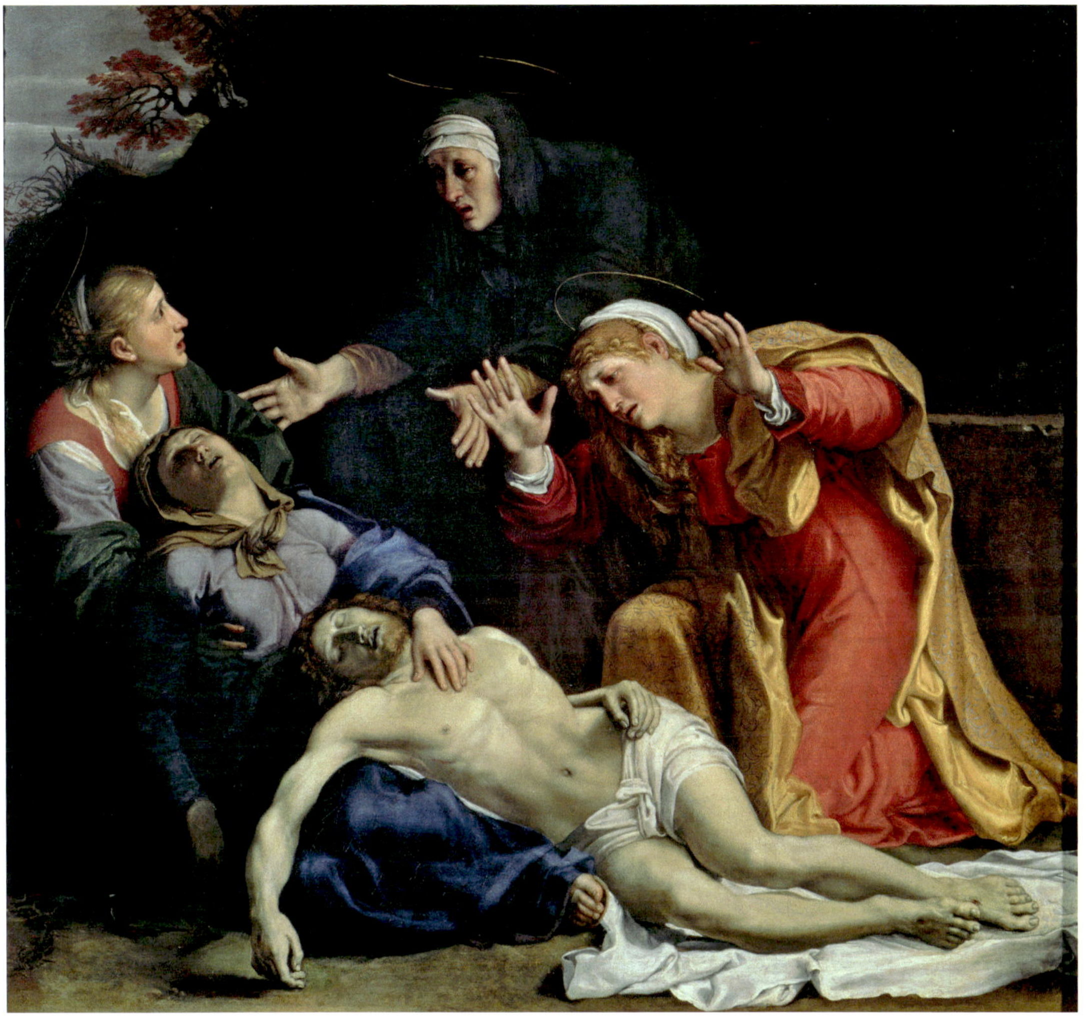

51 ← Jean-Baptiste Marie Pierre, *La Descente de la croix*, 1761, oil on canvas (5.83 × 3.24 metres), Saint-Louis, Versailles.

52 ↑ Annibale Carracci, *Lamentation*, *c*.1604, oil on canvas (92.8 × 103.2 cm), National Gallery, London.

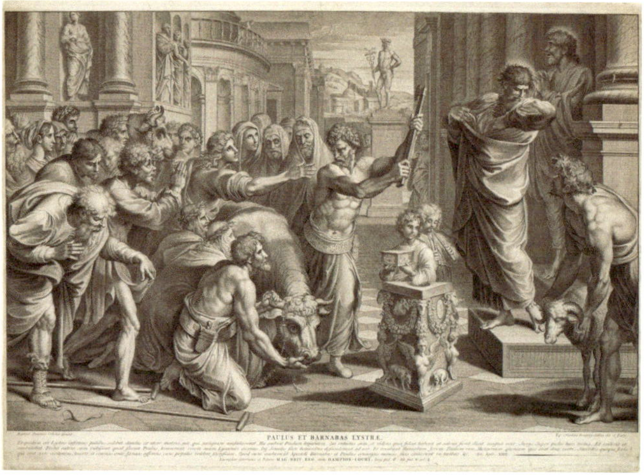

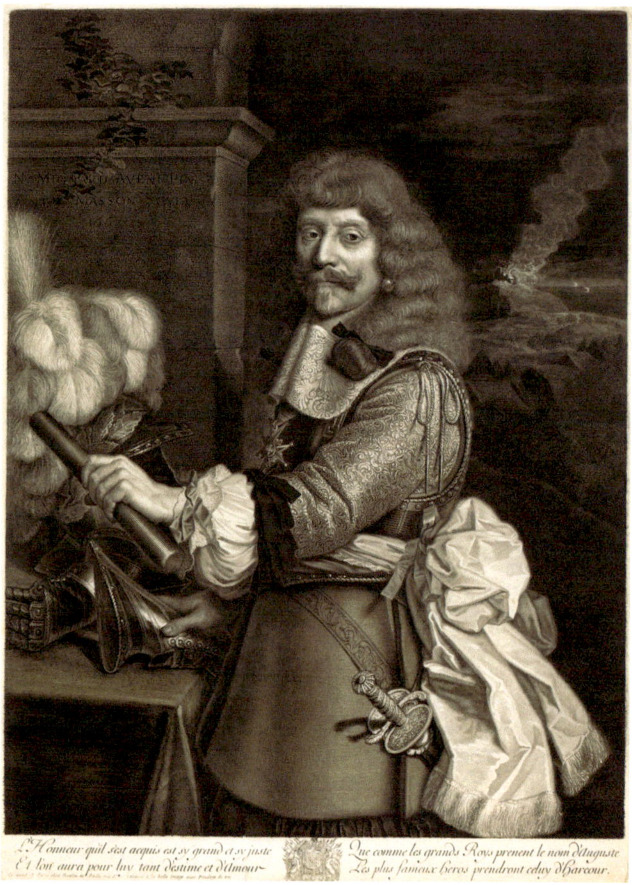

53 ↑ Nicolas Dorigny after Raphael, *Paulus et Barnabas Lystræ*, etching and engraving (534 × 745 mm), pl. 5 from *Pinacotheca Hamptoniana* (1719), Victoria and Albert Museum, London, inv. no. 20288.

54 ↑ Antoine Masson after Nicolas Mignard, portrait of Henri de Lorraine, comte d'Harcourt, engraving, 1667 (517 × 405 mm), National Gallery of Art, Washington, DC.

55 ↗ François-Denis Née and Louis-Joseph Masquelier, *Le Déjeuné de Ferney*, 1770, engraving (111 × 145 mm), Bibliothèque nationale de France, Paris.

56 → Anon., *Le Lever du philosophe de Ferney*, 1770, engraving (145 × 178 mm), Bibliothèque nationale de France, Paris.

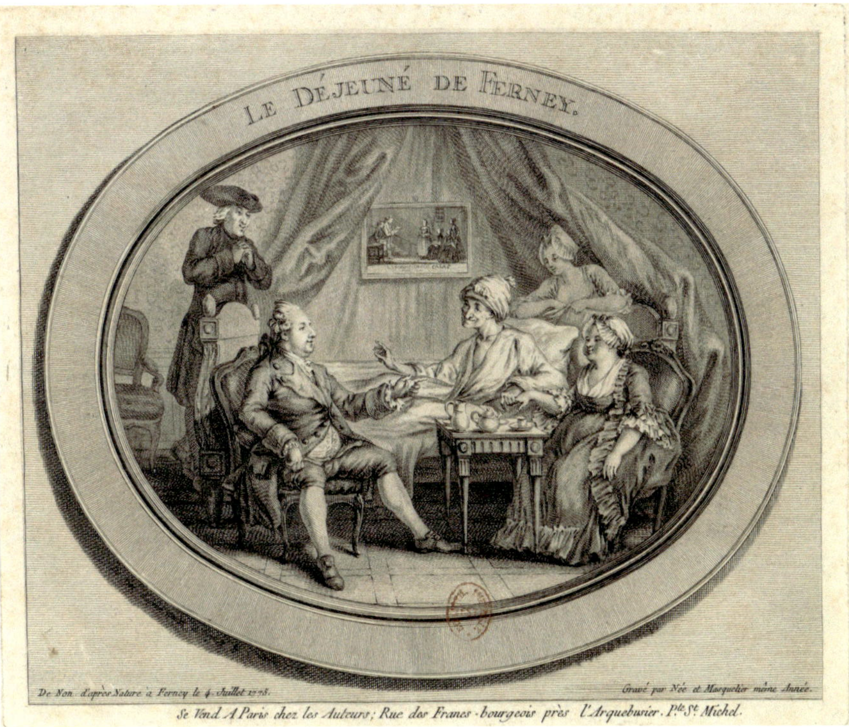
LE DÉJEUNÉ DE FERNEY.
De Non d'après Nature à Ferney le 4 Juillet 1775.
Gravé par Née et Masquelier même Année.
Se Vend A Paris chez les Auteurs; Rue des Francs-bourgeois près l'Arquebusier. Pte St. Michel.

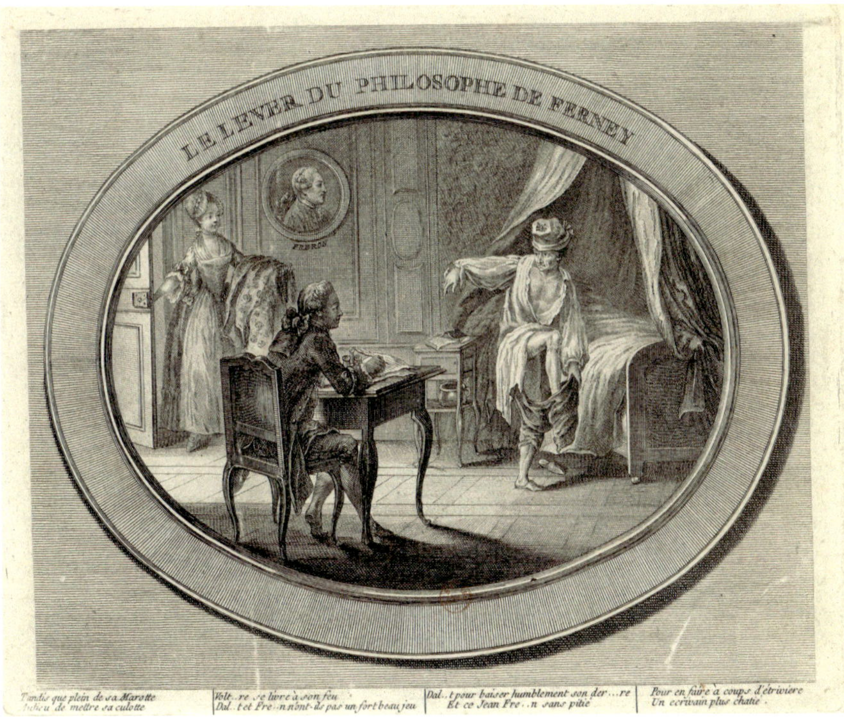
LE LEVER DU PHILOSOPHE DE FERNEY
FRERON
Tandis que plein de sa Marotte
Au lieu de mettre sa culotte
Volt..re se livre à son feu
Dal..t et Fre..n n'ont-ils pas un fort beau jeu
Dal..t pour baiser humblement son der...re
Et ce Jean Fre..n sans pitié
Pour en faire à coups d'étriviere
Un ecrivain plus chatié.

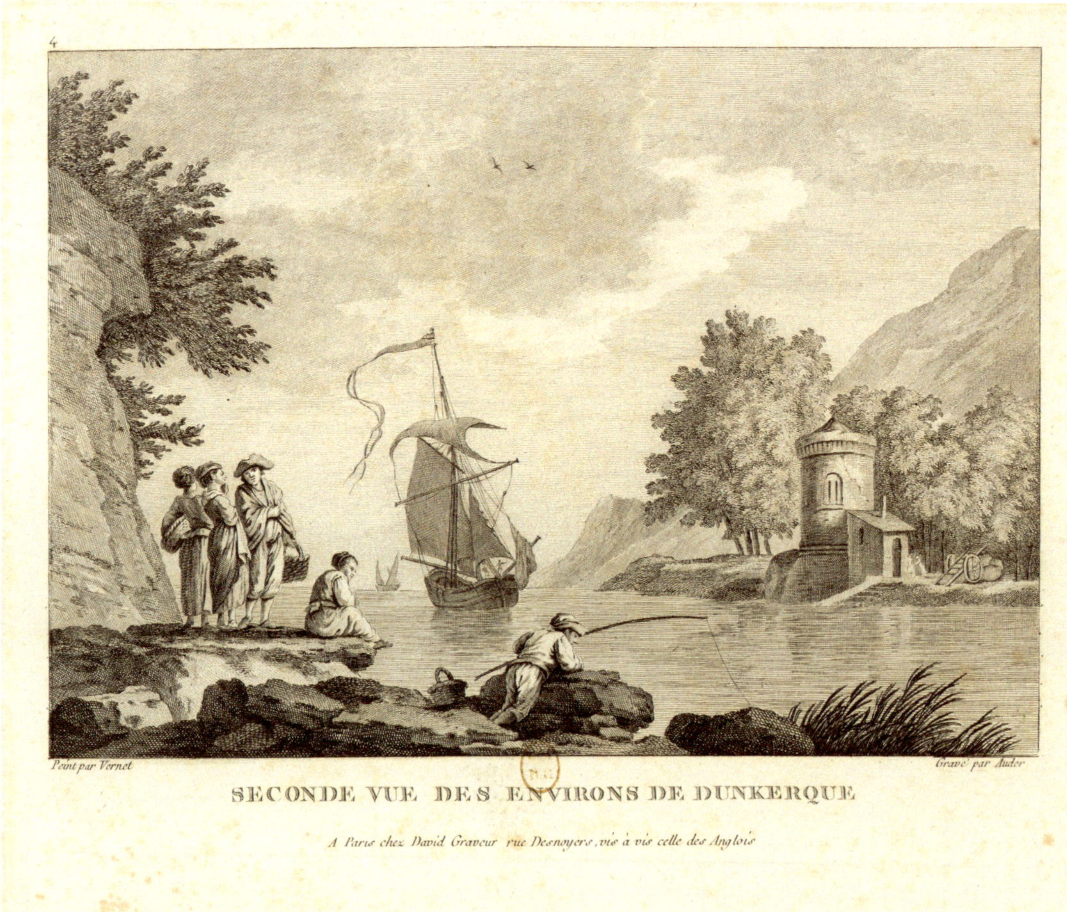

57 ↑ Auder after Claude-Joseph Vernet, *Seconde vue des environs de Dunkerque*, etching and engraving, 1780, Bibliothèque nationale de France, Paris.

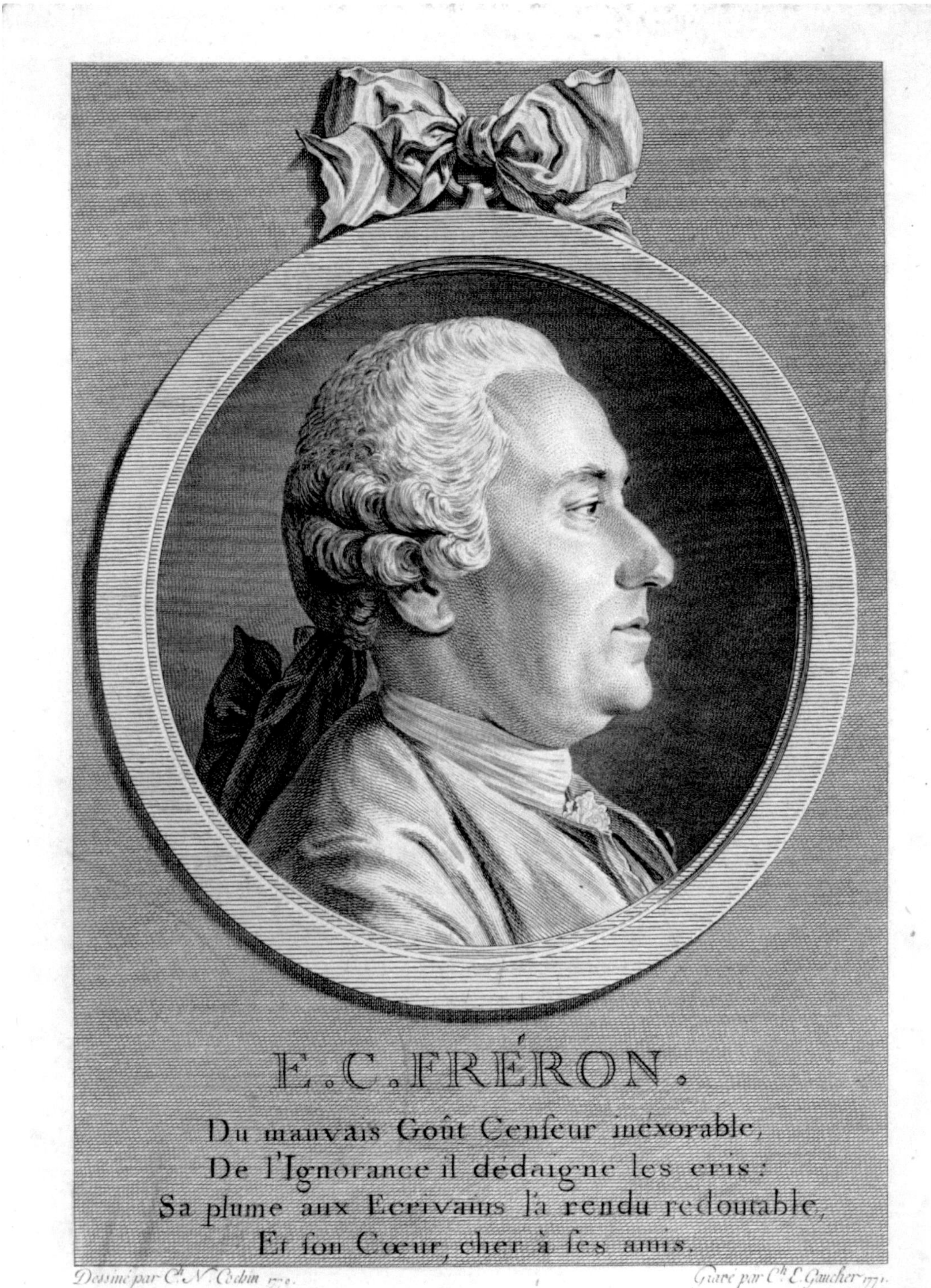

58 ↑ Charles-Étienne Gaucher after Charles-Nicolas Cochin *fils*, portrait of Élie-Catherine Fréron, engraving, 1771 (188 × 136 mm), British Museum, London.

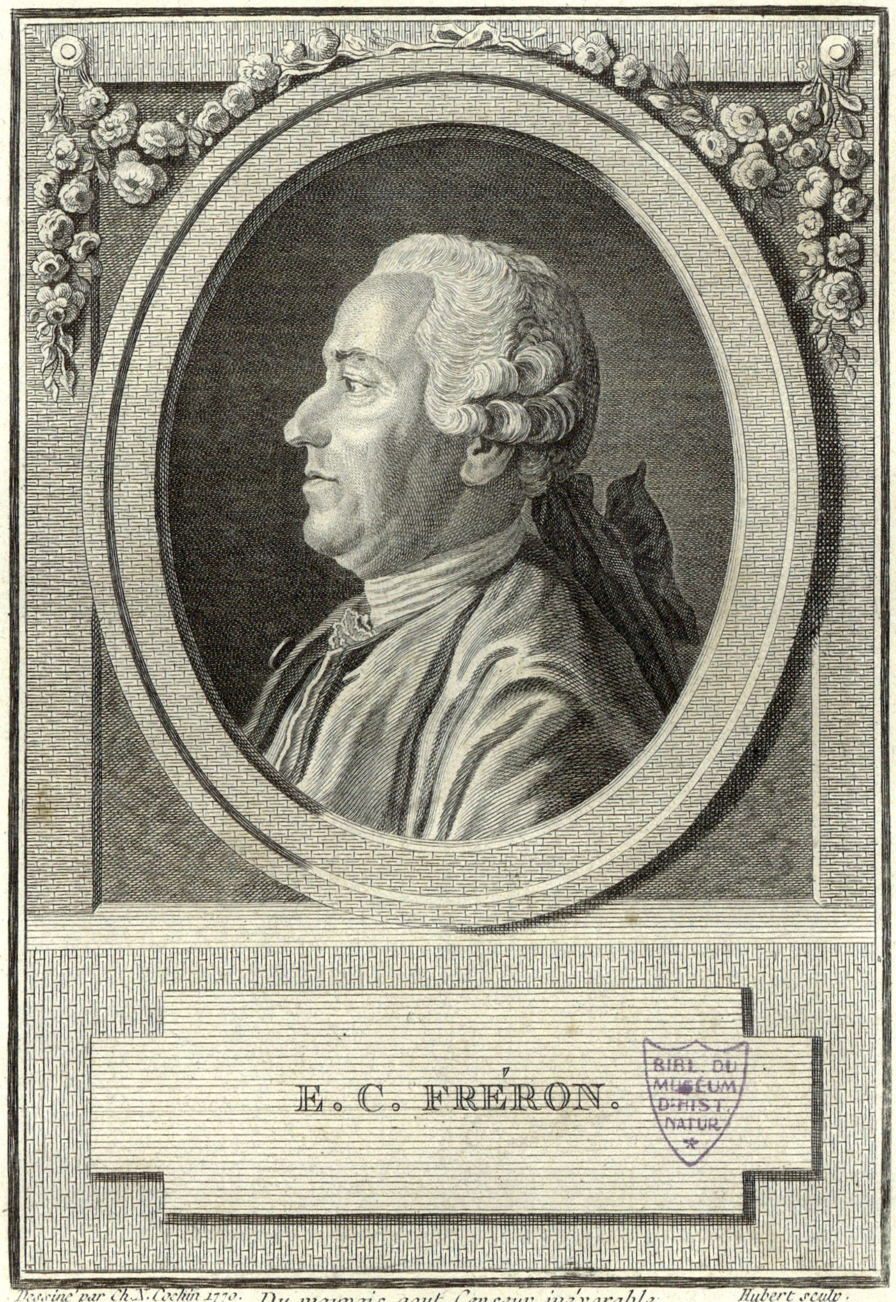

Dessiné par Ch. N. Cochin 1770. Hubert sculp.

Du mauvais gout, Censeur inéxorable,
De l'ignorance il dédaigne les cris:
Sa plume, aux Ecrivains, l'a rendu redoutable,
Et son cœur, cher à ses amis.

A Paris chéz Bligny lancier du Roi cour du Manége aux Thuilleries, Avec Privilége du Roi concedé par le Sr. Gaucher en date du 21 Fevrier 1777, pour cet Article.

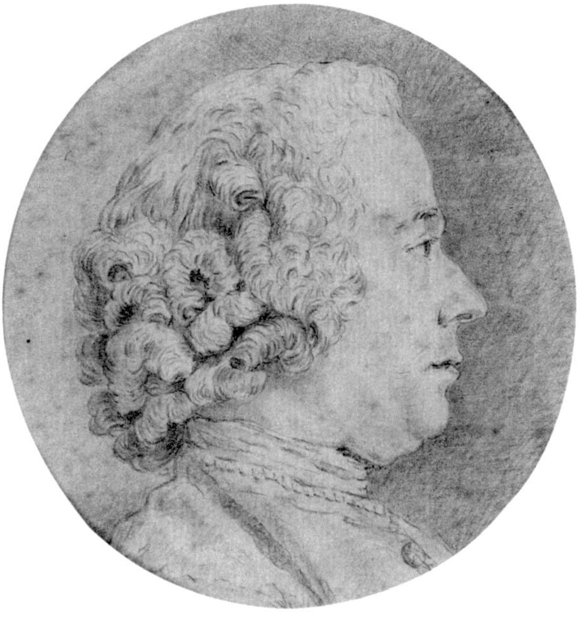

59 ← François Hubert after Charles-Nicolas Cochin *fils*, portrait of Élie-Catherine Fréron, engraving, 1776 (179 × 125 mm), Musée du Louvre, Paris.

60 ↑ Charles-Nicolas Cochin *fils*, portrait of Charles-Antoine Jombert, *c.*1766–70, black lead (dia. 94 mm), private collection.

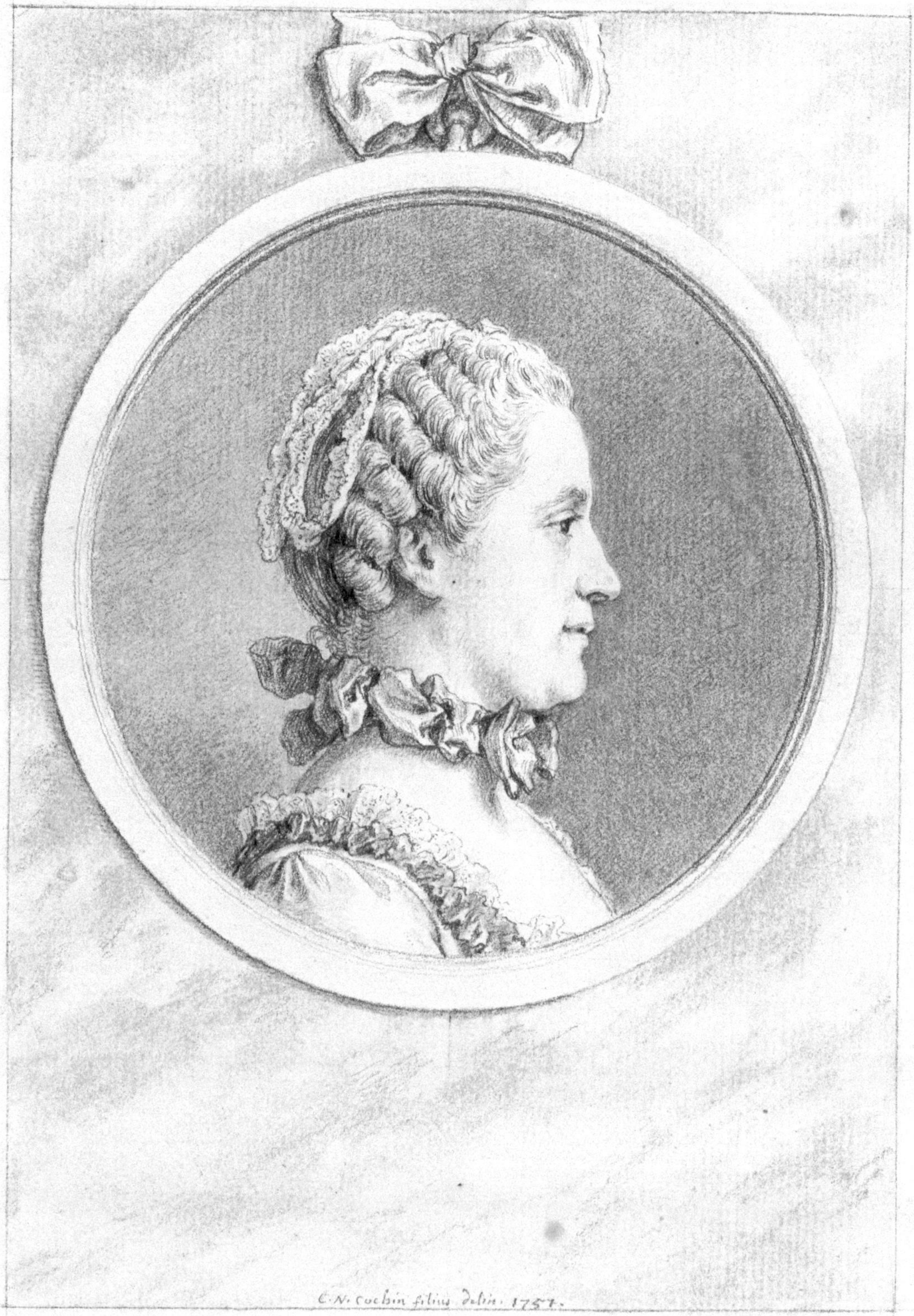
C.N. Cochin filius delin. 1757.

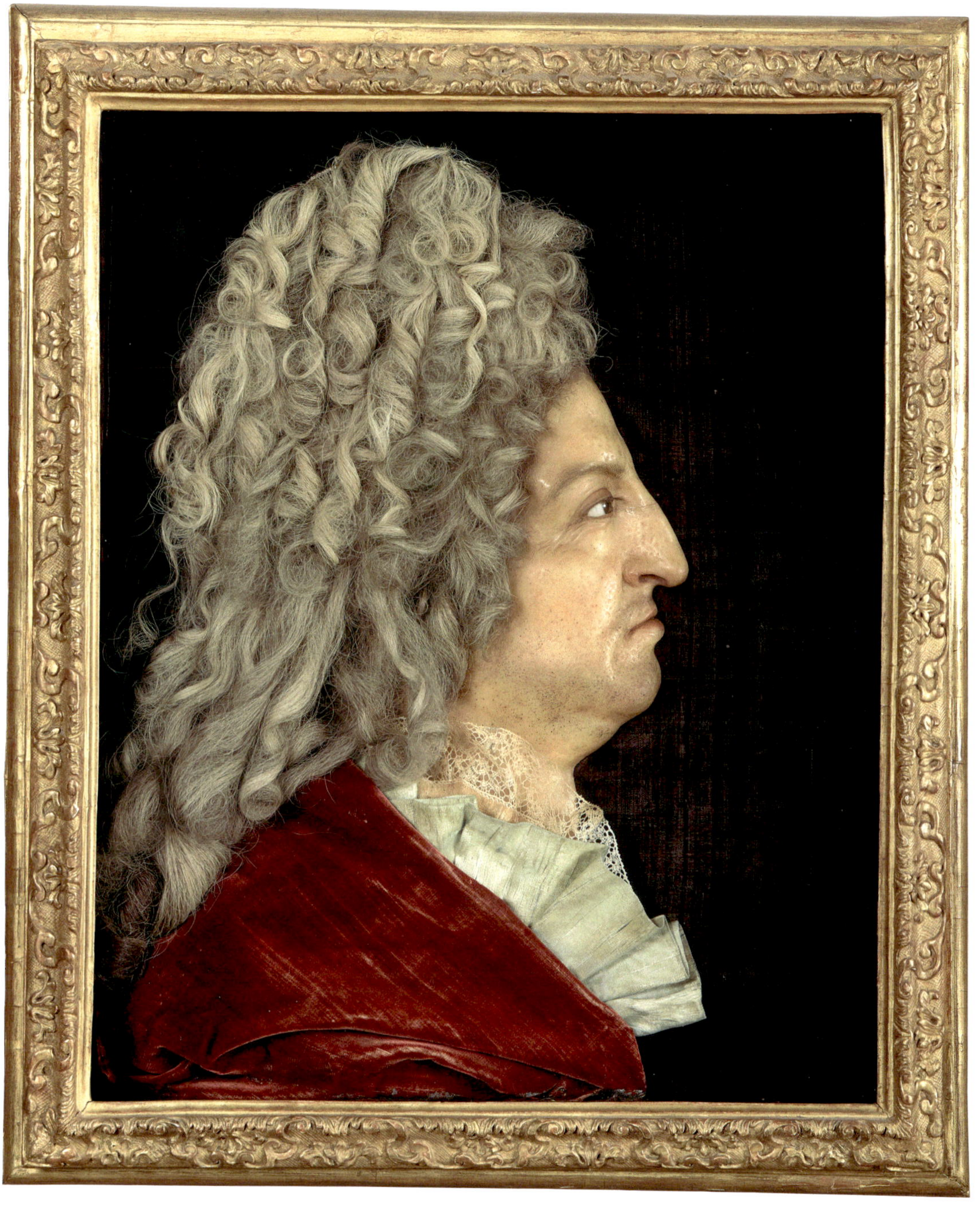

61 ← Charles-Nicolas Cochin *fils*, portrait of Madame Élie Catherine Fréron, née Marie-Thérèse Guyomar, 1757, black chalk (200 × 140 mm), location unknown.

62 ↑ Antoine Benoît, profile portrait of Louis XIV, 1704, wax, hair, glass and textile (520 × 420 mm), Musée du château de Versailles.

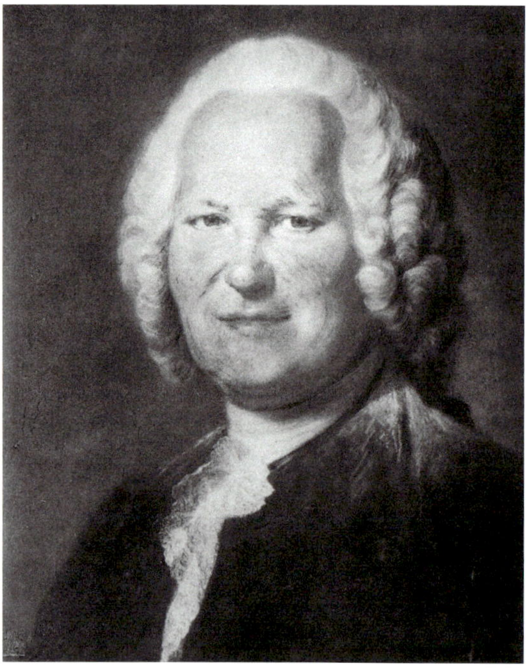

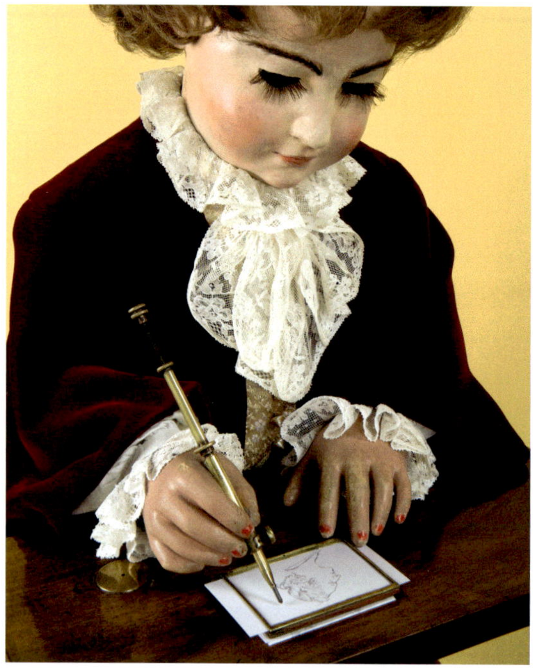

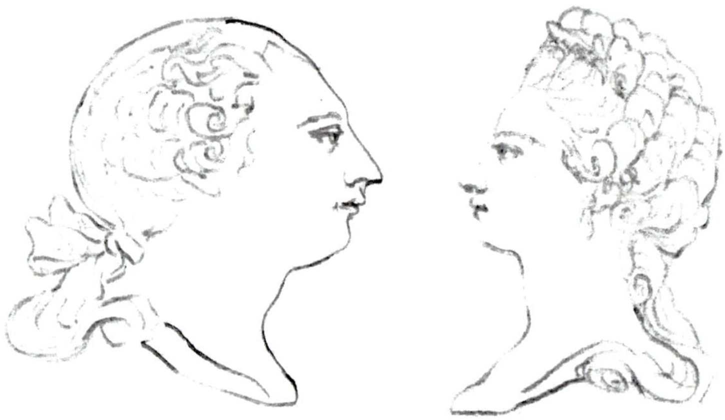

63 ↑ Maurice-Quentin de La Tour, portrait of Pierre Demours, 1767, pastel, location unknown.

65 ↑ Double portrait of Louis XVI and Marie Antoinette by Jaquet-Droz's android *dessinateur*, 1772–4, pencil, Musée d'art et d'histoire, Neuchâtel.

64 ↑ Henri-Louis Jaquet-Droz, *Le Dessinateur*, 1772–4, android (h. 76, w. 39.9, d. 42.6 cm), Musée d'art et d'histoire, Neuchâtel.

66 → Hyacinthe Rigaud, portrait of Pierre Drevet, *c.*1700, oil on canvas (116 × 89 cm), Musée des beaux-arts, Lyon.

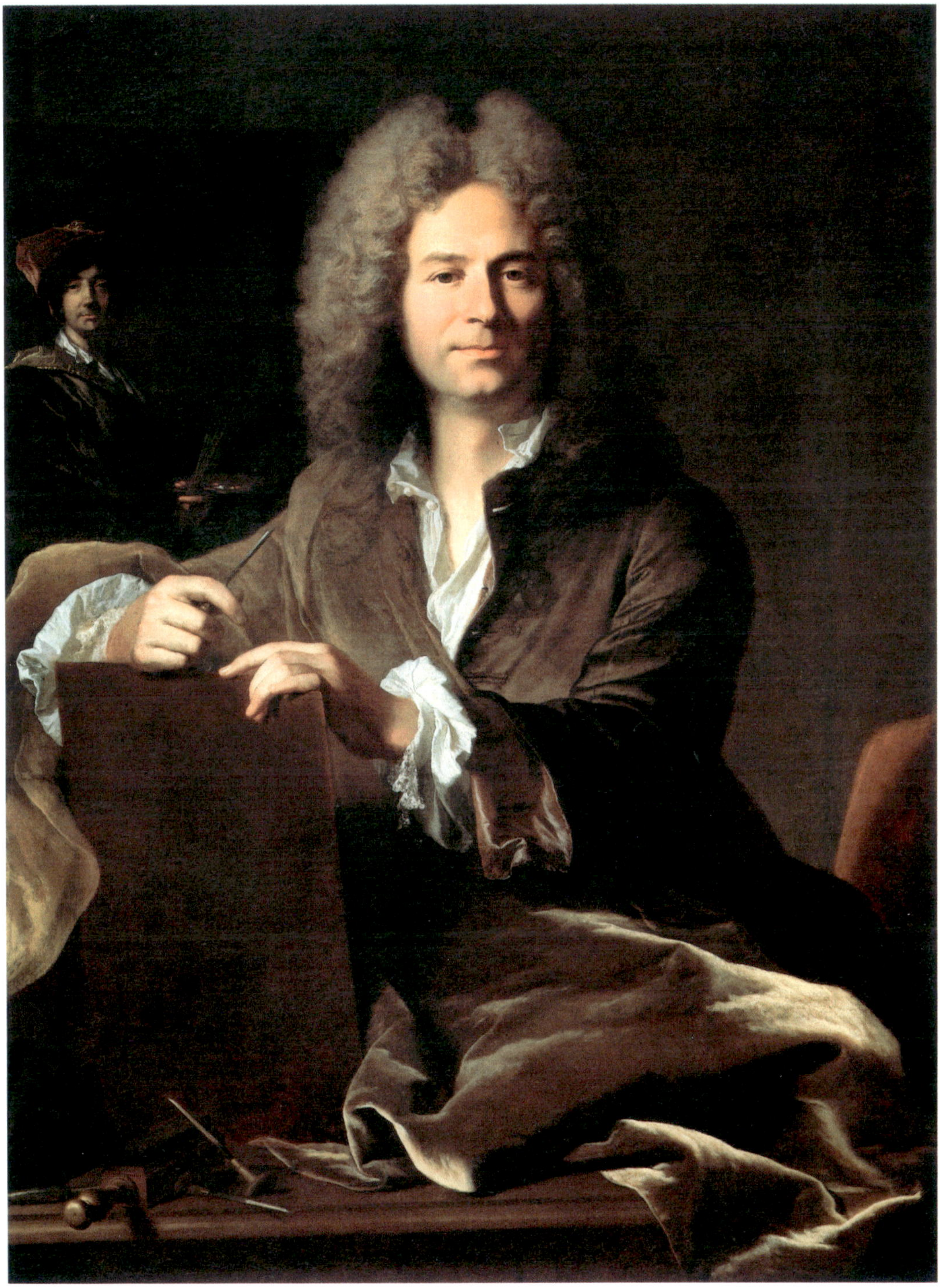

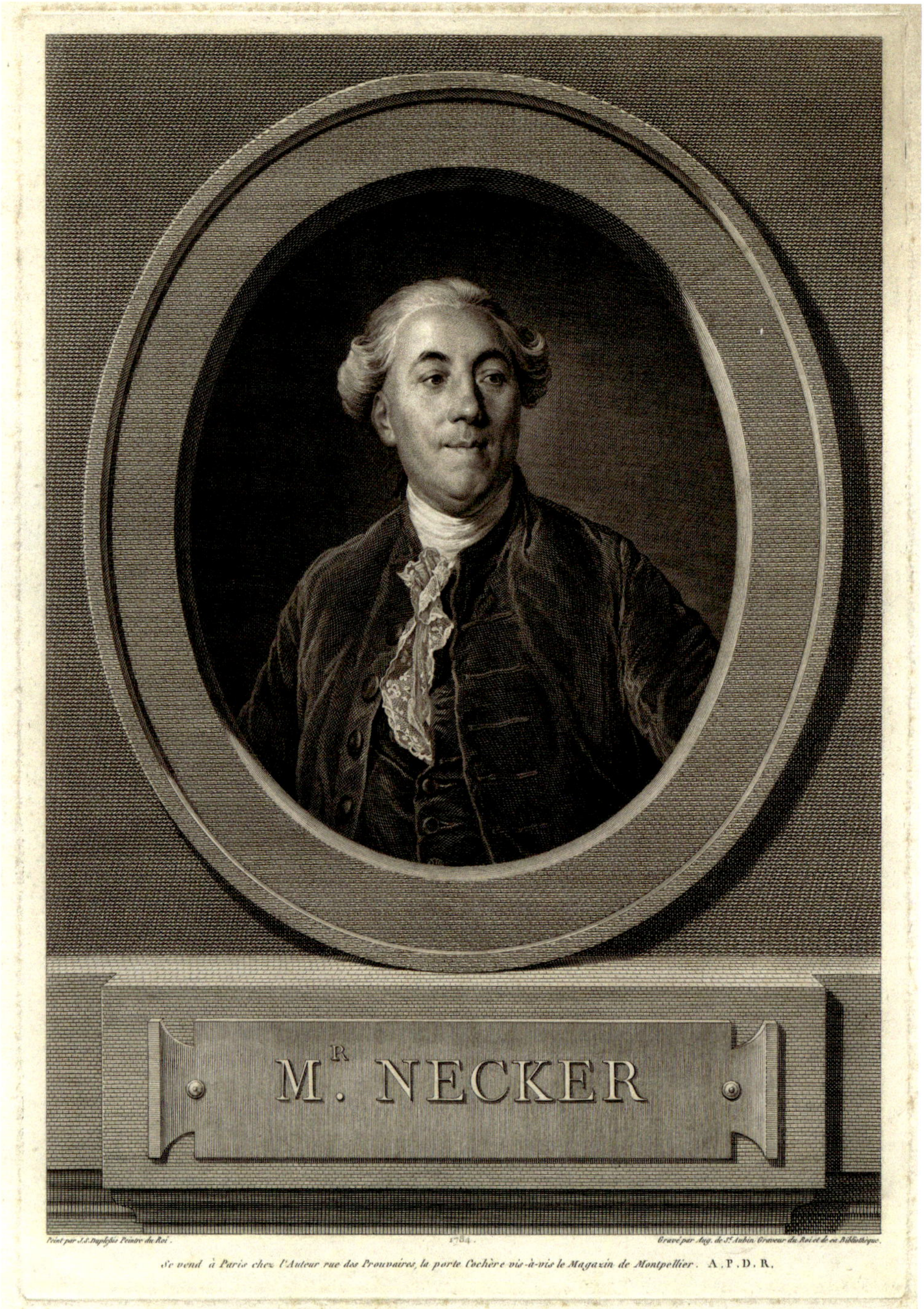

67 ↑ Augustin de Saint-Aubin after Joseph-Siffred Duplessis, portrait of Jacques Necker, etching and engraving, 1784 (335 × 238 mm), British Museum, London.

68 ↗ Nicolas de Launay after Augustin de Saint-Aubin after Joseph-Siffred Duplessis, portrait of Jacques Necker, etching and engraving, 1788 (290 × 220 mm), Bibliothèque nationale de France, Paris.

69 → Antoine-Louis-François Sergent after Augustin de Saint-Aubin after Joseph-Siffred Duplessis, portrait of Jacques Necker, etching and colour printing, 1789 (205 × 140 mm), Waddesdon Manor, Buckinghamshire.

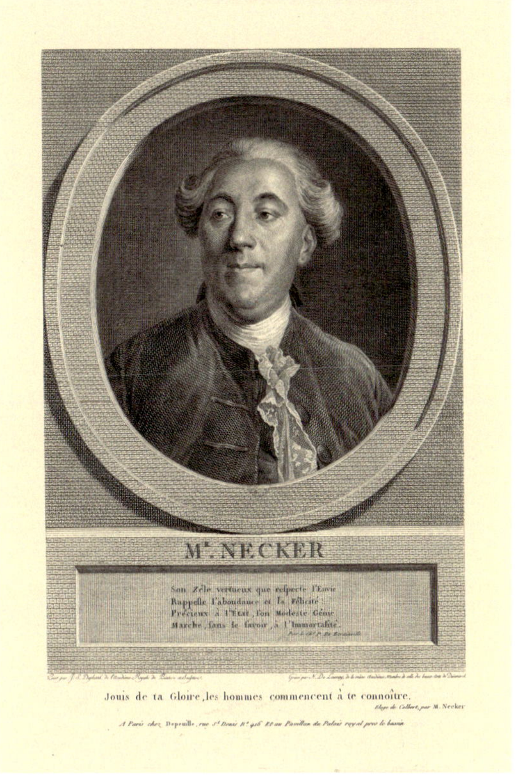
Mr. NECKER
Son Zèle vertueux que respecte l'Envie
Rappelle l'abondance et la Félicité:
Précieux à l'État, son Modeste Génie
Marche, sans le favoir, à l'Immortalité.
Jouis de ta Gloire, les hommes commencent à te connoître.
Eloge de Colbert, par M. Necker
A Paris chez Depeuille, rue St Denis No. 916 Et au Pavillon du Palais royal près le bassin

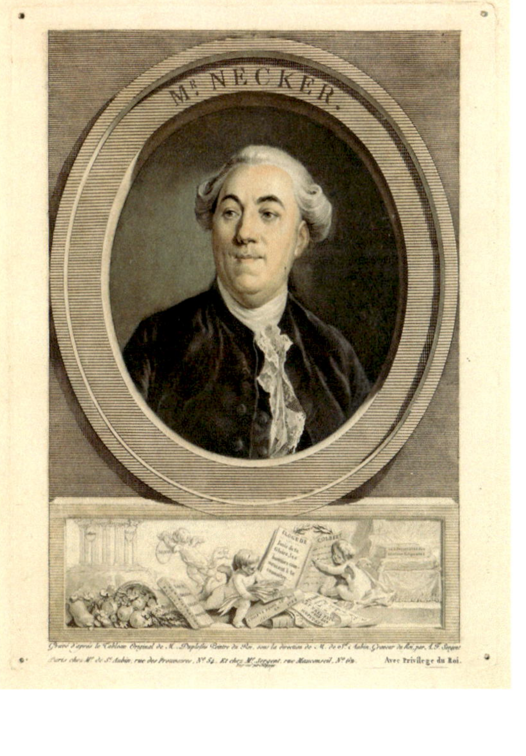
Mr. NECKER.
Avec Privilege du Roi.

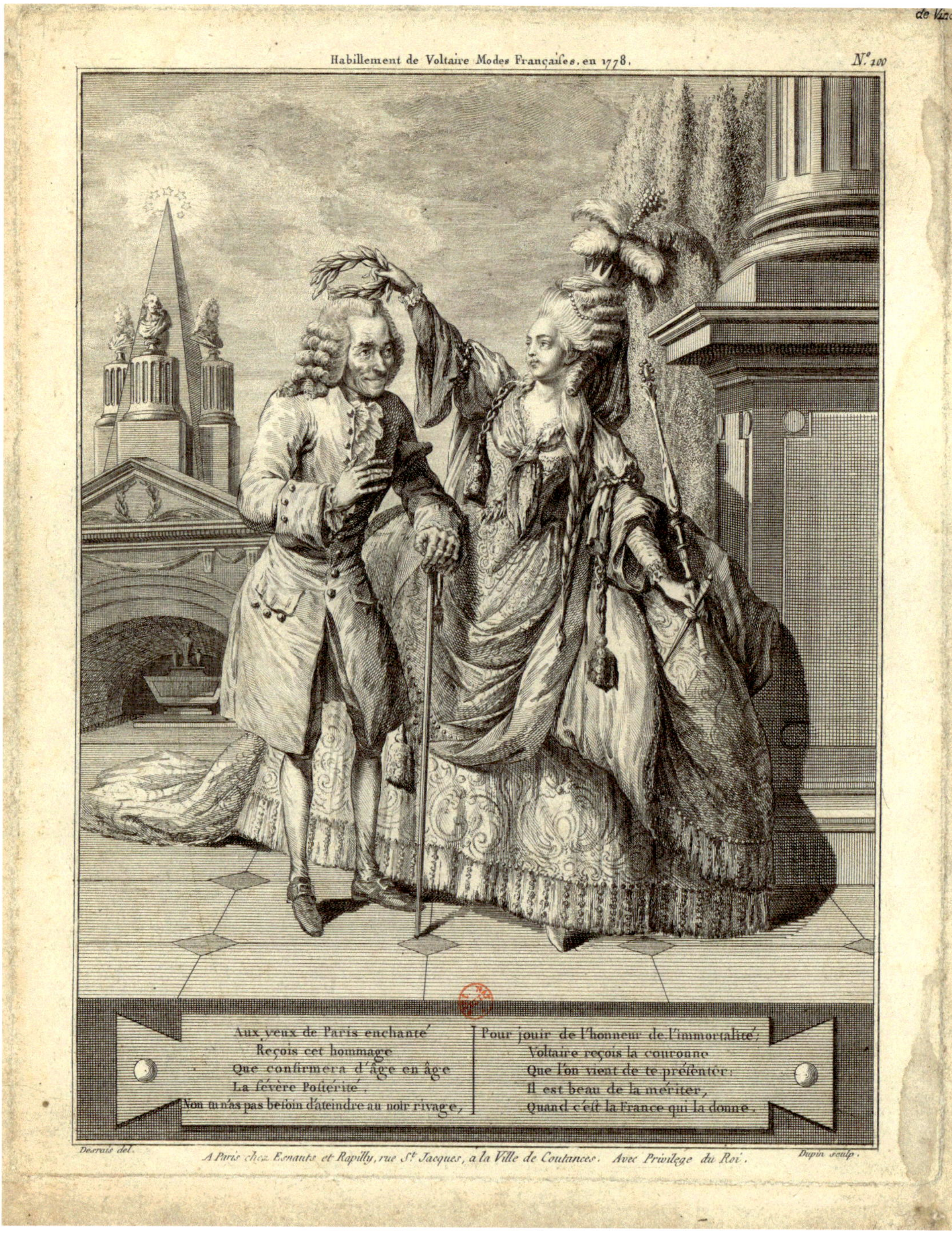

70 ↑ Nicolas Dupin after Claude-Louis Desrais, *Habillement de Voltaire*, etching, *c.*1778 (253 × 196 mm), Bibliothèque nationale de France, Paris.

71 → Anon., four dressed heads, etching with hand-colouring (140 × 220 mm), in Jacques Esnault and Michel Rapilly, *Gallerie des modes et costumes français dessinés d'après nature, gravés par les plus célèbres artistes en ce genre*, 4 vols (1778–87), vol. 1, Cahier 4, D.20, Museum of Fine Arts, Boston.

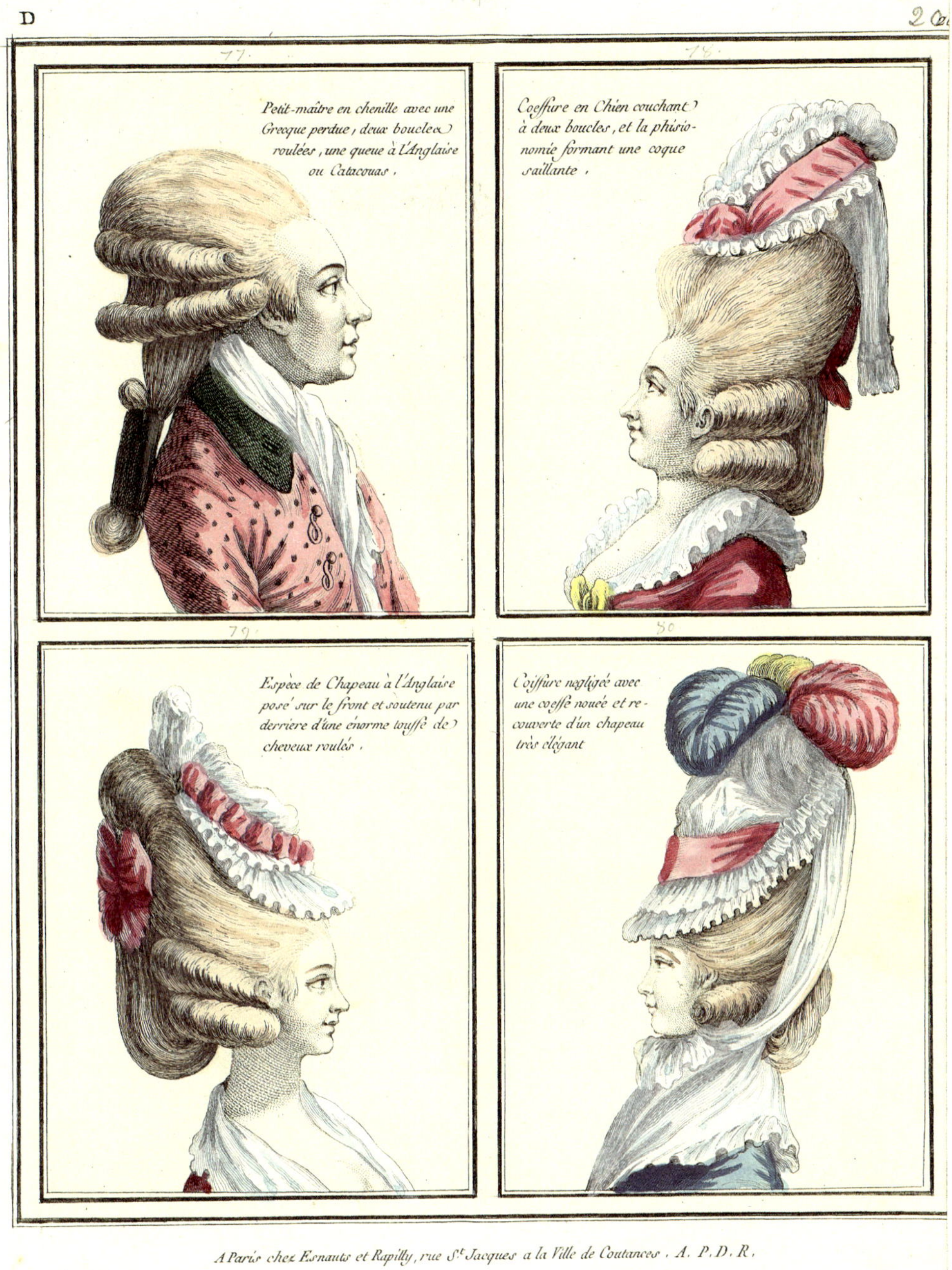
D
77.
Petit-maître en chenille avec une
Grecque perdue, deux boucles
roulées, une queue à l'Anglaise
ou Catacouas.
78.
Coeffure en Chien couchant
à deux boucles, et la phisio-
nomie formant une coque
saillante.
79.
Espèce de Chapeau à l'Anglaise
posé sur le front et soutenu par
derriere d'une énorme touffe de
cheveux roulés.
80.
Coiffure negligée avec
une coeffe nouée et re-
couverte d'un chapeau
très élégant
A Paris chez Esnauts et Rapilly, rue S.t Jacques a la Ville de Coutances. A. P. D. R.

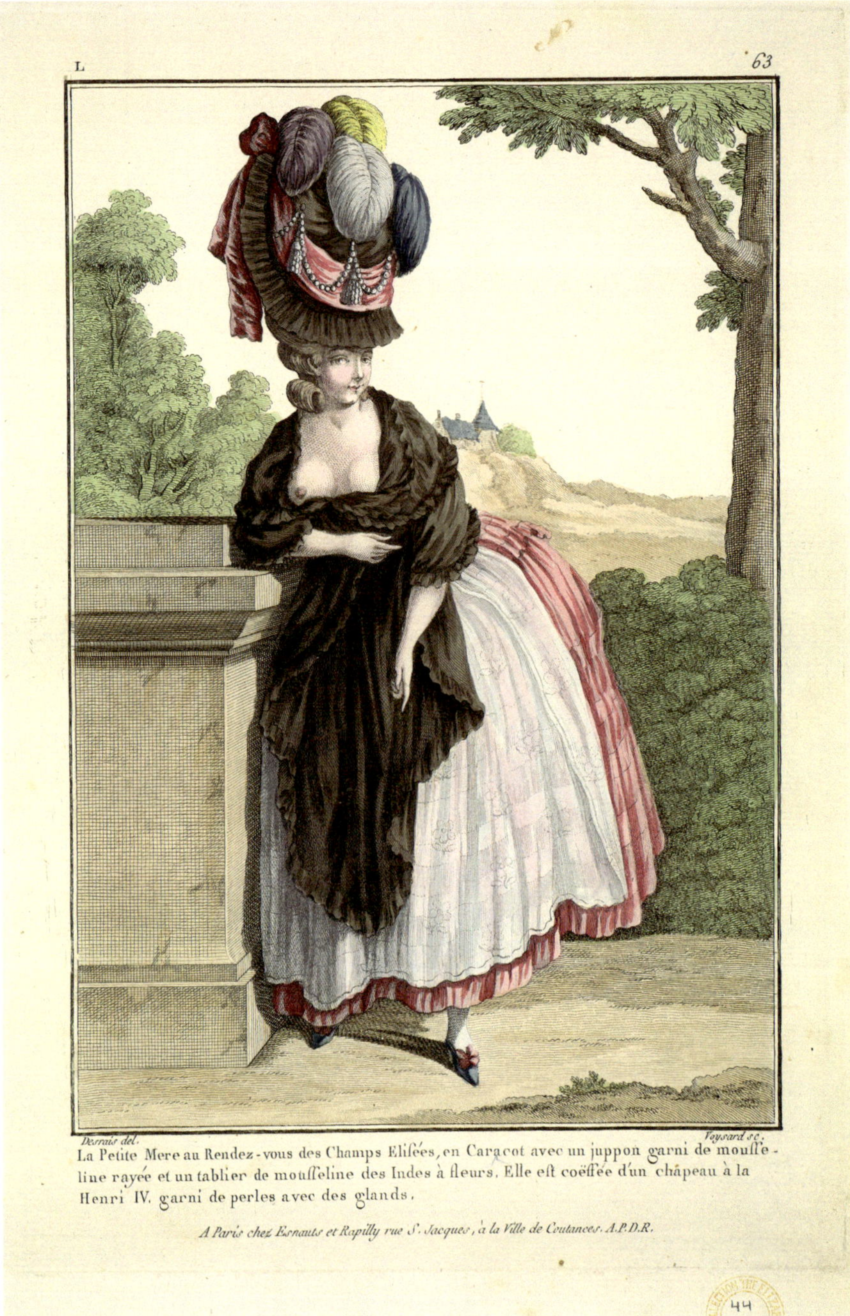

72 ↑ Étienne-Claude Voysard after Claude-Louis Desrais, *Tailleur costumier essayant un cor à la mode*, etching and engraving (140 × 220 mm), in Jacques Esnault and Michel Rapilly, *Gallerie des modes et costumes français dessinés d'après nature, gravés par les plus célèbres artistes en ce genre*, 4 vols (1778–87), vol. 2, Cahier 9, P.85, Museum of Fine Arts, Boston.

73 ↗ Villeneuve, *Matière à reflection pour les jongleurs couronnées*, Louis XVI guillotined, 1793, lithograph (215 × 172 mm), British Museum, London.

74 → Jacques-Louis David, portrait of Jean Bon Saint-André, 1793, pen and black ink with black and grey wash, with pale yellow wash and white gouache highlight over graphite (252 × 182 mm), Art Institute of Chicago.

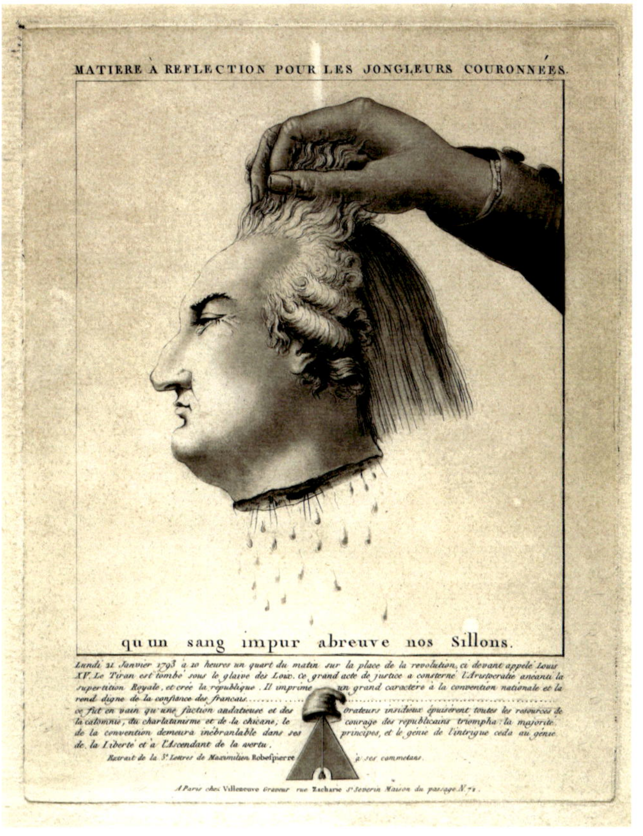
MATIERE A REFLECTION POUR LES JONGLEURS COURONNÉES.
qu un sang impur abreuve nos Sillons.
Lundi 21 Janvier 1793 à 10 heures un quart du matin sur la place de la revolution, ci devant appelé Louis XV. Le Tiran est tombé sous le glaive des Loix. Ce grand acte de justice a consterné l'Aristocratie aneanti la supertition Royale, et créé la république. Il imprime un grand caractere à la convention nationale et la rend digne de la confiance des francais.
ce fut en vain qu'une faction audatieuse et des orateurs insidieux épuisérent toutes les resources de la calomnie, du charlatanisme et de la chicane; le courage des republicains triompha: la majorité de la convention demeura inébranlable dans ses principes, et le génie de l'intrigue ceda au génie de la Liberté et à l'Ascendant de la vertu.
Extrait de la 3e Lettres de Maximilien Robespierre à ses commetans.
A Paris chez Villeneuve Graveur rue Zacharie St Severin Maison du passage N.o 72.

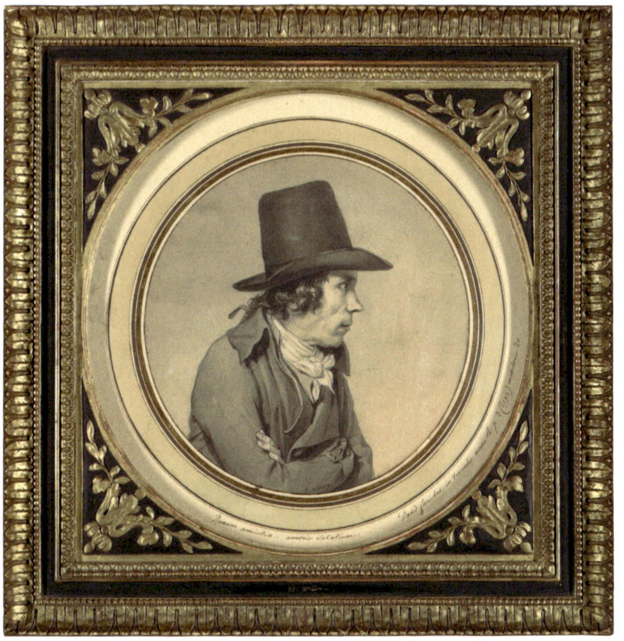

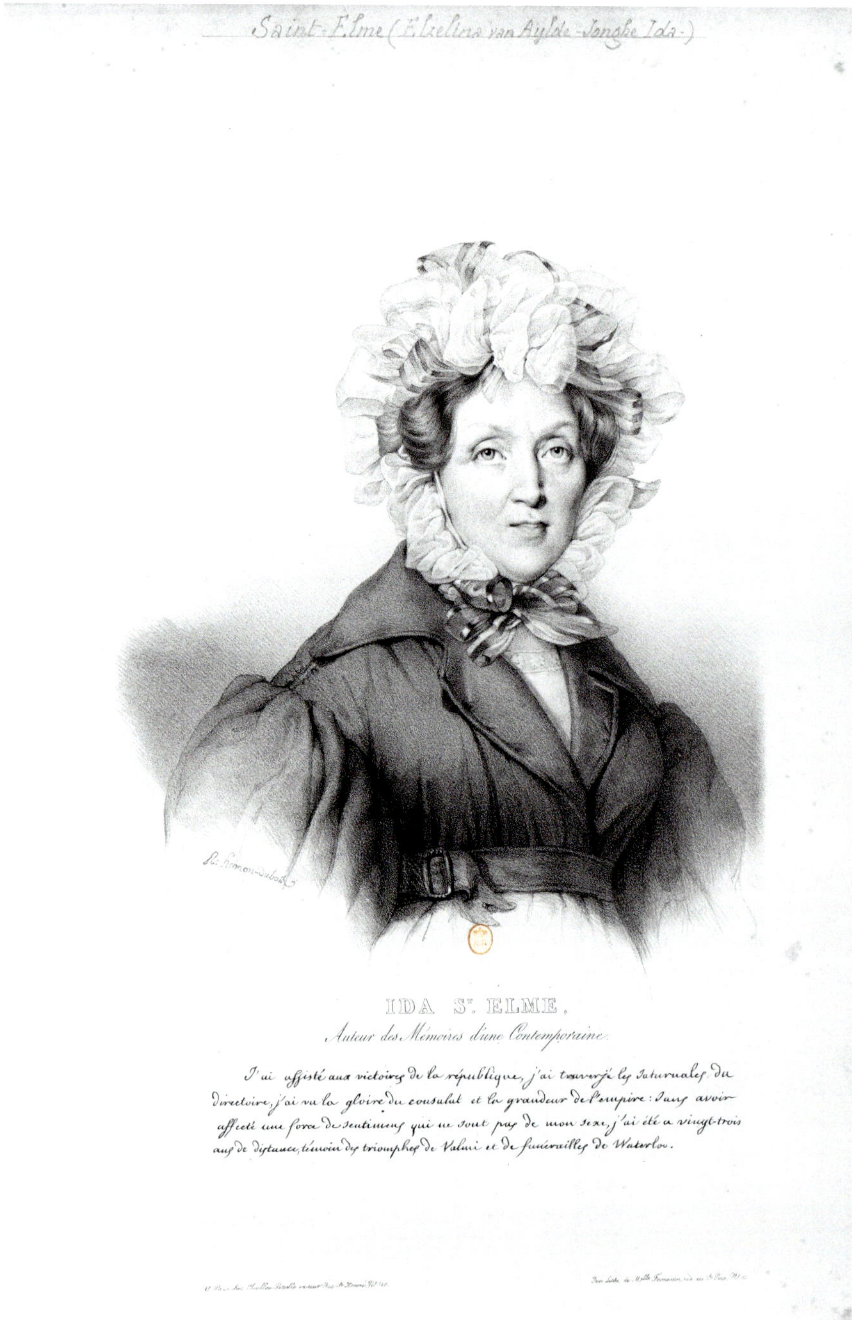

75 ↑ Joseph Planat, portrait of Ida Saint-Elme, 1828, lithograph, Bibliothèque nationale de France, Paris.

76 → Pierre-Louis 'Henri' Grévedon, portrait of Ida Saint-Elme, La Contemporaine, 1828, lithograph, Österreichische Nationalbibliothek, Vienna.

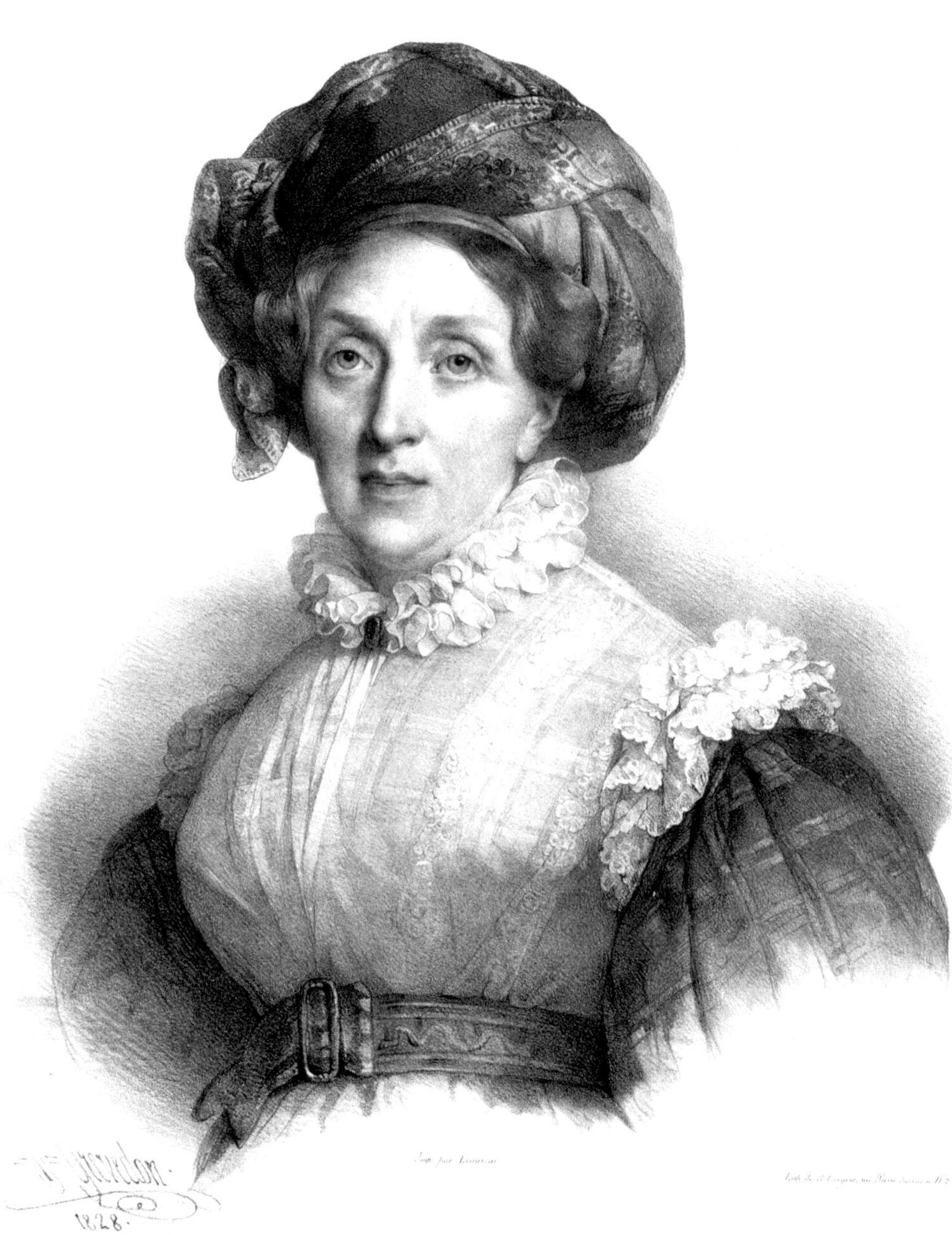

IDA Sᵗ ELME,

Auteur des Mémoires d'une Contemporaine.

Lithographiée d'après nature à l'âge de 50 ans, époque de son départ pour l'Egypte.

J'ai assister aux victoires de la republique j'ai traversé les saturnales du directoire j'ai vu la gloire du consulat et la grandeur de l'empire et sans avoir jamais affecté une force et des sentiments qui ne sont pas de mon sexe j'ai été a vingt trois ans de distance témoin des triomphes de Valmy et des funerailles de Waterloo

Ida St Elme
auteur des mémoires
d'une contemporaine

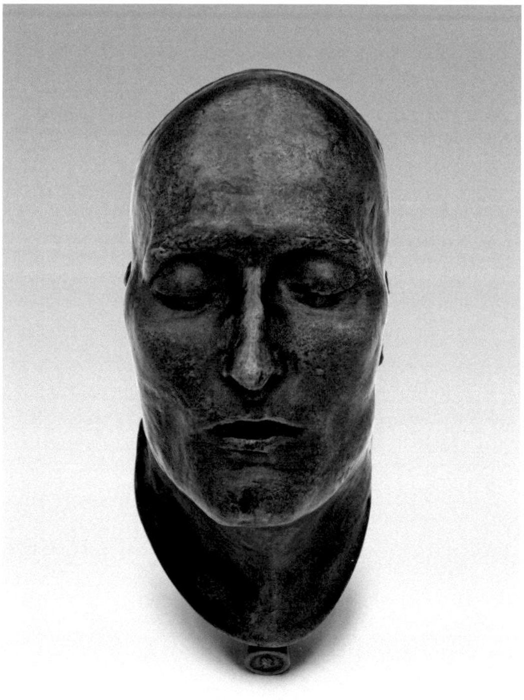

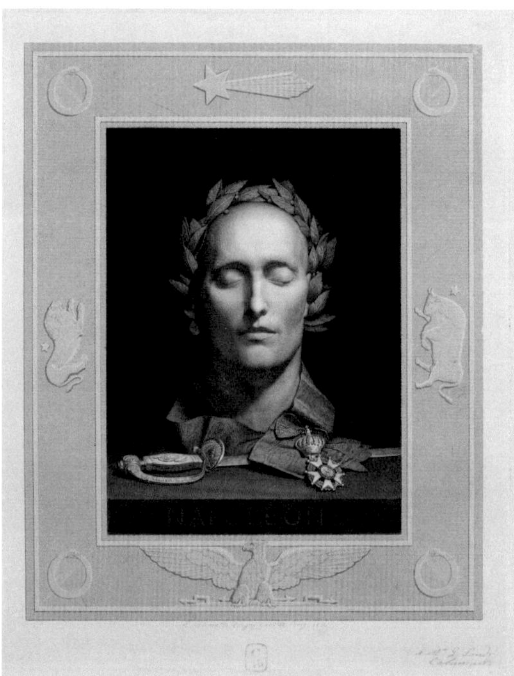

77 ↑ Francesco Antommarchi, death mask of Napoleon, modelled in 1821, cast in 1833, bronze (34.9 × 35.6 × 15.2), Art Institute of Chicago.

78 ↑ Luigi Calamatta, *Masque mortuaire de Napoléon*, 1834, engraving (386 × 312 mm), Fogg Museum, Harvard Art Museums, Cambridge, MA.

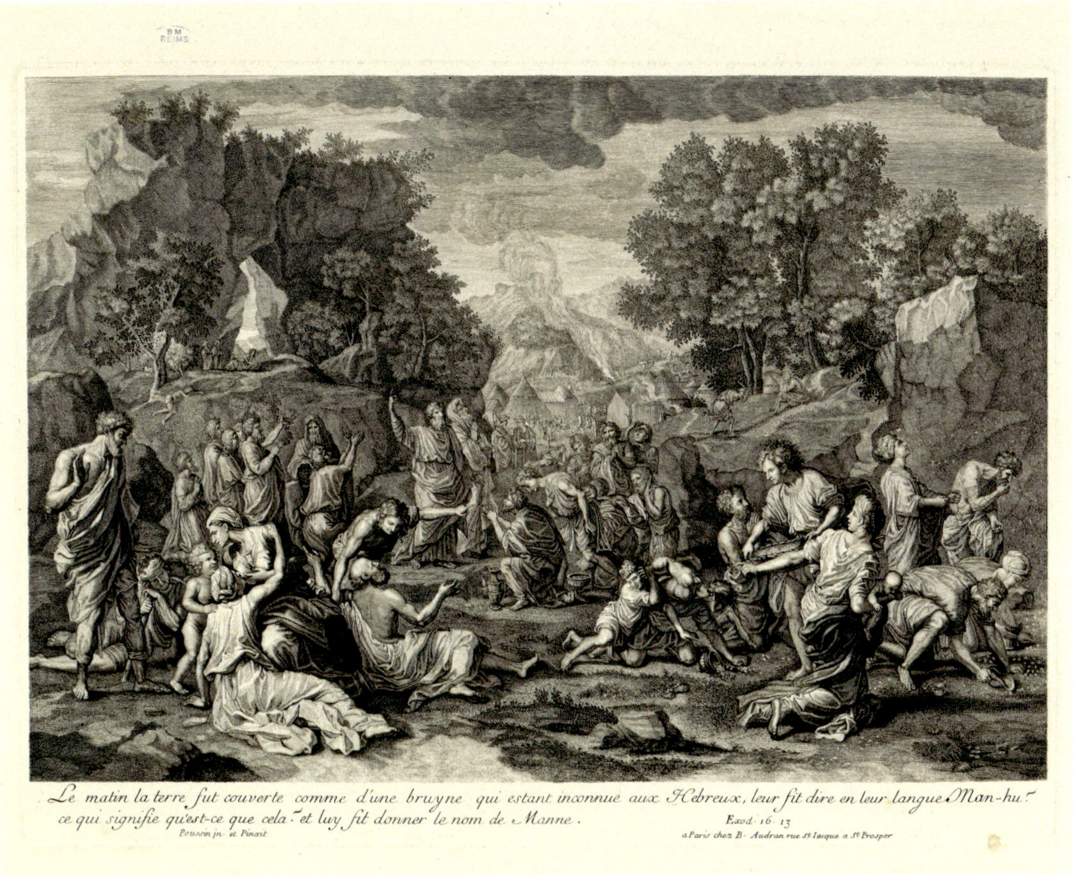

79 ↑ Benoît I Audran after Nicolas Poussin, *Les Israélites recueillant la manne*, engraving, 1686 (278 × 380 mm), Bibliothèque municipale, Reims.

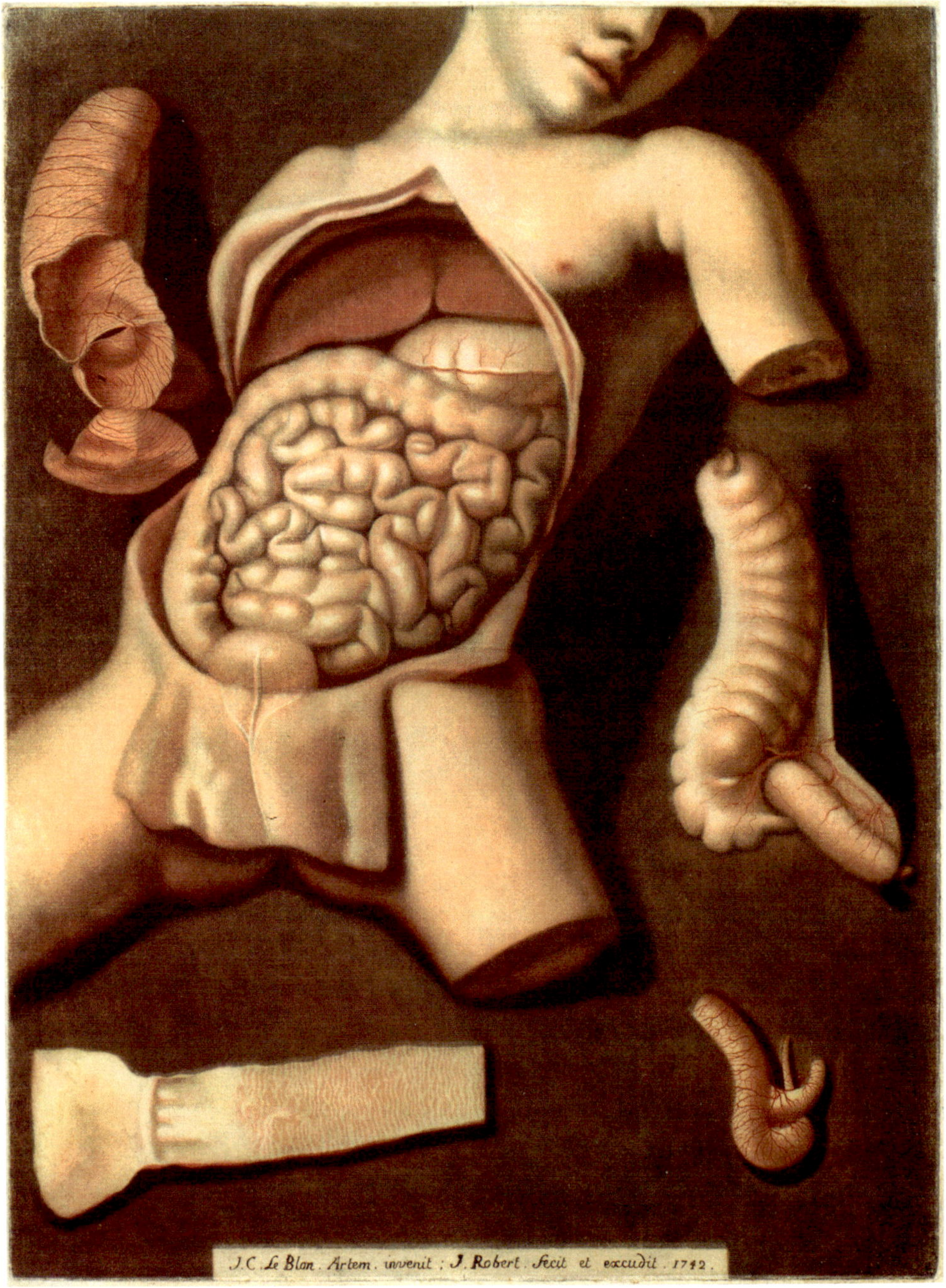

80 ↑ Jean Robert after Jacob Christoph Le Blon, anatomy, colour mezzotint, 1742 (614 × 462 mm), private collection.

81 → Pieter Stevens van Gunst after Gérard de Lairesse, thoracic cavity: anatomy and histology, engraving (813 × 533 mm), for Govert Bidloo, *Anatomia humani corporis* (1685) (Amsterdam, 1690), pl. 73, College of Physicians of Philadelphia Digital Library.

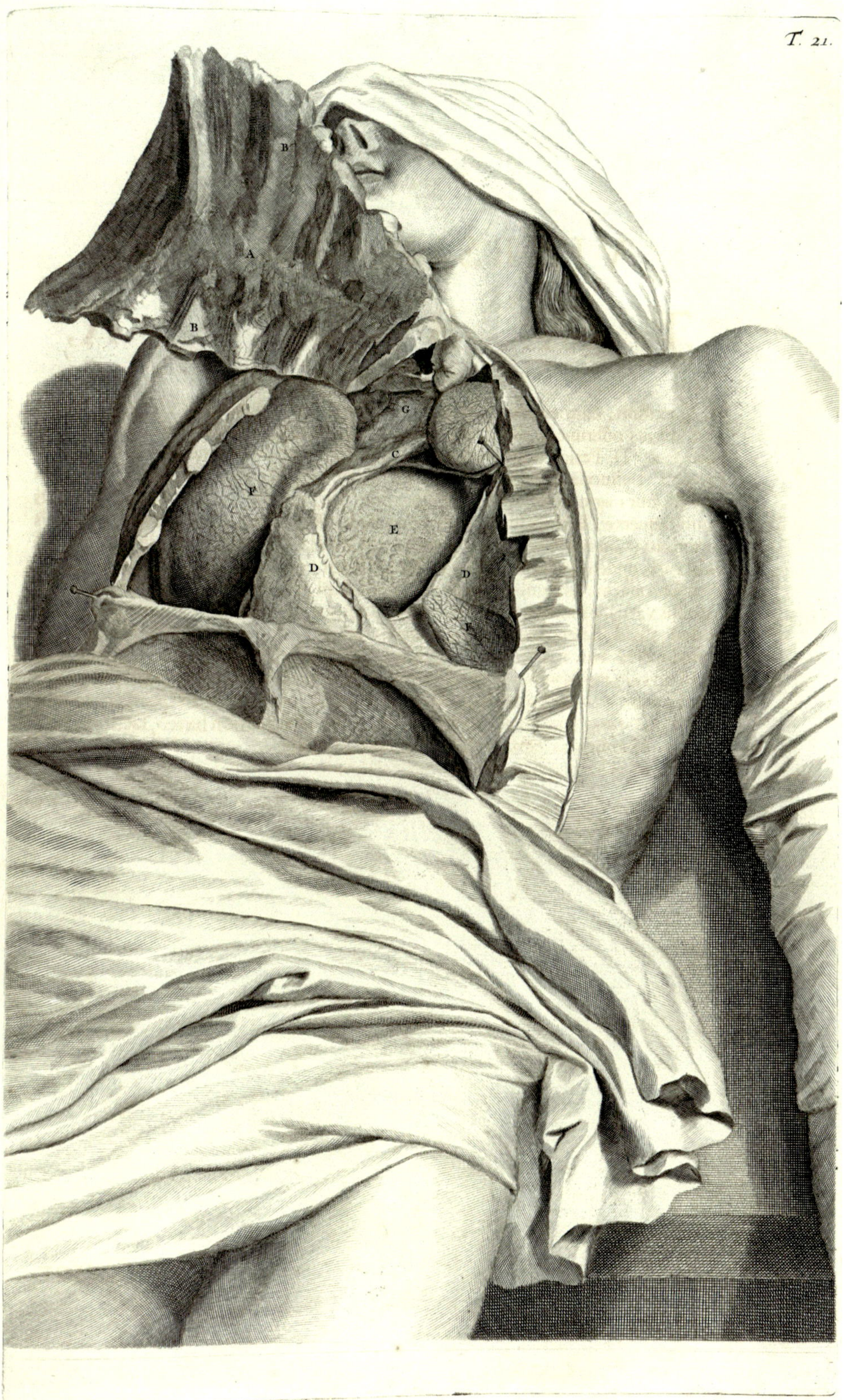
T. 21.
B
A
B
G
C
F
E
D
D
E

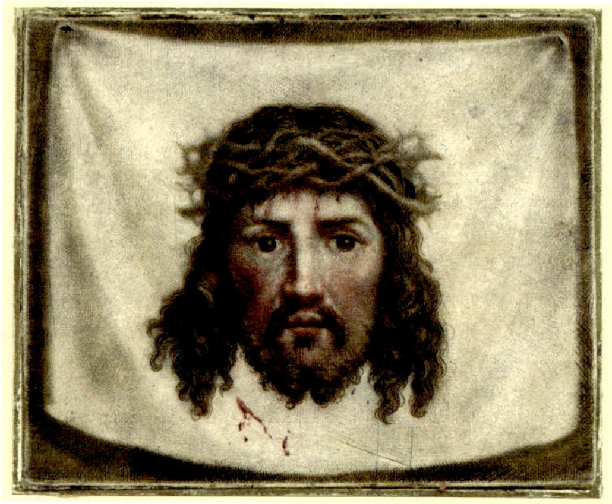

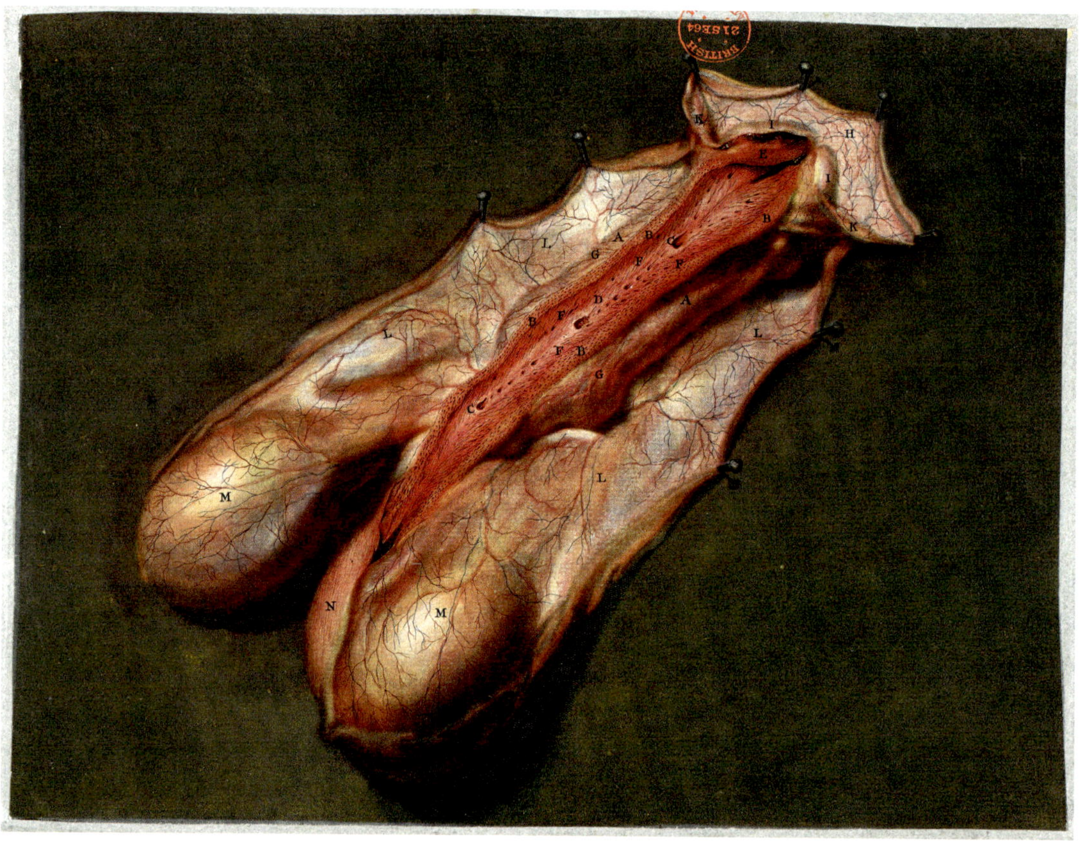

82 ↑ Jacob Christoph Le Blon, *Saint Veronica's Veil*, c.1721, mezzotint (87 × 110 mm) British Museum, London.

83 ↑ Jacob Christoph Le Blon, *Anatomical preparation of Male Genitalia*, c.1722, mezzotint (200 × 270 mm), for William Cockburn, *The Symptoms, Nature, Cause, and Cure of a Gonorrhoea* (1728), British Library, London.

84 ↗ Jacob Christoph Le Blon, *Le Voile de Sainte Véronique*, 1719, oil on canvas (438 × 595 mm), Christ Church, Oxford.

85 → Claude Mellan, *Le Linge de Sainte Véronique: Formatur unicus una*, 1649, engraving (429 × 317 mm), Bibliothèque nationale de France, Paris.

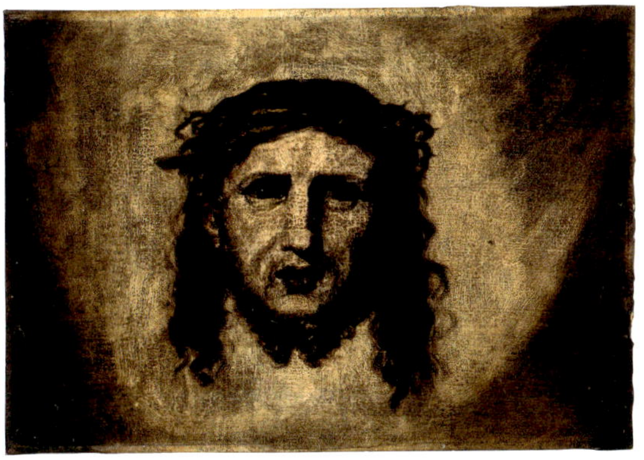

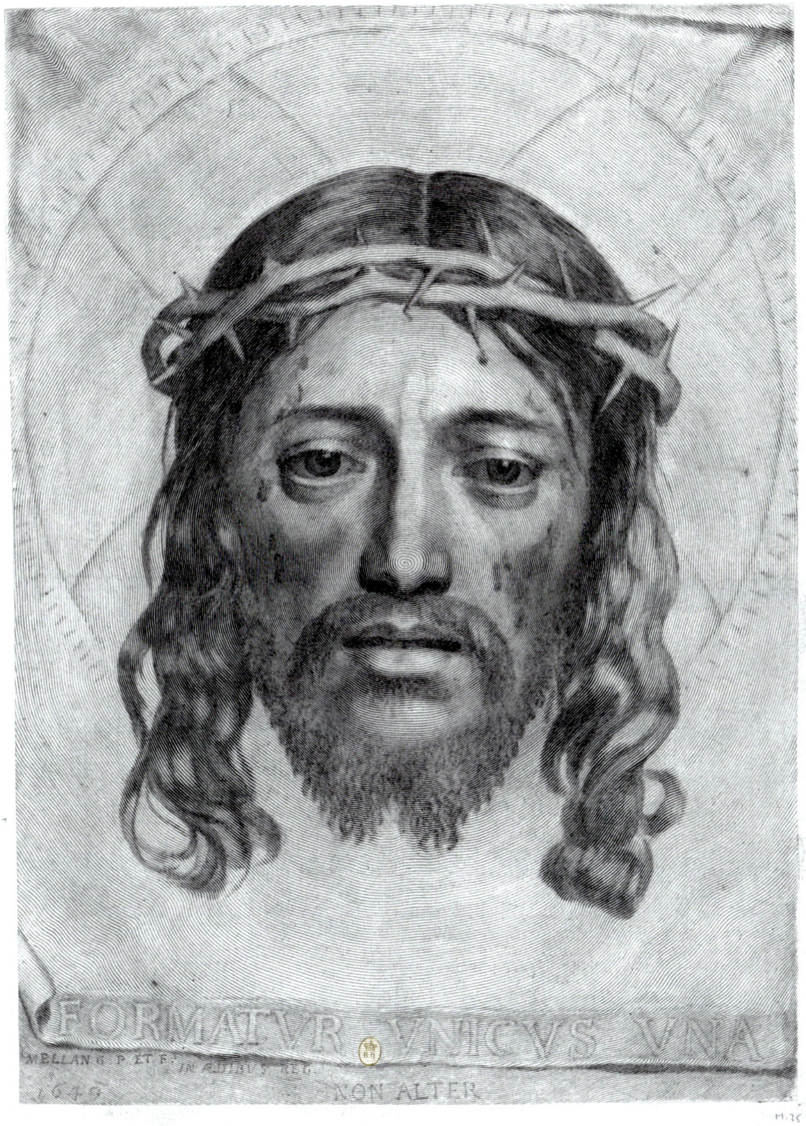
FORMATVR VNICVS VNA
MELLAN G. P. ET F.
IN ÆDIBVS REG.
1649
NON ALTER

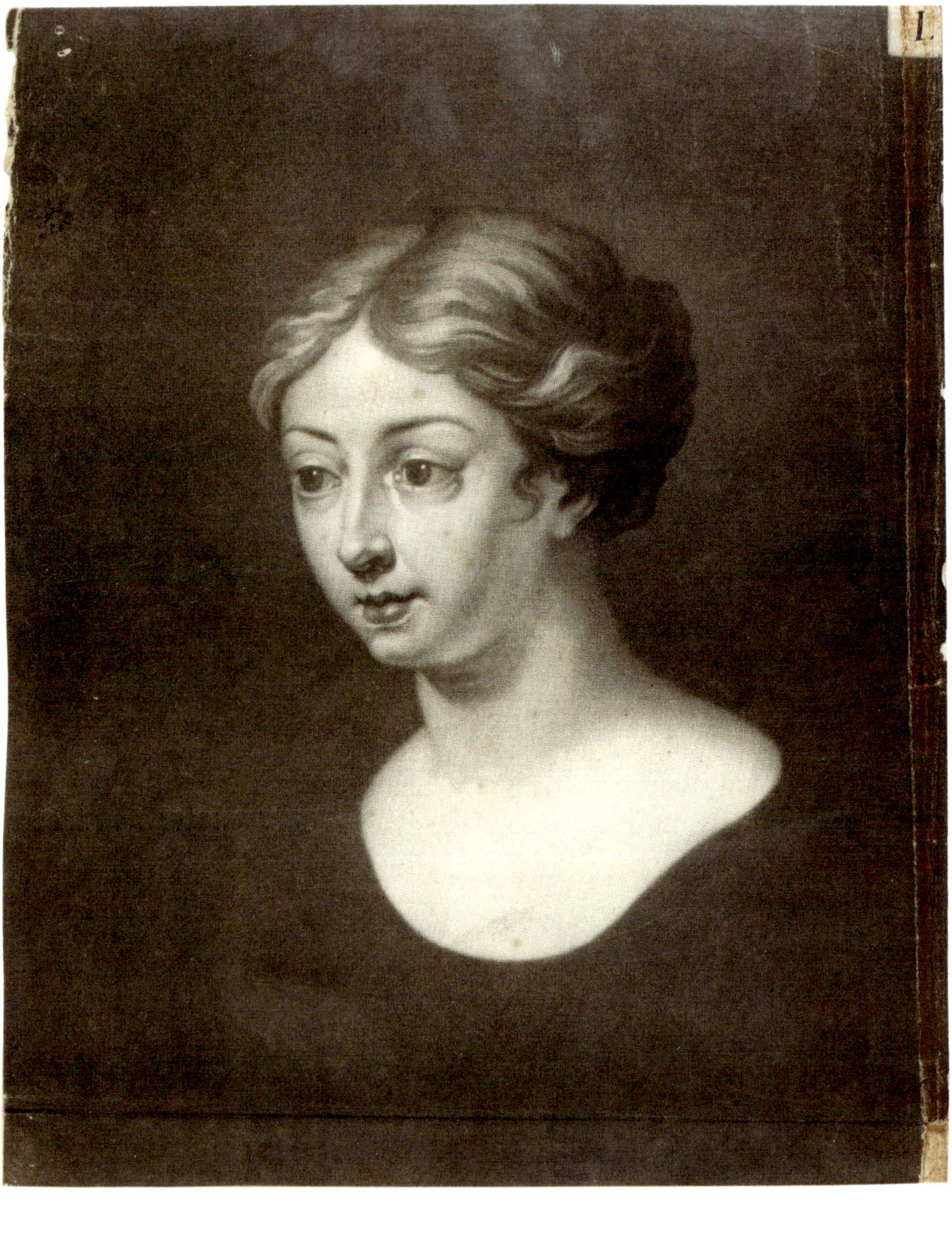

86 ↑ Jacob Christoph Le Blon, head of a young woman, mezzotint (280 × 220 mm), for *L'Harmonie du coloris* or *Coloritto* (n.d. [1725]), plate I, Bibliothèque nationale de France, Paris.

87 ↗ Jacob Christoph Le Blon, head of a young woman, mezzotint (280 × 220 mm), for *L'Harmonie du coloris* or *Coloritto* (n.d. [1725]), plate III, Bibliothèque nationale de France, Paris.

88 → Jacob Christoph Le Blon, head of a young woman, mezzotint (280 × 220 mm), for *L'Harmonie de coloris* or *Coloritto* (n.d. [1725]), plate VI, Bibliothèque nationale de France, Paris.

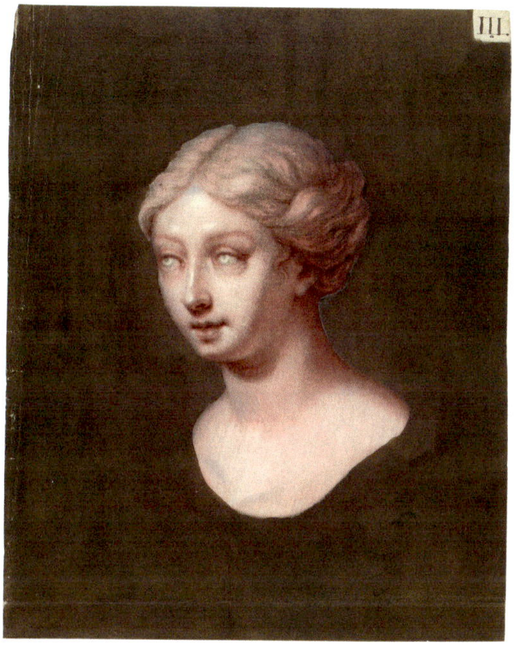
III.

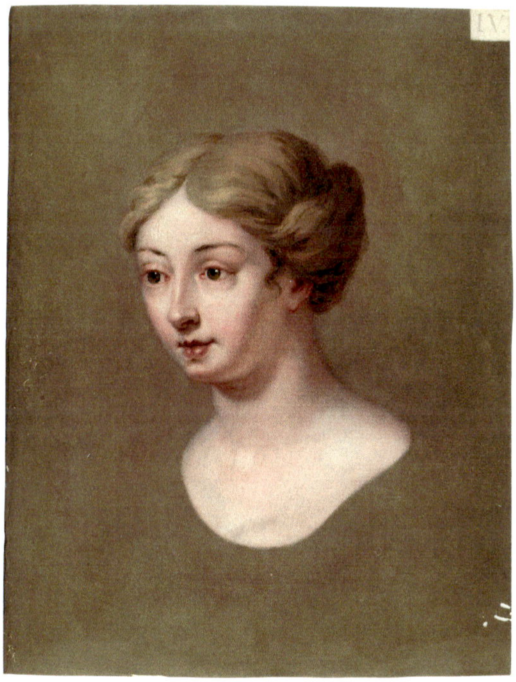
IV

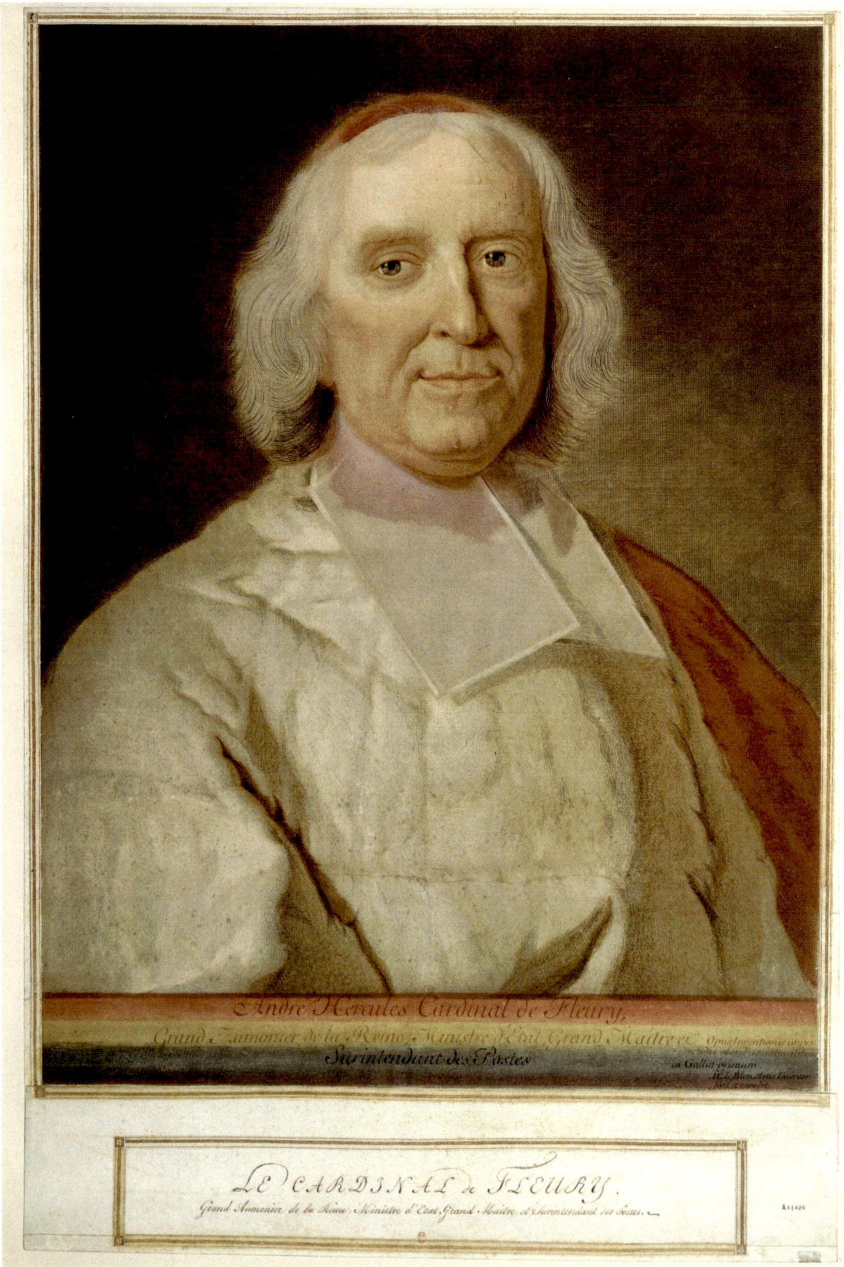

89 ↑ Jacob Christoph Le Blon, portrait of Cardinal André-Hercule de Fleury, 1738, mezzotint (601 × 456 mm), Bibliothèque nationale de France, Arsenal, Paris.

90 ↗ Pierre-Imbert Drevet after Hyacinthe Rigaud, portrait of Cardinal André-Hercule de Fleury, engraving, 1730 (501 × 375 mm), Département des estampes et de la photographie, Bibliothèque nationale de France, Paris.

91 → Antoine Hérisset after Jean Chaufourier, illustration of a light experiment, engraving (245 × 186 mm), headpiece in Isaac Newton, *Traité d'optique sur les réflexions, réfractions, inflexions et couleurs de la lumière*, trans. Pierre Coste, 2nd edn (Paris, 1722), p. 1 (detail), British Library, London.

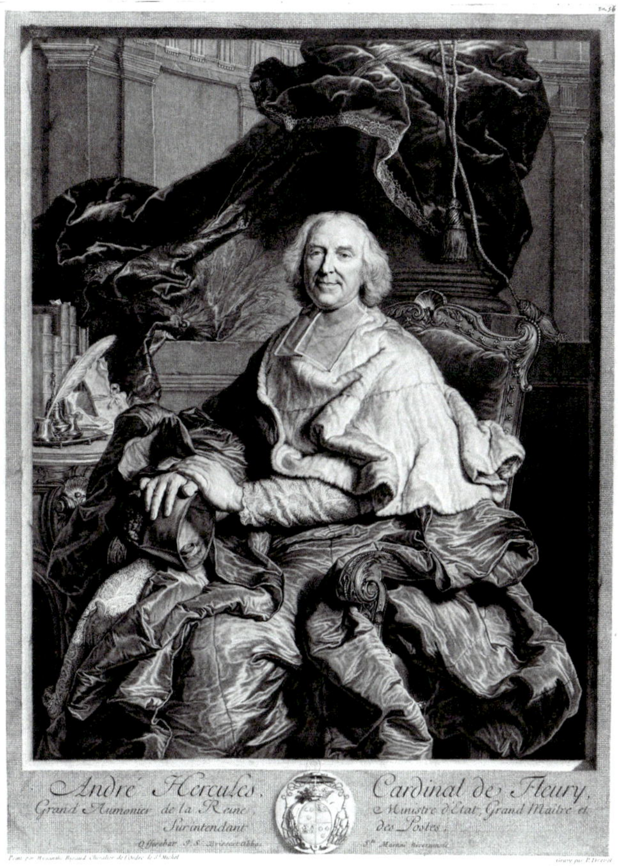

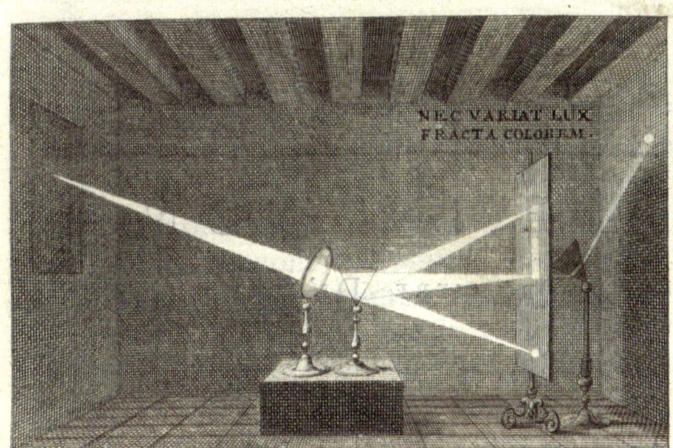

TRAITÉ
D'OPTIQUE,
SUR
LA LUMIERE
ET LES COULEURS.

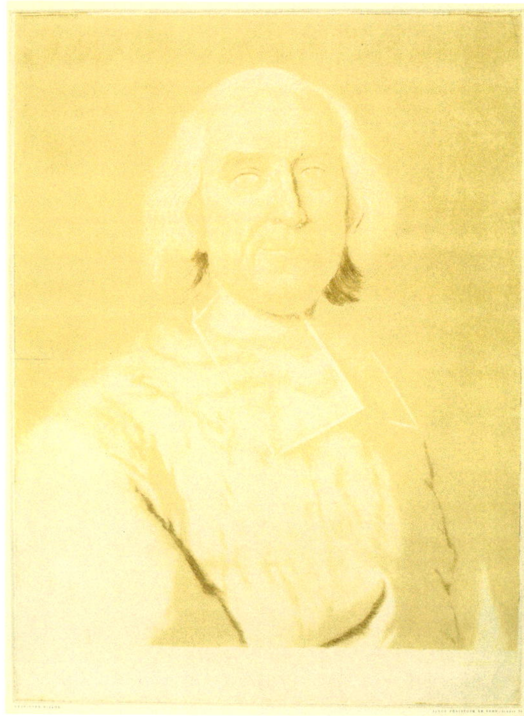

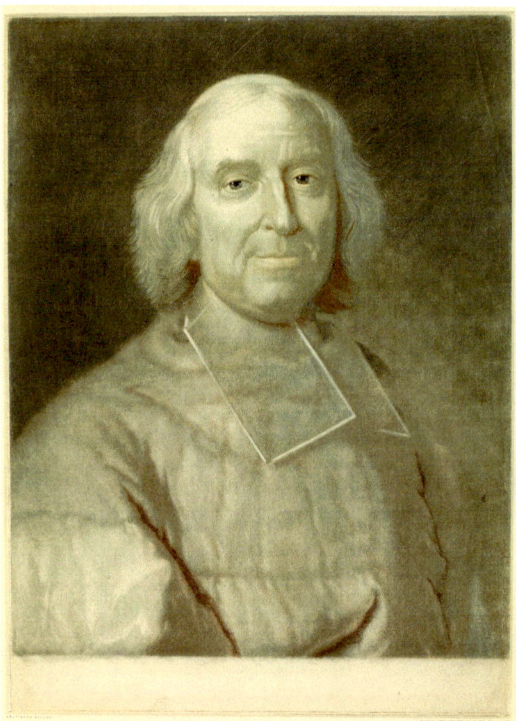

92 ↖ Jacob Christoph Le Blon, portrait of Cardinal André-Hercule de Fleury, 1738, mezzotint (612 × 459 mm), blue proof, British Museum, London.

93 ↑ Jacob Christoph Le Blon, portrait of Cardinal André-Hercule de Fleury, 1738, mezzotint (612 × 458 mm), yellow proof, British Museum, London.

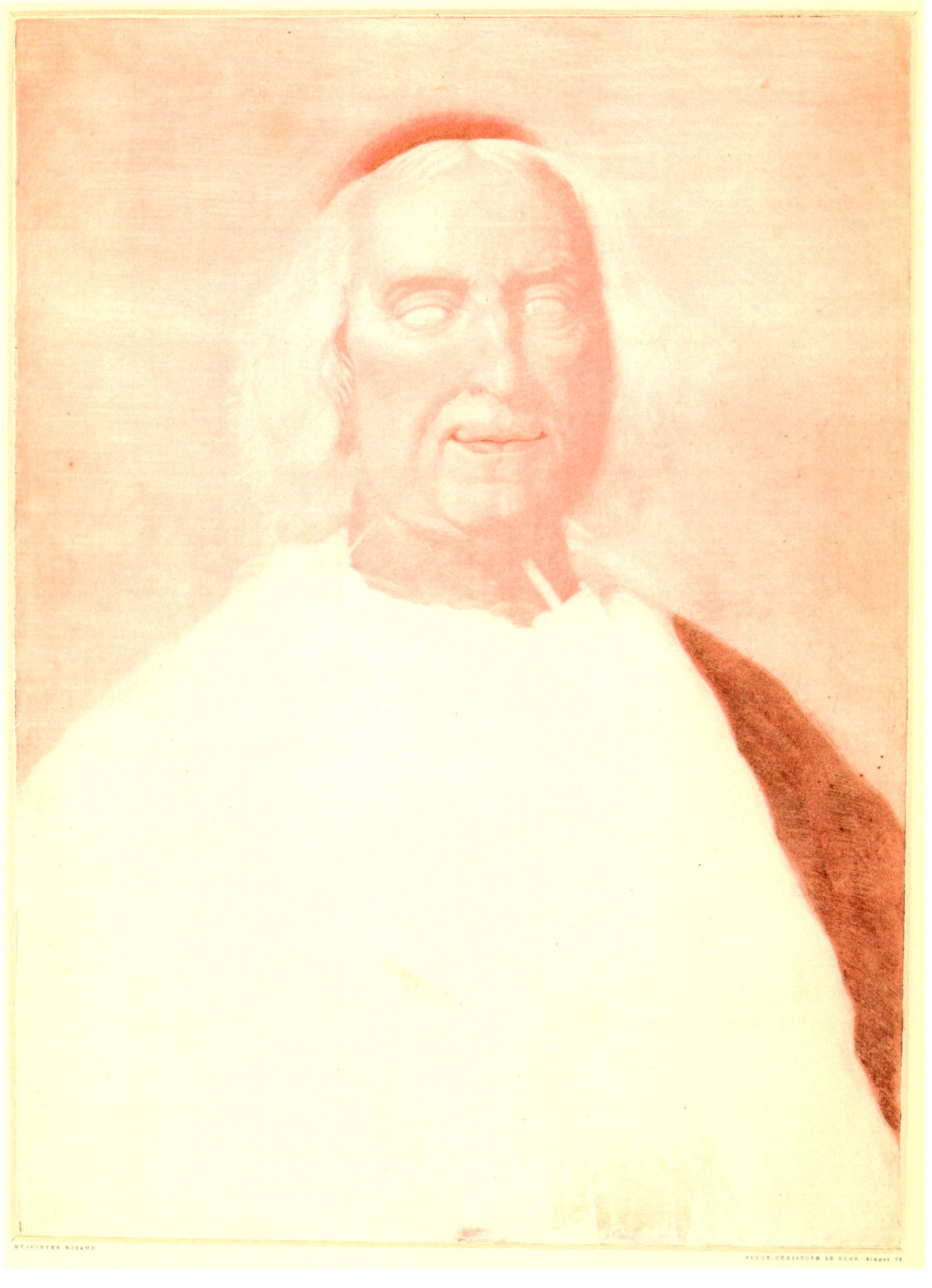

94 ← Jacob Christoph Le Blon, portrait of Cardinal André-Hercule de Fleury, 1738, mezzotint (612 × 458 mm), blue and yellow proof, British Museum, London.

95 ↑ Jacob Christoph Le Blon, portrait of Cardinal André-Hercule de Fleury, 1738, mezzotint (612 × 458 mm), red proof, British Museum, London.

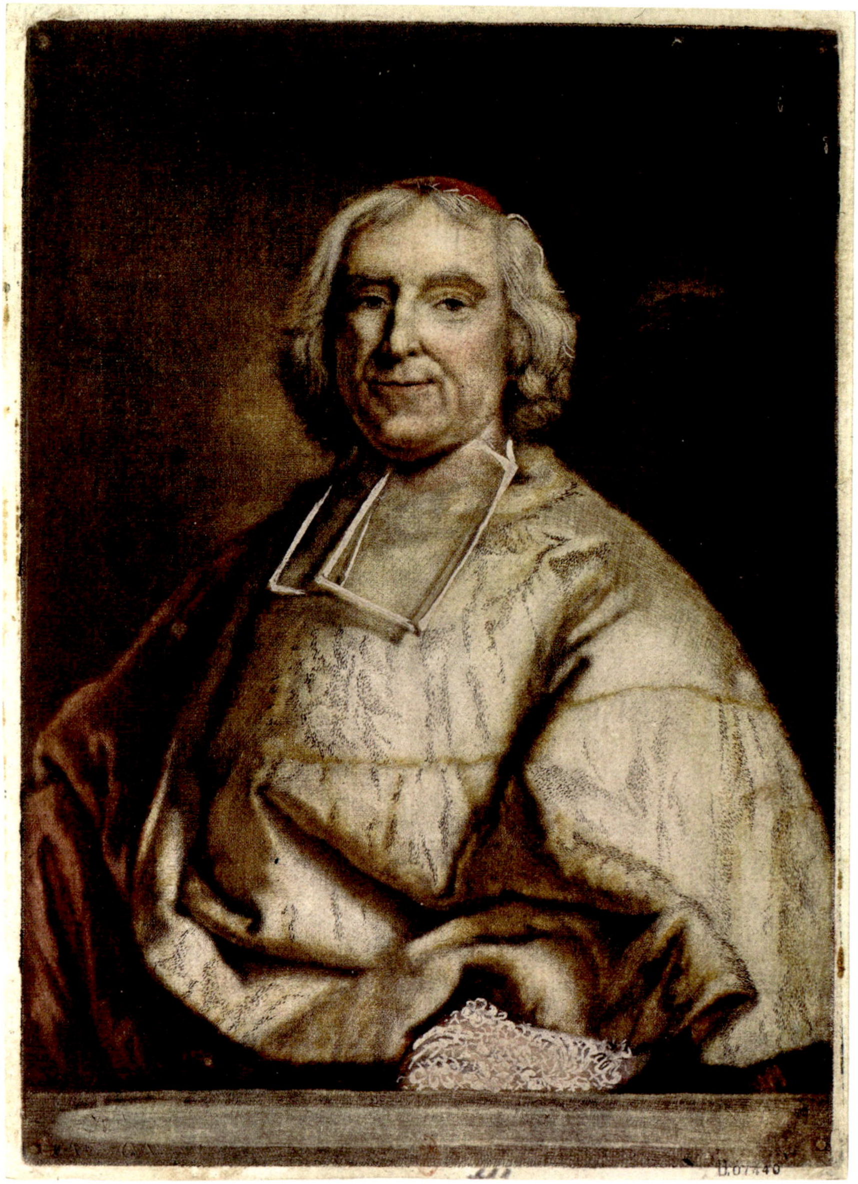

96 ↑ Jacques Gautier, portrait of Cardinal André-Hercule de Fleury, *c*.1743, mezzotint (212 × 156 mm), Bibliothèque nationale de France, Paris.

97 → Agostino Carracci after Paolo Veronese, *La Sacra Famiglia con i Santi Giovanni Battista, Caterina et Antonio Abate*, engraving, *c*.1582 (474 × 317 mm), British Museum, London.

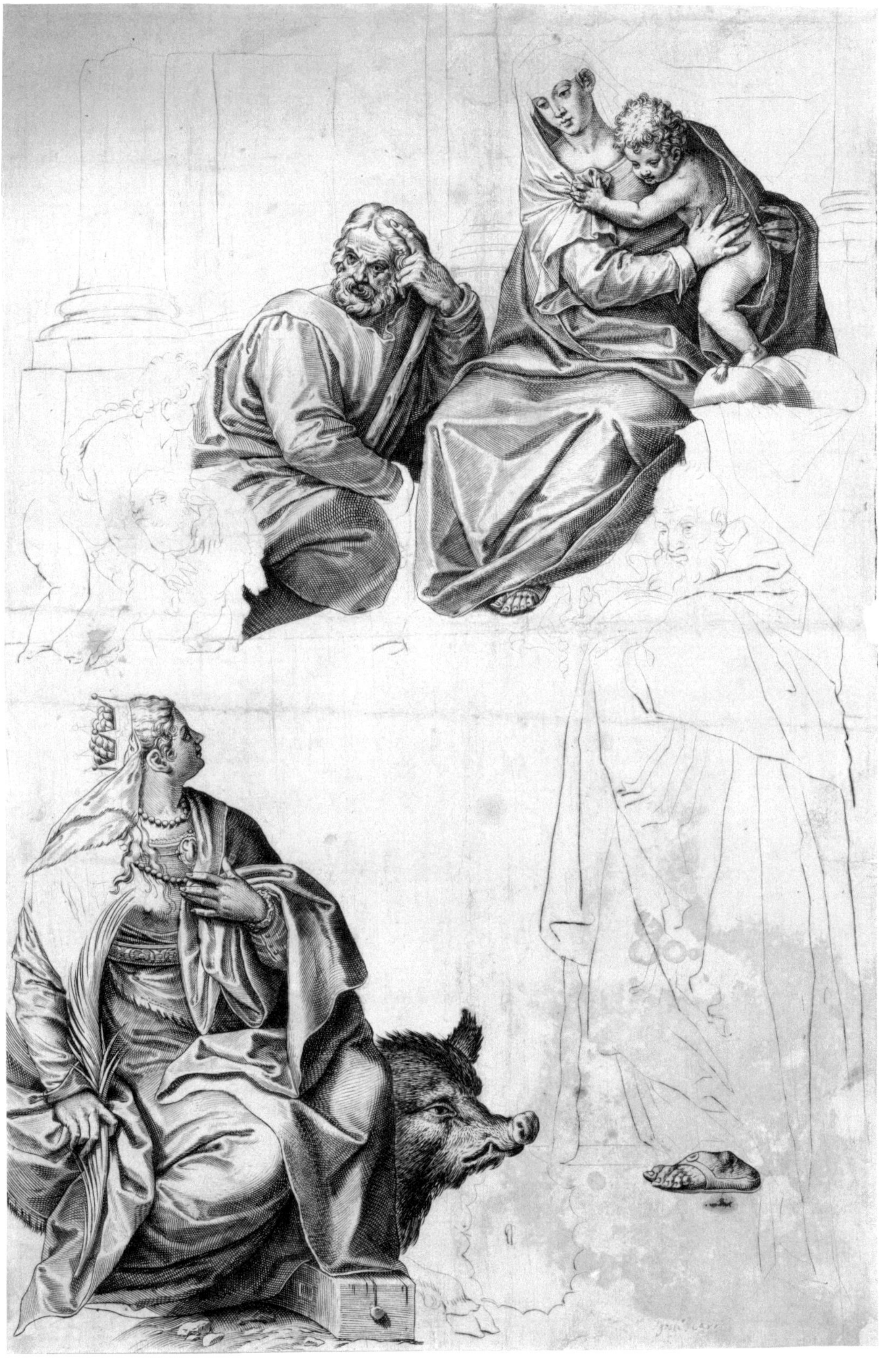

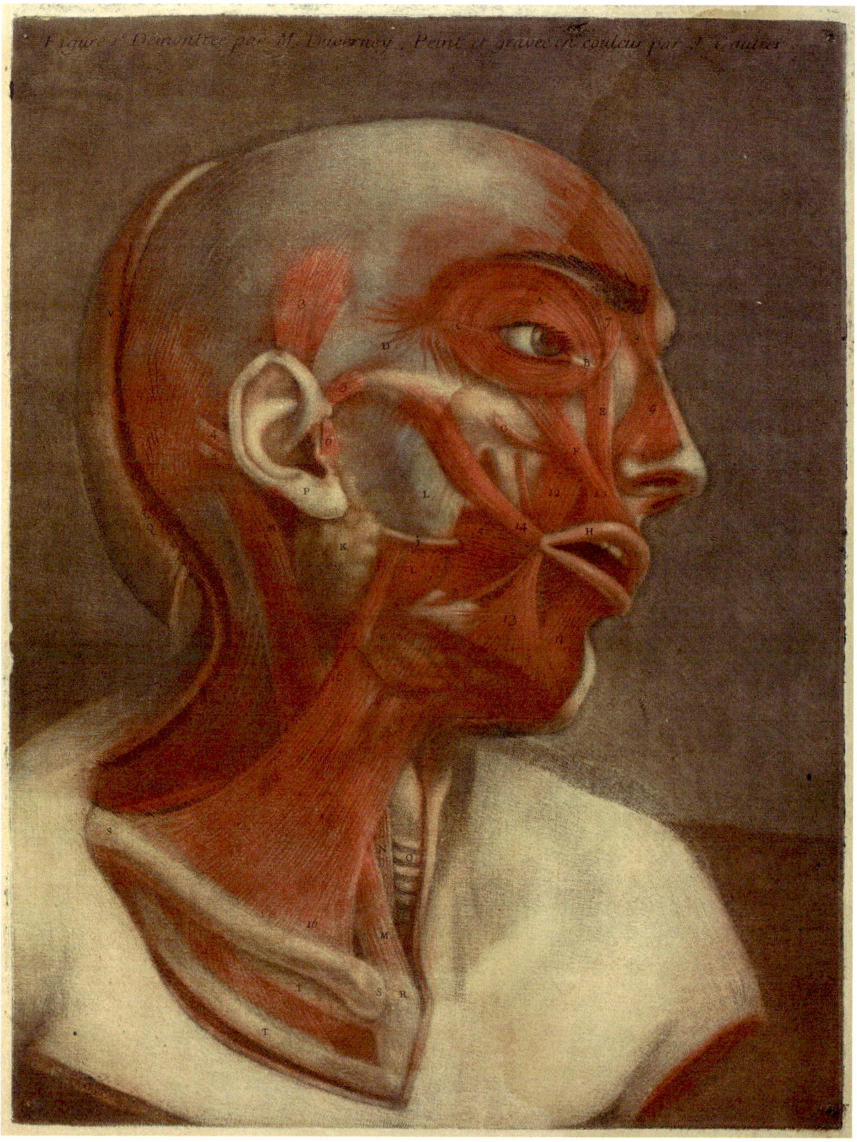
Figure 1 Démontrée par M. Duverney, Peint et gravé en couleur par J. Gautier

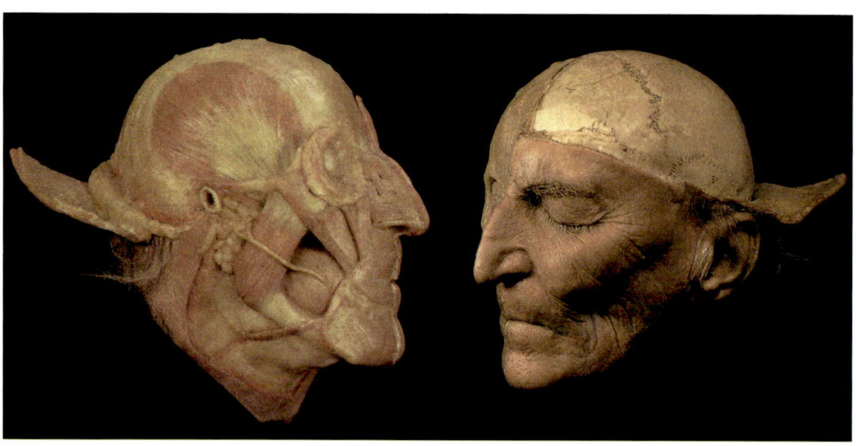

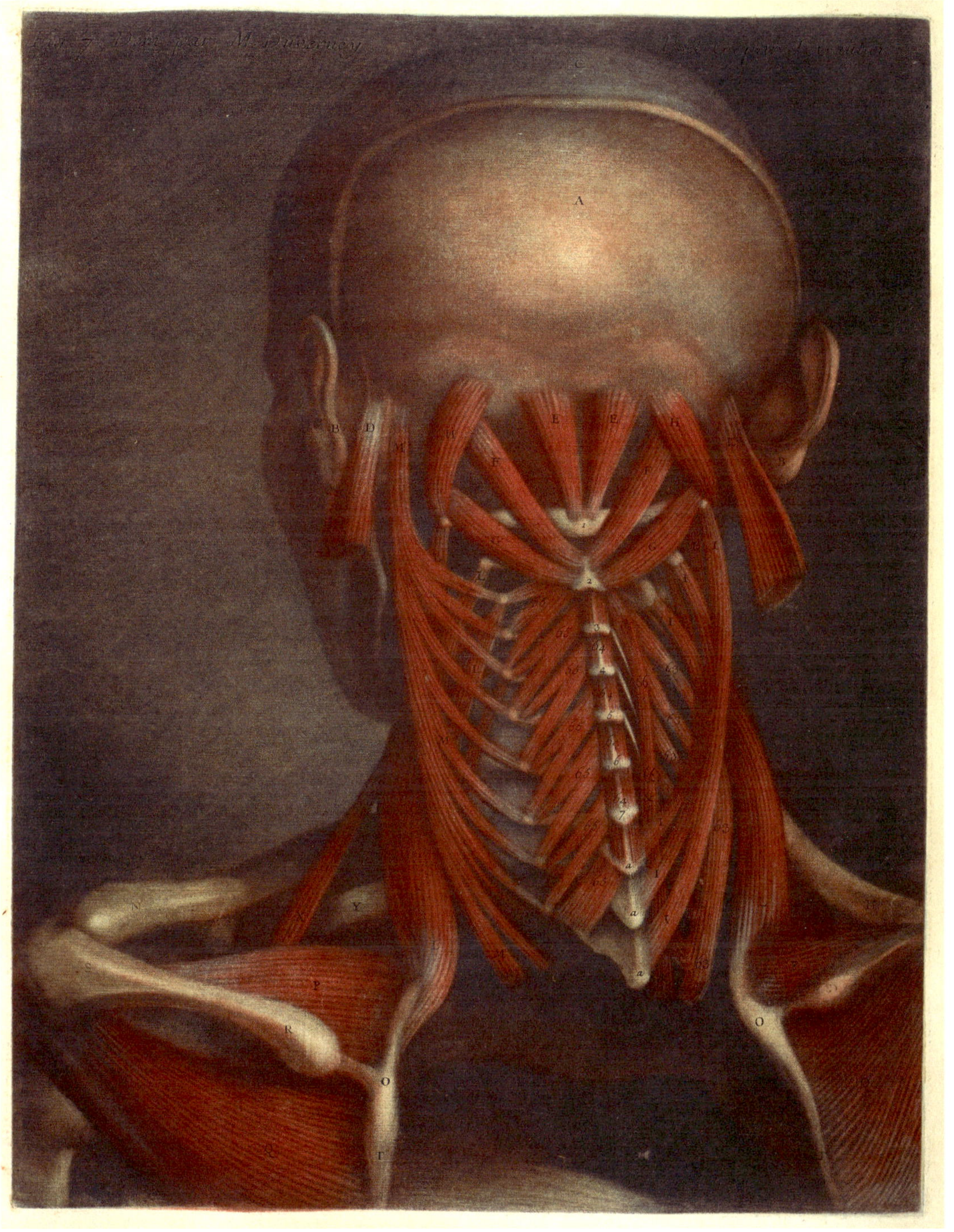

98 ↖ Joseph-Guichard Duverney and Jacques Gautier, the muscles of the head, mezzotint (403 × 317 mm), in *Myologie complette en couleur et grandeur naturelle* (1746), pl. 1, British Library, London.

99 ← Gaetano Zumbo, anatomy of the head, c.1710, wax, Musée d'histoire naturelle, Paris (formerly in the Cabinet du roi).

100 ↑ Joseph-Guichard Duverney and Jacques Gautier, the muscles of the back of the head and neck, mezzotint (403 × 317 mm), *Myologie complette en couleur et grandeur naturelle* (1746), pl. 7, British Library, London.

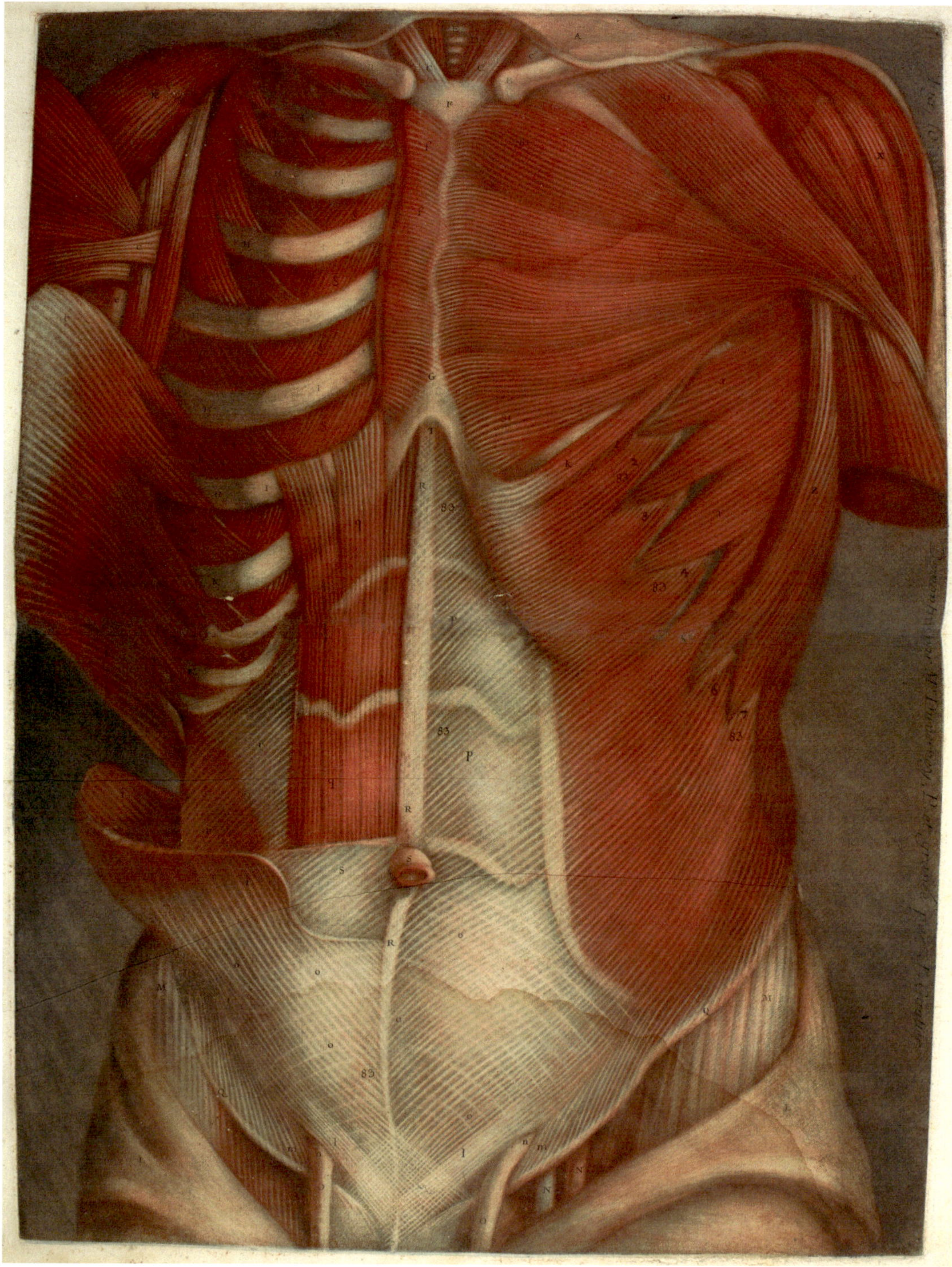

101 ↑ Joseph-Guichard Duverney and Jacques Gautier, the muscles of the front of the male torso, mezzotint (608 × 458 mm), in *Myologie complette en couleur et grandeur naturelle* (1746), pl. 10, British Library, London.

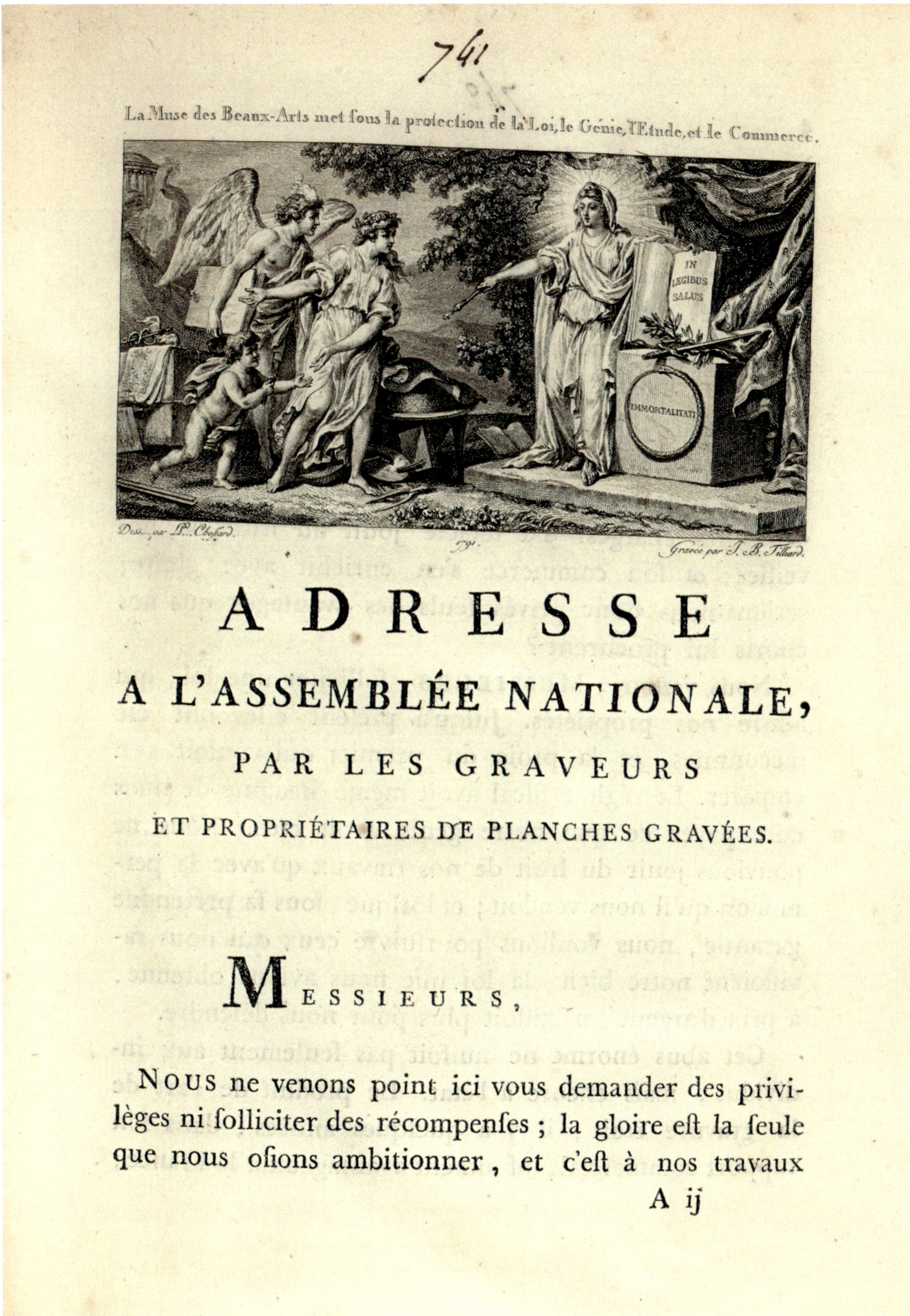

741

La Muse des Beaux-Arts met ſous la protection de la Loi, le Génie, l'Etude, et le Commerce.

ADRESSE

A L'ASSEMBLÉE NATIONALE,

PAR LES GRAVEURS

ET PROPRIÉTAIRES DE PLANCHES GRAVÉES.

MESSIEURS,

NOUS ne venons point ici vous demander des privilèges ni ſolliciter des récompenſes ; la gloire eſt la ſeule que nous oſions ambitionner, et c'eſt à nos travaux

A ij

102 ↑ Jean-Baptiste Tillard after Pierre-Philippe Choffard, *La Muse des Beaux-Arts met sous la protection de la Loi, le Génie, l'Etude, et le Commerce*, etching (65 × 120 mm), headpiece for *Adresse à l'Assemblée nationale, par les graveurs et propriétaires de planches gravées* (Paris, 1791), Bibliothèque nationale de France, Paris.

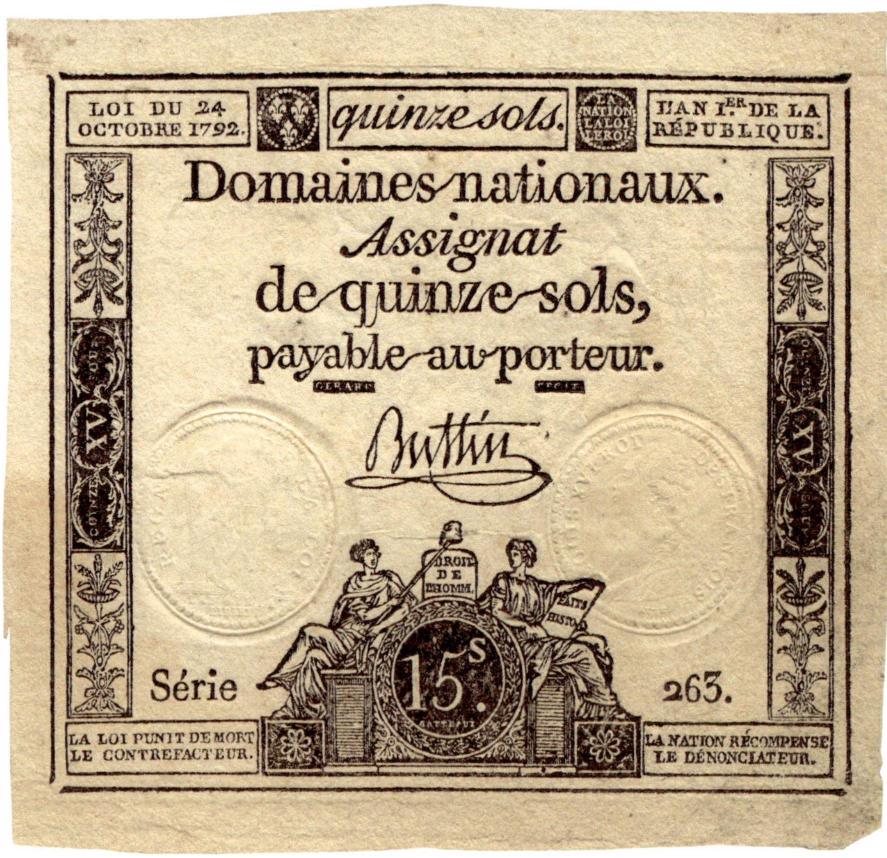

103 ↑ Nicolas-Marie Gatteaux, *Assignat de quinze sols*, 1792, engraving, letter engraving, typography and dry seal (75 × 83 mm), Bibliothèque nationale de France, Paris.

104 → A. Tardieu after Nicolas-Marie Gatteaux, *Assemblage de divers papiers monnaies et assignats*, 1797, etching and hand-colouring (571 × 475 mm), Bibliothèque nationale de France, Paris, Collection Michel Hennin.

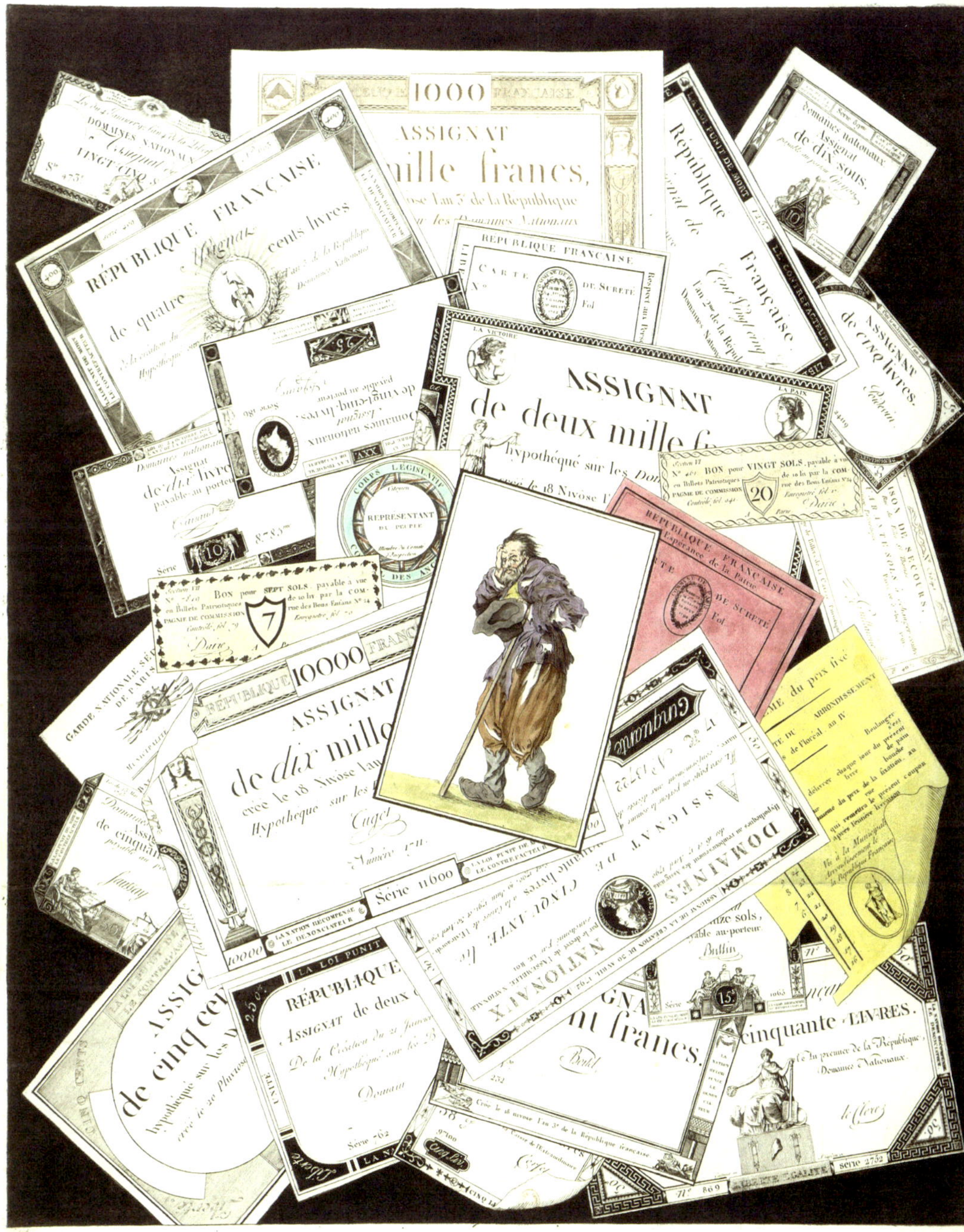

1000
ASSIGNAT
mille francs,
RÉPUBLIQUE FRANÇAISE
de quatre cents livres
ASSIGNAT
de deux mille fr
hypothéqué sur les Dom
BON pour VINGT SOLS payable à vue
20
REPRESENTANT DU PEUPLE
BON pour SEPT SOLS payable à vue
7
10000
ASSIGNAT
de dix mille
Série 11600
LA NATION RÉCOMPENSE LE DÉNONCIATEUR
LA LOI PUNIT DE MORT LE CONTREFACTEUR
DOMAINES NATIONAUX
RÉPUBLIQUE
Assignat de deux
cinquante LIVRES.
Domaines nationaux
RÉPUBLIQUE FRANÇAISE
CARTE DE SURETE

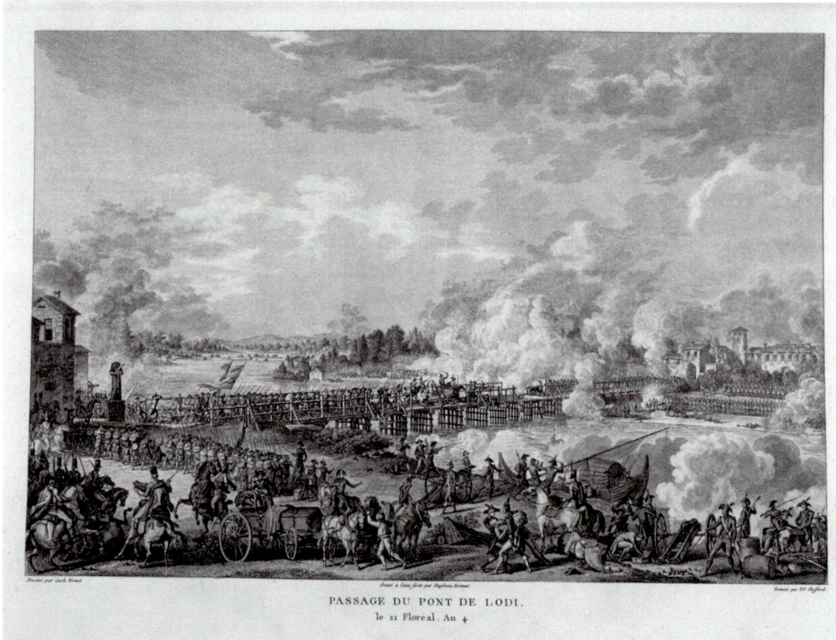

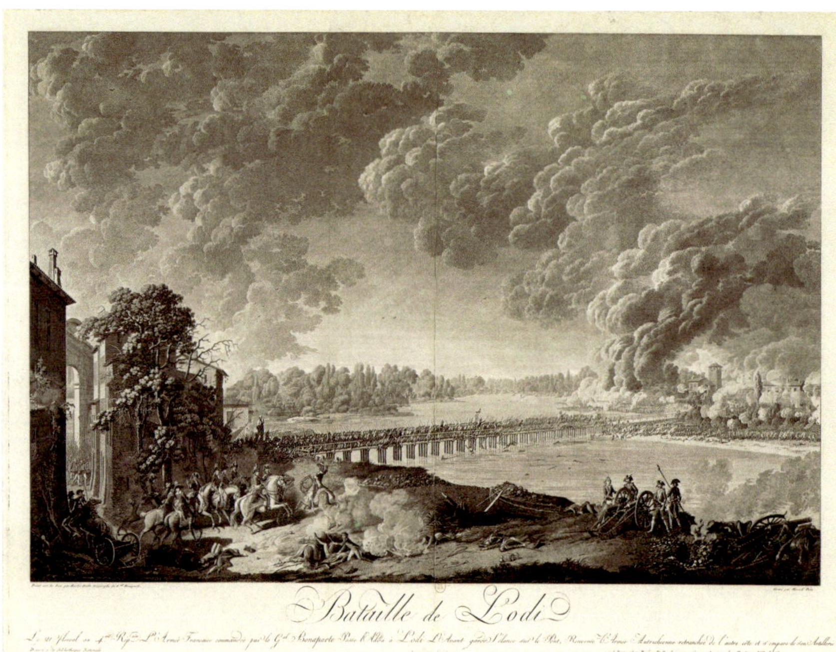

105 ↑ Jean Duplessi-Bertaux after Carle Vernet, *Passage du Pont de Lodi*, etching, with engraving by Pierre-Philippe Choffard, 1799 (285 × 380 mm), published by Auber in *Tableaux historiques des campagnes d'Italie* (Paris, 1806), pl. 4, Bibliothèque nationale de France, Paris.

106 ↑ Michelangelo Mercoli, *Bataille de Lodi*, after Louis Albert Ghislain Bacler d'Albe, *Le Pont de Lodi*, engraving, *c*.1797–1800 (515 × 700 mm), Bibliothèque nationale de France, Paris.

107 ↗ François Boucher, Gilles Demarteau and Hubert Robert, five prints and four drawings of pastoral subjects, *c*.1765–70, crayon-manner etching, red chalk, and pen and ink (356 × 423 mm), Courtauld Institute of Art, London.

108 → Louis-Joseph Mondhare, *La Bataille de Fontenoy. . . le 11 Mai 1745*, *c*.1745, hand-coloured print (290 × 450 mm), Bibliothèque nationale de France, Paris.

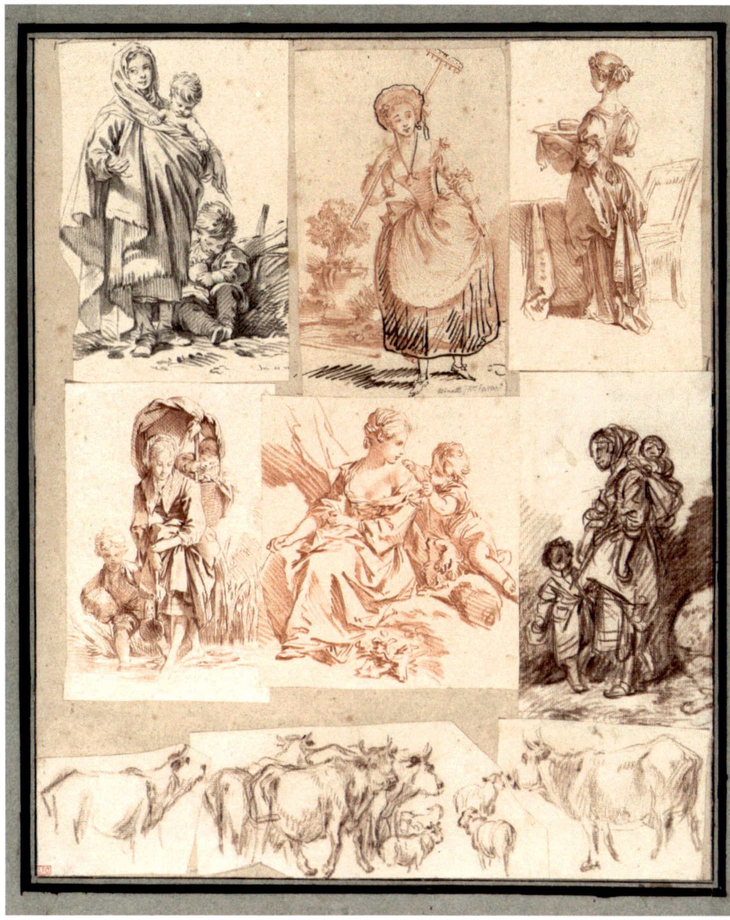

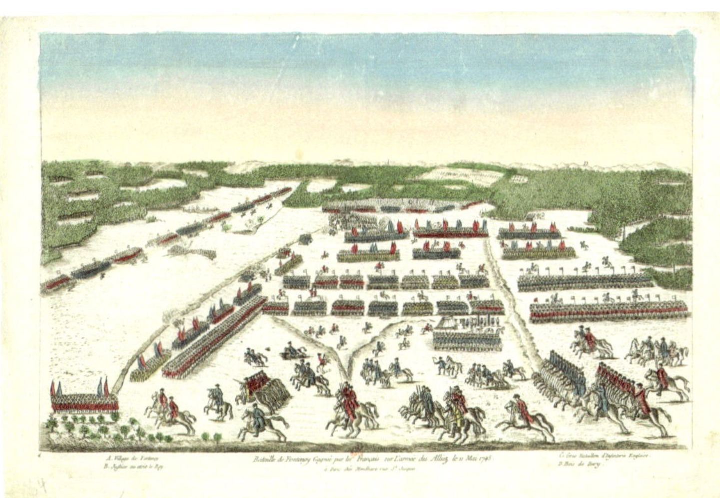
Bataille de Fontenoy Gagné par les François sur l'armée des Alliez le 11 Mai 1745

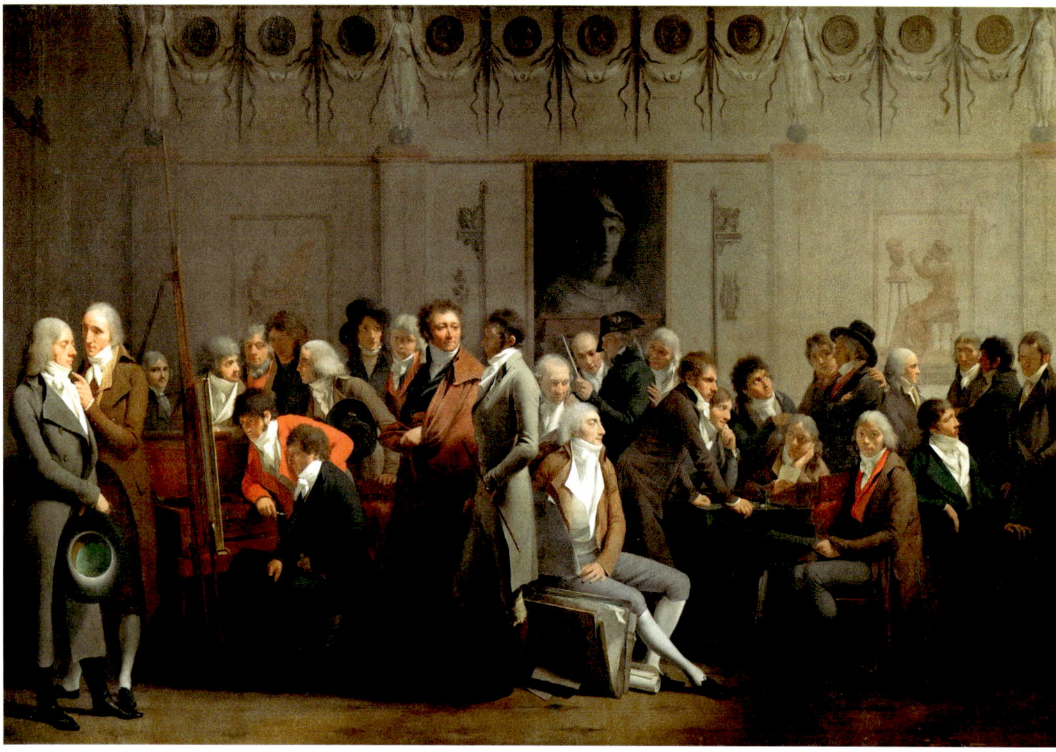

109 ↑ Louis-Léopold Boilly, *Réunion d'artistes dans l'atelier d'Isabey*, 1798, oil on canvas (71.5 × 111 cm), Musée du Louvre, Paris.

110 ↗ Henry Gérard after Marguerite Gérard, *L'Élan de la nature*, etching and engraving, *c*.1798 (760 × 815 mm), Bibliothèque nationale de France, Paris.

111 → Joseph Dufour after Henry Gérard, *L'Élan de la nature*, woodblock-printed wallpaper, *c*.1798, private collection, Saône-et-Loire, France.

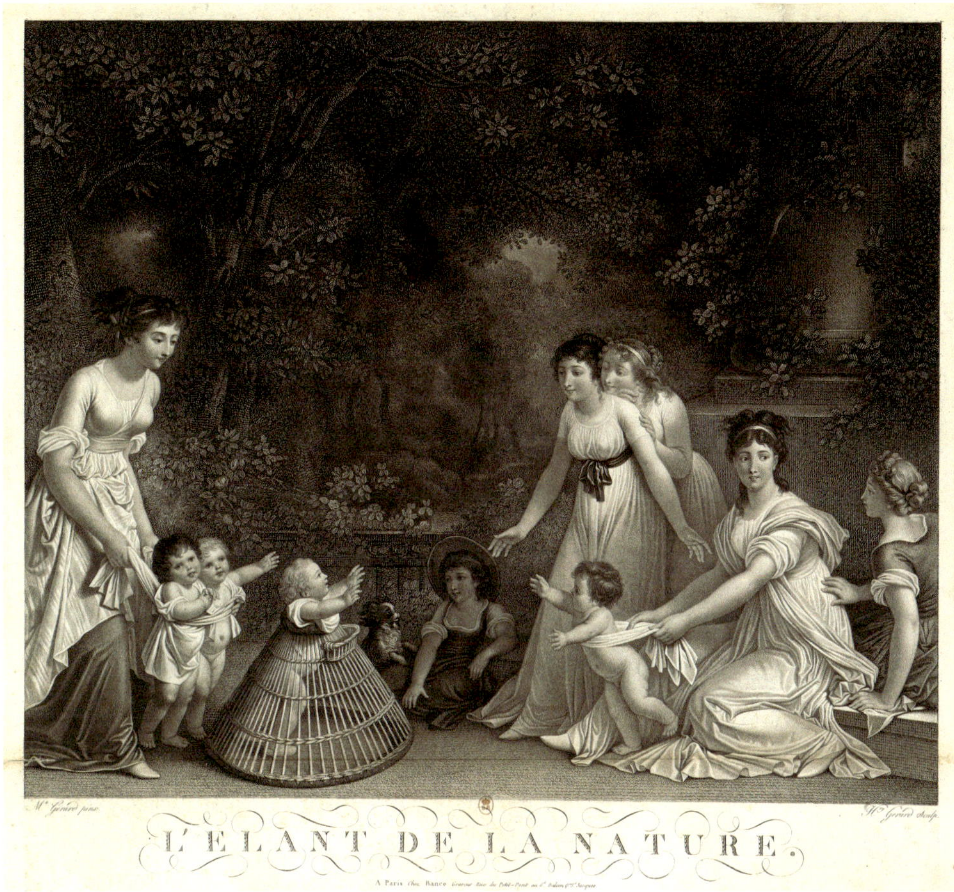
L'ELANT DE LA NATURE.

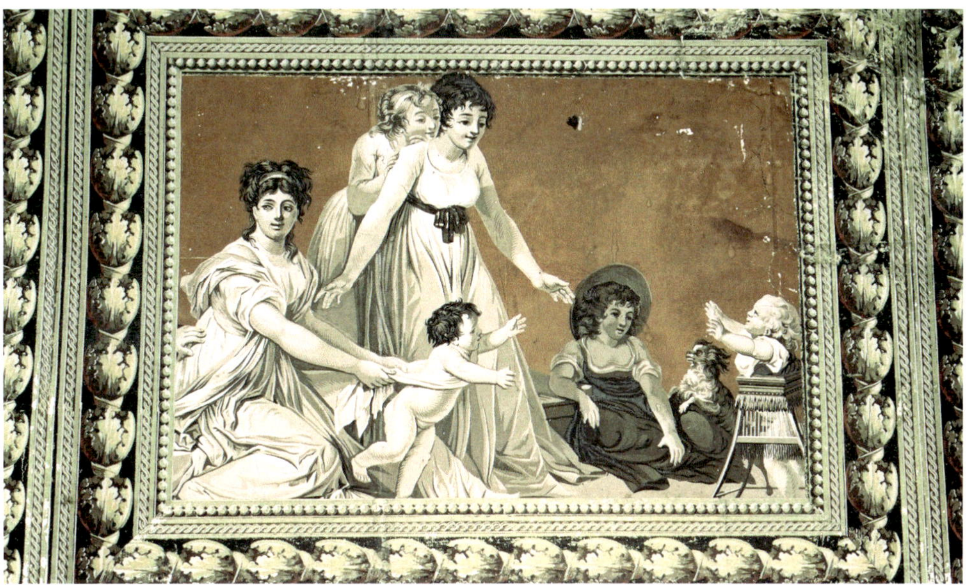

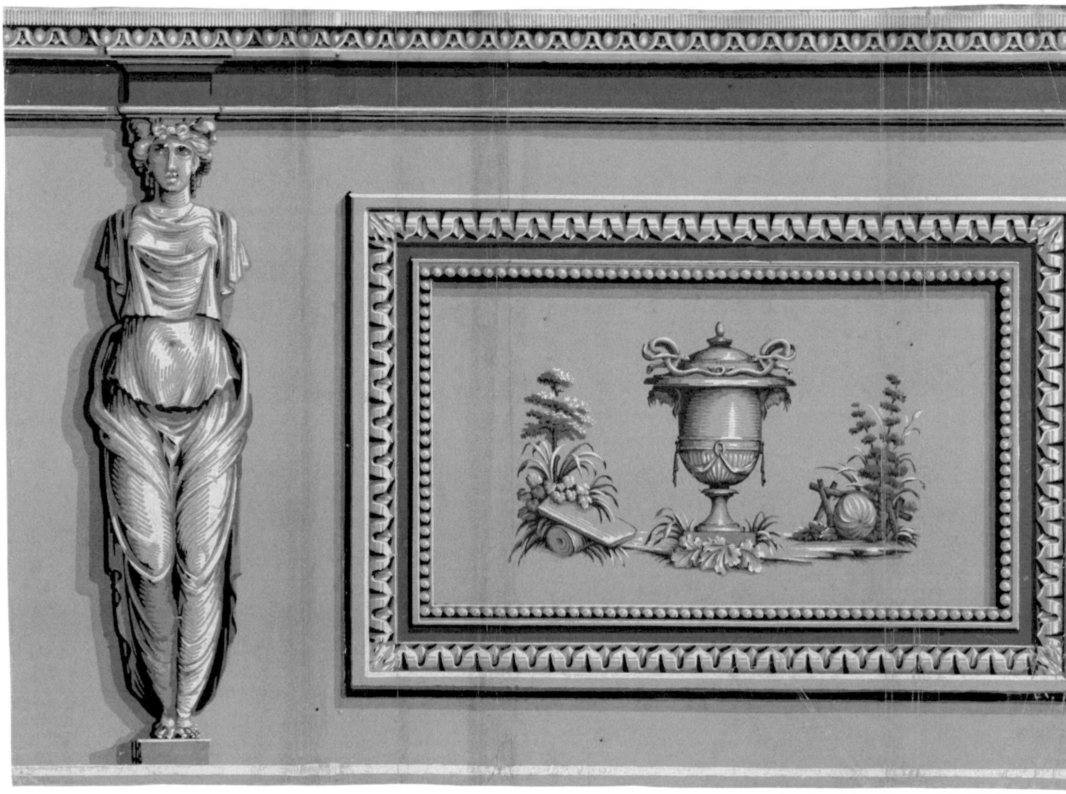

112 ↑ Manufacture Jacquemart et Bénard, repetitive pattern with caryatid and urn in cameo, 1799, woodblock-printed wallpaper, Bibliothèque nationale de France, Paris.

IMITATION: CRIMES OF LIKENESS

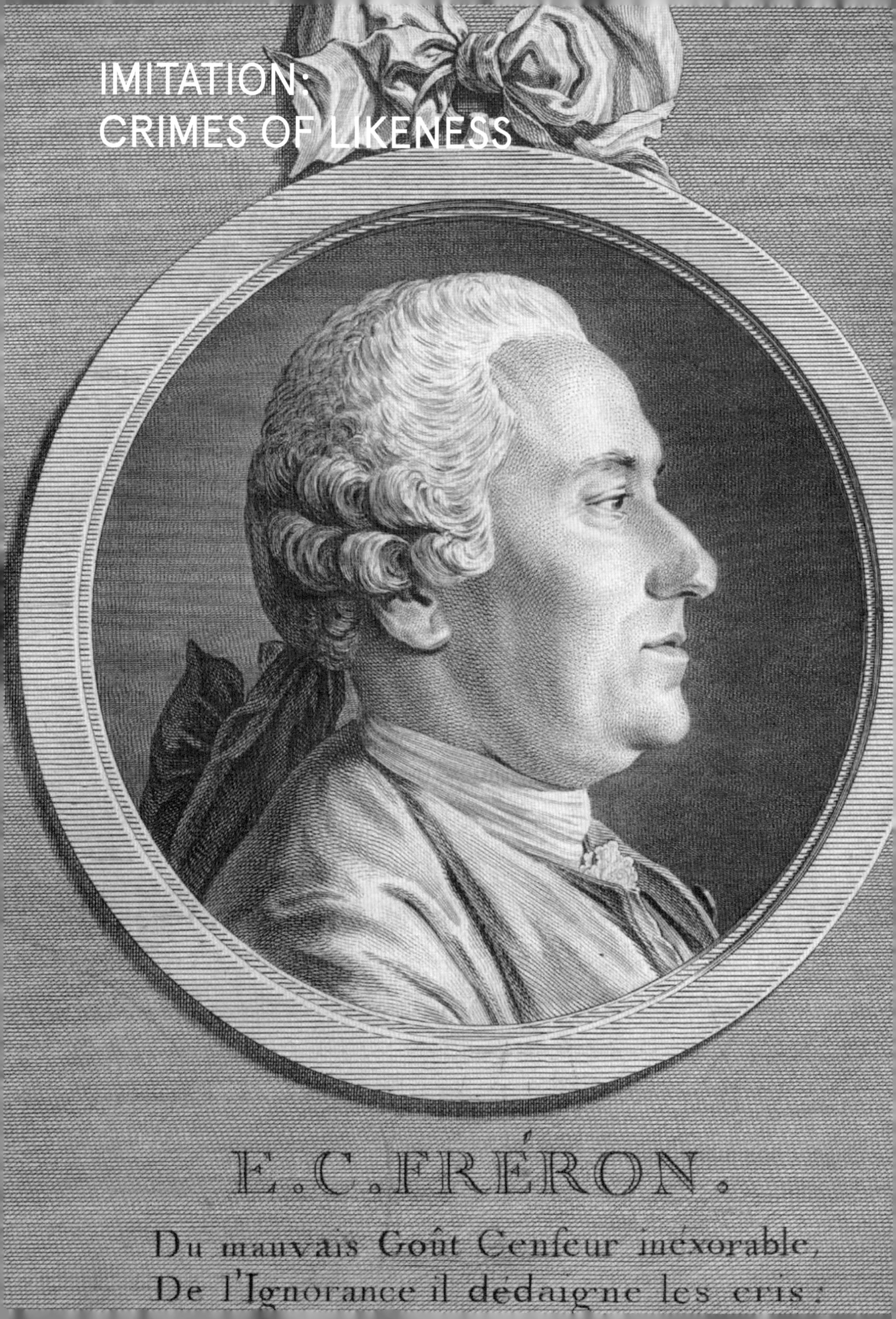

The title of this chapter contains a pun, a play on the word 'likeness': gathered under the one word are references to the genre of art in question – portraiture – and to an artistic practice – copying. Crime occurs in the case of likeness in the second sense, where the law is violated by the infringement of an author's right in his or her work. This is not to say that likeness in the first sense was not also sometimes felt as criminally offensive – Jean-Jacques Rousseau certainly believed that all, or almost all, of the portraits painted of him were libellous.[1] But such portraits were, in the eighteenth century, generally violations of self-esteem and not breaches of law.[2] However, the two senses of likeness are often difficult to untangle. Since portraiture is defined by Renaissance and post-Renaissance art theory as an art of the copy,[3] the question arises, can one copyright a copy? And if so, is the right upheld a prerogative over mere likeness or over nature itself? The title's pun is therefore intended to draw attention to the instability of definitions of artistic representation in both art theory and law.

This chapter focuses on two types of medium. One is comparatively rare and marginal (both as effigy then, and as object now): wax. The other was ubiquitous and normative: the portrait print. Today wax is most readily associated with anatomical preparations, such as those of the late seventeenth-century Sicilian abbot Gaetano Giulio Zumbo, or those, a century later, of the military surgeon André-Pierre Pinson for Louis-Philippe, duc d'Orléans.[4] However, at the beginning of the eighteenth century wax thrived as a medium for portraiture in the hands of the ageing academician Antoine Benoît, who bore the title, 'Peintre ordinaire du roy [Louis XIV] et son unique sculpteur en cire coloriée'.[5] Benoît took casts directly from the body, from which he made moulds and cast heads for medallions, busts and full-length figures, either on commission or speculatively for display at his showroom in the rue des Saints-Pères and at the Paris fairs.[6] While later Bourbon monarchs did not continue to include wax modellers in their retinue and wax virtually disappeared as an artistic medium, the tradition of taking death masks survived, becoming in the nineteenth century an occasional practice for many sculptors when commemorating the illustrious dead.[7] The boundary in law and in aesthetics between these waxes and portraiture – that is, between freehand and mechanical copies – was often extremely fine.

Portrait prints, meanwhile, had been a highly important branch of the French print trade since the early seventeenth century.[8] Quantitative analysis by genre of the print holdings of the Cabinet des estampes at the Bibliothèque nationale de France has suggested that portraiture moved from second place, behind devotional imagery, in the seventeenth century to first place, ahead of genre and landscape, in the eighteenth century, accounting for almost one-third of all printed images produced and sold.[9] Moreover, the prestige of the genre was officially guaranteed in 1704 when the Académie royale de peinture et de sculpture required engravers seeking admission to its ranks to submit, as *morceaux de réception*, two engravings after the portraits of its members, thus also establishing the Académie as the guardian of the grand formal portrait.[10] Meanwhile, in the marketplace, portrait prints of all kinds, from large and expensive single sheets to smaller, cheaper portrait series, were very largely the specialisation of particular printshops – notably, the Drevets' (expensive) and Michel Odieuvre's (cheap) at the beginning of the century, and Augustin de Saint-Aubin's (mid-range) at the end. The particular vulnerability of portrait prints to piracy, recycled and adapted from art print to book or magazine illustration, fashion plate, fan leaf or popular memento, is and was widely recognised.

Both waxes and prints are, or are potentially, multiples. The moulds and copper plates from which they are drawn promise a seemingly endless outpouring of replicas. Those who copied them anticipated considerable financial gain. In the context of a buoyant and competitive eighteenth- and early nineteenth-century print market, it is therefore surprising to find in the registers of the Corporation des libraires et maîtres imprimeurs relatively few entries granting print privileges for single portraits, or for so-called portrait 'galleries'. Pierre Drevet and his son, Pierre-Imbert Drevet, made no applications for protection of their works, apparently; Odieuvre obtained one privilege in 1754 for prints illustrating Jean-François Dreux du Radier's *L'Europe illustre* (1755–65); and the one privilege obtained for a portrait by Saint-Aubin was granted not to the printmaker but to the patron.[11] Although the number of applications rose in the second half of the eighteenth century, it rarely exceeded one per year, or just one-fifth of the total applications for print privileges.

Waxworks, meanwhile, were not subject to protection in quite the same way. That is to say, there was no established procedure by which to obtain protection, no self-designating authority to which to apply. From 1676, Benoît was eligible for an Académie privilege.[12] However, having obtained authorisation in 1668 to exhibit his waxes publicly in Paris and throughout France, he decided instead to convert his *permission simple* into an exclusive, 30-year privilege in 1688. Infringers were threatened with confiscation, costs and a hefty fine of 6,000 *livres*.[13] In 1701, Zumbo followed suit, obtaining a privilege for some of his waxworks, those that skirted Benoît's privilege – namely, his 'anatomical parts of the human and animal body'.[14] Finally, during the July Monarchy (1830–48), Francesco Antommarchi attempted to defend his workshop monopoly of Napoleon's death mask by means of the Literary and Artistic Property Act of 1793. These applications for privilege, and in Benoît's case the importance of the fines, indicate that real commercial interests were at stake.[15]

Although the status and remit of Chancellerie privileges were generally limited, and artists' applications for them, and for Académie privilege, were little short of exceptional, the 1770s and 1780s saw a handful of legal disputes over the piracy of portraits that brought questions of imitation and law from the margins to the centre of debate for the first time. The cases became matters of public as well as artistic concern, thanks to the publication of the lawyers' briefs or memoranda and comment in the press. The prosecuting lawyer in one such suit remarked, in fact, that artists, connoisseurs and all manner of *honnêtes gens* were following his case closely, and anxiously awaited the verdict.[16] Moreover, the first histories of copyright, published in the 1830s by jurists Adrien Gastambide and Augustin-Charles Renouard, confirm portraiture's special status in questions of art copyright by citing litigation over portraits as their illustrative examples of choice.[17]

The crux of the matter was mimesis, or the relation of the copy to its model, a relation of similarity to which some perceived or supposed minimal component of difference is essential in order for imitation to stand clear of duplication. To use the term 'mimesis' is to invoke the concept historically. In humanist theory, it signifies the performance-centred 'emulation' discussed in chapter 2 – that is, both the learning of art as a practice, and the ethical stance of the artist in whom the desire for academic recognition and reputation is repeatedly enacted before peers and the public through exhibition and reproduction – and it also refers to the representation of things and events in the world.[18] Insofar as portraiture was conceptualised in early modern France as the literal imprinting of likeness on a material support, its imitations took the narrowest artistic form of structured resemblance, and not the broader autonomous form of verisimilitude, which creates or composes convincing fictional worlds within the picture. Precision in the definition of portrait-like imitation, far from rationalising its discourse, however, exposed it to contradiction, particularly in cases of portraits where the desire to see the model actualised in the copy, to take it for real, was especially strong. Judgment of the execution of imitation in given instances, whether legal or criminal, was hampered by theoretical reflection, in which the ideal copy comes to life and is indistinguishable from the original in nature. The case of wax effigies, of maximal likeness, cast directly from the body, radically draws attention to the point around which imitation and repetition turn, and to the role of that minimum of difference, that slight gesture of creativity that makes modern, possessive definitions of authorship legally possible. Consequently, the cast portrait will form a bracketing function in what follows, containing the examination of privilege and imitation, as well as marking off the chronological boundaries of the study. Within this framework I set a number of disputes that ended up before the Châtelet or the Tribunaux de police correctionelle (which replaced the Châtelet after the Revolution), and I analyse how the parties pleaded and protested, litigated and lobbied, and how they manipulated artistic discourse on art and imitation in order to achieve the desired legal and commercial outcomes.

GAUCHER *c.* ESNAULT AND RAPILLY

At stake in this case was a medallion portrait print of the critic, man of letters, police spy and anti-*philosophe* Élie-Catherine Fréron (fig. **58**), engraved in 1771 by Charles-Étienne Gaucher after a drawing by Charles-Nicolas Cochin *fils* of 1770. It was pirated five years later by François Hubert (fig. **59**) for the publishers and print dealers Jacques Esnault and Michel Rapilly.[19] Unable to obtain redress in private, and encouraged by fellow engravers who had suffered like ills, Gaucher initiated proceedings against Esnault and Rapilly with a search and seizure of their premises by the police in June 1776.

Esnault and Rapilly originated from Normandy and had started their careers in Paris as street vendors, no doubt peddling the mix of pornography and prohibited works for which the stalls by the Seine were notorious.[20] However, by 1770 they had graduated to the respectability of a shop, À la croix de Lorraine, in the rue Saint-Jacques, and at the time of the lawsuit, they were listed among the print dealers in abbé Le Brun's *Alamanach historique et raisonné des architectes, peintres, sculpteurs, graveurs et cizeleurs*. According to Le Brun, they sold Old and Modern Master prints, 'among the latter many small Portraits'.[21] Le Brun also recorded Gaucher's residence in the street, noting that he too 'engraves small-scale Portraits', prints that Gaucher advertised in the fashionable gazettes of the day, starting in the mid-1760s.[22] Not a member of the Académie in Paris, Gaucher nevertheless promoted his affiliation to the Society of Arts in England and pursued a parallel career as a writer. He was responsible for the 'lives' of over 100 printmakers in the abbé de Fontenay's *Dictionnaire des artistes*, also published in 1776.[23] In short, Gaucher was not only talented but also an educated man, articulate and able to defend himself.

In the case that unfolded at the Châtelet in May and June 1776, the strategy of the defence consisted, initially, in denying that copying had occurred. First, Esnault and Rapilly alleged that they were merely sellers of the Hubert print, which had been lawfully commissioned by a Flemish agent for sale abroad.[24] That argument having failed, they pointed out that Hubert's print differed in essential ways from Gaucher's in size, format and composition. It was smaller, the head faced the other way, the format was oval and not round, and the frame was ornamented with flower garlands not tied with a ribbon.[25]

Gaucher refuted these arguments as specious and argued instead that the allegedly significant differences merely masked a fundamental likeness rendered criminal by the terms of his privilege, which prohibited copies in part as well as in full.[26] In his memorandum for Gaucher, Maître Hecquet, Gaucher's lawyer, implied, indeed, that the defence was endeavouring to exploit the judge's lack of technical expertise, and that anyone familiar with the print trade knew that, in reproduction, images are readily scaled up or down with the help of squaring and the use of a pantograph, and that the printing process necessarily delivers the image in reverse unless a mirror were used to right it. As regards the frame, the prosecution did not acknowledge it as an artistic entity and component of the composition. Rather, aware that the design was standard for Esnault's and Rapilly's portrait prints, Gaucher exposed it as a ruse, the commercial strategy by which Fréron had been smuggled into an ongoing, legitimate and highly successful portrait series, *Suite des hommes illustres*.[27]

The notion that the frame often served to disguise appropriation of its content was strengthened by the case brought simultaneously against the same printsellers by François-Denis Née and Louis-Joseph Masquelier for the piracy of *Le Déjeuné de Ferney* (fig. **55**), a case in which a secondary offence was committed by the replication of the *Déjeuné*'s frame to counterfeit a pendant, *Le Lever du philosophe de Ferney* (fig. **56**).[28] Ironically, the publishers Esnault and Rapilly restored the portrait of Fréron to its original shape when they used the portrait to decorate the background of the *Lever* and to balance Louis Carrogis de Carmontelle's *La Malheureuse Famille Calas*, which hangs above Voltaire's bed in *Le Déjeuné*.[29] Original or copy, the frame was allowed no power potentially to redeem, by its proper originality, the imitation of that which it framed. Indeed, Hecquet denied that a defence could ever be mounted by way of it: 'This frame is only an accessory to the portrait, and I have been told that, following a principle of law, the accessory always yields before the principal: *res accessoria, principali cedit*.'[30]

Having finished cross-examining the visual evidence, Gaucher's lawyer next turned his attention to the sequence of events that led up to the publication of the piracy, reconstructed from the testimony of some of those involved, notably the printmakers Hubert and François Queverdo. Queverdo gave evidence that Esnault and Rapilly had asked him to copy Gaucher's portrait, for which they supplied the necessary impression of the print. He refused. He even claimed to have begged the partners to abandon their illegal venture. Hubert, to whom Esnault and Rapilly applied next, with better success, insisted, however, that he had worked from a drawing, not a print.[31] But when it was pointed out to him that 'the distribution and angle of the incised lines are exactly the same in the original and the copy', he retracted his statement.[32] Intaglio printmaking follows its own traditions and conventions of imitation, ones not usually anticipated by the medium of the original. Thus, for instance, the contract between Gaucher and Charles-Joseph Panckoucke for a portrait of the comte de Vergennes after Jean-Michel Moreau *le jeune* stipulated that it should be executed not in the manner of Moreau's original drawing but in the 'style' of Gaucher's own engraved portrait of Maria Leszczinska.[33] The exact line-for-line equivalence between the Gaucher and the Hubert could not therefore be explained by their respective adherence to a common prototype; Hubert's so-called original was a red herring. It had to have been copied from Gaucher's print simply in order to manufacture evidence for the defence.

Direct reference and indirect allusion to squaring, pantographs, mirrors and tracing paper serve in Hecquet's memoranda to emphasise the appropriative and mechanical aspects of imitation.[34] Such technologies emptied mimesis of all trace of a subjective inscription. So much so, indeed, that not only Hubert, but the entrepreneurs Esnault and Rapilly – the owners, that is, of the means of production – were held accountable for the infringement of the Fréron portrait. It was by their coercive authority that the copy had been made, according to a regime of imitation that was, arguably, itself repressive: slavish copying for a literal likeness. This, in summary, was the case for Gaucher.

Esnault and Rapilly ultimately stopped denying both responsibility for their print of Fréron and its identity as a copy. Instead, they tried to change the terms of the dispute and make it exclusively one about trade, to which only the realities of the market were relevant. To that end they invoked the Edict of Saint Jean-de-Luz (1660) as a regulation of business and not a law on the institution and organisation of an artistic practice – free, that is, not incorporated.[35] The objective of the *arrêt*, they argued, was first and foremost to create a resource of copy-free images for publishers to exploit, and also for young printmakers to copy at will in order to learn the fundaments of their trade.[36] All printmakers, without exception, made copies.[37] Esnault and Rapilly were, they implied, part of the mainstream and not renegades in a moral economy, as Gaucher alleged.[38] Rather, Gaucher and his 'cohort' of 'Artistes' were hypocrites, none more so than Cochin, whose father was, they noted, infamous for having pirated two prints by the great Sébastien Le Clerc for money.[39] Confident on their own ground, Esnault and Rapilly were reluctant to engage with matters of art, and strongly contested Cochin's right to intervene in the affair.[40]

However, Maître Molé, in defence of Esnault and Rapilly, was ultimately drawn into a discussion of the nature of portraiture. To argue that Hubert's copy had not infringed Cochin's portrait, Molé argued that portraiture was like mapmaking, its authority deriving exclusively from the object of representation, accurately and impersonally transcribed upon paper.[41] The analogy was almost certainly formulated opportunistically, pieced together from arguments readily to hand in a lawyer's library, yet it has an unmistakable vividness about it.[42] Not only did the commitment to accuracy transfer easily across these fields of depiction, but the simile further invoked procedural compatibilities between the portraitist and the cartographer, each imagined as surveying the features respectively of face and land, before mapping contours, depressions, elevations, curves and angles in paper patterns of similitude. Both the technologies and the tropes of the copy related to the portrait as an imprint or impression of a sitter's identity and not the expressive trace of the artist's invention.

Up to now, the arguments of the defendants have been to the fore. Esnault and Rapilly were obliged to defend themselves. The plaintiffs were to a greater extent content to rely on the evidence: the original drawing, an endorsed proof and the first state of the original print (the last inscribed 'Avec Privilège du Roi'), and signed witness statements, including written confirmation from Fréron *fils* that Cochin had given his original for reproduction to no one besides Gaucher.[43] To get a fuller and more balanced picture of the issues, I now want to look at the visual evidence in the context of eighteenth-century artistic debates on portraiture.

PARADOXES OF PORTRAITURE

Law and art theory see representation differently, mediated through their own categories of the copy and the real. Each asks its own questions. Law asks where is the boundary between the original and the copy – that is, between nature and representation, and also between reproduction and repetition? Art theory asks: what is the order of the portrait, or rather, what are its imperatives, its rules and internal organisation? Between law and art theory there are significant areas of overlap or transparency, but there are moments, too, of imperfect registration.

Gaucher's print is signed 'Dessiné par Ch. N. Cochin 1770', indicating not only that it reproduced a drawing but that it did so directly. There was no intermediary stage of translation, no mediating hand between the original and the reproduction, as there had been, for instance, in Oudry's illustrations of the *Fables*. 'Dessiné par' or 'delineavit' usually indicated that print was the intended target of the design in question. This was not, however, the case with Cochin's portraits. He started making them in the late 1740s, though it was not until the following decade that he came systematically to develop his talent for them.[44] The small, circular images of profile heads, around 100 mm in diameter, executed with delicate and diligent precision in black chalk and/or graphite, were miniature mementos of friendship (fig. **60**), and condensed records of acquaintance.[45] Although the original portraits of Fréron himself are lost, the survival of a profile of his wife, Marie-Thérèse Guyomar, signed and dated 1757 (fig. **61**), suggests by its date and tender sensitivity a long-standing, quasi-familial relationship between the portraitist and his sitter.[46] It was only in the aftermath of the successful reception of 25 of the drawings at the Salon of 1753, and the encouragement of critics to make them more widely known by print that Cochin began to think of them less as an *honnête* pastime to perform at social gatherings *chez* the *salonnière* Mme Geoffrin and others, and more as a commercial venture for launch on the international print market.[47] But he did not think to obtain a privilege for them, either from the Chancellerie or the Académie.

By virtue of their number, perhaps, and the fact that the majority depicted artists and amateurs, Cochin's drawings were widely noticed by the critics in 1753. Cochin's friend and recent companion in Italy, the abbé Le Blanc, praised them for their 'striking resemblance', a judgment reiterated by another establishment critic and *amateur-honoraire*, the comte de Caylus, who added, for the sake of emphasis, that they had been made 'after nature'.[48] Such opinions aroused no controversy; Étienne La Font de Saint-Yenne, the Académie's bête noire in the late 1740s and 1750s, recognised, likewise, portraits drawn 'au premier trait' that afforded 'the true physiognomy of man'.[49] In the decades that followed, puffs announcing publication of the reproductions took up the refrain: Chardin's likeness was 'happily taken', Charles-Marie de La Condamine's 'very like' and Guillaume-Thomas Raynal's 'perfect'.[50] Assembled in this way, the response, though certainly positive, seems slight, conventional, repetitive, even predictable.

In a brilliant essay on early modern portraiture, Harry Berger, Jr, argues that this 'fiction of objectivity', as he calls it, this illusion of solid reality and unprejudiced transcription, was the peculiar effect of the profile format: predictable in fact.[51] At right-angles to the painter and the viewer, the sitter poses without appearing to do so. He both surrenders himself to the artist's pencil and denies himself control of the viewer's response. Time and movement are arrested. A deathly precision steals over the features of the face with every touch of the artist's tool. Cold waves of sculpted hair scroll over Fréron's ears; his nose and brow rise outcropped on the ridged planes of his face; and his eye and mouth rest in peace. The format works, apparently, as a mould, impressing the likeness with that striking individuality noted by the critics. Esnault and Rapilly had used the analogy of a map not a mould, but a map, as opposed, for example, to a landscape view, also delivers truth by virtue of conventions specifically devised to guarantee the illusion of it. Resemblance, which in individual instances was recognised and appreciated without doubt, raised unsettling questions about its cause and effects – questions touched upon in the Esnault and Rapilly defence but explored more thoroughly with regard to wax sculpture a century earlier.

In the later 1660s – indeed, within two years of each other – André Félibien used wax images to illustrate a sustained and important discussion on the nature of grace in painting, and Antoine Benoît obtained the right to display his wax portraits to the public. It is clear from the way that Félibien introduced his example to the readers of the first of his *Entretiens sur les vies et sur les ouvrages des plus excellens peintres* (1666) that he anticipated their familiarity with wax portraits, very possibly Benoît's, and their approval of the resemblance they found in them. The profile bust of Louis XIV (1704; fig. **62**), the only surviving example of Benoît's work in wax, preserved an uncanny record of Louis's mortal, pock-marked face, and demonstrated the extraordinary lengths of the sculptor's pursuit of 'realism' by its incorporation of human hair to stubble the royal chin.[52] Response to Benoît's effigies in the round, grouped and displayed standing and seated, their life-cast faces bright-blanched, their bodies sumptuously dressed from the wardrobes of the originals, was enthusiastic.[53] To quote one epigram composed in celebration of the so-called Cercle de la reine:

> *Le cercle est-il vivant? On diroit qu'il respire.*
> *Benoît ton art ingénieux*
> *Par un secret nouveau semble animer la cire.*[54]

The 'new secret' of acute life-likeness or animation gave rise, in fact, to instances of substitution and mistaken identity. According to the abbé de Choisy, the widower prince de Guéméné visited the *montage* at Benoît's showroom in the rue des Saints-Pères the day after his second marriage and, overcome with grief at seeing his first wife there, was reduced to platitudes: 'Alas! poor woman! Had she not died, I should never have married again!'[55] Félibien's paradox was a more perfectly like likeness than the one cast directly on the body:

> though these wax images have the same features as the person on whom they have been cast, though the mix of colours is observed with such particular care, and such exact precision that one sees all the nuances of the skin, the veins, the fibres, even the pores, and though great pains have been taken to imitate the brilliancy of that crystalline humour which renders the eyes so bright, yet I have remarked ... that this resemblance surprises the eye rather than persuades the mind, and that it does not constitute a real image of the person it purports to represent.[56]

By 'real' Félibien meant a likeness in which corporeal beauties were united by a 'nœud secret' (a secret knot) to spiritual graces, graces that the process of mask-making could not capture.[57] An undercurrent of horror runs unmistakably beneath Félibien's account of making the mould for the wax. Matter is prepared. It is smeared to cover the features of a motionless subject. As it advances across the sitter's surfaces it 'chases away' and 'repels' the spirit, the inner movements of the soul, which shrink from its touch. It imprints a resemblance 'dead and inert'.[58] Félibien's horror, like Guéméné's anguish, was provoked by a failure to recognise the image as a representation, by blindness to the artist's intervention. Guéméné saw life in one he knew to be dead; Félibien apprehends death in the place of the living. The eye is not so much surprised as shocked, and shocked by sight's imposition, however fleetingly, of error on the mind.

Félibien refused to pass judgment on the makers of portraits and wax masks, though he called the first 'excellent' and admitted to setting at nought the 'science' of the latter.[59] By startling contrast, Benoît's privilege was granted, said the king, in order that he should enjoy the fruits of his 'invention'.[60] Startling not just because Louis and his official historiographer should have come to such diametrically opposed estimations of the value of the wax sculptor's skill, but also because of the definition of that skill as invention. The titles of the works for which protection was specifically sought were duly listed: *Les Cercles de la reine*, *Les Cours d'Europe*, *Les Ambassadeurs de Siam, du Maroque, de l'Algérie*, 'and other extraordinary figures'.[61] They appear generic, which increases the confusion in locating the source of invention. In the individual likenesses? In the secret of the medium used for the cast (a mixture of powdered marble, ground-up eggshell and plaster)?[62] In the idea to cast from life? Or, in the selection and arrangement of the sets – what we might properly call the composition and design?

The instability of privilege is apparent in Robert Nanteuil's abortive attempt, also in the late 1660s, to obtain a monopoly for medallion portrait prints on the scale of life that, according to Pierre-Jean Mariette, he claimed to have invented.[63] Nanteuil was forced to drop his application when Nicolas I Pitau engraved a portrait of Chancelier Séguier after Nicolas de Plattemontagne to the same template, and what Nanteuil had thought his own unique achievement, his proper possession, turned into the *res communis* or the common fund. The distinction between what can be discovered, made, or acquired and transmitted as private property and what is held in common for the use of all (light, air, the sky, the sea, mankind – in short, nature), a distinction between goods and things, of which copyright is one articulation, had yet to be clearly established.[64] In the uncertainty about the scope and rule of *ancien-régime* privilege, artists looked perhaps to take possession of the processes and the conventions of imitation, of a genre (wax portraiture) or format (medallion portraits on the scale of life), with the same assertiveness they expended on the defence of a particular likeness. The advantage in court of deploying definitions of duplication as invention was not, however, fully exploited until the following century. Esnault and Rapilly argued that the possession of a privilege of their own for depictions, present and to come, of *hommes illustres*[65] gave them copyright not only over the portraits they published but also of the 'originals' or subjects these portraits represented, and by logical consequence 'since M. Fréron is an illustrious man, they have a right to engrave his portrait'.[66] In law, likeness seemingly had the potential to make the author an owner of nature.

The boldness with which Esnault and Rapilly tried in 1776 to impose rights assigned to art on life itself suggests the strengthening currency of definitions of portraiture, to which resemblance was not only a necessary but also a sufficient condition. The article on wax in volume three of Diderot and d'Alembert's *Encyclopédie*, published in the same year that Cochin exhibited his first drawings – 1753 – spoke positively of Benoît as a household name, of his 'ingenious invention' of the circles and his 'secret' of imparting 'a kind of life' to his wax effigies.[67] The entry on portraiture in a later volume, published in 1765, identifies 'effigy' as a synonym of 'portrait', alongside 'image' and 'figure': 'An *effigy* takes the place of the thing itself. An *image* represents only an idea. A *figure* exhibits an attitude and draughtsmanship. A *portrait* is only for likeness.'[68] Although the author of the article, the chevalier Louis de Jaucourt, went on to describe the function of the effigy and the portrait differently, the relation of similarity between sign and referent was nevertheless definitional to both: 'In *all* portraits, one cannot say too often, *resemblance is the essential perfection*. Everything that conspires to weaken or disguise it is absurd; thus, all ornament introduced into a portrait to the detriment of the head is inconsistent ... and a mistake.'[69] This certainty of opinion is due, in part at least, to the influence of Roger de Piles, especially his *Cours de peinture par principes* (1708) in which the theorist insisted on painting's unique role as simulacrum: 'The other arts no more than awaken an idea of absent things, while Painting substitutes for them entirely and renders them present by her essence which consists not only in pleasing the eye but in tricking it.'[70] The portraits by the renowned ancient Greek painter Apelles, allegedly so truthful that a spiritualist had been able to cast horoscopes from them, are cited by de Piles as the supreme example of a 'vrai simple', which yields works in which the figures 'seem ... to be able to detach themselves from [the ground of] the picture in order to enter into conversation with those looking at them'.[71]

Echoes of de Piles ring also in Diderot's Salon criticism, notably in his comments on Maurice-Quentin de La Tour's pastel portraits. In 1767, he remarked of the (now lost) portrait of the abbé Gabriel-Charles de Lattaignant, 'it is the man himself thrusting his head through the small black frame'.[72] Gone, however, is de Piles's polite conversationalist, to be replaced by a rude projection, a sitter who obtrudes his presence upon the viewer and interrupts the flow of conversation. Gone, too, is grace as the context for discussing comprehensive likeness. Of La Tour's other portrait at the Salon, the portrait of Pierre Demours (fig. **63**), Diderot remarked, 'hideous figure, beautiful piece of painting'.[73] The paradox is not, however, one of portraiture, but derives from a classical and Renaissance tradition of encomia to absurd or unworthy subjects.[74] It arose because, by the mid-eighteenth century, portraiture had ceased, even notionally, to be the exclusive preserve of the court and those of noble birth – Benoît's royal *cercles* – and had become *bourgeois*. Demours was a celebrated optician, Lattaignant a notorious songster and libertine.[75] Such models had few claims on either painter or public to be regarded with the eyes of love. Their physiognomy was their only distinguishing and substantive trait. Though not peculiar to the portrait, the paradoxical relation of the beautiful and the abject, the high and the low, nevertheless has something important to say about the changing order of portraiture. For Félibien the challenge of likeness had consisted in animating an external reality by an inner truth. Diderot, for whom man was all flesh and blood, his face itself an 'impression' (*empreinte*) or mask of character and class,[76] the problem of portraiture was, by contrast, not one of depth but rather one of surface and time. The problem, as he related famously in *Essai sur la peinture* (1765), is

> that [flesh] comes to life, that it withers, in the blink of an eye; it is that, while the eye of the painter is fixed on the canvas, and his brush is occupied with representing me, I move on; and when he turns round, he no longer finds me. The abbé Le Blanc comes to my mind, and I yawn with boredom. He is followed by the abbé Trublet; my expression becomes ironical. My friend Grimm or my Sophie appears before me; my heart races, and my face is suffused with tenderness and serenity; my joy issues through the pores of my skin, my heart dilates, the little blood capillaries vibrate, and the imperceptible nuance of the fluid that has escaped it [my heart] has flooded incarnation and life on all sides. Fruit, flowers, change under the attentive gaze of La Tour and Bachelier. What torture must not the face of man therefore be to them, that canvas which stirs, moves, stretches, relaxes, flushes, pales according to the infinite vagaries of that light and mobile breath we call the soul![77]

In short, portraiture demanded sight not insight.[78]

This is not to say that in the place of the epistemological uncertainties about the nature and status of the portrait (raised most radically by waxworks) Diderot saw mere technical difficulties, but rather to suggest that those anxieties were displaced in his writing from the relation between the portrait and its referent to the relation between the portrait and its author. He asked, why could history painters make such poor portraitists? Why could an ignorant hack from the Pont Notre-Dame take a better likeness than a professor of the Académie? His answer is equivocal.

It seems deliberately to fall short of resolving the paradox. Thus, while appearing to defend the Académie and a higher truth, his explanation that Academicians were not concerned with the scrupulous imitation of nature but, on the contrary, were committed to 'exaggerating', 'attenuating' and 'correcting' their models according to the many rules of decorum, taste and the antique with which their heads were crammed, rendered that defence of the Academician's liberal status, notionally free from slavery and ignorance, ironic.[79] Moreover, by defining the academic portrait (and Cochin was an Academician) as more than a copy, yet dubbing it a 'caricature en beau', Diderot implied that, in not being very like, such a portrait was in danger of not being very likeable.[80]

Diderot's equivocation may be attributed partly to his admiration of La Tour, an Academician altogether in a different mould from Cochin. Although Diderot insisted of his portraits that resemblance 'is neither their principal, not their only merit', and that 'All the parts of painting are there also', he nevertheless described them in terms of an accuracy of reproduction that breaks every rule of symmetry and proportion.[81] 'In the works of La Tour we see nature herself; it is the system of her in-corrections just as we see them daily.'[82] The logical paradox of La Tour's portraits lay not, however, in an incongruous relation of skill to effect: La Tour was no ignorant dauber. Rather, it was that, while 'his imitation is hot' (lively), 'he is cold'.[83] Death, and by implication coldness, were assigned to wax effigies by Félibien; François Fénelon had imagined a society without artists, in which portraits reflected in golden bowls of water were magically frozen in perpetuity.[84] Coldness was the mark of the perfectly like but authorless portrait. And Diderot may have been prompted to take up the thermal metaphor by La Tour's decision in 1767 to exhibit incognito; his portraits are not listed in the Salon *livret*. However, Diderot reversed the simile, and the chill of similarity is attached to means, not ends, which by virtue of absolute perfection were both like and lively. La Tour's coldness was thus not a matter of temperament but of vocation: the coldness of the autonomous, objective observer committed to maximal imitation.

In contrast to the ambitious Academic insider, either enthused by desire to emulate the great, or tormented by personal genius, the 'modeleur enthousiaste' (evoked at the Salon of 1763 in relation to Falconet),[85] Diderot juxtaposed the simple portraitist: quiescent, unresponsive, unfeeling, a 'marvellous *machiniste*', a 'genius of *technique*'. He elaborated: 'When I say that he is a machinist, it is as I say it of Vaucanson, and not as I would say it of Rubens.'[86] Peter Paul Rubens was, in this context, the author of *grandes machines* ('prodigious compositions'), notably the Medici cycle at the Palais de Luxembourg. Jacques de Vaucanson was a maker of automata: the duck, the drummer boy and, most famously, a faun playing the flute, an automated copy of Antoine Coysevox's statue in the Tuileries.[87] But it was not primarily by their works (though we may note that Jean de La Bruyère had also described Benoît as a maker of marionettes)[88] so much as by the nature of their creativity that the analogy between painting and mechanics held good. Diderot's choice of Rubens to embody his 'modeleur enthousiaste' owes something, no doubt, to a passage from the *Conversations sur la connoissance de la peinture* (1677), in which Roger de Piles had remarked that, because the idea, the 'tout ensemble', of the painting was so strongly present in Rubens's mind, 'he *thought* more about how to make the machine work, than [he] took pains *to polish* the wheels'.[89] Polishing the wheels, in the sense of a 'long', 'unrelenting' study of nature and an attention to detail, was, according to Diderot, precisely the foundation of La Tour's merit, and the wonder of his achievement lay, as with Vaucanson's automata, in its hidden inner machinery: its technique.[90]

But to say that La Tour was a *machiniste* – that is, a machine operator – was also to imply a lack, an emptiness.[91] Sarah Kofman has discussed the riddling resemblance between Diderot's characterisation of La Tour and his description of the actor in *Le Paradoxe du comédien* (1777).[92] Both actor and portraitist made an instrument of the body, converted, in other words, the mechanical impression of the mask or mould into a mechanical gesture of representation. Success demanded negation of the self – in the case of reproduction, a double negation, for the printmaker must be 'Rigaud with Rigaud, Netscher with Netscher',[93] just as before him the portrait painter (Hyacinthe Rigaud, Caspar Netscher, La Tour, Cochin) sacrificed himself to his sitter. So to evacuate the painter of both original idea and proper feeling was, as Diderot was perfectly aware, to sunder the famous Horatian simile, which from the Renaissance had secured painting's liberal status: of La Tour's portraiture he said, 'It is *not* poetry; it is *only* painting' (my emphasis).[94]

The Salons and the *Essai* remained, of course, largely unknown in the eighteenth century, but in 1775 Henri-Louis Jaquet-Droz brought to Paris an android draughtsman (fig. **64**).[95] Set in motion, the young fellow's enamel eyes followed the strokes with which his right hand drew the familiar likeness of Louis XVI in profile (fig. **65**), his left hand holding the paper still, his pale porcelain features fixed in concentration. The task finished, he lifted his hand and blew away the grains of chalk from the surface of the sheet, that he might better admire his handiwork. Marcia Pointon has drawn attention to the positive, aesthetic connotations of this and other Enlightenment automata,[96] yet it is not unreasonable to suppose that, on such spectacular demonstration of the apparently mechanical nature of imitation, of the mimetic accomplishments of mere levers and cams, Esnault and Rapilly could have depended for a sympathetic hearing of their defence.

* * *

According to Rosalie Colie, paradoxy flourishes during periods of intense intellectual activity, when different systems of knowledge and competing ideas about the world come up sharply against one another.[97] However, paradox does not resolve difference; rather, it comments critically on the limitations and rigidity of the conceptual categories with which it is engaged. Why should truth in painting be limited to the copy, or to the effect of matter on matter? Why should a bourgeois subject not make a beautiful painting? Why should rigid correspondences pertain between art and resemblance, feeling and representation? That paradox works to blur distinctions between categories and between values is evident from Diderot's critique of 1767, in which paradox proliferates. He seemingly raised the academic above the real and set La Tour as the standard of excellence. He praised his portraits unreservedly and denied him passion and invention in the matter. He acknowledged himself susceptible to the magic of imitation and no less susceptible to categorising it as mere repetition. In him, both positive and negative discourses on imitation found articulation. But it was the negative discourse, or rather the negative within the positive (the machine-like heart of imitation) that is the most striking.[98] Insofar as imitation, defined in the material terms of Jaquet-Droz's *Le Dessinateur* and Johann Curtius's new generation of automated waxes,[99] enjoyed discursive currency, Gaucher, and Maître Hecquet on his behalf, were under a degree of pressure belied by the balance of evidence and the rule of the law in privilege.

IMITATION, 'VRAISEMBLANCE', FETISHISM

It seems likely that it was left to Cochin, an expert witness at the trial, to argue the case for a different definition of portraiture. Cochin had known and collaborated with Fréron since the 1750s, publishing regularly in the *Année littéraire*, and was perhaps moved to defend the image of his old friend as an expression of active commemoration in the year of the latter's death. Cochin was also on terms of intimacy with Gaucher, having collaborated with him on the illustrations for the engraved edition of *Télémaque* published by Drouet, which in 1775–6 had run into copyright difficulties of its own.[100] Obligation mixed with self-interest prompted Cochin's oratory for the prosecution.[101] We do not know exactly what he said, but his views on portraiture had been aired in two essays published in the *Mercure de France* some 20 years earlier. In *De la diversité des jugements sur la rassemblance des portraits* (1759), Cochin addressed not the nature but the value of likeness. He observed that conflicting interests subtended arguments about the respective merits of truth and beauty in portraiture: those of the sitter and the public on the one hand, and those of artists on the other. 'The public appears to regard the talent of taking a likeness as [portraiture's] principal and virtually its only merit, while artists, by the faint praise with which they damn works that have only that advantage, appear scarcely to award it second place.'[102] Resemblance mattered, Cochin implied, only insofar as it mattered to someone, a point that he later reinforced by describing the expectation of likeness as a 'private interest' (an 'intérêt personnel').[103] To put it another way, the value of likeness in portraiture was relational: a social value not an intrinsic one. Though perfectly conventional, the high premium that the general public set upon likeness stood, he alleged, in explicit opposition to the public priorities pursued by artists on behalf of posterity.

Cochin's essay aimed to expose the public's error and goad it into a different, an enlightened, mode of thinking. He construed the priority of likeness as an over-estimation, an excess, one that occurred in a particular context – in relation, that is, to gender and class. In female portraiture, likeness conventionally played second fiddle to beauty.[104] It was in male portraiture that resemblance commonly constituted the only merit.[105] To be more precise, it was 'les grands' who filled their houses with literal likenesses ('bad pictures'), likenesses that Cochin tellingly scorned as mere 'pieces of heraldry'.[106] By conflating portraits and coats of arms, Cochin pointed to the dependence of imitation as value, on specific institutional systems: on a legally defined society of estates, on legally enforced privilege, on genealogy and laws of heredity. Portraits as coats of arms assumed a status comparable to the ancestral death masks or wax effigies that, according to Pliny, had congregated in the dignity of the Roman atrium,[107] and which, according to Julius von Schlosser, continued to afford European court societies a quasi-juridical inscription of noble identity.[108] In such a context, the value of resemblance lay in its double function: to replicate *and* to differentiate.[109] It particularised the social essence of the sitter, locating identity in the body and in the blood. It individualised likeness, and secured deference, respect, even admiration – that is, actual social benefits for the sitter. Even briefly to unpack Cochin's slighting analogy is therefore to identify characteristics in the *ancien-régime* portrait – its parade of particular attributes, the homology of prestige between bodies and objects, the social value of likeness – which anthropologists identify with the discourse on the fetish.[110] Moreover, the fixation with likeness, of which Cochin accused sitters and the general public alike, suggests a kind of psychical investment in material objects (portraits) with which the psychoanalytic discourse on fetishism is especially concerned.

Cochin did not, of course, use the terms 'fetish' or 'fetishism', which were first coined by Charles de Brosses in 1757 in his *Du culte des dieux fétiches*. Nor did he especially emphasise the materiality of the 'realist' portrait, an abiding truth of the fetish.[111] However, support for the argument that the concept of fetishism may have informed contemporary discourse on the cult of likeness in portraiture is to hand in the famous exchange of letters between Julie and Saint-Preux in Rousseau's epistolary novel *Julie, ou La Nouvelle Héloïse* (1761). Julie describes the portrait she is to send her lover as 'a sort of amulet', a 'talisman', and she anticipates that this embodiment of herself will have tangible effects: contemplation of it will penetrate and infuse the lover's flesh and blood with tenderness; application of it to his eyes, mouth and heart will serve as a prophylactic against lovers' woes; possession of it will establish an 'electric' circuit for communication of the press (*impression*) of the faithful lover's kiss across more than one hundred leagues' distance.[112] Julie's hope is initially fulfilled: Saint-Preux is literally charmed by this 'unexpected object' (the materiality of the sign is emphasised by both donor and recipient), and he bears the erotic brunt of what Bernard Vouilloux has summarised as the portrait's empathetic, sympathetic and telepathic powers.[113] These powers or virtues and their ability to fix and gratify Saint-Preux's desire are, however, exactly proportionate to the portrait's likeness, to its ability to duplicate Julie's presence.[114] But the initial oscillation of Saint-Preux's belief in its being her, and yet not being her, gradually gives way to the disenchanted knowledge of its status as fiction not fetish.[115] The only possibility of reinstating the portrait's original charm lies in the retrenchment of artistic conventions (the flowers in the hair, the dress, the *décolletage*) and the reinstatement of the 'real' (the nearly imperceptible stain on the skin under her right eye, the one on the left side of her neck, the small scar beneath the lip, the slight irregularity to the shape of the jaw);[116] the fetish portrait is logically a natural sign, a reflection.

The fetishisation of likeness has two important consequences for the matters in hand, consequences that Cochin endeavoured to reverse. The first concerns the authority of the author and the second the autonomy of art.

A fetish cannot properly be said to have an author, only an owner, user or worshipper. Of the painter of the portrait of Julie we learn only that he was 'a miniaturist on his way back from Italy'.[117] Described positively as an 'artist', a 'skilful man', and less so as an insensitive *homme de bronze*,[118] he is never named. Moreover, he was never an author, first because the several versions of the portrait he painted are ordered in the text not according to *his* life and activity – according, that is, to some notion of the original[119] – but in relation to their resemblance to *her*, the sitter; and second because Saint-Preux's prime version was not fixed by the artist's signature but was further improved in likeness by a second anonymous hand at Saint-Preux's direction.[120]

The Saint-Preux *pentimenti* primarily involved the revision or addition of lines, because for Rousseau it was drawing, and not colour, that served the practice and constituted the force of imitation. In the *Essai sur l'origine des langues*, written in the 1750s, Rousseau argued that 'The interest and seductiveness of the picture does not stem from the colours.[121] We will still be moved by the outline [*les traits*] of a painting that has been reduced to a print, but if we remove the outline the colours will lose their power.'[122] His critique of the use of colour in Julie's portrait thus included lamentation over the omission of 'ramifying violet lineaments' under the skin at her temples and the overflow of the blush of her cheeks beyond the contours appointed by her face.[123]

Rousseau's refusal of the independent, sensuous life of the signifier is precisely that which Cochin affirmed in his essay. He noted that the portraits of Titian, Tintoretto, Van Dyck, Rembrandt, Philippe de Champaigne and Rigaud were admired in the absence of all knowledge of their likeness.

> It is the great art of painting that has consecrated their worth, and not the advantage ... of having more or less successfully flattered the pride of those who commissioned them; it is *the beauty and the preciousness of the colours* that give portraits their greater or lesser value, and affords them a place in celebrated collectors' cabinets [my emphasis].[124]

In the struggle between the portraitist and the sitter, Cochin insisted that, for the sake of art, loss of authority and identity can be the fate only of the latter. Colour refers not just to a dimension of painting but serves Cochin as a figure for art, for its autonomy, its separate and superior epistemic regime, in implicit rhetorical contrast to the degraded and commonplace values of sitter, likeness and, by implication, line. Colour also stands for the status of the artist, insofar as Cochin argued that a linear likeness was not only within the scope of the most ignorant painter but underneath the skilled artist's work: his *ébauche* or preliminary sketch.[125] 'It is the desire for a more perfect execution which, leading to the acquisition of discrimination and refinement, requires a softening of exaggerated though striking features in order that a learned likeness [*rassemblance savante*] may be achieved.'[126] Cochin's portraitist is an author because he augments (the root of the noun and the verb is the same), because he moves beyond the primitive outline of resemblance to embellish his model. (In the absence of the original we can no more than speculate on the subtle amelioration that Cochin may have brought to Fréron's countenance: refinement to a bulbous nose perhaps, elevation to a subsiding brow?) The ideal likeness would find its ideal viewer in the 'knowledgeable man', or connoisseur;[127] by contrast, *resemblance grossière*, which we can translate as 'primitive likeness', had constituted a kind of primitive religion for those, like the grandee, obsessed by the genealogical features of aristocratic visual identity, or the lover, perversely fixated by details, the divine lineaments (in Saint-Preux's case, blemishes, scars) of the beloved.[128]

Cochin experienced none of Diderot's later equivocation before these two, seemingly distinct, orders of the portrait. On the contrary, in an early satire he used the device of time travel mordantly to narrate the disjunction between a culture in thrall to the false objective values of likeness and the society of the enlightened satirist by whose critique fetishism is exposed. Monsieur Findfault, a citizen of the future, embarks on a study of portraits for evidence of the manners and dress of the 'ancient French'.[129] He assumes that he is dealing with a familiar world, one in which a perfectly indexical relation exists between the sign and its referent. The joke turns on recognitions, which are in fact misrecognitions. Mythological and allegorical portraits, read literally, afford easy targets for ridicule; it is the relatively uncoded details of the 'realist' Baroque portrait, those that afford little semantic information beyond their literal denotation, that are truly 'scandalous'.[130] Seduced by the rich stuffs in the portraits of Hyacinthe Rigaud, for example, by the velvets of all colours, and the gold and silver embroidery, Monsieur Findfault commends, as 'a fashion favourable to painting', the wearing of large sashes of material across the arms and around the shoulders, and recognises as opulent a society in which men of letters and artists are conspicuously rich (fig. **66**).[131] Convinced, likewise, by the contrapposto poses, he concludes that an eighteenth-century man rarely walked facing forward. Rather, he sketched an elegant arabesque by the perpetual twist of his body to look over his left shoulder.[132] Refusing to allow the descriptive to remain at the level of a natural, tacit understanding,

Cochin, via the absurdly innocent eye of Monsieur Findfault, exposed likeness as artificial, constructed, a matter of convention; not true, merely *vraisemblable*. When the contract of mutual recognition between the painter and the viewer breaks down, portraits commended for their truthfulness no longer make sense.

By defamiliarising the conventions of likeness in the satire and by challenging its intrinsic worth in the essay, Cochin rendered contemporary attachment to resemblance problematic, construing it as a fixation on an irrationally invested object. The conditions of this critique require explanation. According to William Peitz, the 'problem-idea' of the fetish arose, and could only have arisen, in association with the emergent articulation of the ideology of the commodity form.[133] Thus he argues that in seventeenth- and eighteenth-century Europe the mysterious valuation of objects in non-capitalist societies, labelled fetishism, provided the terms against which commodity value defined itself rationally.[134] If the *term* had developed in the cross-cultural situation to which trade between Dutch merchants and African tribes of the gold and slave coasts had given rise, the *idea* surely also drew substance from the confrontation of feudal and commercial systems of value within early modern society itself. Portraiture had traditionally stood outside the exchange economy.[135] That is to say, portraits, post-manufacture, belonged not to the market but to the ethical domains of honour and friendship; they were a means of maintaining personal relationships between individuals, groups and generations, and they were transferred by inheritance or gift.[136] In *Julie, ou La Nouvelle Héloïse*, Julie gives portraits of herself not only to Saint-Preux, but also to her mother and to her cousin Claire.[137] Likewise, Cochin had taken likenesses at Mme Geoffrin's only, apparently, to give them back to the habitués of her famous *lundi* gatherings.[138] Meanwhile, in the probate inventories of the period, family portraits are rarely valued as goods but rather are itemised as heirlooms, 'for the record' (*pour mémoire*).[139] Moreover, the several testimonies of the academician Hendrik van Hulst and the publisher Jean Mariette indicate that, even in the context of the print market, love and prestige primarily motivated the decision to reproduce the portraits of a Rigaud, a Largillière and a de Troy in the first half of the eighteenth century.[140]

However, Cochin touches, in his essay, on two circumstances that were to disrupt this cult of likeness profoundly: the inauguration of public art exhibitions and the advent of celebrity. In 1688, La Bruyère had sketched Benoît's character as that of an *arriviste*, a painter upstart, made rich and newly noble by the commercial success of his regular shows of waxworks.[141] Although the official Salons at the Louvre did not transform the economic conditions of portraiture along the same lines, since the exhibitions were free and the portraits exhibited not generally for sale, the Salons' expansion of the audience for portraiture significantly beyond the sitter's circle of acquaintance – beyond, that is, those for whom likeness constituted an indispensable utility – did, nevertheless, revolutionise the reception of portraits. The exhibition viewer's attention and judgment were solicited on grounds extra to those of 'primitive' imitation.[142] Likewise, but by a dislocation of time rather than place, posterity would – indeed, could – value portraits of the illustrious and the celebrated, only on the basis of their aesthetic appeal, of their general 'fund of resemblance', you could say, rather than by the exact correspondence of a literal likeness, which it was in no position to judge.[143] Portraits under these conditions were increasingly compared for likeness with other portraits – that is, in terms of a reduction to the common, abstract constituents of the labour of imitation. In other words, Cochin's essay implies that portraits at an exhibition were 'consumed' primarily in the commodity form and not in the process of use.

Although Cochin had nothing explicitly to say on this point, the conditions under which portraits were made in the later eighteenth century, as well as those under which they were seen, changed significantly. Portraits, especially portrait prints, were increasingly produced for exchange before ultimate consumption; undertaken, that is, as commercial speculations.[144] They were commissioned not only by sitters, but with mounting frequency by merchants who, like Esnault and Rapilly, gambled on making sizeable profits from the likenesses of those known to the market only by reputation. Likeness might be secured by the simple expedient of appending a printed name to the printed face. The odds of success were shortened, that is to say, not by the quality of likeness, the fitness to function, but by the volume of exchange and the size of profit margins. To return to Cochin one last time, it is worth noting that phonetically *fond* (a fund of knowledge) is indistinguishable from *fonds* (an exploitable asset). Therefore, when Cochin attributed to great artists a 'fond de rassemblance fine' (though likeness in their portraits might be wanting), the possibility arises, textually at least, that resemblance, likeness, imitation, call it what you will, constituted the 'capital' or social value by which portraits were, in fact, produced as commodities, becoming, to use Marx's phrase, 'citizens of the world'.[145]

Under Cochin's pen, resemblance was put both on the market and into the hands of the artist. It was the artist's inscription, rather than a property derived from the sitter. Notwithstanding the vigour and radical acuity with which Cochin argued his case, the proposition he advanced – that in portraiture likeness 'is not essential ... indeed, thinking only of the future, one may say it is the least essential'[146] – was unavoidably paradoxical. However, for Cochin and the Académie it was paradoxical in appearance only because, to follow the *Encyclopédie*'s definition, though the statement was 'contrary to received opinion', it was nevertheless 'fundamentally true'.[147] Jaucourt, the author of the *Encyclopédie*'s definition of 'paradox', cited as an example of it Copernicus' hypothesis of a solar system which, in the context of the prevailing view of astronomy in the sixteenth century, had appeared absurd to the general public *and* convincing to the scholarly community. Gradually, over time, such hypotheses lose their paradoxical raiment and become orthodoxy.

GAUCHER *c.* ESNAULT AND RAPILLY: AFTERMATH

Had such a revolution in the theory of portraiture occurred by 1776? Gaucher certainly won his case. On 29 October, Esnault and Rapilly were found guilty of *contrefaçon*, fined 50 *livres*, charged costs of 326 *livres* 9 *sous* 6 *deniers*, required also to pay for 300 public announcements of the judgment to be posted in the capital and, finally, ordered to surrender the copper plate and the remaining impressions of the pirated Fréron.[148] It is, however, far from certain that victory was achieved by Cochin's oratory. Dealers from the provinces who muscled in on the trade in the rue Saint-Jacques were deeply resented, and privilege law may have provided locals with one means of curtailing their trade.[149] Additionally, the support of the comte d'Angiviller, Directeur des bâtiments du roi[150] and a director of the Académie, must have weighed heavily in Gaucher's favour.[151]

When a similar dispute arose some ten years later between the printmakers Augustin de Saint-Aubin and Nicolas de Launay, both Academicians, over a portrait of Jacques Necker after Joseph-Siffred Duplessis, the engravers, as befitted their status, settled matters *à l'aimable*. Saint-Aubin limited his outrage to repudiating de Launay's piracy before a meeting of the Académie and in the newspapers.[152] Advertising his 1784 print (fig. **67**) anew in September 1788, a mere month after Louis XVI's minister of finance had been triumphantly returned to office,[153] Saint-Aubin begged the editor of the *Journal de Paris* to alert the public that, 'this Portrait, the only one to be reproduced after the original Painting, should not be confused with another recently put on sale ... This last is but a copy traced from his [Saint-Aubin's] print, altered only by simplification of the frame.'[154] De Launay's copy (fig. **68**), undertaken in such a hurry to be topical that the matter of reversing the details of the dress (the buttons and buttonholes) alongside those of the body was forgotten, had been advertised the week before at roughly half the price of Saint-Aubin's print.[155]

Did Saint-Aubin avoid acting against de Launay because, given universal praise of Duplessis's portrait for its 'perfect' likeness,[156] he anticipated difficulty in arguing the case for portraiture as difference not copy? Whatever his reasoning, he evidently decided that a better course of action against such pirates – a more effective response, that is, to free competition – lay in the re-production and upgrading of his portrait print in colour by Antoine-Louis-François Sergent (fig. **69**), in order to establish, by a fuller resemblance between copy and original, a greater difference between his and the various other copies on the market.[157] Esnault and Rapilly were not so daunted. Within three years of their conviction they were back in court, but this time as appellants, against the printmaker and *marchand mercier* Paul-André Basset, whom they accused of infringing a copyright of theirs by his piracy of a set of heads modelling hairstyles, and a portrait by Claude-Louis Desrais, etched by Nicolas Dupin, of the coronation of Voltaire entitled *Habillement de Voltaire* (fig. **70**).[158] Indeed, Basset supposed that those 'hard and hot-headed' pirates had cynically secured the tested services of Gaucher's and Née and Masquelier's lawyer in the hope of better results this time.[159]

Although Basset was wrong in his supposition, Maître Molé, Esnault and Rapilly's actual lawyer, was certainly familiar with the arguments used in court at the earlier trial, and drew significantly on matters of art to build their case, an indication of the importance of case law in the 1770s in litigation about print piracy. The disputes were not, however, otherwise related, for Esnault and Rapilly *c.* Basset concerned fashion plates, the so-called *Gallerie des modes et costumes français* (1778–87), for which Esnault and Rapilly had obtained a privilege in August 1778.[160] The question of imitation in the narrow sense of portraiture did not, therefore, present itself, though a portrait was involved.

However, broader issues of portrayal were addressed, both in its definitional artistic sense of animation, or life-liveliness (as opposed to still life), and in its social conventions: can fashion really form a gallery,[161] equivalent – that is – to Rubens's famous Medici gallery at the Luxembourg, for example? Moreover, Basset, in his counterattack on Esnault and Rapilly, used the conceit of a portrait gallery to undermine the credibility of his opponents: he invited his readers to visit Esnault and Rapilly's shop-gallery and gave them a guided tour of pirated portraits of the abbé Terray, the prince de Condé, the duc and duchesse de Bourbon, copied after prints by Pierre-Adrien Le Beau, and the copies of Gaucher's Fréron and Louis XVI.

The tour ended with the pirated portraits of Voltaire, Beaumarchais and Linguet, copied after Augustin de Saint-Aubin.[162]

Satire aside, Basset's defence, which he fought on many fronts, set aside the central jurisprudential question of the Gaucher case: can one copyright a copy? Instead, he asked can fashion be an object of privilege? The question implied that fashion's triviality, and its emphemerality, the profile pose of many of the heads notwithstanding (fig. **71**), disqualified it, in principle, from the law's protection.[163] In relation to the particulars of the charges against him, he asked, additionally, can a copy be simultaneously 'degraded' and 'servile'? By implication, does not incompetence in fact constitute a difference, a kind of originality? He no doubt hoped by sustained derision of his own work, especially the hair-dressed heads, to allay the threat they presented in the eyes of the law. However, his line of defence has an importance beyond the tactical: it indicates the difficulty of evacuating privilege of the social and aesthetic values attached to the word, of abstracting the legal concept.

With regard to the *Habillement de Voltaire*, Basset disputed whether it could be properly classed as a fashion plate and thus fall under the remit of Esnault and Rapilly's privilege. Raising questions of genre drew the attention of the court to the artistic conventions by which imitation creates its effects. In exact reversal of the arguments about wax sculpture, about the dead hand of portraiture, Basset argued that Esnault and Rapilly's *Gallerie* offended by the likeness, animation and action of the figures, which exceeded what was proper in a representation concerned with hair and dress, with inanimate stuffs and defined as fashion.[164] In this case mannequins, not models or sitters, were appropriate and sufficient to the appointed task.[165]

Basset was responding to the case made for Esnault and Rapilly in which Me Molé dressed up their practice in terms of art. He drew, almost certainly, on the text of the *Gallerie des modes*, in which Esnault and Rapilly described their project as portraiture and explained how it had graduated over time from hairstyles to genre and portraits, drawn from life by 'Artists' and hand-coloured. They called the plates 'Tableaux'.[166] The organic development, or artistic incoherence, of the gallery, which had allowed Basset to question Voltaire's inclusion, Me Molé justified by reference to both trade and law. Esnault and Rapilly as authors were in complete possession of their work, free to include in their gallery whom they chose, and the consumer was equally free to buy their goods or not.[167] Esnault and Rapilly had no obligations, no social relations to determine their choice. They were, that is to say, producers of commodities, which privilege protected in all its forms.

Esnault and Rapilly won. The engravers and printsellers Jacques-François Chéreau and Pierre-François Basan had been appointed to review the works and had judged copying to have taken place.[168] The court was, moreover, apparently unconvinced by arguments about genre, arguments not only about the hierarchy of figure and fashion but also about the coherence of sets. Basset had not only argued that Voltaire at his coronation did not belong to *la mode* because the portrait and action exceeded the plate's function, he also alleged that the *philosophe*'s reputation was compromised by the *galanterie* that otherwise defined Esnault and Rapilly's particular discourse on fashion (fig. **72**).[169] The court resisted Basset's invitation to find the *Gallerie des modes* in breach of censorship law by offence of pornography; moreover, its ruling upheld as privileged images bound together by non-sensuous similarities of fashion, sex and celebrity – that is to say, it defended the emergent exchange value of the commodity-portrait.

CRIMES OF LIKENESS: 1793 AND BEYOND

Although commercial monopolies established by privilege were consistently upheld at the Châtelet during the *ancien régime*, insecurity about the autonomy of portraiture, about its originality, persisted – hence the conspicuous measure of defensiveness in the legislation proposed by Basan, Gaucher and

Ponce to replace the system of privileges swept aside with the suppression of the guilds in 1791 (discussed in chapter 5). In the memorandum they addressed to the Assemblée nationale in that year, Basan used portraiture, as traditionally the most transparent form of representation, to illustrate their claims that all acts of depiction, whether original or reproductive, were essentially and individually creative and therefore worthy of legal protection from theft.[170]

However, when in 1793 the Convention passed the first national copyright act, its jurisdiction fell short of the degree of inclusiveness for which Basan and the others had lobbied. The arguments concerning the portraits of Fréron and Voltaire notwithstanding, the piecemeal and sometimes conflicting *arrêts* that enforced the system of privileges during the *ancien régime* had made little or no reference to entitlements (as against terms) of privilege. The Literary and Artistic Property Act of 19 July 1793, on the other hand, specifically addressed genius: 'productions of genius', men 'of genius', 'rights of genius'.[171] Genius, in this context, distinguishes works (*œuvres*) from mere working, authors from makers, and liberty from constraint, thereby constituting the aesthetic as an autonomous domain in law. Article 1 of the Act identifies as included in the category of genius 'painters' and 'draughtsmen', their 'paintings' and their 'drawings' without further qualification of genre or pictorial mode; however, according to Watelet and Levesque's *Dictionnaire des arts de peinture, sculpture et gravure* (1788–91) – the beaux-arts section of the *Encyclopédie méthodique* (1782–1832) and a landmark of art theory in the Revolutionary period – between genius and imitation there was opposition not analogy.[172] Conventional eighteenth-century wisdom assigned to genius the attributes of liberty, vigour and novelty, attributes that Watelet rejected and for which he substituted expression, invention and originality; but both formulations explicitly or implicitly precluded from their realm the objective and servile transcription of nature.[173] The Revolutionary rights of genius were, therefore, not ones to which Esnault and Rapilly could, in principle, have laid claim in the context of the direct and successful manner in which they purchased, exploited and defended their royal privileges: first because, as Basset had been quick to point out, they were dealers with commercial interests but no authorial claims[174] – at best, they would have been cessionaries to the rights of others – and second because portraiture as imitation belonged not to the universal and natural authority of genius but rather to the learned and particular 'talent' of the specialist.[175] A case might have been made after 1793 for the genius of fashion in the *Gallerie des modes et costumes français* but not, apparently, for the originality of likeness in the *Suite des hommes illustres*.

No case of copyright fraud involving portraiture was, in fact, pursued in the 1790s and early 1800s, though portraiture flourished and piracy along with it.[176] Does this suggest an overturning of idealist theories of portraiture, and resurgence after the Revolution of the idea of the portrait as perfect copy? Levesque's definition of portraiture for the *Encyclopédie méthodique* suggests not. Although the entry starts conventionally enough, with the talent of the portraitist summarised as that of 'faithfully rendering a characteristic likeness, such that it may be recognised as the person whose features have been the object of the exercise', it swiftly becomes apparent that by 'faithful rendition' Levesque did not mean the extreme care and meticulous detail found in many modern portraits.[177] He seconded Félibien's rejection of the life mask's absolute imitation, and endorsed the latter's claim that the *idea* of the face, if intelligently grasped and artistically conveyed on canvas, will produce 'a more lively, striking and expressive resemblance than the likeness that would result from a [life] cast'.[178] Moreover, Levesque surpassed Cochin in audacity when he argued, in a sequence of logical steps, not only that imitation was unnecessary in portraiture but that invention was essential. Step one: 'In Art everything is idea, everything is magic.' Thus, step two: art 'introduces falsehood into its most accurate representations of truth', portraiture included. Given that portraiture is, therefore, a lie, step three follows: 'it will never be better perpetrated than by the artist who, having practised the genre of history, is familiar with the greatest lies of Art'.[179] This conclusion, coming at the end of an accumulating force of argument, cuts the last binding threads of likeness and seemingly sets the portrait free. Levesque makes no mention of genius as such, but his emphasis on idea and expression at the expense of likeness, and his identification of excellence in portraiture with the work of Raphael, Titian, Holbein, Dürer, Tintoretto, Veronese and Van Dyck, all of them history painters, tends to indicate that both the faculty of genius and various of its incarnations were indispensable to his definition of 'portrait' as belonging to an autonomous sphere of art.

Levesque was acutely conscious that his was not the view that prevailed in practice. Portraiture had long constituted a specialisation, and it was on the commercially expedient move towards specialisation during the *ancien régime* that he laid the blame for portraiture's degeneration from a mode of history to a branch of still life.[180] Changes wrought by the Revolution served, arguably, to reinforce politically these 'ancient' divisions between portraiture as an artistic ideal and as a social practice. The virtual collapse of private patronage at the upper end of the portrait market, and the widespread revulsion for academic forms of portraiture in oil (the grand, formal portrait, the mythological portrait, the portrait allegory),[181] saw other genres of portraiture – notably, graphic genres, to which the rhetoric of literal likeness was central – emerge from secondary and largely derivative or reproductive status and gain significantly in independence and prestige.[182] Meanwhile, the same public thirst for transparency, the same obsession for reading the new society through bodies that gave rise to the various, and ultimately unfulfilled, projects for republican dress,[183] fuelled the market for portraits, especially portrait prints. To give some significant examples: in 1789–90 at least two collections of portraits of deputies of the new Assemblée nationale were published by Nicolas-François Levachez and by Dejabin; between 1793 and 1802 François Bonneville produced four volumes of *Portraits de personnages célèbres de la Révolution*; and in 1798 Jean-Daniel Auber decided to expand the scope of the celebrated series *Tableaux historiques de la Révolution française* with 60 portrait medallions of those who had left their mark on the Revolution, 'soit en bien, soit en mal'.[184]

'For good or ill' assigns to portraiture the function of a tribunal at which judgment is passed on those who come before it for record. In such circumstances, portraits are required to be not merely like but true. They should abandon the courtly artistic conventions of *ut pictura poesis*, which relies on the internal and self-referential rules of art and illusion, and connect with the outer world of representation. According to the *Moniteur universel*, in the portraits proposed for the *Tableaux historiques* 'analogy' would reign between the appearance of the face, 'perfectly like', and the facts of the life, or, to put it differently, an indexical relation would be seen to yoke the physical and social features (*traits*) of the elected subject.[185] The portrait image thus took its place alongside verbal portraits published in the periodical press and in popular pamphlets which, from 1789, vigorously pursued their self-appointed task of affirming or denouncing those in public office by the sustained clear-sightedness of their physiognomic observations.[186] 'The National Assembly unveiled', for instance, appeared naked to readers eager to see the 'portrait of deputies at the Estates General as they reveal themselves there'.[187] The substitution by political discourse of notions of truth and falsehood for ideas of the real and the ideal in portraiture raised the stakes in the debate on likeness, and rendered highly problematic the positive (and legally defensible) construction of the art of portraiture as a lie, an invention.

Daniel Arasse argues that death is the condition of truth in possibly the most extreme form of Revolutionary portraiture, the *portrait guillotiné*:[188] death of the sitter and of the author. The last look on the face of the sitter was charged with the presumption of complete honesty: there was no room for disguise, no time for equivocation, no hope of postponement, no distance between the self and the judgment that lies beyond the grave. This was, in a literal sense, the moment of truth. The infamous portrait of Louis XVI guillotined (fig. **73**) reproduces that moment in word and image: above, the executioner's hand thrusts aloft the guileless head, the neck cut and bloody; below, Robespierre gives us to remember that on 'Monday 21 January 1793 at a quarter past ten in the morning, at the place de la Révolution, formerly [place] Louis XV, the Tyrant fell under the axe of the law.' The profile's 'fiction of objectivity',[189] is redoubled, in truth, by the narrative of the pose, of its absolute finality: no time. Closed to the creative deceits of the sitter, the portrait, by the fiction of its medium, also denied room to the interventions of the artist. Arasse, and more recently Antoine de Baecque, have noted the coincidence, at the end of the eighteenth century, of the desire for transparency in the political sphere and for mechanical means of reproduction in art.[190] The portrait of Louis XVI's severed head combines etching and aquatint. Although aquatint was generally associated with the reproduction of artists' drawings,[191] in this case it seems rather to imitate another medium and connote another genre: the silhouette. The sharp contrast of the darkly shaded profile against the blank, white ground, delimited not framed, invokes the mechanical tracing of the line of the profile around an edge of shadow cast on a screen by the light of a candle. Silhouettes enjoyed something of a vogue in the later eighteenth century.[192] More importantly, they were valued for their accuracy. In his pseudo-scientific reading of identity, known as physiognomy, Johann Kaspar Lavater attributed to the silhouette accuracy far greater than that of any other portrait form.[193] In the *Physiognomische Fragmente*, translated into French in 1781, he accounted for the fidelity of silhouettes by the 'immediacy' of the reproduction, because in them the distance between the projection and reproduction of likeness was reduced to a minimum.[194] It seems reasonable, therefore, to think that the registration of the silhouette's visual codes and the reproduction of some of its effects in Louis XVI guillotined served to substitute for the signature of the artist the anonymity and objectivity of its apparatus. The fitness of the portrait to its Revolutionary function apparently left no hope for the proprietorial interests of the author.

The portrait of Louis XVI guillotined is a single, extreme example. However, it played a powerful role in the political imaginary of the Revolution. In the changed circumstances post-Thermidor, Ewa Lajer-Burcharth has noted ways in which Jacques-Louis David's medallion portraits of fallen Montagnards (fig. **74**) in turn incorporated the Terror as a condition of their truth: the holes and gaps of the dress and the unconventionally low *découpage* of the busts, for example, enforce attention to cutting as such. Moreover, the reinforcing of profiles with a hard line in pen and ink articulated, very possibly, the exaggerations and the crudeness, associated with forms of reproduction believed to be mechanical.[195] What light does this shed on matters of copyright? To return, for a moment, to Robespierre's account of the execution of Louis XVI, he alleged that the king's death 'destroyed royal superstition and created the Republic'. By analogy we might say that the truth, and not (*pace* Cochin and Levesque) the art, of Revolutionary likeness destroyed the fetish portrait of the *ancien régime* and created a new order of the real. It is an irony that realism became an important issue in art and in law at the very moment when the possibility of representing the real was dramatically brought into question. Critical to confidence in the new 'real' was knowledge of the conditions of its realisation. It is a paradox that inquiry into the origin of true likeness occurred in order to establish the absence of the author.

MALO *c.* PLANAT AND CHÂTILLON

If the first copyright cases involving portraits did not arise until after the Restoration, matters of imitation and execution nevertheless bore materially on their resolution. In 1828, the editor and printseller Malo proceeded against Joseph Planat and Jérôme Châtillon, artist and dealer respectively, for the alleged piracy of a portrait by Henri Grévedon of Ida Saint-Elme, better known as La Contemporaine (figs **75**, **76**).[196]

Saint-Elme had apparently commissioned the likeness and it was initially she who disseminated impressions of it. During the Empire she had attained a degree of celebrity, both for her participation in Napoleon's military campaigns and for her conquests in bed – a celebrity that, in her fifties, she sought to sustain through representation. In 1827, the famous publishing house of Camille Ladvocat published the first volume of her memoirs.[197] There was doubt, however, about the flesh and blood reality of the heroine, not least because *mémoires de fantaisie* was a conspicuously successful genre of the period.[198] Upon Grévedon's *ad vivum* portrait, therefore, rested the burden of proof in the truth of the sitter; not the truth about her – difficult to plumb in view of her habit of passing as a man – but the simple truth of her existence in the world. Impressions of the portrait were eagerly sought; it was now that Malo acquired the lithographic stone and started exploiting the portrait commercially.[199] But within days, Planat's rival print appeared on the market to threaten Malo's profits.

Malo's case against Planat and Châtillon rested first and foremost on the exact correspondence of the facial features in the two lithographs, established beyond doubt with the help of tracing paper, and second on the verbatim transcription of the accompanying legend, a quotation from the memoirs. Malo initially won his case,[200] but within months the defendants launched a successful appeal. Central to their case was the argument that 'accuracy in portraiture cannot constitute a breach of copyright' – in other words, that two things may be identical by virtue of their likeness to a third: the sitter.[201]

Maître Moret, acting for Planat and Châtillon, questioned, indeed, the very possibility of copyright in likeness. He noted in support that portraits of generals Suchet, Gouvion-Saint-Cyr, Macdonald, Foy and Kléber had been widely copied without complaint, and, moreover, that portraits had been excerpted, so to speak, from the battle paintings of baron Gros, François Gérard, Horace Vernet, etc., without the authors feeling entitled to redress. Only history painting and caricature were, according to Moret, sufficiently inventive to warrant the title 'original' and thus the protection of the law.[202] With respect specifically to La Contemporaine, he reiterated that it was 'no more than a copy of which the person represented is the original, and invention alone establishes property'.[203] Moreover, he reasoned slyly that Malo, by seeking to protect Grévedon's copy of Saint-Elme as original, was presumably not suggesting that the artist had invented La Contemporaine. He thereby challenged the plaintiff to make the argument for invention in portraiture, in the certain knowledge that in this case any such proposition could undermine the identity of the sitter and, by extension, the commercial value of the print. By some of the same logic, Moret also refuted Malo's allegation concerning the legend. Saint-Elme's words were, he maintained, as much a constituent of her self as her face, and the line, 'without having laid claim to strength of mind or feelings inappropriate to my sex, I was a witness over 23 years to the triumphs of Valmy and the defeat of Waterloo', belonged to her, to her image as an 'amazone', no less than 'È si pur muove' does to Galileo.[204] In quoting the words that appeared at the head of each of the eight volumes of her memoirs, both prints no more than copied an original: in this, too, they were equally imitations.[205]

Arguments about the portrait as copy and as public property, which had not ultimately convinced at the Châtelet under Louis XVI, proved surprisingly persuasive 50 years later at the Cour royale de Paris under Louis XVIII, though not without the support of an additional line of reasoning that reversed a different 'ancient' legal principle. Moret's assertion that 'accuracy in portraiture cannot constitute a breach of copyright' was qualified by 'unless the accessories are of sufficient importance that *they* form the composition'.[206] He argued in defiance of the principle *res accessoria principali cedit*, which had protected Gaucher, that the different ways Grévedon and Planat had chosen to frame the likeness of the sitter – Grévedon in the exotic, twisted folds of a turban, Planat in the everyday bonnet of a Parisienne – constituted an essential difference sustainable in law.

By such an argument, Moret undermined the unity and hierarchy of the Renaissance portrait: he divided it into separate domains – the face and the accessories or framing context – and set the latter above the former as the site of invention.[207] His defence required, in effect, the law's recognition of signs of genius in the frame, whose expanded and expanding empire, brought on by specialisation, had been diagnosed by Levesque as the symptom of portraiture's wretched degeneration.[208] Levesque argued that, in pursuit of the novel, modern portraits prioritised the stuffs and ornaments that accompanied the sitter and had demoted the head to the status of accessory.[209] Planat's defence thus required a rational absurdity of the law: that copyright range its forces on the side of the *parergon*, the subsidiary – that which philosophically the subject should not become.

Invention came to the aid of imitation by bringing *à bord* (to use Jacques Derrida's familiar phrase) that which had formerly been *hors d'œuvre* – that is, by incorporating accessories, ornamentation and detail into legally defined (though not aesthetically sanctioned) likeness.[210] The appeal court accordingly found that the *fidelity* of the faces to nature and the *difference* of the ornaments in the representations together indicated that infringement had not occurred. However, in the process of splicing contradictory lines of argument about imitation and invention, the meaning of one of the terms, 'imitation', was modified significantly.

In relation to likeness proper, 'imitation' had initially meant an unmediated, exact copy; thereafter, it assumed, with respect to the comparative analysis of the compositions as a whole, the significance of a mode of representation. Moret argued that Planat had used his 'talent' simply to record the 'history' of La Contemporaine's features, while 'the poet' Grévedon had composed the 'fiction' of her face. That is to say that imitation, or the exact representation of nature, was made synonymous with a plain, vernacular visual language and the portrayal of the appearance of the everyday. To illustrate his point beyond details of dress, Moret observed that Grévedon had depicted Saint-Elme with teeth, individually visible between her pursed, rosy lips; by contrast, Planat had reproduced the exact appearance of Saint-Elme's false ones: a division-less length of ivory, with which she had been pleased to fill her mouth for the occasion.[211] Planat's rejection of the intended illusion of teeth revealed his imitation as no less rhetorical a stance – that of the unvarnished truth – than Grévedon's beautiful 'lies'. As such, his copy bore the marks, however minor, of an author's mediation: it was, in fact, an invention. Moreover, as its author, Planat was potentially the bearer of rights in law.

Throughout the case, the discussion of the techniques of imitation was confined to a dispute about whether Planat's portrait had been executed *ad vivum*, a dispute resolved at last by Grévedon, who acknowledged – having been induced to give evidence for the defence – that there had, in fact, been 'no tracing, no copying, no reducing, no counterfeiting, no plagiarism'.[212] He thereby confirmed, indirectly, that Planat must have attended Saint-Elme to sketch her likeness freehand. Six years later, a case came to court in which, however, the processes of perfect – that is, mechanical – imitation were central to the issue of copyright.

ANTOMMARCHI *c.* MASSIMINO

In 1834 the case of Napoleon's death mask (fig. **77**) served to test whether 'The author of the cast of a figure, living or dead, has the right of criminal prosecution, granted by the law of 1793 and articles 425 and 426 of the penal code, against him who reproduces, by countercasting the figure that he has himself cast.'[213] By asking a question about casting rather than about a specific copy, imitation was construed as a process, not an object. Moreover, perhaps because it is easier to establish unequivocally facts about the (practical) means than about the (perceptual) effects of imitation, this case resolved the remaining ambiguity of likeness before the law, marked an absolute distinction between authors and mechanics, and established a firm epistemological foundation for portraiture as invention. However, the case was not won without difficulty and regret.

Maître Janvier presented the case for the prosecution conventionally, focusing on the image, its meaning and the motivation that prompted its realisation. Francesco Antommarchi, the appellant, and the emperor's last physician, had, with considerable difficulty, brought back to France from Saint Helena Napoleon's death mask, and, wishing to give copies to members of the emperor's close circle, had had duplicates cast by Massimino.[214] Before long, however, he became aware of rival casts circulating on the market and, although Massimino had fled abroad, Antommarchi nevertheless decided to take action against him and his accomplices, the dealers Mmes Micheli and Hébert.

From the outset Me Janvier emphasised the value of the likeness, insisting on the seriousness of the breach in view of the 'cult' dedicated to Napoleon's memory. Moreover, he argued that the mask enjoyed exceptional status, in relation not only to the nation but also to its 'author'. Napoleon had apparently left 100,000 *francs* to Antommarchi in his will and an annuity of 6,000 *francs*, legacies that never materialised, leaving the doctor to return from Saint Helena with only two things 'which he preserved in a certain sense as relics': his own memoirs, 'in which he describes, day by day, Napoleon's agony', and the mask.[215]

The pairing of the mask and the memoirs served, on the one hand, to emphasise the historically located and authentic character of the mask by the account of the circumstances surrounding its making,[216] and on the other, to invoke the Horatian simile of poetry and painting as a means of imparting the liberal status of a work of the intellect, or of genius, which indisputably belonged to the text, also to the mask. Analogy yoked the fate of two things – two forms of representation – and buried the dissimilarity in the practices that brought them forth. The question of Antommarchi's commercial interests and methods having thus been disguised, Me Janvier concluded by stressing the disinterestedness of his client in the whole affair.

In truth, the historical record differs considerably from the manner in which Antommarchi remembered events and Janvier recounted them. The initiative and the effort of taking the likeness had belonged rather to Francis Burton, the British physician who attended Napoleon, and whom Antommarchi apparently assisted reluctantly.[217] Difficulties in obtaining matter suitable for the casting (gypsum) had had to be overcome before the separate impressions of the face and head could be taken. Shortly thereafter Antommarchi absconded from Napoleon's residence, Longwood, with the stricken face in his luggage. If Burton was ultimately unsuccessful in obtaining the safe return of his property, the legal measures he put in hand had the effect, at least, of rendering Antommarchi circumspect in his diffusion of the mask until after Burton's death in 1828. The coast clear and France ready, after the Revolution of 1830, to acknowledge its imperial past, Antommarchi launched a subscription for the head in July–August 1833, a subscription for which Luigi Calamatta's engraving (fig. **78**), published a year later, served as an eloquent *hors d'œuvre*.[218]

Calamatta's engraving anticipated Me Janvier's rhetoric, even possibly helped to shape it, by representing the mask according to the conventions of portraiture and not still life. Napoleon, erect, obscurely animate, poses for the viewer, eyes closed. The ragged physical boundaries of the likeness are carefully disguised, naturalised: a laurel wreath crowns the outer limit of the head, ears are implied besides, and a sash of the Légion d'honneur wraps the severed neck like a collar. Moreover, so convincing is the fiction of the pose that we attribute to the face a skin with the marmoreal qualities of pallor and stilly coldness; that is, we read the real, the physical, properties of the cast, metaphorically. Finally, the elaborate *trompe l'œil* frame completes the illusion of the portrait. It both raises the status of the cast via its use of conventions reserved for the presentation of works art and it elaborates the presence of the 'sitter' by allusion to the character and duration of his life: the meteoric rise, the imperial rule of Jove, the birth under Leo and the death under Taurus.

Those who were led by such eloquence to subscribe acquired a head in plaster or in bronze, similarly marked by the artistic ambition for likeness.[219] Death masks were often framed or mounted like sculpture;[220] moreover, the bronze casts of Napoleon's head were signed from left to right by the 'author' and the founders in the manner conventional to reproductive prints. One edition of Napoleon's mask was, like Calamatta's print, embellished with a laurel wreath.[221] All incorporated, at the rise of the neck, a medal of Napoleon, a portrait within a portrait. The two effigies were no doubt intended to be read in terms of one another, the medal serving as a kind of hallmark, a gold standard, for the mask, and the mask providing a larger context of likeness, a measure of authenticity, for the medal.[222] Though not conceived with copyright specifically in mind – that is, as defences against the possibility of fraud – the inscriptions and accessories nevertheless made claims for the mask as the outcome of a productive, and not merely a reproductive, imagination.

Maître Sudre, acting for the defence, denied, however, the relevance of the mask's eloquence of likeness. He broke with precedent and avoided both philosophical speculation on the nature of the copy and utilitarian debate about the social value of portraiture. He made his rejoinder not with a critique of imitation understood as a relation between two created things (one natural, one artificial) but with a refutation of casting as a process of creative simulation.[223] Casting, he argued, with the support of expert testimony from members of the Institut de France, notably the sculptors François-Joseph Bosio and James Pradier, was a 'purely manual operation', requiring neither intellect nor genius: 'the least able [*ingénieux*] workman…, the humblest apprentice, can make one [a cast] with the greatest perfection'.[224] Benoît's wax 'inventions' and the powerfully armed privilege that had protected them were forgotten. Sudre's question, 'And what has Dr Antommarchi done?' was conspicuously rhetorical:

clearly, nothing. There could be no genius involved in taking 'by means of plaster, or other comparable material, the cast of the great man's features... He [Antommarchi] is not the author of those features that lend the plaster all its value; in reproducing them, he has no more than plagiarised Nature and Death.'[225]

Inserted into an argument about genius, death was stripped of the complexity it enjoyed in the context of Revolutionary likeness. It served no moral function here, neither as a condition of the sitter's truth, nor as a metaphor for the artist's objectivity. It assigned the image no superior value of resemblance. It simply described a particular state of nature. Sudre was concerned with agency not image. He argued that, in this case, nature, in the guise of death, was the agent. He was careful, however, not to call nature an author because, although her creations have, arguably, the appearance of the very greatest works of art, nature is not a subject in law, and is not endowed with property rights; on the contrary, she is the object of them. Massimino, Micheli and Hébert were innocent according to Sudre, because there was no case to answer.

The court agreed. Bosquillon de Fontenay's ruling repeated Sudre's plea almost verbatim. In the absence of genius, he found Massimino's trade perfectly within the law. The sentence of three months in gaol and 50 *francs* in fines that he handed down to the cast-maker was just penalty for Massimino's appropriation of Antommarchi's signature and not his reproduction of Napoleon's face.

However, summing up the facts of the case prior to judgment, Louis-Napoléon Geoffroy-Château acknowledged the difficulty of estimating the evidential value of the mask. He remarked: 'It is impossible not to be moved by the sight of this terrible and sublime exhibit; when one contemplates this figure where, before plaster, Death had, so to speak, petrified suffering; when one sees those eyes closed and swollen, those brows depressed in pain, those sunken cheeks, that deformed mouth, still half-opened by the last sigh exhaled; when one thinks that *this* was Napoleon, and that between the image submitted for your appreciation and justice, and the dead head of the emperor, there is no other intermediary than plaster, subtle in action, which moulded itself to the features of this great man at Saint Helena in order to reproduce later these images of his agony and death.'[226]

The language Geoffroy-Château brought to bear on the cast bespeaks an almost irresistible subjective response to its sensuous materiality, as if it were indeed a work of terrible and sublime genius. In the speech, the features come to life in a coherent expression of death. Moreover, the fragmentary relic is said to capture a pregnant moment, to invoke the suffering of the whole body before, as well as at, the historic scene of Napoleon's end. At the appointed time, the emperor, a notoriously reluctant sitter,[227] seemingly left a lasting, petrified and petrifying impression of himself which the tribunal was specifically invited not only to register as evidence but to 'appreciate'. The magical power of likeness was poised, it seems, to project genius as the source of its origin. However, what distinguishes Geoffroy-Château's response from that of a fetishist is its self-consciousness, announced by the double negative 'it is impossible not to be moved', and the awareness throughout that the account proceeds 'as if'.[228] Reason and knowledge establish boundaries around illusion and belief. Judgment against Antommarchi marked, additionally, a successful effort to establish the discriminate, informed and rational nature of aesthetic and legal categories.

* * *

The copyright act of 1793 and the cases involving portraits tried in relation to it in 1828 and 1834 resolved some of the long-standing difficulties raised in law by the notion of imitation. From the complex array of arguments about the Grévedon and Planat portraits of Ida Saint-Elme, their parts and their visual codes, emerged the idea of the original copy, the copy that, by virtue of having been made by human hand after nature, or some other object in the public domain,[229] necessarily constituted an invention, a work requiring a minimum input of intellect and genius. The winning comic stroke of the false teeth determined that the original was, in the wake of Grévedon and Planat, always located in the representation, always artificial. The gathering autonomy of the sphere of the fine arts was reinforced by the failure of Antommarchi's case. The positive valuation that accrued to the mechanical and the machine-like in theories of portraiture that prioritised truth evaporated in an aesthetic and legal context that recognised genius and invention as alone definitive. Moreover, the rapid expansion of actual and commercially viable duplicating machines in the early nineteenth century (for example, the pointing machine, photography) stripped the man/machine analogy further of the virtues it had possessed when nature's works had been technically beyond compare.[230] The status of cast likeness was irredeemable for lack of its potential to fabricate, to give more than itself. The discursive consequence of the first case was the relabelling of imitation as invention; the result of the second was the reorientation of debate about the right to copyrights around the idea of the author. The spiriting away of imitation as an issue in copyright brought a stabilisation of the legal category of the portrait: as an invention, it denotes itself, it is utterly self-regarding and thus is secure from loss of identity in its referent. Moreover, as an invention it invokes not merely an agent but an author; it asks the question who made it? It presupposes rights in the non-mechanical reproduction.

The germ of these arguments was present in disputes about portraits and privilege before the Revolution, but it was not until after the passing of the Literary and Artistic Property Act in 1793 that the question of what legally constituted a work of representational art was raised and directly contested in court. I have argued that the successful extension of copy-privilege to likeness was coincident with, in fact dependent upon, changes in the production and reception of portraits at the end of the eighteenth century. If the Act of 1793 had its foundation in the bourgeois economy, the terms of its rhetoric disguised that commercial interest. The reasons for Sudre's condemnation of casting as non-fabricated fabrication were twofold: that the activity was mechanical, and that it was mercenary. Antommarchi, he insisted, was motivated by profit.[231] Genius, by implicit contrast, is creative not only *by* nature but *like* nature.[232] A gift at birth, genius enables the artist to create unaided, unprompted and without end. Derrida, in his reading of Immanuel Kant's *Critique of Judgment* (*Critik der Urtheilskraft*, 1790) describes such theories of pure productivity, of unexchangeable production, as immaculate and poetic. In the light of Marx's critique of the commodity, the poetry of commerce is, however, unmasked as fetishism. Paradoxically, the disavowal of the commodity status of the work of genius is precisely what confirms its appearance and enables its defence in law.

INVENTION:
THE SECRETS OF COLOUR

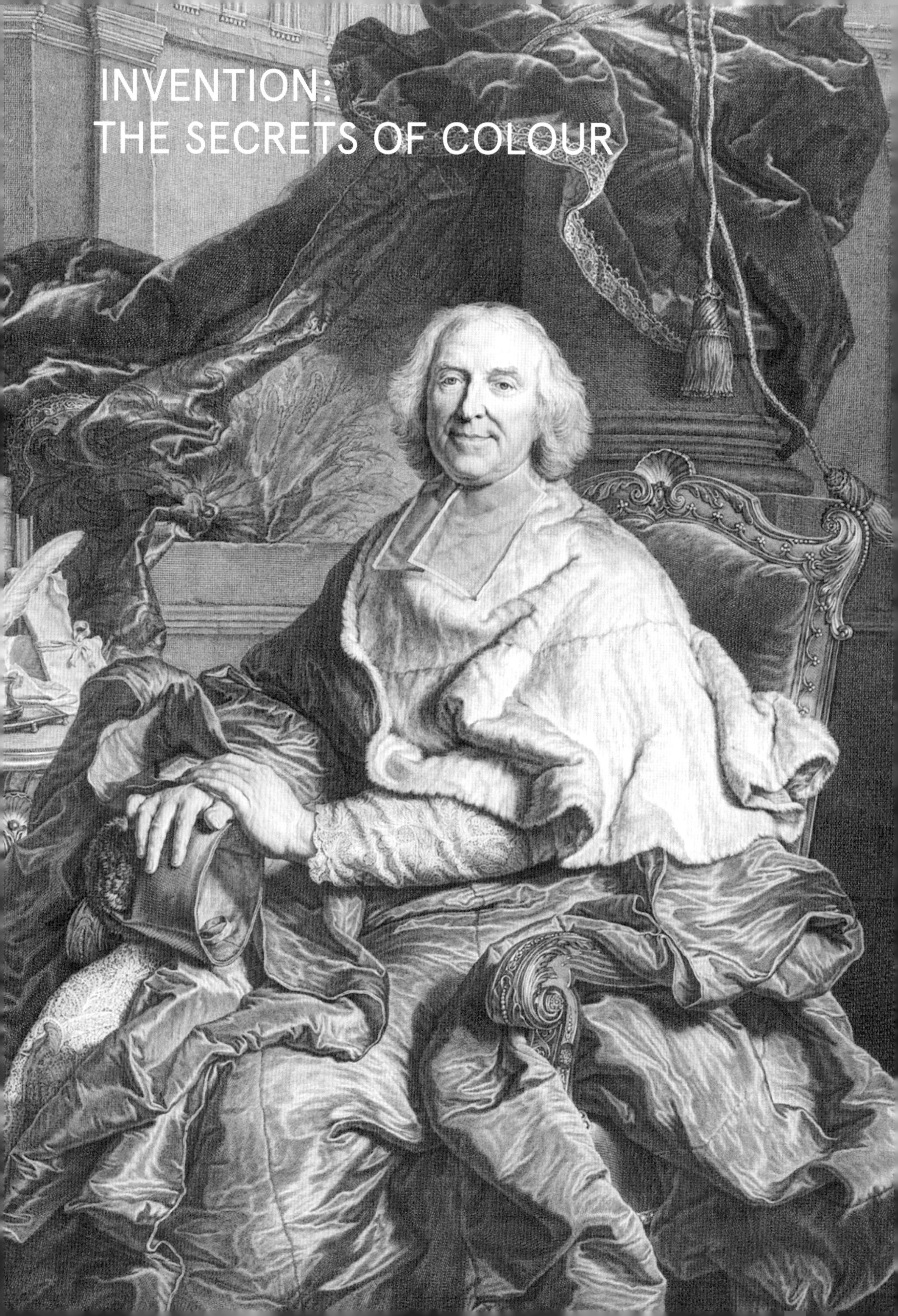

In his defence of the inventive portrait, Charles-Nicolas Cochin *fils* argued that to colour belongs the credit of painting's superior worth and, more importantly in the context of this chapter, that colour is the index of the artist's status and his title to a name.[1] In this chapter we shall be primarily concerned with the artist – in the broadest sense and not only the Academician – and the claims that he or she can make to the status of author in law. We shall explore those claims via the contested authorial rights to colour printing in the first half of the eighteenth century. Arguments set aside at the end of chapter 2 to make way for the investigation, in chapter 3, of the fraught legal nature of the work of art – if copy, how original? – are taken up again, but in the form of first-person claims to unique acts of individual creativity, rather than third-person denouncements of plagiarism and *contrefaçon*. More particularly, the chapter is concerned with the exclusivity of the relationship between the artist and his or her work, captured by the concept of invention in art, science and law. It was invention, according to Roger de Piles, writing at the beginning of the century, that provided opportunities for the artist 'to show' himself.[2] Of course, even for a committed colourist like de Piles, artistic invention was primarily a matter of composition, of new ways of envisioning old stories.[3] Invention in science was something different. Foucault argues that modern science's regime of truth logically precludes (I simplify) authorship based on invention.[4] However, in the *Encyclopédie*, whose self-appointed task it was to record invention's myriad manifestations in both the arts and sciences,[5] invention was construed in conspicuously individualistic ways.[6] The chevalier Louis de Jaucourt peppered his entry with proper names: Thales of Miletus, Alessandro della Spina, Johannes Gutenberg, Flavio Gioja, Julien Leroy,[7] etc. He noted, moreover, that the first eulogies – that most personal form of literary tribute – were written in praise of inventors.[8]

Jaucourt's definition of invention does not, however, acknowledge it as a principle of privilege, and his inventors are not authors in law. No *renvois*, or cross-references, send readers of the *Encyclopédie* from 'invention' to 'privilège exclusif' or from 'privilège exclusif' to 'invention'. Yet, before the 1762 'royal declaration on privileges granted to inventors', a high proportion of those awarded privileges for discoveries were also entrepreneurs; indeed, such celebrated inventors as Blaise Pascale were known to have profited substantially from their inventions.[9] One aim of this chapter is to re-establish the relations edited out by Jaucourt in the case of the science and technologies of art. Links will be made where none are explicitly stated, the qualifications in parentheses that the editors of the *Encyclopédie* used to distinguish between the different domains of invention and privilege will be disregarded, and we shall endeavour to reconnect law and economy, art and science, and technology and rhetoric.[10] Attention will focus on invention's use as a trope in eighteenth-century eulogy and publicity, and on its tendency to exaggerate the subject's claims to originality. Invention is, we shall see, always, as a concept, potentially excessive.[11]

COLOUR PRINTS, COLOUR PRINTING AND PRIVILEGES

The invention, in this case, was the invention of colour printing. Antony Griffiths estimates that roughly 50 per cent of the middle and bottom end of the print market was for coloured prints, a demand met almost entirely by hand-colouring executed by watercolourists working for print publishers and printsellers.[12] The title of Esnault and Rapilly's *Gallerie des modes*, discussed in chapter 3, announced that the plates were 'coloured with the greatest care by Madame Le Beau', the wife of an engraver.[13] Fashion plates were just one of the genres for which a colour finish was regarded as highly desirable; others were maps, botanical illustrations and, later in the century, *vues d'optique* (perspective views). Colour doubled the retail value of prints and accelerated trade. It is therefore not surprising that printmakers and print publishers were on the lookout for a method to print colour directly, and that those who believed they had invented one should have sought to protect it.

In November 1737 Louis XV granted Jacob Christoph Le Blon a 20-year monopoly for his 'secret of reproducing Paintings in print using three plates', giving as his reasons for doing so Le Blon's advanced age, the importance of 'the art he possesses', and the artist's willingness 'to communicate his secret in order that, when he is no longer able to work, use may be made of it'.[14] Le Blon was not the first to have applied for such a monopoly. A century earlier, in January 1637, Abraham Bosse and Charles de La Font successfully obtained a privilege for five years for 'the art of copper printing on paper, parchment, leather and all kinds of fabric ... in colour', an art that, their privilege notes, 'up until now' was 'unknown, though sought by several persons of wit and invention'.[15] There are a number of significant differences between the privileges obtained for this colour technology. First, the 1637 monopoly was for five years, not the 20 of Le Blon's 1737 privilege, which may suggest increasing awareness of the commercial possibilities of colour printing.[16] Charles-François de Cisternay Du Fay, a chemist at the Jardin royal des plantes and dye consultant at the Gobelins, was appointed to head the committee of experts reviewing Le Blon's invention – a significant choice.[17] The terms of Bosse's claims to privilege were also significantly weaker than Le Blon's: Bosse claimed to have developed '*an* art' of colour printing, one implicitly among others. Le Blon's privilege speaks, by contrast, of '*the* secret' (my emphasis), albeit one he was willing, in the right circumstances, to disclose. The use of the definite article and the substitution of a contents for a means, strengthened the claim that Le Blon was able to make.

Histories of technology generally associate secrecy with the closed culture and tacit knowledge of the early modern guilds, craft organisations and practices swept aside by the new 'openness' of seventeenth-century science. In the eighteenth century, what Joel Mokyr has called the Industrial Enlightenment helped to raise openness to the level of government policy, which in turn prioritised access to 'useful knowledge' in the regulation of trade and industry.[18] But the discourse on secrecy did not disappear. On the contrary, it remained a powerful language with which to articulate proprietory-like claims: by withholding its contents, the secret redirects attention towards the person in whom it is embodied. Individuals step forward as more important than arguments, a phenomenon that is reflected in this chapter by the part played by the 'lives' of the inventors concerned: first Le Blon and thereafter Jacques-Fabien Gautier[19] and Jean Robert.

The privileges for colour printing issued to Le Blon and to Bosse and de La Font were granted on the recommendation of different authorities, according to different terms and conditions, and on the basis of different assumptions and priorities. Bosse and de La Font purchased their privilege from the Chancellerie; Le Blon, on the other hand, owed his to the Bureau du commerce (Board of Trade), one of a number of institutions, including the Académie royale des sciences and the Maison du roi, responsible for directing and administering privileges in industry, the forerunners of modern patents.[20] Moreover, Le Blon's monopoly came free of charge. Such royal largesse was justified on the grounds of utility: colour printing extended to the sciences the promise of enhanced detail in scientific representation, and to the textile industries new, potentially cheaper, methods of production.[21] Bosse's art, by contrast, had been promoted by its author as a source merely of pleasure, of 'grâces' satisfying to the eye – that is, as adornment to the paper necessities of social life: 'Almanacs, *thèses*, posters, New Year cards, screens, fans, and all figurative images, both devotional and other.'[22] Bosse's initiative was construed, in short, as an ornament or supplement, an artistic effect, and was attributed a pseudo-existence as form. In granting it a privilege, the king prohibited (intentionally or otherwise) all imitations of such bodies of printed colour; to spell it out, he proscribed all works 'similar to' Bosse's, directly or indirectly 'approaching the manner of' his work, and all imitations 'notwithstanding every disguise'. In short, the privilege erected a prohibition on colour printing so general that, in principle, it ruled out altogether the work of others, whether achieved by use of woodblocks or copper plates, whether at the hands of relief or intaglio printmakers, or painters or illuminators.[23] Such a universal monopoly was not repeated. Le Blon's privilege referred not to colour per se but to the process by which it was made manifest: printing 'à trois planches'.

Le Blon's privilege concerned, then, the 'made-ness' of his images. Conflicts that arose over rights to colour in printmaking could not, therefore, be judged on the basis of the visual evidence, the prints alone (as would have been the case with Bosse and de La Font). It required investigation of the manner of execution, processes not always visible to the naked eye. Imitation in both the realist and idealist traditions tended, by force of literary analogy, to deny facture.[24] It did so by rendering functionally invisible the physical dimension of both the support and the colour raised upon it – its substance as pigment.[25] Privileges like Le Blon's apparently reversed this order of priority. By paying attention to the other side of the ontological 'cut' between the work of art as representation and as material object, it made the image disappear, and brought into focus (in this case) the triple or (disavowed) quadruple layers of colour and tone caught between the rough of the paper and the gloss of the finish.[26] The law's rule of facture, of the doing, making and materials of invention via patent privileges, thus advanced a technical definition of the arts that, by not denying – indeed, by acknowledging and supporting – the connection between painters, printers, dyers and other kinds of commercial colour men, seems to undermine the boundaries of exclusivity that the Académie royale de peinture et de sculpture (intentionally) and the system of copy-privileges (unintentionally) was working simultaneously to erect around art defined as a liberal profession.[27]

While this chapter seeks to draw out the contrasts between the liberal and the technical and between the different regimes of privilege to which they gave rise, it also recognises the contradictions inherent in the very notion of invention: at one level a collection of discrete local narratives about the creation of 'new' pigments, dyes and techniques, at another a meta-narrative about the power of art to imitate not only the appearance of nature but, more audaciously, her very processes, as occasioned, for example, by alchemy.[28] To cast the contradiction of high and low differently and in terms of the artist, Joseph Koerner has noted that, in art, *factura* is at once gross matter and inspired, painterly trace. It is the place, in fact, where the connoisseur most certainly and rapturously expects to locate the subject in the object.[29] It is therefore important to ask, in addition to what kind of art object is the technical novelty, what kind of artistic subject, what kind of author, is to be found in invention as material practice?

To answer these and other questions, the chapter begins with a brief retelling of Le Blon's life, his talent and his search for profitable conditions of business for his invention. Then follows a broader investigation of invention in seventeenth- and eighteenth-century art theory, and of several prints via which Le Blon sought to articulate his position and the status of his new colour technology. Diderot remarked in a letter to Sophie Volland that conversation resembles colour in its seemingly directionless flow and its pooling of freely associated ideas.[30] To reverse the analogy, colour in these contextual settings is a little like conversation: it prompts a sometimes roundabout and digressive discussion. Discussion becomes pointed again with the disputes over the cession of the privilege after Le Blon's death in 1741. I sketch Jacques Gautier's early career in outline before considering the operations and values of secrecy in the context of art. The final act is assigned to the bitter dispute between Gautier and Jean Robert in the late 1740s and 1750s over the proper attribution of the 'real' secret of the technology, and opens out into a wider consideration of the way in which these disputes contributed to the transformation of early modern definitions of the artist by virtue of uncanny skills, skills that resist rationalisation and of which he or she could not be completely dispossessed.

LE BLON

Jacob Christoph Le Blon was born in Frankfurt to a family long and closely associated with the book trade, printmaking and science.[31] After a period of study in Rome, he was persuaded by the Dutchman Bonaventura van Overbeek to settle in Amsterdam, where in 1705 he is mentioned in the city records as a miniature-painter. He became especially interested in colour and started experimenting with colour mixes and colour printing, his progress noted and discussed in the correspondence between the collector Lambert ten Kate and the painter and engraver Hendrik van Limborch.[32] Le Blon's trials seem to have focused particularly on the translucency and opacity of pigments and on the effects that could be achieved by superimposing different colours. His 'discovery' consisted not, as he later implied, in isolating a minimum number of primary or 'primitive' colours from which all others might be mixed – this having become relatively common studio knowledge by the end of the seventeenth century[33] – but in applying his learning of primary and compound colours to printmaking, specifically to painting's graphic analogue, mezzotint.

Mezzotint, unlike engraving or etching, is a tonal process.[34] As such it offers the possibility of colour mixing by over-printing flat areas of colour in such a manner that from layered primaries complex secondary colours – oranges, purples and greens – emerge. For every colour print, three copper plates are therefore required. Each must be 'grounded', or systematically roughened with a spiked tool called a rocker, to create a soft, even and close velvety grain.[35] Each must be worked or 'scraped' using a burnisher to smooth in the design according to its content of red, yellow and blue. The plates must then be carefully inked and wiped, taking particular care with the hollowed highlights; and, finally, each is rapidly printed in reverse order of importance (blue, yellow, red), each one over the last while the inks remain sufficiently wet to mix and blend.[36]

Severally, none of the procedures was novel. Mezzotint had flourished in the hands of Northern printmakers since the mid-seventeenth century, reaching France by the end of the century, and the use of multiple printing surfaces and coloured ink was older and just as familiar.[37] The invention lay, paradoxically, in harnessing *manière noire* (mezzotint) to the cause of colour[38] and in the creation of a palette via the mixture and not the adjacency of pigments transferred from copper plates onto moist paper. Le Blon spent a decade, or the best part of it, developing and perfecting the adaptation of these processes.

In 1716, Le Blon set off in search of a patent. He travelled first to The Hague and then to Paris before arriving, still empty-handed, in Britain.[39] His efforts were finally rewarded by George I, who granted Le Blon two patents, the first, in February 1719, for colour printing, the second, in June 1727, for colour weaving.[40] The facts appear to speak for themselves but there was, actually, nothing self-explanatory about this sequence of events. Before 1750, patenting in the Netherlands, France and Britain was not the usual or established presumption of the inventor.[41] In Britain patents were time-consuming and costly to obtain, and, once secured, additionally expensive and protracted to defend. Moreover, judging specifically by the low annual uptake of patents in Britain in the early 1700s, it seems obvious that the kinds of industrial and economic policies that make strategic use of patents had yet fully to develop. In the last decades of the seventeenth century, and in the unstable climate of the Revocation of the Edict of Nantes (1685), there had, to be sure, been some attempt to use patent as an incentive to encourage the inward migration of Huguenot craftsmen, but the boom in patenting in the early 1690s was, as Christine Macleod has shown, almost entirely speculative; a by-product of surplus liquidity, or risk capital, on the financial markets.[42]

Why, then, did Le Blon seek out a patent in 1718? Notwithstanding the disillusionment occasioned by the aggressive stock-jobbing of invention in the 1690s, patent remained an important means of raising capital. Le Blon's Picture Office, as he named his enterprise, was capital intensive, requiring at least three times the investment of an ordinary printshop by virtue, first, of the threefold multiplication of pigments, plates and labour in the production of each printed image,[43] and, second, because of the ambitious size of the plates planned, which aimed at the facsimile reproduction of Roman and Bolognese paintings. The colour printing patent granted in 1719 enabled Le Blon successfully to sell shares in his invention and set production in motion.[44] Moreover, as an instrument of publicity, this first patent served to promote turnover by its promise of novelty (genuine or assumed),[45] and by its legal guarantee of exclusivity. The early advertisements of Le Blon's prints in the *London Gazette* and *Daily Courant* highlighted 'His Majesty's Letters Patent' for this very purpose.[46]

However, despite Le Blon's energetic campaigns for patents, neither the printing venture at the Picture Office, nor the later weaving project at the Chelsea looms was a success. Bankrupt and fleeing creditors, Le Blon moved to Paris in late 1735 or early 1736 and once more set about obtaining preferential terms of business. His route was smoothed by the enthusiastic advance reports of his invention in London published by the French press from the early 1720s, and by his own foresight in having sent a copy of his treatise on colour, *L'Harmonie du coloris dans la peinture; réduite en pratique mécanique et à des règles sures et faciles* (n.d. [1725]), to Louis de Boullogne, director of the Académie royale de peinture et de sculpture, where it was read at one of the Académie's assemblies.[47]

In 1719, at the very date when Le Blon first won favour in Britain, France, under the financial and economic direction of John Law, was attempting a transfer of British technology on a grandiose and unprecedented scale. John Harris has estimated that some 120 watchmakers, locksmiths, glassblowers and metalworkers and their families – that is, in excess of 200 individuals – were brought over to France in a single concerted campaign and established in protected manufacturing enclaves in and around Paris.[48] Although the viability of so aggressive an industrial policy was undermined in short order by defensive measures taken by Britain, and by the collapse of John Law's 'Système' and the discrediting of his economic policies, French officials continued throughout the 1720s and 1730s to see privileges as opportunities for speculation, and, covetous of developments across the Channel, to welcome with open arms such British know-how as it made its own way into the kingdom.[49]

Le Blon, as an honorary 'Anglois' bringing new technology (a *manière anglaise*), which, it was confidently anticipated, would prove 'important', particularly in the domains of anatomy, botany and natural history, was, without much further ado, granted a *privilège exclusif* for the duration of 20 years starting from 12 November 1737.[50] *Privilèges exclusifs*, the precursors to patents, had been introduced in France at the same time as those for publishing and the book trade, and by the eighteenth century constituted for the Crown a significant, though increasingly contentious, regulatory instrument to advance trade and industry.[51] A *privilège exclusif* freed the holder to work not only (as the term, indeed, makes clear) free from competition but also outside the limits of legally determined conventional practice, or, to put it another way, undisturbed by the guilds.

Printmaking was not, of course, an incorporated trade. On the contrary, it had been confirmed in law as a liberal art by the Edict of Saint Jean-de-Luz (1660). Inventors of print technologies had no need, therefore, of such negative defence of their freedom to innovate. However, in 1692 the copper-plate printers formed themselves into a guild with a monopoly of print jobs in the capital.[52] It is highly likely that one of the advantages Le Blon hoped to secure with his privilege was the right to train and retain his own specialised printers and circumvent the prerogatives of the city's master printers. Mezzotint printing required a specific set of skills – ones not ready to hand in Paris's printshops at that date.[53] More importantly, in sending plates out from the studio to be printed, Le Blon knew he ran the risk of disclosing knowledge of his new method of printmaking. That he failed finally in the attempt to exercise complete control of the production process[54] does not detract from the tendency of exclusive privilege to enclose the studio workshop, allowing and announcing its self-sufficiency, and thereby promoting the possessive relation between inventor and invention.[55]

Once located and attributed – once in the hand, so to speak – invention confidently entered the market. Within short months of receiving his privilege and before having met all the conditions, Le Blon had sold a half-share of his enterprise to Antoine Gautier de Montdorge for 4,000 *livres*, the sum thereafter constituting the company's working capital.[56] With money for materials and labour now safely in his pocket, and lodgings at the king's expense promised at the Marbrerie,[57] Le Blon was set to exploit an invention legally determined as exclusively his.

INVENTION: SLIPPERY CONCEPTS

'Invention' has referred above to a number of different things: new mechanical and chemical processes, a legally determined monopoly, an industrially exploitable resource, a national asset, and, finally, a bone of contention. The specific inflections of the term arose historically from the particulars of time and place:[58] London in the 1720s, Paris in the 1730s. In the latter case, context could be refined further: invention was there shaped respectively by the milieux of the workshop, the Conseil du roi, and the notary's office.[59] But however detailed this historical relativism may be, it has tended to ignore the nature of the objects at issue. These might as reasonably have been munitions and diving bells as colour printing in the case of Britain, or stocking-looms and paper mills in that of France.[60] Although printmaking in France had, in the sixteenth and early seventeenth centuries, been widely understood as mechanical, and therefore little different in principle from loom or mill technology, by the end of the seventeenth century, it was, thanks to books by Abraham Bosse, André Félibien and others, earning its place among the arts of *disegno*.[61] Invention in relation to graphic media thus additionally engaged with the aesthetic, if only to stand opposed to it in subtle contradistinction. Our examination will therefore need to be attentive to the overlaps in the discourses of art theory, technology and law.

Invention in painting, as Roger de Piles explained in his *Cours de peinture par principes* (1708), concerned the envisioning of the subject of a composition, typically its historical or allegorical narrative, and the disposition of figures and forms.[62] Thus, to take a specific example, the inscription 'N. Poussin Invenit et Pinxit' ('N. Poussin invented and painted [this]') below Benoît I Audran's engraving of *Les Israélites recueillant la manne* (fig. **79**) draws attention to Poussin's inventive pictorialisation of the text, tacitly inviting comparison with other actual or possible visualisations of the scene.[63] By contrast, the first anatomy colour print produced in France (fig. **80**) was inscribed within the image 'J. C. Le Blon. *Artem. invenit*: J. Robert. *fecit et excudit*. 1742.' ('J. C. Le Blon invented the art; J. Robert made and executed [this print]').[64] Invention here apparently has nothing to do with what is viewed – with the composition or design as such. It does not invoke or encompass the graceful balance of the axially articulated body, or the tenderly mirrored curves of cheek and shoulder, or the aestheticisation of dissection by analogy with the truncations effected by the *mise-en-page*, or, even, the disconcerting ways in which the marginal specimens of intestinal tract relate to the central figure, either as phallic objects or as prosthetic limbs. Rather, invention is explicitly identified with 'art' – that is, with Le Blon's idea for the colour printing process, and the skills (and not the lines) by which the executant, the mezzotinter Jean Robert, manipulated the technology to reproduce the flesh and viscera of the corpse.[65] The inventiveness or artfulness of art is interior, concealed, dissimulated, made to look other than itself (like brushwork); only its outcome or product is beheld.

Although both definitions are essentially modern – which is to say that invention is construed as productive of knowledge and not as an unveiling or discovery of truth[66] – they nevertheless bisected the work of art along traditional lines: into liberal and mechanical parts. To these parts corresponded different regimes of legal privilege, referred to rather clumsily in this chapter as 'copy-privilege' and 'patent-privilege' to avoid confusion between them. Copy-privilege, like artistic composition, was monochromatic.[67] It offered protection to design: that is, to dark marks – outlines, contours, hatchings, cross-hatchings, dashes, lozenges, dots, etc.[68] – in their intricate distribution across a light surface. It noted for possible reference not only the broad parameters of the motif, its lines of beauty, but local detail: the direction and pressure of the incised strokes by which intention was made fully material.[69] Moreover, narrative, that other dimension of artistic invention highlighted by theory, was and is figuratively linked to line: that is to say, it could be represented in terms of line – 'lines of communication', 'life-line', 'line of conduct', 'in a straight line', 'line of attack', 'line of defence', 'line of writing', 'between the lines', 'on the line', 'draw to an end', etc.[70] Charles Le Brun's famous 1667 reading of Poussin's *Israélites* makes significant and forceful use of this vocabulary of line: the composition 'retraces', 'follows' the thread of the biblical text; it articulates 'lines' of action or movement that 'link', 'join together', chains of figures and events, 'relating' them to the main subject, preventing attention's escape, safeguarding, in short, the moral end of the story, the *dénouement*.[71] In detail: on the left, the old woman to whom 'Roman' charity is dispensed and the tear-stained child from whom it is withheld stand as 'the chain and the link' to the agonised mother whose destiny is crossed (X) by the conflicting duties of filiation.[72] Moreover, to the family bonds, generational connections and social ties Le Brun added the circulation of rhetorical gesture, and the various lineaments of character and expression. Amply capacious, then, in its recognition of all manner of lines, copy-privilege had, by contrast, nothing to say about colour, or the substance of paint, or the constituents of printers' ink, or the work that preceded the final articulations and concluding touches of the image. Copyright was both superficial and timeless: superficial because it dealt with surface, resolution and finish, and timeless because it did not recognise the invented work as process – that is, as constituted in and over time.

By contrast, the invention recognised by *privilège exclusif*, or patent, addressed both time and space: it plumbed the colour of lines and it looked beyond resolved surface patterns to acknowledge the processes of becoming. Chromatic invention is not, in this sense, to be confused with de Piles's argument for *coloris*, or the 'intelligence' of colour, by which, he claimed, the artist makes an inspired and self-defining choice of hues for art, but must rather be identified with Le Brun's unredeemed *couleur*, the province of colour-grinders, dyers and weavers.[73] Indeed, only that which in a painting, print or printed textile is locally mixed and gradually built up in layers was the stuff of patent-privilege. Specific instances of red, yellow and blue, so-called 'rouge turc d'Andrinople', Nankeen yellow and Prussian blue, all received patents in the eighteenth century,[74] or, more precisely, not the colours as such (for lack of a precise enough terminology to designate their physical and chemical substance) but the technologies of their manufacture and the properties that made them solid: tangibly and permanently locatable on or in things.[75] We know Le Blon experimented with inks. For trichromacy, inks needed, first of all, to be composed of pigments that would not corrode the copper plates or oxidise on contact with them,[76] and they needed to have properties both of coverage (depositing a body of colour across the paper) and of transparency (to mix with other, superimposed pigments to form secondary colours).[77] While Gautier de Montdorge's account of Le Blon's practice suggests that the printmaker's choice of yellow and red lakes conformed to standard studio practice, his preliminary use of indigo and his finish in Prussian blue were novel, and may explain the early association of the colour blue with his 'invention'.[78]

To simulate oil painting, the paper was wholly saturated with pigment, such that, at a representational level, the things depicted appeared not to alight from the mind via the tip of the tool but to rise from depths of shadow. They have substance and body. Comparing Le Blon's anatomy plate (fig. **80**) with one by Gérard de Lairesse for Govert Bidloo's acclaimed *Anatomia humani corporis* (1685) (fig. **81**), we note, moreover, that colour obscures or hides line. In contrast to Lairesse's precisely edged organs, anchored within the thoracic cavity by the broken relief of cut ribs, the outlines of Le Blon's fleshy forms are pulled partly under cover of darkness. In places, edges of skin dissolve and become fuzzy and difficult to read. Gautier de Montdorge counselled those attempting a colour print to approach the contour of their idea or design with caution, to hold back from approaching it too nearly with the burnisher because a margin of error and adjustment, a temporary parergonal void, was needed for the adequate registration of the three plates.[79] The anxiety of the edge in tonal processes often led to dark enfoldings of line by colour. For Cochin *fils*, the lack of 'firmness', or vigorous linearity, undermined mezzotint's (and, by extension, trichromacy's) suitability and 'propriety' for elevated narrative subjects like history painting.[80] By contrast, the bluntly factual content of Le Blon's eviscerated hermaphrodite was defined at all three levels – legal, technological and representational – by its coverage, its coloured, opaque raiment, not its curves.

Colour's capacity to blind the viewer to design finds a parallel in the propensity of technological innovations in art to dissimulate, and to hide in conventional forms. Colour prints looked painted; crayon-manner etchings looked drawn; aquatints looked penned and washed. Thus, in order for the consumer of technical marvels not to be deceived he or she needed to bring into play senses additional to sight. Jacques Gautier explained in one of the many announcements in the *Mercure de France* for his later colour prints that, to avoid the confusion of his works with common or garden hand-coloured ones, he always offered them unvarnished in order that the sceptic might test their status as genuine.[81] Just as *trompe l'œil*, the illusion of the real, calls forth the hand for verification by touch, so colour printing, the illusion of paint, demanded an analogous process of validation; Gautier recommended spitting, followed by the subtle rub of inquiring fingers. Colour fastness was proof that the pigment was printed, integral to the image, and not superficially applied.[82] Antoine-Joseph Loriot's invention of a fixative for pastels in 1753 similarly attracted an abrasive testing by touch,[83] while encaustic or wax painting, the controversial sensation of the following year, invited trial by water: a surreptitious smear of saliva or a more candid drenching, sponge in hand.[84] Moreover, the connoisseur or purchaser wishing to know which of the several encaustic methods under development was in use before him must be alert to smell. Diderot observed a *savant* nosing out Jean-Jacques Bachelier's 'secret', betrayed by the odour of white spirit, in which the wax for encaustic had been dissolved.[85] The necessary revival of the lower offices of mouth, hand and nose for the appreciation of images in the context of technology and patent-privilege inevitably exposed technical invention to ridicule. André Rouquet's *L'Art nouveau de la peinture en fromage ou en ramequin, inventée pour suivre le louable projet de trouver graduellement des façons de peindre inférieures à celles qui existes* (1755) satirised the pretensions and modishness of inventors by advertising an outlandish concoction of cheese mixed with beaten egg for application onto a dough-like support. By attending to ingredients, the cooking and mixing of colours and media, and the processes of their application onto surfaces, invention and patent highlighted continuities between the studio and the kitchen that art theory worked so hard to deny.

There are here a number of interwoven threads: the thread of Le Blon's life; the thread that connects *artistic* invention to line, copy-privilege, surface, finish, sight and elevated narrative; and the thread that links *technical* invention to patent, colour, depth, process, the senses and the low. One might add to this series of contrasts one last (counterintuitive) observation that while copy-privilege could be said to lend a fictive weight to ideas, recognising both their significance and their likeness to tangible property, patent-privilege, for all its concern with density and matter, registered, by contrast, the lightness and fragility of the art object. Talking of Maurice-Quentin de La Tour's pastel portraits at the Salon of 1767, Diderot made the following melancholy reflection:

> one bat of Time's wing will leave nothing to justify (his) reputation... The precious dust will fall from the canvas [*sic*], half of it dispersed into the atmosphere, the other half caught on aged Saturn's long feathered wings ... Oh La Tour! *memento homo, quia pulvis es et in pulverem reverteris* ['Remember, man, that dust thou art, and unto dust shalt thou return'].[86]

Loriot's invention was designed to frustrate Saturn's dry rot, encaustic aimed to counter his wet, other inventions transferred unstable paintwork onto firmer ground[87] and printmaking preserved faint originals by copper-plated reproduction.[88] The pleasures of paint and of colour were haunted by fear of the corruptibility of matter; technological inventions such as these offered themselves as so many bulwarks against loss.

If the meanings of invention in art practice were as many and complex as those in art theory, they served nevertheless to confirm the status of useful knowledge as mechanical not liberal. How then did the inventor articulate claims not just to agency but to authorship?

Pamela Long has noted that patent differed from copyright by the value it placed on priority (coming first) and on novelty. These, she argues, surpassed notions of originality (that which finds its origin in a particular author) that were increasingly central to definitions of copyright.[89] The claims of the new brought about an important distinction between the discursive functions of 'inventor' and 'author'. While, as Michel Foucault has shown, originals were and are attributed to authors according to the logic of coherence in the construction of an enduring artistic subjectivity,[90] novelties presuppose no such obviously affective ties of personhood with their makers. Indeed, by the early nineteenth century, the inventor was defined by the diversity, the seemingly random nature of his or her creations.[91] Something of the inventor's later, de-centred, scattered self is anticipated in the manner in which Le Blon's invention and his early corpus of work were reported in France. Pierre Desmaizeaux, in his second letter written to the *Journal des sçavants* about Le Blon's activities in London, published in January 1722, recounts the miniature-painter's experiments with colour and colour printing in some detail before discussing impressions of two prints since dispatched to Paris for the inspection of the 'curieux': *Saint Veronica's Veil* (*c.*1721; fig. **82**) and *Anatomical Preparation of Male Genitalia* (*c.*1722; fig. **83**).[92] Desmaizeaux notes that connoisseurs compared the prints closely. He says nothing of their curious, not to say potentially blasphemous, conjunction as pendants. They are, of course, not real pendants – conjoined by visual play or narrative thread. The disconcerting discrepancy in scale alone prohibits such interrelation. Indeed, so bare are the facts, the low plumbing, of incarnation, that the dissected penis all but pricks the sacred mystery of the Passion. The implicit repeal of the hierarchy of genres on the one hand made the comparison possible, but on the other necessarily precluded explanations grounded in constructions of a rational and coherent artistic personality. How could the 'author' of the high one also be responsible for the low other? Rather, the relation between the images made sense in the context of a history of technological progress. They represented steps in the quest for the perfect reproduction or simulacrum. Comparison thus yielded not meaning but technical knowledge.

Following Desmaizeaux, modern scholars tend to discuss Le Blon's oeuvre in terms of its technical merit: his work executed in England is, for example, invariably judged superior to what he subsequently produced in France.[93] Much less attention, by contrast, is paid to the subjects of the prints, beyond the general observation that the preponderance of 'masterpieces' by renowned artists, portraits of the great and works with erotic élan, indicates an astute concern for business. Florian Rodari even goes so far as to suggest that it was shareholders not the artist who directed the Picture Office's output.[94] Such complete disregard for Le Blon's authorial investment in his work, for the possible attempts to fashion an identity for inventor and invention in the oeuvre, no doubt seems justified in light of the fact that so many of Le Blon's works can be classified as illustrative or reproductive. The *Anatomical Preparation of Male Genitalia*, for instance, was intended for an edition of William Cockburn's *The Symptoms, Nature, Cause, and Cure of a Gonorrhoea*, and *Saint Veronica's Veil* (fig. **82**) reproduced one of Le Blon's own compositions in oil (fig. **84**).[95] However, there is a case for saying that the print of *Saint Veronica's Veil* is not, in fact, secondary, but primary, original, and that the painting stands in relation to it as preparatory sketch, in the same way and manner that drawings and *grisailles* have often served so-called painter-etchers and engravers.[96]

The napkin of Saint Veronica, the *vera icona*, was after all the ur-print. On the road to Calvary, Veronica accepted the very first impression, fixed upon her veil, for which the Holy Face served as the printing surface and Christ's sweat and blood as ink.[97] This being so, depiction of the miraculous relic properly spoke to the origins of printmaking not painting. There was a close identification of the icon with the origin of colour printing, moreover, because, according to Gautier de Montdorge, use of a 'veil' was recommended as the best means to transfer the outline of the original onto each of the trinity of plates involved.[98] Martin Kemp has argued that in Claude Mellan's *Le Linge de Sainte Véronique: Formatur unicus una* (1649; fig. **85**) – to which Le Blon's treatment is possibly indebted – a graphic demonstration of near magical skill was put at the service of the sacred. The single engraved line by which Mellan conjures up the coiled shade of the expiring Christ stands metaphorically for the 'oneness' of Christ, the only Son of God, who, in the words of the Communion, 'by his one oblation of himself, once offered, made a full, perfect and sufficient sacrifice ... for the sins of the whole world'.[99] However, in the case of Le Blon, whose print was in the first instance marketed to a Protestant audience, the metaphor surely operates in the opposite direction. The coloured, bloodstained veil stands metaphorically for the mystery and miracle of composite facsimile production and for the power of its appearance of unity to enchant and mystify us.

Saint Veronica's Veil was only the first of a number of images through which, in the beginning, Le Blon attempted to invent, or at least appropriate, a tradition for his innovation and to attach his name to it. He refrained at this stage from a show of hand – that is to say, from an exhibition of the technique as such – and chose rather to allegorise his art in narratives not only elevated and poetic but apt. Beautiful Narcissus, whose fatal story of mirrored perfection had, since Alberti, served as a figure for the invention of painting, was the subject of another print of the 1720s.[100] The mythical huntsman crouches by the water's edge, artfully attempting to embrace the surface of the pool; his perfect, seductive reflection, spoiled by touch, escapes in streams through his fingers. So far, so traditional, but the viewer has in his or her hand a flawless reproduction, its bodies of colour and tone safely and forever arrested and satisfyingly palpable. Failure to distinguish between original and reproduction, painting and printed copy brings this beholder fulfilment not death.[101]

In *L'Harmonie du coloris* or *Coloritto*, privately published and choicely circulated by Le Blon to advertise his 'discoveries',[102] allusion is further made to the myth of Pygmalion. Five illustrations inserted at the end, and intended to summarise Le Blon's rules concerning colour, plot its advent via a sequence in which the inert, abstracted, black-on-white features of a girl (fig. **86**), are gradually, magically, transfused with life-giving pigment (figs **87**, **88**).[103] The myth is, of course, thoroughly and complexly reworked. The story here focuses on Galatea not Pygmalion. Where Ovid's hero lovingly created an ideal of her, Le Blon is manifestly concerned with the dispassionate, empirical observation and record of the real her.[104] Moreover, the layered stages in the productive process differ markedly from the chain of events in the fulfilment of narrative. Each phase in the coming into colour supersedes, covers over and obliterates, the stages before. Consequently, where, in Ovid's tale, beauty and narrative unfold together in a smooth linear progression, Le Blon's technological progress coils, loops back, in such a way that, although the absolute perfection of polychrome finally stands in the place of the relative merits of monochrome, during the interval Galatea falls into abjection.[105] In plate III (fig. **87**) she appears as a fleshy sculpture, flushed to the ends of her hair, the half-life of her pallid stare exposing her former inanimate state as death not art. Pygmalion as a tale of technology thus uses the myth's promotion of life over the aesthetic and its advocacy of carnality, not sublimation, to mount an argument for the superiority of painting over sculpture, for full colour not line.[106] The technology directly in question was, of course, not trichromacy but painting; only in the dedication of the book to Robert Walpole does Le Blon mention the ramification of the discovery of his harmonic rules for printmaking.[107] However, insofar as the plates, as prints, obliquely register the arrival of colour printing, they work to attach their *invenit* to painting, forsaking the traditional twinning of printmaking and sculpture connoted by *sculpsit*. In so doing, the printmaker is apparently dispensed with; Le Blon assumes the role of *peintre-graveur*, directly and absolutely in charge of his own original work.[108] In the hierarchy of the visual arts, invention had the potential to promote some arts and some artists over others.

Allegoricalisation of pagan and Christian myth was commonplace in the early modern period, especially in France under Absolutism. Like Louis's use of Apollo, Le Blon's exploitation of Christ, Narcissus and Pygmalion served both to ennoble and to enchant. Myth illustrated the sophistication of his new technology, equal to reproducing the most ambitious genres, in a formal register that removed the idea of technological innovation from the concoction of recipes and the vulgar self-promotion of advertising to the sacred site of fable. At the same time, what allegory made public by convention it also concealed through metaphor, enhancing the mystery of what it ostensibly revealed.[109] By conflating the origins of colour printing with the origins of art (the veil, the reflective surface), Le Blon established his claim to priority without disclosing its basis. Mythography articulated his ideas on colour for an elite audience versed in modes of indirect learning, while concealing the mechanism of its reproduction from competition. Moreover, by variously casting himself in the role of Veronica, Narcissus and Pygmalion, Le Blon implied that his pursuit of perfect imitation was, like the Academician's, motivated by love not profit. The laws of privilege and the market were thus poetically disguised.

LE BLON, GAUTIER

Reviewing *L'Harmonie du coloris* in the *Mémoires pour l'histoire des sciences et des beaux-arts* in August 1737, the Jesuit scientist Louis-Bertrand Castel pointed, none too charitably, to the snail-paced progress of Le Blon's invention: 'The Author arrived in Paris a year ago, with his book and several Examples of his work barely more advanced, indeed perhaps even less so, than when he left 20 years ago.'[110] A year elapsed without response before Antoine de La Roque published in the *Mercure de France* a letter that Le Blon had sent him, as editor, in which the inventor apologised for the non-appearance of the marvels the arrival of his new technology in France had seemed to promise. Defending himself against the delay, Le Blon deflected responsibility in three directions: first towards the *rallentando* of the king's pleasure in matters of *privilège*, second to the time-consuming business of securing investment, and last to the gap in the local skills' market. He had had to 'train Pupils in a form of printmaking which it seems that France has feigned to neglect, namely *Art Noir*, or *Manière Noire*' (mezzotint).[111] One of these 'pupils' was Jacques-Fabien Gautier, who entered Le Blon's studio in 1738, joining at least one other, Pierre-François Tardieu. It was, probably, for their work on the portrait of Cardinal Fleury after Hyacinthe Rigaud and the self-portrait after Van Dyck that Le Blon begged indulgence at the close of his letter, describing these very first prints of the Paris workshop as 'études', mere preliminaries to the serious and perfected work to follow.[112] Gautier did not, however, stay to see it realised. Within weeks he had moved on, his place filled by Jean Robert.

Our knowledge of Gautier's early life and career is somewhat sketchy and not wholly reliable. Unlike Le Blon's other apprentices, Gautier was neither a Parisian nor from a printmaking background. He originated from Marseille and from the not unrelated world of *indiennage* – the printed-cotton trade.[113] As such, we may assume that he had a primary knowledge of relief printing, and, more importantly perhaps, a basic grasp of the chemistry and manipulation of pigments for the purposes of dyeing – skills that possibly directed him towards experimentation in colour printing independently of Le Blon.[114] The reasons for Gautier's migration to the capital are unclear, though it is not unreasonable to suppose that renewed efforts in the mid-1730s to enforce the prohibition on *indiennes* may have had something to do with it.[115]

Concerning Gautier's activities between his brief sojourn *chez* Le Blon and 1741, the year of the latter's death, the documentary evidence is once more frustratingly silent. 1741, however, decisively marks Gautier's arrival on the scene. On 5 September, a bare four months after Le Blon was buried at Saint-Séverin, Gautier was granted a 30-year privilege for 'the art of printing Pictures with three plates'.[116] In December a long notice in the *Mercure de France* reproduced the pertinent extract from the registers of the Conseil d'état granting the new dispensation, and followed it by a list of 21 colour prints by Gautier; one of these, the *Coquille turbinite*, was included *gratis* with the issue of the journal, and the rest, the reader was informed, could be purchased directly from the workshop on rue Saint-Honoré, opposite the Oratoire.[117] Gautier's inaugural confidence, expressed not only in the volume of his oeuvre but in the range of his subject matter (history, portraiture, landscape, still life, anatomy, natural history) and the prestige of the cited collections to which some of the works he reproduced belonged (Charles-Guillaume, marquis de Broglie, and Joseph Bonnier de La Mosson), stands in contrast to Le Blon's earlier diffidence. That confidence was almost immediately put to the test.

On 2 January 1742 Maître Perrin, a lawyer representing Marguerite Le Blon and Claude-François Le Marchand Descatillon (Gautier de Montdorge's clerk, whose name served his master as a cover), successfully registered their opposition to Gautier's *arrêt*,[118] and on the 12th of the following month Gautier's tools, press and plates were seized, putting an end to all activity.[119] Thick, impassioned and often indignant memoranda were drafted by lawyers on both sides. The matters in contention were only finally resolved on 12 May, when Gautier, his right having been upheld by the court, finally agreed to buy the privilege from Le Blon and 'Descatillon' for 6,403 *livres*, a tidy sum.[120] So far as the law was concerned, the crucial issue related to the nature of the privilege, whether personal favour or private property – in practical terms, that is, whether it had expired along with the patentee or whether, by virtue of having been divided and willed, it survived respectively in the persons and interests of the partner and the daughter. The arguments presented on behalf of the cause of Le Blon's heirs thus necessarily relied for support on the exact wording of the original privilege and particularly on the *arrêt du Conseil* (1 April 1738), by which Le Blon was enabled to cede shares in the privilege to whomsoever it pleased him to do so.[121]

The challenge mounted by Maître Jean de La Clef for Gautier, however, forced a wider debate. It opened up a case dominated by questions of legal semantics to broader considerations of priority, of the respective values of theory and practice (of knowing and knowing-how) and of the justification for and benefits of privilege. To elaborate a little, the memorandum for the defence – that is to say, for the heirs of Le Blon – presented their case in terms of genealogy.[122] Theirs was a double line of direct, legitimate descent: the biological and pseudo-biological relations of fathers and daughters, and brothers-in-partners, to whom privilege and property were carefully entrusted, running parallel to institutional relations between master and pupil, to whom 'all the information and knowledge [*lumières*] regarding [the master's] art' had been properly and fully imparted. Gautier, variously styled in the *mémoire* 'worker', 'basic worker' and 'workshop boy', and apparently tied to the studio by no more than relations of exchange, fell outside this intimacy; he had no place in the family tree.

For his part Gautier conceded to the other side no more than the legalities, the bare facts of privilege. He presented himself as Le Blon's peer, not his pupil. On the issue of priority, he was thus able stubbornly to maintain, against clear evidence to the contrary, that he and Le Blon had discovered the art of colour printing at the same time and in the same place – in the colour theory of *père* Castel – and were thus reflections of each other.[123] The only difference he allowed at this stage concerned not the origins of the invention but its subsequent development: Le Blon's jump-started pursuit of legal monopoly is contrasted to Gautier's stay-at-home application to perfecting the technology. From this perspective, the transfer of the privilege to Gautier had resulted not from the opportunistic 'surprise' of the king's justice (as Me Perrin alleged) but rather from the fulfilment of proverbial wisdom: 'tout vient à celui qui sait attendre'.

By reassigning the origin of trichromacy to Castel's colour theory, Gautier sought not only to absolve himself of theft but also to shift the parameters of the debate. For, if colour printing consisted merely in the reasoned application of (Castel's) science, privileges should self-evidently follow and protect operational principle and practical competence, since advances in knowledge *tout court* cannot be secured by privilege as such.[124] Where quality and output were concerned, Gautier felt assured. In evidence for the bold assertion that 'The sieur Gautier… has considerably surpassed the sieur Le Blon in the Practice of this Art which he has brought to the greatest height of perfection', Me de La Clef cited letters from Castel and de Montdorge that apparently acknowledged without equivocation the superiority of Gautier's *Saint Pierre* (*c*.1738) to Le Blon's *Fleury* and *Van Dyck*.[125] Additionally, Me de La Clef drew attention to the score and range of Gautier's oeuvre: 21 with landscapes to Le Blon's three without.[126] Moreover, since 'the public good' had always been the aim of the 'concession' initially granted to Le Blon, Me de La Clef argued that this end would now more profitably be served by support of Gautier's assured capacities and certain delivery than by faith in those merely promised by the Le Blon workshop – a reference to the long-announced *Cours d'anatomie* which had yet to materialise.[127] Left unworked or under-exploited, privilege became monopolistic and an obstacle to progress.

Me de La Clef was able to make a case for the coincidence of his client's interests and the public good because, although Gautier had requested a *privilège exclusif*, he had in fact been granted only the lesser *permission simple* – that is to say, leave to practise without let or hindrance, to trespass legally on Le Blon's purported exclusivity. Turning the weakness of Gautier's prerogative into strength, Me de La Clef argued that Gautier's example would promote emulation, encourage competition, precisely because it did not prevent others from seeking identical permissions.

In winning the case, Me de La Clef demonstrated that by the early 1740s, that is to say before the appointment of Daniel Trudaine at the Bureau du commerce, government policy already inclined towards protecting the exploitation of invention rather than the rights and interests in secrets.[128] Whether from conviction or by shrewd insight the Bureau acted rightly. The deed of sale by which Gautier bought Le Blon's privilege states quite candidly that the sale was taking place because '[neither] the sieur Des Castillons [*sic*], nor the said minor can by themselves draw any profit or advantage from the said privilege … given that they possessed neither the art nor the secret of printing Paintings using three plates'.[129]

SECRETS: ELUSIVE FACTS

'Secret' was a word used routinely to describe Le Blon's contested invention. As we have seen, the text of the privilege, the puffs in the paper, the lawyers' rhetoric all made pointed reference to secrets – to knowledge set apart and more or less consciously concealed.[130] Indeed, 'secret' is peculiar to the vocabulary of patent-privileges and patenting. Unlike copy-privileges that protected the *expression* of an idea – that is, its openly forged forms and coherently composed narratives – secrecy, and the patent-privileges that recognised it, protected the *idea* itself. By stealth, and/or by law, the idea remained private, elusive, only its effects were known to the public for certain. Secrecy enters the argument here in two specific ways: as an object of and sign in the ongoing litigation between Gautier and Le Blon's heirs, and as a contested value in progressive discourse on science and technology. By attending to the discursive drama of secrecy – to the logics of concealment and the temptations to disclosure – we shall, I hope, discover whether secrecy and patent-privilege participated in the formation of Enlightenment notions of art and the artist, notions independent, that is, of academic endorsement and status.

Secrecy, in the context of eighteenth-century arts and manufactures, referred to a number of different things: to secrets that varied according to whether they were individual or corporate, communicable or non-transferable.[131] Jean-Baptiste Oudry, when speaking of colour at the Académie in 1749, referred to his 'stock' of knowledge as a *bien* inherited from his master, Nicolas de Largillière, a stock to which he added from his own lifetime's experience without, in the last analysis, being able to distinguish his ideas from his master's: 'it is so long since they formed a common entity'.[132] Since professional secrets were, by this account, collectively and corporately engendered, they ought, Oudry argued, also to be shared: 'In an art like ours I know nothing so low as to have petty secrets and not to render those services rendered unto us to those who follow.'[133] By contrast, technique, or that which critics and theorists called 'touch', was widely regarded as both individual and inimitable.[134] The critic Baillet de Saint-Julien spoke in 1755 of the eye's obsessive search for Chardin's 'secret' in precisely this sense.[135] It was more than a figure of speech. Although Chardin was described as generous and open in his counsel on colour, he was notoriously secretive about his methods in the studio; none was allowed to see him paint.[136] Where the 'secrets' confided by Oudry were those of the trade and were transferable in principle, and where the 'magic' of handling or technique, personified by Chardin, was deemed so individual that it brooked no imitation, a third kind of secret, the invention of processes – colours, encaustics, varnishes, fixatives, printing processes, etc. – combined, by contrast, transferability and personal title. This kind of secret, by virtue of being intangible, absolutely distinct from the labour of execution – a formula, recipe, or set of instructions – was highly susceptible to dissemination, licensed or otherwise. It was also novel,[137] a breaking step with tradition – in other words, a highly idiosyncratic intervention.

It was only the last type of secret to which *privilèges exclusifs* or patents applied, the first being insufficiently particular to be claimed by any one, and the second insufficiently separate to be threatened by any other. Le Blon himself wrote of his enterprise as a quest after just such a secret, one once known to the ancients.[138] Moreover, having successfully discovered it, he not only patented the *arcanum*, he also seemingly re-encrypted it in images that conspicuously assume secrecy as their subject. *Saint Veronica's Veil*, opus no. 1, proclaims the presence of mystery. Behind the image's modest, seemingly simple surface, a complex division of labour and a significant novelty in production (among other, arguably nobler, secrets) lie hidden, indeed veiled. 'Secret' not only guards, in this instance, it also commends an unknown thing of value, raising the keeper and initiate to the status of exception. To say this is to recognise that the discourse on secrecy, by itself alone, doubles claims to possession. Colour printing belonged to Le Blon; it belonged not to others. Privilege merely lent formal status and legal force.

Unlike British patents, however, *privilèges exclusifs* were granted on condition that inventions were fully disclosed. By the *arrêt* of 12 November 1737 Le Blon was required to communicate his invention to a panel of experts in order to establish both its priority and its efficacy. Disclosure would additionally ensure that, on expiry of the privilege, the secret was not lost but released into the public domain. Mario Biagioli has argued that the notion of public domain is historically anachronistic with regard to patent-privileges in early modern Europe. He notes that, whereas in modern patent systems disclosure is a value involving commitment to an ideal of openness, in the sixteenth and seventeenth centuries it was a practice – that is, an exchange between specific individuals (in this instance, Le Blon and officials of the royal administration) – operating in a particular political economy: mercantilism.[139] Whereas modern patents are assigned by a right of property to any inventor so long as the invention is genuinely his or hers, a privilege was granted in the *ancien régime* by royal prerogative and consequently only when consistent with the Crown's economic policies. It was, possibly, in anticipation of the particular interest of trichromacy to the Imprimerie royale and the Gobelins, and to the print and textile industries more generally, that Le Blon endeavoured to constrain disclosure and to protect his invention as if it were, in fact, his private property. The expert members of his panel – the painter Madeleine Françoise Basseporte, the scientists and Academicians Henri-Louis Duhamel du Monceau and Charles Du Fay – were expressly forbidden 'to claim any part of the profit that could result from the implementation of the privilege' were they to disclose it themselves.[140]

Le Blon was happily positioned, apparently, to insist on strict confidentiality in the disclosure of his secret; this was by no means generally the case. The Académie royale des sciences, formally put in charge of providing expertise for the verification of inventions for privilege in 1699, held to the view that technological progress was incremental; each small advance built on the foundations of that which came before.[141] In order to avoid error and the needless duplication of effort, it was, in its view, essential to foster communication and cooperation wherever possible, notably through publication in its own *Histoire et mémoires de l'Académie royale des sciences*.[142] In principle, at least, the view of secrecy held by the Académie royale des sciences was therefore wholly negative, classically instanced by the short, shuttered social circuits and veiled, figurative language of alchemy.[143] Commitment to an enlightened and therefore liberalist dissemination of knowledge not only distinguished science from magic, it also raised academies above guilds: the statutes and regulations of the Académie royale de peinture et de sculpture, for instance, had from the beginning laid openness as a duty on its members.[144] Industry, likewise, imposed its laws, its *privilèges exclusifs*, according to a double and contradictory logic: protection of the petitioner's interest for the sake of encouragement, and also limitation of that interest for the general good. Privilege was certainly a practice open to the arbitrariness of the king's pleasure; in the eighteenth century the policy of that legal practice was, however, informed by openness as a value – one thought conducive to the progress of knowledge and thus of public utility. By inviting a response and a responsibility in law, possession of the secret became conditional.[145] A limited public authority of exception was substituted for the perpetual and occulted personal one.

Should not our concern, then, be with openness? With proven and verified 'facts', not elusive ones? The answer at a technical and evidential level must be evasive because, despite official pursuit of openness, secrecy remained, in this case, invention's ubiquitous sign: the Bureau du commerce sought reassurance that the invention really was a secret, a novelty, before privileging it;[146] notwithstanding the terms of Le Blon's privilege, Gautier alleged that disclosure was never made, that a change of status never, in fact, took place.[147] Consequently, the content of Le Blon's secret remained open to speculation – so much so, indeed, that Gautier was able later to argue that he, not Le Blon, was the keeper of the 'real' secret.[148] Instead of putting a case for either one as the significant context, I want, rather, to shift attention to 'disclosure', to that moment when (following the *Oxford English Dictionary*'s definition of the word) the cover or veil is lifted and the secret exposed to view; a moment when openness and secrecy collide. It is a point of absolute contradiction, therefore, during which the secret-as-secret is perfectly beheld. Secrecy, I suggest, instead of being dispelled under the emerging regime of Enlightenment, was, in fact, re-routed to serve new, unforeseen purposes.

Disclosure could take many forms, though by the eighteenth century the scientific communities of Europe favoured two: demonstration and publication. Le Blon avoided neither. In London, he published his discovery in the *Philosophical Transactions of the Royal Society*.[149] In Paris he demonstrated his process not only to the official committee of experts but, according to *père* Castel, to all those who expressed an interest.[150] Turning his back on allegory, a genre under attack,[151] Le Blon also *performed* disclosure in at least one of his prints.

When Le Blon dismissed the portrait of Cardinal Fleury and the self-portrait of Van Dyck as mere 'studies', he was being disingenuous. The qualities of the rocking, burnishing, inking and printing may have fallen below his professional standards, but the choice of subjects and the components of the designs were deliberate and considered. To take the simpler of the two first: in the eighteenth century Van Dyck embodied imitation, or the creation of perfect likeness.[152] To seek to replicate perfection was, quite simply, to lay claim to that standard. The portrait of Cardinal Fleury (fig. **89**) repeats its pendant's audacity. Likewise, it insists – insofar as Rigaud, whose work it reproduces, was widely acclaimed as Van Dyck's like and heir[153] – on the highest achievements of imitation. But it does much more. By force of its inscription and the identity of the sitter, the portrait of Cardinal Fleury takes priority over, even eclipses, its companion. 'In Gallia primum' reads the right fringe of the third line in blue. This, then, was the *first* impression of a *first* coming into printed colour in France, represented by, and implicitly addressed in honour to, the king's *first* minister, 'André Hercules Cardinal de Fleury, Grand Aumonier de la Reine, Ministre d'État, Grand Maître et Surintendant des Postes.' A first in time finds its match, the expression of its consequence, in a prime of dignity and power.

To know more of this 'first', we must look again at the fringe. Jostling with Fleury's titles, a statement in yellow and blue unfolds: 'Opus Inventionis imprimendi Coloribus naturalibus', which may be translated as 'A Work of Invention printable in natural Colours', or, alternatively, 'A Work of Invention that should be expressed in natural Colours'. According to the first translation, the invention is located straightforwardly in the colour printing, which allows a greater mimetic accuracy, a fuller copy. In the second, the gerundive 'imprimendi' assumes an imperative function, implying, perhaps, that on other occasions this 'work of invention' or portrait, had not been so naturally tinted. Those other occasions would refer to the portraits of Fleury after Rigaud, engraved in black on white by François I Chéreau in 1726 and Pierre-Imbert Drevet in 1730 (fig. **90**). Indeed, from the latter, Le Blon took the exact wording of Fleury's titles. No direct acknowledgement is made, however, of the painting or print that served Le Blon as model. No other 'author' shares the glory of the margin – 'J.-C. le Blon Artis Inventor fecit et excudit' – no other maker, that is, no studio assistance in rocking and burnishing, either. The caption thus reveals and conceals. It reveals and extols the effect of the invention; it conceals its cause and allows its moment of origin in France to overshadow the origin of the French design. Allusion to an engraved source is obscurely packed into the Latin text, the double sense of certain words serving not so much to attribute honour where it is due, but to impress by the difference invoked between pied artifice and natural colour.

'Natural colour' is the effect of the invention, a point seemingly overmade by the complete saturation of the print in it, including those parts where conventionally colour had no referential value. Red, yellow and blue cut up the textual border into stripes, along which ambiguous words float in parallel. There is more to this than extravagance and excess. It is in this space, where the artist is most conspicuously at work in words and colour, that the moment of revelation occurs, a moment according to Georg Simmel that 'constitutes the acme in the development of the secret; all of its charms are once more gathered in it and brought to a climax – just as the moment of dissipation lets one enjoy with extreme intensity the value of the object'.[154] The 'charms' accumulated here can be enumerated as follows: first, the technological charm of a facsimile reproduction of painting; second, the economic charm of maximum output delivered by minimum investment – the vast array of nature's subtleties of hue conveyed with the primitive economy of the primaries; third, the commercial charm that such economy made possible by bringing an elite work of beauty to a large, discriminating middle market.[155] Are there not also, finally and more controversially, semantic charms arising from correspondences between traditional forms of 'forbidden knowledge', nature's secrets and state secrets: that is, between Le Blon's colour and Fleury's politics (or the so-called *secret du roi*),[156] between Le Blon's hermetic surfaces and Fleury's serenely composed façade?

It was not always and only thus. The duc de Saint-Simon vividly describes a fraught moment at court when, out of respect for the king's grief and his own political hide, Fleury had endeavoured to suppress his joy at news of the duc d'Orleans's death and 'could be observed sweating under the need for concealment'.[157] 'Secret as secretion', to quote Gilles Deleuze and Félix Guattari's memorable phrase. This is an epigrammatic way of saying that secrets are on the move, dynamic, and inevitably betray themselves as secrets; they 'ooze from the box'.[158] Here, however, the secret does not so much ooze as explode at the lower border of the print. Propelled by the energy formerly dedicated to containing it – the dew on the brow – its contents are released publicly in an almost carnivalesque display of striated colour.[159] It was greeted by connoisseurs and consumers with matching intensity, born of anticipation.

As others have been quick to realise, the secret revealed by the print consists in the relation between the primaries separated out in the border below and their mixture in the portrait above to produce all the gradations of natural colour required by the likeness of life.[160] Such a secret, as already noted, was scarcely rated secret by the 1730s; it was, as the French say, a 'secret de Polichinelle'. Le Blon, however, reintroduces a touch of mystery to the commonplace by the outer edge of darkness at the bottom, the 'black' that results from the mixture of all three primaries. In *L'Harmonie du coloris*, Le Blon had been at pains to emphasise that his colour theory concerned only 'material colours' – that is, pigments – 'Because the mix of all the immaterial Colours produces not *Black* but precisely the reverse, *White*, as the incomparable Sir Isaac NEWTON has demonstrated in his *Opticks*.'[161] Le Blon's theory, by reversing Newton's, by styling itself a negative replica, invoked the composition of Newton's white light with his black. The stripes become rays, a 'spectrum' of unequally refrangible rays, from the least (red) at the top to the most (blue) at the bottom. Newton's *Opticks* was widely read and debated in France, a French translation by Pierre Coste having first been published in Amsterdam in 1720.[162] For a second French edition Newton was asked to provide a *vignette* to serve as headpiece to the several parts (fig. **91**).[163] In a dark, empty room, white light comes in through a high hole in a blanked out window, passes via a lens through a prism and is broken.

The fractured rays come to rest on a screen, where they hang in a bar of separated colour. It was the discovery of the elongated form of the spectrum that distinguished Newton's experiments with a prism from those of his predecessors.[164] At a time when the colour circle had yet to impose itself as the model for visualising colour relationships, it seems likely that Le Blon's border stripes were designed precisely to invoke the new rectilinear configuration of hues. Moreover, the parallel lines and triumvirate colours may have suggested not just the shape of the projected refraction but the form of the instrument that accomplished it – that is, the geometric properties of the prism, its edges and angles, which, according to *père* Castel, were an essential component of the instrument's authority, and of the fetishistic admiration that it commanded.[165]

Although Newton's 'New Theory of Light and Colour' was perhaps not 'tight', not yet universally approved[166] – as were the rules of colour mixing – it was nevertheless public knowledge. By the time Le Blon was granted a privilege, the experiments of consequence related in the *Opticks* had long since been successfully replicated at the Académie royale des sciences and elsewhere.[167] It was, therefore, not his 'secret', his disclosure, that Le Blon was joyfully telling. Rather, it was an unforeseen application of Newton's theory, the grasping of which required the viewer to read the rainbow rim of the portrait simultaneously as rays and strata. A cross-section of light *and matter*, the sequence of colours represents a marriage of the universal laws of refraction and the particularities of colour printing, in this instance. Separated colours are over-printed from separate plates, the order of service following the fall of the spectrum and building from blue at the base towards red on the surface. This is the 'Opus Inventionis', the 'Artis' of which Le Blon was 'Inventor', and to which he drew attention by its intellectual beauty.[168]

Notwithstanding the compound links carefully established between stripes, rays and strata, Le Blon seems to have doubted the success of his disclosure, if disclosure it was, and not the mere appearance of it. The previous year, Castel had published the following judgment of Le Blon's verbal exposition of his colour theory: 'This little Book [*L'Harmonie du coloris*] is so concise, so inarticulate, so Theoretical, so new, and seems to relate from such a distance to the new art of which it is the key, but a key that itself requires a key, that the like of Oedipus is needed to make it out.'[169] Since the striped border exhibited the same qualities of concision, abstraction and novelty as the booklet, it was unlikely that this 'key' would prove any more successful at unlocking the secrets of Le Blon's *œuvre-prison*. It resembled, rather, the anagrams or ciphers used by scientists, Newton among them, to announce a discovery while making it known only to the persistent and insightful.[170] Le Blon, would in any case, have confidently anticipated that viewers would focus on the portrait and the narratives of identity, prestige and power foregrounded by the conventions of the genre. He expected few to look beyond the obvious, the ostensible meaning, and discover the other story in the stripes: the secret of the image-as-reproduced-object. For the vast majority of 'under-readers',[171] specifically for those *curieux* inattentive to material properties of particular prints but nevertheless 'wanting to deepen their knowledge of the Mechanics of the new art of printing Colour Prints' in general, Le Blon consequently redoubled his efforts, repeating himself in a series of 'separates', published and sold alongside the finished work: blue (fig. **92**), yellow (fig. **93**), a proof uniting the blue and the yellow to make green (fig. **94**) and finally red (fig. **95**).[172] At first glance the separates merely maximise the border: a minimised line of colour unfolds in grand folio. However, considered again, it is clear that where the border represented Le Blon's secret, the separates reproduce it step by step: blue plus yellow equals green, plus red equals the naturally coloured impression of the finished product. Setting theory aside, the sequence of separates conjures up for the viewer the scene of practice in the studio, and he or she becomes a virtual witness to the invention in process.

In summary, the secret of colour printing is told not once but three times in Le Blon's portrait of Cardinal Fleury: alluded to by the inscription, disclosed by the stripes, performed by the separates. This prolixity was, moreover, not confined to the portrait. Le Blon had earlier broached the theory behind colour printing in *L'Harmonie du coloris* (1725). A brief account of the technical process had appeared in the *Mercure de France* over the winter of 1727, and the invention had seen full and official publication in the internationally circulated *Philosophical Transactions of the Royal Society* in the summer of 1731.[173] A strong impression of ebb and flow is created: of a contents released, seemingly recouped, only to be released once again. Such repeated recourse to self-revelation may have been forced by a lack of receptivity to the new product, but it also suggests that important benefits were secured at that paradoxical moment when the secret was at once fully beheld and utterly undone. Confession thrusts an 'I', the I to whom the secret uniquely belongs, before the eyes of witnesses, and, in the case of technology, thereby vigorously establishes priority and property in the invention. Le Blon's repeated and clamorous disclosures should, therefore, have left the question of the content, origin and authorship of the secret beyond doubt. How was it then that Gautier was able so swiftly and successfully to stake a claim of his own?

Gautier's own portrait of Cardinal Fleury (fig. **96**), provides one possible answer. It is a unique instance of Gautier's directly repeating Le Blon, and of Gautier's visibly interposing himself between his former master and the fame that was his due. At first glance, Gautier's portrait appears modest, unassuming, an altogether more reticent image. Although we cannot be certain, surviving proofs before letterpress indicate no planned revelations for the margin of the finished state.[174] Nor did Gautier issue separates for this or any other of his works. In his case, secrecy was practised not breached. Which is not to say that the portrait was silent on all matters of manufacture. If the not inelegant way the print draws Le Blon's earlier version into balanced comparison by reversing the composition was almost certainly unintended – a gratuitous by-product of the technology – the differences in detail were just as certainly planned. The cardinal's formerly bloody neck has been restored by Gautier to a healthy pallor below the crisply rendered starched tapes of his white collar. The ermine cloak extends more fully into deeply shadowed folds, from beneath which emerges the intricate tracery of a bobbin-laced cuff.

These conspicuous 'improvements' and adornments take on sense in the context of the accounts of colour printing that prefaced the sale notices for Gautier's prints in the *Mercure* in 1742 and 1745. The first plots a dense 'ancient' history for colour printing, crowded with forebears inventing and perfecting first engraving and etching and then, more pertinently, the art of chiaroscuro woodcut.[175] Against this background, Le Blon's trichromacy was proclaimed an invention not for its dramatic discontinuity with the past – that is, because it replaced a technology based on tone by one based on colour – but because it advanced by a step a common objective: in short, because his works 'sustain the comparison with Painting' more successfully. By so defining invention as a matter of ends, or effects, and not means, Gautier's account allowed for the possibility of further improvements, further discoveries. Le Blon's prints, by virtue of their novelty, were, according to Gautier, necessarily crude.[176] They lacked subtlety. The 'harsh contrasts' and 'dry handling' bespoke the unyielding copper plates and the savage tools from and by which the images were wrought; or so he implied.[177] By contrast, Gautier claimed as his own achievement the imparting to reproductive prints of 'the vigour and unctuousness' of brushwork:[178] the bold, starched crispness of the cardinal's cuff and the soft, folding pallor of his ermine cape served as visual proof of that claim. The invention of the facsimile reproduction of painting was thus narrated in three related parts, and traced a line of technological transmission by descent: part 1, the reproduction of tone pioneered by Ugo da Carpi; part 2, the reproduction of colour discovered by Le Blon; and, finally, part 3, the reproduction of medium invented by Gautier.[179] The dispute between Le Blon and Gautier was not a matter just of 'facts' but also of conflicting discourses.

If Gautier's triumph in presenting himself, provisionally at least, as the fulfilment of colour printing rested largely on the superior currency of 'progressive' arguments about technological development, it also owed something to Le Blon's failure to communicate his invention successfully. Or, to put it another way, it resulted also from the scant willingness of people to understand and accept a technique based on natural philosophy (laws of nature) that seemingly commanded neither complete confidence nor absolute consensus.[180] Castel spoke, as we have heard, of the riddle of *L'Harmonie du coloris*; later, as a witness at one of Le Blon's demonstrations, he wrote of the first blue stage of the printing of a Madonna and Child as a realisation in pellucid, 'Virgin' blue.[181] The use of the word 'virgin' suggests two things and betrays two impulses: first, a reluctance to de-symbolise colour, to release it from deep meaning, in the manner necessary to grasp fully colour's constitutive role in the optical 'real'; and, second, a desire to mend the unity of light that Newton's experiments had shattered – 'Virgin blue' stands for all that the Virgin is.[182]

Such misreadings of Le Blon's process may have resulted from his description of the separates as 'épreuves', or trial proofs. In conventional printmaking, an 'épreuve' was an impression of the plate printed during its working, in order to monitor progress. In the case of engraving, the engraver began by outlining the composition on the copper plate in drypoint before working it up with a burin, section by section. As Antony Griffiths explains, this was because the engraver could not see whether his results were consistent with creating a sense of volume by the intersection of lines unless an area was engraved more or less completely.[183] In Agostino Carracci's reproduction of Paolo Veronese's *La Sacra Famiglia con i Santi Giovanni Battista, Caterina et Antonio Abate* (fig. **97**) we see the Virgin and Child, top right, more or less fully formed, and the imagination easily supplies the missing details: her forehead and veil. It is unlikely that even connoisseurs would have seen a proof impression such as this one. However, all those familiar with portrait prints would have been aware of the conventional stages through which they progressed from proof to finished state: head in drypoint, fully engraved head before the addition of the frame, and head and frame before the lettering.[184] Progress was doubly linear: the repeated laying in of lines and a simple one-way movement from part to whole.

The relationship between 'separates' is not sequential and progressive in quite this sense. Each plate is complete in itself, a perfectly engineered mechanical component, which, operating in parallel with others, produces an integrated image in print. It is well nigh impossible for the uninitiated, faced with a yellow or red separate, to resolve the unfinished image imaginatively. Reading 'separates' awry as proofs – that is, simultaneously as representations and simple, surface technical information, as both image and work – induces what, in a different context, Brian McHale has termed an 'ontological flicker' between the mimetic and material realities of the 'text'.[185] The resulting effects – the familiar face of the cardinal defamiliarised by the primaries and the strangely embodied colour of the painter's familiar palette – disturbed settled notions of optics and technology but afforded no clear understanding of the invention in question, even, apparently, among the scientifically informed. There was room, rhetorically, for Gautier to appropriate and 'improve'.

However, when Gautier's position was challenged in 1748 by Jean Robert, another of Le Blon's former apprentices, Gautier rapidly abandoned the title of 'perfector', to which Robert could also reasonably lay claim,[186] for that of 'originator', taking up lines of argument first developed in the litigation with Le Blon's heirs in 1741. Me de La Clef had then asserted that Le Blon and Gautier had coincidentally discovered the art of colour printing in the colour theory of *père* Castel; Gautier now insisted that he alone had enjoyed Castel's patronage for an invention he, Gautier, brought with him from Marseille.[187] While the dispute reveals, in general, the weakness of proprietory arguments based on Francis Bacon's ideas of collective invention and collaborative progress,[188] the details of conflicting, indeed opposed, sources – no longer Newton but the anti-Newtonian Castel – suggest, in particular, that despite all efforts at disclosure Le Blon's secret had remained locked in his images and texts.

LE BLON, GAUTIER, ROBERT

In November 1748 the *Mercure de France* broadcast the publication, 'Avec Privilège du Roi', of a 'New Print' in 'the new manner' of colour printing in oil by Jean Robert after a Crucifixion by Nicolas Delobel.[189] Having noted that the print was to be had at Robert's studio in Montmartre and, more centrally, at an address in rue Saint-Honoré, the newspaper went on to add that Robert had been a pupil of the late Le Blon 'to whom France owes this technique of printmaking', and that his, Delobel's, work was distinguished by its sharpness of focus.

Gautier's response to this assault on the uniqueness of his status as Le Blon's pupil and heir was immediate. The following month, in the same paper, he counterclaimed that Robert had no personal title in the privilege but one merely derived from the residual rights of Messrs Viguier and Villars, Gautier's former partners, trading, as it turned out, from his former address in the rue Saint-Honoré.[190] Robert's print was, Gautier alleged, no more than a 'trial attempt', and, since it had been realised using four copper plates not three, was in fact a copy after his, Gautier's, process, and not in the manner of Le Blon's *tri*-chromacy.[191]

In an advertisement for anatomical prints in April the following year, Gautier styled his technology, more emphatically still, '*another system* with four plates' (my emphasis): not a modification of Le Blon's practice but an 'other system' altogether.[192] The relationship with Le Blon, or rather with the tradition of colour printing, was still acknowledged but increasingly Gautier represented his part in its invention as decisive, not incremental – as that which alone made Le Blon's discovery 'practicable'.[193] What prompted this change in rhetorical mode, this substitution of claims to invention of a 'door-opening' rather than a 'gap-filling' kind? Part of the answer lies in Gautier's business dealings: first, in the specific terms of the settlement with his former partners, Viguier and Villars, and, second, in the decision to exchange partnership arrangements for public subscriptions as the means to finance operations.

Viguier, a clerk in the office of the Contrôleur général des finances, Philibert Orry, and Villars, a *bourgeois de Paris*, had been in partnership with Gautier since January 1745.[194] They had equal shares in the privilege, secured in their case by substantial capital funds and in Gautier's by 'the secret' and a commitment to labour. Within 18 months, however – that is, by 6 August 1746 – Villars had lost confidence in the enterprise, daunted by the extraordinary capital outlay required by Gautier's myological studies on the scale of life.[195] Viguier and Gautier agreed to buy him out, dividing his share equally between them.[196] However, the problems did not end there. Viguier was a troublemaker. As one of the partners in an earlier company formed by Gautier, he had apparently sowed strife sufficient to force a buyout.[197] With Villars's departure, Viguier appointed a certain La Bory to watch over his interest.[198] Before the month of August had fully run its course, La Bory, suspecting Gautier of fraud, had closed the workshops and brought production to a standstill.[199] Gautier, later exonerated by the courts, was convinced by the experience of the impossibility of an accommodation, and thus of the need to cut and run. An anonymous memorandum on the dispute, drawn up at the time for Malesherbes, provides a chronicle of unfolding events, lists the grievances on both sides, sets out proposals for winding up the partnership and reveals, moreover, the extent to which 'the secret', and secrecy more generally, was recognised as intrinsically related to the failure of the enterprise.[200]

From the outset, the partnership was fatally undermined by lack of trust. Not having been privy to the secret, Viguier and Villars were prey to almost paranoid suspicions;[201] they believed Gautier guilty of operating clandestine presses elsewhere in the capital to run off impressions exclusively for his own profit,[202] and they daily anticipated that he would abscond with the secret, leaving them indebted and empty-handed.[203] They had introduced procedures to secure themselves a greater measure of control over the means of production: the workshop was to be secured by two locks and the two keys, entrusted respectively to Gautier and to Viguier and Villars. Moreover, the copper plates and impressions were to be counted in and out at the beginning and end of every working day.[204] Keys and accountancy, however, failed to quiet anxiety. And, meanwhile, Gautier had become increasingly impatient with the bureaucracies that he said hampered the profitable exercise of trade.[205]

The author of the memorandum expressed himself firmly on the side of artistic invention and contemptuous of Philistine capital, but he noted that: 'The King granted Letters of Privilege for colour printing with the intention of making so useful an art common practice throughout the Kingdom; [but] up until now this Privilege has had the opposite effect, making it more mysterious, more hidden, more inaccessible to the host of clever Artists of which France is filled.'[206]

A division of the privilege at the dissolution of the Gautier, Viguier and Villars partnership would achieve for the government what its granting had not, and pressure was doubtless applied to end monopoly in the public interest. Initially, Viguier had wanted Gautier either to take over the privilege in its entirety or to abandon it completely,[207] but Gautier was in no position to assume the partnership's liabilities. Unwilling also to forfeit his trade and invention, Gautier proposed dividing the company's assets along with the privilege. Viguier was originally offered the anatomical plates and prints – that is, the most recent output of the business – but in 1746, with the project as yet unfinished, costs mounting and output at a standstill, the anatomical atlas did not look an attractive proposition.[208] Believing that more reliable profit was to be found in the reproduction of works of art than in the speculative pursuit of science, Viguier finally accepted as his share the stock of copper plates and impressions of all genres except anatomy, including the plates bought from Le Blon's estate in 1742.[209] The market for colour prints thus became competitive overnight. Gautier rightly anticipated that Viguier would try to harness the talents of another of Le Blon's former pupils.[210] The advertisement in the *Mercure de France* in November 1748 for Robert's Crucifixion is proof of his success.[211]

Wary of partnerships, Gautier, meanwhile, had turned to alternative forms of finance. In October 1745, he had launched a subscription for the first eight plates of his anatomy of the superficial musculature of the head after dissections prepared by the late Joseph-Guichard Duverney, anatomist and celebrated demonstrator at the Jardin royal des plantes.[212] Between May and September of that year, when the subscription closed, Gautier had sold 200 subscriptions, each at 24 *livres*, raising sufficient capital, apparently, fully to underwrite the publication.[213] However, where subscription had been an additional source of revenue in 1745–6, by 1747, when Gautier was acting alone, it had become his sole mode of finance. Subscription transformed the role of privilege in the market for invention. No longer exclusive property by which to raise investment, privilege functioned rather as a sign, by force of which consumers would be persuaded to commit payment for a book or print in advance of publication.[214] Already in October 1745, when Gautier first advertised subscription to his anatomical prints, he made a particular point of the fact that these were not 'a repetition of other Authors, not old prints [newly] hand-coloured', but 'original works representing Nature herself, after whom they have been drawn using the new Art of colour printing'.[215] The incorporation into the advertisement of a brief history of the privilege served to reiterate officially the novelty of the process, which Gautier claimed as his own by virtue of his 'discoveries'.[216]

Having lost monopoly of the privilege and exclusive right to the secret, and being determined to rely henceforth on subscription, Gautier was compelled to adopt a more aggressive marketing strategy for his work. In these changed circumstances and stripped of its legal muscle, privilege served Gautier as a rhetorical figure, as hyperbole in his address to potential consumers. Battles over the profit in invention thus took place not in court but in the newspapers, and not with 'facts' for weapons, but fictions.[217]

In July 1749 the *Mercure de France* published a second exchange of letters between Robert and Gautier. Robert countered Gautier's claim that he had discovered the 'real' system of colour printing by insisting that Le Blon's trichromacy had, in fact, depended on more than three plates – the portrait of Cardinal Fleury and a portrait of Louis XV had each required four – and that Le Blon had even envisaged manipulating up to five or six plates for the highest quality results.[218] Gautier's reply, addressed not to the editor of the *Mercure* but to Claude Gros de Boze, whom the king had appointed to resolve the dispute between Gautier and his partners in 1747, insisted, however, that the function of these additional plates, which he dubbed 'contre-planches', had been merely superficial: to add finishing detail – strands to a mane of hair, definition to the edge of a collar, intensity to the colour of a sash.[219] They were not necessary to the process of colour printing as such. Gautier's fourth plate, by contrast, played a fundamental part in what he called his 'système pratique des quatres primitives'.[220] 'Primitive' was the word by which the Latin *primarius* was translated in the French edition of Newton's *Opticks*, and Gautier may well have intended the allusion and welcomed the association.[221] However, the emphasis on practice in 'système pratique' also suggests a break with Newtonianism at the moment of its application.

Newton had established an absolute theoretical distinction between chromatic colours or hues on the one hand and a scale of brightness from white to black on the other. Gautier's account of his method of printing colour reinstates, however, a traditional modification theory of colour that combined tonal and chromatic indices.[222] The following passage from the letter finds him ordering colours in the Aristotelian fashion, *between* black and white: 'I use four colours to reproduce pictures painted in oil: that is, black, blue, yellow & red; these four colours & the white of the paper generate all the colours imaginable.'[223] Gautier performs, in effect, a chiasmus: things that had once been linked with the secret (invention, colour, Le Blon) now appear opposed to it; and things that had earlier stood apart from the secret (convention, tone, Gautier) have become closely identified with it. They are revealed as the 'true' secret and Gautier's exclusive property.

Invited by the editor of the *Mercure*, Pierre Rémond de Saint-Albine, to arbitrate in the dispute, Gautier de Montdorge, Le Blon's former partner, upheld Robert's contention that he had learned all the secrets of the art from Le Blon.[224] Le Blon had, he confirmed, systematically used a fourth plate to deliver black (not finish) to the printing process. He had not admitted as much because the laws of light and colour held it unnecessary; it was, rather, the business of practice that rendered it desirable. The black plate yielded economies of material, skill and time; made colour printing more 'expedite' and 'reliable'.[225] A daily routine of the studio, it was precisely the evidence that confirmed Robert as Le Blon's pupil, and put Gautier's own claims to the invention of an 'other system' in jeopardy.

Undaunted, Gautier advertised more subscriptions: four in all between 1745 and 1749. Moreover, to allay disappointment at the inevitable delays in the delivery of promised prints, in 1751 Gautier published a ten-page recapitulative 'Projet général' of his anatomical works, which recounted in sequence and in detail the output of his workshop from the earliest flayed heads to the anticipated full-length anatomical portraits of a man and a woman on the scale of life.[226] Confident that 'no-one doubts any longer that M. Gautier has first made practicable the technique of colour printing', the author forbore to talk further about the invention and its history. Rather, he stressed the particular utility of trichromacy for the science of anatomy, and the advances in general knowledge that the reproductive process allowed in its new perfection.[227]

His extravagant talk of 'triumph', of royal 'rewards' and of 'public esteem' apparently drew no comment from the competition until several years later, when he attempted to re-establish himself in the market for art prints. In 1755, he announced in his recently founded periodical the *Observations sur l'histoire naturelle, sur la physique et sur les beaux-arts* his intention to furnish colour reproductions of paintings in the collection of Claude Alexandre de Villeneuve, comte de Vence, the first two of which, *La Toilette du soir* after Arnold Boonen and *Le Magister hollandois* after Gerard ter Borch, were advertised in the *Mercure de France* in November of the same year.[228] An anonymous correspondent was provoked to write to the *Mercure* the very next month and contest Gautier's categorical reiteration that he was 'the inventor of the art of colour printing with four plates', and to insist that, in fact, his was the lesser honour of having 'by means of a *privilège exclusif*, alone perfected the art of colour printing using four plates'.[229]

In a final bitter exchange the following year, Gautier argued that in saying he had invented colour printing he was not attempting to deny that others had tried, but was insisting that he alone had been perfectly successful. He claimed his success as the success of an inventor by the same reasoning that the one to discover the philosopher's stone would earn the title, notwithstanding the many who had failed in the attempt before.[230] As such, Gautier appeared to be saying that his discovery belonged to matters of fact, to the physical laws of nature, ones that had always existed but which he alone had grasped. The anonymous critic was quick to point out that such a 'secret', once broadcast, might as easily be acted upon by the ignorant as by the learned; in short that, as a law and not a practice, such a secret entailed no 'art'.[231] Consequently, it could not be attributed to a particular subjectivity, nor, by extension, was it indubitably the object of private property.[232]

This exchange occurred in the very years that Bachelier and the comte de Caylus were embroiled in a parallel dispute over priority and originality in the invention of encaustic. In 1755, Diderot published a memorandum on the wax affair that is strikingly similar in tone and argument to the letters of Gautier's nemesis. The lengthy, scholarly 'history' of a secret seemingly little worth keeping brings into contempt the parties involved:[233] big names, Academicians both. Diderot exposed the conceit of Bachelier's and Caylus's respective claims to the distinction of inventor. Bachelier's discovery is revealed as the product of chance; Caylus's as the outcome of philological and historical inquiry. Moreover, the development of their respective versions of encaustic emerges as heavily dependent on collaboration with others – notably chemists – and on making connections across different fields of knowledge – between, for instance, encaustic painting and resist printing.[234] In an instance where art was more conspicuously at issue, Diderot found reasons nevertheless to undermine the right of any individual to monopolise knowledge and the profit in it.

'Nothing', insisted Diderot in his opening sentence, 'is so contrary to the progress of knowledge as secrecy', and from the outset he judged it 'a crime to deprive one's fellow men of knowledge of the useful arts'.[235] Indeed, he later argued that civil law should punish those who took their 'secrets' to the grave as severely as canon law prosecuted those clergy who left accumulated fortunes.[236] The public is construed as having rights to know that lay waste the inventor's entitlement to property in his invention, and Diderot delighted in the Enlightenment 'malady' that had him 'burning' to disclose inventions the moment they came to his attention.[237]

Ironically, Gautier was forced by market circumstances, by competition, to learn to articulate an exclusive, personal stake in invention at precisely that historical moment when his prior arguments on invention as a collaborative process in the public interest were helping to reshape the government's policy on *privilèges exclusifs*. The arrival in 1749 of Daniel Trudaine at the Bureau du commerce brought a decisive shift away from regulation and *privilèges exclusifs*. The royal declaration of 24 December 1762 envisaged privilege as a reward – that is, as an instrument of industrial and commercial policy; it was not a right.[238] Privileges were henceforth not to stand in the way of competition; on the contrary, they had to stimulate it.[239]

Wounded by the *Mercure*'s assault on his reputation, anticipating further blows with the imminent publication of Gautier de Montdorge's revised edition of *L'Harmonie du coloris* and his article 'Gravure en couleur' in the *Encyclopédie*, both of which were certain to promote Le Blon at Gautier's expense, and there being no prospect in sight of improving the legal defence of his process, Gautier retreated.[240] He retired to Marseille, hoping for better success with his anatomical publications in the provinces.[241]

HYPERBOLE: UNCANNY EFFECTS

'Hyperbole' was not a word used to describe Gautier's work in the way that 'secret' had denoted Le Blon's. Nor was it a synonym for privilege. Unlike secrecy, in other words, it was not a strategy, actual or rhetorical, for securing property in an idea. Rather, Gautier deployed hyperbole from the late 1740s to describe the value of his invention. By exaggeration of what was actually true – the discontinuity of his four-plate system with other, earlier colour-printing technologies – Gautier aimed to establish a proper understanding of the 'true', extraordinary nature of his work.[242] At a time when the Bureau du commerce was becoming increasingly disenchanted with monopolies, hyperbole seemingly justified those rare instances of patent-privilege. Moreover, Gautier not only amplified his claims to authorship through the copious newspaper articles and advertisements he published in the 1740s, he also repeated his addresses to privilege in all its legal forms. In 1745, it was he who supplemented the *privilège exclusif* by purchase of a 20-year *privilège général* for the anatomies from the Paris Corporation des libraires et maîtres imprimeurs.[243] Such apparent instances of redundancy are a reminder that hyperbole, overreaching, may be both positively and negatively construed. Critics were quick to agree that Gautier overstated his claims in word and image. But if hyperbolic tropes are relatively easy to identify in Gautier's writing, his prints demand a more inferential reading. Unlike Le Blon, Gautier did not directly articulate his invention via traditional myths of origin (Veronica, Narcissus, Pygmalion, etc.); nor did he parade a visual deconstruction of his technology by means of separates. There is no surviving black proof. Rather, it was by recourse to the aesthetics of the Sublime – of which hyperbole is a significant figure, following Longinus[244] – that Gautier chose to dramatise, by intensity, the uniqueness of his invention. The egotistical insistence – in red, so to speak – of *his* art and *his* presence in the work suggests a Romantic rather than an Enlightenment construction of the author, by which I mean one not only possessing but also possessed by invention. Gautier's visual overstatement produced uncanny effects. Critics described his black-based 'inventions' as 'sales' (dirty).[245] The secret had become a lie, a lie about priority and authenticity, one that was obscurely, indirectly felt (as filth) rather than knowingly registered, and by virtue of remaining partially hidden continued to disrupt and render problematic Gautier's creations. Examination of the nature of the authorial uncanny is the final stage of this investigation of the *ancien-régime* artist as inventive author.

The anonymous critic of the 1755–6 articles in the *Mercure* justified his remorseless assault on Gautier's reputation on the grounds that the latter invited criticism by the self-regarding nature of his many newspaper articles. It was, he further asserted, for works of art to stand on their own merits and not for artists to make claims on their behalf.[246] For this writer, Gautier's hyperboles were unhappy; like so many falsehoods, they opened up an inadmissible gap between what was claimed and what was actually (believed to be) the case.[247] For Gautier, on the other hand, the very *topos* of invention, of the hitherto impossible, seemed to license hyperbole: a double hyperbole, of the self and of its imaginings. The 'Lettre à M. de Boze', Gautier's definitive statement on colour printing, is marked by the frequent occurrence of the personal pronoun, which by constant repetition in the context of everyday events and feelings – '*I* arrived in Paris ... *I* was careful to keep my ideas to *myself* ... *I* did not, however, wish to be ignored ... *I* sought the means to make *myself* known ... and *I* found them'[248] – amplifies the authorial subject of the text, the specifically inventive 'I', and works to make credible the assumptive statements 'I engraved 22 different pieces *according to my system in four colours* ... I have since executed *even greater subjects which can compete with real paintings.*'[249] Meanwhile, adjectival hyperbole establishes the proper scale of Gautier's achievement: '*Great* projects', he asserts, 'can be achieved only in *great* Cities, and I imagined to myself being able to realise mine only in Paris.'[250] The gigantic proportion of the capital served as a metaphor for the grandeur of Gautier's innovation and the status of his system. That system, succinctly described, is characterised, moreover, by categoricals – 'I use four colours to imitate *all* oil paintings ... these four colours and the white of the paper create *all* the colours imaginable' (my emphasis throughout)[251] – that lend it an incontrovertible universality. Repetition, magnification and deterministic assertion are just some of the hyperbolic strategies used by Gautier to promote recognition of his invention in the ordinary language of publicity. That he was successful is strongly suggested by the anonymous critic's admission that he had been disposed initially to believe the unbelievable, had indeed been blind to the operations of hyperbole and transfixed by the self-effacing illusion of a unique and great personal achievement.[252]

What of Gautier's images? In what extravagant terms do the various anatomies refer to the origin or the nature of colour printing? How do they promote and extol Gautier's invention as exclusively his? The questions are not idle. In relation to the first, Barbara Stafford has argued for the paradigmatic value of dissection in Enlightenment thought. In a literal and a figural sense, dissection both accomplished and represented the 'investigative method that uncovered the duplicity of the world': in this instance, its riot of colour hidden beneath the surface of white light.[253] Moreover, she draws attention to the parallels between the 'cutting' involved in printmaking and in surgery, finding deployed in Giambattista Piranesi's *Vedute di Roma antica e moderna* (1745) specifically 'surgical' lines of incision.[254] In mezzotint, however, the tender action of the burnisher, which smoothes a light path through rough planes of darkness, has evidently not the incisiveness and decisiveness to spark the chain of associations between anatomy, dissection, refraction, colour that the analogy demands. And Gautier, who was garrulous in all matters concerning his art, was conspicuously silent in respect of the stories his prints might tell concerning their technology. Not the subject matter, not the intaglio process but the pictorial mode is significant here.

In 1747, Charles Lefebvre de Saint-Marc offered a new edition of Nicolas Boileau's literary works, volume 4 of which contains the poet's long since definitive translation of Longinus. In the mass of prefatory materials on the Sublime are gathered the thoughts of Louis-Bertrand Castel, the same Jesuit scientist upon whose practical and theoretical assistance in matters of light and colour Gautier admitted depending for his 'system'. According to Castel, the Sublime is to poetry what discovery or invention is to natural philosophy: both deal with the new, the marvellous, the great and the curious.[255] As an example of this correspondence Castel juxtaposed Virgil's hyperbolic description of Aeneas' descent into the underworld, where 'rebus nox abstulit atra colores' ('night stole the colour of things'), with Descartes's discovery that 'colours are only modified light, and that night, in chasing away light, chases away colour'.[256] If Descartes's experiments substantiated Virgil's sublime metaphor by exposing its truth, poetry, Castel argued, plays an important role in rendering admissible – pleasurable, even – the extraordinary and shocking discoveries of science.[257] In short, the Sublime is the language proper to invention.

Le Blon had, as already noted, published separates to make *known* his invention but in order that reason may be enlightened, the senses suffer a shock, are even revolted, when confronted, for example, by the red impression of Cardinal Fleury (fig. **95**). Antoine Furetière recorded conventional opinion when he noted in his dictionary definition of that colour that 'it is a beauty in lips to be intensely red; it is a great defect in eyes'.[258] Scarlet, at Le Blon's direction, seeps into crevices and invades surfaces of the cardinal's body from which it ought properly to have been outlawed: the crack of the smile (at the expense of the flesh of the lips), the albinotic gaze. Gautier, by contrast, settled for making *sensible* the invention of colour printing. In plate 1 of the *Myologie complette en couleur et grandeur naturelle* (1746; fig. **98**), in which a head is posed in a manner made classic by Gaetano Zumbo's wax (fig. **99**), and the first layer of muscle exposed, the horror of colour separation vanishes; red returns to its adjectival function, sinking into the abject only below the body's surface.[259] The lips are subtle shades of candy pink. Enveloped in what Castel would have described as 'poetic raiment', invention's 'bright spark' is here glimpsed indirectly as novelty, appearing only to disappear again.[260]

In an article for the *Mercure de France* in October 1749, which advanced a theory of pictorial 'keys' inspired directly by Castel's famous ocular harpsichord,[261] Gautier classified his anatomies with Roman and Bolognese painting, on the grounds of grandeur and of the balance of sombre tones.[262] He cited the sublime Salvator Rosa among those whose works he had reproduced in this key.[263] In concert with Italian Baroque painting and in contrast with the conventions of anatomical illustration of the day, Gautier's prints are densely coloured and on the scale of life, characteristics picked out in red on the title-page of the *Myologie complette*. The impression of vast, even monumental size is exaggerated, moreover, in many of the plates – for example, the head and neck viewed from the back (fig. **100**) and the front view of a male torso (fig. **101**) – by the tight cropping of the specimens, such that they appear to overpower the physical constraints of the page. However, the equally excessive body of colour is what strikes the viewer first. Roger de Piles's defence of the study of anatomy for artists, published as a prefatory text to François Tortebat's *Abrégé d'anatomie* in 1667, had singled out its importance to the proper definition of the contours of the human figure, to the line of the silhouette.[264] From the point of view of artists, therefore, a public to whom Gautier's prints were certainly addressed, colour had in the past been absent from the anatomical study of the body; it continued, in the eighteenth century, to be regarded as superfluous.[265] But that which was pedagogically marginal, in the *Myologie* was also artistically central: not only are the specimens illuminated, the prints are covered with colour. The abstract space of conventional anatomies – denoted by an empty page, or in Vesalius's illustrations (which were re-used by de Piles and Tortebat) by a classical landscape – is replaced in Gautier's work by the particular conditions of an actual place, where real light highlights (the back of the skull in fig. **100**) or obscures in shadow. Moreover, the obscurity of the background radicalises the *éclat* of the red, the predominant hue of the prints and, according to Castel, the dominant colour of nature.[266] The muscles throb into three dimensions, assume a livid liveliness that in some instances aligns with a narrative of pain and suffering (fig. **98**) and in others seemingly occasions an uncanny insouciance at the body's casual dismemberment.[267]

Gautier paraded invention in the sublimity of nature. The 'uniqueness' of his achievement, upon which he also insists in the title of his book (we come on here to the second question, the question of authorship), thus arose first from the referential value of his plates in a field dominated by copies: de Piles had justified the recycling of Vesalius's illustrations in the *Abrégé d'anatomie* on the grounds that they were, in his view, 'impossible to improve upon'.[268] Direct imitation of nature, perfectly or imperfectly achieved, was proof of originality, of the difference of this myology from every other – a difference that justified Gautier's authorial priority over the anatomists Duverney and (later) Pierre Tarin, whose dissections, executed, respectively, at the Jardin royal des plantes and the Charité, he reproduced.[269] It was Gautier's name that appeared on the title-page, in red.[270] Moreover, Gautier's name did not only *appear* in red but, in a certain sense, his name *was* red. To make the same point differently, red in the anatomies performed an indexical as well as a descriptive function; it pointed to the author. By the mid-eighteenth century, it was common knowledge that the eye is stimulated by colour, independent of all signification, and that red light by virtue of the speed and relative directness of its travel, 'strikes the retina with great force, excites the most sensible vibrations, and moves us with the most vivid sensation of colour'.[271] Red, in a certain sense, stands for colour, for its autonomy, because red is never completely located or absolutely adjectival. By force of impact it insists on its presence as such. Thus, emblematic of colour in a world of black and white, red served Gautier in the manner of a trademark, a mark that implicitly guaranteed the uniqueness of his work in a second, technological sense, but without disclosing how it was done. That, figuratively speaking, Gautier was red to Le Blon's blue finds a measure of support in dye technology and the structure of the eighteenth-century textile industry: indigo and madder dyeworks operated independently – were, indeed, mutually exclusive – before mid-century.[272]

The critics' response to Gautier's *Myologie* and its extravagant articulations of difference was almost as hostile as their reaction to his tall tales (*contes jaunes*)[273] of originality and priority in invention. Brief, unstudied and intended merely to discredit Gautier's pretension to invention by means of an assault on his taste, their remarks nevertheless have the intensity and pointedness of overreaction; in fact, they reveal anxiety beneath the avowed contempt. Gautier de Montdorge dismissed anatomy as a horror, noting that he had abandoned Le Blon's projected *Cours d'anatomie* (of which fig. **80** is the first and only known plate) after the artist's death because, 'to speak frankly, I discovered that there are a hundred more pleasing occupations in life than arranging and rearranging the entrails or the heart of a hanged man'.[274] The anonymous writer of the 1755–6 articles likewise scorned Gautier's anatomy, though not so much because of its transgressions – the violations of law and the body upon which, as de Montdorge noted, it depended for its primary materials[275] – but because it addressed itself merely to the body and natural history and not to humankind and history painting.[276] That opposition implies that the source of the critics' discomfort before Gautier's works was in part related to their conspicuous concern with the material and the mechanical – that is, with the physical properties of both the body and its reproduction. The printers' inks lie in uneven distribution across the fibrous mesh of the rag paper, accentuating its textured, corrugated surface,[277] and draw attention from the contours to the fibres (fig. **101**) of the body. In this, Gautier's *Myologie* was absolutely consistent with the most advanced vitalist and materialist trends in eighteenth-century physiology. The shift of focus in the 1740s and 1750s from organs to fibres, which, according to the *Encyclopédie*, particularly characterised 'mechanical anatomists' – those, that is, who conceived of the body by analogy with a machine – undermined the dualisms upon which the anonymous critic's critique depended for its impact. It was precisely because, following the Swiss anatomist Albrecht von Haller, traditional properties of liveliness and ensoulment, such as motility, were discovered by observation and experiment to belong to the body that humankind emerged, according to Julien Offray de La Mettrie, Haller's notorious French disciple, as not merely like a machine but actually no more than a machine.[278] Modern, mechanical man was not the heroic subject of history painting; rather, he was the anonymous and paradoxically lively cadaver of anatomy.

It was not only the subject matter, however, that provoked dread; the anonymous critic repeatedly abrogated Gautier for the dirtiness of his prints.[279] According to Le Blon, this displeasing effect was caused by an imbalance in the manipulation of the primaries, specifically by an excess of red,[280] the very colour with which Gautier was most closely identified. For the anonymous critic, however, dirt was linked with black, and not so much with technical incompetence as with desire: desire for exclusive authorship of the invention or secret, desire to emulate painting, and desire for the subjectivity that the status of painter (as opposed to reproductive printmaker) would confer.

Taken together, Gautier's work and the critics' responses expose an unexpected collision of the Sublime and the uncanny. In an essay published in 1919, Sigmund Freud defined the uncanny not only taxonomically, in relation, that is, to a class of phenomena that 'arouse dread and horror' and to which Gautier's anatomies appear related – waxworks, automata, detached body parts, especially those that 'prove capable of independent activity', ghosts – but also philologically, as a concept that 'develops in the direction of ambivalence, until it finally coincides with its opposite': *heimlich* (the familiar, the homely) becomes *unheimlich* (the unfamiliar, the strange).[281] A similar movement of inversion seems to occur in the way the controversy over Gautier's claim to invention, instanced in the anatomies, was played out. Thus, while Gautier commended them to the public for their realism 'minus the horror that the subject ordinarily inspires, and without its pestilential odour'[282] – that is, as a horror tamed – the critics apparently experienced that same realism, that uncanny life-likeness of figure and fibre, with fear and disgust. In the critics, it seemingly aroused the return of an early, 'primitive' belief in animism, in the possibility of living dolls (or, in this case, living anatomies), which reason ordinarily surmounts and keeps at bay.[283] And, while Gautier vaunted the dark key of his anatomies as solid, substantial and constitutive (you might say 'grand', both in balance and in weight), the anonymous critic read the same hues as dark products of an occult process: specifically of the effect of the fourth, black plate in four-plate colour printing. In the terms of the formalist discourse of the time, the Sublime failed in its rescue of invention and Gautier's prints struck the critics rather as instances of indecorum – examples, that is, of hyperbole overshooting its mark and, as Longinus had warned, swinging round into its contrary, producing, in this case, an uncanny effect.

Scholarly attention has tended to focus on the formal rather than the social or political aspects of Freud's uncanny, and, until recently, little consideration had been given to the historical conditions of its emergence. However, in a collection of essays published in 1995, Terry Castle related the uncanny to Enlightenment: speaking metaphorically, she argues that it is what confronts us 'after a certain light has been cast'. Speaking historically, she claims it is that which 'comes to light' during the Enlightenment.

> At numerous points in 'The Uncanny,' ... it is difficult to avoid the conclusion that it was during the eighteenth century, with its confident rejection of transcendental explanations, compulsive quest for systematic knowledge, and self-conscious valorization of 'reason' over 'superstition,' that human beings first experienced that encompassing sense of strangeness and unease Freud finds so characteristic of modern life.[284]

Elaborating Freud's reading of E. T. A. Hoffmann's tale 'The Sandman', she connects the return of the repressed wish (primitive or infantile) for animism, figured by the 'lovely' automaton Olympia, with actual advances in mechanics, which had, by the eighteenth century, made possible the production of convincingly life-like 'dancing dolls', such as Vaucanson's flautist, and Jaquet-Droz's *Le Dessinateur* (fig. **64**).[285] By a parallel line of argument, a case could be made for locating the origin of the uncanny in Gautier's anatomies in seventeenth-century advances in optics and in the subsequent rationalisation of the primaries. In Charles-Nicolas Cochin's account of colour printing, we find an unexpected and telling tension between the colourless and systematic description of the repetitive stages of the rational printing process and the visual evocation of the effect of the red plate, singled out as exemplary precisely because red is actually and figuratively the sanguine colour of lips, cheeks, skin – in short, of human life – and, by implication, also of the 'primitive' belief in the magical power of images.[286] However, the case I want to make is rather that the disquiet provoked by the prints is, in fact, more fully and satisfactorily explained in relation to the emergent notions of possessive authorship. To put it another way, that the uncanny in the anatomies is black (not red), and that, insofar as it constitutes a return to an earlier state of mind, it is to an infantile narcissism rather than a primitive animism. Finally, that the uncanny is more an effect of Gautier's conscious, but ultimately thwarted, drive for differentiation than it is the 'toxic side effect' of increasingly higher levels of mastery and control in print technology.[287]

Black, defined by Furetière as 'an opaque and porous body [*corps*] that absorbs [*imbibe*] light and reflects not one part of it', is matter that hides inside itself. It is, as a colour, its own negation.[288] Thus, to argue for the uncanny-ness of black in Gautier's prints is to argue for the importance of a property that, in accordance with the etymology of 'secret', is simultaneously discerned (from the Latin verb *cerno, cernere*) and set apart (by the prefix *se-*) – in this case, from sight.[289] Black was the 'real' secret, the fourth element, secreted behind the ostensible and officially avowed secret of *tri*-chromacy. Its presence, merely sensed, was, however, later vigorously asserted and contradicted in the course of the dispute between Gautier and the disciples of Le Blon. With provocative hyperbole – that is, with a distinctly unsettling and narcissistic overestimation of his own creative powers – Gautier insisted on both the exclusivity and the technical efficacy of his invention. In so doing, he did violence to Le Blon, violence that, according to Robert, amounted to plagiarism, the 'theft of his [Le Blon's] reputation', an attack not only on Le Blon's property but also on his posthumous 'body'.[290] The Oedipal aggression of which Gautier stood accused in relation to his father-master is unmistakable. Yet, it is not the return of Gautier's repressed fear of castration that is experienced as uncanny in the prints since, according to Gautier de Montdorge, Gautier was not told, and therefore may not have known, of Le Blon's use of a black plate at the time of his apprenticeship.[291] To understand the haunting effects of Le Blon's secret on Gautier's anatomies, we need to borrow analytical tools not from Freud but from Nicolas Abraham and Mária Török, specifically from their theory of the phantom.

The concept of the phantom allows Abraham and Török to explain how influences outside a person's immediate, lived experience can determine their psychological development; how, in this case, Le Blon's secret modification of the technology of trichromacy could produce a disturbance at the level of representation in Gautier's work. It presupposes a model of psychic development in which individuation is achieved by a gradual process of separation rather than a moment of dramatic rupture, a separation that is, moreover, neither absolute nor complete because the child's emerging ego ('shell') carries with it part of the mother's unconscious ('kernel'), a residue of its original union with her.[292] The relationship with the mother is therefore simultaneously the arena in which separation is played out and the conduit via which 'family history' is transmitted. A 'phantom' occurs when this process of individuation becomes malignant as a consequence of a gap or hiatus in the parent's psyche, which prevents the child's normal repression of the parental unconscious, specifically when an 'unspeakable' family secret is silently passed on.

In 'The Phantom of Hamlet or The Sixth Act' (1975) Abraham uses his theory to account for the 'uneasiness' provoked by Shakespeare's play, in particular its ambivalences of plot and character.[293] In his own words, he aims 'to cure' the public of its fascination, release it from its thrall, by tracing back the uncanny 'phantom effect' of the play to its origin. That origin turns out to be a shameful secret, one that Hamlet's father takes to his grave but which his son unconsciously inherits. The legacy inhibits the younger Hamlet's ability to act, specifically to exact filial retribution on Claudius. What is significant in the present context is, first, the suggestion that the effect of the uncanny may be explained by a particular conformation in which a thing unknown (Abraham's *nescience*, Freud's *unheimlich*) to a subject in one generation is secretly known (*heimlich*) to an other in an earlier one; and, second, that the consequence of this trans-generational haunting is failure of the new subject to develop as an autonomous individual.[294] By this logic, the uncanny in the *Myologie complette* finds its explanation in Gautier's unaware awareness of Le Blon's secret: his unawareness of Le Blon's invention of the black plate, his ignorance too of the shameful compromise that profit can exact on art and science, and, simultaneously, his conscious and knowing use of black in the fabrication of his own designs. The theory of the 'phantom' thus seems to offer a resolution to the paradox of Gautier's failure ever to dispossess his father–master of his secret, notwithstanding the red assertions of authorship, the black practice of emulation and the early transfer of the privilege. Caught by a secret, the content of which he appears never fully or consciously to have reconstructed, Gautier remained ever mastered by and never master of the invention of another.

Abraham is not concerned with the haunting of Hamlet as a historical problem. He has nothing to say about the codes of honour and the taboos that in sixteenth-century England determined the encrypting of knowledge of those fictive actions and events whose secret existence he infers. By contrast, the challenge here is to move beyond the examination of the phantom as the driving force in an actual individual, beyond, too, explanations in the light of it of his rhetoric and his state of mind (satirised by the anonymous critic as voluntary amnesia),[295] and to relate the haunting to changing conditions of invention in eighteenth-century France. Freud, unlike Abraham and Török, historicised his account of the uncanny to the degree that he related its invention to the rise of the novel and to 'realist' modes of writing, having noted the absence of uncanny effects in myth, legend, and fairy tales – that is, in those archaic forms of oral storytelling that, by their avowed fantasy, are necessarily exempt from the 'reality testing' that gives rise to 'a conflict of judgement as to whether things which have been surmounted and are regarded as incredible may not, after all, be possible'.[296] The shift in Freud's argument from a nameless, very probably collective, archaic storyteller to an unnamed and singular modern author marks the passage in institutional terms from guilds and the silent husbanding of unsystematic knowledge and skills to academies and the self-conscious articulation, publication and dissemination of rationally ordered knowledge by individuals.[297]

Printmakers did not, of course, belong to guilds, but, in common with incorporated trades, early modern printmaking was founded on the face-to-face transmission by example of an amorphous body of technical know-how.[298] It was defined, that is, by its relative lack of a literature.[299] By the eighteenth century, scientists and natural philosophers, many of them members of royal academies, had, according to Stephan Epstein, become suspicious of the predominantly mute and largely unlettered culture of craft, to the point of wilfully assimilating it to alchemy, to its secrecy and its unreliability.[300] It was, no doubt, in an effort to stand above and apart from artisanal 'illiteracy' that Le Blon purported repeatedly to reveal in word and image how facts about colour and about printing, merely contiguous facts in the minds of fellow printmakers, had been systematically ordered and related by him to produce trichromacy. Le Blon wanted words because he knew that words gave his invention clarity, brought it reason; he used images – the separates – because they gave it shape. Words made him an author in the conventional sense of the word. However, his choice of words and images bent the facts like sticks in water. The pertinent facts in the application of the laws of optics to colour printing were chemical, not physical and mechanical as the separates alleged. They concerned the efficacy and economy of colour mixes. The scientific basis of these chemical arts was, however, poorly understood before the end of the eighteenth century and almost impossible to codify: first, for lack of a standard nomenclature and, second, because of significant variability in the quality and the kind of ingredients and in the conditions of production.[301] Gautier, who recognised colour printing as a problem of colour combination, merely published recipes, ones dubbed 'according to his system', though the system lacked persuasive principle and intellectual structure. It amounted to no more, indeed, than a patterning of pigments arranged by hue from white to black.[302] He drew attention to the *problem* of the secret, but the revelation concerning black did not ultimately locate it. Gautier's was a learned ignorance of trichromacy, assimilated unconsciously because the influence was not comprehended; its source was unnoticed.[303] Under heuristic conditions, visual models and descriptive accounts of inventions were of very little practical use.[304] The 'reverse engineering' of Le Blon's separates proposed a rhetorical figure of invention rather than a deconstruction of its secret substance. The apparent articulation of the process – in both senses of the verb 'articulate': to express distinctly in verbal (or, in this case) visual units, and to mark with apparent joints – actually registered the limits of language, and thus of reason and openness. When everything had been revealed, a certain irreducible something remained hidden: the tacit knowledge or 'blindsight' of the artist, and his or her personal knacks and skills.

If Enlightenment marks a presumed movement from an age of tradition and secrecy in technology defended by guilds to one of discovery and invention promoted by academies, the passionate social drama surrounding the origins of colour printing in France suggests that that movement was fractured and incomplete. All the (tall) talk of priority and authorship, the (straight) talk for purposes of privilege and its defence, the (sweet) talk to gain academic respectability – Gautier was actually elected an *associé correspondent* at the Académie de Dijon in 1753, only to be expelled shortly thereafter[305] – could not disguise the extent to which the art of colour printing remained inviolate to exhaustive verbal exposition. Haunted by the archaic 'mystery' of skill, a mystery that attached invention indissolubly to the body of the artist and to the tools and materials into which he poured himself, authorship, newly minted as open and articulate, owed the strength of its possessiveness, its subjectivity, precisely to this ghost. The unresolved contradictions between heuristics and theory, the unadmitted anxieties about tacit knowledge, and the blatantly incompatible assertions over priority produced areas of semantic slippage, discontinuities of meaning, phantoms, all of which generated powerful effects in Gautier's works, giving the viewer an inaugural sense of the uncanny.

* * *

In this chapter the conventional artistic meaning of invention has been set aside. In contrast to chapters 2 and 3, in which we examined emulation and imitation at the intersection of the legal and the artistic in order to plot art's informing of privilege and law's transformation of art, in chapter 4 we have analysed invention in the context of privilege alone. Science's culture of openness, and privilege's condition of disclosure did, to be sure, prompt Le Blon to create a number of inventively self-aware images, but, in general, imitation was the ground on which instances of invention in art were tested. It was also, in the case of colour printing, the prime referent for judging the invention's success. When Gautier turned reviewer of the artistic inventions of others, reviews he published in his journal, *Observations sur l'histoire naturelle*, he took his realist paradigm with him. His 'scientific' eye judged Oudry exceptional. So perfectly real was the painter's *Un Lapereau et une perdrix grise pendus par les pattes*, exhibited in 1751, that Gautier wanted to pluck the bird and discover if the skin beneath was as soft as the feathers.[306] At the 1753 Salon he preferred Oudry's 'truthful' handling of light to François Boucher's artifice – that is, the history painter's indiscriminate distribution of light and colour to create, and to be seen creating, *éclat*, rather than the real.[307] The point I am making is that, while invention had to prove itself institutionally in terms of making up novel technological processes, the law's ratification through privilege transformed invention into truth, into matters of fact, or the real in an epistemological sense. Academic history painters were not dependent on the law for such endorsement. Their reputations were made from the creative acts seen in their work, whether in the form of Boucher's idiosyncratic use of colour and light, or his artful re-use of themes, figures and motifs from antiquity and the Modern School. The Académie's privileges were purely defensive, and not constitutive of possession in the artistic sense. Academic work was personal because the artist was seen as embodied in it and could not therefore be completely alienated from it. Le Blon's and Gautier's invention, once verified by the Académie royale des sciences and privileged by the Bureau du commerce, lost visibility as a process, of making and making up, to became a matter of fact, a thing. And in not being present in their invention, in the way that artists were in theirs, Le Blon and Gautier could not invoke a moral right to it. It was in this sense that colour printing was like property, a thing distinct from the self that could be, and was in this case, inherited, divided, bought and sold, and, of course, allegedly stolen.

The property-like nature of patent-privilege did, however, leave the inventor vulnerable. His or her relation to the works was always a claim, articulated to the law and before the public. It was never self-evident. In this chapter, we have retraced Gautier's agonies as he pursued his legal entitlement to call himself the author of colour printing. In order to compel others to recognise his right, Gautier had to take possession of it over, and over, and over again. Claims and counterclaims that rehearsed the creative process and kept it in view were almost as important to maintaining his property right as his privilege, and the science of the invention itself. Ellipsis enabled Le Blon to disclose less than he claimed, and hyperbole allowed Gautier to claim more than he knew. For neither of them, however, did privilege yield the anticipated economic dividend: in fact, Gautier was bankrupt at his death in 1785. The state, meanwhile, identified the kingdom's advantage with the sharing, not the keeping, of technological secrets, the dissemination, not the ownership, of intellectual property. The royal declaration of 24 December 1762 thus set a limit of 15 years for all privileges issued by the Bureau du commerce.[308] Moreover, possession of such a privilege did not automatically entail its renewal or its transferability; if not worked within twelve months of issuance, the privilege became null and void, and royal dispensation was required for the privilege to pass from one generation to the next. Thus, while invention's discourse of possession was largely uncontested in principle, its legal condition as property was limited. Paradoxically, as Liliane Hilaire-Pérez has observed, the status of the inventor, his genius, was rising at the very same time that confidence in privilege as a juridical lever for national betterment and progress was falling.[309]

ART AND INDUSTRY: INTELLECTUAL PROPERTY AND THE FRENCH REVOLUTION

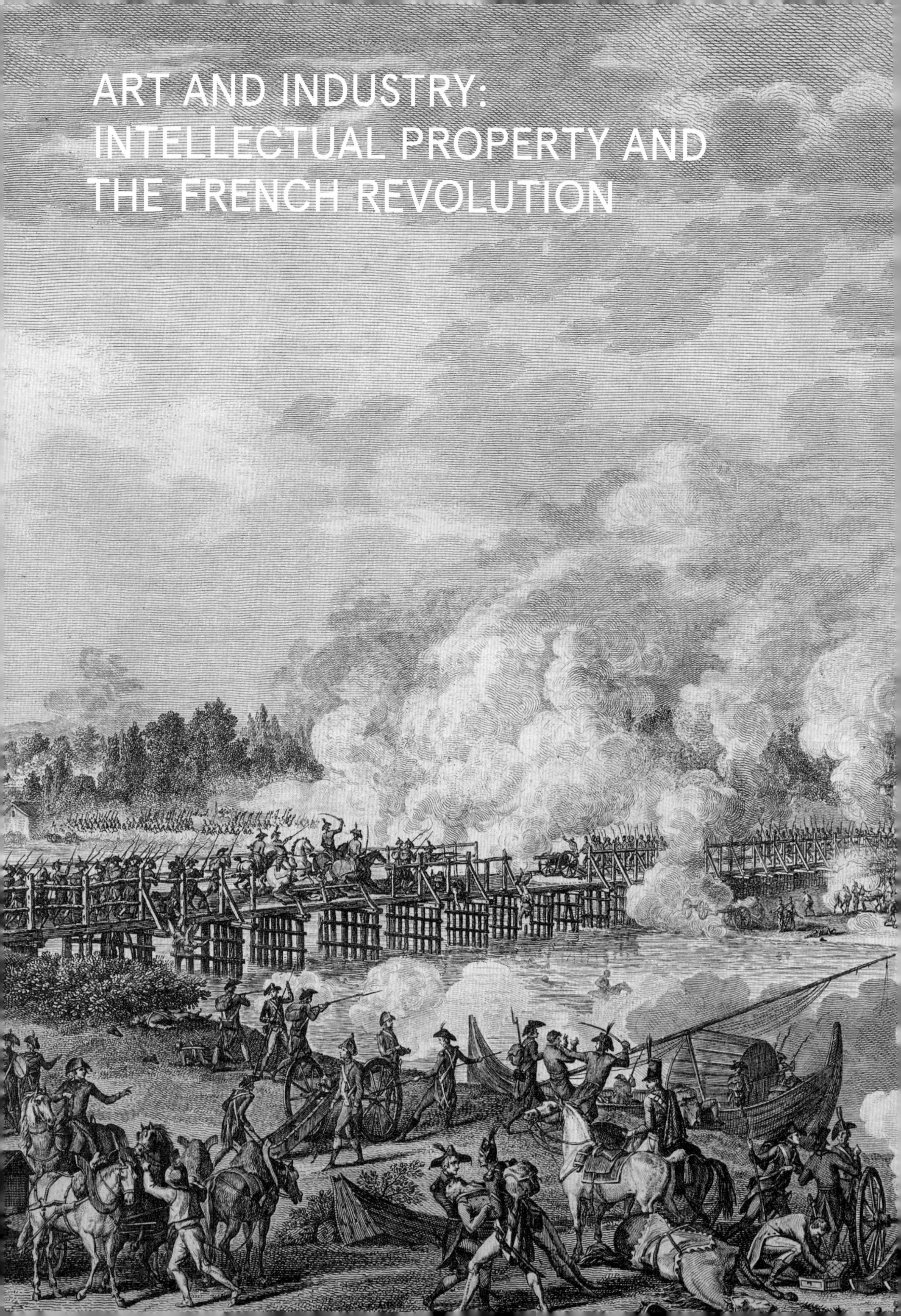

On 19 July 1793, the National Convention passed the *Décret… relatif aux droits de propriété des auteurs d'écrits en tout genre, des compositeurs de musique, des peintres et des dessinateurs* (Literary and Artistic Property Act). The opening article decreed that:

> Authors of all kinds of writing, composers of music, painters and draughtsmen who have their paintings reproduced in print shall enjoy a lifetime and exclusive right to sell, authorise for sale and distribute their works in the territory of the Republic, and to transfer that property in full and in part.[1]

It was the first time that a law on the commercialisation of works of art through reproduction had acknowledged, in so many words, both the rights of authors and the intellectual property in their work, on condition, nevertheless, of fulfilling the formalities of deposit and registration.[2] The politician Joseph Lakanal, reporting on the bill moments before its passing, stressed its property-like nature as follows: 'Of all properties the least subject to dispute, the one whose increase can neither injure republican equality nor offend liberty, is without doubt the property in the creations of genius.'[3] More often quoted than the Act itself for the feeling with which it voices the prerogatives of authorship, Lakanal's statement frames the so-called 'Act of the Rights of Genius' as the realisation of the natural rights of authors, first articulated by Louis d'Héricourt in 1725, reiterated by Diderot and the Paris book guild in 1763–4 and crucially not admitted as such in the *arrêt* of 1777. An Enlightenment ideal of authorship fulfilled and a bourgeois form of intellectual property enshrined in law, the Act serves as the fitting end to this book. In becoming property, art and its authors were brought into being and assume their modern identities.

While marking the end of the book, this chapter is not, however, a conclusion in the conventional sense of drawing the disparate arguments about privilege together and summarising the main points of the preceding chapters. This would be to suggest that in the Act the tension between the different meanings and terms of privilege, as either reputational and personal or like property, as assigning belonging and attribution or denoting ownership, as arising from originality or produced by invention were finally resolved and rationalised in conjunction with the Revolution's other intellectual property laws. There is certainly a temptation to do so. The writer Stanislas-Jean de Boufflers's address to the Assemblée nationale in 1790 on the reasons to establish the first national patent act in France anticipated the terms later used by Lakanal. Boufflers also insisted on the primacy of thought as a property beyond challenge. 'Invention, which is the origin of the arts, is', he asserted, 'also the origin of property; it is property's inaugural form. All other kinds are merely so by convention.'[4] Moreover, the first jurists to write about copyright in the 1820s and 1830s drew on Boufflers's text as much as on Lakanal's.

However, for these jurists the French Revolution marked not the fulfilment of the artists', inventors', writers' and publishers' aspirations for privilege. On the contrary, it broke decisively with the legal past. Only in civilised societies where liberty reigns can the notion of intellectual property emerge, Adrien Gastambide argued in his *Traité théorique et pratique des contrefaçons en tous genres* (1837).[5] This explained, he remarked, the lack of legal literature on the subject up to that moment. Gastambide contrasted modernity's bright spectacle of rights with an obscure, old regime, without public law in the arts and trades, and only particularistic regulations imposed 'secretly' and 'abusively' by guilds and other corporate bodies. By the time of Boufflers's 1790 address on patents for inventions, the legitimacy of the guilds had been thoroughly undermined, first by the revocation of all privileges on 6 May 1789, and months after, on 26 August, by the *Déclaration des droits de l'homme et du citoyen*.[6] The capital's printmakers, like the book publishers, the inventors and other interested parties, immediately began to petition the Assemblée nationale for intellectual property laws to replace the *privilèges en librairie* and those formerly issued by the Bureau du commerce. This chapter begins by reviewing the printmakers' petition, among the first to be submitted in 1790 and much the longest and most detailed such petition made by the print trade in the eighteenth century, vastly exceeding in scope and ambition those sent to the Directeur de la librairie, Antoine de Sartine, in the 1760s. In it, they referred to the Engravers' Act in Britain (1735), an act crucially by, as well as for, printmakers, and they asserted their right to write a law of their own to secure the liberty of the art of printmaking and the inviolability of their property.

Having discussed the extent to which the aspirations of printmakers were met by the 1793 Literary and Artistic Property Act, the chapter concludes with two of the first court cases tried under the Act, which are analysed in order to clarify the agency of a law articulated in just seven articles. The first concerns prints after Carle Vernet's depictions of Napoleon's Italian campaigns, published by Jean-Daniel Auber in 1799 and allegedly pirated in 1801 at the instigation of Pierre Jean, another Paris print publisher. The second concerns the purported *contrefaçon* in wallpaper of two engravings after genre scenes by Marguerite Gérard. The publisher of the prints, Jacques-Louis Bance, took action against the vendor of the Dufour wallpapers, Pierre Simon, in 1802. The issues are different in each case. In the first, I re-examine the arguments about copying, imitation, artistic reputation and property rights familiar from our study of litigation during the *ancien régime*. Were they articulated differently after the Revolution? Did the Revolution reshape the relation between the artistic author and the work in significant ways? The questions are not only important in themselves, but additionally relevant because the suppression of the guilds in 1791 and of the academies in 1793, destroyed the institutional distinction between the fine and the mechanical arts. Law emerged, arguably, as a newly important means by which that hierarchy could be partially reinstated. The status of art and artist provides a link to the second case, which considers whether a copy in wallpaper of a fine-art print constituted infringement. Did wallpaper deprive engraving of sales it might otherwise reasonably have expected to secure? Was wallpaper, in short, a print in the conventional sense, or was it a product of industry? And if the latter, under which of the different intellectual property laws (copyright or patent) did it fall?

These questions take us into new territory. Progress, economic growth and national prosperity were, and are, thought to be predicated on creativity and invention, and were encouraged by privilege, and are promoted by copyright. But they are also and equally facilitated by secondary imitation of those primary creations and inventions. In the *ancien régime*, the conflict of interests between the respective prerogatives of the individual and of the public pitted different corporations (notably guilds and academies) and different localities (Paris and the provinces) against one another, which law and regulations proper to specific trades aimed to resolve. In the Revolution, the issue of interests was raised to the level of political and ideological as well as legal principle.[7] In literary copyright and in patent, justice balances and settles individual and public claims temporally, by fixing the duration of copyright's time in order that the author is rewarded and society not unduly deprived. Copyright and the public domain were, in this way, co-produced by the 1793 Act, as Jane Ginsburg has observed.[8] In art, the question of interests presents itself differently. It was more a matter of space. It was about the extent to which copyright, in upholding the right of the author, simultaneously foreclosed an artistic domain and prohibited translations of designs native to it into other, apparently non-artistic media. Did the law allow the reprinting of a reproductive print published in May as a printed textile or wallpaper in June? The conceptual parameters of intellectual property constructed art in law from the outside, setting art apart from its others, notably industry. How and on what basis it did so in *c.*1800 will be our concluding concern.

COPYRIGHT AND REVOLUTION

The various forms of copy-protection granted by the *ancien régime*'s corporate and royal bodies – its Chancellerie, Bureau du commerce, guilds and academies – though not specifically targeted by the Revolution, were rendered politically moot by the suppression of privileges and the *Déclaration des droits de l'homme*. They were left legally null and void by the dissolution of the guilds and the Bureau du commerce in 1791 and of the academies in 1793.[9] These events radically transformed the art world. Painters, sculptors and engravers were stripped of their elite corporate identity. They were required to obtain an occupation licence, called *patente*, in common with the vast body of urban artisanal trades from whom they had formerly been distinguished by their exemptions and privileges, and with whom they were now equated as citizens.[10] Inventors and artists, along with writers, responded promptly by lobbying the Assemblée nationale constituante with petitions and draft decrees in an effort to reclaim their commercial monopolies.[11] Not all the proposals originated from within the arts and trades. The first, by the abbé Emmanuel-Joseph Sieyès, dated January 1790, was written in the context of the freeing of the press and in response to the urgent need to police 'crimes that can be committed by means of printing, and by the publication of writings and prints'.[12] It took the form of a single clause in government legislation drafted otherwise to counter the threat of sedition. Other petitions that soon followed did, however, express the concerns, interests and opinions of inventors, playwrights, printmakers and writers.

The emigration of those who had formerly patronised the arts and the interruption in state commissions raised printmaking to new prominence in the 1790s. This graphic turn was shadowed by a rapid rise in print piracy. To tackle the issue, the printmakers and publishers Pierre-François Basan, Charles-Étienne Gaucher and Nicolas Ponce addressed a petition for copyright to the Assemblée nationale in May 1790.[13] Who were these spokesmen and by what right did they speak? All three brought detailed experience of privilege to the task: in the 1750s Basan had been involved in struggles with the Paris *libraires* over deposits, in the 1770s Gaucher was caught up in a case of piracy involving his engraved portrait of Fréron, and Ponce, the youngest of the three, was in the 1780s closely in touch with the book trade as an illustrator.[14] Of the three, it was probably Ponce, on the brink of publishing *Fastes de la Révolution française*, who, in 1790, could most legitimately claim, as the petition did, to represent the interests of the nation's 'printmakers and copper-plate owners'.[15] Basan, officially the 'president' of the assembly of printmakers and print publishers convened and consulted in preparation of the document, was by that date retired. Gaucher's part is more uncertain. His output as an engraver was modest by the 1790s,[16] but since we know him later to have acted, like Ponce, as an expert witness in important copyright trials in the early 1800s it seems likely that his role as secretary of the assembly was significant.

Did the petition argue for reinstatement of privilege under another name? Or did it help to bring about a revolution in the legal culture of the copy? In scope, length, depth and complexity, the petition was unprecedented. The imagery of its elegant headpiece (fig. **102**), designed by Pierre-Philippe Choffard, suggests new beginnings.[17] Choffard depicts the moment when the Muse of the Fine Arts places Genius (the winged youth), Education (the putto) and Commerce (invoked by Mercury's caduceus, the globe and the crates) under the protection of Law, and thereby secures artists their immortality. Law, a composite figure with attributes both of Commandment (tablets) and of Justice (sword), is not allegorised as a *lieu de mémoire*, or repository of earlier decrees and judgments; rather she symbolises pure instrumentality. Sceptre-like, she will create history, not reflect it and record it.[18] Precedent is also absent from the text of the *Adresse*.[19] Former regulations feature merely as detail in the sorry story of the abuses printmakers had suffered at the corrupt hands of the Corporation des libraires et maîtres imprimeurs.[20] The political symbolism of such discursive erasure of the archive was later also manifest materially. In October 1793, weeks after the passage of the Copyright Act into law, the printmaker François-Anne David, whose name had in the 1770s and 1780s appeared regularly in the registers of the Paris *libraires*, surrendered to the Commune des arts for destruction 'several' privileges obtained in the king's name.[21] Such actions assimilated print privileges to other feudal titles, notably landed ones, ritually destroyed at the time on Revolutionary bonfires. In its repudiation of history and precedent, and in its articulation of its demands according to 'principles', the *Adresse* consciously broke new ground because the said principles were avowedly rooted in the *Déclaration des droits de l'homme* (1789).[22]

First, and most importantly, Basan, Gaucher, Ponce and Choffard claimed the right to contribute as citizens and representatives to the formation of law, specifically to the law regarding property.[23] Alexis de Tocqueville famously argued that the Revolutionaries inherited the centralised state,[24] but in 1790–91 petitioners like Basan and the others imagined that a new state was in the process of legal and administrative invention, and, believing themselves entitled, they were determined to participate in its constitution. Liberty and property, rights enshrined by the *Déclaration*, were the structuring principles that they identified as necessary to the creation of a new kind of engravers' Act. They noted that 'The sacred right to speak, write and communicate our ideas' freely had already been recovered, and the matter did not therefore long detain them. It was sufficient that free speech raised questions about to whom the law belonged and in whose interests it had formerly been exercised.

> Despite the declarations of some of our kings, all of whom recognised the unrestricted liberty of our art, we were subject to inquisitorial censorship, to a police as destructive as it was unpredictable and vexatious; we were allowed to undertake anything except that which might displease Mr Noble, Mr Powerful or Mr Rich; frequently the interests, the whims, of a minor despot or one of his most despicable minions, deprived us of the reward of a work endorsed by a royal sanction, [and] obtained as always for cash.[25]

The owners of copper plates in whose name the authors wrote implicitly set themselves apart from the landed and *rentier* classes invoked in this passage, self-interested abusers of the law; they represented themselves instead as an artisanal and commercial bourgeoisie with capital in their workshops and rights in their art. Under the law proposed by Basan, Gaucher, Ponce and Choffard, those rights were to be obtained without lobbying and protected free of any charge, precisely because they were rights, not privileges. For the same reason they would be unlimited and transferable in full by sale, gift or inheritance. The engravers were not looking to restore the regulations of the *ancien régime*, especially not the decree on privileges of 1777, but to institute a new copy*right* regime of their own.

In advancing their work as property of a special kind, Basan, Gaucher, Ponce and Choffard were no more than reiterating the contention of jurists since the late seventeenth century and the unqualified assertion of first the nation's petitioning inventors and later the capital's playwrights.[26] However, the mixed, if not muddled terms deployed in the engravers' address – terms such as 'positive right' – indicate the absence of legal counsel in its drafting, and ignorance too, possibly, of the erudite natural-law tradition.[27] Property, they argued, was a right simultaneously both legal and negative: legal because *positively* created by the Revolution's laws, and negative because those same laws could no more than defend it.[28] In addition to this definitional contradiction in the legal context, the meaning of 'property' in the petition was further confused by the retention of its non-legal, colloquial meaning. On the one hand, this led the petitioners to describe in physical as well as metaphorical detail the various property-like forms that printmaking assumed and, on the other, it resulted in a confrontation between the abstract concept of property deployed by analogy in privilege discourse and the real state of property brought about by the Revolution.

According to the *Adresse*, there was property of two distinct kinds in print, one public and the other private, because 'any subject incised on a copper plate is necessarily engraved after either a public or a private property'.[29] Note that property is here located in the original – painting, sculpture, print – and not in its reproductions. 'National' they conceded was for them a synonym of 'public'; 'public' thus designated specifically all those things that belonged to the state after 1789 and were amenable to reproduction, such as 'all national monuments, buildings and palaces', and all 'the paintings, drawings, statues and bronzes they contain'.[30] In contrast, therefore, to the royal works and collections, which from 1667 Colbert had reserved by privilege for reproduction exclusively at the king's command and by his own printmakers, the Revolution had, the *Adresse* implied, overnight created a 'vast and fertile field in which artists *all equally* have the *right* to harvest' designs to copy and sell (my emphasis).[31] The wealth of works of art and architecture freely available for the first time for reproduction that the authors of the *Adresse* conjured up was used by them to obscure the fact that the only public property of freely exploitable designs in the sphere of graphic art that they were willing to recognise was in those relatively rare instances where 'the copper plate no longer exists'. Only if the copper plate was destroyed or irretrievably lost, they argued, was a printmaker at liberty to re-engrave its composition for profit from an original impression. Thus, in the petition, an unconditional property right over the printed image was rendered politically compatible with liberty, equality and fraternity by offsetting absolute private ownership against the yield of the Revolutionaries' policy of compulsory nationalisation, or *biens nationaux*.[32]

If Basan and his fellow petitioners mitigated request for legal monopolies in their reproductive works by indexing a condition of public ownership for the originals in the making, they did not presume that in so doing their claims would necessarily prevail. They also rehearsed arguments for intellectual property. These were mostly tried and tested and characterised by partisan defensiveness on the question of the author-function of the reproductive printmaker.[33] They were original, however, in at least two respects. First, the petitioners proposed a new solution to the problem that the concept and practice of imitation poses to copyright and that so vexed portraitists; and, second, they substituted the *assignat*, the paper currency introduced in 1789, for land as the figure of property to compare to art by analogy. Resolution of the imitation problem entailed long and considered argument; by contrast, the change of metaphor appears hasty and merely expedient. Both were, however, significant.

Imitation presents a problem for copyright based on a labour theory of property because it has nothing to say about labour as such; it merely indexes the author, leaving unanswered the questions of whether author-function can properly belong to makers of imitations, and whether copies can be copyrighted. In their petition, Basan, Gaucher, Ponce and Choffard addressed the problem by substituting personality for originality, in its legal sense of having origin in. Taking as their example a bust of the young soldier André Désilles,[34] they argued 'exact copy' logically into impossibility by asserting that no two reproductions of it by different authors could ever be the same. What belongs exclusively to each individual is his or her particular and intrinsic mode of 'expression', which is inevitably manifest even when artists share an object of depiction.[35] It was 'morally and physically impossible', they asserted, contra the premise of emulation, for artists collectively drawing before a motif in common to produce good and like copies; to do so they would have to become one another. Basan, Gaucher, Ponce and Choffard were making an ontological claim about pictorial representation; they were not reiterating Locke's epistemological argument about the origins of property in labour.

The reason the authors of the *Adresse* chose Désilles to illustrate their redefinition of imitation was primarily commercial: like the portrait of the king before 1789, the market for an image of so celebrated a Revolutionary martyr was highly competitive. The reasons informing the selection of the *assignat* to denote intellectual property are not so immediately obvious. Land had traditionally served that purpose under privilege because of origin's importance in Locke's labour theory of property: agriculture is logically work's inaugural form. By setting aside the Lockean view, Basan, Gaucher, Ponce and Choffard liberated the discursive field to alternative metaphors. After the night of 24 August 1789, political expediency also dictated the end to explicit reference to feudalism in the wake of its abolition by the Assemblée nationale. Analogy of artistic property to a kind of *fief en l'air*, as in the Esnault and Rapilly *c.* Basset case (1779), for instance, was now both inaccurate and potentially dangerous.[36] If these matters, one philosophical, the other political, informed the authors' choice, they did not, however, say so. Rather, it seems more likely that they chose the *assignat* (fig. **103**) because it resembled print. In being the *assign*ment of a value (secured on the national domain of expropriated church lands), it was, like a print, a representation. Furthermore, it was mechanically reproduced and multiple – in short, actually a print. Basan, Gaucher, Ponce and Choffard were therefore able to argue that, in the same way that one could give, trade, sell or destroy an *assignat* but not forge one, because to do so made a private claim on the portion of the national wealth represented, so one could give, trade, sell or destroy prints but could not pirate them, because to do so was criminally to appropriate a portion of the author's wealth.[37] Owing to the congruencies of medium and technology, the analogy between reproductive prints and paper money made the proposition that prints constituted a form of intangible intellectual property easier to grasp and arguably more persuasive. Moreover, since no one disputed the criminality of counterfeiting currency notes, the analogy strengthened the case for civil action against piracy and for the imposition of heavy penalties.[38] The petitioners could obviously not have foreseen that within five years the symbolic value of the *assignat* would be undermined utterly by forgery and hyperinflation, and that the notes, far from signifying wealth, were – as a medley print attributed to Nicolas-Marie Gatteaux, a designer of *assignats*, made particularly clear – synonymous with destitution (fig. **104**).[39] Nevertheless, it successfully transformed the discourse on copyright from one based on the grant of privilege and shaped by the seigneurial metaphor of land tenure, to one based upon rights of bourgeois property, and characterised, seemingly, by profound similarities between macro- and micro-levels within the economy. Such alleged compatibilities, in turn, served to mask the fact that the interests that Basan, Gaucher, Ponce and Choffard were trying to secure were private interests, analogous possibly to national interests but also, arguably, contrary to the public good.

The response of the Assemblée nationale to the *Adresse* is unknown. It seems likely that the petition was referred to the Comité d'agriculture et de commerce, to which François Hell's later *projet de loi* for the rights of writers was redirected. Both belonged to what Carla Hesse has called the lobbying phase of the pre-history of the 1793 Act, a phase in which specialist groups petitioned separately on behalf of their professions and trades.[40] They followed Sieyès's first proposal for copyright law as an instrument primarily of censorship, and preceded the third and last phase, when the matter was transferred to the Comité d'instruction publique. The change of committee in 1792, as Hesse has noted, re-contextualised the intellectual property question yet again, this time as an issue of education, in relation to which the production and public dissemination of knowledge was a priority to help meet the economic needs of the nation.[41] Choffard's headpiece indicates that education was a context for copyright also envisaged by the printmakers. Choffard had depicted Study (the putto with the burin) among copyright law's imagined beneficiaries. But the benefit to Study was indirect. Basan, Gaucher and Ponce insisted in the text of the *Adresse* that the human right to subsistence did not ever legitimise the sale of students' copies.[42] In a perpetual copyright economy for which they appealed, students would no longer copy to support themselves and would be compelled to be creative from the start. To the drafters of the 1793 Act, Choffard's putto probably stood for education narrowly defined as training, which was not exclusively their brief. The Comité d'instruction publique was concerned more broadly with the political, social and moral education that inducts men and women into the just and proper relation of their individual rights to the general good. They were concerned, that is, with the dissemination side of the intellectual property right question no less than its production side. For Lakanal and the committee, intellectual property and public domain were not ontologically distinct, as they had been defined in the *Adresse*, but mutually determining products of justice: the one became the other ten years after the author's death.[43]

The very day the Act was passed, the Commune des arts – from 4 July 1793 officially the Académie royale's replacement – minuted in its records the company's satisfaction with it.[44] The fact that the decree's effect, 'to preserve artists' property [in their works] by preventing all manner of copies', had required some explanation to the assembled members, indicates, perhaps, less than perfect awareness and concern about the matter. Certainly the time-limited protection the Act afforded did not provoke the outrage that had met the 1777 decree on the duration of privileges.[45] The surviving business correspondence of Basan's sons, who had succeeded their father in the print trade, with a bookseller in the Netherlands, Joseph de Busscher, makes no mention of copyright; of much greater concern in the mid-1790s was the rapid rise in the wages of copper-plate printers and bookbinders and the equally rapid devaluation of the *assignat*.[46] It was thus not, apparently, the conditions of copyright but the definition of the law's scope that troubled artists in the wake of 1793. The Act of that year refers generally and generously to authors of 'works of the mind, or of genius', specifically denominating as examples in the field of the visual, 'painters and draughtsmen who have their work reproduced'.[47] Thus, unlike the draft decrees of the lobbyists, the Act did not interpolate particular makers and trades; rather, and cutting across these corporate divisions, it constituted a class of intellectual property owners for the first time. That artists initially had difficulty in recognising themselves as belonging to that legal class is suggested by the case of the plaster-casters. In March 1794, they sent a petition to the Convention nationale to correct an 'omission' in the Act: neither sculptors nor casters were specifically nominated by it.[48] They argued their case for protection under the Act on the grounds of the general and long-standing recognition of the injury they suffered from counter-casting, but they simultaneously and naively described the art of the cast-maker as requiring 'neither the gifts of genius, nor a talent for imitation, nor the study of Nature'. Basan, Gaucher, Ponce and Choffard had insisted defensively on the inventiveness of imitation in printed reproduction precisely to forestall refusal on grounds of genius; the casters' open acknowledgement of the mechanical nature of their work sealed their rejection from their own mouths. Not until Antoine-Joseph Romagnesi's successful suit against Gabrielle Robin's unauthorised cast of his bust of Louis XVIII at the Restoration did three-dimensional art make its claim to genius, and to interpolation under the 1793 Act.[49]

The ambiguity of genius stemmed not only from its blindness to skills, materials and tools – the indices by which the arts and trades had formerly been categorised – but also from its indifference to dignity and function. The Académie had defined and subdivided art according to its public utility and the register of its discourses: public and universal (history), or private and particular (genre). Questions on the nature of the intellectual property right and the character of the object of its protection came together in the early nineteenth century in disputes involving changes of medium. The draft decree of the engravers Basan, Gaucher, Ponce and Choffard incorporated an article that prohibited copies in all reproductive media.[50] The 1793 Act did not. Was there infringement in cases where a high-art figure sculpture was reproduced as an ornament for a clock or vase? Or when an engraving was copied and reproduced as a *vue d'optique* ('optical view'), or on a handkerchief, or a sweet wrapper? If the suppression of privilege in 1789 had cut art off from its former titles of nobility, legal disputes of this kind over the position of the legal line dividing the fine and the industrial arts, or copyright and design patent, seemingly separated bourgeois property owners from their working-class imitators. The copyright question was not only about rights; it was also about hierarchy and status. In that sense, parallels can be drawn with the controversies about professional licences.[51] Some, possibly many, members of the Académie found the *patente* not only costly but humiliating. Jacques-Louis David was not among them. He willingly paid for his in 1792. Although some historians of copyright have proposed that the 'Act of the Rights of Genius' was specifically tailored to meet David's needs, it seems altogether more consistent with his stance on the *patente* that he actually deposited no copies of the engraved reproductions made after his paintings and neither affirmed nor sought to safeguard his private property in them.[52]

AUBER *c.* JEAN, 1801

The case between Auber and Jean, heard first at the criminal court in Paris in the late summer of 1801, and then on appeal in the winter of the same year, was not the first such case to be tried after 1793, but for the art world it was among the most important. Auber accused Jean of pirating three prints of Napoleon's Italian campaigns that he, Auber, had published two years earlier. What made the case remarkable, as we shall see, was the judgment – Auber won[53] – and the reliance of the judge in making it on the expert testimony of artists: painters, draughtsmen, printmakers and sculptors. Ten gave evidence at the first trial, a further 37 at the appeal. The list is a roll call of the leading lights in 1800: painters Jacques-Louis David, Pierre-Narcisse Guérin, Philippe-Auguste Hennequin, Pierre-Paul Prud'hon, Jean-Jacques-François Le Barbier, Jean-François Peyron, Jean-Honoré Fragonard, Hubert Robert, Jean-Baptiste Greuze, Louis-Léopold Boilly, Martin Drolling and others; and printmakers, notably Gaucher, Ponce, Choffard, authors of the 1790 petition, but also Charles-Clément Bervic, Louis-Joseph Masquelier, Alexandre Tardieu, Jean-Joseph Tassaert, Jacques Swebach-Desfontaines, François Robert Ingouf, Maurice Blot and others. It would scarcely be an exaggeration to say that the case, which coincided with the 1801 Salon, became a *cause célèbre*.

The evidence we have to reconstruct the case is both incomplete and one-sided. No copies of Auber's memorandum, published on the eve of the appeal, have survived, but we do have copies of Jean's three memoranda responding to it.[54] The 'facts' are therefore largely as Jean recorded and presented them. Meanwhile, Auber's prints are well known. They are three of the first four plates of his *Tableaux historiques des campagnes d'Italie*, etched by Jean Duplessi-Bertaux after drawings by Carle Vernet, first published in 1799 as sheets and in 1806 collected together and issued as a book, with the rest of the set, a frontispiece, a map of Italy and a descriptive text.[55] Of Jean's copies, by the little-known draughtsman Claude-Louis Desrais and engraved by Pierre-Adrien Le Beau, I have found no trace.[56] From what we have, we can nevertheless draw some provisional conclusions about the relationship between authors and their works after the Revolution, about the legal nature of intellectual property and piracy after the 1793 Act and more generally about the practices and structure of the print trade at the turn of the century.

The events leading up to the case were briefly these.[57] In the wake of Napoleon's rapid and sensational victories at the head of the Republican army in Piedmont in April 1796, and in Lombardy in May, Auber had the happy idea for a print series depicting the Battle of Mondovi, the crossing of the river Pô at Piacenza and the taking of the town of Lodi. To that end he sent his correspondent Louis Chicoilet de Corbigny to Milan, who on arrival was directed to the topographical office of Bacler d'Albe, military engineer and close companion of Napoleon.[58] Corbigny was told by Bacler that an identical project was already well in hand. Bacler showed him his own finished topographical views of the battles, together with a new map of Italy and the manuscript of an accompanying text. He strongly advised Corbigny to abandon his mission. Undeterred, Corbigny apparently recruited the services of the Turinese court painter Giuseppe Bagetti and Pierre-Athanase Chauvin, a pupil of David, to draw the sites of the battles in situ.[59]

Back in Paris these sketches and a map were given by Auber to Carle Vernet to serve as the basis for his 'pictures', reproduced and published in May and August 1799.[60] Jean was allegedly approached by Desrais some months later with sketches of the same battles, sketches that Jean decided to buy and have engraved.[61] His three prints were published in January, April and July 1801.[62] A bare two months later, the drawings, copper plates and impressions were seized and Auber started formal proceedings against Jean for copyright infringement.[63]

Auber's case relied heavily on the visual evidence and on a particular interpretation of the 1793 prohibition to copy in full or in part. Jean opened up his more complex defence on several flanks: he denied, of course, that his prints were copies of Vernet, but he also accused Auber and Vernet of having themselves followed not Bagetti's sketches so much as Michelangelo Mercoli's prints after Bacler d'Albe's battle paintings, first published in Milan and then again in Paris.[64] Jean also noted that Auber had registered his own copyright only at the end of July 1801, less than a week before he took action against Jean and well after Jean's prints had been published.[65] He denied liability on that count. Moreover, he argued that were there a case to answer in law it was against Desrais, the artist, not against himself, the publisher and printseller. Finally, Jean used a copyright case then also in progress, in which Auber was the defendant, to undermine his credibility as a reputable print publisher.[66]

• Copying and *contrefaçon* •

Not since Gaucher's case in 1776 had the outcome of a copyright dispute depended so heavily on the question of copying, and the legal definition of *contrefaçon*. And it is no surprise to find that Gaucher was a key witness at the trial. Jean's defence made much of the disagreements and inconsistencies in the definitions of copying and infringement advanced by Auber and his artist witnesses. The meaning he proposed instead was simple and predictable: exact reproduction achieved by mechanical means.[67] But he also recognised that the forensic use of tracing to map his prints onto those of Vernet and thereby to demonstrate the lack of perfect coincidence between the two was not alone sufficient to see off the charge.[68]

From Jean's first memorandum we can infer that Auber and Vernet rested their case on broad compositional similarities between the corresponding pairs of prints. Jean, by contrast, argued that battle scenes consisted of combinations of fixed and given parts on the one hand and mobile and chosen elements on the other. The fixed parts were the site, the background, the perspective and the subject matter; the mobiles were the trees, ordnance and figures.[69] Conceding similarities with regard to the first, he excused them as inevitable because of the given data, the science of representation and because Napoleon's victories were national property that all were free to represent.[70] In answer to Auber's specific accusation that the bridge of Lodi in Desrais's image was identical with the one in Vernet's (fig. **105**) and must therefore have been copied directly, the painter Le Barbier observed, for Jean, that the Ponte Molle in Raphael's and Le Brun's depictions of the Battle of the Milvian Bridge was the same, but no one would think to indict Le Brun for plagiarism.[71] Moreover, the treatment of the figures in the two prints was completely different; not one soldier, not one horse corresponded exactly.

The personal and individual performance of taste, which Jean assigned exclusively to the choice and distribution of the figures, Gaucher and Ponce, witnesses for Auber, identified in the setting too, specifically in the atmospheric effects and the distribution of light and shade.[72] They argued against Jean's definition of the landscape as inert given background, and for a lively, integrated and creative conception of setting, and for landscape as the very subject of the work. According to them, Desrais's deliberate alteration or variation of the figures was motivated by his need cynically to disguise his copy of the landscape composition to avoid prosecution.[73] In Gaucher's and Ponce's testimony, the figures are mere accessories that frame the subject proper.

The arguments of the litigants and the opinions of the witnesses were informed, clearly, by the academic hierarchy of genres, but not perhaps as we would expect. Auber and the history painter Vernet built their case around landscape and the notion of documentary imitation as nevertheless inventive. It was rather Jean and the fashion-plate designer Desrais who mustered the support of history, in which only the figures signified and counted as relevant. Artist privileges at the Académie had been dominated by history; for modern French landscape, privilege had been an exception.[74]

At Jean's appeal, Bacler d'Albe was the key witness. Having expressed feelings of injury at the hands of the Société Auber, Bacler nevertheless acknowledged that Vernet's and Jean's prints did not infringe his own copyright, even though there was 'a striking resemblance' between their depictions of Lodi and his own. The figures were too obviously dissimilar.[75] The other history painters among the witnesses, such as Le Barbier, and including David, Guérin, Prud'hon and others, agreed.[76]

• Copyright and authorship •

The judgment in Vernet's and Auber's favour is surprising, the more so given that the legal case was weak. Auber had registered his copyright only two years after the publication of his prints and some time too after Jean had published his. According to Jean, such was the delay that Auber had tacitly renounced his title to an exclusive right, and by implication freed the works for others to appropriate and use.[77] Auber's explanation was that he was waiting to complete the set of 23 *Tableaux* before depositing to register his copyright.[78]

Jean's memoranda do not allow us to follow Auber's argument, except in snatches, according to the specific points that Jean's lawyer chose to contest. These clustered around the question of moral rights rooted in natural law: Auber had accused Jean of a *vol moral* of Vernet's property.[79] It was Vernet who had instigated legal action. It was he who had discovered Jean's copies on the *quais*, and he who had compelled Auber to take action against Jean for infringement by refusing to continue to produce the *Tableaux* unless Auber sought legal redress.[80] His reputation was, he said, at stake.

Jean defended his position in a scatter-gun fashion. The artist's property is created, he said, by statute, and its legal force depends, as with other forms of conventional property, on the exact fulfilment of the conditions specific to it, notably registration.[81] Moreover, were the case, in fact, one of natural right, then it properly concerned authors, not retailers. On these grounds, Jean argued successfully for Desrais's annexation as a co-defendant in the trial.[82] Jean also sought to put the question of reputation to rest by pointing out that his prints were not attributed to Vernet. Indeed, such was their lowly artistic status that they were unsigned. Neither Desrais nor the printmaker Le Beau had wanted to acknowledge authorship of them.[83] Anonymity, in short, forestalled injury to reputation; Vernet's, Desrais's and Le Beau's.

In finding for Auber, the court was evidently swayed by the argument from natural law. The plaintiffs had presumably made a case for authorial property based on absolute artistic sovereignty over the work. It is also safe to presume that the case was articulated more in terms of invention than in those of creative imitation, which had served portraitists in the 1770s, and informed also by the 1790 petition to the Assemblée nationale. 'Safe' because Vernet had not confronted nature directly in making his works: unlike Bagetti, he had not visited the sites, and unlike Bacler, he had not witnessed the battles.[84] Moreover, according to Jean's lawyer, when Bagetti's sketches were produced in court it was evident to the defence that Vernet's compositions bore a closer resemblance to Bacler's prints (fig. **106**) than to Bagetti's drawings.[85] Jean argued, in fact, that Vernet's creative method had closely resembled Desrais's, since both had created their works in the studio.[86]

In court, Desrais acknowledged his title as 'author and inventor' of the sketches presented in evidence for Jean's prints, and he described to the court the draughtsman's habitual method of working. 'He takes various ideas suitable to his subject here and there where he finds them and uses them without, for all that, being a pirate [*contrefacteur*].'[87] To demonstrate, Desrais opened his sketchbooks filled with 'engraved battle pictures'. '"Here", he said, "is all you need to create all manner of battle pictures, by selecting and adapting the uniforms that you find everywhere in them."'[88] The pages of Desrais's notebook may have looked something like one of the sheets from a Hubert Robert sketchbook, now at the Courtauld Institute (fig. **107**), where we see gathered and pasted down a group of five crayon-manner prints and four drawings after François Boucher's pastoral figures, which, throughout his career, Robert culled for rural types to populate his own landscapes.

In contrast to this piecemeal recycling and rearrangement of modified motifs, gathered over time, I think we have to assume that Vernet defined and described authorial invention as a unique and instantaneous visualisation of a composition, one closer to Le Blon's idea for colour printing than to practices of emulative following. Drawing on seventeenth-century art theory, Vernet probably defined composition as the immaterial conceptualisation of a picture in all its parts, and all at once, prior to its execution on paper or canvas. It is surely significant that Vernet's *Tableaux* realised after Auber had won the case are signed not simply 'dessiné par…', in the way they had been up to that moment, but 'composé & dessiné par Carle Vernet'.[89]

To argue that Vernet's notion of his authorial right was informed by seventeenth-century art theory is not, however, to argue for continuity in its definition with the privileges of the *ancien régime*. Composition did not feature prominently as a conceptual category in earlier privilege disputes and has not, therefore, been a particular focus of our analysis of them. Moreover, unlike seventeenth-century theories of composition, Vernet's did not apparently hold with a hierarchical understanding of *ordonnance* in the distribution and arrangement of the figural components, one which distinguished the main figures bearing the narrative from the accidental and accessorial parts of the picture. It was Jean and Desrais who had unsuccessfully made arguments of this kind. Moreover, Vernet's ethical case, voiced as a defence of his reputation, was not predicated on belonging to an institutionalised artistic elite such as the former Académie and to a visual tradition. His authorial self-realisation was not achieved through emulation and choice reference to the great works of the past – Raphael's, Le Brun's or anyone else's. His history paintings were implicitly without precedent, because they represented the now. And, finally, the right he claimed was more comprehensive than any privilege: it encompassed imitations of all kinds, free as well as exact, low as well as high.

Vernet's copyright, ceded to Auber, was distinct as the product of the 1793 Literary and Artistic Property Act. It is an instance of what Bernard Edelman has termed in law the 'author-as-individual', which is to say that it interpreted the rights of 'man' as preceding, encompassing and taking precedence over those of the 'citizen'.[90] It construed the author as unique and individual: creative genius alone invented fully formed pictorial ideas, whose materialisation in paint via the artist's brush was little more than a symptom. To paraphrase Edelman, the 'work' was considered not a creation of privilege law, nor the product of abstract labour but a sacred and inviolable intellectual property, and the law's duty was to organise, or rather reorganise itself in its defence. According to the *Journal du palais*, Jean was fined 8,000 *francs*, or the equivalent of the sale of 3,000 copies of Auber's 'originals' – a punitive sum, given the unlikelihood that Jean would have sold this number of 'copies' in the period of two to four months between Auber's deposit and the trial.[91]

The interpretation of the 1793 Act in Auber *c.* Jean was not the only one possible. It did, however, prevail in spite of the support of Le Barbier, David and the majority of painters for Jean and Desrais. The judgment recognised a new kind of author, one stripped of the social and artistic hierarchies that had formerly defined him or her at the Académie; Vernet was a genius *tout court*. Like Jacques Gautier in the dispute over colour printing, Vernet had overstated his claims to invention, but unlike Gautier, Vernet's hyperbole did not court ridicule, despite Jean's efforts to expose them as false. The author-subject construed by the Revolution's Act was one constituted not on the basis of skill, social relations or public function, but by his or her property imprinted, however minimally, by the expression of his or her artistic self.

AUTHOR AND NATION, ART AND INDUSTRY

The dispute between Auber and Jean was primarily a dispute between print publishers, notwithstanding the roles played by Vernet and Desrais. It would be naive to suppose that commercial issues were not, therefore, the priority, even though Jean's memoranda have so much more to say about authorship than about trade. In court, Jean caricatured Auber as a simple publisher of portrait prints on the edge of commercial respectability.[92] But we know that Auber was a big player in the publication of prints during and after the French Revolution. In 1794, he had taken over editorial control of Jean-Louis Prieur and Pierre-Gabriel Berthault's *Tableaux historiques de la Révolution française*, which he expanded in two new editions, in 1798 and 1802, and to which he brought new talent, notably Duplessi-Bertaux. It was, in fact, in relation to the portraits that Auber planned to add to the 1798 second edition (mentioned in chapter 3), that François Bonneville, the author of portraits pirated by Auber, had taken the publisher to court, a trial that Jean exploited at every turn in his own defence.[93] The pictures of the *Campagnes d'Italie* were, in many respects, a continuation of the pictures of the *Révolution française*, involving many of the same printmakers. Like the Revolution series, the *Campagnes d'Italie* was a managerially complex, capital intensive and artistically ambitious publishing project. Susan Siegfried has described the excitement caused by new forms of battle painting exhibited at the Salon of 1801 and the critical applause enjoyed by the soldier–painter Louis-François Lejeune for his 'documentary' portrayal of the Battle of Marengo, a mode of representation that integrated the exact and vivid impression of landscape with the events of war rendered in hallucinatory detail, as she puts it.[94] It was a mode that Auber, Vernet and Duplessi-Bertaux were developing along parallel lines in print. The stakes were high both financially and artistically.

Pierre Jean's business was more diverse. He had inherited a stock of reproductive copper plates from his father-in-law, the print publisher Louis-Joseph Mondhare, which included Old Masters, notably Rembrandt, and Moderns from the French School.[95] In particular, he had an important corpus of plates after the paintings of Claude-Joseph Vernet, which no doubt informed his provocative suggestion that for the *Tableaux historiques* Carle Vernet had supplemented his borrowings from Bagetti's sketches and Mercoli's prints with recycled backgrounds from his father's oeuvre.[96] Mondhare had also traded in so-called *demi-fine* prints, aimed at a non-connoisseurial, middle market of general consumers. He had made a speciality of *vues d'optique* of cityscapes and contemporary events (fig. **108**), intended for viewing with a perspective glass or peepshow, a genre that flourished in the period 1770–1820. Unit cost was low and turnover was brisk for such prints.[97] They were habitually, indeed almost by convention, piracies of up-market prints: Claude-Joseph Vernet's ports of France, Jacques Rigaud's royal palaces and gardens and so forth. Jean alleged that Le Beau's three prints of Napoleon's campaigns were intended for inclusion in this category of his stock.[98] From these modest beginnings, Pierre Jean's shop developed in scope and volume into one of the most important print firms under the Directoire, Consulat and Empire.[99]

When Jean argued that his prints were not piracies because they were not identical with Auber's he intended more than a difference of appearance; he also referred to material variations in the works. His lawyer, Delavigne, argued that *contrefaçon* was defined not just by pictorial resemblance but also by identity in the physical substance of the work, because piracy is theft of the revenue that the author can reasonably expect from the sale of his or her work. It is, in short, the theft of a market. Jean was not, therefore, being disingenuous when he argued that differences in the size and quality of the prints were significant factors in this case. He described the larger format of his prints and also the stronger phenomenological effects they create through rough and ready handling of line and additions of primary colour. These qualities were 'planned', in the knowledge that clumsy drawing is smoothed by the illuminator's brush and errors of rendering disappear when the print is viewed with a perspective glass.[100] In Mondhare's *Bataille de Fontenoy gagnée par les français sur l'armée des alliez le 11 mai 1745* colour seems, in fact, to create the visual excitement of future triumph. It reinterprets, that is, the lines describing the respective positions of the mustered forces of Saxe and Cumberland before the battle. Jean's point was *not* Basset's in the case of fashion prints in the 1770s, or to argue that poor quality and ugliness are forms of originality, but rather clearly to demarcate the range of specialities in printmaking and the graded levels of its several markets. Consumers who bought his prints, Jean maintained, positively wanted Desrais's images; they were not duped into imagining they had acquired Vernet's at a fraction of the cost.

Jean's arguments were more than special pleading. They convinced the majority of artists at the trial, and in numbers that require explanation. Was Delavigne proposing a different interpretation of the 1793 Act? He noted that when Desrais depicted Napoleon's victories and when Jean reproduced them, neither had imagined himself in danger from 'enemies of the *patrie*' and at risk of ruin for having wanted, according to his own merits and means, to raise 'trophies' in honour of the French army.[101] The judgment of the trial had represented, Delavigne said on appeal, not a victory for truth and justice, but the success of intrigue and petty private interests – that is, not *droit d'auteur* but 'vanité d'auteur'.[102] Vernet's obsession with reputation was, Delavigne implied, not a disinterested concern for posterity but the personal egoism of one in pursuit of celebrity, an interpretation that calls to mind Boilly's *Réunion d'artistes dans l'atelier d'Isabey* (fig. **109**), in which Vernet poses at the front and centre, in a portrait that had caused sensation at the Salon of 1798 and memory of which was still fresh. Delavigne did not advance a counter-characterisation of the author. Instead, in Jean's memoranda authorial rights were offset implicitly against the entitlement of the nation, of those citizens wishing to supply versions of Napoleon's campaigns to that portion of the nation unable or disinclined to buy Auber's refined and expensive prints. In this scenario, the author was, legally and politically speaking, what Edelman terms the 'author-as-nation', an author whose rights and duties as a citizen precede, encompass and curtail those of the 'man'.[103] Author-as-nation constructs man socially as the product of the nation. Such an author draws from the collective culture, makes with it a personal contribution from which to derive an income under the law's protection, but then returns that contribution to the nation, having satisfied his or her immediate private needs. In the case of the writer, the bargain was struck by a temporal limit to the author's right: the writer's lifetime, plus ten years. In the case of the visual arts, Delavigne attempts to negotiate the right in relation, additionally, to its material scope: by limiting the author's property claim to works similar as physical things and manufactured goods – in this case, to fine art prints, but not to *vues d'optique*.

The reunion of artists at Jean's appeal represented, I suggest, a divided nation – divided not, in this case, along the generational lines of Isabey's collective portrait but into factions.[104] The intrigue to which Jean and Delavigne referred was the mobilisation by Auber of witnesses who were directly or indirectly implicated in his venture: the engravers Masquelier and Choffard, who added finish to Duplessi-Bertaux's etchings, and François-Étienne Joubert, Auber's one-time partner in the *Tableaux historiques de la Révolution française*, who raised the power of his positive testimony of *contrefaçon* in court by reiterating it in a pamphlet published in 1801.[105] Insofar as they, along with Vernet and Auber, were unpatriotic, their actions were regarded as counter-Revolutionary. The faction for Jean – the Le Barbiers, the Davids, the Hennequins, the Vincents – was not completely, or even primarily, made up of former Jacobins; however, its blindness to likeness, to copying, promoted the interests of equality and fraternity above those of the artist's liberty to exploit the property in his or her work unreservedly.

Isabey's fashionable studio, as seen in Boilly's painting, had been designed in the Etruscan manner by the architects Percier and Fontaine. The walls, though identified by the architects as panelling, have the matte, flat aesthetic feel of wallpaper. In 1801, the Louvre was host not only to the Salon but also to the state-sponsored exhibition of the products of French industry, at which wallpaper manufacturers, among others, exhibited to mark and celebrate the foundation of the Republic, and to index, by juxtaposition of the works displayed in the Salon carré and in the courtyard, the national benefits to be derived from the fraternal relations between art and industry.[106] It was in respect of wallpaper that the arguments over the nature and scope of the artist's authorial right, personal or civil, individual or collective, were taken up in earnest in a copyright trial that immediately followed Jean's failed appeal.

JACQUES-LOUIS BANCE *c.* PIERRE SIMON, 1802

In February 1802 the stipple engraver and print publisher Jacques-Louis Bance brought a copyright case before the same Tribunal de police correctionelle in Paris that had tried Auber *c.* Jean.[107] He accused Pierre Simon of selling wallpapers that infringed his property in two reproductive prints after paintings by Marguerite Gérard.[108] The case was in many ways a reprise of Auber *c.* Jean, and Bance urged artists to pack the court because the outcome touched them closely.[109]

Like Auber, he rallied expert witnesses to his side; indeed, some of those instrumental in determining the result of the earlier case also gave expert testimony for Bance: Gaucher, Ponce and Masquelier.[110] Bance won, and on 11 June 1802 Simon was fined 6,000 *francs*.[111] Like Jean, Simon appealed at the Tribunal criminel du département de la Seine. Unlike Jean, Simon was successful. On 4 January 1803 the sentence of the Paris court was overturned. Unwilling to accept the verdict as final, Bance took his case to the Cour de cassation (the supreme court of appeal), only to abandon it. He was right nevertheless in his assessment of the importance of his cause: the stakes were higher, the language was correspondingly more aggressive and exacting, and the political context was more overtly brought into play.

We have for reference, in this case, lawyers' briefs for both sides, as well as most of the visual evidence. The memoranda were republished in 1806 in Ambroise Falconnet's corpus of exemplary cases and became key reference points in nineteenth-century legal histories of copyright.[112] The reproductive engravings, titled *L'Élan de la nature* (fig. **110**) and *Le Baiser de l'innocence*, are well known and were the work of the engraver Henry Gérard.[113] Of the wallpaper overdoors copied from the prints and produced in the very early days of Joseph Dufour et Cie's manufactory at Mâcon and supplied to Simon,[114] one, *L'Élan de la nature*, survives in situ in a private house in Sâone-et-Loire.

The events leading up to the case were these. In 1795, Bance, at the very beginning of his career, bought two paintings by Marguerite Gérard, with a view to having them engraved.[115] The time entailed by engraving meant that the copper plates were not finished until three years later. By then the market for such a 'luxury enterprise' was badly depressed. Bance therefore decided not to publish the prints immediately but rather to offset his investment by selling Gérard's paintings. While continuing to wait for trade to pick up, Bance deposited impressions of the prints at the Bibliothèque nationale to confirm the copyright ceded by Gérard.[116] In the meantime, he was surprised to discover copies of his prints in wallpaper (fig. **111**).[117] Having identified their source, Bance initiated proceedings against Simon in January 1802. A receipt established that the wallpapers had been supplied by Dufour, and since only 16 remained of the original order of 24, it was a fair assumption that a number had been sold.[118] Initially, Simon agreed to settle out of court, but when he and Dufour failed to produce their wares for arbitration, relations rapidly degenerated. Bance had, he said, no alternative but to pursue matters at the police tribunal.

• Copies and translations •

The crucial difference in this case was that Simon and Dufour more or less readily acknowledged that their overdoors were wallpaper copies of Bance's prints. Matters of artistic quality, so crucial to Jean's defence, consequently had no role to play. In fact, Bance himself said he admired them.[119] Since the wallpapers did not travesty Gérard's work, the question of her moral or reputational right was also marginal to the case. Little was said about Marguerite Gérard, nothing about Henry. The point of overlap between the two cases is rather the scope of the author's right under the 1793 Act.

Lépidor, Simon's barrister, opened his memorandum with praise of the courts' strict enforcement of the 1793 Act. He alleged, however, that authors had interpreted that diligence as evidence of favour, and were determined to extend the authority of their 'privilege' beyond its intended limit.[120] More especially, he alleged that Bance had been put up to fight the case by a 'coalition' of printmakers, who wanted to establish themselves as a 'privileged corporation', having executive authority over all manufactories dependent on design and with the right to arrest the progress of industries other than their own.[121]

To represent the artist's point of view, Bance responded with a hypothetical. Imagine that Louis-Simon Boizot, an artist who worked both as a fine-art sculptor and as a designer for Sèvres, sculpts a bas-relief that attracts public attention.[122] Imagine also that one of the visitors to his studio admires it to the point of wanting to make a copy, which Boizot authorises. The copyist is so pleased with his handiwork that he decides to sell it and it falls into your entrepreneurial hands. You recognise not only its artistic merits but also its commercial potential. You have a woodblock print made and you put the resulting wallpaper on sale. The difference between sculpture and wallpaper does not excuse the copy because the composition is independent of its actual and possible materialisations. In the progress from his original to your imitation, you have robbed Boizot of his intellectual property, now and in the future. That future and all the potential it contains for exploitation and reward, and which the artist does not necessarily grasp initially, is, Bance argued, what the 1793 Act protects.

From such examples, Bance extrapolated a typology of copies, differentiated not by appearance but by the intentions of the copyist and the agency of the image. Copies were of three kinds: first, the innocent copy made for study and pleasure; second, the copy in the same medium as the original done for sale – what he called the plagiarised copy; and third, the criminal copy produced using a technology that multiplies the original faster, more plentifully and at a fraction of the cost. A copy of the last kind travelled quicker and further than the original, easing its way cheaply into exchange, and could saturate the potential markets for the original by its affordability.[123] The onus on the witnesses was to testify to the near limitlessness of the impressions that could be pulled from woodblocks, which they did.[124]

Lépidor, for Simon, noted with surprise the prosecution's reluctance to discuss matters of execution. It was execution that, according to Simon, constituted and defined the art work and was protected by the law, not, as Bance contended, the compositional idea or image. Both Agostino Carracci and Domenichino had, he pointed out, each painted a *Comunione di San Girolamo*, works known to the members of the tribunal, he confidently supposed, because having been captured during Napoleon's Italian campaigns, they were on display side by side at the Louvre.[125] The composition was the same, the disposition of the figures similar, yet connoisseurs judged Carracci's original work beautiful and Domenichino's variation Sublime – Sublime in the Burkian sense and denoting a superiority of achievement. It followed, he concluded, that 'it is not the composition of the work that constitutes its originality', but the handling. Simon, in effect, co-opted the discourse on the artist's touch – the mark of genius according to connoisseurs – to undermine the very idea of intellectual property in art.

In place of Bance's typology of copies, Simon substituted the metaphor of translation, one commonly used in discussions of reproductive printmaking.[126] His wallpaper, he argued, was a translation of Gérard's prints and therefore innocent of the charge of *contrefaçon*.[127] To judge by Bance's extended reply to this hijacking of an artistic metaphor, he registered it as a serious threat to his copyright claim. Bance itemised no fewer than six interrelated artistic, moral, political and legal reasons why the analogy did not hold.[128] Quite apart from noting that both wallpaper and engraving were prints, and that in this regard copyright had indeed been infringed, Bance vigorously refuted suggestions that the benefits derived by the author and the public from textual translation spring also from reproductions of visual art. Given that pictorial representation is a universal language, 'translation' does not promote the artist's reputation in ways that are inaccessible to the original. For the same reason, public knowledge and Enlightenment are not served by pictorial translations in the manner of literary ones, which transplant and indigenise otherwise alien cultural ideas, facts and opinions.

Bance's aim was, he said, to clarify the legal meaning of the terms 'copy' and *contrefaçon*, terms that had remained ambiguous in Auber *c.* Jean. He shifted the argument from matters of imitation to the question of the copyist's intentions, and from discussion dominated by art and authorial reputation to one focused on intellectual property and commerce. His strategy was initially successful, but the question of the public's claim was not finally resolved. It came to dominate discussion on appeal, ultimately reversing the initial outcome.

• Rights and privileges •

Both sides described the relation of the creator to his or her work as possessive. That, as such, it derived from natural law is implied but never stated in Bance's first memorandum. Bance chose rather to talk about the uniqueness of the artist's creation and the personal character of imagination. He noted that Gérard's domestic scenes, unlike Vernet's battles, were purely the product of her free invention, and her property was thus beyond all challenge.[129] Insofar as he discussed the author's reward, it was in the context of the disinterestedness that art demands. Society compensates the painter at the point of sale with an honorarium (not a salary), and the law protects the author's property for the future.[130] Only in the memorandum written for the Cour de cassation, and not taken forward, did Guégnet, Bance's barrister, articulate the natural-law argument: '[artists] draw the property of their ideas, not from positive laws, nor from institutions, which are purely conventional, but from a law of a superior kind, from a law that pre-exists all conventions, and derives from the very nature of things. *Non scripta sed natal ex*... Positive laws have been able to recognise and make public this property; but they have not yet been able to bestow it. It exists independently of them.'[131] The 1793 Act, Guégnet argued, artificially limited the artist's right by restricting its duration to the life of the artist plus ten years.[132]

Lépidor challenged the liberty Bance assigned to the author and questioned the extent to which creativity was ever, in fact, personal. He contended that art works were not freely conceived but were, rather, the product of exchanges of ideas – at the extreme, in the prescriptive terms of the contract between the artist and the patron.[133] He implied that art was no different in this from other forms of work. In regard to the dispute, he drew attention to the artist's studio and the liaison between master and pupil, noting that *L'Élan de la nature* owed much to an earlier work, Marguerite Gérard's *Le Premier Pas de l'enfance*, for which the reproductive etching by Géraud Vidal and Nicolas-François Regnault recorded the joint authorship of Gérard and Fragonard, Gérard's teacher and brother-in-law.[134] Were anyone to be compensated for Simon's 'copies', he argued, it was not Bance but Fragonard, 'who first sketched this touching scene of domestic life'.[135]

More broadly, Lépidor contested Guégnet's interpretation of the author's liberty under the 1793 Act to possess and dispose of his property. He interpreted the Act in a manner that emphasised the claims of equality and fraternity, though not in so many words. He insisted that so-called 'authors' rights' were not natural but were the creation of statute, and that the Act's purpose was to limit those rights in the national and collective interest. He portrayed Bance and engravers more generally as intent on re-establishing a despotic control over industry in the name of art, an aim achieved, in the first instance, by Bance's use of expert witnesses and by his abduction of the common language of law, which he invested with new, specialist meaning by assimilating it to elite artistic jargon ('composition', 'artistic idea', etc). Like Apollo's punishment of Marsyas for his 'emulation', Bance had, Guégnet alleged, erected a scaffold for those who infringed the cessionary printsellers' 'sacrilegious' rights. Rights so interpreted were, in substance, privileges and 'a derogation from universal law'.[136]

To establish the limits of the author's 'privilege', Lépidor developed an argument from Auber *c.* Jean. The property of the artist resides in the work, not the image, and the law protects the artist from exact imitations that threaten the specific market to which her work is addressed. It does not assign rights in all possible markets for the image. To find otherwise would, Lépidor argued, infringe the 'natural rights' of the citizen–imitator to imitate. The imitator 'employs his materials, his time and his industry', less brilliantly, perhaps, than the author, but he is equally and no less certainly the proprietor of his imitation than the inventor is of her invention.[137] Were the judgment of the Tribunal de police correctionelle to be upheld, Simon foresaw the destruction of countless manufactories for the sake of the 'isolated art' of intaglio, from which French commerce benefited little.[138] Ironically, Lépidor was led to deploy an *ancien régime* definition of copy-privilege, determined by positive law and written statute, in support of a public domain of images for appropriation and industrial exploitation to the benefit and betterment of the Republic and its citizens, while the legislation of the Revolution was engaged by Guégnet to protect an elite art world of formerly 'noble' and now propertied and bourgeois artists armed with their rights.

• *Droit exclusif* and fair use •

Simon mounted his appeal on two contentions: first, on the existence of a hierarchy of quality in creative works, and, second, on the divisions this hierarchy opened up in the exchange and in the uses of them. The legal equality of citizen-inventors and imitators that Guégnet had proclaimed was paradoxically dependent on social hierarchy, but a hierarchy not of man but of the products of his or her work. Simon emphasised the difference between the fine and mechanical arts, identifying intaglio printmaking with the first and wallpaper with the second. Wallpaper was the product of a labour force of carvers, not of individual author-engravers; it was a labour of disparate hands, whose blocks were brought together and were manually printed in a combination of colour and glue. In contrast to the personal and integrated creations of an Edelinck, a Strange or a Bartolozzi, these makers of the various woodcut components needed in wallpaper production were anonymous and worked, by implication, without expression.[139]

Differences of product extended into differences of use. Art prints were bought at a price by artists, scholars, amateurs, speculators and the fashion conscious. They were preserved in portfolios or expensively framed.[140] Wallpaper served as decoration, and was exposed naked to the injuries of air, damp and smoke and to the careless destruction of servants and children. It was never worthy of a frame.[141] From the moment it was hung, it depreciated in value, counting for so little that it was abandoned readily when a tenant moved house.

From this absolute difference in technology, value and use, Lépidor went on to argue that printsellers were, in fact, getting from wallpaper manufacturers what in modern copyright law is termed a 'free ride'. In the seventeenth and eighteenth centuries, large-scale figure tapestries had discouraged the display of prints. The interiors of today, Simon contended, had plain wallpaper surfaces of a kind particularly appropriate for the hanging of prints. He estimated that with the advent of wallpaper, the sale of prints in France had quadrupled.[142]

Moreover, like Jean, who claimed as a right the commemoration of Napoleon's victories for those who could not afford Vernets, Simon argued that the imperfect multiplication of masterpieces by industry democratised art, and put works of genius within the reach of all. By this means, taste for beauty spread and desire for the originals was enhanced.[143]

At the Cour de cassation, which reconsidered appeals where legitimate questions remained about the interpretation of the law and its correct application, Bance had planned to counter that the possession of wallpaper Gérards not only extinguished desire for the engraving, but further that, even in instances where no such wallpaper purchase was made, mere knowledge of the existence of a wallpaper picture in a neighbouring house was sufficient to stall the impulse to buy the original.[144] Moreover, wallpaper's capacity to shame was not restricted to the consumer. Authors, too, experienced humiliation from the marketing of vulgarisations of their work.[145] In Bance's view, there was, therefore, nothing fair in industry's use of the creations of genius. If free rides were to be had, they were entirely on the side of the *fabricants*, who exploited the reputation of art and artists for their own commercial ends.

Bance argued that art and industry were, in practice (though not in art theory), closely overlapping spheres, and that, in order to pay just tribute to the progress of Enlightenment, which was art's achievement alone, law should set them apart and establish limited and equitable dealings between them. Failure to do so would result in despair and discouragement for artists and a vulgarisation of the national culture as a whole. For Simon, by contrast, there was nothing naturally intimate in the relationship between the *beaux-arts* and the *arts mécaniques*. Each sphere was utterly distinct,[146] and it was the duty of the law to withdraw, to *laissez faire*, and to allow a productive and profitable traffic to develop between them. We cannot know what led Bance to abandon his case. Simon thus had the last word. Moreover, the case was settled, you could say, not only in favour of industry but also in vindication of the conceptualisation of the author-as-nation.

To support his claim that wallpaper was a print not a wallcovering, Bance had referred the court to Diderot and d'Alembert's *Encyclopédie*, in which wallpaper was subsumed under the general heading 'Print' and alluded to in the subsection 'Woodcut', which otherwise recounted the early history of printmaking and its first triumphs in the works of Altdorfer, Durër and Mantegna.[147] He could also have appealed to law. *Ancien-régime* privilege did not discriminate between wallpapers and art prints: in 1739 the manufacturer Didier Aubert had obtained a privilege for 'various designs', and in 1779 Jean-Baptiste Réveillon was likewise granted a privilege for 'designs of his own composition and others which he has acquired and which are destined for wallpaper'.[148] Study of the ledgers in which copyright deposits were entered at the Bibliothèque nationale after 1793 indicates, moreover, that wallpaper manufacturers continued to register designs for copyright. In fact, Simon had deposited a sample of an arabesque wallpaper on 2 November 1799 for that very purpose.[149] But there was doubt on the point. That the Tribunal de police correctionelle had not allowed Dufour to stand alongside Simon as the 'genius' who had ceded him his rights, in the way Desrais had stood by Jean, suggests that it did not recognise him as an author, or rather that it did not attribute authorship and personality to industrial design.

The court was not the first to take this line. When the guilds had been reorganised in 1776, wallpaper was amalgamated with bookbinding in the new Communauté des relieurs et papetiers-colleurs en meubles, and in 1778 it drew up fresh regulations for privilege in wallpaper in response to an epidemic of piracy.[150] Comparison of these regulations and the 1793 Act is revealing. The guild did not recognise a wallpaper design as the author's intangible property. Draughtsmen and woodblock cutters made things – drawings – in which they had no inalienable rights either as employees or as piece-workers; their interests ended at the point of sale. Only the owners of the drawings – that is, the entrepreneurs and manufacturers – were eligible for protection by privilege.[151] The designers were, therefore, expressly prohibited from reproducing, multiplying and reselling designs already sold.[152] Industry, as Molly Nesbit has observed, does not want authors in its ranks; rather it wants 'control over property rights at every stage of production, from the technical drawing to the finished commodity' in order to maximise profit.[153] The post-1793 deposits at the Bibliothèque nationale confirm her analysis. The authors of the designs produced for the larger Parisian firms are anonymous. It was not they who signed the samples registered for copyright but the manufacturers, the firms themselves. But where the regulation of 1778 determined that, for the benefit of trade, privileges should be short – of four years' duration – the 1793 Act offered protection for life, which, in the case of a firm, could logically result in perpetual monopoly.[154]

The appropriateness of the 1793 'Act of the Rights of Genius' to industrial design, and wallpaper manufacture in particular, was coincidentally the subject of complaint and debate within the Ministère de l'Intérieur in the very year that Bance and Simon were deciding their commercial futures in court. In 1802, Eugène Bénard, of the renowned firm of Jacquemart et Bénard,[155] who had been a witness at Bance's and Simon's trial, addressed a written grievance to the Minister, Jean-Antoine Chaptal, alleging that the Act was failing his company's needs. At the trial, Bénard had supported Bance and condemned the secondary imitation that allowed manufacturers to cut costs by not employing designers. To Chaptal, Bénard complained that the legal and administrative procedures required to pursue infringers successfully was burdensome and protracted. Retribution needed to be fast to serve as a deterrent, particularly, we can infer, in design industries, where novelty was at a premium. He complained also that magistrates generally accepted the smallest modifications of layout and detail as proof of invention.[156] The same points were reiterated several years later, in 1808, in a petition submitted by a group of the most important wallpaper manufacturers in Paris. They added, moreover, that the system of depositing samples at the Bibliothèque nationale was counterproductive because, instead of offering protection to designs, it actually served to advertise them.[157] Unlike models and drawings, which came under the *loi des brevets* or patent legislation of 1791 and were deposited sealed, wallpaper samples at the Bibliothèque nationale were available for public inspection and therefore provided a remarkably up-to-date resource for unscrupulous manufacturers to exploit. In Bance *c.* Simon and in these petitions, competition and rivalries within the design industries come to light, rivalries between large and small firms, between those that invested heavily in original design (fig. **112**) and those that economised by adapting popular material in circulation.[158] Copyright had the potential to serve the first; it threatened to hinder the second.

Bénard's complaint provided an opportunity for broader reflection on matters of industrial design. Specifically, it resulted in the head of the Bureau des arts et manufactures, Claude-Anthelme Costaz, writing an extended report to accompany and second their application for legislation more in keeping with their needs.[159] Costaz, who was without vested interests in the matter, was much more searching and wide-ranging in his criticism than Jacquemart et Bénard, and focused on the one aspect of the 1793 law with which the manufacturers were seemingly content: the term of copyright's duration. Costaz argued that if a lifetime's protection plus ten years

> is appropriate for works of great importance, such as the production of a book of literature, a large picture, etc., it should not apply to designs that are mainly the product of a flash of fantasy. A work of literature, a large painting requires several years' work; a moment will often suffice for the making of a design: rarely does a designer have to work at one for months at a time.[160]

In short, the period of protection should be proportionate to the time invested in creation. Costaz suggested that, as with patent, protection should not exceed 15 years and ideally should be in the order of three. Such deregulation would benefit industry in two ways. First, it would encourage progress and growth by stimulating emulation as firms took stock of, perfected and built upon one another's artistic developments. Second, it would significantly reduce the instances of copyright infringement because the brevity of the delay before replication became legal would cease to make it worth anyone's while.

Despite much discussion and concerted efforts to draw up alternative regulations,[161] and despite the unequivocal conclusion of the tribunals of Gien and Loiret in 1804 that the Act of 19 July 1793 did not apply to wallpaper because it was not a work of genius,[162] wallpaper remained a fine art under the law until 1823. By that date, proper provision had been devised for the design of textiles, and it was by the extension of the legislation of 1806 formulated for the Lyon silk industry that wallpaper came under a regime anticipated by Costaz.[163] From that moment, the divergent systems of copyright for art and industry exaggerated and entrenched the perceived differences between art and design that had only begun to surface in the Bance–Simon affair. For the fine arts, copyright was a moral right, lifting it above the market. Copyright in design, by contrast, was an instrument of business and potentially of government, designed to promote trade and national prosperity by protecting the private interest of manufacturers, but to the minimum.

* * *

The cases of Auber *c.* Jean and Bance *c.* Simon stand at the threshold between the old system of privilege and a new system of rights. In winning, Auber and Simon perpetuated long-standing contradictions in privilege law: on the one hand, to protect the prerogatives of authors, and, on the other, to encourage emulation for the sake of all. They did so by mapping those distinctions onto art and industry, which were then separated in law. In recognising the artist's property, the 1793 Act protected the future of his or her compositions – rights not just to remuneration arising from their materialisation, which had been secured in the seventeenth century at the Van Opstal trial (see chapter 2), but also to the profit in their reproduction in other tangible forms by technology. But law also set an artificial limit to those forms. The artist's right ended at the edge of industry. Paradoxically, materiality and technology had a determining role in questions about the immaterial imagination in art. They constructed it from the outside and shaped the rights of artists accordingly. The politics of the Revolution were crucial to this articulation and apportioning of rights. A balance was struck between liberty and equality. Bance abandoned his appeal because, though his art had a case in law, justice was too clearly on the side of Simon's and Dufour's industry. Ultimately, however, Simon's victory was not absolute, for it gave rise to broader reflection on the relations between industry and copyright. Copyright appeared hostile to industry not only in the context of its relation to art but also as a means of regulating the internal affairs of manufactures heavily dependent on design. Prosperity, Napoleon's bureaucrats believed, depended on a finely judged equilibrium between fostering private initiative by safeguarding its reward and facilitating the communication of invention and novelty by setting a limit to the prerogatives conferred by property right.

The cases also touched the art world. Both were widely reported in the press.[164] Reference to Bance *c.* Simon also made its appearance in Salon criticism. In a review of the 1802 Salon, a critic noted as an aside in his applause of Gérard's paintings that they had been the subject of a 'bizarre' and 'absurd' instance of litigation. He was astonished by Bance's initial victory.[165] In his view, wallpaper was to painting what the travesties of the *foires* are to epic: trivialities to be ignored. A review of 1806 is more thoughtful but just as sceptical.[166] The critic argued that, in painting, lifting and transferring figures or motifs from a source is only a beginning. The painter has then alone to fill the traced outline with light and colour, and embed the figure in a composition on canvas. Technique and execution are nine-tenths of that artistic work. A derivative painter is still an artist, though second-rate. An artist with imagination but no practical skills is not one by any definition.[167] Reproduction, which had made viewers more alert and sensitive to repetition, led some to fetishise execution, or the touch of the artist's hand. The 1806 reviewer gave as his example of magical *faire* the work of the troubadour painter Fleury Richard and not that of his more illustrious and inventive master, David. At the very moment that law first recognised genius and the liberal and intellectual status of fine art, matter and transferable skill returned to haunt it.

APPENDIX

Académie print privileges, 1714–1789

The table overleaf lists the privileges granted by the Académie royale de peinture et de sculpture, and minuted in the *Procès-verbaux* of the Académie's bi-monthly meetings (see *Procès-verbaux de l'Académie royale de peinture et de sculpture, 1648–1792*, ed. Anatole de Montaiglon, 10 vols (Paris, 1875–92)); the source column provides a reference for the entry consisting of volume and page numbers. The minutes provide family names for the applicants and artists, to which I have added forenames, but other information – for instance, the identities of printmaker and publisher, and the place of sale – is given as it appears in the minutes, without additional details. The titles of the prints are transcribed from the minutes, except in the case of portraiture. In the case of ambiguous titles, I have substituted the inscription of the print itself. Where multiple artists are listed in a single entry, the works listed are attributed to the artists in the same order. For a table of the privileges granted by the Chancellerie, see <courtauld.ac.uk/katie-scott>.

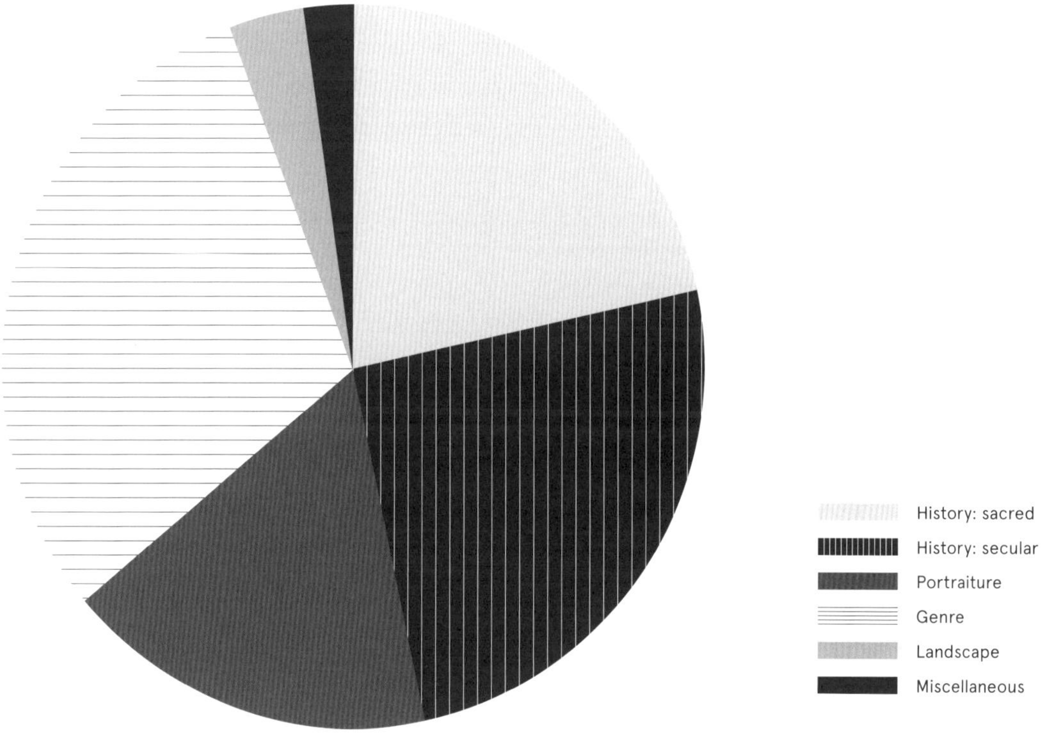

Académie print privileges (1714–89) quantified from the data in the table, according to subject matter and in the order of the hierarchy of genres.

Name of applicant	Author	Printmaker	Title	Sold by	Copies	Application date	Source
Pierre Giffart	Louis Feuillée	Pierre Giffart	*Journal des observations physiques, mathématiques et botaniques faites ... sur les côtes orientales de l'Amérique méridionale, et dans les Indes occidentales*	Pierre Giffart, Paris, 1714		5 Jan. 1715	*P-V*, 4: 195
Nicolas Guérin	Nicolas Guérin		*Description de l'Académie royale des arts de peinture et de sculpture*	Jacques Collombat, Paris, 1715		2 Mar. 1715	*P-V*, 4: 98–9
Louis Joblot	Louis Joblot		*Description et usages de plusieurs nouveaux microscopes tant simples que composez*	Jacques Collombat, Paris, 1718		5 Dec. 1716	*P-V*, 4: 234
Louis Joblot	Louis Joblot		*Histoire des animaux*			28 May 1718	*P-V*, 4: 267
Louis Joblot	Louis Joblot		*Histoire abrégée des insectes qui se trouvent aux environs de Paris*			3 Sept. 1718	*P-V*, 4: 271
Antoine Coypel	Antoine Coypel		unidentified			7 Dec. 1720	*P-V*, 4: 306–7
Jean-Baptiste Fermelhuis	Jean-Baptiste Fermelhuis		*Éloge funèbre de Monsieur Coysevox, sculpteur du roy*	Jacques Collombat, Paris, 1721		29 Mar. 1721	*P-V*, 4: 312, 315–16
Jacques-Philippe Ferrand	Jacques-Philippe Ferrand		*L'Art du feu ou de peindre en émail*	Jacques Collombat, Paris, 1721		30 May 1721	*P-V*, 4: 314–15
Jacques Collombat	Antoine Coypel		*Discours prononcez dans les conférences de l'Académie royale de peinture et de sculpture*	Jacques Collombat, Paris, 1721		30 Aug. 1721	*P-V*, 4: 320
Jean-François de Troy	Jean-François de Troy	Henri-Simon Thomassin	*La Peste de Marseille*	Thomassin, rue Neuve des Petits Champs; Duchange, rue Saint-Jacques	1	31 Dec. 1727	*P-V*, 5: 36
Nicolas-Henri Tardieu	Pierre Dulin	Nicolas-Henri Tardieu	*Saint Carlo Borromeo*	Nicolas Tardieu, rue Saint-Jacques	2	10 Nov. 1731	*P-V*, 5: 95
Gaspard Duchange	Paolo Veronese	Gaspard Duchange	*Christ au tombeau*		2	5 Jan. 1732	*P-V*, 5: 95
Nicolas de Larmessin	Charles Parrocel	Nicolas de Larmessin	equestrian portrait of Louis XV		2	21 July 1732	*P-V*, 5: 105

Charles-Nicolas Cochin *père*	François Le Moyne	Charles-Nicolas Cochin *père*	*Jacob arrive en Mésopotamie, aperçoit Rachel et se fait connoître à elle*	Charles-Nicolas Cochin *fils*, rue Saint-Jacques at 'S. Prosper'	2	27 Sept. 1732	*P-V*, 5: 108
Alexis Simon Belle	Alexis Simon Belle	Jean Daullé	portrait of the dauphin	Alexis Belle, rue du Four; Veuve Chéreau, rue Saint-Jacques		30 May 1733	*P-V*, 5: 120, 124
Jean Audran	Nicolas Poussin; Jean II Restout	Jean Audran	*L'Enlèvement des Sabines*; *L'Extase de Saint-Benoît*		1 of each	28 Nov. 1733	*P-V*, 5: 128
Charles-Antoine Coypel	Charles-Antoine Coypel	Louis Surugue	*Thalie chassée par la Peinture*	Louis Surugue, rue des Noyers	2	6 Feb. 1734	*P-V*, 5: 137
Henri-Simon Thomassin	Jean Thierry	Henri-Simon Thomassin	the fountains at La Granja de San Ildefonso		2	3 July 1734	*P-V*, 5: 141
Jean-François de Troy	Jean-François de Troy	Henri-Simon Thomassin	*La Vierge à l'enfant*			2 Oct. 1734	*P-V*, 5: 145–6
Jean-François de Troy	Jean-François de Troy	Charles-Nicolas Cochin *fils*; Charles-Nicolas Cochin *père*	*La Mort d'Hippolyte*; *Jupiter et Calisto*; *Le Pied de bœuf*	Chez l'Auteur, place des Victoires; Duchange, rue Saint-Jacques		30 Apr. 1735	*P-V*, 5: 157–8
Jean-François de Troy	Jean-François de Troy	Étienne Fessard	*Léda et le cygne*			30 July 1735	*P-V*, 5: 161
Pierre Dulin	Pierre Dulin	Charles-Nicolas Cochin *fils*	*Jésus-Christ guérissant les malades*		2	30 July 1735	*P-V*, 5: 161
Nicolas de Larmessin	Nicolas Lancret	Nicolas de Larmessin	*Les Quatre Âges caractérisés par leurs amusemens*		8	30 July 1735	*P-V*, 5: 161–2
Nicolas de Larmessin	Nicolas Lancret	Nicolas de Larmessin	*Les Amours du bocage*		2	31 Dec. 1735	*P-V*, 5: 168

Name of applicant	Author	Printmaker	Title	Sold by	Copies	Application date	Source
Jean-François de Troy	Jean-François de Troy	Henri-Simon Thomassin	portrait of the dauphin		2	7 Jan. 1736	*P-V*, 5: 170
Hubert Drouais	Hubert Drouais	Jean Daullé	portrait of Mlle Pélissier	Drouais, rue de Richelieu, au Bain royal	2	28 Jan. 1736	*P-V*, 5: 171
Jean-François de Troy	Jean-François de Troy	Étienne Fessard	*La Manne*		2	3 Mar. 1736	*P-V*, 5: 172–31
Jacques-François Courtin	Jacques-François Courtin	Michel Aubert	*La Prêtresse; L'Amant complaisant; Le Hanneton; L'Amant magnifique*		2	7 Apr. 1736	*P-V*, 5: 175–6
Jacques-François Courtin	Jacques-François Courtin	Michel Aubert	*La Belle Danseuse; Les Jeux naïfs*		2	26 May 1736	*P-V*, 5: 177
Charles Dupuis	Carle Vanloo	Charles Dupuis	*Le Mariage de la Vierge*	Veuve Chéreau, rue Saint-Jacques	1	30 June 1736	*P-V*, 5: 178
Charles-Nicolas Cochin *fils*	Jean II Restout		*La Colère d'Armide contre Renaud*		2	28 Sept. 1736	*P-V*, 5: 183
Nicolas de Larmessin	Nicolas Vleughels		*Frère Luce*		2	5 Jan. 1737	*P-V*, 5: 192–3
Nicolas de Larmessin	Nicolas Lancret		*Les Oies du frère Philippe*		2	5 Jan. 1737	*P-V*, 5: 192–3
Jean Moyreau	Philips Wouwermans		unidentified		2	23 Feb. 1737	*P-V*, 5: 196–7
Charles-Nicolas Cochin *père*	Jean II Restout	Charles-Nicolas Cochin *père*	*Laban s'excuse et dit à Jacob que la coûtume du païs étant de marier les aînées avant les cadettes, il a dû lui donner Lia avant Rachel*		2	2 Mar. 1737	*P-V*, 5: 198
Jean Moyreau	Philips Wouwermans		*La Guerre des huguenots*		2	26 May 1737	*P-V*, 5: 202
Jean Moyreau	Jacques de La Joue		*Titres aux morceaux d'après Wouwermans*		2	6 July 1737	*P-V*, 5: 209
Jean Moyreau	Philips Wouwermans		*Le Colombier du maréchal*		2	23 Aug 1737	*P-V*, 5: 211

Charles-Nicolas Cochin *fils*	Giovanni Paolo Panini		*Les Feux d'artifice tirés dans la place de Navonne*		2	28 Sept. 1737	*P-V*, 5: 216
Jean Moyreau	Philips Wouwermans		*Les Baigneurs*		2	28 Sept. 1737	*P-V*, 5: 216
Charles Dupuis	Carle Vanloo		*Énée qui porte son père Anchise*		2	5 Oct. 1737	*P-V*, 5: 217
Charles-Nicolas Cochin *père*	Jacques de La Joue	Charles-Nicolas Cochin *père*	*L'Histoire; La Sculpture; L'Astronomie; L'Optique*		8	26 Oct. 1737	*P-V*, 5: 218
Jean Moyreau	Philips Wouwermans		*Le Quartier de rafraîchissement*		2	31 Dec. 1737	*P-V*, 5: 222
Jean Moyreau	Philips Wouwermans		*La Prédication de Saint-Jean-Baptiste*		2	29 Mar. 1738	*P-V*, 5: 228
Louis Surugue	Charles-Antoine Coypel	Pierre-Louis Surugue	*Roland apprend par les bergers la perfidie d'Angélique*		2	29 Mar. 1738	*P-V*, 5: 228
Charles-Nicolas Cochin *père*	Jacques de La Joue	Charles-Nicolas Cochin *père*	*La Botanique; La Pharmacie*		4	29 Mar. 1738	*P-V*, 5: 228
Gaspard Duchange	Pierre-Jacques Cazes; Jean II Restout; Carle Vanloo	Nicolas-Dauphin de Beauvais	illustrations of the 'mystères du nouveau testament' for *Les Heures nouvelles de Paris*		2 × 16	12 Apr. 1738	*P-V*, 5: 229
Jean Moyreau	Philips Wouwermans		*La Chasse aux éperviers*		2	21 June 1738	*P-V*, 5: 232
Louis Surugue	Jacques Dumont le Romain		*Le Roman comique*		2	2 Aug. 1738	*P-V*, 5: 236
Jean Moyreau	Philips Wouwermans		*Le Présent du chasseur*		2	30 Aug. 1738	*P-V*, 5: 239
Jean Moyreau	Philips Wouwermans		*La Conduite des dames pour la chasse*		2	27 Sept. 1738	*P-V*, 5: 241
Jean Moyreau	Philips Wouwermans		*La Petite Foire au chevaux*		2	8 Nov. 1738	*P-V*, 5: 243

Name of applicant	Author	Printmaker	Title	Sold by	Copies	Application date	Source
Nicolas Delobel	Nicolas Delobel	Charles-Nicolas Cochin *père*	*La Lorraine réunie à la France*		2	31 Dec. 1738	*P-V*, 5: 244
Jean Moyreau	Philips Wouwermans		*L'Écurie hollandaise*		2	28 Feb. 1739	*P-V*, 5: 247
Jean Moyreau	Philips Wouwermans		*Le Vin de l'estrier*		2	25 Apr. 1739	*P-V*, 5: 251
Jacques-François Courtin	Jacques-François Courtin	C. Mathey	*L'Amour médecin*		2	13 May 1739	*P-V*, 5: 252
Charles-Nicolas Cochin *père*	Jean Siméon Chardin		4 prints submitted but only 2 identified: *La Blanchisseuse*; *La Fontaine*		8	27 June 1739	*P-V*, 5: 253
Jean Moyreau	Philips Wouwermans		unidentified		2	27 June 1739	*P-V*, 5: 253
Gaspard Duchange	Charles Le Brun; Eustache Le Sueur	Bernard Picard	*Les Peintures de l'hôtel Lambert*		1	5 Sept. 1739	*P-V*, 5: 257–8
Edme Jeaurat	Edme Jeaurat	Michel Aubert	*Laban qui cherche ses dieux*		2	5 Sept. 1739	*P-V*, 5: 258
Jean Moyreau	Philips Wouwermans		*Les Maquignons à la foire*		2	5 Sept. 1739	*P-V*, 5: 258
Nicolas-Henri Tardieu	Jean II Restout	Jacques-Nicolas Tardieu	*Notre Seigneur qui guérit le paralytique près de la piscine*		2	3 Oct. 1739	*P-V*, 5: 261
Charles-Nicolas Cochin *père*	Nicolas Lancret		*Le Colin maillard*		2	28 Nov. 1739	*P-V*, 5: 263
Jean Moyreau	Philips Wouwermans		*La Petite Chasse aux oiseaux*		2	28 Nov. 1739	*P-V*, 5: 263
Charles-Nicolas Cochin *père*	Jean Siméon Chardin	François-Bernard Lépicié	*La Gouvernante*		2	30 Jan. 1740	*P-V*, 5: 267
Jean Moyreau	Jean Raoux		*L'Enfance*		2	30 Apr. 1740	*P-V*, 5: 271
Louis Surugue	Antoine Coypel		*La Descente d'Énée aux enfers*		2	30 July 1740	*P-V*, 5: 276
Nicolas-Henri Tardieu	Pierre Parrocel		*Christ en croix*		2	30 July 1740	*P-V*, 5: 276

Charles-Nicolas Cochin *père*	Jean Siméon Chardin	Charles-Nicolas Cochin *père*	*L'Écureuse; Le Garçon cabaretier*		4	24 Sept. 1740	*P-V*, 5: 282
Jean Moyreau	Philips Wouwermans		*Le Pillage des titres durant les guerres civiles des françaises*		2	26 Nov. 1740	*P-V*, 5: 284
Charles-Nicolas Cochin *père*	Jean Siméon Chardin		*La Mère laborieuse*		2	7 Jan. 1741	*P-V*, 5: 290
Nicolas de Larmessin	Nicolas Lancret		*Les Quatre Heures du jour*		8	25 Feb. 1741	*P-V*, 5: 293
Jean Moyreau	Philips Wouwermans		*La Famille du maréchal*		2	24 Mar. 1741	*P-V*, 5: 295
Edme Jeaurat	Nicolas Vleughels	Nicolas-Henri Tardieu; Laurent Cars; Nicolas de Larmessin	*Les Pèlerins d'Emmaüs; L'Apparition de Jésus à Marie; La Samaritaine*		6	6 May 1741	*P-V*, 5: 297–8
Jean Moyreau	Philips Wouwermans		*L'Abreuvoir des chasseurs*		2	23 June 1741	*P-V*, 5: 300
Nicolas-Henri Tardieu	Pierre Dulin		*Saint-Jérôme en méditation*		2	30 Sept. 1741	*P-V*, 5: 306
Jean Moyreau	Philips Wouwermans		*Le Marchand de foin*		2	30 Sept. 1741	*P-V*, 5: 307
Louis Surugue		Louis Surugue; Pierre-Louis Surugue	*L'Amour de la chasse; L'Amour du vin*		4	27 Oct. 1741	*P-V*, 5: 308
Jean Moyreau	Philips Wouwermans		*Le Manège*		2	27 Jan. 1742	*P-V*, 5: 313
Nicolas-Henri Tardieu	Peter Paul Rubens		2 prints from *Histoire de Constantin*		4	23 Feb. 1742	*P-V*, 5: 315
Jean Moyreau	Philips Wouwermans		*Le Défilé d'équipages*		2	30 June 1742	*P-V*, 5: 323
Nicolas-Henri Tardieu	Peter Paul Rubens		2 prints from *Histoire de Constantin*		4	28 Sept. 1742	*P-V*, 5: 329

Name of applicant	Author	Printmaker	Title	Sold by	Copies	Application date	Source
Charles-Nicolas Cochin *père*	Pierre-Jacques Cazes		*Saint-Pierre guérissant le boiteux à la porte du temple*		2	27 Oct. 1742	*P-V*, 5: 331
Charles-Nicolas Cochin *père*	Nicolas Bertin		*Le Baptême de l'eunuque par Saint-Philippe*		2	27 Oct. 1742	*P-V*, 5: 331
Jean Moyreau	Philips Wouwermans		*Gardes de cavalerie*		2	27 Oct. 1742	*P-V*, 5: 331
Nicolas-Henri Tardieu	Peter Paul Rubens		from *Histoire de Constantin*		2	1 Dec. 1742	*P-V*, 5: 333
Jean Moyreau	Philips Wouwermans		*Le Marchand de Mitridate*		2	30 Mar. 1743	*P-V*, 5: 341
Carle Vanloo	Carle Vanloo		a set of six Académie figures		2	30 Mar. 1743	*P-V*, 5: 341
Jean Moyreau	Philips Wouwermans		*Le Petit Pont de bois*		2	28 June 1743	*P-V*, 5: 345
Nicolas-Henri Tardieu	Peter Paul Rubens		*L'Entrevue de Constantin et de Crispe après la bataille de Galipoli; Rome*		4	27 July 1743	*P-V*, 5: 347
Gaspard Duchange	Jean Jouvenet		*Résurrection du fils de la veuve de Naïm*		3	3 Aug. 1743	*P-V*, 5: 348
Jean Moyreau	Jean Raoux		*L'Âge virile*		2	8 Sept. 1743	*P-V*, 5: 352
François Boucher	François Boucher	John Ingram	2 suites: *Pastorales; Figures chinoises*		4	31 Jan. 1744	*P-V*, 5: 360
Jean Moyreau	Jean Raoux	Jean Moyreau	*La Vieillesse*		2	25 Apr. 1744	*P-V*, 5: 364
Charles-Nicolas Cochin *père*	Philips Wouwermans	Charles-Nicolas Cochin *père*	*Accident de voyage; Vue de Hollande*		4	29 Aug. 1744	*P-V*, 5: 371
Jean Moyreau	Philips Wouwermans	Jean Moyreau	*L'Embrasement du moulin*		2	26 Sept. 1744	*P-V*, 5: 372
Nicolas-Henri Tardieu	Peter Paul Rubens		*La Défaite de Maxence par Constantin*		4	30 Jan. 1745	*P-V*, 6: 2
Jean Moyreau	Philips Wouwermans		*La Défaite des sarazins*		2	27 Mar. 1745	*P-V*, 6: 6–7

Nicolas de Larmessin	Nicolas Lancret		*Les Quatre Saisons*		8	3 Apr. 1745	*P-V*, 6: 8
Jean Moyreau	Philips Wouwermans		*Les Chasseurs sortant de la forêt*		2	24 July 1745	*P-V*, 6: 12
Gaspard Duchange	Étienne Jeaurat		*Les Mystères de la Trinité; L'Incarnation; La Rédemption*		6	8 Jan. 1746	*P-V*, 6: 22
Jean Moyreau	Philips Wouwermans		*Le Bouffon des chasseurs*		2	26 Feb. 1746	*P-V*, 6: 24
Nicolas-Henri Tardieu	Peter Paul Rubens		from *Histoire de Constantin*		6	26 Mar. 1746	*P-V*, 6: 26–7
Jean Moyreau	Philips Wouwermans		*Les Bohémiens*		2	30 July 1746	*P-V*, 6: 32
Jean Moyreau	Philips Wouwermans		*Le Travail du maréchal*		2	29 Oct. 1746	*P-V*, 6: 38
Nicolas-Henri Tardieu	Jean-Baptiste Oudry		*Vue de la ville de Beauvais*		2	24 Mar. 1747	*P-V*, 6: 49–50
Jean Moyreau	Philips Wouwermans		*La Chaumière*		2	24 Mar. 1747	*P-V*, 6: 50
Jean Moyreau	Philips Wouwermans		*La Diligence hollandaise*		2	23 June 1747	*P-V*, 6: 59
Gaspard Duchange	Charles Le Brun	Gaspard Duchange	*Christ au tombeau*		2	29 July 1747	*P-V*, 6: 61
Louis Surugue	Charles-Antoine Coypel		*La Folie qui pare la décrépitude des agréments de la jeunesse; Une Dame en habit der bal*			5 Aug. 1747	*P-V*, 6: 63
Louis Surugue	Jean Siméon Chardin		*Les Amusements de la vie privée*		6	5 Aug. 1747	*P-V*, 6: 63
Jean Moyreau	Philips Wouwermans		*L'Accident du chasseur*		2	30 Sept. 1747	*P-V*, 6: 70
Jacques-Philippe Le Bas	David Teniers		*Œuvres de miséricorde*		2	30 Dec. 1747	*P-V*, 6: 81–2

Name of applicant	Author	Printmaker	Title	Sold by	Copies	Application date	Source
Jean Moyreau	Philips Wouwermans		*La Fontaine de Neptune*		2	24 Feb. 1748	*P-V*, 6: 92
Jean Moyreau	Philips Wouwermans		*La Grotte du maréchal*		2	31 Aug. 1748	*P-V*, 6: 134
Gaspard Duchange	Charles-Antoine Coypel		*L'Enfant Jésus au berceau*		2	28 Sept. 1748	*P-V*, 6: 137
Jean Moyreau	Philips Wouwermans		*Les Marchands forains*		2	31 Dec. 1748	*P-V*, 6: 145
Jean Moyreau	Philips Wouwermans		*La Barque du pêcheur*		2	12 June 1749	*P-V*, 6: 163
Jean Moyreau	Philips Wouwermans		*L'Abreuvoir hollandois*		2	30 Aug. 1749	*P-V*, 6: 175
Jean-Marc Nattier	Jean-Marc Nattier	Jean-Joseph Balechou	portrait of the duchesse de Châteauroux in the guise of 'la Force'		2	10 Jan. 1750	*P-V*, 6: 191–2
Jean Moyreau	Philips Wouwermans		*La Fontaine du Triton*		2	4 Apr. 1750	*P-V*, 6: 204
Jacques-Nicolas Tardieu	Antoine Coypel		*La Colère d'Achille; Les Adieux d'Héctor*		4	25 Apr. 1750	*P-V*, 6: 208
Jean Moyreau	Philips Wouwermans		*La Fontaine de Vénus*		2	29 Aug. 1750	*P-V*, 6: 227
Charles-Nicolas Cochin *père*	Philips Wouwermans	Charles-Nicolas Cochin *père*	[*Accident de voyage*]			30 Jan. 1751	*P-V*, 6: 250
Charles-Nicolas Cochin *père*	Jean-Baptiste Marie Pierre	Charles-Nicolas Cochin *père*	[*Le Voyage*]		4	30 Jan. 1751	*P-V*, 6: 250
Jean Moyreau	Philips Wouwermans		*Le Conseil des chasseurs*		2	27 Mar. 1751	*P-V*, 6: 265
Jean Moyreau	Philips Wouwermans		*La Récréation militaire*		2	26 June 1751	*P-V*, 6: 276

Jean Moyreau	Philips Wouwermans		*La Marche d'armée*		2	25 Sept. 1751	*P-V*, 6: 286
Jean Moyreau	Philips Wouwermans		*Les Cavaliers du manège*		2	24 Mar. 1752	*P-V*, 6: 311
Jean-Marc Nattier	Jean-Marc Nattier	Michel Aubert	*Un Amant qui verse du vin à sa maîtresse*		2	29 July 1752	*P-V*, 6: 326
Jean Moyreau	Philips Wouwermans		*Les Occupations champêtres*		2	29 July 1752	*P-V*, 6: 327
Laurent Cars	François Le Moyne	Laurent Cars	*L'Enlèvement d'Europe*		2	4 Nov. 1752	*P-V*, 6: 338
Jean Moyreau	Philips Wouwermans		*Port de mer*		2	2 Dec. 1752	*P-V*, 6: 340
Jean-Marc Nattier	Jean-Marc Nattier	Jean-Joseph Balechou	portrait of Mme Infante, the duchess of Parma		2	3 Feb. 1753	*P-V*, 6: 345
Jean Moyreau	Philips Wouwermans		*L'Écurie de la poste*		2	28 Apr. 1753	*P-V*, 6: 349
Jean-Marc Nattier	Jean-Marc Nattier		portrait of Mme Victoire		2	24 Nov. 1753	*P-V*, 6: 370
Jean Moyreau	Philips Wouwermans		*Le Quartier des vivandiers*		2	31 Aug. 1754	*P-V*, 6: 395
Louis Surugue	Rembrandt		*Philosophe en méditation*		2	31 Dec. 1754	*P-V*, 6: 403
Jean-Marc Nattier	Jean-Marc Nattier	Jacques-Nicolas Tardieu	portrait of the queen Maria Leszczinska		2	22 Mar. 1755	*P-V*, 6: 411
Jacques-Nicolas Tardieu	David Teniers the younger		*Le Médecin empirique*		2	22 Mar. 1755	*P-V*, 6: 411–12
Jean Moyreau	Philips Wouwermans		*Le Départ pour la chasse à l'oiseau*		2	31 Dec. 1755	*P-V*, 6: 433
Jean Moyreau	Philips Wouwermans		*L'Écuyer du manège*		2	30 Oct. 1756	*P-V*, 7: 25
Jean-Marc Nattier	Jean-Marc Nattier	Jacques-Nicolas Tardieu	portrait of Mme Henriette		2	1 July 1758	*P-V*, 7: 67
Étienne Fessard	Carle Vanloo	Étienne Fessard	*Jupiter et Antiope*		2	14 Jan. 1759	*P-V*, 7: 81

Name of applicant	Author	Printmaker	Title	Sold by	Copies	Application date	Source
Pierre-Louis Surugue	Rembrandt	Pierre-Louis Surugue	*Le Père de Rembrandt peint par son fils*			7 July 1759	*P-V*, 7: 95
Claude-Henri Watelet	Claude-Henri Watelet		*L'Art de peindre: Poëme, avec Réflexions sur les différentes parties de la peinture*	Hippolyte-Louis Guérin and Louis-François Delatour, Paris, 1760		28 July 1759	*P-V*, 7: 97
Michel-François Dandré-Bardon	Michel-François Dandré-Bardon		*Les Éléments des beaux-arts*			1 Sept. 1759	*P-V*, 7: 102
Jean Moyreau	Claude Lorraine	Jean Moyreau	*Conversation des matelots*		1	28 Sept. 1759	*P-V*, 7: 104
Jacques-Nicolas Tardieu	Nicolas de Largillière	Jacques-Nicolas Tardieu	portrait of Jean-Baptiste Oudry		3	2 Aug. 1760	*P-V*, 7: 140
Pierre-Louis Surugue	Jean Siméon Chardin	Pierre-Louis Surugue	*L'Aveugle*		1	28 Mar. 1761	*P-V*, 7: 160
Étienne Fessard	François Boucher	Étienne Fessard	*La Lumière du monde; L'Amour désarmé*		2	4 Apr. 1761	*P-V*, 7: 161
Michel-François Dandré-Bardon	Michel-François Dandré-Bardon		*Traité de peinture, suivi d'un essai sur la sculpture*	Charles Saillant, Paris, 1765		6 Oct. 1764	*P-V*, 7: 272–3
Michel-François Dandré-Bardon	Michel-François Dandré-Bardon		*Histoire universelle, traitée relativement aux arts de peindre et de sculpter, ou Tableaux de l'histoire*, 3 vols	Joseph Merlin, Paris, 1769		4 June 1768	*P-V*, 7: 390
Nicolas-Henri Tardieu	Étienne Jeaurat	Élisabeth-Claire Tardieu	*Le Joli dormir*			7 Jan. 1769	*P-V*, 8: 1–2
Joseph-Siffred Duplessis	Joseph-Siffred Duplessis		portrait of Christoph Willibald von Gluck			25 Feb. 1775	*P-V*, 8: 180
Michel-François Dandré-Bardon	Michel-François Dandré-Bardon		*Éloge du tombeau du maréchal de Saxe*			26 Apr. 1777 7 June 1777	*P-V*, 8: 263, 269
Michel-François Dandré-Bardon	Michel-François Dandré-Bardon		*Mausolée de feu Mgr le dauphin et de feue Mme la dauphine, ordonné par le roi Louis XV, érigé par Louis XVI dans la cathédrale de Sens, monument sculpté par Coustou*	Louis Cellot, Paris, 1777		2 Aug. 1777	*P-V*, 8: 275–6

Jacques-Philippe Le Bas	Jean-Michel Moreau *le jeune*		*Figures de l'Histoire de France*	Jacques-Philippe Le Bas, 1778		4, 6 June 1778	*P-V*, 8: 331, 338
Charles-Louis Clérisseau	Charles-Louis Clérisseau	Claude René Gabriel Poulleau	*Antiquités de la France*	Charles-Louis Clérisseau; Claude René Gabriel Poulleau; François Joullain, Paris.		4 July 1778	*P-V*, 8: 341, 353
Jacques-Philippe Le Bas	Jean-Michel Moreau *le jeune*		*Figures de l'Histoire de France*, 2e livraison	Jacques-Philippe Le Bas, 1778		25 July 1778	*P-V*, 8: 342
Michel-François Dandré-Bardon	Michel-François Dandré-Bardon		*Éloge historique à Jean-Baptiste Le Moyne, sculpteur du roi*			31 Nov. 1778	*P-V*, 8: 351
Jacques-Philippe Le Bas	Jean-Michel Moreau *le jeune*		*Figures de l'Histoire de France*, 3e livraison			27 Feb. 1779	*P-V*, 8: 368
Antoine-Joseph Loriot	Antoine-Joseph Loriot		*Secret de M. Loriot*			4 Mar. 1780 29 Apr. 1780	*P-V*, 9: 15, 21
Jean-Baptiste Le Prince	Jean-Baptiste Le Prince		*Prospectus pour une suite d'estampes*			23 June 1780	*P-V*, 9: 27
Antoine-Nicolas Dézallier d'Argenville	Antoine-Nicolas Dézallier d'Argenville		*Description sommaire des ouvrages de peinture, sculpture et gravure exposés dans les salles de l'Académie royale*	Jean de Bure, Paris, 1781		1 July 1780 27 Jan. 1781	*P-V*, 9: 29, 49, 78
Jean-Michel Moreau *le jeune*	Jean-Michel Moreau le jeune		*Prospectus pour une suite d'estampes, destinée à décorer la nouvelle édition de M. de Voltaire, proposée par souscription par M. Moreau-le-Jeune, dessinateur et graveur du Cabinet du roi ...*			3 Feb. 1781	*P-V*, 9: 50, 52
Jean-Pierre Houël	Jean-Pierre Houël		*Prospectus pour un voyage pittoresque des isles de Sicile, de Malte et de Lipari*			3 Mar. 1781	*P-V*, 9: 54–5, 89–90, 98–9
Pierre-Antoine de Machy	Pierre-Antoine de Machy		*Prospectus pour ... vues de la ville de Paris*			30 June 1781	*P-V*, 9: 67–8

Name of applicant	Author	Printmaker	Title	Sold by	Copies	Application date	Source
Jean-Pierre Houël	Jean-Pierre Houël		*Voyage pittoresque des isles de Sicile, de Malte et de Lipari*, 3e–4e livraison			31 Aug. 1782	*P-V*, 9: 123
Jean-Pierre Houël	Jean-Pierre Houël		*Voyage pittoresque des isles de Sicile, de Malte et de Lipari*, 5e livraison			9 Nov. 1782	*P-V*, 9: 130
Jean-Pierre Houël	Jean-Pierre Houël		*Voyage pittoresque des isles de Sicile, de Malte et de Lipari*, 6e livraison			22 Feb. 1783	*P-V*, 9: 140–41
Charles-Nicolas Cochin *fils*	Michel-François Dandré-Bardon		*Costumes des anciens peuples*	2nd abridged edn, Alexandre Jombert *le jeune*, 1784–6		27 Sept. 1783	*P-V*, 9: 168–9
Jean-Michel Moreau *le jeune*	Jacques-Philippe Le Bas		*Figures de l'Histoire de France*, 13e livraison	Jean-Michel Moreau *le jeune*, Paris, 1785		4 Dec. 1784	*P-V*, 9: 219, 221
Jean-Joseph Sue	Jean-Joseph Sue		*Précis d'un cours d'anatomie pittoresque à l'usage des élèves*			25 June 1785	*P-V*, 9: 44–5
Jean-Jacques-François Le Barbier	Jean-Jacques-François Le Barbier		*Œuvres de Salomon Gessner*	Jean-Jacques-François Le Barbier; Veuve Hérissant; Pierre Théophile Barrois, 1786–93		1 Apr. 1786	*P-V*, 9: 280–81
Jean-Charles Le Vasseur	François-Guillaume Ménageot		*La Mort de Léonard de Vinci*	Jean-Charles Le Vasseur, rue des Maçons		23 Feb. 1788	*P-V*, 9: 351
Jean-Charles Le Vasseur	Jean-Baptiste Greuze		*Le Testament déchiré*	Jean-Charles Le Vasseur, rue des Maçons		23 Feb. 1788	*P-V*, 9: 351, 359–60
Antoine Renou	Charles-Alphonse Dufresnoy		*L'Art de peindre: traduction libre en vers François du poème latin de Charles-Alphonse Dufresnoy, avec ses remarques*			7 Feb. 1789	*P-V*, 10: 2

NOTES

INTRODUCTION
Artists, authorship and property

1 Michel Foucault, 'What is an Author?' (1969), in *Language, Counter-Memory, Practice: Selected Essays and Interviews*, trans. Donald F. Bouchard and Sherry Simon, ed. Donald F. Bouchard (Oxford, 1977), pp. 113–38. See also Peter Jaszi, 'Towards a Theory of Copyright: The Metamorphoses of Authorship', *Duke Law Journal*, 2 (1991), 455–502.

2 In the case of France see Raymond Birn, 'The Profit of Ideas: *Privilèges en librairie* in Eighteenth-Century France', *Eighteenth-Century Studies*, 4 (1970–71), 131–68; Elizabeth Armstrong, *Before Copyright: The French Book-Privilege System, 1498–1526* (Cambridge, 1990); Carla Hesse, 'Enlightenment Epistemology and the Laws of Authorship in Revolutionary France, 1777–1795', *Representations*, 30 (1990), 109–37; Bernard Edelman, *Le Sacre de l'auteur* (Paris, 2004).

3 In this I follow in the footsteps of Martha Woodmansee and Mark Rose in their respective studies of copyright in Germany and Great Britain. Martha Woodmansee, *The Author, Art, and the Market: Rereading the History of Aesthetics* (New York, 1994); Mark Rose, *Authors and Owners: The Invention of Copyright* (Boston, 1995).

4 Mario Biagioli and Peter Galison, *Scientific Authorship: Credit and Intellectual Property in Science* (New York and London, 2003).

5 Krzysztof Pomian, 'Marchands, connoisseurs, curieux à Paris au XVIIIe siècle', *Revue de l'art*, 43 (1979), 23–36; Colin B. Bailey, *Patriotic Taste: Collecting Modern Art in Pre-Revolutionary Paris* (New Haven, CT, 2002); Charlotte Guichard, *Les Amateurs d'art à Paris au XVIIIe siècle* (Paris, 2008); Charlotte Guichard, *La Griffe du peintre: Essai sur la valeur de l'art (1730–1820)* (Paris, 2018); Kristel Smentek, *Mariette and the Science of the Connoisseur in Eighteenth-Century Europe* (New York and London, 2014).

6 For an introduction to questions of collaboration in the case of writing, see Martha Woodmansee, 'On the Author Effect: Reviewing Collectivity', in *The Construction of Authorship: Textual Appropriation in Law and Literature*, Martha Woodmansee and Peter Jaszi (eds) (Durham, NC, 1994), pp. 15–28.

7 On 22 May 1724 Charles-Antoine Coypel was granted a privilege for the *Histoire de Don Quichotte* for 12 years (BnF, Mss. f.f. 21952); on 2 Mar. 1725 Jean-Baptiste Oudry was granted a ten-year privilege for *La Chasse du cerf* (BnF, Mss. f.f. 21953); on 26 Aug. 1730 Nicolas Lancret was granted a six-year privilege for the portrait of Mlle de Camargo, *Les Mois de l'année*, *Les Saisons*, and eight pictures of 'divertissements' (BnF, Mss. f.f. 21954); on 7 July 1767 Jean-Baptiste Greuze was granted a six-year privilege for *Le Paralitique servi par ses enfants*, *L'Accordée de village*, *La Mère bien aimée*, *La Mort du père de famille*, and *L'Enfant gâté* (BnF, Mss. f.f. 21963).

8 BnF, Mss. f.f. 21953, 5 Aug. 1727. Jullienne's privilege prohibited the copy of 'les dits Tableaux dud. Sr Watteau qui sont en sa [Jullienne's] possession'. Theoretically, engravings after those paintings that were reproduced for the *Recueil Jullienne* but did not belong personally to Jullienne entered the public domain on publication. The privilege was for ten years and fines were set exceptionally high, at 10,000 *livres*.

9 *P-V*, vol. 5, p. 253, 27 June 1739, for *La Blanchisseuse* and *La Fontaine*; vol. 5, p. 282, 24 Sept. 1740, for *L'Écureuse* and *Le Garçon cabaretier*; vol. 5, p. 290, 7 Jan. 1741, for *La Mère laborieuse*.

10 Peter Fuhring, 'The Print Privilege in Eighteenth-Century France, II', *PQ*, 3 (1986), 19–33.

11 Molly Nesbit, 'What was an Author?', *YFS*, 73 (1987), 229–57.

12 Anne Barron, 'Copyright, Art and Objecthood', in *Dear Images: Art, Copyright and Culture*, Daniel McClean and Karsten Schubert (eds) (London, 2002), pp. 277–311; Nadia Walravens, 'The Concept of Originality in Contemporary Art', in ibid., pp. 170–95. See also Martha Buskirk, 'Authorship and Authority', in *The Contingent Object in Contemporary Art* (Cambridge, 2005), pp. 21–56.

13 See, for example, the studies of Joseph Koerner, 'Albrecht Dürer: A Sixteenth-Century Influenza', in *Albrecht Dürer and his Legacy*, exh. cat., British Museum, London, Giulia Bartrum (ed.) (London, 2003), pp. 25–31; Lisa Pon, *Raphael, Dürer and Marcantonio Raimondi: Copying and the Italian Renaissance Print* (London, 2004).

14 The 1515 privilege was for the 'livre & carte'. See Armstrong, *Before Copyright*, pp. 204–5. The only surviving copy of the book with the map bound in is in the Bibliothèque nationale de France (available on Gallica). In 1495 Signot had been asked by Charles VIII to reconnoitre suitable passes across the Alps, in preparation for the latter's invasion of Italy. The resulting 'complete' and 'true' description, with map of the passes, published in Paris by Toussaint Denis, went through four editions between 1515 and 1522.

15 Bernard Edelman, *Le Droit saisi par la photographie: Éléments pour une théorie marxiste du droit* (Paris, 1973); new edn (Paris, 2001).

16 I am drawing here on Raymond Williams's definitions of the dominant, the residual and the emergent: Raymond Williams, *Marxism and Literature* (Oxford, 1978), pp. 121–7.

17 Barron, 'Copyright, Art and Objecthood', pp. 291–2.

18 Édouard Meaume, 'François Collignon', *NAAF* (1876), 298–300.

19 Marianne Grivel, *Le Commerce de l'estampe à Paris au XVIIe siècle* (Geneva, 1986), p. 105.

20 Arguments put forward in 1734 for the right of the engravers and printsellers of Paris to have printing presses in their studios, in opposition to the copper-plate printers' statutory monopoly, cited, in defence of their need for immediate oversight of the printing of their plates, the theft by printers of proofs for resale and for copying; see *Mémoire pour les graveurs et marchands d'estampes, ayant des fonds de planches gravées; contre les syndics ou jurez de la Communauté en taille-douce* (Paris, 1734), pp. 2, 6–7.

21 Thomas Puttfarken, *The Discovery of Pictorial Composition* (London and New Haven, CT, 2000).

22 Roger de Piles, *Cours de peinture par principes* (1708) (Paris, 1989), p. 208.

23 Ibid., p. 211.

24 Abbé Jean-Baptiste Du Bos, *Réflexions critique sur la poésie et la peinture* (1719) ed. Dominique Désirat (Paris, 1993), p. 163.

25 Quoting Pliny, de Piles argued for the conditions prevailing in antiquity where 'Il n'était pas permis de tenir comme prisonier la peinture sur les murailles, elle demeurait indifférent à toutes les villes, et un Peintre était un bien commun à toute la terre.' De Piles, *Cours de peinture par principes*, p. 211.

26 This definition is César Chesneau Dumarsais's in *Traité des tropes* (Paris, 1730); see Dumarsais, *Des tropes, ou Des différents sens: Figure et vingt autres articles de l'Encyclopédie, suivis de l'Abrégé des tropes de l'abbé Ducros* (1730), ed. Françoise Douay-Soublin (Paris, 1988), p. 135.

27 See, for example, Antoine-Joseph Dézallier d'Argenville's lives of Michelle Corneille and Jean Jouvenet in *Abrégé de la vie des plus fameux peintres*, 4 vols (Paris, 1762), vol. 4, pp. 199, 204–5. The copies artists made were often collected and kept. See also Louis Gougenot's 'Vie de M. Galloche' (1767),

in which he recounts Louis Galloche's habit of encouraging his students to make copies by citing the examples of Carlo Maratta and Charles de La Fosse, who continued to copy into old age. Gougenot notes that he could have given himself as an example, since he made a copy after Van Dyck at the Palais du Luxembourg, aged 70. Gougenot, 'Vie de M. Galloche', in *Mémoires inédits sur la vie et les ouvrages des membres de l'Académie royale de peinture et de sculpture*, ed. Louis-Étienne Dussieux et al., 2 vols (Paris, 1854), vol. 2, p. 298.

28 For a discussion of these issues in the Renaissance, see Jacqueline T. Miller, *Poetic License: Authority and Authorship in Medieval and Renaissance Contexts* (New York, 1986), esp. ch. 4. For Petrarch, the portrait was the antithesis of proper, or creative imitation.

29 Peter Kelly in 'Notes from the Field: Materiality', *Art Bulletin*, 95 (2013), 18–21.

30 Foucault, 'What is an Author?', p. 126.

31 Grivel, *Le Commerce de l'estampe*, pp. 104–12; Peter Fuhring, 'The Print Privilege in Eighteenth-Century France, I', *PQ*, 2 (1985), 174–93; Fuhring, 'The Print Privilege, II'; Antony Griffiths, *The Print before Photography: An Introduction to European Printmaking, 1550–1820* (London, 2016), pp. 99–107.

32 Stef Van Gompel, '*Les formalités sont morts, vive les formalités!* Copyright Formalities and the Reasons for their Decline in Nineteenth-Century Europe', in *Privilege and Property: Essays on the History of Copyright*, Ronan Deazley, Martin Kretschmer and Lionel Bently (eds) (Cambridge, 2010), pp. 157–206.

33 It is worth noting here that the vast majority of copyright requests were made by printmakers in Paris; this was not true of inventions, even inventions in art materials and technologies, which were submitted to the Bureau du commerce and the Académie royale des sciences from all over France.

34 Ernest Coyecque, *Inventaire de la Collection Anisson sur l'histoire de l'imprimerie et de la librairie*, 2 vols (Paris, 1900).

35 BnF, Mss. f.f. 22071/141. Henri Falk dated it 1677; Falk, *Les Privilèges de librairie sous l'ancien régime: Étude historique du conflit des droits sur l'œuvre littéraire* (Paris, 1906), pp. 74–6.

36 The memorandum mentions submission only to the Chancellor. In the 15th and 16th centuries, submissions to the king were made directly; this practice continued, on occasion, until the end of the *ancien régime*. The engraver Charles-Étienne Gaucher recorded that he was granted a privilege for his engraved portrait of Louis XV following presentation of a proof of the print to the sitter; see BnF, Mss. f.f. 22121/34.

37 For an account of the transfer of a manuscript back and forth between the Chancellerie and the censor see Antoine-François Mormoro, *Traité élémentaire de l'imprimerie, ou Le Manuel de l'imprimeur* (Paris, 1793), pp. 282–3.

38 On the function and institution of the Conseil du roi see the special issue of *Revue administrative*, 3 (1999), *Le Conseil d'état avant le Conseil d'état*, esp. Bernard Babiche, 'Le Conseil du roi dans tous ses états', pp. 20–26; Michel Antoine, 'Qui entrait au Conseil du roi?', pp. 70–76.

39 That Gilles-Marie Oppenord had a marked interest in, and good knowledge of, the book trade has been noted by Peter Fuhring in *Bulletin monumental*, 171/2 (2013), 19–20. On Oppenord's Ripa see Jean-François Bédard, *Decorative Games: Ornaments, Rhetoric, and Noble Culture in the Work of Gilles-Marie Oppenord (1672–1742)* (Newark, DE, 2011).

40 Oppenord roughly sketched the scene at the end of the *espitre*, and incorporated de Bie's printed signature. He then drew a finished version on a separate sheet, which he pasted over the first version, secured by a flap. Oppenord also decorated the opening page of the dedication. It is framed with attributes, among them the casket of seals, easily identified by the fleur de lys pattern across its surface. On such dedications see Roger Chartier, 'Princely Patronage and the Economy of Dedication', in *Form and Meanings: Texts, Performances, and Audiences from Codex to Computer* (Philadelphia, 1995), pp. 25–42.

41 Mormoro, *Traité élémentaire*, p. 283, mentions that the letters of privilege were written on parchment.

42 On the history of the booksellers' registers and for the first substantial and systematic examinations of this source with a table of results, see Fuhring, 'The Print Privilege, II'.

43 In the case of François Chauveau's *lettres patentes*, issued on 27 Feb. 1667, 'pour quinze ans de designer, graver et imprimer les œuvres de sa main', see Maxime Préaud, 'L'Inventaire après décès de François Chauveau, 20–28 février, 1676', *AAF*, 26 (1984), 91–104, at 102; in the case of Robert Nanteuil see, most recently, Audrey Adamczak, *Robert Nanteuil (ca. 1623–1678)* (Paris, 2011), p. 49.

44 *Confirmation des statuts pour la Communauté et Académie de Saint-Luc*, Mar. 1730, AN, K 1032/1.

45 *Arrêt de la Cour de parlement, portant homologation d'une délibération de la Communauté des maîtres fondeurs, pour la sureté des modèles*, 30 July 1766, reproduced in full in Svend Eriksen, *Early Neo-Classicism in France* (London, 1974), Appendix X, pp. 271–6, arts. 1, 5.

46 See, in greater detail, chapter 5.

47 The registers do not survive, but among the Académie's papers is a recapitulative list of privileges granted between 1727 and 1749; *Estampes admises au privilège de l'Académie et de chacunes desquelles lui appartiennent deux exemplaires*, ENSBA, Ms. 38.

48 Liliane Hilaire-Pérez, 'Invention and the State in Eighteenth-Century France', *Technology and Culture*, 32 (1991), 911–31; Liliane Hilaire-Pérez, *L'Invention technique au siècle des Lumières* (Paris, 2000).

49 Maps and wallpaper occupied an indeterminate place in the intellectual property field in the *ancien régime*. Maps were both technical instruments and prints; wallpaper was both a print and an industrial product.

50 BnF, Mss. f.f. 22120/14, 17. The documents relating to the affair were first published by Fuhring in 'The Print Privilege, I'.

51 The Lyonnais' memoranda indicate that they were neither surprised, nor indeed especially concerned by Charpentier's copies as such. Their anxiety arose from the danger that his privilege presented to their legitimate and established business with their regular correspondents. The best the Chancellor was able to do to mitigate that risk was to exert sufficient pressure on Charpentier to compel him to share the prerogatives of his privilege with the Lyonnais, thereby enabling them to continue to trade the *découpures* without exposing themselves to the danger of pursuit for infringement of their own works. See the letter of 19 Nov. 1746 from the Chancellor to Perrichon, the Prévôt des marchands at Lyons, conveying the news; BnF, Mss. f.f. 22120/18.

52 See the example provided by the print publisher François Langlois, who, in 1639, contracted François Collignon to execute a set of eight copies after marine prints by Stefano della Bella published in Florence in 1634; Collignon was to be paid 100 *livres* with the condition that he should not make further copies of his copies or variants for other French publishers. See Meaume, 'François Collignon'; Grivel, *Le Commerce de l'estampe*, p. 105.

53 An example of the kind of prints in question is published by Fuhring in 'The Print Privilege, I', fig. 99; they were inscribed with the partners' *execudit*.

54 The extra requirement to give the date of the privilege was imposed by an *arrêt* of 16 Dec. 1704, in the wake of a trial

over print piracy between mapmakers Gaspard Bailleul and Jean Besson; see Mireille Pastoureau, 'Contrefaçon et plagiat des cartes de géographie et des atlas français de la fin du XVIe siècle au début du XVIIIe siècle', in *Les Presses grises: La Contrefaçon du livre (XVIe–XIXe siècles)*, François Moureau (ed.) (Paris, 1988), pp. 275–302.

55 *Lettres patentes du roy pour le règlement des libraires, imprimeurs et relieurs de cette ville de Paris*, in *PSC*, France, 1618, art. 12; Martin-Dominique Fertel, *La Science pratique de l'imprimerie* (Saint-Omer, 1723), p. 119.

56 For further discussion of privilege and the frame see Katie Scott, 'Maps, Views and Ornament: Visualising Property in Art and Law', in *Privilege and Property: Essays on the History of Copyright*, Ronan Deazley, Martin Kretschmer and Lionel Bently (eds) (Cambridge, 2010), pp. 254–88. On the clasp, see Scott, 'Motifs et métaphores de l'ornement sous l'ancien régime', *Perspective* (2010–11), no. 1, 15–18.

57 Grivel, *Le Commerce de l'estampe*, pp. 112–16.

58 *Arrest du Conseil d'état privé du roy qui ordonne à tous les auteurs, libraires, imprimeurs et graveurs du royaume de remettre aux syndics et adjoints des libraires huit exemplaires de chacun des livres, feuilles et estampes*, 17 Oct. 1704, AN, AD IX/19. See also Grivel, *Le Commerce de l'estampe*, p. 114.

59 See chapter 2.

60 See the memorandum 'concernant la gravure' by the printer-publisher Claude-François Simon on the malpractices of engravers, 7 Jan. 1757, BnF, Mss. f.f. 22120/35; and the reply of the engraver and print publisher François Basan, *Exposé du sieur Basan et autres ses confrères graveurs en taille-douce, contre la communauté des libraires, Septembre 1757*, BnF, Mss. f.f. 22076/73.

61 In the collection of Jacques Doucet, INHA, Paris.

62 Claude-Marin Saugrain, *Code de la librairie et imprimerie de Paris* (Paris, 1744), 'Avertissement'. See also, Yves-Bernard Brissaud, 'Pistes pour une histoire de l'édition juridique française sous l'ancien régime', *Histoire et civilisation du livre*, 1 (2005), 33–136.

63 'Privilège', in *Le Dictionnaire de l'Académie françoise*, 2 vols (Paris, 1694), vol. 2.

64 Jacques Savary des Bruslons, 'Privilège', in *Dictionnaire universel de commerce*, 4 vols (Geneva, 1744), vol. 3.

65 Only a handful of women appear in the registers of print privileges of the Corporation des libraires et maîtres imprimeurs. The majority were widows of print publishers and printsellers: Veuve Chéreau, on 7 June 1730, for a miscellany of prints after Poussin, Vanloo, Lancret, Watteau and others, BnF, Mss. f.f. 21954; Veuve Chéreau again, on 20 Jan. 1757, for the works of Hubert Boucher, BnF, Mss. f.f. 21957; Veuve Henry Bonnart, on 19 July 1731, for a Don Quixote series, BnF, Mss. f.f. 21954. Others were widows of printmakers: Coussinet, widow of François Chauveau, on 6 Sept. 1711, for Chauveau's prints of the Saint Bruno cycle, BnF, Mss. f.f. 21950; Veuve Baudoin, on 26 Mar. 1772, for prints after her husband's *Le Lever* and *La Toilette*, BnF, Mss. f.f. 21965. Three women artists did, however, obtain privileges, directly or indirectly. On 8 May 1706, Élisabeth-Sophie Chéron was granted a privilege for prints after her drawings after Raphael, BnF, Mss. f.f. 21948; on 26 Aug. 1769, the Academician Nicolas-François Regnault acquired a privilege for his sister Geneviève's illustrated book *La Botanique mise à porter de tout le monde*, BnF, Mss. f.f. 21965; and on 8 Aug. 1786, Mlle Veni, 'graveur', secured a privilege for her prints of 'antiquités d'Angleterre', BnF, Mss f.f. 21969.

66 BnF, Mss. f.f. 21963, 20 Aug. 1765. The privilege was for nine years and fines were fixed at 3,000 *livres*.

67 In August 1768 the Paris printsellers Jacques Esnault, Jean Alibert and Michel Rapilly were found guilty of pirating Delafosse's print: the pirate was identified as a certain Laurent and the copper-plate printer was Richomme. 290 impressions of the contrefaçon had been pulled; 41 remained at the time of the arrest. See BnF, Mss: f.f. 22099/73–74, discussed in Casselle, 'Le Commerce des estampes à Paris dans la seconde moitié du XVIIIe siècle', PhD diss., École nationale des chartes, Paris, 1976, p. 27. Bernard Gagnebin has identified two different pirate prints, one published by Pierre Gleich at Augsburg in 1766, and the other published anonymously in London at around the same date. However, in the absence of international copyright agreements, neither of these constituted an infringement of the Calas privilege. See Gagnebin, 'La gravure de "La Malheureuse Famille Calas"', *GBA* (1978), 197–202, figs 2 and 3.

68 'Privilège', in Antoine Furetière, *Dictionnaire universel*, 2nd edn, 3 vols (The Hague, 1701), vol. 3.

69 'Droit', in *Le Dictionnaire de l'Académie françoise*, 5th edn, 2 vols (Paris, 1798), vol. 1.

70 Today the term is fixed at 70 years *post mortem*, or the author's life plus those of his or her heirs for two generations. It was increased from 50 years, set in 1908, on grounds of extended life expectancy. The Copyright, Designs and Patents Act (1988) brought British copyright law into alignment with that of the EU in terms of duration.

71 The wrappers were published *chez* Bulla in Paris; see Adrien Gastambide, *Traité théorique et pratique des contrefaçons en tous genres* (Paris, 1837), p. 295.

72 For one example of augmentation by means of a frame see Jacques-Philippe Fagniani's edition of Jacques Callot's *Les Misères et les malheurs de la guerre* (1713), discussed in Scott, 'Maps, Views and Ornament'.

73 See, for example, the 15- and 20-year prolongations granted to Nicolas Langlois for a range of devotional and profane images in 1675, BnF, Mss. f.f. 21732, 14 June 1675; and the 15-year 'continuation de Privilège' granted to François II Poilly on 11 Sept. 1738 for an extensive stock of images, 'de sa Composition' and 'de celles de ces Ancestres et de son Père', BnF, Mss. f.f. 21957.

74 Peter Baldwin, *The Copyright Wars: Three Centuries of Trans-Atlantic Battle* (Princeton, 2014).

75 Lynn Hunt, *Inventing Human Rights: A History* (New York, 2007). On law and emotion see Susan Bandes (ed.), *The Passions of the Law* (New York, 1999), and more specifically in relation to property, H. Conway and S. Stannard, 'Property and Emotions', *Emotion Review*, 8 (2016), 38–43.

76 On the print see Nathanael Weiss, 'À propos de Calas: Histoire de l'estampe de Carmontelle', *Bulletin de la Société du protestantisme français*, 62 (1913), 257–65; Gagnebin, 'La gravure de "La Malheureuse Famille Calas"'. See also the opening of Élie de Beaumont's *Mémoire pour Dame Anne-Rose Cabibel, Veuve Calas, et pour ses enfants* (Paris, 1765), in which he claims that citizens of France and other nations were concerned with the matters arising in the case.

77 Élie de Beaumont was one of a number of lawyers to become involved in the case at the instigation of Voltaire; see Sarah Maza, *Private Lives and Public Affairs: The causes célèbres of Pre-Revolutionary France* (Berkeley, 1993), pp. 27–33.

78 'Fabulation' is Bernard Edelman's word for the 'reality' that law constructs. In relation to rights, see Edelman, *Quand les juristes inventent le réel* (Paris, 2007), pp. 206–12, 285–7.

79 'Privilège', in *Le Dictionnaire de l'Académie françoise* (1694), vol. 2. Elaine Scarry fully articulates the argument for the connection between beauty and being fair that is merely suggested in the Académie's dictionary; Scarry, *On Beauty and Being Just* (Princeton, 2006).

80 'Contrefaire', 'Contrefait', in *Le Dictionnaire de l'Académie françoise* (1694), vol. 1. *Contrefait* signified deformed and misshapen, as well as copied, and thus suggested something qualitatively, if not legally, improper. See also Furetière, 'Contrefait', in *Dictionnaire universel*, vol. 3. Cf. 'Contrefaire', in ibid., in the legal sense: 'c'est imprimer un livre, une

image, un dessein, pour frustrer l'Auteur du droit du privilège qu'il a obtenu de le faire imprimer tout seul'.

81 Peter Parshall, '*Imago Contrafacta*: Images and Facts in the Northern Renaissance', *Art History*, 16 (1993), 554–75.

82 François-Étienne Joubert, *Définition des mots 'copie' et 'contrefaçon' en gravure* (Paris, 1801).

83 Lawrence Liang, 'Beyond Representation: The Figure of the Pirate', in *Making and Unmaking Intellectual Property: Creative Production in Legal and Cultural Perspective*, Mario Biagioli, Peter Jaszi and Martha Woodmansee (eds) (Chicago, 2011), pp. 167–80; Adrian Johns, 'The Property Police', in ibid., pp. 199–213.

84 See Grivel, *Le Commerce de l'estampe*, p. 110, on the destruction of Jacob Honervogt's piracies of prints after Peter Paul Rubens. Comparable penalties in the case of casts for sculpture seem not to have been imposed. On rare occasions the plaintiff asked for leniency. See also Pastoureau, 'Contrefaçon et plagiat', fig. 15, for the scored and sealed impression of the map used during the case.

85 Signature takes at least three different forms in the context of copies: (1) the *contrefaçon* is unsigned, in which case the publisher is held responsible for infringement; (2) the pirate signs in place of the original engraver and risks prosecution for infringement; (3) the pirate copies the author's signature and risks prosecution for counterfeit and fraud. In the case of the last, see Laurent Pfister, 'L'Usage illicite du signe d'autruit: Quelques observations sur les enseignes et marques de l'ancien droit', *Mémoires de la Société pour l'histoire du droit et des institutions des anciens pays bourgignons, contois et normands*, 65 (2008), 171–93.

86 Joseph-Nicolas Guyot, *Répertoire universel et raisonné de jurisprudence civile, criminelle, canonique et bénéficiale*, 64 vols (Paris, 1775–83), vol. 4, pp. 647–8. See also 'Jurisprudence', in Charles-Joseph Panckoucke, *Encyclopédie méthodique par ordre de matières*, 216 vols (Paris, 1782–1832), vol. 3, pp. 295–8.

87 'Contrefaçon', in Joubert, *Définition des mots 'copie' et 'contrefaçon'*, vol. 2: 'le mot seul fait la chose'.

88 In a case between the cartographer Guillaume Delisle and the mapseller Jean-Baptiste I Nolin discussed below, the Registres du Conseil d'état privé du roy (BnF, Mss. f.f. 21733/61–68) record that in order to obtain certainty in a case of copies involving maps, red ink was use to trace Delisle's map onto an impression of Nolin's, and yellow was added to those areas where the maps coincided.

89 On the Châtelet see Richard Mowery Andrews, *Law, Magistracy and Crime in Old Regime Paris, 1735–1789* (Cambridge, 1994), pp. 56–75. See Émile Campardon, 'Saisie et destruction de gravures représentants *Les Modes et coiffures françoises* (1779)', *NAAF*, 9 (1882), 300–09, for an account of the process by which those accused of piracy were arrested and tried.

90 On the *procureurs* see Charles Bataillard and Ernest Nusse, *Histoire des procureurs et des avoués, 1483–1816*, 2 vols (Paris, 1882).

91 For those in the Bibliothèque nationale, see Augustin Corda, *Catalogue des factums et d'autres documents judiciaires antérieurs à 1790*, 7 vols (Paris, 1890–1936).

92 Maza, *Private Lives and Public Affairs*; and on the *mémoires judiciaires* see esp. pp. 116–30.

93 On this case see Numa Broc, 'Une Affaire de plagiat cartographique sous Louis XIV: Le Procès Delisle–Nolin', *Revue d'histoire des sciences et de leurs applications*, 23 (970), 141–53; Pastoureau, 'Contrefaçon et plagiat', pp. 298–302; Christine Marie Petto, *When France was King of Cartography: The Patronage and Production of Maps in Early Modern France* (Lanham, MD, 2007), pp. 143–76.

94 However, he and his father, Claude Delisle, had obtained a privilege on 17 Feb. 1698 'pour graver leur Globes & leurs six Cartes générales', under the protection of which they might have hoped to draw Guillaume's world map; BnF, Mss. f.f. 21733/61–68.

95 Nolin had obtained a privilege for this map, among others, on 5 May 1690.

96 The experts were the mathematicians Joseph Sauveur and François Chevalier. They not only compared the maps, they also interrogated the parties and noted that only Delisle knew and understood what he was talking about. There could be no better proof that the first was the author and the second the plagiarist. By a ruling of the Conseil du roi, Nolin was condemned to have his copper plates seized and broken, and was fined 50 *livres* for 'injures et calomnies'. In the event, the plates were scored and scraped to erase the cartography but Nolin was allowed to keep the frame elements, designed and engraved by Nicolas Bocquet. See fig. 15 in Pastoureau, 'Contrefaçon et plagiat', for Nolin's *Le Globe terrestre représenté en deux plans-hémisphères*, 1700, BnF, Cartes et Plans, GE AA-1259 (RES), also available on Gallica.

97 See the letter from Chancelier d'Aguesseau to M. Perrichon, 23 Apr. 1747, BnF, Mss. f.f. 22120/24, quoted in Fuhring, 'The Print Privilege, I', pp. 191–2.

98 *Confirmation des statuts pour la Communauté et Académie de Saint-Luc*, Mar. 1730, arts. 69–70, AN, K 1032/1. The fine was set at 1,000 *livres*.

99 The point is made by Griffiths, *The Print before Photography*, p. 115. When, in *c.*1743, Hendrik van Hulst was preparing a catalogue of the prints after Hyacinthe Rigaud's portraits, he recommended the excision of copies of Gérard Édelinck's print after Rigaud's portrait of Jean-Baptiste Boyer, from Rigaud's oeuvre, 'à moins qu'on voulût grossir de toutes les copies et arrières-copies de plusieurs autres estampes y rassemblées'. See Hendrik van Hulst, 'Catalogue de l'œuvre gravé du sieur Hyacinthe Rigaud', in *Mémoires inédits*, ed. Dussieux et al., vol. 2, p. 172.

100 Although literary satires were few, Jean-Baptiste Crépy published a game of the goose in the same spirit, engraved by Jeanne Chapoulard in 1687, and entitled *L'Escole des plaideurs*. There are no lucky or bonus squares – indeed, it is a game impossible to win.

101 *MdF* (Jan. 1731), 138–9. The advertisement identifies both painter and engraver as Academicians, and addresses its recommendations of the invention of the composition and the quality of the engraving to 'connoisseurs'. The print was sold *chez l'Auteur*, quai de la Mégisserie.

102 All the court documents are published in Georges Wildenstein, *Lancret* (Paris, 1924), pp. 49–52.

103 There are at least four autograph copies and variants of the portrait of Mlle de Camargo dancing: Wallace Collection, London; National Gallery of Art, Washington, DC; Musée des beaux-arts, Nantes; State Hermitage Museum, St Petersburg.

104 Wildenstein, *Lancret*, p. 52.

105 Jules-Joseph Guiffrey, *Nicolas Lancret: Sa Vie et son œuvre, 1690–1743* (Paris, n.d.), p. 76.

106 David Lefranc, 'Historical Perspective on Criminal Enforcement', in *Criminal Enforcement of Intellectual Property: A Handbook of Contemporary Research*, Christopher Geiger (ed.) (Cheltenham, 2012), pp. 101–27.

107 *MdF* (Dec. 1735), 2685–8. Cochin notes that the closest and most pernicious of these *contrefaçons* take copying to the limit of reproducing dedications and 'le nom même de M. Le Clerc'. He does not mention that he was himself responsible for copies of *L'Académie des sciences* and *L'Entrée d'Alexandre à Babylone*. See Christian Michel, *Charles-Nicolas Cochin et l'art des Lumières* (Rome, 1993), pp. 24–5.

108 *Journal de Paris* (7 Jan. 1789), 441: 'Chaque épreuve ... sera remise au souscripteur numérotée et signée de moi.' See also Maurice Fenaille, *L'Œuvre gravée de P.-L. Debucourt (1755–1832)* (Paris, 1899), pp. 24–5. I have not been able to trace an impression of the print signed and numbered. This

form of signature, directed at the collector, and exceptional in the 18th century, is not to be confused with those on the verso of prints, which relate rather to the contracts between the author of the image and the printmaker; a signature on the verso served to confirm the fulfilment of the terms of the contract between author and printmaker, and to ensure that extra impressions (proofs or final states) were not being illicitly pulled and sold by the printmaker for his or her own profit. For an example and extended discussion of this kind of signature, see Antony Griffiths, 'Greuze et ses graveurs', *NE*, 52–3 (1980), 9–11. For other instances of signature for authentication purposes see Casselle, 'Le Commerce des estampes', p. 29.

CHAPTER 1
'UT PICTURA POESIS': Matters of privilege and property

1 The 16th-century printer Robert Estienne defines privilege as 'une loy particulière, pour ou contre aucun'. See 'Privilegium', in Robert Estienne, *Dictionarium latinogallicum*, 3rd edn (Paris, 1552). On Estienne's privileges see A. E. Tyler, 'Robert Estienne and his Privileges, 1526–1550', *The Library*, 5 (1950), 225–37.

2 'Privilège', in Joseph-Nicolas Guyot, *Répertoire universel et raisonné de jurisprudence civile, criminelle, canonique et bénéficale*, 64 vols (Paris, 1775–83), vol. 47, pp. 326–44.

3 So called because they are open and public, in contrast to *lettres de cachet*, which are sealed and private.

4 They were related by date, by intended readership and anticipated market, by technology and by selection of some of the contributing artists: Jean-Baptiste Papillon was responsible for the woodcut decoration in both publications; Charles-Nicolas Cochin *fils* had overall charge of the illustration of the *Fables* and designed the frontispiece for the *Encyclopédie*; the intaglio printmaker Defer worked on the illustrations of both books. They were also connected by the simultaneous participation of one publishing partner – Laurent Durand – in both ventures; see Frank A. Kafker and Jeff Loveland, 'The Elusive Laurent Durand, a Leading Publisher of the French Enlightenment', *SVEC*, 12 (2005), 259–81. They were also related by the objection of another partner – Charles-Antoine Jombert – to the publication of the *Encyclopédie* on grounds of trespass; see Charles-Antoine Jombert, *Requête au Chancelier Malesherbes... relative à la concurrence que lui créent les traducteurs de Chambers*, n.d., BnF, Mss. n.a.f. 3347, fols 199–200.

5 According to the historian of the printing trade André Chevalier, 'gravure' invariably followed 'imprimerie', in everything, the bad as well as the good. See André Chevalier, *L'Origine de l'imprimerie de Paris: Dissertation historique et critique* (Paris, 1694), p. 224.

6 Michel Foucault, 'What is an Author?' (1969), in *Language, Counter-Memory, Practice: Selected Essays and Interviews*, trans. Donald F. Bouchard and Sherry Simon, ed. Donald F. Bouchard (Oxford, 1977), pp. 113–38.

7 Carla Hesse, 'Enlightenment Epistemology and the Laws of Authorship in Revolutionary France, 1777–1795', *Representations*, 30 (1990), pp. 109–37. See also Raymond Birn, 'The Profit of Ideas: *Privilèges en librairie* in Eighteenth-Century France', *Eighteenth-Century Studies*, 4 (1970–71), 131–68; Bernard Edelman, *Le Sacre de l'auteur* (Paris, 2004). For comparison with Britain and Germany see Mark Rose, *Authors and Owners: The Invention of Copyright* (Boston, 1993); Martha Woodmansee, *The Author, Art, and the Market: Rereading the History of Aesthetics* (New York, 1994); Brad Sherman and Lionel Bently, *The Making of Modern Intellectual Property: The British Experience, 1760–1911* (Cambridge, 1999).

8 The existing literature on this subject is quite extensive. See François Courboin, *L'Estampe française: Graveurs et marchands* (Paris, 1914), pp. 146–8; Pierre Casselle, 'Le Commerce des estampes à Paris dans la seconde moitié du XVIIIe siècle', PhD diss., École nationale des chartes, Paris, 1976, pp. 7–30; Peter Fuhring, 'The Print Privilege in Eighteenth-Century France, I', *PQ*, 2 (1985), 174–93; Peter Fuhring, 'The Print Privilege in Eighteenth-Century France, II', *PQ*, 3 (1986), 19–33; Marianne Grivel, *Le Commerce de l'estampe à Paris au XVIIe siècle* (Geneva, 1986), pp. 83–122; Antony Griffiths, *The Print before Photography: An Introduction to European Printmaking, 1550–1820* (London, 2016), pp. 99–107.

9 Louis d'Héricourt, *Mémoire en forme de requête à M. le Garde des sceaux*, in Édouard Laboulaye and Georges Guiffrey, *La Propriété littéraire au XVIIIe siècle: Recueil de pièces et de documents* (Paris, 1859), pp. 13–40 at p. 24; *PSC*, France, 1725–6.

10 Denis Diderot, *Lettre sur le commerce de la librairie* (1763), ed. Michel Parfenov (Paris, 2001), pp. 17–18, 20, 21. Diderot explained that publishers managed their business by balancing quick returns on 'little jobs' against investment in long-term ambitious ventures. For historical confirmation of this practice see Henri-Jean Martin, *Print, Power and People in Seventeenth-Century France*, trans. David Gerard (Metuchen, NJ, 1993), pp. 161–75; Peter Stallybrass, '"Little Jobs": Broadsides and the Printing Revolution', in *Agent of Change: Print Culture Studies after Elizabeth L. Eisenstein*, Sabrina Alcorn Baron, Eric N. Lindquist and Eleanor F. Shevlin (eds) (Amherst and Boston, 2007), pp. 315–41.

11 According to André Chevalier, privilege originated from the scandal and injustice created by pirate editions of Ulrich Gering's first French edition of the works of Virgil. See Chevalier, *L'Origine de l'imprimerie*, pp. 205–6.

12 See Johann Speyer's printing monopoly, in *PSC*, Latin, 1469. For those that followed elsewhere in Europe, see Christopher Witcombe, *Copyright in the Renaissance: Prints and the Privilegio in Sixteenth-Century Venice and Rome* (London, 1991), pp. 326–44.

13 On the first press set up at the Sorbonne see Jean-Marc Chatelain, *La Naissance du livre moderne (XIVe–XVIIe siècles): Mise en page et mise en texte du livre français* (Paris, 2000), pp. 116–31.

14 Jeanne-Marie Dureau, 'Les Premiers Ateliers français', in *HEF*, vol. 1, pp. 163–75; Henri-Jean Martin and Jeanne-Marie Dureau, 'Années de transition, 1500–1530', in *HEF*, vol. 1, pp. 217–25.

15 David T. Pottinger, *The French Book Trade in the ancien régime, 1500–1791* (Boston, 1958), pp. 179–83; Annie Parent, *Les Métiers du livre à Paris au XVIe siècle (1535–1560)* (Geneva, 1974), pp. 155–96. Speyer may have been attracted to Venice by the availability of good printing paper; see Juraj Kittler, 'From Rags to Riches: The Limits of Early Paper Manufacturing and their Impact on Book Print in Venice', *Media History*, 21 (2015), 8–22.

16 Lucien Febvre and Henri-Jean Martin, *The Coming of the Book: The Impact of Printing, 1450–1800*, trans. David Gerard (London, 1976), pp. 109–17.

17 Elizabeth Armstrong, *Before Copyright: The French Book-Privilege System, 1498–1526* (Cambridge, 1990).

18 Ibid., pp. 165–90.

19 On the revival of the Roman law school in France in the early 16th century see Peter Stein, *Roman Law in European History* (Cambridge, 1999), ch. 4.

20 The directness of enunicatory writing and personal address is sometimes represented in print by the use of italic type for the reproduction of letters patent in books. See, for example, Robert Estienne's edition of Luigi Alamanni's *La coltivatione* (Paris, 1546).

21 The literature on the gift and commodities is extensive. I have found especially helpful James Carrier, 'Gifts,

Commodities and Social Relations: A Maussian View of Exchange', *Sociological Forum*, 6 (1991), 119–36; James Carrier, *Gifts and Commodities: Exchange and Western Capitalism since 1700* (London, 1995); John Frow, 'Gifts and Commodities', in *Time and Commodity Culture: Essays in Cultural Theory and Postmodernity* (Oxford, 1997), pp. 102–217; Natalie Zemon Davis, *The Gift in Sixteenth-Century France* (Madison, WI, 2000); Christopher Gregory, *Gifts and Commodities*, 2nd edn (Chicago, 2015). All are variously informed by, or engage with, Marcel Mauss's theory of the gift in *The Gift: The Form and Reason for Exchange in Archaic Societies* (1950), trans. W. D. Halls (London, 1990).

22 See Eloy d'Amerval's privilege, in *PSC*, France, 1507: the musician and poet d'Amerval appealed for Louis XII's 'grâce et liberalité'.

23 Mark Rose makes a similar case for privilege as patronage in England in the 16th and 17th centuries. See Rose, *Authors and Owners*, pp. 16–17.

24 Elizabeth Armstrong, *Robert Estienne: Royal Printer* (Cambridge, 1954), p. 38. Henri-Jean Martin, 'Le Temps de Robert Estienne', in *HEF*, vol. 1, pp. 231–4. Geoffroy Tory had been appointed Imprimeur du roi by François I in 1533.

25 Mauss, *The Gift*, pp. 10–23.

26 See, for instance, the privilege granted for, and reproduced in Geoffroy Tory, *Champfleury* (Paris, 1529). It mentions that Tory had given a copy of the book to the king before making his petition: 'Lequel Livre il nous a faict veoir & presenter'.

27 Armstrong, *Robert Estienne*, p. 39. A gathering, or bifolium, is a single folded sheet, making two leaves and four sides.

28 Eloy d'Amerval's privilege, in *PSC*, France, 1507.

29 Elizabeth Armstrong, *Robert Estienne*, pp. 142–5.

30 Robert Estienne, Preface, *Les Censures des théologiens de Paris, par lesquelles ils avoyent faussement condamné les Bibles imprimés par Robert Estienne* (1552), quoted in Antoine-Augustin Renouard, *Annales de l'imprimerie des Estienne*, 2nd edn (Paris, 1843), p. 545.

31 Ian Maclean, *Scholarship, Commerce, Religion: The Learned Book in the Age of Confessions, 1560–1630* (Cambridge, MA, 2012), pp. 159–61.

32 A royal ordinance was distinctive in its address to the whole kingdom; an edict, by contrast, was aimed at a specific group of individuals and/or a particular part of the country.

33 *Recueil général des anciennes lois françaises depuis l'an 420 jusqu'à la révolution de 1789*, ed. Athanase-Jean-Léger Jourdan et al., 29 vols (Paris, 1821–33), vol. 14, pp. 210–11.

34 See the printer's mark of Guillaume Eustache, reproduced in Armstrong, *Before Copyright*, fig. 1.

35 Robert Estienne threatened to pursue infractions of his privileges, but did not do so – probably for reasons of time and expense. See Tyler, 'Robert Estienne and his Privileges'.

36 Pierre Bourdieu, *Outline of a Theory of Practice*, trans. Richard Nice (Cambridge, 1977), ch. 4, esp. p. 180.

37 Armstrong, *Before Copyright*, pp. 21–62.

38 Foucault, 'What is an Author?', p. 130. For a review of the scholarly literature on authorship from the 16th to the 19th centuries see Christine Haynes, 'Reassessing "Genius" in Studies of Authorship: The State of the Discipline', *Book History*, 8 (2005), 287–320.

39 The figure is Michel Pastoureau's, from 'L'Illustration du livre: Comprendre ou rêver?', in *HEF*, vol. 1, pp. 501–29.

40 Armstrong, *Before Copyright*, p. 80. On Gringore see especially Cynthia Jane Brown, *Poets, Patrons and Printers: Crisis of Authority in Late Medieval France* (Ithaca, NY, and London, 1995), pp. 35–8.

41 *Geoffroy Tory: Imprimeur de François Ier, graphiste avant la lettre*, exh. cat., Musée national de la Renaissance, Grand Palais, Paris (Paris, 2011), pp. 34–46.

42 On the collaboration see Kay Amert, 'The Humanization of a Medieval Form: Geoffroy Tory's and Simon de Colines's Books of Hours', in *The Scythe and the Rabbit: Simon de Colines and the Culture of the Book in Renaissance Paris* (New York, 2012), pp. 167–74.

43 Armstrong, *Before Copyright*, p. 205. See also Désiré Guilmard, *Les Maîtres ornemanistes, dessinateurs, peintres, architectes, sculpteurs et graveurs*, 2 vols (Paris, 1880), vol. 1, p. 27; Félix Herbet, *L'École de Fontainbleau*, exh. cat., Grand Palais, Paris (Paris, 1972), p. 685; Peter Fuhring, 'Estampes d'ornement de la Renaissance: L'Apport de la France', in *La Gravure française de la Renaissance à la Bibliothèque nationale*, Marianne Grivel (ed.) (Paris, 1995) , pp. 162–3.

44 Danièle Sansy, 'Texte et image dans les incunables français', *Médiévales*, 22–3 (1992), 47–70; cf. Pascale Chiron and Philippe Maupeu, 'L'Utilisation des bois gravés: Arbitraire et signification dans les premiers textes imprimés', in *Le Discours du livre: Mise en scène du texte et fabrique sous l'ancien régime* (Paris, 2011), pp. 43–78.

45 Eloy d'Amerval, *Le Livre de la déablerie* (1508), ed. Robert Deschaux and Bernard Charrier (Geneva, 1991), p. 37. See also, Sansy, 'Texte et image', p. 67.

46 For a description of the re-cuts in Estienne's *De la dissection*, see Hélène Cazes, 'Théâtres imaginaires du livre et de l'anatomie: La Dissection des parties du corps humain, Charles Estienne, 1545–1546', *Fabula: La Recherche en littérature* (2004) <www.fabula.org/colloques/document103.php> (accessed 30 Sept. 2016). For the practice in general, see Sansy, 'Texte et image', pp. 58–9.

47 Charles Estienne, Preface, *De la dissection des parties du corps humain* (Paris, 1546) (unpaginated).

48 Armstrong, *Before Copyright*, p. 204.

49 On 16th-century manuscripts and their relation to printed books see Myra Orth, 'French Renaissance Manuscripts and l'histoire du livre', *Viator: Medieval and Renaissance Studies*, 32 (2011), 245–78.

50 See the copies at the Bibliothèque nationale de France and the Arsenal, Paris.

51 Laurent Pfister, 'Author and Work in the French Print Privileges System: Some Milestones', in *Privilege and Property: Essays in the History of Copyright*, Ronan Deazley, Martin Kretschmer and Lionel Bently (eds) (Cambridge, 2010), pp. 115–36.

52 For what follows see Marta Madero, '*Tabula picta*: L'Écriture, la peinture et leur support dans le droit médiéval', *Annales: Histoire, sciences sociales*, 56 (2001), 831–47; Marta Madero, *Tabula picta: La Peinture et l'écriture dans le droit médiéval* (Paris, 2004).

53 Madero, *Tabula picta*, pp. 81–96.

54 Madero, '*Tabula picta*: L'Écriture'.

55 'Privilege du roy, nostre cire', Geoffroy Tory, *Horæ in laudem beatiss. semper virginis Mariæ, secundum consuetudinem curiæ Romanæ* (Paris, 1525) (unpaginated).

56 For an account of the relatively easier task of detecting copy frauds in print see Chevalier, *L'Origine de l'imprimerie*, pp. 205–20.

57 Charles Talbot, 'Prints and the Definitive Image', in *Print and Culture in the Renaissance: Essays on the Advent of Printing in Europe*, Gerald P. Tyson and Sylvia S. Wagonheim (eds) (Newark, NJ, and London, 1986), pp. 189–207.

58 Jean-Gérard Lapacherie, 'Typographic Characters: Tension between Text and Drawing', *YFS*, 84 (1994), 63–77, esp. 66–7. See also Olivier Halévy, 'À travers Champ fleury: Norme typographique et imagination visuelle', in *Geoffroy Tory: Imprimeur de François Ier*, pp. 70–105.

59 On printers see Lisa M. Maruca, 'Bodies of Type: The Work of Textual Production in English Printers' Manuals', *Eighteenth-Century Studies*, 36 (2003), 321–43.

60 Estienne, Preface, *De la dissection* (unpaginated).

61 Peter Parshall, 'Imago contrafacta: Images and Facts in the Northern Renaissance', *Art History*, 16 (1993), 554–79.

62 On the case for the privilege consciousness of writers see Brown, *Poets, Patrons and Printers*, esp. ch. 2.

63 Griffiths, *The Print before Photography*, p. 82.

64 Armstrong, *Beyond Copyright*, p. 82.

65 Brown, *Poets, Patrons and Printers*, ch. 1.

66 On Nyverd see Philippe Renouard, *Imprimeurs et libraires parisiens du XVIe siècle*, 2 vols (Paris, 1964), vol. 1, p. 70; William Kemp, 'Transformations in the Printing of Royal Entries during the Reign of François Ier: The Role of Geoffroy Tory,' in *French Ceremonial Entries in the Sixteenth Century*, Nicolas Russell and Hélène Visentin (eds) (Toronto, 2007), pp. 120–21.

67 On the declining status of *labeur* in the later 16th century see Laure Chantrel, 'Les Notions de richesse et de travail dans la pensée économique française de la seconde moitié du XVIe siècle et au début du XVIIe siècle', *Journal of Medieval and Renaissance Studies*, 25 (1995), 129–58.

68 Pierre Bourdieu, *Outline of a Theory of Practice*, p. 175.

69 Simon Marion, *Plaidoyez second sur l'impression des Œuvres de Sénèque, reveuës et annotées par feu Marc Antoine de Muret* (1586), in *PSC*, France, 1586, p. 12.

70 Maclean, *Scholarship, Commerce, Religion*, p. 135.

71 Roland Mousnier, *Le Conseil du roi de Louis XII à la Révolution* (Paris, 1970), pp. 18–20. On state formation, see Pierre Bourdieu, 'Rethinking the State: Genesis and Structure of the Bureaucratic Field', *Sociological Theory*, 12 (1994), 1–18.

72 On the difference between the two types of ordinance, see Norbert Rouland, *L'État français et le pluralisme: Histoire politique des institutions publiques de 476 à 1792* (Paris, 1995), p. 202.

73 Jane McLeod, *Licensing Loyalty: Printers, Patrons and the State in Early Modern France* (Philadelphia, 2011); on Séguier as a patron see Yannik Neyon, 'Le Mécénat du Chancelier Séguier', in *L'Âge d'or du mécénat (1598–1661)*, Roland Mousnier and Jean Mesnard (eds) (Paris, 1985), pp. 49–57.

74 The Chancellor presided over the Conseil d'état privé, which then issued *arrêts simples*.

75 Du Sault, *Nouveau Stile des lettres des chancelleries de France, comme elles sont à présent en usage* (Paris, 1666), pp. 36–42.

76 However, important legislation on privilege – for example, the code of 1723 – was promulgated by an *arrêt en commandement* made in the Conseil des dépêches and in the king's presence. See Giles Barber, 'French Royal Decrees Concerning the Book Trade, 1700–1789', *Australian Journal of French Studies*, 3 (1966), 316–17.

77 Michel Foucault offers a broad-brush historical account of the economy as a *lieu de justice*, in 'Leçon du 17 janvier 1979', in *Naissance de la biopolitique: Cours au Collège de France (1978–1979)*, François Ewald, Alessandro Fontana and Michel Senellart (eds) (Paris, 2004), pp. 29–51; and in 'Governmentality', in *The Foucault Effect: Studies in Governmentality*, Graham Burchell, Colin Gordon and Peter Miller (eds) (Chicago, 1991), pp. 87–104, esp. pp. 91–2. The historical validity of his exposition, and the main points in his argument on significant shifts in fiscal policy up to the French Revolution are to a large extent not dependent on whether one accepts his alleged neo-liberalism. For an alternative, 'left' reading of Foucault's late work on the state, see the essays in Daniel Zamora and Michael C. Behrent (eds), *Foucault and Neoliberalism* (Cambridge, 2014), especially that by Behrent. For the once much debated issue of *embourgeoisement* of the state or *féodalisation* of the bourgeoisie, see Ralph E. Giesey, 'State Building in Early Modern France: The Role of Royal Officialdom', *JMH*, 55 (1983), 191–207.

78 The Sorbonne supposedly controlled the book trade through 24 authorised booksellers. By some estimates there were more than 60 booksellers in Paris, of which over half were therefore outside its control.

79 *Lettres patentes du roy pour le règlement des libraires, imprimeurs et relieurs de cette ville de Paris* (1618), in *PSC*, France, 1618. In the booksellers' 'remonstrance' to the king that prefaces the statutes, mention is made of the 'beaux privilèges et immunitez' they had traditionally enjoyed and that had distinguished them from the 'arts méchaniques', and of the difficulty the university's authorised booksellers had in governing the trade. For background to the regulations see Bernard Babiche, 'Le Régime et l'édition', in *HEF*, vol. 1, pp. 367–78.

80 *PSC*, France, 1618, p. 8.

81 Ibid., p. 10.

82 Ibid., pp. 10–11.

83 'Privilège', in Guyot, *Répertoire... de jurisprudence*, p. 337. The duration of *privilèges réels* lasted as long as the institutions to which they belonged. It is possible that publishers and printers in the 17th century came to envisage their privileges as without temporal limit, having recognised privilege as derived from corporate membership.

84 Séguier both directly appointed the syndics in elections and also altered the terms of such elections so that only former syndics and guards could elect new officers to those posts. See Henri-Jean Martin, 'Renouvellement et concurrences', in *HEF*, vol. 1, pp. 379–403.

85 The terminology is Bruno Latour's. See his *Reassembling the Social: An Introduction to Actor-Network Theory* (Oxford, 2005).

86 The book trade regulations of 1649 restricted the number of publishers, printers and bookbinders admitted to membership each year to one of each. It also required printers to have a command of Latin and Greek. These measures were designed specifically to reduce the number of printshops in the capital. In 1666–7, on the advice of the Paris book trade, Colbert further sought to reduce the number of printers in the provinces. See McLeod, *Licensing Loyalty*, pp. 37–67.

87 *Lettres obtenuës par aucuns des imprimeurs et libraires de Paris* (1649), in *PSC*, France, 1649, p. 10, clause 26.

88 *Arrest et règlement du Conseil touchant les privilèges et continuation d'iceux* (1665), in *PSC*, France, 1665, pp. 11–12.

89 Marion, *Plaidoyez second sur l'impression des Œuvres de Sénèque*, in *PSC*, France, 1586, p. 12; cited in Pfister, 'Author and Work', p. 125.

90 Marion, *Plaidoyez second sur l'impression des Œuvres de Sénèque*, in *PSC*, France, 1586, p. 12.

91 Antoine Vitré, *S'il est advantageux pour le public d'accorder aux libraires des continuations de privilèges* (n.d.), in *PSC*, France, 1650s.

92 On *privilèges généraux* see Henri Falk, *Les Privilèges de librairie sous l'ancien régime: Étude historique du conflit des droits sur l'œuvre littéraire* (1906) (Geneva, 1970), pp. 71–4.

93 Birn, 'The Profit of Ideas', p. 137. They found support for their cause in the Parlements.

94 Ibid., pp. 138–9.

95 *Statuts et règlemens des imprimeurs et libraires de Paris*, 21 Aug. 1686 (1687), in *PSC*, France, 1687.

96 Ibid., pp. 15–16.

97 Jean Valdor, 'Préface au lecteur', *Les Triomphes de Louis le juste, XIII* (Paris, 1649).

98 Valdor, 'Privilège du roi', ibid.

99 'Privilège du roy', *Les Images ou tableaux de platte peinture des deux Philostrates sophistes Grecs*, trans. Blaise de Vigenère (Paris, 1614). The privilege was issued in 1609 and at least one of the 68 plates is dated 1609, but, the publishers having died, it was left to their widows to publish the illustrated edition in 1614. So successful was it that five editions were printed between 1614 and 1637. On the illustrations see William McAllister Johnson, 'Prolegomena to the *Images ou tableaux de platte peinture* with an Excursus on Two Drawings of the School of Fontainebleau', *GBA* (1969), 277–304.

100 For a discussion of the survival of legal norms, see Karl Renner, *The Institutions of Private Law and their Social Functions* (1904), ed. Otto Kahn-Freund, trans. Agnes Schwarzschild (London, 1976).

101 'Avertissement', *Les Images ou tableaux*.
102 'Privilège du roy', ibid.
103 'Privilege du roy', Pierre Corneille, *Les Quatres Livres de l'Imitation de Jésus Christ* (Rouen, 1656): 'il ne pourroit être remboursé en si peu de temps [five years] des dépenses qu'il lui convient faire pour ledit Impression et pour lesdites Figures en taille-douce'. Corneille had obtained a privilege for the first two books on 22 Sept. 1651, but the privilege had made no reference to the 'Figures de taille-douce sur chaque Chapitre, contenans chacune quelque exemple tiré de l'Écriture Sainte, ou de la Vie des Saints.' He wished to remedy that omission in order to prevent other publishers from copying them, seemingly legitimately, for illustation of the Latin edition of the text or other translations. The illustrations are by François Chauveau, though the engraver is not named in the letters of privilege or in the preface, which stresses rather the text's simplicity and lack of ornament.
104 Alain Guéry, 'Le Roi dépensier: Le Don, la contrainte, et l'origine du système financier de la monarchie française sous l'ancien régime', *Annales ESC*, 39 (1984), 1241–69.
105 Claire Lévy-Lelouch, 'Quand le privilège de librairie publie le roi', in *De la publication: Entre Renaissance et Lumières*, Christian Jouhaud and Alain Viala (eds) (Paris, 2002), pp. 139–59.
106 Lévy-Lelouch's conception of the public is not consistent with Jürgen Habermas's bourgeois public sphere, a sphere defined above all by its autonomy from the state; rather, it overlaps with Christian Jouhaud's notion of *publicité*, a mode of representation and disclosure through literature in the contiguous spaces of Crown and court, described in *Les Pouvoirs de la littérature: Histoire d'un paradoxe* (Paris, 2000).
107 Roland Mousnier, 'L'Édition parisienne au XVIIe siècle: Quelques aspects économiques', *Annales ESC*, 7 (1952), 308–18; Martin, *Print, Power and People*, pp. 296–320.
108 See esp. Alain Viala, 'La Triple Économie du littéraire', in *Art et argent en France au temps des premiers modernes (XVIIe–XVIIIe siècles)*, Martial Poirson (ed.), Studies on Voltaire and the Eighteenth Century (Oxford, 2004), pp. 19–34.
109 Grivel, *Le Commerce de l'estampe*, pp. 104–12.
110 On the community of Flemish printmakers and printsellers in Paris see Roger-Armand Weigert, 'Graveurs et marchands d'estampes flamands à Paris sous le règne de Louis XIII', *NE*, 10 (1969), 445–56.
111 André Thevet, 'Au bénévole lecteur', *Les Vrais Pourtraits et vies des hommes illustres grecz, latins et payens* (Paris, 1584) (unpaginated).
112 Griffiths, *The Print before Photography*, pp. 28–35.
113 On the collaboration made necessary by this division of tasks see Roger Gaskell, 'Printing House and Engraving Shop: A Mysterious Collaboration', *Book Collector*, 53 (2004), 213–51.
114 Griffiths, *The Print before Photography*, p. 129.
115 Grivel, *Le Commerce de l'estampe*, p. 87.
116 On the Tavernier family see Roger-Armand Weigert, *Le Commerce de la gravure en France au XVIIe siècle: Les Tavernier* (Antwerp, 1975).
117 On this case see Jeanne Duportal, *Étude sur les livres à figures édités en France de 1600 à 1660* (Paris, 1914), pp. 11–15; Grivel, *Le Commerce de l'estampe*, pp. 87–8. The seized stock included copies of the first account by a Cape Horner, Guillaume Schouten's *Journal, ou Description du merveilleux voyage* (Amsterdam, 1618), illustrated with intaglio prints and maps; an unknown edition of the collected works of the military surgeon Ambroise Paré, which were, from 1598, illustrated with woodcuts; an edition of the *Commentaires* (1592) of the Catholic hero of the Wars of Religion Blaise de Montluc; *De la vocation des prestres* (Sedan, 1618) by the Protestant preacher Pierre Du Moulin; a French translation of Lucius Florus' history of Rome (Paris, 1615); and an edition (unspecified) of the essays of Michel de Montaigne. Tavernier conceded that none of these could, in a strict sense, legally be termed an illustrated book, though some contained plates; he denied that the books were, in fact, for sale.
118 Louis Servin, *Arrest de la Cour de parlement donné en l'audience de la Chambre de l'édict le sixième iour de mars mil six cents vingt; entre les syndics et gardes des marchands livraires, imprimeurs, relieurs de cette ville de Paris, appelants de l'entherinement de lettres par le prévost de Paris le vingtième novembre mil six cents dix huit, et sentence du dixhuitième janvier ensuivant d'une part; et Melchior Tavernier, imprimeur en taille douce d'autre, maître* [Louis] *Servin* (n.p., n.d. [1620]), BnF, Mss. f.f. 22119/12, p. 4.
119 Ibid., pp. 3–4.
120 Louis Servin, *Actions notables et plaidoyez de Messire Louys Servin* (Paris, 1639), pp. 951–6. The library of the Garde des sceaux Germain-Louis Chauvelin contained a copy. See *Catalogue des livres de feu Monsieur Président Chauvelin* (Paris, 1754), no. 1319.
121 Tavernier's lawyer, Labbé, argued that book publishers, printers and booksellers should, in fact, be legally restrained from selling illustrated books of any kind 'when the value of the figures exceeds that of the printing'. See *Labbé plaidant pardevant nos seigneurs tenans la Cour de parlement, en la Chambre de l'édict à Paris, pour Melchior Tavernier maistre graveur, imprimeur en taille-douce, deffendeur, opposant et demandeur à la fin de main levée de la saisie sur lui faicte le premier décembre dernier passé à la requeste de Laurent Sonius, Gabriel Clopjot, Jean Daumale, et François Julliot, se disans scindics et gardes des marchands libraires, imprimeurs, et relieurs de cette ville de Paris* (n.p., n.d. [1621]), BnF, Mss. f.f. 22119/13, p. 1. So self-evidently legitimate did Tavernier regard his case that he interpreted the guild's action as malicious. It was noted that Jean Le Clerc, whose stock was comparable to Tavernier's, had not been troubled by the officers of the booksellers' guild. Tavernier had, it seemed, been singled out; ibid., p. 13. On the division of rights in illustrated books see also Griffiths, *The Print before Photography*, pp. 181–94, esp. pp. 188–91.
122 Servin, *Arrest de la Cour de parlement*, p. 6.
123 *Labbé plaidant*, pp. 1–2. To reinforce the distinction, the memorandum was illustrated with a plate showing the two, different, presses. See Grivel, *Le Commerce de l'estampe*, pl. 5.
124 Servin, *Arrest de la Cour de parlement*, p. 5. On privilege for type see Herman de La Fontaine Verwey, 'Les Débuts de la protection des caractères typographiques au XVIe siècle', *Gutenberg Jahrbuch* (1965), 24–34.
125 *Labbé plaidant*, p. 9: 'l'ouvrage de l'esprit surpasse l'ouvrage de la main'.
126 Compare, for example, Pierre Gringore, *Les Fantasies de mère Sotte* (1515), Jean Chapelain, *La Pucelle* (1656) and Hippolyte-Jules Pilet de La Mesnardière, *Poésies* (1656).
127 *Labbé plaidant*, p. 10.
128 Labbé related that Louis XIII, fascinated by the new intaglio, came to watch the process for himself, and invited Tavernier to engrave and print René d'Anjou's 'Le Livre des tournois', one of the Bibliothèque royale's most impressive 15th-century manuscripts. Ibid., p. 18.
129 Ibid., p. 8.
130 'Extraict du privilege du roy', in Pierre d'Hozier, *Les Noms, surnoms, qualitez, armes, et blasons des chevaliers et officiers de l'Ordre du S. Esprit* (Paris, 1634).
131 Nicolas Schapira, 'Quand le privilège de librairie publie l'auteur', in *De la publication: Entre Renaissance et Lumières*, Christian Jouhaud and Alain Viala (eds) (Paris, 2002), pp. 121–37.
132 Schapira quotes from a letter from Jean Chapelain to Jean-Louis Guez de Balzac, in which the former tells the latter that it is more 'honourable' for the author to obtain the privilege and then cede it to the publisher than for the publisher to do so on the text's behalf. Ibid., p. 125.

133 BnF, Imprimés F5001/171. See William McAllister Johnson, *French Royal Academy of Painting and Sculpture Engraved Reception Pieces, 1672–1789*, exh. cat., Agnes Etherington Art Centre, Kingston, Ontario, and other venues (Kingston, 1982), p. 23. Peter Fuhring, who first published the privilege in printed form, has suggested that it may have been intended for pasting on the wall of printshops, Le Brun's own workshop included. See Fuhring, 'The Market for Prints under Louis XIV: Charles Le Brun', *PQ*, 19 (2002), 3–11 at 5.

134 BnF, Imprimés F5001/171, and Fuhring 'The Market for Prints', fig. 1. The incorporation of eulogy into privilege in the 1630s and 1640s can be seen as a manifestation of, and a contribution to, its rehabilitation as a serious literary form in that period. See Mark Bannister, 'Heroic Hierarchies: Classical Models for the Panegyric in Seventeenth-Century France', *International Journal of the Classical Tradition*, 8 (2001–2), 38–59.

135 Du Sault, *Nouveau Stile*, p. 39.

136 For example, in 1656, the year of the privilege, the *libraire* Antoine de Sommaville published a volume of Hippolyte-Jules Pilet de La Mesnardière's poetry with a frontispiece designed by Le Brun and engraved by Gilles Rousselet. See Véronique Meyer, *L'Œuvre gravé de Gilles Rousselet, graveur parisien du XVIIe siècle: Catalogue général avec les reproductions de 405 estampes* (Paris, 2004), p. 286, cat. no. 330.

137 Daniel Wildenstein, 'Les Œuvres de Charles Le Brun d'après les gravures de son temps', *GBA* (1965), 1–58.

138 Véronique Meyer, 'Le Brun éditeur: Étude d'après les inventaires du peintre et de sa veuve', in *Curiosité: Études d'histoire de l'art en honneur d'Antoine Schnapper*, Olivier Bonfait, Véronique Gerard-Powell and Philippe Sénéchal (eds) (Paris, 1998), pp. 103–14; Antoine Schnapper, 'La Fortune de Charles Le Brun', *Revue de l'art*, 114/4 (1996), 17–22.

139 Roger-Armand Weigert, 'Testament inédit de Charles Le Brun', *AAF*, 21 (1949), 9–17.

140 Schnapper, 'La Fortune de Charles Le Brun'; Weigert, 'Testament inédit'.

141 The petition is published along with Le Brun's *scellé* by Jules Guiffrey, *Scellés et inventaires d'artistes français du XVIIe et du XVIIIe siècle: Documents inédits tirés des Archives nationales*, 3 vols (Paris, 1883–5), vol. 1, pp. 152–4: 'Il y a principalement entre les desseins une estude particulière dud. s. Le Brun sur la Phisionomie et sur les Passions qu'il a fait avant d'estre au Roy, peu utile à Sa majesté, que la famille regarde comme une chose qui loy est très chère et très précieuse' (p. 154).

142 Ibid. pp. 153–4.

143 In the 16th century the average term for a privilege was three years. In the 17th century this had risen to six to ten years. Author privileges were often in the range 15–20 years. Abraham Bosse's for *Traicté des manières de graver en taille douce sur l'airin* (Paris, 1645) was, for instance, for 20 years.

144 Marianne Grivel's research has revealed that in the 27 years between 1635 and 1651 and 1653 and 1664 for which the registers of the Paris *libraires* survive, 125 print privileges were registered by print publishers and engravers, or just over four per year, rising to five per year in the period 1684–1725. Between 1664 and 1684 she found just one. See Grivel, *Le Commerce de l'estampe*, pp. 107–9. She thinks that these figures are conservative and that the number was possibly much higher, calling privilege in the 17th century 'une pratique habituelle.' I am not so sure.

145 The documents relating to the case were published by Alexandre Tutey in *BSHAF* (1918), 31–41, and are discussed by Grivel in *Le Commerce de l'estampe*, pp. 109–10, and by Nico Van Hout, 'Copyright Rubens: Cum privilegiis', in *Rubens et l'art de la gravure*, exh. cat., Koninklijk Museum voor schone kunsten, Antwerp, and Musée nationale des beaux-arts, Quebec (Ghent, 2004), pp. 30–39.

146 Before Le Brun, Simon Vouet, had also made reproductive printmakers part of his studio and had applied for privileges. See Marianne Grivel, '*Execudit* et privilège: Les Éditeurs de Simon Vouet', in *Simon Vouet: Actes du colloque internationale*, Stéphane Loire (ed.) (Paris, 1992), pp. 307–29; Alvin L. Clark, Jr, 'Vouet and his Printmakers', in *French Prints from the Age of the Musketeers*, exh. cat., Boston Museum of Fine Arts (Boston, 1998), pp. 28–42.

147 Armstrong, *Before Copyright*, pp. 63–77.

148 Fuhring, 'The Print Privilege, I', 178.

149 See Introduction, p. 27, and Grivel, *Le Commerce de l'estampe*, pp. 112–16.

150 The document is published in full in Préaud, *DEE*, pp. 15–19. See also Grivel, *Le Commerce de l'estampe*, pp. 84–5.

151 On the booksellers' dispute see *Mémoire sur la contestation qui est entre les libraires de Paris et ceux de Lyon au sujet des privilèges et des Continuations que le Roy accorde pour l'impression des livres* (n.d. [1690s]), in *PSC*, France, 1690s. On the dispute about deposits see *Arrest du Conseil d'état privé du roy qui ordonne à tous les auteurs, libraires, imprimeurs et graveurs du royaume de remettre… aux syndics et adjoints des libraires… huit exemplaires… de chacun des livres, feuilles et estampes*, 17 Oct. 1704, AN, ADIX/19. See also Grivel, *Le Commerce de l'estampe*, p. 114.

152 *Arrest du Conseil d'état privé du roy*, p. 5. See also Fuhring, 'The Print Privilege, I', 179–80.

153 There was a second attempt in 1644 and a third in 1660. See Grivel, *Le Commerce de l'estampe*, pp. 93–4, 96–9.

154 The reading I offer here of events preceding the Edict of Saint Jean-de-Luz of 1660 differs from Grivel's important analysis insofar as it does not assume, first, that incorporation would necessarily have been disadvantageous for all printmakers and, second, that printmakers in 1660 constituted a homogeneous social body and a unanimity of opinion. Just as painters and sculptors were divided in their allegiance between the Paris Corporation des maîtres peintres et sculpteurs and the more recently founded Académie royale de peinture et de sculpture, it seems possible, even likely, that there were those, led by Michel Lasne, who genuinely believed that they had something to gain by establishing a trade guild.

155 Robert Nanteuil, 'Abrégé de quelques raisons contre l'établissement d'une maîtrise', 1660, in Eugène Bouvy, *Le Portrait gravé et ses maîtres: Nanteuil* (Paris, 1924), pp. 18–20. See also René-Henri d'Allemagne, 'Histoire de la corporation des graveurs', *Bulletin de la Société archéologique, historique et artistique, Le Vieux Papier* (1908), 81–100; Grivel, *Le Commerce de l'estampe*, p. 99; Audrey Adamczak, *Robert Nanteuil (ca. 1623–1678)* (Paris, 2011), p. 52.

156 The ruling arose from an action by the booksellers against the engraver Jacques Auernault and the printer-publisher Jean Vierne for selling as a 'print' a book of some 250 pages with 36 illustrations entitled, *Le Miroir des prestres*. See BnF, Mss. f.f. 22119/19, 12 Oct. 1650.

157 BnF, Mss. f.f. 22119/24, 26 Oct. 1661. On the king's portrait see Neil Jeffares, *Dictionary of Pastellists before 1800* (London, 2006), p. 385; Adamczak, *Nanteuil*, p. 49, and cat. no. 175.

158 Kineret S. Jaffe, 'The Concept of Genius: Its Changing Role in Eighteenth-Century French Aesthetics', *Journal of the History of Ideas*, 41 (1980), 579–99.

159 In contrast, see the 1618 regulations and act of incorporation of the Paris book trade, in *PSC*, France, 1618. The preamble gives as reason for the foundation of the book guild the ignorance of publishers and printers, many of whom, it says, do not know how to read and 'n'ay[ent] la cognoissance requise de l'impression, ny la vente & Relieure des livres' (p. 7). The second two clauses of the regulations concern apprenticeship.

160 Ibid., p. 2.

161 *Arrêt du Conseil d'état qui maintient et garde l'art de la Gravûre de Taille-douce, au burein et à l'eau forte, et autre manière telle qu'elle soit, et ceux qui font profession d'icelui... en la liberté qu'ils ont toûjours eûe de l'éxercer dans le royaume sans qu'ils y puissent être réduits en maîtrise ni corps-de-métier*, 26 May 1660, in *PSC*, France 1660, p. 2 [modified translation]. In the 17th century, 'manière' denoted practice differentiated by level of skill, rather than personal idiosyncrasy. See Abraham Bosse, *Sentimens sur la distinction des diverses manières de peinture, dessein et graveure , et des originaux d'avec leurs copies* (Paris, 1649), pp. 38–54 (painting), pp. 73–81 (engraving). By the end of the century the meaning of 'manière' had shifted from imitation of nature to imitation of other artists, and referred to personal style in the modern sense. See Philippe de Champaigne, 'De l'éducation de la jeunesse suivant son génie naturel (Contre les copistes des manières)', conférence, 11 June 1672, in LM*Con*, vol. 1, pp. 461–3.

162 BnF, Mss. f.f. 22119/33. On Nicolas de Poilly, an important print publisher 'à la Belle Image' on the rue Saint-Jacques, see José Lothe, *L'Œuvre gravée de François et Nicolas de Poilly d'Abbeville: Graveurs parisiens du XVIIe siècle* (Paris, 1994); Préaud, *DEE*, pp. 264–5.

163 There were of course exceptions: in Valdor's *Les Triomphes de Louis le juste, XIII*, the intaglio headpieces are by Stefano della Bella and signed.

164 The great exception in the field of sheet prints was portrait engravings. See chapter 3.

165 'Extraict du privilège du roy', in Thevet, *Les Vrais Pourtraits*.

166 This was, of course, a simplification of production that erased the contribution of the letter engraver and the printer. On these aspects of printmaking, which remain relatively obscure, see Griffiths, *The Print before Photography*, pp. 44–7, 78–87.

167 See, for example, 'Extraict du privilège du roy', in Thevet, *Les Vrais Pourtraits*.

168 The range of author inscriptions is discussed in Griffiths, *The Print before Photography*, pp. 78–87.

169 In 1714, for instance, Jean II Berain successfully solicited a privilege, which was granted both because this subject was 'particularly known' to the king – he held the royal office of draughtsman to the Cabinet du roi – and because the works in question, while 'ouvrages de sa composition', owed their original execution to the king's order. They reproduced some of the court entertainments and ballets for which Berain had designed costumes and sets. See BnF, Mss. f.f. 21950/849–50 (Appendix 1). Berain's *Œuvres*, in a calf-bound volume, formed part of the king's personal library at Versailles until 1746. See *État des livres et autres remis à Messieurs de la Bibliothèque du roi suivant les différents départements*, BnF, Mss. f.f. 22033, fol. 11.

170 BnF, Mss. f.f. 21950, 22 Sept. 1711.

171 Roger de Piles, *Cours de peinture par principes* (1708) (Paris, 1989), pp. 7–9, 19–26.

172 William Ivins, *On the Rationalisation of Sight* (New York, 1938), p. 9.

173 Jean-Claude Passeron and Jacques Revel, 'Penser par cas: Raisonner à partir de singularité', in *Penser par cas*, Jean-Claude Passeron and Jacques Revel (eds) (Paris, 2005), pp. 9–44; Lauren Berlant, 'On the Case', *Critical Inquiry*, 33 (2007), 663–72.

174 Michel Foucault, 'Questions of Method', *The Foucault Effect: Studies in Governmentality*, Graham Burchell, Colin Gordon and Peter Miller (eds) (Chicago, 1991), pp. 73–86.

175 To give some examples from the first decades of the 18th century: abbé Jean-Louis Cordemoy, petitioned for a privilege for his *Nouveau traité d'architecture*, 17 Feb. 1706, BnF, Mss. f.f. 21949; Robert de Cotte for a suite of prints of the renovated choir of Notre-Dame, 7 Apr. 1714, BnF, Mss. f.f. 21930; and Claude-Nicolas Du Buisson for a set of designs for ecclesiastical altar furnishings, 14 July 1716, BnF, Mss. f.f. 21951.

176 In 1710 the privilege, originally granted to Le Jeune de Boulencourt for a description with plates of the Invalides, was renewed for the painter and print publisher Giles Demortain, who had bought the plates and wanted to reprint them, adding views of the interior of the chapel to the plan of the original edition. And six years later, the same Demortain applied for a six-year privilege for a large collection of views of Versailles, its gardens and fountains, for which he had 'selected the best draughtsmen and engravers' and with which he hoped 'to satisfy the taste of *curieux*, both French and foreign'. See BnF, Mss. f.f. 21950, 14 Sept. 1710, 30 Jan. 1716.

177 A rough calculation of the publishers and printsellers listed in Préaux, *DEE*, would indicate a 50 per cent increase in number in the second half of the 17th century. That figure almost doubles again between the end of the 17th century and the end of the 18th century.

178 See chapter 5 for the competition of England from the 1780s.

179 BnF, Mss. f.f. 21949, 2 Sept. 1709, three-year privilege for an anonymously illustrated account of the funeral of the prince de Conti at Saint André-des-arts; BnF, Mss. f.f. 21952, 22 Dec. 1722, three-year privilege for the print of the crown used at Louis XV's coronation, engraved by Sébastien Antoine after Augustin Duflos; BnF, Mss. f.f. 21954, 18 Mar. 1729, three-year privilege for the anonymous 'Tableaux où sont représentés la passion de N.S. J. Christ et les actions du Prestre à la Messe'; BnF, Mss. f.f. 21950, 22 Jan. 1713, 20-year privilege for new editions of the works of Jacques Callot and Stefano della Bella; BnF, Mss. f.f. 21958, 31 Aug. 1745, for a 'suite de planches d'anatomie' by Jacques Gautier d'Agoty.

180 It is impossible to be categorical because of the poor survival rate of prints at the lower end of the market.

181 Henri-Jean Martin, 'La Direction des lettres', in *HEF*, vol. 2, pp. 67–8.

182 For the *arrêt* of 6 Dec. 1700 ordering the national survey see BnF, Mss. f.f. 21748. See also Claude Lannette-Claverie, 'La Librairie française en 1700', *Revue française d'histoire du livre*, 3 (1972), 3–43.

183 The regulations were issued for Paris by the Conseil du roi on 28 Feb. 1723; they were extended and implemented for the whole kingdom, again by act of the Conseil du roi, on 24 Mar. 1744. See Barber, 'French Royal Decrees', p. 314; Frédéric Rideau, 'Commentary on the *Code de la librairie* (1723)', in *PSC*, France, 1744.

184 Rideau, 'Commentary on the *Code de la librairie* (1723)', in *PSC*, France, 1744.

185 Pierre-Jacques Blondel, *Mémoire sur les vexations qu'exercent les libraires et imprimeurs de Paris* (Paris, n.d. [1725]), p. 2, in *PSC*, France, 1725–6. The memorandum caused quite a stir and is mentioned both in Matthieu Marais's journal and in the magistrate Jean Bouhier's correspondence. It was to have been followed by a second memorandum by Bernard de Montfaucon, but of that there is no trace.

186 He alleged that *libraires* exaggerated the financial risks of publishing, that they used privilege to manipulate the price of books and that they falsified counts of editions in order to disguise the huge profits made possible by privilege. Ibid., pp. 2–10.

187 Blondel contrasted the learning and practical knowledge of the journeymen with the ignorance of the publishers: all they know 'selon le bon mot d'Arlequin, c'est que le blanc est le papier, & le noir est l'impression.' Ibid., p. 14. He denounced at length the 'rude servitude' imposed by the master *libraires* on their journeymen, which reduced them to the lowest kind of skivvies. Ibid., pp. 13–66. Blondel's *Mémoire* chimes with Nicolas Contat's account of the printer's shop in the 1730s, as analysed by Robert Darnton in *The Great Cat Massacre and Other Episodes in French Cultural History* (New York, 1984).

188 The first edition of Moréri's *Grand dictionnaire historique* was published by Jean Girin and Barthélemy Rivière at Lyon in 1674. The title of Frézier's book was *Relation du voyage de la mer du Sud, aux côtes du Chili, du Pérou et de Brézil, fait pendant les années 1712, 1713 et 1714* (1717); Frézier's illustrations were engraved by Nicolas Guérard and the publishers were J.-G. Nuyon, E. Ganneau and J. Quillau.

189 The preamble notes that the king ordered the ruling, having been made aware that the 'avarice' of some had led them to misuse privilege, create artificial scarcity and proportionately inflate the price of existing stocks of books. See *PSC*, France, 1725, clause 4 and *passim*. The *arrêt* also defined (clause 3) the legal conditions for subscription in order to eliminate abuses, specifically poor quality in production and failure to deliver.

190 On Louis d'Héricourt see the editor's preface on his life in *Œuvres posthumes de maistre Louis d'Héricourt*, 4 vols (Paris, 1759), vol. 1, pp. iii–xx.

191 *Avocats* (barristers) such as d'Héricourt were, in fact, barred from taking evidence (the role of the *procureurs*, or prosecutors). The role of the barrister was rather to draw the judge's attention to the relevant legal principles of the case. See Philip Dawson, 'The *bourgeoisie de robe* in 1789', *French Historical Studies*, 4 (1965), 1–21.

192 According to a handwritten note at the bottom of the copy of the memorandum belonging to the Chancellor's office, the memorandum so enraged the Garde des sceaux that he insulted warden Mariette and his adjoint and had them dismissed from office. See Louis d'Héricourt, *Mémoire de Louis d'Héricourt à Monseigneur le Garde des sceaux* (Paris, n.d. [1725]), in *PSC*, France, 1725–6, p. 2.

193 Rideau, 'Commentary on the *Code de la librairie* (1723)', in *PSC*, France, 1744.

194 The *acte de cession*, 15 May 1752, was signed by Aumont, Barbon, Bordelet, Brocas, Veuve Brocas, Cavellier (in the interest of his mother), Damonville, David *l'aîné*, David *père*, David *le jeune*, Despilly *père*, Durand, Huart, C. Le Clerc, Moreau, Nyon *fils*, Quillan *fils* and Savoye, between whom interests in the privilege were by then divided. Only if the quarto and folio editions failed did the cession allow de Montenault to launch, after a lapse of time of more than 12 months, an octavo edition likewise illustrated and decorated with prints after Oudry and Bachelier. See Louis-Jean Regnard de Montenault, *Mémoire sur l'édition des fables de La Fontaine, avec copie de la cession faite par les libraires*, undated, BnF, Mss. n.a.f. 3345, fol. 406. For a discussion of the first editions of La Fontaine's *Fables choisies*, see Gervais E. Reed, *Claude Barbin, libraire de Paris sous le règne de Louis XIV* (Geneva, 1974), pp. 24, 48. Barbin and Thierry's first edition was a highly priced quarto, several hundred copies of which were still in stock at the time of Barbin's sale in 1695; profit was made rather on the duodecimo edition launched in October 1668 with the same illustrations. Two important collections of documents relating to the publication of this book are to be found at BnF, Mss. n.a.f. 3345, and f.f. 12495. According to de Montenault's draft *Notes et avis différens sur la nouvelle édition des fables de La Fontaine* (BnF, Mss. f.f. 12495, fol. 3v), preparations for the project had started in 1751.

195 Oudry's drawings were bound into two volumes, one of which was broken up and dispersed after the Raphaël Esmerian sale at the Palais Galliera, Paris, 6 June 1973, lot 46. The other was bought by the British Rail Pension Fund; it was later sold at Sotheby's, London, 3 July 1996, lot 96. On the history of the Regnard de Montenault–Oudry edition see Roger Gaucheron, 'La Préparation et le lancement d'un livre de luxe au XVIIIe siècle: L'Édition des Fables de La Fontaine, dite d'Oudry", *Arts et métiers graphiques*, 2 (1927), 77–82; Hal N. Opperman, *Jean-Baptiste Oudry*, 2 vols (New York, 1977), vol. 1, pp. 99–101, 128, 143; vol. 2, pp. 682–710, D221–359; *J.-B. Oudry, 1686–1755*, exh. cat., Grand Palais, Paris (Paris, 1982), cat. nos 76–85; Alain-Marie Bassy, *Les Fables de La Fontaine: Quatre Siècles d'illustration* (Paris, 1986), pp. 90–93, 110–14, 174–81.

196 For the Salon *livret* for 1753 see J.-J. Guiffrey, *Collection des livrets des anciennes expositions depuis 1673 jusqu'en 1800*, 5 vols (Paris, 1869–71), vol. 2, pp. 18–19. The engravings are not itemised, or given a catalogue number or heading in the *livret*, but are incorporated into the list of Oudry's painted exhibits. At the following Salon (1755) Laurent Cars exhibited three of his prints after Oudry's designs: *L'Âne chargé de reliques* (2: 10), *Le Chasseur, le pâtre et le lion* (6: 1), and *Le Meunier, son fils et l'âne* (3: 1); see Salon *livret* for 1755, ibid., vol. 2, p. 35, cat. no. 166. On 31 May 1755 de Montenault had been granted a special dispensation from the *lieutenant de police*, Nicolas-René Berryer, to instal printing presses at his address in rue Sainte-Anne to print Oudry's plates. The printers Thévenard and later J.-B. Dutertre were charged with the task. See BnF, Mss. f.f. 12495, fol. 34.

197 *MdF* (Aug. 1754), 118.

198 For a transcript of the contract 'sous seignes privés' between de Montenault and Desaint and Saillant and Durand, dated 10 Dec. 1754, see BnF, Mss. f.f. 21495, fols 90–91.

199 According to Gaucheron, the enterprise had financial backing from the banker Darcy. Further funds were raised through subscription. See Gaucheron, 'La Préparation et le lancement', pp. 77, 79. The subscription was launched in *Année littéraire* (1754), no. 4, 190–93; *MdF* (Aug. 1754), 117–20; *Mémoires de Trévoux* (Sept. 1754), 2295–302. In February 1758 de Montenault approached the Directeur des bâtiments du roi, the marquis de Marigny, indirectly with a proposal that the woodland at the Champs-Élysées announced for public auction be awarded to Miger, *marchand de bois*, who, in return for the right to fell the timber, would finance volume 4 of the *Fables*. See de Montenault, *Mémoire*, BnF, Mss. n.a.f. 3345, fol. 462. Additional subscriptions were also being solicited for volume 4 by the *Année littéraire*, (1760), no. 7, 46–8, even though the subscription had officially closed on 30 June 1755.

200 In the second of his memoranda, de Montenault identified the cessation of international trade during the war as a contributing factor to his financial difficulties. See de Montenault, *Mémoire sur l'édition des fables de La Fontaine*, BnF, Mss. n.a.f. 3345, fols 420–24 at fol. 422v; de Montenault, *Notes et avis différens sur la nouvelle édition des fables de La Fontaine*', BnF, Mss. f.f. 12495, fols 39–43v at 41v.

201 Five memoranda and other papers related to the vexed nature of the publication are to be found in BnF, Mss. n.a.f. 3345. In the first (fol. 382), de Montenault suggested that Louis XV buy 200 copies of the printed volumes, or buy Oudry's drawings for the royal collection – both measures, as he noted, that had been taken in the case of Jean-Baptiste Massé's *Grande galerie de Versailles* (1723–53). He also proposed a cash donation or an interest-free loan, comparing the scale and importance of his project to César-François Cassini's map of France, published from 1756 (fol. 381). He itemised the costs as follows: printmakers – 24,500 *livres*; letter engravers – 10,000 *livres*; drawings – 6,000 *livres*; prints – 15,000 *livres*; paper – 6,247 *livres* 10 *sous*; copper plates – 3,000 *livres*; woodcut printers' flowers, the portrait of the author and other sundry expenses – 8,000 *livres*; total – 72,747 *livres* 10 *sous* (fol. 386).

202 At the time de Montenault was writing, cheaper, octavo editions of the *Fables* had already been reprinted by important publishers in Dresden (*chez* Georg Konrad Walther, publisher of Winckelmann), Leyden (*chez* Frères Élie Luzac, publishers of La Mettrie) and Copenhagen, but it was protection

against the anticipated piracies in the French capital that de Montenault's petition was intended to secure. He proposed a fine of 10,000 *livres* as a deterrent, considerably in excess of the average. See de Montenault, *Mémoire sur l'édition des fables de La Fontaine*, BnF, Mss. n.a.f. 3345, fols 420–24 at fol. 422; *Projet du privilège du Roy à accorder*, fols 406v–407; de Montenault, *Notes et avis*, BnF, Mss. f.f. 12495, fol. 40v.

203 I repeat here Jacques Derrida's assertion that, to be just, decisions must be 'both regulated and without regulation… must conserve the law and destroy it'. See Derrida, 'The Force of Law', trans. Mary Quaintance, in *Deconstruction and the Possibility of Justice*, Drucilla Cornell, Michel Rosenfeld and David Gray Carlson (eds) (New York, 1992), pp. 3–67.

204 De Montenault, *Mémoire… avec copie de la cession faite par les libraires*, BnF, Mss. n.a.f. 3345, fols 403–8 at fol. 403.

205 The typeface was subjected to anonymous critique by the punchcutter, type designer and founder Pierre-Simon Fournier *le jeune* in two letters published in the *Journal des sçavants*: 'Lettre sur l'imprimerie, à Messieurs les amateurs du *Journal des sçavants*' (Jan. 1756), 13–23; 'Seconde lettre sur l'imprimerie, à Messieurs les amateurs du *Journal des sçavants*' (Feb. 1756), 73–83. These provoked replies from the printer and *libraire* Austin-Martin Lottin, in *Journal des sçavants* (May 1756), 298–305; (June 1756), 425–35.

206 'Prospectus', BnF, Mss. n.a.f. 3345, fols 387–9. In his *Traité historique et pratique de la gravure en bois*, 3 vols in 2 (Paris, 1766), Papillon claimed that Le Sueur delegated to a pupil, Le Fevre, the cutting of some of 'les plus délicates & déliées tiges de fleurs', which he, Le Sueur, found 'ennuyantes à graver' (vol. 1, p. 335, see also p. 413).

207 The prospectus explicitly stated that 'il ne faut pas confondre' these 276 plates, reproduced at the same size as the drawings and which may be regarded as 'des Tableaux finis', with 'les vignettes dont on a coutume d'orner la pluspart des Livres' (BnF, Mss. n.a.f. 3345, fol. 388). On Chauveau's earlier campaign of illustration, see Raymond G. LePage, 'The 1668 Edition of the Fables, Book VI: An Iconographic Interpretation', *L'Esprit créateur*, 21/4 (1981), 66–77; Bassy, *Les Fables de La Fontaine*, pp. 41–88, 146–8. That the superior impact of the illustrations was not merely the allegation of a self-promoting publisher but the actual experience of some readers is suggested by a review in the *Journal des sçavants*. The reviewer, Pierre-Simon Fournier, noted the assignment of priority to the illustrations in the arrangement of the book: image occupies the recto pages from the beginning, and the fables, which are, or should have been, according to this critic, 'the principal object of the edition', and therefore the most conspicuous and advantageously placed part, often have to be content with the verso pages. See [Fournier], 'Seconde lettre sur l'imprimerie', p. 78.

208 Claude Marin Saugrain, *Code de la librairie et imprimerie de Paris* (Paris, 1744), art. 101, p. 361. See also Rideau, 'Commentary on the *Code de la librairie* (1723)', in *PSC*, France, 1744.

209 For a discussion of Michel de Montaigne's *Essais* as open form, and of revision and augmentation as authorial strategies developed in response to the privilege regime, see Georges Hoffmann, 'The Montaigne Monopoly: Revising the *Essais* under the French Privilege System', *PMLA*, 108 (1993), 308–19; repr. in Georges Hoffmann, *Montaigne's Career* (Oxford, 1998), pp. 108–29.

210 In some instances Oudry followed Chauveau's composition closely, changing only details – his figures are given contemporary dress – (e.g. Book 1, *Fable* XIII) or format (Book 1, *Fable* XXII). In other instances Oudry used Chauveau's illustration as a point of departure (e.g. Book 3, *Fable* I: Oudry's first plate followed Chauveau but he then added four more to finish the story), and in others he decomposed Chauveau's design and redistributed the parts in more than one plate (e.g. Book 3, *Fable* VIII). Oudry certainly knew Chauveau's illustrations, though there is no evidence that he owned a copy. See Oudry's *inventaire après décès*, ANMC, LIII/345 7/v/1755.

211 Jean de La Fontaine, *Fables choisies*, Regnard de Montenault (ed.) 4 vols (Paris, 1755–9 [1760]) (hereafter RdM (ed.)), vol. 1, p. xxix: 'Vie de La Fontaine'. See BnF, Mss. f.f. 12495, for drafts of de Montenault's 'Vie' and transcriptions of lives of La Fontaine by other writers. For a different perspective on La Fontaine's practice of imitation, see Antoine Houdart de La Motte, 'Discours sur la fable', in *Fables nouvelles*, 2 vols (Paris, 1719), vol. 1, pp. ix–x. On La Fontaine's concern to make himself present in the text by accenting his intervention in tradition see John Lyons, 'Author and Reader in the Fables', *French Review*, 49 (1975), 59–67.

212 La Fontaine, *Fables*, RdM (ed.), vol. 1, pp. iii–iv: 'Avertissement'. De Montenault was here re-using a topos that had earlier served André Félibien to describe the relationship between Chauveau and La Fontaine: *Entretiens sur les vies et sur les ouvrages des plus excellens peintres anciens et modernes*, 6 vols (Paris, 1666–88), vol. 5, p. 182.

213 Oudry had a reputation by then as great painter of animals. In the introduction, de Montenault goes further and denies that the pictorialism immanent in the *Fables* had ever been fully exploited by the great poet. By contrast, Jacques-Nicolas Tardieu's engraved portrait of Oudry (the adoption of which as a frontispiece for the *Fables* de Montenault encouraged from 1762) suggested via its elaborate frame that the still-life painter possessed not only *disegno* and *colore* but poetry and music too – a self-sufficiency, in fact, in the lyric arts for this project. In the absence of an actual relationship of production between the book and the portrait, an announcement, no doubt by de Montenault, in the *Mercure de France* built up the connections between the two by arguing for the identification of the volumes depicted in the portrait with volumes of the *Fables*, and for an interpretation of the model as belonging to that stage of maturity during which Oudry was known to have composed the designs for them. See *MdF* (Oct. 1762), 152–3.

214 W. J. T. Mitchell, *What do Pictures Want? The Lives and Loves of Images* (Chicago, 2005), ch. 2.

215 See Denis Diderot's definition of 'naïf' in the *Pensées détachées sur la peinture*, in *Œuvres esthétiques*, ed. Paul Vernière (Paris, 1965), 884–5. See also Alain-Marie Bassy, 'Le Paradoxe du réalisme et du merveilleux dans l'illustration des *Fables* de La Fontaine au XVIIIe siècle', *Bulletin du bibliophile*, 10 (1979), 216–38.

216 'Regardez bien, ma soeur; / Est-ce assez? dites-moi; n'y suis-je point encore? / Nemmi. – M'y voici donc?– Point du tout. – M'y voilà? / Vous n'en approchez point', in Jean de La Fontaine, *Fables*, ed. Antoine Adam (Paris: Garnier, 1966), pp. 52–3.

217 La Fontaine, *Fables*, RdM (ed.) vol. 1, pp. vii–viii: 'Vie d'Ésope le phrygien'. On La Fontaine's life of Aesop, see Marie-Christine Bellosta, '"La Vie d'Ésope le Phrygien" de La Fontaine, ou Les Ruses de la vérité', *Revue d'histoire littéraire de la France* (1979), 2–13. On the alleged episode of the figs see Louis Marin, 'The "Aesop" Fable-Animal', in *On Signs*, Marshall Blonsky (ed.) (Oxford, 1985), pp. 334–40.

218 Mitchell, *What do Pictures Want?*, pp. 33–34.

219 The memorandum by Labbé was still in circulation in the 18th century; Papillon referred to it in his *Traité*, vol. 2, pp. 78–80. It is possible that it was known to de Montenault.

220 'Le monde est plein de gens qui ne sont pas plus sage: / Tout bourgeois veut bâtir comme les grands seigneurs, / Tout petit prince a des ambassadeurs, / Tout marquis veut avoir des pages.' La Fontaine, *Fables*, ed. Adam, p. 53.

221 See, for example, the definition of 'privilège' in Antoine Furetière's *Dictionnaire universel*, 2nd edn, 3 vols (The Hague,

1701), according to which 'se dit en général de toutes sortes de droits, prerogatives, d'avantages attachez à de certaines conditions, à de certains états, à de certains emplois'. As an example he cites the condition of husband and the privileges he enjoys in his wife.

222 De Montenault, *Mémoire... avec copie de la cession faite par les libraires*, BnF, Mss. n.a.f. 3345, fol. 403.

223 For a short discussion of positive and natural law in the context of Enlightenment see Ernest Cassirer, *The Philosophy of the Enlightenment*, trans. Fritz C. A. Koelln and James P. Pettegrove (Princeton, NJ, 1951), pp. 234–5.

224 The 'benefits' he proposed were purchase of the original drawings for 25,000–30,000 *livres*, or failing that a pre-order of 100 copies (reduced from 200 in the first memorandum). See de Montenault, *Mémoire sur l'édition des fables*, BnF, Mss. n.a.f. 3345, fol. 424. See BnF, Mss. f.f. 12495, fols 48–9, for a copy of the signed receipt for the 100 copies of the *Fables* (50 printed on 'très grand papier', 50 on 'grand papier'), delivered to the Cabinet du roi on 21 Apr. 1761.

225 Walter Benjamin, 'Critique of Violence', in *Reflections: Essays, Aphorisms, Autobiographical Writing*, trans. Edmund Jephcott, ed. Peter Demetz (New York, NY, 1986), pp. 277–300.

226 De Montenault, *Mémoire... avec copie de la cession faite par les libraires*, BnF, Mss. n.a.f. 3345, fol. 405.

227 De Montenault, *Projet de privilège du Roy à accorder*, BnF, Mss. n.a.f. 3345, fol. 407: 'etant informés d'ailleurs des soins qu'il a pris, des recherches, des dépenses considérables qu'il a faites pour la perfection de cette édition... et des Risques que peut courrir sa fortune dans cette enterprise, s'il n'étoit *authorisé et maintenue dans la possession de cet ouvrage dont il est juste qu'il jouisse paisiblement*]: à ces causes...' (my emphasis). Significantly, the passage in square brackets was not retained in the final text of the privilege. For another copy, see also fols 411–12.

228 In 1725 Jean-Baptiste Oudry had successfully petitioned to obtain a ten-year privilege for the reproduction of his *Chasse de cerf*. In the letters patent he was addressed as 'notre bien amé... peintre' – that is, in a manner more consistent with that used in relation to Le Brun. BnF, Mss. f.f. 21953, 2 Mar. 1725.

229 La Fontaine, *Fables*, RdM (ed.), vol. 1: 'Avertissement'. The reviewer for the *Mémoires de Trévoux* noted that in such moments of inspiration the artist is not troubled by business matters, nor by 'la voix impérieuse de l'intérêt', nor by 'la présomption de l'amour propre.' He is entirely given up to art. See *Mémoires de Trévoux* (Sept. 1754), 2297.

230 The claim is made, of course, in defiance of the prologue to the fable 'Le Vieux Chat et la jeune souris', dedicated to the duc de Bourgogne, 'qui avait demandé à M. de La Fontaine une fable qui fût nommée "Le Chat et la Souris"'. On the tension between invention and commission, see Patrick Dandrey, *La Fabrique des fables: Essai sur la poétique de La Fontaine* (Paris, 1991), pp. 79–90. To emphasise La Fontaine's wittily insubordinate nature, de Montenault quoted, out of context, a poem addressed by La Fontaine to his patron Mme de La Sablière, in which he famously said of himself: 'je suis volage en vers comme en amours'. La Fontaine, *Fables*, RdM (ed.), vol. 1, p. xxx: 'Vie de La Fontaine'.

231 La Fontaine, *Fables*, RdM (ed.), vol. 1, p. xxix: 'Vie de La Fontaine'.

232 De Montenault, ibid.: 'Le soin de les retirer [de sa tête] fut tout son travail'.

233 Ibid., p. iv. See also *Mémoires de Trévoux* (Sept. 1754), 2298, and the set of paintings realised for Versailles in 1747: *Le Loup et l'agneau, Le Renard et la cigogne, La Lice et sa compagne* and *Le Cerf se mirant dans l'eau*.

234 John Locke, *The Two Treatises of Government* (1689), Book II, ch. 5, §27.

235 Locke had in his library modern editions of *Corpus iuris civilis* and Justinian's *Institutiones*. On the debt he may have owed to the classical legal notion of *ferruminatio* see Roger T. Simonds, 'John Locke's Use of Classical Legal Theory', *International Journal of the Classical Tradition*, 3 (1997), 424–32. See also on Locke's mixtures Wolfram Schmidgen, 'The Politics and Philosophy of Mixture: John Locke Recomposed, *Eighteenth Century*, 48 (2007), 205–23.

236 Locke, *The Two Treatises*, Book II, ch. 5, §27.

237 D'Héricourt, *Mémoire*, in Laboulaye and Guiffrey, *La Propriété littéraire*, p. 23; *PSC*, France, 1725–6, p. 2.

238 Ibid., in Laboulaye and Guiffrey, *La Propriété littéraire*, p. 22; *PSC*, France, 1725–6, p. 1.

239 Oren Bracha, 'The Political Economy of Copyright: Writing Copyright's History in the Shadow of the Reason/Power Dichotomy', paper given at the conference to launch the Arts and Humanities Research Council's *Primary Sources on Copyright History*, 19–20 Mar. 2008.

240 D'Héricourt, *Mémoire*, in Laboulaye and Guiffrey, *La Propriété littéraire*, p. 22; *PSC*, France, 1725–6, p. 1. On the importance of narrative in definitions of property, see esp. Carol Rose, *Property and Persuasion: Essays on the History, Theory, and Rhetoric of Ownership* (Boulder, CO, and Oxford, 1994), pp. 11–45.

241 D'Héricourt, *Mémoire*, in Laboulaye and Guiffrey, *La Propriété littéraire*, p. 23; *PSC*, France, 1725–6, p. 2.

242 Bernard Edelman, *Ownership of the Image: Elements for a Marxist Theory of Law* (London, 1979), p. 70.

243 De Montenault, *Projet de privilège du Roy à accorder*, BnF, Mss. n.a.f. 3345, fols 406–8.

244 *Année littéraire* (1760), no. 7, 46–8. See also BnF, Mss. f.f. 12495, fol. 46v: a marginal note on a memorandum records that de Montenault sold impressions of the 276 plates for 400 *livres* when printed on 'très grand papier', 348 *livres* on 'grand papier' and 300 *livres* on 'papier ordinaire'.

245 *MdF* (Nov. 1760), 165–7. According to the *Mercure*, de Montenault, in fact, ceded his rights to the *cul-de-lamps* to Choffard. Pirate copies of the woodcuts were already widely in circulation. Papillon acknowledged possession of a copy by Leprote of one of the *fleurons* (Papillon, *Traité*, vol. 1, p. 336). Printed below the puff for the Choffard prints in the *Mercure de France* was the following: 'cet Artiste avertit MM les Imprimeurs-Libraires, & tous autres, de cesser une pareille contrefaction [of the ornaments] aussi préjudiciable à la chose par sa mauvaise exécution, qu'à ses intérêts particuliers.' The editor commended Choffard for this course of action, given that he could have sought legal redress. He urged artists not to copy but to invent 'desseins agréables' and 'belles gravure de bois' for the publishing trade. A second set was published two years later, see *MdF* (Dec. 1762), 151. Choffard's prints were described as 'une traduction fidelle en Taille-douce des chefs d'œuvre de Gravure en bois consacrés dans l'original'. Both sets were for sale *chez* Veuve Chéreau for 20 *sous*.

246 La Fontaine, *Fables*, RdM (ed.), vol. 1, p. iii: 'Avertissement'.

247 Philibert Secretan, *L'Analogie* (Paris, 1984); on metaphor in legal discourse see also William Patry, *Moral Panics and Copyright Laws* (Oxford, 2009), pp. 43–55.

248 La Fontaine, *Fables*, Book 3, *Fable* X: 'Le Lion abbatu par l'homme'; Book 9, *Fable* VI: 'Le Statuaire et la statue de Jupiter'. Note the emphasis on the material in the second: 'Qu'en fera, dit-il, mon ciseau / Sera-t-il dieu, table ou cuvette?'

249 See de Piles, *Cours de peinture par principes*, p. 211, on decorative painting and notions of private property in antiquity. For an expanded discussion of the relation of framing and *trompe l'œil* to privilege, see Scott, 'Maps, Views and Ornament: Visualising Property in Art and Law', in *Privilege and Property: Essays on the History of Copyright*, Ronan Deazley, Martin Kretschmer and Lionel Bently (eds) (Cambridge, 2010), pp. 254–88.

250 For a comparison of natural and positive law, informed by the terms *espace striée* and *espace lissée* in Gilles Deleuze and Félix Guattari, *Mille Plateaux* (Paris, 1980), see Leif Dahlberg, 'Achilles' Foot and the Law: Legal Space(s), Striated and Smooth', in *Practising Equity, Addressing Law: Equity in Law and Literature*, Daniela Carpi (ed.) (Heidelberg, 2008), pp. 119–39.

251 D'Héricourt, *Mémoire*, in Laboulaye and Guiffrey, *La Propriété littéraire*, p. 36; *PSC*, France, 1725–6, pp. 8, 10.

252 The memoranda reveal nothing about the terms or date of the purchase. *Mémoire détaillé de ce qui reviendroient des fables de La Fontaine en figures et caractères gravez au burin* estimates for the drawings and engraving of the first 142 'sujets' 12,100 *livres*. The drawings in question, however, are likely to be those made by Cochin specifically for the printmakers, not Oudry's 'originals'. See BnF, Mss. n.a.f. 3345, fols 391–3.

253 In *Mémoire*, in Laboulaye and Guiffrey, *La Propriété littéraire*, p. 30; *PSC*, France, 1725–6, p. 8, d'Héricourt claims for the purchaser: '[Il] doit demeurer perpétuellement propriétaire du Texte de cet Ouvrage, lui & ses descendans, comme d'une terre ou d'une maison qu'il auroit acquise, parce que l'acquisition d'un heritage ne diffère en rien par la nature de l'acquisition de celle d'un manuscript.'

254 De Montenault, *Mémoire... avec copie de la cession faite par les libraires*, BnF, Mss. n.a.f. 3345, fol. 403.

255 De Montenault, *Mémoire sur l'édition des fables de La Fontaine*, Bnf, Mss. n.a.f. 3345, fol. 420v.

256 De Montenault, *Notes et avis*, BnF, Mss. f.f. 12495, fol 8v.

257 Ibid., fol 40v. De Montenault notes that his difficulties in delivering volume 2 on time to subscribers were caused almost entirely by Cochin's failure to make the necessary redrawings for the printmakers. According to Charles-Antoine Jombert, Cochin eventually redrew all the illustrations, and so extensive were his 'corrections' that 'il se les est rendu propres' and 'on y reconnoît aisément sa touché et manière'. Jombert, *Catalogue de l'œuvre de Charles-Nicolas Cochin fils* (Paris, 1770), p. 89. See also *Mémoires de Trévoux* (Sept. 1754), 2299, and Christian Michel, *Charles-Nicolas Cochin et l'art des Lumières* (Rome, 1993), p. 103. As early as 1751 Cochin had designed a 'fable... en forme de vignette in-quarto' for de Montenault, illustrating 'The rich man and the shoemaker'. In 1746 he had also been involved in another edition of the *Fables* for which he provided a frontispiece and two *vignettes*, engraved by Fessard. See Jombert, *Catalogue de l'œuvre de... Cochin*, pp. 55, 78.

258 For de Montenault's lists of the names and addresses of the printmakers, see BnF, Mss. f.f. 12495, fols 96–102; on the printing presses at his house, see ibid., fol. 34; see also Gaucheron, 'La Préparation et le lancement', p. 78.

259 De Montenault, *Notes et avis*, BnF, Mss. f.f. 12495, fols 7–8.

260 Malesherbes had given copies of the first two volumes of de Montenault's edition to the Mlles de La Fontaine in 1755, for which they thanked him by a letter of 7 June, in which the edition is described as 'fort chere pour les embellissemens' and as having given very great pleasure. See BnF, Mss. n.a.f. 3345, fol. 400. On the *affaire* La Fontaine, see BnF, Mss. f.f. 22178/16, f.f. 22073/57, *PSC*, France, 1761. The sorry plight of La Fontaine's granddaughters had become the subject of newspaper attention. In September 1759 the *Mercure de France* published a letter by the abbé de Breteuil, on behalf of the duc d'Orléans making generally known the 'misfortunes' of the family of 'l'un des plus grands Poètes que la France ait vû naître' and holding out the promise of a pension. *MdF* (Sept., 1759), 143–4. It seems likely that its 18th-century publishers lost the privilege in La Fontaine by the combined pressure of de Montenault and the La Fontaine heirs. On the more famous case of the granddaughters, see E. Rodocanachi, 'Les Petites-filles de La Fontaine et la propriété littéraire', *Séances et travaux de l'Académie des sciences morales et politiques: Compte rendu* (1930), 95–104; Birn, 'The Profit of Ideas', pp. 150–51; Frédéric Rideau, 'Commentary on the La Fontaine case (1761)', in *PSC*, France, 1761.

261 In the draft privilege, de Montenault has the king articulate emulation as his principal aim. See *Projet de privilège du Roy à accorder*, BnF, Mss. n.a.f. 3345, fol. 407.

262 La Fontaine, *Fables*, RdM (ed.), vol. 4. Note that the reference is to men of letters and amateurs, precisely those who were prohibited from printing and publishing books since they were not members of the Corporation des libraires et maîtres imprimeurs.

263 See, for instance, the privilege for Bernard de Montfaucon's *Antiquité expliquée et représentée en figure* (Paris, 1719).

264 La Fontaine, *Fables*, RdM (ed.), vol. 1, p. v. The lawyer Simon Marion had, in the 16th century, argued that publication automatically delivered works into the public domain unless effort was made to prevent it through privilege. See Marion, *Plaidoyez second sur l'impression des Œuvres de Sénèque*, in *PSC*, France, 1586.

265 Edelman, *Le Sacre de l'auteur*, pp. 157–72.

266 See Augustin Courbé's 1649 edition of *Les Fables d'Ésope*.

267 Rideau, 'Commentary on the La Fontaine case (1761)', in *PSC*, France, 1761.

268 Rose, *Property and Persuasion*, pp. 105–62.

269 Hesse, 'Enlightenment Epistemology'.

270 In *The Business of the Enlightenment: A Publishing History of the Encyclopédie, 1775–1800* (Boston, 1979), Robert Darnton calls the *Encyclopédie* the 'supreme work' of the time (p. 4).

271 On 23 Jan. 1759 the *Encyclopédie* was examined and condemned by the Parlement; on 8 Mar. 1759 the 1746 privilege was revoked. See Arthur Wilson, *Diderot* (New York, 1972), pp. 335–6; Henri-Jean Martin, 'Malesherbes et la librairie', *Actes du colloque Malesherbes*, Claude Goyard (ed.) (Paris, 1995), pp. 43–67; Jacques Proust, *Diderot et l'Encyclopédie* (1962) (Paris, 1995), p. 65. The publishers, Le Breton et al., had, in fact, taken out three privileges for the text: in April 1745, January 1746 and April 1748. Each corresponded to a stage in the elaboration of the original plan to publish a four-volume translation of Ephraim Chambers's *Cyclopaedia, or Universal Dictionary of the Arts and Sciences* (London, 1728). Malsherbes arranged for the *Encyclopédie* to be granted a *permission tacite*, which allowed the project to continue. Martin notes that for the project to have failed would, because of the number of partners and investors, have brought the whole Paris book trade into crisis.

272 'Privilège d'impression', in Denis Diderot and Jean Le Rond d'Alembert, *Encyclopédie, ou Dictionnaire raisonné des sciences, des arts et des métiers* (Paris and Neuchâtel, 1751–72), vol. 13, pp. 389–91: 'pour avoir *seul* la permission d'imprimer ou faire imprimer tel livre' (my emphasis).

273 On the *Encyclopédie*'s relations to luxury in the pursuit of knowledge, see Mary Sheriff, 'Decorating Knowledge: The Ornamental Book, the Philosophic Image and the Naked Truth', *Art History*, 28 (2005), 151–73. The quality of the decoration tails off over the volumes and Papillon cut costs by re-using blocks from other publications, but overall the *Encyclopédie* is still closer to the quality of the *Fables* than to André Félibien's *Des principes de l'architecture, de la sculpture, de la peinture et des autres arts qui en dépendent* (Paris, 1676), with which it is often compared.

274 The subscription was for ten volumes of which two were of plates: 60 *livres* was due in advance, 36 *livres* on receipt of the first volume, 24 *livres* on receipt of each of the rest until the seventh, and 40 *livres* each for the volumes of plates, making a total of 296 *livres*. On the subscription scheme for the *Encyclopédie*, see Proust, *Diderot et l'Encyclopédie*, pp. 51–2, and for the costs, p. 51, n. 33. See also Darnton, *The Business of the Enlightenment*, p. 273.

275 Proust, *Diderot et l'Encyclopédie*, pp. 49–51. The number of subscribers had passed the 2,000 mark by the time of the *arrêt*, 7 Feb. 1752, which banned retrospectively the publication of the first two volumes. In total 4,225 copies of the 17 volumes of the *Encyclopédie*'s text were sold and about 4,000 copies of the 11 volumes of plates.

276 'Privilège du Roy', in Denis Diderot, *Recueil de planches, sur les sciences, les arts libéraux, et les arts méchaniques, avec leur explication*, vol. 1 (Paris, 1762), p. 6.

277 Pierre Patte, 'Dénonciation d'un plagiat à M. Fréron', *Année littéraire* (1759), no. 7, 341–51. See also Georges Huard, 'Les Planches de l'*Encyclopédie* et celles de la *Description des arts et métiers* de l'Académie des sciences', in *L'Encyclopédie et le progrès des sciences et des techniques* (Paris, 1952), pp. 35–46; Jacques Proust, 'La Documentation technique de Diderot dans l'*Encyclopédie*', *Revue d'histoire littéraire de la France*, 57 (1957), 335–52; Madeleine Pinault, 'À propos des planches de l'*Encyclopédie*', *SVEC*, 254 (1988), 351–61; Geraldine Sheridan, 'Views of Women at Work by the Royal Academicians: The Collection *Descriptions des arts et métiers* (1761–1789)', *Studies in Eighteenth-Century Culture*, 32 (2003), 155–91.

278 Patte was advertising himself in the *Mercure de France* from 1754 as an engraver with a new method for the better reproduction of architecture. See *MdF* (Feb. 1755), 172–4; (Apr. 1755), 153–4.

279 Patte, 'Dénonciation', pp. 341–2.

280 On the illustrations for the *Description des arts et métiers*, see Martine Jaoul and Madeleine Pinault, 'La Collection "Description des arts et métiers": Étude des sources inédites de la Houghton Library Université Harvard', *Ethnologie française*, 12 (1982), 335–60; Madeleine Pinault Sørensen, 'Les Dessinateurs de l'Académie royale des sciences', in *Règlement, usages et sciences dans la France de l'absolutisme*, Christiane Demeulenaere-Douyère and Éric Brian (eds) (Paris, 2002), pp. 147–67.

281 Patte alleged that Diderot, aware that printmakers habitually kept proofs of all their prints, sought out and suborned Réaumur's engravers (Claude Lucas, namely) and offered them 10 *louis* per person for their works, thereby amassing copies of Réaumur's corpus at a fraction of his cost. Patte claims that Réaumur had invested 100,000 *livres*, naming Lucas as his source. Meanwhile, thanks to Françoise Gardey's research we know that Diderot also borrowed impressions of the *Description des arts et métiers* from the Beringhen collection at the Cabinet des estampes, part of the Bibliothèque du roi. See Françoise Gardey, 'Quelques planches des *Descriptions des arts et métiers* de l'Académie des sciences, au Cabinet des estampes', *NE*, 5–6 (1964), 166–9. Her source, the Garde du Cabinet des estampes de la Bibliothèque du roi, Hugues-Adrien Joly, noted that Réaumur had received a subvention from the king of 12,000 *livres* for the project.

282 Patte, 'Dénonciation', p. 345.

283 Of the company of publishers, Briasson was the one charged with the material business of production and sale. See Frank A. Kafker and Jeff Loveland, 'Antoine-Claude Briasson et l'*Encyclopédie*', *RDE*, 35 (2003), 131–42.

284 From the 'Extrait des régistres de l'Académie royale des sciences: Rapport concernant les planches de l'*Encyclopédie*', quoted from Pierre Patte, 'Lettre de M. Patte, architecte à M. Fréron', *Année littéraire* (1760), no. 1, 246–57 at 251.

285 Patte, 'Lettre de M. Patte', p. 245.

286 *MdF* (Jan. 1760), 176.

287 See esp. George B. Watts, 'The *Encyclopédie* and the *Descriptions des arts et métiers*', *French Review*, 25 (1952), 444–54; Maurice Daumas and René Tresse, 'La *Description des arts et métiers* de l'Académie des sciences et le sort de ses planches gravées en taille douce', *Revue d'histoire des sciences et de leurs applications*, 7 (1954), 163–71; Huard, 'Les Planches de l'*Encyclopédie*; Proust, 'La Documentation technique'.

288 For this purpose Diderot may have recruited new draughtsmen. See Madeleine Pinault Sørensen, 'Sur un collaborateur énigmatique de l'*Encyclopédie*: Jean-Michel Moreau, dit le jeune', *RDE*, 43 (2008), 2–6.

289 Gardey, 'Quelques planches des *Descriptions*'.

290 Bibliothèque de l'Institut, Ms. 1064, XX(A), XX(B). Patte's critique is to be found in his advance review of Duhamel de Monceau's *L'Art du Charbonnier* (Paris, 1761) in *Année littéraire* (1760), no. 8, 51–60 at 59. Patte reworked Lucas's engraving for Duhamel's text, but, as Françoise Gardey has noted, he was careful, in light of the *affaire des plagiaires*, to sign the plate 'Patte Correxit 1760'. Gardey, 'Quelques planches des *Descriptions*', p. 168.

291 Patte, 'Lettre de M. Patte'; *Année littéraire* (1760), no. 6, 192–203; *Année littéraire* (1760), no. 8, 51–61.

292 *L'Observateur littéraire*, 5 (1759), 216; *MdF* (Jan. 1760), 176.

293 Diderot and d'Alembert, *Encyclopédie*, vol. 5, p. 365.

294 Ibid.

295 'Particulier' here is both the opposite of 'general' and the opposite of 'public'.

296 Diderot expressed this view in the complementary and not unrelated entry 'Éclectisme'; see *Encyclopédie*, vol. 5, pp. 283–4. The text of the *Encyclopédie* alone consisted of 71,818 articles written by some 160 authors.

297 The point is made specifically with respect to the dispersed publications of the Académie royale des sciences; see 'Encyclopédie', in Diderot and d'Alembert, *Encyclopédie*, vol. 5, p. 635a.

298 'Receuil', in Diderot and d'Alembert, *Encyclopédie*, vol. 13, pp. 868–9. For a wider-ranging account of the meanings of *recueil* in the 18th century, see Jean-Gérald Castex, 'D'un mot et de ses usages: Le Recueil gravé', in *À l'origine du livre d'art: Les Recueils d'estampes comme entreprise éditoriale en Europe, XVIe–XVIIIe siècles*, Cordélia Hattori, Estelle Leutrat and Véronique Meyer (eds) (Milan, 2010), pp. 141–9.

299 A distinction should, however, be made between the interior decorations of the book and the volumes of plates – that is, between the woodcut ornament and the engraved frontispiece on the one hand and the illustrations on the other. The first were designed and executed by some of the same artists involved in the *Fables*; indeed, Papillon's figure of Apollo for the title-page, dated 1747, indicates his prior involvement with that project. But neither he nor Cochin was much employed in the realisation of the *Recueil*.

300 The original intention had been to increase the number and quality of illustrations in Ephraim Chambers's *Cyclopaedia* (1728), of which the *Encyclopédie* was to have been a translation; Chambers's 19 were to have been increased to 120. On the relation of the *Encyclopédie* to Chambers's earlier publication see Proust, *Diderot et l'Encyclopédie*, pp. 45, 47; Philip Stewart, 'Illustrations encyclopédiques: De la *Cyclopaedia* à l'*Encyclopédie*', *RDE*, 12 (1992), 71–98.

301 Madeleine Pinault, 'Diderot et les illustrateurs de l'*Encyclopédie*', *Revue de l'art*, 66 (1984), 17–38; Madeleine Pinault, 'À propos des planches de l'*Encyclopédie*'. For a more positive evaluation of the plates see François Moureau, *Le Vrai Roman de l'Encyclopédie* (Paris, 2001). Rare were those like Harguiniez who had had an academic training (see Madeleine Pinault Sørensen, 'Harguiniez: Élève de l'Académie royale de peinture et de sculpture et dessinateur pour l'*Encyclopédie*', *RDE*, 44 (2009), 229–33); most of the *dessinateurs* and engravers employed more than occasionally on the illustrations of the *Encyclopédie* were from artisanal backgrounds. Goussier has even been described as the one working-class collaborator on its text and its illustrations. On Goussier see Georges Dulac, 'Louis-Jacques Goussier, Encyclopédiste et "original sans principes"', *Recherches nouvelles sur quelques écrivains des Lumières*, Jacques Proust (ed.) (Geneva, 1972), pp. 63–110. For a collective dictionary of

those involved see Frank A. Kafker and Madeleine Pinault Sørensen, 'Notices sur les collaborateurs du Recueil de planches de l'*Encyclopédie*', *RDE*, 18–19 (1995), 201–30.

302 For the 2,885 plates only 43 drawings are known to have survived. Those by Goussier at the Conservatoire national des arts et métiers were deposited by the artist himself. On drawings produced for the plates in the wake of the scandal, see Dorothy P. Arthur and David Smith, 'Sur un collaborateur énigmatique de l'Encyclopédie: Jean-Michel Moreau dit le jeune', *RDE*, 43 (2008), 145–57. De Montenault was meanwhile offering to sell Oudry's drawings to the king for 30,000 *livres*. See BnF, Mss. n.a.f. 3345, fol. 381 (undated memorandum sent by de Montenault to Malesherbes).

303 Desgerantins had produced six drawings in all. On the two discussed here see Madeleine Pinault Sørensen, 'À propos des planches de l'*Encyclopédie*', *RDE*, 15 (1993), 143–52.

304 It is rarely possible to identify those involved in any given instance. In the case of Chaufourier's drawing of charcoal manufacture for the *Description*, we know his design to have been based on a drawing by *père* Sébastien Truchet, and informed by members of the Académie royale des sciences. In the case of Desgerantins's design, those participating included Diderot and possibly the author of the *Encyclopédie*'s text article 'Plumassier'. On the composite and collaborative nature of such illustrations, see Madeleine Pinault Sørensen, 'La Fabrique de l'*Encyclopédie*', in *Tous les savoirs du monde: Encyclopédies et bibliothèques, de Sumer au XXIe siècle*, exh. cat., Bibliothèque nationale de France, Paris, Roland Schaer (ed.) (Paris, 1996), p. 237, no. 10.

305 In a letter of 23 Feb. 1756 to the *philosophe* and cleric Johann Heinrich Samuel Formey, Réaumur claimed to have experienced the plagiarism himself as a personal loss. See Proust, *Diderot et l'Encyclopédie*, p. 189.

306 'Discours préliminaire', in Diderot and d'Alembert, *Encyclopédie*, vol. 1, p. xl.

307 Denis Reynaud, 'Pour une théorie de la description au 18e siècle', *Dix-huitième siècle*, 22 (1990), 347–66.

308 Diderot and d'Alembert, *Encyclopédie*, vol. 4, p. 878.

309 Ibid., p. 879.

310 Ibid., p. 878. I have, for my own different purposes, very crudely summarised the complex and evolving relation between description and definition patiently and subtly tracked by Reynaud, 'Pour une théorie'. We can note that Daubenton, who was from 1745 *garde-démonstrateur* in natural history in the section of the Cabinet du roi at the Jardin royal des plantes, may have collaborated on volume 6 of the plates; see Kafker and Pinault Sørenesen, 'Notices', p. 210.

311 'Discours préliminaire', in Diderot and d'Alembert, *Encyclopédie*, vol. 1, pp. xxxix–xli.

312 Georges-Louis Leclerc, comte de Buffon, *intendant* of the Jardin royal des plantes, argued that, in scientific projects, 'il faut tâcher d'arriver à ce haut degré de connoissances où nous pouvons juger que les effets particuliers dépendent d'effets plus généraux, où nous pouvons comparer la nature avec elle-même dans ses grandes opérations.' See Alain-Marie Bassy, 'Typographie, topographie, "outopo-graphie": L'Illustration scientifique et technique au XVIIIe siècle', in *Die Buchillustration im 18. Jahrhundert* (Heidelberg, 1980), pp. 206–33 at p. 209.

313 Françoise Teynac, Pierre Nolot and Jean-Denis Vivien, *Wallpaper: A History* (London, 1982), pp. 28–34.

314 'Marbreur de papier', in Diderot and d'Alembert, *Encyclopédie*, vol. 10, pp. 72–4. See also Richard J. Wolfe, *Marbled Paper: Its History, Techniques and Patterns* (Philadelphia, 1990), 32–47.

315 Tellingly, in the article 'Dictionnaire' in the *Encyclopédie*, d'Alembert compares the writing of an encyclopaedic dictionary to the description of a complex machine: 'on commenceroit par *démonter* cette machine, pour en faire voir *séparément & distinctement* toutes les pièces', and thereafter one would explain the relation of the *parties* one to another but 'sans même être obligé de la remonter'; Diderot and d'Alembert, *Encyclopédie*, vol. 4, p. 968. At the level of particular arts, Goussier pursued those strategies of deconstruction and analysis visually that Diderot and d'Alembert championed textually for the dictionary as a whole.

316 Jacques-André Naigeon, *Mémoires historiques et philosophiques sur la vie et les ouvrages de Diderot* (Paris, 1821), p. 70, on Diderot as exceptionally gifted, drawing the most 'results' from eclectic knowledge.

317 Diderot and d'Alembert, *Encyclopédie*, vol. 5, pp. 284–5. In the article 'Éclectisme', Diderot argues for the foundation of an academy of the mechanical trades, sponsored by the state, precisely to advance knowledge by the critical record and analysis of their arts.

318 Daniel Rosenberg, 'An Eighteenth-Century Time Machine: The Encyclopedia of Denis Diderot', in *Postmodernism and the Enlightenment: New Perspectives in Eighteenth-Century French Intellectual History*, Daniel Gordon (ed.) (New York and London, 2001), pp. 45–66.

319 'Système figuré des connoissances humaines', in Diderot and d'Alembert, *Encyclopédie*, vol. 1, unpaginated.

320 'Encyclopédie', in Diderot and d'Alembert, *Encyclopédie*, vol. 5, p. 645.

321 'Plagiarisme, ou selon d'autres Plagiat', in Diderot and d'Alembert, *Encyclopédie*, vol. 12, p. 679.

322 The *vignettes* had in fact been drawn by Lucotte and survive at the Cooper Hewitt, Smithsonian Design Museum, New York.

323 Denis Diderot, *Diderot Salons*, ed. Jean Seznec and Jean Adhémar, 4 vols (Oxford, 1957–67), vol. 3, Salon 1767, p. 279.

324 'Encyclopédie', in Diderot and d'Alembert, *Encyclopédie*, vol. 5, pp. 365–6. The matter of the dictionary of the Académie française, whose 25 privileges had prevented the publication of other French dictionaries at the end of the 17th century, had been a key issue in the dispute between the Paris booksellers and their provincial counterparts. See *Mémoire sur la contestation qui est entre les libraires de Paris et ceux de Lyon au sujet des privilèges et des continuations que le roy accorde pour l'impression des livres*, in *PSC*, France, 1690s. On Diderot's critique of *Le Dictionnaire de l'Académie françoise* (Paris, 1694) see Rosenberg, 'An Eighteenth-Century Time Machine', pp. 51–2.

325 On the matter of disclosure and secrecy in the mechanical arts see Denis Diderot, *L'Histoire et le secret de la peinture en cire* (Paris, 1755); and see, at greater length, chapter 4.

326 Diderot and d'Alembert, *Encyclopédie*, vol. 12, p. 680.

327 Bernard Siegfried Albinus, *Tabulae sceleti et musculorum corporis humani* (Leyden, 1747); Govert Bidloo, *Anatomia humani corporis* (Amsterdam, 1685); Andreas Vesalius, *De humani corporis fabrica libri septem* (1543).

328 Jean Le Rond d'Alembert, *Dictionnaire de synonymes en langue françoise*, cited in Émile Littré, 'Continuation', *Dictionnaire de la langue française*: 'On donne continuation de l'ouvrage d'un autre et la suite au sien' (<littre.reverso.net/dictionnaire-francais/auteur/d'alembert/39>, accessed 9 Jan. 2017).

329 *Déclaration du roy, concernant les privilèges en fait de commerce*, 24 Dec. 1762, in *PSC*, France, 1762, and Frédéric Rideau's commentary.

330 Pinault, 'Diderot et les illustrateurs'.

331 For the bee as an image or metaphor of imitation, see George W. Pigman III, 'Versions of Imitation in the Renaissance', *Renaissance Quarterly*, 33 (1980), 1–32. On 18th-century borrowings from the *Recueil* see Madeleine Pinault, 'Les Métamorphoses des planches de l'*Encyclopédie*: Quelques questions', *RDE*, 12 (1992) 99–112; Raymond Birn, 'Words and Pictures: Diderot's Vision and Publishers: Perceptions of Popular and Learned Culture in the *Encyclopédie*', in *Popular Traditions and Learned Culture in France from the Sixteenth to the Twentieth Centuries*, M. Bertrand (ed.) (Saratoga, NY, 1985), pp. 73–92.

332 Diderot, *Lettre sur le commerce de la librairie*.
333 Ibid., pp. 37–39, 41, 51, 59, for La Fontaine.
334 It was, in fact, renewed in the 1770s; see Rideau, 'Commentary on the La Fontaine case (1761)', in *PSC*, France, 1761.
335 'Droit de copie', in Diderot and d'Alembert, *Encyclopédie*, vol. 5, pp. 146–7.
336 Benjamin, 'Critique of Violence'.
337 On first possession, see Rose, *Property and Persuasion*, pp. 11–23. See Proust, *Diderot et l'Encyclopédie*, pp. 434–5, on the feudal nature of this story of property, as opposed to the story of its institutionalisation advanced by Locke.
338 Gaultier de Biauzat appears to allude to the *Encyclopédie* affair in his 1776 memorandum on privilege, when he argues against its use in relation to scientific publications and the establishment of facts through research and direct observation. See Jean-François Gaultier de Biauzat, *Mémoire à consulter pour le libraires et imprimeurs de Lyon, Rouen, Toulouse, Marseille et Nîmes* (1776), in *PSC*, France, 1776, p. 32.
339 Paul Oskar Kristeller, 'The Modern System of the Arts' (1951–2), repr. in *Renaissance Thought*, vol. 2: *Papers on Humanism and the Arts* (New York, 1965), pp. 163–227. For a recent critical debate on this foundational text see James I. Porter, 'Is Art Modern? Kristeller's "Modern System of the Arts" Reconsidered', *British Journal of Aesthetics*, 49 (2009), 1–24; Peter Kivy, 'What Really Happened in the Eighteenth Century: The "Modern System" Re-Examined (Again)', *British Journal of Aesthetics*, 52 (2012), 61–74.
340 *Représentations et observations en forme de mémoire sur l'état ancien et actuel de la librairie, ses règlements, ses privilèges et autres objets relatifs à son commerce et aux gens de lettres, présentées à M. de Sartine, Maître des requêtes, Directeur général de la librairie et imprimerie, par les syndics et adjoints en charge au mois de mars 1764* (1764), in *PSC*, France, 1764. Malesherbes had left office when his father, Chancelier Guillaume de Lamoignon de Blancmesnil, was exiled in 1763.
341 Diderot, *Lettre sur le commerce de la librairie*. On the history of the two texts see Louis Brunel, 'Observations critiques et littéraires sur un opuscule de Diderot', *Revue d'histoire littéraire de France*, 10 (1903), 1–24; Jacques Proust, 'Pour servir à une edition de la *Lettre sur le commerce de la librairie*', *Diderot Studies*, 3 (1961), 321–45; and most recently, Isabelle C. Demarte, 'Détournements d'auteur: Les Surprises de l'épistolarité dans la *Lettre sur le commerce de la librairie* de Denis Diderot', in *Architecture, Cultural History, Autobiography*, Jonathan Mallinson (ed.), Studies on Voltaire and the Eighteenth Century (Oxford, 2008), 127–66; and Isabelle C. Demarte, 'Échanges à trois: Les Dessous romanesques de la *Lettre sur le commerce de la librairie*', *RDE*, 43 (2008), 71–90.
342 Rideau, 'Commentary on the La Fontaine case (1761)', in *PSC*, France, 1761.
343 *Représentations et observations*, in *PSC*, France, 1764, pp. 74–5.
344 Ibid., pp. 53–4.
345 Diderot, *Lettre sur le commerce de la librairie*, p. 43.
346 *Représentations et observations*, in *PSC*, France, 1764, pp. 63, 66, 68–9, 71–2. Opposition arose from the Parlements, both in Paris and the provinces.
347 Ibid., pp. 56, 58, 65, 67, 68, 74, 87–8, etc. For context see Jean-Claude Perrot, 'L'Économie politique aux XVIIe et XVIIIe siècles (vocabulaire, contenu, postulats)', *Revue européennes des sciences sociales*, 26 (1988), 45–56.
348 *Représentations et observations*, in *PSC*, France, 1764: 'l'homme entreprenant et habile' is contrasted with 'l'homme inepte et rapace' (p. 61); 'l'homme inventif et entreprenant' is juxtaposed with 'la populace du corps' (p. 64).
349 For examples see ibid., p. 73.
350 On the publisher's *fonds* see ibid., pp. 84–5. He also needed a corpus of cheaper publications guaranteed to sell quickly, widely and well in order to offset the slower returns on the greater works. This argument was used to justify the issuance of privilege for books of all kinds.
351 Ibid., p. 94.
352 Montfaucon's was one of the examples cited (ibid., p. 73). According to the preface, it contained approximately 1,120 plates depicting some 3,000–10,000 figures, which were 'd'une utilité merveilleuse'; but the privilege makes no mention of them. The booksellers estimated advance costs on such publications at 100,000 *livres*.
353 Ibid., p. 87.
354 Ibid., pp. 116–17.
355 A note on Sartine's copy, annotated by his assistant, Joseph d'Hémery, an inspector of the book trade, asked rhetorically how, after the example of the Mariette memorandum, the wardens had dared 'repeat the same ideas and leave themselves open to the same punishments?' See Brunel, 'Observations critiques et littéraires', p. 7. D'Hémery's marginal comments consistently advised caution on the question of legislative reform. See [Joseph d'Hémery] (ed.), *Représentations et observations en forme de mémoire sur l'état ancien & présent de la librairie et particulièrement sur la propriété des privilèges, présentées à M. de Sartine par les syndics et adjoints, et au marge les observations que M. Marin a faites sur chaque article d'après les notes instructives que je lui ai remises par ordre du magistrat*, BnF, Mss. f.f. 22183, *passim*.
356 Thierry Rigogne, *Between State and the Market: Printing and Bookselling in Eighteenth-Century France*, Studies on Voltaire and the Eighteenth Century (Oxford, 2007), pp. 18–20.
357 Roger Chartier, 'L'Imprimerie en France à la fin de l'ancien régime: L'État général des imprimeurs de 1777', *Revue français de l'histoire du livre*, 3 (1973), 253–79.
358 The concept of 'governmental rationality' and the neologism 'governmentality' are Michel Foucault's. See Foucault, 'Governmentality', in *The Foucault Effect*.
359 Foucault, 'Leçon du 17 janvier 1979', in *Naissance de la biopolitique*. On the usefulness of the concept of governmentality in the case of law, see Nikolas Pose, Pat O'Malley and Mariana Valverde, 'Governmentality', *Annual Review of Law Society and Social Science*, 2 (2006), 83–104.
360 Simon Clicquot-Blervache, *Considérations sur le commerce et en particulier sur les compagnies, sociétés et maîtrises* (Amsterdam, 1758). For context see Simone Meyssonnier, 'Vincent de Gournay (1712–1759) et la "Balance des hommes"', *Population*, 45 (1990), 87–112, esp. 93–100. On physiocracy see T. J. Hochstrasser, 'Physiocracy and the Politics of Laissez-Faire', in *The Cambridge History of Eighteenth-Century Political Thought*, Mark Goldie and Robert Wokler (eds) (Cambridge, 2006), pp. 419–42.
361 Malesherbes contradicted the *libraires*' claim that privilege quickened trade, and argued instead that it was a means of passively harvesting 'fruit' without care or effort, 'as one enjoys a property that returns a vast rent'. See Guillaume-Chrétien de Lamoignon de Malesherbes, *Mémoires sur la librairie, Mémoire sur la liberté de la presse*, ed. Roger Chartier (Paris, 1994), p. 159. On the *Mémoires* see David Pepperkorn, 'Malesherbes on the Rights and Duties of Authors', in *Intellectual Property and Information Law: Essays in Honour of Herman Cohen Jehoram*, Jan J. C. Kabel and Gerard J. H. M. Mom (eds) (The Hague and London, 1998), pp. 223–39.
362 Clicquot-Blervache, *Considérations*, pp. 14–15, 22. The essay opens with the question of relative French weakness in trade by comparison with the free economies of the Netherlands and Britain (pp. 3–4). On 18th-century conceptualisation of growth and the role of governmental intervention see Jean-Yves Grenier, 'La Notion de croissance dans la pensée économique française au 18e siècle (1715–1789)', *Review (Fernand Braudel Center)*, 13 (1990), 499–549, esp. 533–7.
363 Vincent de Gournay's *Remarques*, cited in Meyssonnier, 'Vincent de Gournay', pp. 95–6.

364 Clicquot-Blervache, *Considérations*, p. 49.

365 Foucault, 'Leçon du 17 janvier 1979', pp. 33–4.

366 Complaints about the use of privilege to manipulate the price of books had been made since the beginning of the century. See Blondel, *Mémoire sur les vexations* (n.d. [1725]), in *PSC*, France, 1725–6, p. 3. Such protests were renewed in the 1750s and 1760s. See Rigogne, *Between State and the Market*, ch. 2. The Paris booksellers contested the view that, in the absence of privilege, prices would fall, claiming that if it happened at all, it would be only a momentary drop, and would be followed by bankruptcies. See *Représentations et observations*, pp. 96–7, in *PSC*, France, 1764.

367 Jean-Claude Perrot, 'Premiers aspects de l'équilibre dans la pensée économique française', *Annales: Histoire, sciences sociales*, 38 (1983), 1058–74.

368 See, for example, the acknowledgements made by Claude Bourgelat, inspector of the book trade at Lyon, to Sartine in 'Lettre de M. Bourgelat, inspecteur de la librarie de Lyon à M. de Sartine, 24 décembre, 1763', *Revue d'histoire de Lyon*, 13 (1914), 52–64 at 61.

369 *Représentations et observations*, in *PSC*, France, 1764, p. 103.

370 Henri-Jean Martin, 'La Librairie française en 1777–1778', *Dix-huitième siècle*, 11 (1979), 87–112; Henri-Jean Martin, 'À la veille de la Révolution: Crise et réorganisation de la librairie', in *HEF*, vol. 2, pp. 681–93.

371 Gaultier de Biauzat, *Mémoire à consulter*, p. i.

372 *Arrest du Conseil d'état du roi, portant règlement sur la durée des privileges en librairie*, 30/08/1777, BnF, Mss, f.f. 22073/146, in *PSC*, France, 1777.

373 *Représentations et observations*, in *PSC*, France, 1764.

374 *Arrest du Conseil d'état du roi, portant règlement sur la durée des priviléges en librairie, du 30 août 1777*, in *PSC*, France, 1777, clauses 2 and 6.

375 Foucault, 'Leçon du 17 janvier 1979', 29–47.

376 *Arrest du Conseil d'état du roi… du 30 août 1777*, in *PSC*, France, 1777.

377 Blondel, *Mémoire sur les vexations*, *passim*. Their avarice was manifest especially in their relation to writers and their ignorance in their relation to their journeymen. According to Blondel, 'tout ce qu'ils savent, selon le bon mot d'Arlequin, c'est que le blanc est le papier, & le noir est l'impression' (p. 14).

378 Diderot, *Lettre sur le commerce de la librairie*, pp. 44–5, 60–62. See also Geoffrey Turnovsky, 'Conceptualising the Literary Market: Diderot and the *Lettre sur le commerce de la librairie*', in *Voltaire, Diderot, Demography, Women's Studies, Poètes et versificateurs, the Influence of the Enlightenment*, Studies on Voltaire and the Eighteenth Century (Oxford, 2003), pp. 135–70; Geoffrey Turnovsky, 'The Enlightenment Literary Market: Rousseau, Authorship, and the Book Trade', *Eighteenth-Century Studies*, 36 (2003), 387–410.

379 On the status of the publisher in the later 18th century see Sabine Juratic, 'Du Livre à l'écriture: Libraires-auteurs à l'âge des Lumières en France', *Revue française du livre*, 114–15 (2002), 181–204; Véronique Sarrazin, 'L'Auteur-éditeur de ses œuvres à la fin du XVIIIe siècle: Aspects légaux et économiques', *Travaux de littérature*, 14 (2001), 335–60.

380 Courboin, *L'Estampe française*, ch. 4; Casselle, 'Le Commerce de l'estampe à Paris', ch. 2; Griffiths, *The Print before Photography*, ch. 17.

381 Charles-Nicolas Cochin's *Projet d'arrest du Conseil pour les graveurs*, BnF, Mss. f.f. 22120/68, is marked 'qui m'a été remis par M Cochin. Juin 1764'. The statement is ambiguous. It is not clear whether or nor the proposal was requested.

382 On Cochin's responsibilities, see Michel, *Charles-Nicolas Cochin*, pp. 63–74, 487–505

383 Gabriel Huquier, *Projet en forme de mémoire pour l'assurance et le renouvellement des privilèges accordés à l'art de la gravure en taille-douce, et pour l'établissement d'une commission à l'effet d'empêcher aucune copie ou contrefaçon des ouvrages de gravure en taille-douce quelconque dans toute l'étendue du royaume*, Jan. 1764, BnF, Mss. f.f. 22120/60, fol. 195.

384 *Copie de la saisie fait par les libraires*, BnF, Mss. f.f. 22120/33.

385 *Exposé concernant la saisie faitte par les officiers de la Chambre sindicale des libraires chez M. Ledoux, le 10 janvier 1758*, BnF, Mss. f.f. 22120/35, fol. 96.

386 Huquier, *Projet en forme de mémoire*, BnF, Mss. f.f. 22120/60, fol. 195v.

387 The question of the number of proofs that an engraver could legitimately pull before the print was officially published and the plate handed over to the publisher gave rise to intense debate, because proofs competed directly for the same market as prints themselves. Pirate copies, on the other hand, were aimed at a different market from the original – the popular as distinct from the connoisseurs' market. On the debates about proofs in the 1750s and 1760s, see Antony Griffiths, 'Proofs in Eighteenth-Century French Printmaking', *PQ*, 21 (2004), 3–17.

388 On 9 Apr. 1757, Veuve Chéreau applied for a six-year privilege for a vast miscellany of works published from plates purchased from the stock of Veuve Moulinet, and including military subjects, landscapes, portraits, hunting scenes and topographical views; on 7 Oct. 1757 Gilles Demarteau applied for a ten-year privilege for 'Des livres d'ornemens et de fleurs gravées'; on 7 July 1759 Philippe Lebas obtained a 15-year privilege for 'les traits de l'Histoire universelle sacrée et profane d'après les plus grands Maîtres d'Italie'; and on 12 Dec. 1760 Jacques Rigaud requested a six-year privilege for 'Ses œuvres représentans des vuës des maisons royales, et autres différens paysages, vuës de marine, entrées d'Ambassadeurs, feux d'artifices et autres fêtes'. BnF, Mss. f.f. 21961–21962.

389 Cochin does not once feature in the register of privileges; Huquier appears only once, on 9 Jan. 1738, for unspecified 'desseins pour la gravure'. See Fuhring, 'The Print Privilege, I', 181.

390 The proposed update of Charles Perrault's *Les Hommes illustres de France* appears not to have been published at all. The application was made by the collector and amateur La Live de Jully. The other was for Pierre Patte's *Monumens érigés en France à la gloire de Louis XV* (Paris, 1765).

391 On 6 Feb. 1764 Charles-Antoine Jombert applied to renew privileges on five titles: Jacques-François Blondel's *Architecture françoise*, Augustin-Charles Daviler's *Cours d'architecture*, François Tortebat's *Abrégé d'anatomie accommodé aux arts de peinture et de sculpture*, Sébastien Leclerc's *Pratique de la géométrie*, and Alexandre Le Blond's *La Théorie et la pratique du jardinage*. BnF, Mss. f.f. 21963.

392 *Exposé du sieur Basan et autres ses confrères graveurs en taille-douce contre la communauté des libraires, Septembre 1757*, BnF, Mss. f.f. 22076/73; published first by William McAllister Johnson, 'Documents', *NE*, 45 (1979), 10–11. See also Fuhring, 'The Print Privilege, I', 178.

393 Fuhring 'The Print Privilege, I', 178. To put these costs in context, at mid-century Pierre-François Basan estimated the cost of a copper plate at 20–24 *livres*. Even with additional costs of ink, paper, printing and design, the cost of production was significantly below the cost of the privilege.

394 *Mémoire concernant la gravure*, BnF, Mss. f.f. 22120/35. A marginal note gives the date 7 Oct. 1757: 'C'est Simon la médaille [Claude-François Simon] qui est l'auteur de cette mémoire qui a été donnée à M. Malesherbes dans la vue de se procurer la censure [de la gravure].' He calls such privileges 'purement imaginaires' (fol. 88v).

395 Gaultier de Biauzat, *Mémoire à consulter*, in *PSC*, France, 1776, p. 45.

396 One of the last to incorporate particular praise of the author was the privilege granted in 1724 to Charles-Antoine Coypel

'de l'Académie Royale de Peinture et de Sculpture, Peintre de nostre tres cher & tres amé oncle le duc d'Orléans', for his 'Tableaux sur l'histoire de Don Quichotte... qui ont eu tout le succes qu'on pourroit en attendre'. Thus 'voulant marquer aud. Coypel nostre estime et le mettre en estat de donner au public des ouvrages dont l'Excellence et la beauté meritent son applaudissement & ses éloges', the king granted him a 12-year privilege and set fines for infraction at 10,000 *livres*. BnF, Mss. f.f. 21952.

397 Only a handful of other painters made such applications in the second half of the 18th century. On 28 Aug. 1767 Jean-Jacques Bachelier applied for a six-year privilege for 'Une suite d'Études de desseins de toutes sortes de genre de sa Composition', BnF, Mss. f.f. 21964. On 30 Oct. 1769, Nicolas-François Regnault applied also for a six-year privilege for *La Botanique mise à porté de tout le monde*, realised with his sister Geneviève de Nagis Regnault, ibid. And on 27 Mar. 1772 the widow of Pierre-Antoine Baudoin applied for a six-year privilege for reproductions of her husband's *Le Lever de la mariée* and *La Toilette*, in the wake of the success of Jean-Michel Moreau *le jeune*'s engraving of *Le Coucher de la nouvelle mariée*, for which he obtained a privilege on 16 Oct. 1770 (BnF, Mss, f.f. 21965). On 1 Dec. 1778 the printmaker Moreau *le jeune* applied for a ten-year privilege for 'Des ouvrages Définis et gravés de sa composition', BnF, Mss. f.f. 21968. On 13 June 1780 Jacques Gamelin applied for a one-year privilege for his *Nouveau recueil d'ostéologie et myologie* (Toulouse, 1779), BnF, Mss. f.f. 21968. And on 26 June 1789 Philibert-Louis Debucourt applied for a ten-year privilege for two scenes for *Annette et Lubin* and for *Le Bon Papa avec son enfant* and its pendant, BnF, Mss. f.f. 21971.

398 On Babuty, see the entry in Frédéric Barbier, Sabine Juratic and Annick Mellerio, *Dictionnaire des imprimeurs et gens de livre à Paris, 1701–1789*, vol. 1: *A–C* (Geneva, 2007).

399 For an example where the address is especially prominent, see Jean-Jacques Flipart after Jean-Baptiste Greuze, *Jeune fille qui pleure son oiseau mort* (1766), where Greuze's address is centred immediately below the coat of arms of the duchesse de Grammont.

400 See, for example, *MdF* (1 Apr. 1767) p. 142 (*Le Paralytique*, engraved by Jean-Jacques Flipart), Greuze's address is rue Sorbonne; *MdF* (1 Apr. 1770) p. 187 (*L'Accordée de village*, engraved by Jen-Baptiste Tilliard), Greuze's address is rue Pavée; *MdF* (Apr. 1781) pp. 187–8 (*La Belle-mère*, engraved by Jean-Charles Le Vasseur), Greuze's address is Rue Notre Dame des Victoires.

401 *MdF* (Apr. 1767), vol. 2, 139–42.

402 Pierre-Étienne Moitte's reproductions of Greuze's *Le Donneur de sérénade* and *La Paresseuse* were each advertised at 3 *livres* (*MdF* (Apr. 1765), vol. 1, 174–5), and Pierre-Charles Ingouf's engraving after Greuze's *Petite Fille tenant un capucin de bois* was priced at 1 *livre* 4 *sous* (*Avant-coureur* (16 June 1766), 370). These were all, of course, much smaller works.

403 Pierre-Jean Mariette, *Abecedario de P. J. Mariette*, ed. Philippe de Chennevières and Anatole de Montaiglon, 6 vols (Paris, 1853–62), vol. 2, p. 331.

404 The occasion was Greuze's divorce from his wife. Among his grievances against her, he listed her alleged appropriation of the income from his prints. The figure, which he acknowledged was only a rough estimate, is likely therefore to be on the high side. See Philippe de Chennevières, 'Mémoire de Greuze contre sa femme', *AAF*, 2 (1852–3), 153–72 at 163.

405 On Greuze's partnerships with his engravers and the terms for sharing profits and losses, see Maurice Tourneux, 'Greuze et ses graveurs', *Courrier de l'art* (11 Oct. 1883), 485–87; Henri Macqueron, 'Procès d'artistes', *Bulletin de la Société d'émulation d'Abbeville*, 8 (1911), 315–20; Georges Wildenstein, 'Quelques documents sur Greuze', *GBA*, 56 (1960), 227–34; Françoise Arquié-Bruley, 'Documents notaires sur Greuze', *BSHAF* (1981), 125–54.

406 *Lettres d'un voyageur à Paris, à son ami Sir Charles Lovers, demeurant à Londres: Sur les nouvelles estampes de Monsieur Greuze* (London, 1779), p. 37.

407 *Lettres d'un voyageur*, p. 68. Flipart is criticised for his 'extrême docilité' in acquiescing to Greuze's demands. Greuze is portrayed as imposing his artistic identity, in a reversal of the classic topos of the printmaker voluntarily assuming the artist's identity.

408 *Lettres d'un voyageur*, pp. 14–15, on the sameness of Greuze's figures, as if they were all from the same family, and for the criticism that he failed to understand how details of colour are translated in print; see *Lettres d'un voyageur*, p. 68, for the reproduction of Greuze's prints as if after grisaille.

409 *Diderot Salons*, vol. 1, p. 236.

410 Ibid., pp. 229–30. The subject was taken from Jean-François Marmontel's hugely successful *Contes moraux* (1761). At the 1767 Salon Diderot remarked in more general terms on the folly of patrons – here, a poet prescribing compositions to artists: in this instance, Saint-Lambert's commission of illustrations for his poem *Les Saisons*. See *Diderot Salons*, vol. 3, pp. 108–9.

411 Huquier, *Projet en forme de mémoire*, BnF, Mss. f.f. 22120/60, fols 198v–199r.

412 Jean-François Forty, *Livre d'orfèvrerie* (n.d.), 13 Dec. 1765, BnF, Mss. f.f. 21963; Jean Lamour, *Recueil des ouvrages en serrurerie que Stanislas le Bienfaisant, roy de Pologne, duc de Lorraine et de Bar a fait posés sur la place royale de Nancy* (1767), 11 Jan. 1768, BnF, Mss. f.f. 21963; Jean-Charles Delafosse, *Nouvelle Iconologie historique* (1768), 24 Feb. 1768, BnF, Mss. f.f. 21963.

413 Cochin, *Projet d'arrest*, BnF, Mss. f.f. 22120/68.

414 Huquier, *Projet en forme de mémoire*, BnF, Mss. f.f. 22120/60, fol. 195v.

415 *Arrest du Conseil d'état du roi ... du 30 août 1777*, in *PSC*, France, 1777, art. 5.

416 Jean-Luc Nancy, *Le Regard du portrait* (Paris, 2000).

417 Jean-Michel Moreau *le jeune* on 1 Dec. 1779 for 'Des Ouvrages définis et gravés de sa composition', BnF, Mss. f.f. 21968; Nicolas de Launay on 20 Feb. 1784 for prints after Étienne Aubry, Jean-Honoré Fragonard, Nicolas Lavreince and Antoine Borel, BnF, Mss. f.f. 21969; Noël Le Mire on 9 July 1784 for a portrait of La Fayette after Jean-Baptiste Le Paon, BnF, Mss. f.f. 21969; Nicolas Ponce on 26 Mar. 1785 for 'ses œuvres', BnF, Mss. f.f. 21969; Jean-François Janinet on 27 Jan. 1787 for 'une Collection d'estampes représentans différens sujets d'après Lavreince', BnF, Mss. f.f. 21970; Philibert-Louis Debucourt on 26 June 1798 for *Annette et Lubin*, BnF, Mss. f.f. 21971.

418 Of particular note are: the Le Campion brothers' application on 1 May 1781 for a privilege for their prints *Le Repas de la Rosière* and *Le Couronnement de la Rosière*, BnF, Mss. f.f. 21968; the British painter George Carter's application on 19 July 1781 for his prints *The Battle between HMS Quebec and the French Frigate La Surveillante, 6 October 1779*, and *The Death of Captain Cook*, BnF, Mss. f.f. 21968; Charles-François Macret's application on 28 June 1782 for a privilege for *L'Arrivée de J. J. Rousseau au Champs Élisées* and *La ville de Beauvais assiégée et défendue par Jeanne Hachette* after Jean-Jacques Le Barbier, BnF, Mss. f.f. 21968; and Louis-Charles Ruotte's application for a privilege for *Vénus parée par les Grâces* by Francesco Bartolozzi, BnF, Mss. f.f. 21969.

419 Claude-François Berthelot, *La Mécanique appliquée aux arts, aux manufactures, à l'agriculture et à la guerre*, 2 vols (Paris, 1782), 21 Oct. 1781, BnF, Mss, f.f. 21968; Jean-Pierre Simon, *Les Figures des Fables de La Fontaine*, 6 vols (1787), 7 Dec. 1784, BnF, Mss, f.f. 21969.

420 See BnF, Mss, f.f. 21968, 5 Jan. 1781, for *Antiquités étrusques, grecques et romaines* (Paris, 1785); BnF, Mss, f.f. 21969, 3 June 1785, for *Histoire de Russie, représentée par figures* (Paris, 1785); BnF, Mss, f.f. 21969, 20 June 1786, for *Le Muséum de Florence*.

421 Cochin expressed the view in a memorandum drawn up in a later case over the publication of Ignatius Mouradgea d'Ohsson's *Le Tableau général de l'empire Othoman*, 3 vols (Paris 1788–1820). See Christian Michel, '*Le Tableau général de l'empire Othoman*: Une Entreprise de gravure à la veille de la Révoution', *NE*, 84 (1985), 6–25.
422 *Copie de la lettre écrite le 12 mars 1774 par le Sr Jombert père, libraire à Paris, au Sieur Robert, libraire à Toulouse*, BnF, Ms f.f. 22127/116.
423 Charles-Nicolas Cochin to Jean-Baptiste Descamps, 27 Nov. 1777, see Christian Michel, 'Lettres adressées par Charles-Nicolas Cochin fils à Jean-Baptiste Descamps, 1757–1790', *AAF*, 28 (1986), 30–32 (Lettre XXXII). On the correspondence see also Aude Henry-Gobert, 'La Correspondance de Jean-Baptiste Descamps: De l'intérêt partagé au réseau de solidarité (1738–1791), in *Réseaux de correspondance à l'âge classique (XVIe–XVIIIe siècles)*, Pierre-Yves Beaurepaire, Jens Häseler and Antony McKenna (eds) (Saint-Étienne, 2006), pp. 301–18. On Jombert see Catherine Bousquet-Bressolier, 'Charles-Antoine Jombert (1712–1784): Un Libraire entre sciences et arts', *Bulletin du bibliophile*, 2 (1997), 299–333. On Jombert's other son, Claude-Antoine Jombert, see Annie Parent-Charon, 'Quel public pour le livre maritime dans le Paris du XVIIIe siècle? Le Livre maritime chez Claude-Antoine Jombert', in *Le Livre maritime au siècle des Lumières*, Annie Charon, Thierry Claerr and François Moureau (eds) (Paris, 2005), pp. 85–98.
424 In the case of Cochin, *Lettre sur les peintures d'Herculanum* (1751), *Voyage pittoresque d'Italie* (1756), *Projet d'une salle de spectacle* (1765), *Réponse de M. Jérôme* (1769), etc.; in the case of Descamps, *La Vie des peintres flamands, allemands et hollandois* (1753–64).
425 Michel, *Charles-Nicolas Cochin*, pp. 103, 104. Jacqmin was the king's jeweller.
426 Cochin to Descamps, 27 Nov. 1777, in Michel, 'Lettres', p. 31 (Lettre XXXI).
427 Ibid., pp. 31–32.
428 'Encyclopédie', in Diderot and d'Alembert, *Encyclopédie*, vol. 5, p. 636.
429 Cochin to Descamps, 27 Nov. 1777, in Michel, 'Lettres', p. 31 (Lettre XXXI).
430 Cochin to Descamps, 16 June 1778, in Michel, 'Lettres', p. 41 (Lettre XLI).
431 Ibid.
432 Cochin later offered to send Pluquet's first and second letters to Descamps. See Cochin to Descamps, undated, in Michel, 'Lettres', p. 39 (Lettre XXXVII).
433 François-André-Adrien Pluquet, *Lettre à un ami sur les arrêts du Conseil du 30 août 1777 concernant la librairie et l'imprimerie* (Paris, 1778), in *PSC*, France, 1778. Surprisingly, perhaps, given Simon-Nicolas-Henri Linguet's interest in the arts, Cochin did not mention his slightly earlier pamphlet. Cochin was suspicious of Linguet's radicalism. See Cochin to Descamps, 30 Jan. 1772, in Michel, 'Lettres', p. 19 (Lettre XIII).
434 Pluquet, *Lettre à un ami*, *PSC*, France, 1778.
435 Jean Quéniart, *L'Imprimerie et la librairie à Rouen au XVIIIe siècle* (Paris, 1969), pp. 172–8; Robert L. Dawson, 'The French Book Trade and the "Permission Simple" of 1777: Copyright and Public Domain', *SVEC*, 301 (1992), 18–60. For complaints from Rouen in 1776 see Gaultier de Biauzat, *Mémoire à consulter*, in *PSC*, France, 1776.
436 Cochin to Descamps, 20 Jan. 1778, in Michel, 'Lettres', p. 33 (Lettre, XXXIV).
437 Ibid., p. 34.
438 Cochin to Descamps, 27 Nov. 1777, in Michel, 'Lettres', p. 32 (Lettre XXXI). On Cochin's role as censor see Richard Wrigley, 'Censorship and Anonymity in Eighteenth-Century French Art Criticism', *OAJ*, 6 (1983), 17–28.
439 By the *Décret de la Convention nationale du dix-neuf juillet 1793 relatif aux droits de propriété des auteurs d'écrits en tout genre, des compositeurs de musique, des peintres et des dessinateurs*, the duration of the author's right when ceded to a publisher was the life of the author plus ten years (instead of the lifetime of the author), or ten years, whichever was the longer.

CHAPTER 2
EMULATION: Privilege and plagiarism

1 *P-V*, vol. 8, pp. 287–8.
2 Daniel McClean, 'Piracy and Authorship in Contemporary Art and the Artistic Commonwealth', in *Copyright and Piracy: An Interdisciplinary Critique*, Lionel Bently, Jennifer Davis and Jane C. Ginsburg (eds) (Cambridge, 2010), pp. 311–39.
3 Antoine Furetière, 'Émulation', in *Dictionnaire universel*, 2nd edn, 3 vols (The Hague, 1701), vol. 1: 'Noble jalouise entre les gens de sçavoir ou de vertu, qui les font disputer à qui acquerera plus de gloire.'
4 This was so even when the patron was responsible for commissioning the copy, as was often the case in the 17th and 18th centuries. For an example of commissioned copies see Daniel Conström's account of his transaction with Jean Berain over a design for a border, Cronström, letter to Nicodemus Tessin *le jeune*, 20 Sept. 1696 in *L'Art en France et en Suède, 1693–1718: Extraits d'une correspondance entre l'architecte Nicodème Tessin le jeune et Daniel Cronström*, Roger-Armand Weigert and Carl Hernmarck (eds) (Stockholm, 1964), p. 148.
5 On personhood and property, see Margaret Jane Radin, *Reinterpreting Property* (Chicago and London, 1993), pp. 35–71.
6 Furetière, 'Plagiaire', in *Dictionnaire universel*, vol. 3: 'C'est l'épithète qu'on donne aux Auteurs qui prenn[ent] effrontément les ouvrages d'autrui pour se les appliquer, et s'en attribuer la gloire.'
7 This point is made by Marilyn Randall in *Pragmatic Plagiarism: Authorship, Profit and Power* (Toronto and London, 2001), esp. pp. 99–125.
8 For the view promoting the relationship between the origins of copyright and Romanticism, see Randall, *Pragmatic Plagiarism*; see also Michel Schneider, *Voleurs de mots: Essai sur le plagiat, la psychanalyse et la pensée* (Paris, 1985); Tilar Mazzeo, *Plagiarism and Literary Property in the Romantic Period* (Philadelphia, 2007); Marie Darrieussecq, *Rapport de police: Accusations de plagiat et autres modes de surveillance de la fiction* (Paris, 2010).
9 Abraham Bosse, *De la manière de graver à l'eau forte et au burin. Et de la gravure en manière noire*, with additions by Charles-Nicolas Cochin *fils* (Paris, 1745), pp. 97–9, 106–17.
10 On the Académie engravers see Christian Michel, 'Les Graveurs à l'Académie royale de peinture et de sculpture au XVIIIe siècle', in *L'Estampe au Grand Siècle: Études offertes à Maxime Préaud*, Peter Fuhring, Barbara Brejon de Lavergnée, Marianne Grivel, Séverine Lepape and Véronique Meyer (eds) (Paris, 2010), pp. 483–92.
11 They included Jean Audran, Nicolas-Dauphin de Beauvais at the Image de Saint-Nicolas, François I Chéreau at the Deux Piliers d'or, Pierre Drevet at L'Annonciation, Gaspard Duchange at the Deux Anges couronnés, Gérard Edelinck at the Séraphin, Edme Jeaurat at the Livre d'or and Jean de Poilly at the Belle Image. See Préaud, *DEE*.
12 Walter Benjamin, 'The Work of Art in the Age of Mechanical Reproduction' (1936), repr. in *Illuminations*, ed. Hannah Arendt, trans. Harry Zohn (London, 1973), pp. 217–51.
13 *Arrest du Conseil portant deffenses de copier et mouler les ouvrages des sculpteurs de l'Académie* (1676), in *PSC*, France, 1676. See also *P-V*, vol. 1, pp. 87–8.
14 *P-V*, vol. 1, p. 91, 24 July 1676: the meeting decided that the 'marque' would be the Académie's seal and that the *secrétaire* of the Académie would keep the registers. I have

been unable to trace these registers in the archives of the Académie at the École nationale supérieure des beaux-arts.

15 For the text of the *arrêt* see *PSC*, France, 1714. I have translated *estampes* as 'prints', though strictly speaking only engravers were admitted to the Académie royale de peinture et de sculpture.

16 Although I have not been able to find trace of these lawsuits, the Comptes des bâtiments du roi and the correspondence between Daniel Cronström and the architect Nicodemus Tessin *le jeune* do allow the identification of plaster workers at this time, including Bertrand, Philippe Buister, Guillaume Cassegrain, Grenon, François Langlois, Thibaut Poissan and Pierre Robert. See Jules Guiffrey (ed.), *Comptes des bâtiments du roi sous le règne de Louis XIV*, 5 vols (Paris, 1881–1901), vol. 3, p. 359 (Buister); pp. 150, 207, 242, 276, 305, 550, 1070, 1230 (Cassegrain); p. 553 (Langlois); pp. 105, 359 (Poissan); pp. 105, 359, 469 (Robert); Roger-Armand Weigert, *Les Relations artistiques entre la France et la Suède, 1693–1718: Nicodème Tessin le jeune et Daniel Cronström correspondance* (Stockholm, 1964), pp. 130, 133, 182 (Cassegrain); pp. 92, 118 (Robert).

17 *P-V*, vol. 2, p. 33, 28 Sept. 1674.

18 *PSC*, France, 1714.

19 *P-V*, vol. 2, p. 87.

20 *Arrest du Conseil du roi*, BnF, Mss. f.f. 21732, 22 Dec. 1667, registered by the Paris Parlement on 7 Feb. 1670; repr. in Claude Marin Saugrain, *Code de la librairie et imprimerie de Paris* (Paris, 1744), p. 460. See also Marianne Grivel, *Le Commerce de l'estampe à Paris au XVIIe siècle* (Geneva, 1986), p. 100.

21 Nicolas Boileau, 'Discours au roi', in *Satires, épîtres, art poétique*, ed. Jean-Pierre Collinet (Paris, 1985), p. 64. The *discours* is a satire on literary panegyrics. Cited by Grivel in *Le Commerce de l'estampe*, p. 100, n. 55.

22 On the Cabinet du roi see Georges Duplessis, 'Le Cabinet du roi: Collection d'estampes commandées par Louis XIV', *Bibliophile français*, 3 (1869), 87–105; Marianne Grivel, 'Le Cabinet du roi', *Revue de la Bibliothèque nationale*, 15 (1985), 36–67; Jean-Gérald Castex, 'De la collection du marquis de Beringhen au Cabinet des estampes de la Bibliothèque royale: L'Histoire du volume des Tableaux gravés du roi', in *L'Estampe au Grand Siècle: Études offertes à Maxime Préaud*, Peter Fuhring, Barbara Brejon de Lavergnée, Marianne Grivel, Séverine Lepape and Véronique Meyer (eds) (Paris, 2010), pp. 507–14.

23 *P-V*, vol. 4, p. 231, 5 Sept. 1716. On the Coysevox bust see *The Frick Collection: An Illustrated Catalogue*, vol. 9: *Drawings, Prints and Later Acquisitions* (Princeton, 2003), pp. 460–65. On the leakiness of sculptors' studios and the fears of copying see the regulations of the bronze-casters' workshops, 1766, discussed in Katie Scott, 'Authorship, the Académie and the Market Place in Early Modern France', *OAJ*, 21 (1998), 29–41.

24 Trade interest also probably informed the applications made between 1733 and 1736 by Alexis Simon Belle and Jean-François de Troy for protection of engravings after their respective portraits of the dauphin, born in 1729. See *P-V*, vol. 5, pp. 120, 124, 30 May 1733; *P-V*, vol. 5, p. 170, 7 Jan. 1736. Jean Daullé engraved Alexis Simon Belle's portrait and Henri-Simon Thomassin engraved de Troy's.

25 *P-V*, vol. 1, pp. 44–6, statutes of the Académie, 27 May 1651, art. 9: 'Que tous ceux desd. Corps, qui ferront des desseins pour faire graver ou pour graver eux-mêmes, seront obligés de les faires voir à l'Académie avant de les mettre au jour pour y estre mis le visa, afin qu'il ne ce mette rien en public de deshonneste, et en cas de manquement il y aura amande arbitraire.'

26 Granted on 6 Apr. 1699 and renewed in 1715; BnF, Mss. f.f. 21950, 27 Feb. 1715.

27 The Académie had moved to the Louvre a decade earlier, in 1692. This first move was marked by a *conférence* by Georges Guillet de Saint-George addressed to the Académie on 15 Mar. 1692, in LM*Con*, vol. 2, pp. 427–30. In 1714 the Académie was granted better and more spacious accommodation in the same palace.

28 *P-V*, vol. 4, p. 170, 19 Aug. 1713. On Coypel's preparatory drawing see Nicole Garnier, *Antoine Coypel (1661–1722)* (Paris, 1989), no. 474, fig. 381. In the event, the book was printed in octavo because of shortage of funds. On the Académie's finances under the directorship of the duc d'Antin see Christian Michel, *L'Académie royale de peinture et de sculpture (1648–1793): La Naissance de l'école française* (Geneva, 2012), p. 80.

29 *P-V*, vol. 4, p. 180, 3 Feb. 1714. Initially the Académie had resolved to leave charge of the printing in Guérin's hands and at his expense (*P-V*, vol. 4, pp. 176–7), but for reasons unknown it had a change of heart.

30 On the abbé Bignon see Jack Clark, 'Abbé Jean-Paul Bignon, "Moderator of the Académies" and Royal Librarian', *French Historical Studies*, 8 (1973), 213–35.

31 *PSC*, France, 1714.

32 Georges Guillet de Saint-George, *Sur le portrait du roi de Henry Testelin (1667), conférence*, 6 Oct. 1691, in LM*Con*, vol. 2, pp. 409–16.

33 *P-V*, vol. 4, pp. 198–9, 2 Mar. 1715.

34 'Approbation de l'Académie royale de peinture et de sculpture', in Jacques-Philippe Ferrand, *L'Art du feu ou de peindre en émail* (Paris, 1721); 'Approbation de l'Académie royale de peinture et de sculpture', in Antoine Coypel, *Discours prononcez dans les conférences de l'Académie royale de peinture et de sculpture* (Paris, 1721). When Coypel's *Discours* was reviewed in the *Mercure de France* in December 1721, the approbation was reproduced in full, as a public endorsement. See *MdF* (Dec. 1721), 69. Censorship as a positive not a negative force during the *ancien régime* was discussed by Robert Darnton in the first of his Panizzi Lectures in 2014, 'Censors at Work: Bourbon France, Imperial India, and Communist Germany', British Library, London, 6 Jan. 2014. On Ferrand see the obituary in *MdF* (Mar. 1732), 550–52. On Coypel's *Discours* see René Démoris, 'La Parole d'un savant peintre en 1721: Les *Discours* d'Antoine Coypel', in *Estetica e arte: Le concezione dei 'moderni'*, Stefano Benassi (ed.) (Bologna, 1991), pp. 11–32.

35 On 'owning as belonging' in discussions of surrogacy, on which I have drawn, see Jeanette Edwards and Marilyn Strathern, 'Including our Own', in *Cultures of Relatedness: New Approaches to the Study of Kinship*, Janet Carsten (ed.) (Cambridge, 2000), pp. 149–66.

36 For an introduction to the *procès-verbaux* as a genre and practice of writing see Anatole de Montaiglon's brief comments in *P-V*, vol. 1, pp. viii–xiii.

37 For examples picked from many to illustrate the ubiquity of both gifts and the language of giving see *P-V*, vol. 1, pp. 325, 31 Dec. 1667 (Tortebat); vol. 2, pp. 26–7, 30 Dec. 1673 (Audran, Baudet); vol. 2, p. 270, 16 Mar. 1684 (Edelinck); vol. 3, p. 192, 28 July 1696 (Le Clerc); vol. 4, p. 93, 26 Oct. 1709 (Chéron); vol. 4, p. 240, 9 Jan. 1717 (Audran, Simonneau); vol. 5, p. 36, 31 Dec. 1727 (de Troy); vol. 5, p. 108, 27 Sept. 1732 (Cochin); vol. 5, p. 308, 27 Oct. 1741 (Surugue); vol. 6, p. 403, 31 Dec. 1754 (Surugue); vol. 7, p. 251, 26 May 1764 (Massé).

38 See Pierre Richelet's definition of *présent* as a mark of friendship, esteem and respect: Richelet, 'Présent', in *Dictionnaire de la langue françoise ancienne et moderne*, 2 vols (Amsterdam, 1706), 644. Furetière gives as the defining condition of *présent* that it must be put 'in the hand of a present person'. Giving presumes presence. Furetière, 'Présent', in *Dictionnaire universel*, vol. 2: 'On dit proverbialement, que les présents valent mieux que les absents; faisant equivoque du don avec la présence de quelqu'un.'

39 *P-V*, vol. 5, p. 141, 3 July 1734. Thierry carried out the work at La Granja between 1721 and 1728. It included not only the two fountains – *Le Triomphe d'Amphitrite* and *Le Triomphe*

d'Apollon, engraved by Thomassin – but also four figures – *L'Europe*, *La Gloire des princes*, *L'Hyver* and *Flore*. Impressions of these last four were not, however, given to the Académie. On the sculpture see François Souchal, *The Sculptors of the Seventeenth and Eighteenth Centuries: The Reign of Louis XIV*, 3 vols (Oxford, 1987), vol. 3, pp. 304–25, nos 43, 106, and nos 58–61.

40 *P-V*, vol. 5, p. 144, 28 Aug. 1734; vol. 5, p. 146, 30 Oct. 1734. The preparatory drawing for the print is in the collection of the École nationale supérieure des beaux-arts, inv. no. 1157. Nicolas de Largillière's portrait is in the collection of the Musée des beaux-arts, Lyon.

41 *P-V*, vol. 5, p. 157, 13 April 1735.

42 For example, in 1696 Jean Jouvenet gave the Académie a portrait drawing of Cardinal de Mazarin, a former protector of the Académie, to be engraved; and in the same year Sébastien Le Clerc gave impressions of five of his engravings of the works of Le Brun, including those of the battles of Alexander the Great, to remember him by. See *P-V*, vol. 3, p. 191, 9 July 1696; vol. 3, p. 192, 28 July 1696.

43 Michel, 'Les Graveurs à l'Académie royale', pp. 483–92.

44 The ceremony can be dated to the time of the Académie's definitive break with the *maîtrise* in 1654. The casket with the documents survives in the collections at the École nationale supérieure des beaux-arts.

45 On the ritual of becoming a member of the Académie see Hannah Williams's excellent *Académie Royale: A History in Portraits* (Farnham, 2015), ch. 2.

46 *P-V*, vol. 5, p. 56, 26 Feb. 1729.

47 *P-V*, vol. 4, pp. 284–5, 29 July 1719; p. 286, 26 Aug. 1719; p. 287, 30 Sept. 1719.

48 On the primary importance of social position and status as a determinant of identity, and the fetishisation of social relations under feudalism, see Karl Marx, *Capital: A Critique of Political Economy*, trans. Ben Fowkes, vol. 1 (Harmondsworth, 1976), pp. 63–82. With the transition to capitalism, fetishism assumes, Marx argues, the form of commodity fetishism. See also Slavoj Žižek, *The Sublime Object of Ideology* (London and New York, 1989), pp. 18–22.

49 *P-V*, vol. 5, p. 229, 12 Apr. 1738; pp. 257–8, 5 Sept. 1739. On Gaspard Duchange see Préaud, *DEE*, pp. 111–13. On the breviary see *MdF* (Apr. 1738), 740.

50 No Academician engraver appears to have applied for a privilege for a print of his own invention (*invenit*), only his own execution (*sculpsit*).

51 Of the requests for privilege, 65 were to protect works by Old Masters and 59 works by Modern Masters. Of the eight Old Masters whose particular submitted works were assigned a privilege, two were from the French School: Poussin and Claude.

52 *P-V*, vol. 5, p. 95, 10 Nov. 1731. Henri-Simon Thomassin's engraving of Jean-François de Troy's *La Peste de Marseille* was given as a *présent* to the Académie on 31 December 1727 and subsequently listed in its records as having received the first print privilege, but no mention of the *arrêt* was made in the minutes. *P-V*, vol. 5, p. 36, 31 Dec. 1727.

53 *P-V*, vol. 5, p. 108, 27 Sept. 1732; *MdF* (Oct. 1732), 2214–15.

54 Peter Fuhring, 'The Print Privilege in Eighteenth-Century France, I', *PQ*, 2 (1985), 174–93.

55 On such *privilèges réels* see Joseph-Nicolas Guyot, *Répertoire universel et raisonné de jurisprudence civile, criminelle, canonique et bénéficale*, 64 vols (Paris, 1775–83), vol. 47, p. 337.

56 Georges Guillet de Saint-George, *Mémoire sur Gérard Van Opstal*, 2 Aug. 1692, in LMCon, vol. 2, 454–62. For biographical information and a discussion of his works see Geneviève Bué-Akar, 'Éléments nouveaux concernant la vie et l'œuvre de Gérard Van Opstal, sculpteur ordinaire du roi', *BSHAF* (1975), 137–46.

57 According to LMCon, vol. 1, pp. 207–29, the statute of limitation was actually 30 years, but it was given as one year in the court brief, and the case was fought on that basis.

58 [Henri Bessé de La Chapelle], *Plaidoyer pour le sieur Gérard Van Opstal, un des recteurs de l'Académie royale de la peinture et de la sculpture*, in LMCon, vol. 1, pp. 208–29, esp. pp. 223–6.

59 Ibid., p. 224.

60 *P-V*, vol. 1, p. 328, 4 Feb. 1668; p. 332, 2 June 1668. Henri Bessé de La Chapelle later went on to become an *inspecteur des beaux-arts* under the *surintendance* of Édouard Colbert, marquis de Villacerf, in the 1690s. The *plaidoyer* was reprinted 'par les soins de François Roumier, sculpteur des Bâtimens du roi' by the publisher Paulus-du-Mesnil (Paris, 1733).

61 Radin, *Reinterpreting Property*, pp. 35–71.

62 [La Chapelle], *Plaidoyer pour... Van Opstal*, in LMCon, vol. 1, pp. 209–10.

63 Ibid., p. 210.

64 Ibid.

65 *P-V*, vol. 3, p. 67, 4 Aug. 1691; p. 69, 18, Aug. 1691.

66 *MdF* (Mar. 1755), 145–6. On the prints see Pierrette Jean-Richard, *L'Œuvre gravée de François Boucher dans la collection Edmond de Rothschild* (Paris, 1978), nos 933–7. See also Scott, 'Authorship, the Académie and the Market Place', p. 36.

67 On the specific case of François Boucher see Katie Scott, 'Reproduction and Reputation: François Boucher and the Circulation of Identity in Eighteenth-Century France', in *Rethinking Boucher*, Melissa Hyde and Mark Ledbury (eds) (Los Angeles, 2006), pp. 91–132.

68 Marie-Claude Phan, 'Les Déclarations de grossesse en France (XVIe–XVIIIe siècles), *RHMC*, 22 (1975), 66–81.

69 On the trope of the work of art as artist's offspring see Ernst Kris and Otto Kurz, *Legend, Myth and Magic in the Image of the Artist: A Historical Experiment*, trans. Alastair Laing and Lottie M. Newman (New Haven, CT, 1979). André Félibien said of Nicolas Poussin 'Le Poussin... n'a pas été assez heureux pour faire passer aux siens ce qu'il avait acquis d'honneur & de bien: mais ses ouvrages lui tiennent lieu d'enfants qui ne lui ont jamais donné que du plaisir & qui conserveront son nom avec bien de la gloire pendant plusieurs siècles.' See Claire Pace, *Félibien's Life of Poussin* (London, 1981), p. 128. For a comparable 18th-century example, see the abbé Louis Gougenot, 'Vie de Monsieur Oudry' (1761), in *Mémoires inédits sur la vie et les ouvrages des membres de l'Académie royale de peinture et de sculpture*, ed. Louis-Étienne Dussieux et al., 2 vols (Paris, 1854), vol. 2, pp. 365–403, and Diderot's epistolary debate with Falconet on posterity, in which the *philosophe* presumes to describe the sculptor's works, such as *Pygmalion* (1763), as 'precious children'. See Diderot to Falconet, 22 Jan. 1766, in Denis Diderot, *Correspondance*, ed. Laurent Versini (Paris, 1997), p. 592.

70 Coypel, *Discours*, p. 62.

71 Michel, *L'Académie royale de peinture et de sculpture*, p. 207.

72 *Les Publications de l'Académie royale des sciences de Paris (1666–1793)*, ed. Robert Halleux, James McClellan, Daniela Berariu and Geneviève Xhayet, 2 vols (Turnhout, 2001).

73 *PSC*, France, 1714.

74 The only drawing lessons provided at the Académie in Paris were in the life class. The elementary stages of drawing after prints and casts were the students' own responsibility and took place in the studio of their master, or in their own time. For the privilege for Élisabeth-Sophie Chéron's *Livre à dessiner* see BnF, Mss. f.f. 21949, 28 May 1706; for the presentation of a copy to the Académie see *P-V*, vol. 4, p. 30, 3 July 1706, when she gave six sheets of heads; p. 93, 6 Oct. 1709, when she gave a further 12 heads and one foot.

75 Colbert to Errard, 15 Sept. 1679, *CDR*, vol. 1, p. 18; Colbert to Errard, 17 Nov. 1679, ibid., p. 92.

76 Christian Michel, 'La Peinture peut-elle être réduite en art?', in *Réduire en art: La Technologie de la Renaissance aux Lumières*,

Pascal Dubourg Glatigny and Hélène Vérin (eds) (Paris, 2008), pp. 133–48.

77 *Statuts et règlements que le roy veut et ordonne estre observés dans l'Académie royale de peinture, sculpture et architecture, que Sa Majesté a résolu d'establir dans la ville de Rome pour l'instruction des jeunes peintres, sculpteurs et architectes françois, qui y seront envoyés pour estudier*, 11 Feb. 1666, in *CDR*, vol. 1, pp. 8–11.

78 Matthieu La Teulière, director of the Académie de France, wrote to Édouard Colbert, marquis de Villacerf, Surintendant des bâtiments du roi, of the difficulty of obtaining access to the Stanze after the appointment of Carlo Marrata as keeper of the Vatican collection; 28 Aug. 1691, *CDR*, vol. 1, p. 209. See La Teulière's reiteration of the difficulties to Villacerf, 9 July 1696, *CDR*, vol. 2, pp.244–6; and René-Antoine Houasse to Jules Hardouin-Mansart, 21 Nov. 1702, *CDR*, vol. 3, p. 94. According to Nicolas Vleughels, Charles-François Poerson's inadequacies and bad temper as a director were largely owing to the necessity of courting those with collections for the *pensionnaires*; Vleughels to d'Antin, 26 Sept. 1724, *CDR*, vol. 7, p. 63. Much later, the marquis de Marigny advised new director Charles-Joseph Natoire to try bribery when good manners failed; Marigny to Natoire, 2 Apr. 1752, *CDR*, vol. 10, p. 382. On the scaffolding needed for copying in the Stanze see *Inventaire général* (1684), in *CDR*, vol. 1, pp. 129–42 at p. 137; and La Teulière to Villacerf, 16 Oct. 1691, *CDR*, vol. 1, p. 228. Vleughels made the obvious point to d'Antin that in order to make good copies, the students needed to be able to see; Vleughels to d'Antin, 8 June 1729, *CDR*, vol. 8, pp. 31–2. On copying using a veil see La Teulière to Villacerf, 7 Oct. 1692, *CDR*, vol. 3, p. 328.

79 In the first years of the Académie's foundation, Colbert commissioned professional copies of the Borghese and Medici vases and urged Errard to ensure that the students copied continuously. On student obligations see Colbert to Errard, 15 Sept. 1679, *CDR*, vol. 1, p. 88; on the vases see Colbert to Errard, 29 Feb. 1680, *CDR*, vol. 1, p. 94.

80 In the case of Gilles-Marie Oppenord, La Teulière reported to Villacerf that he lent him prints and books to make copies for himself; La Teulière to Villacerf, 23 Nov. 1694, *CDR*, vol. 2, p. 85; La Teulière to Villacerf, 1 Nov. 1695, *CDR*, vol. 2, p. 169; La Teulière to Villacerf, 25 May 1696, *CDR*, vol. 2, p. 231. Vleughels distinguished between 'copies' for the king and 'études', copies that the students made for their own 'advancement'; Vleughels to d'Antin, 29 Oct. 1727, *CDR*, vol. 7, p. 377.

81 Emmanuel Coquery, 'L'Anatomie d'une académie', in *L'Idéal classique: Les Échanges artistiques entre Rome et Paris au temps de Bellori (1640–1700)*, Olivier Bonfait (ed.) (Paris, 2002), p. 141. In the specific case of sculpture, see Geneviève Bresc-Bautier, 'Les Transports vers Paris des sculptures de l'Académie de France à Rome (1667–1689)', in ibid., pp. 327–62. The extent to which the students were little more than disposable skill sets is especially apparent when Villacerf refers to weak *pensionnaires* as a 'meuble[s] inutile[s]', good only for sending back home; Villacerf to Le Teulière, 10 May 1694, *CDR*, vol. 2, p. 20.

82 In the 1720s d'Antin renewed requests for copies for the royal palaces; d'Antin to Poerson, 28 Aug. 1724, *CDR*, vol. 7, p. 53; d'Antin to Poerson, 16 Oct. 1724, *CDR*, vol. 7, pp. 76–7. In the *Instruction pour la régie de l'Académie de Rome* (1737) imposed by Philibert Orry on his appointment as Directeur des bâtiments du roi in 1737, the main object of the students' study was still copies for the king, though their purpose and destination were left undetermined; see *CDR*, vol. 9, pp. 315–18, art. 2.

83 Vleughels to d'Antin, 2 Aug. 1725, *CDR*, vol. 7, pp. 191–2. For the reaction of a visitor to the Académie on the feast day of Saint Louis in 1725 see Pressiat to Charles-Jean-Baptiste Fleuriau, comte de Morville, 30 Aug. 1725, *CDR*, vol. 7, pp. 204–5. On such painted copies see Claire Aubaret, 'Les Copistes du Cabinet des tableaux de la surintendance des bâtiments du roi au XVIIIe siècle', *Bulletin du Centre de recherche du château de Versailles*, 18 Dec. 2013, <crcv.revues.org/12223> (accessed 12 Nov. 2017).

84 Bernard Hercenberg, *Nicolas Vleughels: Peintre et directeur de l'Académie de France à Rome (1668–1737)* (Paris, 1975), pp. 13–30; Pierre Arizzoli Clémentel, 'Les Envois de la couronne à l'Académie de France à Rome au XVIIIe siècle', *Revue de l'art*, 68 (1985), 73–84; Stéphane Loire, 'Raphaël au palais Mancini: Les Copies des pensionnaires (1725–1753)', in *L'Académie de France à Rome au XVIIIe siècle. Le Palais Mancini: Un Foyer artistique dans l'Europe des Lumières (1725–1792)*, Marc Bayard, Émilie Beck Saiello and Aude Gobet (eds) (Rennes, 2016), pp. 207–56.

85 The remark was made specifically with reference to Edme Bouchardon's drawings after the antique; Vleughels to d'Antin, 2 Sept. 1728, *CDR*, vol. 7, p. 451. Student rooms sometimes formed part of a guided tour: on the visit of the duc d'Harcourt see Vleughels to d'Antin, 25 Feb. 1736, *CDR*, vol. 9, p. 231. The question of to whom drawings executed in Rome actually belonged was moot. In a letter to La Teulière about Oppenord's drawings executed in Rome, Surintendant Colbert de Villacerf reminded the director of the Académie de France that 'les pensionnaires estant logez, nourris et ayant une pension du Roy, les ouvrages qu'ils y font appartenent à S.M. Ainsi, quand Oppenordt reviendra, il faudra m'envoyer *tous* les ouvrages qu'il aura faits', though he expresses conviction that the king will give them back to the artist for 'safe keeping' (my emphasis), 22 July 1697, *CDR*, vol. 2, p. 325. The implication is that all copies and drawings belonged to the king even as they remained in the possession of the author.

86 The exception is, of course, the case of Queen Christina of Sweden's collection: see [Guilbert], *Mémoire ou remarques concernant les tableaux du célèbre cabinet de la feue reint Christine de Suède*, in *CDR*, vol. 5, pp. 340–45.

87 Coypel, *Discours*, p. 12.

88 Philippe de Champaigne argued in *De l'éducation de la jeunesse suivant son génie naturel (contre les copistes des manières), conférence*, 11 June 1672, in *LMCon*, vol. 1, pp. 461–3, that 'slavish' copies were forgivable only in the very young student, 'qui est encore sous l'aile du maître'. For an example of continuing 'servitude' in maturity, see Dézallier d'Argenville's life of Jean-Baptiste Santerre, which describes an artist who was narrow in his intellectual horizons, concerned primarily with the mechanical aspects of his craft, and whose work was consequently monotonous and whose pupils – among whom was Geneviève Blanchot – remained copyists. See Antoine-Joseph Dézallier d'Argenville, *Abrégé de la vie des plus fameux peintres*, 3 vols (Paris, 1745), vol. 2, p. 386.

89 Coypel, *Discours*, 13. Dézallier d'Argenville, in his life of Nicolas Lancret, noted that Watteau, his master, warned him that masters were useful only up to a certain point, and that in relying exclusively on them 'on court le risque de n'être qu'un copiste', a warning that distinguished Watteau as a good master. See Dézallier d'Argenville, *Abrégé*, vol. 3, p. 290.

90 *CDR*, vol. 1, pp. 8–11. In 1695 Villacerf reiterated to La Teulière that 'un homme qui est logé, nourri dans l'Académie du Roy, et son Pensionnaire' was not allowed 'de travailler pour autruy'; Villacerf to La Teulière, 5 Dec. 1695, *CDR*, vol. 2, p. 183. La Teulière noted the ease with which it was possible for students to get away with moonlighting in Rome; La Teulière de Villacerf, 27 Dec. 1695, *CDR*, vol. 2, pp. 190–91.

91 Villacerf to La Teulière, 10 May 1694, *CDR*, vol. 2, p. 20; La Teulière to Villacerf, 1 June 1694, *CDR*, vol. 2, p. 33. In La Teulière's case he referred, for instance, to René Frémin as

a 'disciple' of François Girardon'; Le Teulière to Villacerf, 25 Oct. 1695, *CDR*, vol. 2, p. 168; La Teulière to Villacerf, 15 Nov. 1695, *CDR*, vol. 2, p. 175.

92 Colbert to Errard, 29 Feb. 1680, *CDR*, vol. 1, p. 94; Colbert to Errard, 16 Mar. 1680, vol. 1, p. 95; Colbert to Errard, 5 June 1680, *CDR*, vol. 2, p. 98; Colbert to Errard, 27 Aug. 1682, *CDR*, vol. 2, p. 117. On the copies, three of each vase, for the Bassin de Latone at Versailles see Francis Haskell and Nicolas Penny, *Taste and the Antique: The Lure of Classical Sculpture, 1500–1900* (New Haven, CT, and London, 1981), pp. 37–42, esp. p. 39, and nos 81–2.

93 This is not to say that economic considerations were not acknowledged. Charles-François Poerson argued that the students' 'love' of their work justified the king's expense; Poerson to d'Antin, 31 Aug. 1717, *CDR*, vol. 5, p. 96; Poerson to d'Antin, 11 July 1719, *CDR*, vol. 5, p. 252. He singled out Saussard as a student whose copies were marked by love and care; Poerson to d'Antin, 23 Apr. 1720, *CDR*, vol. 5, p. 322.

94 'Devoir' is defined in the 17th and 18th centuries as an obligation by law, necessity or custom either to say or to do something. It is both morally and socially coded: obligations are owed to a person or institution of superior rank. See Furetière, 'Devoir', in *Dictionnaire universel*, vol. 1; Richelet, 'Devoir', in *Dictionnaire*, p. 520. Colbert urged Errard to maintain the *pensionnaires* in their *devoirs*; Colbert to Errard, 24 Sept. 1683, *CDR*, vol. 1, p. 119.

95 The directors of the Académie de France, La Teulière, Houasse and Poerson, used the word *devoir* interchangeably with 'copy' in a general sense; for example, La Teulière to Villacerf, 22 Aug. 1691, *CDR*, vol. 1, p. 208; Houasse to Hardouin-Mansart, 18 July 1702, *CDR*, vol. 3, p. 86; Poerson to d'Antin, 28 Feb. 1719, *CDR*, vol. 5, pp. 209–11.

96 On Blanchard *fils* see Poerson to d'Antin, 8 Sept. 1708, *CDR*, vol. 3, p. 229; on Goupil see Poerson to d'Antin, 4 Apr. 1711, *CDR*, vol. 3, p. 458; Poerson to d'Antin, 5 Sept. 1711, *CDR*, vol. 4, p. 15; on Gaultier see Poerson to d'Antin, 24 Nov. 1722, *CDR*, vol. 6, p. 200.

97 By copying, students were cured of their mannerisms; Poerson to d'Antin, 26 Nov. 1712, *CDR*, vol. 4, p. 170; Vleughels to d'Antin, 22 Oct. 1733, *CDR*, vol. 8, p. 17. De Troy was, however, less sure that a cure was possible or desirable; de Troy to Orry, 30 Oct. 1744, *CDR*, vol. 10, p. 79.

98 La Teulière to Villacerf, 22 Aug. 1691, *CDR*, vol. 1, p. 203. On La Teulière, a man of letters and protégé of the La Rochefoucauld family, see Bénédicte Gady, 'L'Étrange Monsieur La Theulière', in *L'Idéal classique: Les Échanges artistiques entre Rome et Paris au temps de Bellori (1640–1700)*, Olivier Bonfait (ed.) (Paris, 2002), pp. 161–85.

99 André Bélanger, *The Ethics of Catholicism and the Consecration of the Intellectual* (Liverpool, 1997), pp. 75–84. See also Elena Russo, 'Virtuous Economies: Morality and Noble Expenditure from Montesquieu to Caillois', *Historical Reflexions*, 25 (1999), 251–78.

100 Vleughels to d'Antin, 31 Oct. 1726, *CDR*, vol. 7, p. 297. The history painter Dandré-Bardon, also in Rome as a student in the later 1720s, later recommended diligence in copying in his treatise on painting for Académie students; see Michel-François Dandré-Bardon, *Traité de peinture, suivi d'un essai sur la sculpture*, 2nd edn, 2 vols (Paris, 1765), vol. 1, p. 17. Dandré-Bardon quoted Nicolas Boileau's *L'Art poétique* (1674) in support, translating advice for poetry into the terms of art: '... sans perdre de courage / Vingt-fois d'un crayon sûr retouchons notre ouvrage, / Polissons-le sans cesse & repolissons; / Ajoutons quelquefois & cens fois effaçons.'

101 On Jean-François de Troy and Charles-Joseph Natoire, both directors of the Académie de France in Rome, see Christophe Leribault, *Jean-François de Troy (1679–1752)* (Paris, 2002), pp. 111–61; Susanna Caviglia-Brunel, *Charles-Joseph Natoire, 1700–1777* (Paris, 2012), pp. 115–43.

102 The three drawings at the Département des arts graphiques at the Louvre have been analysed in detail by Françoise Joulie in *L'Appel de l'Italie: Artistes français et nordiques dans la péninsule. Dessins des XVIIe et XVIIIe siècles*, exh. cat., Musée de Grenoble, Jean-Claude Boyer et al. (eds) (Montreuil, 2006), cat. nos 70–72. Joulie argues, to the contrary, that the personality of each of the draughtsmen 'les conduit à un résultat différent'. See also Sonia Couturier, *Drawn to Art: French Artists in Eighteenth-Century Rome*, exh. cat., National Gallery of Canada, Ottawa (Milan, 2011), cat. no. 6. On the Natoire, see Caviglia-Brunel, *Natoire*, p. 177, no. D24.

103 Natoire to Marigny, 11 June 1755, *CDR*, vol. 11, p. 93.

104 Caviglia-Brunel, *Natoire*, p. 174, no. D11. These different responses of painter and sculptor are also subtly evident in the copies after Luti: Dumont le Romain and Natoire are more attentive to the balance of chiaroscuro and instances of reflected light; Bouchardon's copy gives priority to mass and plane.

105 See, in the case of the 16th-century Netherlands, Walter Melion, 'Hendrick Goltzius's Project of Reproductive Engraving', *Art History*, 13 (1990), 458–87. For imitation as a leitmotif in engravers' lives see 'Vie de Gérard Edelinck', in *Mémoires inédits*, ed. Dussieux, et al. vol. 2, pp. 46–60 at p. 52; François-Bernard Lépicié's obituary of the Academician engraver Henri-Simon Thomassin in *MdF* (Mar. 1741), 568.

106 A *pensionnaire* with a vocation for printmaking, not painting was, according to Poerson, better sent back to Paris; Poerson to d'Antin, 21 May 1712, *CDR*, vol. 4, p. 96; Poerson to d'Antin, 7 Apr. 1713, *CDR*, vol. 4, p. 194. A French printmaker, Pierre-Jacques Gautier, petitioned for a place at the Académie de France in Rome because Italian printmaking was so mediocre; l'Hôpital to Orry, 15 May 1742, *CDR*, vol. 10, pp. 12–14.

107 Perrin Stein, 'Diplomacy, Patronage and Pedagogy: Etching in the Eternal City', in *Artists and Amateurs: Etching in Eighteenth-Century France*, exh. cat., Metropolitan Museum of Art, New York (New York, 2013), pp. 103–35.

108 On the copies see Jean-François Méjanès, *Pierre-Charles Trémolières (1703–1739)*, exh. cat., Musée d'art et d'histoire, Cholet (Paris, 1973), Dessins, cat. nos 13–16, Gravures, cat. nos 9–10; Stein, 'Diplomacy, Patronage and Pedagogy', p. 106.

109 Leribault, *Jean-François de Troy*, pp. 200–3 and nos P286, P287.

110 The inventories of the school's property drawn up by Errard in 1684 and Poerson in 1709 both mention a roller press for printing copper plates and a number of copper plates by Thomassin; see *CDR*, vol. 1, p. 137; *CDR*, vol. 3, pp. 350 (press), 356 (plates).

111 *CDR*, vol. 1, pp. 153–5, 12 June 1686. See also Mignard's note to Villacerf on Colbert's copy policy, *CDR*, vol. 1, pp. 222–3. Vleughels saw it as one of his principal tasks to procure works that were unknown in France for the students to copy; he described his efforts in terms not of conquest, however, but of harvest; Vleughels to d'Antin, 6 May 1735, *CDR*, vol. 9, p. 162; Vleughels to d'Antin, 3 Dec. 1735, *CDR*, vol. 9, p. 211. Marigny, on the other hand, was not receptive to the idea of novelty in the choice of models for the students to copy; Marigny to Natoire, 22 Apr. 1752, *CDR*, vol. 10, p. 381, in reponse to Natoire to Marigny, 15 Mar. 1752, *CDR*, vol. 10, p. 373.

112 Carol Rose, *Property and Persuasion: Essays on the History, Theory, and Rhetoric of Ownership* (Boulder, CO, and Oxford, 1994), pp. 11–23.

113 Colin Bailey notes, in relation to Carle Vanloo's 1729 painting of the same subject, that the subject of Aeneas and Anchises was a topos for French artists in Rome; see Colin Bailey (ed.), *The First Painters of the King: French Royal Taste from Louis XIV to the Revolution*, exh. cat., Stair Sainty Matthiesen Gallery, London, and other venues (New York, 1985), pp. 92–94, cat. no. 12.

114 *CDR*, vol. 2, p. 223, 16 Apr. 1696. Le Pautre's earlier project for a Hercules and Cacus group was judged unfit for Versailles and *Énée et Anchise* was being considered instead. In the *Aeneid*, Anchises carries the palladium, the image of Pallas Athene that protected the household, but Lepautre here substitutes Minerva, the Roman goddess of the arts, a reference to Louis XIV's art patronage. On the work see Gertrude Rosenthal, 'Pierre Lepautre and his Aeneas Group', *Journal of the Walters Art Gallery*, 6 (1943), 70–81; Rosenthal, 'Additional Bozzetti for the Aeneas Group', *Journal of the Walters Art Gallery*, 7–8 (1944–5), 127–30; François Souchal, 'Le Pautre', *French Sculptors of the Seventeenth and Eighteenth Centuries*, 3 vols (1977–87), vol. 2, no. 9.

115 D'Antin to Polignac, 23 Aug. 1708, *CDR*, vol. 3, p. 226.

116 See, for instance, Laurent Guiard's treatment of the theme, of which a small terracotta is at the Louvre and the full-size plaster at the Musée Granet, Aix-en-Provence.

117 From the evidence of the drawings, it seems unlikely, because all three were drawn from exactly the same point of view, with no lateral variation.

118 Deanna Petherbridge, *The Primacy of Drawing: Histories and Theories of Practice* (New Haven, CT, and London, 2010), p. 270. Portraiture was another means of supporting interpersonal relations at the Académie de France in Rome. The *pensionnaires* decorated the dining room at the Palazzo Mancini with their portraits: 'Les pensionnaires ont accommodé la salle où on mange; ils l'ont décoré de leurs portraits d'une grandeur uniforme et ils s'en rencontrent parmi qui sont fort bien; c'est un amusement qui leur est avantageux, car il n'est rien tel pour notre métier que se familiariser avec le naturel; cela embellit cette chambre, et, dans la suite, elle délaissera pas d'avoir sa curiosité. On ne perd point ici de temps et on tâche que les divertissemens puissant devenir proffitables.' Vleughels to d'Antin, 19 May 1735, *CDR*, vol. 9, pp. 171–2.

119 When sending cases of copies back to France, Vleughels noted, 'on trouvera dans la caisse le nom de ceux qui les ont copié', which indicates that lists had to be included for lack of individual signatures; Vleughels to d'Antin, 1 July 1734, *CDR*, vol. 9, p. 95.

120 Stéphane Loire, 'Poussin chez Raphaël, 1627: Sur quelques graffiti d'artistes français à Rome', in *Mélanges en hommage à Pierre Rosenberg: Peintures et dessins en France et en Italie, XVIIe et XVIIIe siècles*, Anna Cavina et al. (eds) (Paris, 2001), pp. 264–74; Charlotte Guichard, *Graffitis: Inscrire son nom à Rome, XVIe–XIXe siècles* (Paris, 2014), ch. 2. See also La Teulière to Villacerf, 6 May 1692, *CDR*, vol. 1, p. 283, in which La Teulière alleges, defensively, that it was Italian artists, not French, who were responsible for the graffiti in the Stanze.

121 On the souvenir see Susan Stewart, *On Longing: Narratives of the Miniature, the Gigantic, the Souvenir and the Collection* (Durham, NC, 1996), pp. 132–51.

122 In Colbert's correspondence with Errard, works of genius constitute the pay-off for the copies; Colbert to Errard, 16 Mar. 1682, *CDR*, vol. 1, p. 111; Colbert to Errard, 10 July 1682, *CDR*, vol. 1, p. 126. The directors of the school, on the other hand, recognised that students were not sent to become copyists, and works of genius, insofar as they are successful, mark independence and maturity and not just private interest; see, for instance, Poerson to d'Antin, 21 May 1712, *CDR*, vol. 4, p. 96; Vleughels to d'Antin, 8 Aug. 1724, *CDR*, vol. 7, p. 47; Vleughels to d'Antin, 10 Aug. 1725, *CDR*, vol. 7, p. 197.

123 Aristotle, *On Rhetoric*, Book 2, part 11; Poerson to d'Antin, 20 July 1717, *CDR*, vol. 5, p. 89.

124 For Lepautre see La Teulière to Villacerf, 25 May 1694, *CDR*, vol. 2, pp. 29–30; for Bouchardon see Vleughels to d'Antin, 10 Mar. 1729, *CDR*, vol. 8, p. 14, and Vleughels to d'Antin, 11 July 1730, *CDR*, vol. 8, p. 124.

125 See the especially harsh assessment of the sculptors Robert Le Lorrain and Pierre Le Gros, who capitalised on their positions as *pensionnaires*, La Teulière to Villacerf, 15 June 1694, *CDR*, vol. 2, p. 41; La Teulière to Villacerf, 27 July 1692, vol. 2, p. 55; Villacerf to La Teulière, 5 Dec. 1695, vol. 2, p. 183.

126 Aristotle, *Aristotle's Ethics: Writings from the Complete Works*, ed. Jonathan Barnes and Anthony Kenny (Princeton, 2014), pp. 245–6.

127 In painting, Bon Boullogne's artistic identity was precisely as a 'Protée en peinture'. Paradoxically Boullogne was, according to Dézallier d'Argenville, only ever fully autograph when imitating others, notably Poussin and Guido Reni. When producing his own work, he delegated much of the painting to his 'disciples'. See Dézallier d'Argenville, *Abrégé*, vol. 2, pp. 373–9. In print, Marcantonio's copies of Dürer established the latter's *Life of the Virgin* (1502–5) as a testing ground of talent for, among others, Charles-Nicolas Cochin; see Véronique Meyer, 'Les Copies de Nicolas Cochin', *NE*, nos 179–80 (2001–2), 33–52. Meanwhile, Bernard Picart, in emulation of Hendrick Goltzius, etched, published and, it appears, innocently passed off as original work pastiches and copies in the signature styles of other artists; see Bernard Picart, *Impostures innocentes, ou Recueil d'estampes d'après divers peintres illustres* (Amsterdam, 1734), pp. 4–5 and nos 41, 44. On Picart's work see Christophe Henry, 'Les *Impostures innocentes* de Bernard Picart ou la revanche du "marchand forain"', in *Théorie des arts et création artistique dans l'Europe du nord du XVIe au début du XVIIIe siècle*, Michèle-Caroline Heck, Fréderique Lemerle and Yves Pauwels (eds) (Lille, 2001), pp. 313–32. Charles-Nicolas Cochin *fils*'s earliest prints also included copies after Goltzius (see Charles-Antoine Jombert, *Catalogue de l'œuvre de Charles-Nicolas Cochin fils* (Paris, 1770), 1729, nos 5, 7), and Pierre-Louis Surugue *fils*'s first advertised print was a reproduction of Goltzius' *Le Jugement de Pâris*, 'très heureusement gravée... dans le goût de Goltzius.' *MdF* (June 1741), vol. 2, 1421.

128 Vleughels to d'Antin, 2 Sept. 1728, *CDR*, vol. 7, pp. 450–52. I thank Edouard Kopp warmly for drawing my attention to this passage. For his analysis of Bouchardon's Italian copies see Edouard Kopp, *The Learned Draftsman: Edme Bouchardon* (Los Angeles, 2017).

129 See, for instance, Dézallier d'Argenville's account of Hyacinthe Rigaud's mistake in taking one of his own early works for a Van Dyck, in *Abrégé*, vol. 2, p. 410.

130 Although Bouchardon's case is not like Chardin's, staged at the determining moment of inclusion/exclusion, Vleughels sets the scene for Bouchardon's humiliation by saying that his ego had been inflated by the admiration of 'le tout Rome'; the school is the restricted group in which value is truly judged. Vleughels to d'Antin, 2 Sept. 1728, *CDR*, vol. 7, pp. 450–52.

131 It differs from a trademark insofar as its signifying function was directed as much at other members as at other audiences, and its purpose was not exclusively, or even primarily, commercial.

132 W. J. T. Mitchell, *What do Pictures Want? The Lives and Loves of Images* (Chicago, 2005), esp. ch. 9, pp. 188–96.

133 Louis Réau, *Étienne-Maurice Falconet*, 2 vols (Paris, 1922), vol. 1, pp. 127–33.

134 Jean Seznec, 'Diderot et les plagiats de Monsieur Pierre', *Revues des arts*, 5–6 (1955–6), 67–74.

135 See, for instance, Christian Michel on the Falconet affair in *L'Académie royale de peinture et de sculpture*, pp. 227–8.

136 Susan Stewart, *Crimes of Writing: Problems in the Containment of Representation* (Durham, NC, and London, 1994), p. 24.

137 *Dictionnaire de l'Académie française*, 3 vols (Paris, 1694), vol. 2, p. 254.

138 Julie Hayes, 'Plagiarism and Legitimation in Eighteenth-Century France', *Eighteenth Century*, 34 (1993), 115–31.

139 Jean-Baptiste-Claude Robin, 'Éloge de Falconet, sculpteur', *Revue universelle des arts*, 15 (1862), 245–56. On the Académie

in the late 1740s and 1750s see Élisabeth Lavezzi, 'Appelle en Arlequin: À propos d'un manuscrit de Caylus: *De l'avantage des vertus de société*', in *Le Comte de Caylus: Les Arts et les lettres*, Nicholas Cronk and Kris Peeters (eds) (New York, 2004), pp. 125–47.

140 Tomas Macsotay, *The Profession of Sculpture in the Paris Académie* (Oxford, 2014), pp. 43–86. I warmly thank the author for generously allowing me to read the manuscript of his book before its publication.

141 On the two-stage process of election to the Académie in the 17th and 18th centuries, by submission first of a *morceau d'agrément* and then of a *morceau de réception* see *Les Peintres du Roi, 1648–1793*, exh. cat., Musée des beaux-arts, Tours, and Musée des Augustins, Toulouse (Paris, 2000); Michel, *L'Académie royale de peinture et de sculpture*, pp. 176–243. Geneviève Bresc-Bautier and Guilhem Scherf are currently preparing a catalogue of the *morceaux de réception* by the king's sculptors at the Louvre.

142 Robin, 'Éloge de Falconet', pp. 247–8.

143 A small model was exhibited at the Salon in 1745 and a full-scale terracotta cast in 1746. See the Salon *livrets* for 1745 and 1746 in Jules-Joseph Guiffrey, *Collection des livrets des anciennes expositions depuis 1673 jusqu'en 1800*, 5 vols (Paris, 1869–71), vol. 1. See also the object file at the Victoria and Albert Museum, London, inv. no. A.5-1957. That versions of *Le Génie de la sculpture* were in circulation by no later than 1749 indicates that by *c.*1750 Falconet had almost certainly opted for the Milo as his reception piece.

144 Réau, *Étienne-Maurice Falconet*, vol. 1, pp. 133–4; George Levitine, *The Sculpture of Falconet* (Greenwich, CT, 1972), pp. 25–7; Alexander Schenker, *The Bronze Horseman: Falconet's Monument to Peter the Great* (New Haven, CT, and London, 2003).

145 *P-V*, vol. 5, p. 371, 29 Aug. 1744.

146 Michel, *L'Académie royale de peinture et de sculpture*, pp. 201, 217–22.

147 Ibid., pp. 227–28.

148 *P-V*, vol. 5, p. 373, 3 Oct. 1744; vol. 6, p. 12, 24 July 1745; Macsotay, *The Profession of Sculpture*, pp. 29–42.

149 Harold Bloom, *The Anxiety of Influence. A Theory of Poetry* (1973), 2nd edn (New York and Oxford, 1997). See, also Hall Bjørnstad (ed.), *Borrowed Feathers: Plagiarism and the Limits of Imitation in Early Modern Europe* (Oslo, 2008).

150 Guiffrey, *Collection des livrets*, vol. 1: *Salon 1745*, no. 171.

151 The distinction between recollection and repetition is Kierkegaard's and is mobilised by Bloom when discussing *kenosis*, the third of his six ratios of influence, in *Anxiety of Influence*, pp. 77–92, esp. pp. 82–3.

152 For use of the frame as a metaphor for textual citation see abbé Jean-Baptiste Du Bos, *Réflexions critiques sur la poésie et la peinture* (1719), ed. Dominique Désirat (Paris, 1993), pp. 186–97.

153 For a discussion of plagiarism as palimpsest see Schneider, *Voleurs de mots*, pp. 57–64.

154 Louis Petit de Bachaumont, *Essai sur la peinture, la sculpture et l'architecture* (1751), 2nd edn (n.p., 1752), pp. 38–9.

155 On the size of *morceaux de réception* in painting and sculpture see Michel, *L'Académie royale de peinture et de sculpture*, pp. 215–22.

156 Bloom, *Anxiety of Influence*, p. 30.

157 For an extended discussion of the *morceaux* as an institution, see Michel, *L'Académie royale de peinture et de sculpture*, pp. 177–230.

158 Ibid.

159 Du Bos, *Réflexions critiques*. I should note that Bloom always denied the inference of the Oedipal in his concept of the 'anxiety of influence'.

160 See Michel on taste as one of the Académie's criteria of judgment; Michel, *L'Académie royale de peinture et de sculpture*.

161 Guiffrey, *Collection des livrets*, vol. 1: *Salon 1745*, no. 171.

162 Geneviève Bresc-Bautier, *Pierre Puget: Milon de Crotone* (Paris, 1996).

163 On the models and cast see Nina Kosareva, 'Maserpieces of Eighteenth-Century French Sculpture', *Apollo*, 101 (1975), 443–51, at 445–6; cf. Macsotay, *The Profession of Sculpture*, pp. 37–8.

164 For an overview, see Luc Georget, 'La Fortune critique', in *Pierre Puget: Peintre, sculpteur, architecte, 1620–1694*, exh. cat. Musée des beaux-arts, Marseille and Paris, 1994, pp. 381–7.

165 Comte de Caylus, *Vie de François Girardon*, 2 May 1750, in LM*Con*, vol. 5, p. 496. Caylus based his characterisation of Girardon as servile on Pierre-Jean Grosley, *Mémoire sur la vie et les ouvrages de François Girardon*, read at the Académie on 4 Aug. 1742, in LM*Con*, vol. 4, pp. 509–21.

166 [Charles Léoffroy de Saint-Yves], *Observations sur les arts et sur quelques morceaux de peinture et de sculpture exposés au Louvre en 1748* (Leyden, 1748), pp. 125–6.

167 On Puget's identification with the Milo, see *Pierre Puget: Peintre, sculpteur, architecte, 1620–1694*, pp. 381–7.

168 Du Bos, *Réflexions critiques*, p. 187.

169 The allusion I make here is to Jacques Lacan's reading of Freud's essay on the ego and the id, in which Lacan describes how the subject introjects an exterior image or ego ideal, and adds thereby a new stratum to his own ego (like layers of an onion). The subject is thus provided with a secondary, stabilising identification in which to take form. See Jacques Lacan, *The Seminar of Jacques Lacan, Book I: Freud's Papers on Technique, 1953–1954*, ed Jacques-Alain Miller, trans. John Forrester (New York, 1991), pp. 170–71.

170 [Saint-Yves], *Observations*, p. 125. For a fuller discussion, see Aline Magnien, *La Nature et l'antique, la chair et le contour: Essai sur la sculpture française du XVIIIe siècle*, Studies on Voltaire and the Eighteenth Century (Oxford, 2004), pp. 292–333. See also Falconet's own assessment of Puget in *Réflexions sur la sculpture* (Paris, 1761), p. 33.

171 According to the *livret*'s description: 'Et comme la connoissance de l'Histoire & des Mathématiques, fait encore partie de cet Art, son Génie s'assure aussi sur des Livres de l'une & de l'autre espèce.' See, Guiffrey, *Collection des livrets*, vol. 1: *Salon 1745*, no. 171.

172 Bloom, *Anxiety of Influence*, *passim*. Bloom describes the anxiety of influence as a 'mode' of melancholy.

173 The Académie's alleged initial objection to the Milo in 1744 may partly have rested on the scale of Falconet's ambition. Falconet, the most unprecocious student-apprentice, of humble origin – his father was a journeyman joiner – and without the necessary training in Rome, appeared perhaps to be making unacceptably high claims to a place in the Académie. Ten years later, his success assured by a royal commission and work for Madame de Pompadour at Crécy and Bellevue, Falconet was altogether a more credible heir. With the passage of time, attention may have shifted from the indices of surrender to those of masterly control. Moreover, Falconet's reputation had caught up with his self: the mimetic touch of the marble having become part of Falconet's own signature.

174 Klaus Herding, *Pierre Puget: Das bildnerische Werk* (Berlin, 1970), pp. 14–26. Note that Falconet had direct access to the sculpture since his master, Jean-Baptiste Le Moyne, was at that time working on the Bassin de Neptune at Versailles. See Réau, *Falconet*, vol. 1, pp. 57–8.

175 *P-V*, vol. 6, pp. 394–5, 31 Aug. 1754.

176 Étienne La Font de Saint-Yenne, *Réflexions sur quelques causes de l'état présent de la peinture en France* (The Hague, 1747), pp. 141–2.

177 Ibid., p. 132 (Le Moyne's sketch for a Narcissus: 'tout y est feu & génie'), p. 142 (Vinache's sketch-model for a Saint Theresa).

178 *Lettre sur le Salon de 1755, adressée à ceux qui la liront* (Amsterdam, 1755), pp. 75–7.

179 Falconet's Milo is also mentioned in: [Joseph de La Porte], *Sentimens sur plusieurs des tableaux exposés cette année dans le grand Salon du Louvre* (n.p., 1755), p. 18; [Pierre Estève], *Lettre à un partisan du bon goût sur l'exposition des tableaux dans le grand Salon du Louvre* (n.p., 1755); *Réponse à une lettre adressée à un partisan du bon goût, sur l'exposition des tableaux fait dans le grand Salon du Louvre* (n.p., 1755), p. 25; and in newspaper reviews in the *MdF* (Oct. 1755), 184, and *Année littéraire* (1755), no. 3, 61.

180 The standard and yet to be bettered history of the Salon is Thomas Crow, *Painters and Public Life in Eighteenth-Century Paris* (London and New Haven, CT, 1985).

181 *MdF* (Oct. 1737), 2013.

182 Guiffrey, *Collection des livrets*, vol. 1: *Salon 1737*, preface.

183 Ernst Cassirer, *The Philosophy of the Enlightenment*, trans. Fritz C. A. Koelln and James P. Pettegrove (Princeton, 1951), pp. 93–133. Specifically on the writings of Albrecht von Haller, Étienne Bonnot de Condillac and Charles Bonnet at mid-century, and associated with sensationalism by modern scholars, see Anne C. Vila, *Enlightenment and Pathology: Sensibility in the Literature and Medicine of Eighteenth-Century France* (Baltimore, 1998), pp. 13–42.

184 Lambert-Sigisbert Adam, *Collection de sculptures antiques grecques et romaines trouvées à Rome dans les ruines des palais de Néron et de Marius* (Paris, 1755).

185 *MdF* (Apr. 1755), 156; *MdF* (June 1755), vol. 2, 309–10.

186 [Charles-Nicolas Cochin *fils*], 'Lettre à M. l'abbé R*** sur une très mauvaise plaisanterie qu'il a laissé imprimer dans le *Mercure* du mois de décembre 1754, par une société d'architectes, qui pourroissent bien aussi prétendre être du premier mérite et de la première réputation, quoiqu'ils ne soient pas de l'Académie', *MdF* (Feb. 1755), 148–71.

187 Ibid., p. 168.

188 'Lettre à M.*** sur la peinture encaustique', *MdF* (Mar. 1755), 146–51 at 146.

189 On Cochin and Raynal see Christian Michel, *Charles-Nicolas Cochin et l'art des Lumières* (Rome, 1993), pp. 122–3. On Raynal as editor of the *Mercure* see Jean Sgard (ed.), *Dictionnaire des journalistes (1600–1789)* at <dictionnaire-journalistes.gazettes18e.fr/dictionnaires-presse-classique-mise-en-ligne> (accessed 22 Dec. 2017). Raynal left the *Mercure* in January 1755, so, although addressed to him, the letter would have been received by the new editor, who was Jean-François de Boissy.

190 *MdF* (Sept. 1755), 202. The pendant, *Tempête*, also engraved by Balechou, was advertised in the same journal with a more expansive endorsement by Vernet. The editor asked rhetorically: 'qui mieux que lui est en état de juger de traduction d'après ses tableaux?' See *MdF* (June 1757), vol. 1, 163–4.

191 *MdF* (Mar. 1755), 45–6; *MdF* (May 1756), 131–3.

192 Guiffrey, *Collection des livrets*, vol. 2: *Salon 1755*, nos 167, 173. For other prints awarded privilege see the Appendix to this book. In 1737 Thomassin exhibited his portrait of Jean Thierry (fig. **35**) and Cochin *père* his *Jacob arrive en Mésopotamie, aperçoit Rachel et se fait connoître à elle* (fig. **36**).

193 *MdF* (Sept. 1737), 2015–16. Famously, La Font de Saint-Yenne also insisted on the disinterestedness of his criticism (*MdF* (Sept. 1749), 186–90), although the *Mercure* later condemned, on the grounds of personal injury, pamphlet criticism of his type (*MdF* (Nov, 1755), 185–6).

194 Denis Diderot, *Diderot Salons*, ed. Jean Seznec and Jean Adhémar, 4 vols (Oxford, 1957–67), vol. 3, Salon 1767, p. 52.

195 Nicolas Lesur and Olivier Aaron, *Jean-Baptiste Marie Pierre, 1714–1789: Premier peintre du roi* (Paris, 2009), p. 213.

196 *MdF* (Oct. 1761), vol. 1, 148.

197 Seznec, 'Diderot et les plagiats'. For a much more positive evaluation of Pierre's act and career, see Lesur and Aaron, *Jean-Baptiste Marie Pierre*, pp. 128–32 and *passim*.

198 Seznec, 'Diderot et les plagiats', 68. On the theory of invention as a combinatory strategy see Anne Le Pas de Sécheval, 'L'Abeille et le pinceau: Théorie et pratique de l'éclectisme chez Antoine Coypel', *Revue d'esthétique*, 31–2 (1997), 237–52. Antoine Coypel's *conférences* continued to be delivered at the Académie well into the 1740s and 1750s; see LM*Con*.

199 On Diderot and genius see Herbert Dieckmann's classic article, 'Diderot's Conception of Genius', *Journal of the History of Ideas*, 2 (1941), 151–82; in a wider context, see Kineret S. Jaffe, 'The Concept of Genius: Its Changing Role in Eighteenth-Century French Aesthetics', *Journal of the History of ideas*, 41 (1980), 579–99.

200 It is worth noting that the plagiarist serves as a foil to the genius in part 2 of Du Bos, *Réflexions critiques*, pp. 171–212.

201 *Diderot Salons*, vol. 1, p. 113.

202 Du Bos, *Réflexions critiques*, p. 199.

203 Réau, *Falconet*, vol. 1, p. 60.

204 'État de la vaisselle portée à la Monnoie de Paris', *MdF* (Jan. 1760), 217–81 at 236. Other artists included the architects Ange-Jacques Gabriel and Germain Soufflot and the miniaturist Jean-Baptiste Massé. Pierre's donation was the largest in this group.

205 Du Bos, *Réflexions critiques*, p. 198.

206 *Diderot Salons*, vol. 1, p. 113.

207 Ibid.

208 See chapter 1, pp. 69–76.

209 Diderot makes no mention of Carracci's *coloris* or brushwork. Later, when reviewing the work of Charles-Amédée-Philippe Vanloo, he noted that a painter's reputation could be transmitted only according to the values registered by print, '[a]insi le mérite du coloris disparaît'. *Diderot Salons*, vol. 1, Salon 1761, pp. 123–4. It is possible that Diderot knew of Carracci's *Lamentation* primarily via Jean-Louis Roullet's 1689 print, on which see Christine Raimbault, 'Jean-Louis Roullet (1645–1699), interprète d'Annibal Carrache: Le Contrat de 1686 avec Pierre Le Tessier de Montarsy', *NE*, no. 220 (2008–9), 33–41.

210 For plagiarism as excision, see *Diderot Salons*, vol. 2, Salon 1765, p. 186. Scissors also served the critic. Diderot suggested that the viewer mentally cut Philippe-Jacques de Loutherbourg's landscape *Rendez-vous de chasse du prince de Condé* vertically in two to reveal that each half was traced along the contours of the other; ibid., p. 166.

211 See, for example, Charles-Antoine Jombert, 'Contenant diverses pratiques et inventions pour copier un dessin ou tableau', *Méthode pour apprendre le dessin* (Paris, 1784), ch. 7, pp. 123–36.

212 Michel Delon, 'Les Essais sur la peinture, ou la place de la théorie', *Diderot Studies*, 30 (2007), 31–51, esp. 39–41.

213 *Diderot Salons*, vol. 1, Salon 1761, pp. 133–4. In his 1765 *livret*, Diderot asserted that, while plagiarism was also possible in sculpture, 'il est rare qu'il soit ignoré. Il n'est ni aussi facile à pratiquer, ni aussi facile à sauver qu'en peinture.' *Diderot Salons*, vol. 2, Salon 1765, p. 212.

214 *Diderot Salons*, vol. 1, Salon 1761, p. 120. Abbé Jean-Bernard Le Blanc, in the *Mercure*, defended Deshays against those connoisseurs who had claimed that his *La Dernière Communion de Saint Benoît* was after Agostino Carracci's famous *San Girolamo*, arguing instead that 'comme objet d'émulation, la communion de S. Jérôme a pu servir à élever l'imagination du Peintre François'. *MdF* (Oct. 1761), vol. 1, 152.

215 We can note that Diderot's scanning repetitions appropriately imitate verse in the Bible, notably the Psalms.

216 Denis Diderot, *Lettre sur le commerce de la librairie* (1763), ed. Michel Parfenov (Paris, 2001), p. 42.

217 Ibid., p. 41.

218 However, the formal application made by a student in 1761 (*P-V*, vol. 7, p. 139, 26 Feb. 1761) to copy *morceaux de réception* was not well received. See Cochin's discussion with Marigny, Cochin to Marigny, 3 Mar. 1761, in *Correspondance de M. de Marigny avec Coypel, Lépicié et Cochin*, ed. Marc

Furcy-Raynaud, 2 vols, *AAF*, 19–20 (1903–4), vol. 1, 195–6: 'L'orsqu'il leur a été permis de copier les ouvrages de réception... il s'en est ensuivi qu'on a vu le pont Notre-Dame étaler de mauvaises copies à en faire la parodie et devenoient pour eux une mortification.' See also *P-V*, vol. 7, p. 197, 19 Mar. 1761.

219 Lavezzi, 'Appelle en Arlequin'; Michel, *L'Académie royale de peinture et de sculpture*, ch. 3.

220 See eulogies to Pierre published in the *Mercure de France*, first in 1749 by Jean-Claude Gaspard de Sireuil (which begins 'Ami, dont le brillant génie / Des grands maîtres d'Italie / Nous promet les talents divers' and ends 'Poursuis de si nobles travaux, / Ils font honneur à ta Patrie: / C'est en surpassant tes rivaux / Que tu feras faire l'envie'), and, after the execution of his ceiling at Saint-Roch, by Anne-Marie du Boccage, the translator of Milton; *MdF* (Jan. 1749), 78–9; *MdF* (Dec. 1756), 182–3. On oppositional factions at mid-century see Crow, *Painters and Public Life*, pp. 104–33.

221 Anne Fastrup, 'Mediating *le philosophe*: Diderot's Strategic Self-Representations', in *This is Enlightenment*, Clifford Siskin and William Warner (eds) (Chicago, 2010), pp. 265–83.

222 Diderot *Salons*, vol. 2, Salon 1765, p. 186 (plagiarism), pp. 225–30 (engraving).

223 Ibid., p. 186. The altarpiece in question was François-Bernard Lépicié's *Saint-Crépin et Saint-Crépinien, distribuant leur bien aux pauvres*, for the church of the Carmelites at Chalon-sur-Saône.

224 Ibid., pp. 225–6. Diderot's remarks are made in the context of arguments about the authenticity and individuality of handwriting, and specifically in light of Louis Pierre Vallain's *Traité sur la preuve par comparaison d'écritures* (Paris, 1761), in which the author insisted on the knowledge and skill of a *maître-expert*, or writing master, in determining real from false signatures.

225 William M. Ivins, *Prints and Visual Communication* (Cambridge, MA, 1953), pp. 71–93 at p. 73. On translation as a metaphor for reproduction see Christian Michel, 'Réflexion sur la comparaison entre gravure et traduction au XVIIIe siècle', in *Delineavit et sculpsit: Dix-neuf Contributions sur les rapports dessin-gravure du XVIe an XXe siècle. Mélanges offerts à Marie-Félicie Perez-Pivot*, François Fossier (ed.) (Lyon, 2003), pp. 151–61.

226 *Diderot Salons*, vol. 2, Salon 1765, p. 227.

227 The critic abbé de La Porte argued, in relation to Pierre's *Descente*, that when an altarpiece fulfilled the needs of the faithful it had succeeded in its (artistic) aim. See Joseph de La Porte, 'Observations d'une société d'amateurs sur les tableaux exposés au Salon', *Observateur littéraire* (1761), 19.

228 *MdF* (Mar. 1755), 145–6.

229 Benjamin, 'The Work of Art in the Age of Mechanical Reproduction', pp. 224–5.

230 *Diderot Salons*, vol. 2, Salon 1765, p. 227.

231 William M. Ivins, *How Prints Look: An Illustrated Guide*, rev. edn (London, 1988), p. 66.

232 *Diderot Salons*, vol. 2, Salon 1765, p. 226.

233 The loss of marble's dazzle and prestigious glow Falconet counted a gain for the purposes of study. See Giuseppe Pucci, 'Les Moulages de sculpture anciennes et l'esthétique du XVIIIe siècle', in *Les Moulages de sculptures antiques et l'histoire de l'archéologie*, Henri Lavagne and François Queyrel (eds) (Geneva, 2000), pp. 45–55.

234 André Malraux, *La Psychologie de l'art*, 3 vols (Geneva, 1947), vol. 1, pp. 18–52.

235 *Diderot Salons*, vol. 1, Salon 1761, p. 123.

236 Ibid., p. 124.

237 See this view for example in 'Réflexions sommaires sur les ouvrages exposés au Louvre cette année', *MdF* (Nov, 1755), 186.

238 Crow, *Painters and Public Life*, pp. 175–209

239 Richard Wrigley, 'Censorship and Anonymity in Eighteenth-Century French Art Criticism', *OAJ*, 6 (1983), 17–28.

240 *Dialogue sur la peinture* (n.p., 1773), pp. 4–7. On the pamphlet and the political context of the 1770s see Crow, *Painters and Public Life*, pp. 180–81.

241 *Dialogue sur la peinture*, p. 6. The chapel in question was the chapelle de Saint-Grégoire. Originally decorated by Michel Corneille in the 17th century, it had been irreparably damaged by damp and Carle Vanloo had been charged with its redecoration, but he died before undertaking it. Doyen was his replacement. See *Peinture de la coupole de la chapelle Saint-Grégoire* (1771), Collection Deloynes, vol. 49, no. 1323: 589–609 (Gallica); Marc Sandoz, 'La Chapelle Saint-Grégoire de l'église de Saint-Louis des Invalides', *GBA*, 77 (1971), 129–44.

242 *Dialogue sur la peinture*, p. 99. For a full discussion of the political context see Crow, *Painters and Pubic Life*, pp. 175–91.

243 For other accusations of plagiarism see, for example, the case of Jean-Jacques Lagrenée *le jeune*, *Saint Michel terrassant les anges rebelles* (cathedral of Saint-Étienne, Auxerre), exhibited at the Salon of 1773, whose composition, according to the author of the *Dialogue sur la peinture*, 'n'est pas de lui' but rather derived from a print after Antoine Rivalz's altarpiece of the same subject for the cathedral of Saint-Just and Saint-Pasteur, Narbonne. *Dialogue sur la peinture*, p. 15. The critic found such indebtedness forgivable only in old age.

244 *Sur la peinture: Ouvrage succinct qui peut éclairer les artistes sur la fin originelle de l'art* (The Hague, 1782), p. 74.

245 On Doyen's self-fashioning see Anne Leclair, 'Lettres d'un artiste à un amateur: La Correspondance de Doyen avec le marquis de Voyer d'Argenson (1770–1772)', in *Curiosité: Études d'histoire de l'art en honneur d'Antoine Schnapper*, Olivier Bonfait, Véronique Gerard-Powell and Philippe Sénéchal (eds) (Paris, 1998), pp. 139–58; Laetitia Pierre, 'Le Fonds d'estampes de Gabriel-François Doyen', in *La Gravure: Quelles problématiques pour les temps modernes?* Isabelle Michel-Évrard and Pierre Wachenheim (eds) (Bordeaux, 2009), pp. 143–52.

246 *Le Dictionnaire de l'Académie françoise*, 4th edn, 2 vols (Paris, 1762), vol. 1, p. 614.

247 D'Angiviller to Pierre, 17 Sept. 1777, *P-V*, vol. 8, pp. 281–3.

248 *Mémoire à consulter et consultation, pour le sieur Gaucher, graveur en taille-douce, de l'Académie des arts d'Angleterre; contre les sieurs Esnauts et Rapilly, marchands d'estampes* (Paris, 1776), AN, AD XI/18; *Précis pour le sieur Gaucher, graveur en taille-douce, de l'Académie des arts d'Angleterre; contre les sieurs Esnauts et Rapilly, marchands d'estampes et le sieur Hubert; et encore par les sieurs Née et Masquelier, graveurs en taille-douce; contre lesdits sieurs Esnauts et Rapilly, le sieur Dupin, et le sieur André* (Paris, 1776), BnF, Mss. f.f. 22121/34.

249 According to the *Précis pour le sieur Gaucher*, p. 7, a large number of Academicians were also present at the trial.

250 *Mémoire à consulter*, p. 3.

251 *Précis pour le sieur Gaucher*, p. 19.

252 Ibid., p. 26.

253 Ibid., p. 22.

254 Ibid., pp. 23–4. Cochin also distinguished between the legitimate copying of the Old Masters and the criminal copying of the Moderns.

255 *Jugement rendu par Monsieur Lenoir, commissaire d'état, lieutenant-général de police, commissaire du Conseil*, 29 Oct. 1776, BnF, Mss. f.f. 22121/35.

256 D'Angiviller to Lenoir, 17 Jan. 1777, AN, O1 1914/34.

257 *P-V*, vol. 8, pp. 285–6.

258 In greater depth see Scott, 'Authorship, the Académie and the Market Place', pp. 37–8.

259 *Journal de Paris*, no. 76 (16 Mar. 1780), 313–24.

260 Ibid., p. 314.

261 *Précis pour le sieur Gaucher*, pp. 19–20. Esnault and Rapilly had allegedly sold 200 copies of *Le Déjeuné* at 15 *sous*.

262 See chapter 1, pp. 87–90.

263 *Journal de Paris*, no. 76 (16 Mar. 1780), 314.

264 Charles-Nicolas Cochin *fils*, *Project d'arrest du Conseil pour les graveurs*, June 1764, BnF, Mss. f.f. 22120/68.

265 Marcle Plaisant and Olivier Pichot, *La Conférence de Rome: Commentaire pratique de la nouvelle convention pour la protection internationale de la propriété littéraire et artistique* (Paris, 1934), pp. 50–51; quoted from David Saunders, *Authorship and Copyright* (London, 1992), p. 31.

CHAPTER 3
IMITATION: Crimes of likeness

1 Jean-Jacques Rousseau, *Rousseau juge de Jean-Jacques: Dialogues*, in *Œuvres complètes*, ed. Bernard Gagnebin and Marcel Raymond, 5 vols (1959–95), vol. 1, pp. 778–82; Douglas Fordham, 'Allan Ramsay's Enlightenment, or, Hume and the Patronizing Portrait', *Art Bulletin*, 88 (2006), 508–24.

2 On the different ways art can offend, see Anthony Julius, 'Art Crimes', in *Dear Images: Art, Copyright and Culture*, Daniel McClean and Karsten Schubert (eds) (London, 2002), pp. 473–503.

3 See, among others, Richard Brilliant, *Portraiture* (London, 1991); Georges Didi-Huberman, 'Rassemblance mythifiée et rassemblance oubliée chez Vasari: La Légende du portrait "sur le vif"', *Mélanges de l'École française de Rome, Italie et Méditerranée*, 106 (1994), 383–432; Édouard Pommier, *Théories du portrait: De la Renaissance aux Lumières* (Paris, 1998); Hans Belting, *Face and Mask: A Double History*, trans. Thomas S. Hansen and Abby J. Hansen (Princeton, 2017)

4 For Zumbo see *Mercure galant* (May 1701), 325; (June 1701), 252–61; (Sept. 1701), 403–9; (Jan. 1702), 185–7; Ronald Lightbown, 'Gaetano Giulio Zumbo, II: Genoa and France', *Burlington Magazine*, 106 (1964), 563–7, 569; E. J. Pyke, *A Biographical Dictionary of Wax Modellers* (London, 1973). For Pinson see Michel Lemire, 'Les Modèles en cire colorée du XVIIIe et du XIXe siècle: Instruments de démonstration anatomique', in *L'Image et la science*, René Ginouves (ed.) (Paris, 1992), pp. 165–71.

5 He was so styled on his death certificate, 8 Apr. 1717. On Benoît see Anatole de Montaiglon and Jules-Joseph Guiffrey, 'Antoine Benoît, sculpteur en cire: Lettres de relief de dérogeance à noblesse en faveur d'Antoine Benoist (1706), et Débat sur un portrait de Mademoiselle de Noailles (1711)', *NAAF* (1872), 301–11; Eugène Vaudin, 'Antoine Benoist de Joigny, peintre et sculpteur en cire de Louis XIV', *Bulletin de la Société des sciences historiques et naturelles de l'Yonne* (1886), 313–38; Henri Stein, 'Nouveaux Documents sur le peintre sculpteur Antoine Benoist', *Réunion des sociétés des beaux-arts des départements à la Sorbonne* (1895), 791–804; Antoine Dutilleux, 'Antoine Benoist, premier sculpteur en cire du roi Louis XIV', *Revue de l'histoire de Versailles et de Seine-et-Oise* (1905), 81–97, 198–213; Stanislas Lami, *Dictionnaire des sculpteurs de l'École française sous le règne de Louis XIV* (Paris, 1906).

6 *Mercure galant* (Apr. 1684), 174–6; Antoine-Nicolas Dézallier d'Argenville, *Voyage pittoresque de Paris* (Paris, 1752), p. 355; J.-A. Piganiol de La Force, *Description de Paris, de Versailles, de Marly* (Paris, 1765), p. 291.

7 Antoinette Le Normand-Romain, *Mémoire de marbre: La Sculpture funéraire en France, 1804–1914* (Paris, 1995), pp. 240–45.

8 On the French portrait print in the 17th and 18th centuries, see George Duplessis, *De la gravure de portrait en France* (Paris, 1875); Richard Campbell, 'The Portrait Print: Tradition and Transformations', in *Regency to Empire: French Printmaking, 1715–1814*, exh. cat., Baltimore Museum of Art, Victor I. Carlson and John W. Ittmann (eds) (Baltimore, 1985), pp. 28–35; Marianne Grivel, *Le Commerce de l'estampe à Paris au XVIIe siècle* (Geneva, 1986), esp. pp. 141–3; Véronique Meyer, 'Le Portrait gravé sous le règne de Louis XIV', in Emmanuel Coquery et al., *Visages du Grand Siècle*, exh. cat., Musée des beaux-arts, Nantes, and Musée des Augustins, Toulouse (Paris, Nantes and Toulouse, 1997), pp. 163–78.

9 Grivel, *Le Commerce de l'estampe*, p. 135.

10 William McAllister Johnson, *French Royal Academy of Painting and Sculpture Engraved Reception Pieces, 1672–1789*, exh. cat., Agnes Etherington Art Centre, Kingston, Ontario, and other venues (Kingston, 1982).

11 BnF, Mss. f.f. 21960, 27 May 1754 (Odieuvre); BnF, Mss. f.f. 21971, 19 Nov. 1788 (Saint-Aubin); the latter portrait was of the actor Henri-Louis Le Kain.

12 See chapter 2, pp. 96–8.

13 *Lettres patentes*, 23 Sept. 1668, repr. in *BSHAF* (1874), 167.

14 AN, O1 45/156, 163–4. According to Louis de Jaucourt, however, Benoît also made anatomical waxes, which were no less memorable for their beauty than his portraits. See Denis Diderot and Jean Le Rond d'Alembert, *Encyclopédie, ou Dictionnaire raisonné des sciences, des arts et des métiers* (Paris and Neuchâtel, 1751–72), vol. 3, p. 471.

15 The relatively low value of Benoît's stock at the time of his death suggests that value inhered less in the objects as commodities than as exhibits. For Benoît's *inventaire après décès* see Mireille Rambaud, *Documents du Minutier central concernant l'histoire de l'art*, 2 vols (Paris, 1964–71), vol. 2, pp. 206–7. The *permission simple* to exhibit, granted by Gabriel Nicolas de La Reynie in August 1685, fixed Benoît's entry charges as 5 *sous* per person. See Dutilleux, 'Antoine Benoist', 93.

16 *Précis pour le sieur Gaucher, graveur en taille-douce, de l'Académie des arts d'Angleterre; contre les sieurs Esnauts et Rapilly, marchands d'estampes et le sieur Hubert; et encore par les sieurs Née et Masquelier, graveurs en taille-douce; contre lesdits sieurs Esnauts et Rapilly, le sieur Dupin, et le sieur André* (Paris, 1776), p. 2, BnF, Mss. f.f. 22121/34.

17 Adrien Gastambide, *Traité théorique et pratique des contrefaçons en tous genres, ou de la propriété en matière de littérature, théatre, musique, peinture, dessin, gravure... sculpture* (Paris, 1837), p. 279; Augustin-Charles Renouard, *Traité des droits d'auteurs, dans la littérature, les sciences et les beaux-arts*, 2 vols (Paris, 1838), vol. 2, p. 78.

18 On mimesis see Eric Auerbach, *Mimesis: The Representation of Reality in Western Literature*, trans. Willard Trask (Princeton, 1971); Louis Marin, 'Mimesis and Description', *Word and Image*, 4 (1988), 25–36; John D. Lyons and Stephen G. Nichols, Jr (eds), *Mimesis: From Mirror to Method, Augustine to Descartes* (Hanover, NH, 1982); Gunter Gebauer and Christoph Wulf, *Mimesis: Culture–Art–Society*, trans. Don Reneau (Berkeley, CA, 1995); and more narrowly in relation to pictorial representation Jacques Thuillier, 'La Notion d'imitation dans la pensée artistique du XVIIe siècle', in *Critique et création littéraires en France au XVIIe siècle* (Paris, 1974), pp. 361–74; Peter Parshall, '*Imago contrafacta*: Images and Facts in the Northern Renaissance', *Art History*, 16 (1993), 554–79; Claudia Swan, 'Ad vivum, naer het leven, from the Life: Defining a Mode of Representation', *Word and Image*, 11 (1995), 353–72; and the multi-authored 'Notes from the Field: Mimesis', *Art Bulletin*, 95 (2013), 190–211.

19 Gaucher's print was announced in the following journals: *Avant coureur* (22 July 1771), 450; *MdF* (Aug. 1771), 181; *Journal des beaux-arts*, 4 (Oct. 1771), 188; *Gazette de France* (2 Dec. 1771). Hubert's print was advertised in the *Gazette de France* until 7 Mar. 1777.

20 On Esnault and Rapilly, active between *c.*1770 and 1804, see Pierre Casselle, 'Recherches sur les marchands d'estampes parisiens d'origine cotentinoise à la fin de l'ancien régime', *Bulletin d'histoire moderne et contemporaine*, 11 (1978), 75–93.

21 Abbé Le Brun, *Almanach historique et raisonné des architectes, peintres, sculpteurs, graveurs et cizeleurs*, 2 vols (Paris, 1776–7), vol. 2, pp. 171–2.

22 Ibid., p. 159. For Gaucher's portrait prints see *MdF* (Aug. 1766), 208; (June 1770), 205; (Dec. 1772), 180; (April 1773), 175; (July 1782), 186; (Aug. 1782), 46; (Nov. 1783), 235. On Gaucher

see Roger Portalis and Henri Draibel, *Charles-Étienne Gaucher, graveur: Notice et catalogue* (Paris, 1879); for the print in question see ibid., p. 85, cat. no. 64.

23 Louis Abel Bonafous, abbé de Fontenay, 'Preface', in *Dictionnaire des artistes*, 2 vols (Paris, 1776), vol. 1. In the same year he also published the pamphlet *Désaveu des artistes* in defence of Cochin, and in 1782 and 1783 obituaries of the printmakers Jean-Jacques Flipart and Jacques-Philippe Le Bas in the *Journal de Paris* (3 Aug. 1782), 880; (12 May 1783), 554–5. For a brief account of Gaucher's other literary works see Charles Fournier, 'Correspondance entre le graveur Étienne Gaucher et le Baron de Heineken', *NAAF* (1872), 392–9; Anatole de Montaiglon, 'Charles-Étienne Gaucher, 1788', *NAAF* (1874–5), 360–63.

24 *Mémoire à consulter et consultation pour le sieur Gaucher, graveur en taille-douce, de l'Académie des arts d'Angleterre; contre les sieurs Esnauts et Rapilly, marchands d'estampes* (Paris, 1776), p.6. This is the first of two briefs; the second, *Précis pour le sieur Gaucher*, is cited above, note 16. The briefs for Esnault and Rapilly have not survived. Their contents can only be inferred from the summaries contained in the brief for the prosecution.

25 Ibid., p. 13. The significance of the last point about the originality of the frame was, had the defendants but known it, readily to hand in Charles-Antoine Jombert's *Catalogue raisonné* of Cochin's *œuvre*, published in 1770, which included among the portraits one attributed to the artist by virtue not of the portrait or the etching work but of the design of the frame. See Charles-Antoine Jombert, *Catalogue de l'œuvre de Charles-Nicolas Cochin fils* (Paris, 1770), p. 129, cat. no. 95.

26 See Gaucher's privilege for six years for 'différens Portraits de sa composition', BnF, Mss. f.f. 21965, 2 May 1771.

27 *Mémoire à consulter*, pp. 13–14.

28 *Précis pour le sieur Gaucher*, pp. 18–20.

29 *La Malheureuse Famille Calas* by Jean-Baptiste Delafosse after Carmontelle was a print that, a decade earlier, Esnault and Rapilly were accused of having pirated; see BNF, Mss. f.f. 22099/73, 21 Aug. 1768. See Pierre Casselle, 'Le Commerce des estampes à Paris dans la seconde moitié du XVIIIe siècle', PhD diss., École nationale des chartes, Paris, 1976, p. 27; and Introduction p. 29.

30 *Mémoire à consulter*, p. 13.

31 On the difference between working from a drawing or a print, in cases of reprinting and plagiarism, see chapter 1, pp. 70–71.

32 *Mémoire à consulter*, p. 21.

33 Charles Fournier, 'Traité entre Gaucher et Panckoucke pour la gravure du portrait du comte de Vergennes d'après le dessin de Moreau, juillet 1784', *NAAF* (1872), 385.

34 In the print jargon of the period the ability of the printmaker to copy with precision and to scale the image up and down was known as 'posséder le dessein'. See Daniel Cronström to Nicodemus Tessin *le jeune*, 1696, in *L'Art en France et en Suède, 1693–1718: Extraits d'une correspondance entre l'architecte Nicodème Tessin le jeune et Daniel Cronström*, Roger-Armand Weigert and Carl Hernmarck (eds) (Stockholm, 1964), p. 117.

35 This interpretation of the Edict of Saint Jean-de-Luz is in marked contrast to the circumstances that gave rise to its formal confirmation in 1734 and 1742 and informal affirmation in 1757, when first the Corporation of copper-plate printers and then the *libraires* attempted to impose on the liberty of printmakers to own presses and to publish and sell prints freely. See *Arrests du Conseil d'estat du roy, qui permettent aux graveurs d'avoir des presses chez eux*, 13 and 27 July 1734, AN, AD XI/18; *Arrest du Conseil d'état du roy qui maintient et garde les graveurs en taille-douce, au burin et à l'eau-forte dans le droit et possession de vendre et débiter dans tout le royaume les ouvrages de gravûre dont ils sont les auteurs ou propriétaires*, 23 Jan. 1742, AN AD XI/18; the book publisher, Claude-François Simon's, *Mémoire concernant la gravure* (1757), BnF, Mss. f.f. 22120/32; and Pierre-François Basan's response, *Exposé du sieur Basan et autre ses confrères graveurs en taille-douce à Paris contre la communauté des libraires, Septembre 1757* (1757), BnF, Mss. f.f. 22076/73.

36 *Précis pour le sieur Gaucher*, pp. 7, 22, 25, 26.

37 Esnault and Rapilly named Le Bas, Saint-Aubin, Flipart and René Gaillard; ibid., pp. 28–9, 31.

38 Gaucher made the case for probity, not competition, as the engine of trade. See *Mémoire à consulter*, p. 5.

39 *Précis pour le sieur Gaucher*, pp. 29–30, with Cochin's defence of his father's sin of youth.

40 Ibid., p. 7: Esnault and Rapilly reportedly tried to prevent Cochin's and the Académie's intervention in their case, on the grounds that they were not 'compétens pour fixer l'usage des Marchands d'Estampes'.

41 Ibid., pp. 16–17. The analogy was drawn specifically between this case and a case involving the 1769 map of Reims by Jean Lattré. Me Hecquet counterclaimed that, while map-making was an exact science and therefore two maps might, indeed, be exactly the same without one necessarily having been copied from the other, in the case of portraits this was not so.

42 See the brief discussion in the Introduction (pp. 33–4) of an early and important infringement case related to maps.

43 *Jugement rendu par Monsieur Le Noir*, 29 Oct. 1776, p. 1, BnF, Mss. f.f. 22121/35 (another copy, AN, O1 1914/36).

44 The following discussion of the portraits draws on Christian Michel, *Charles-Nicolas Cochin et l'art des Lumières* (Rome, 1993), pp. 172–4.

45 The circular frames later assigned to the drawings by printmakers – suspended from rings by bows of ribbon – may have recalled that origin in drawing. That style of frame was devised for the presentation of Old Master drawings under glass; the amateur Pierre-Jean Mariette had half a dozen sheets of Van Dyck heads so mounted. See Martin Eidelberg, 'The Comte de Caylus's *tête-à-tête* with Van Dyck', *GBA*, 131 (1998), 1–20.

46 On the relationship between Cochin and Fréron see Madeleine Pinault Sørensen, 'Élie-Catherine Fréron et le dessin', in *Élie Fréron: Polémiste et critique d'art*, Sophie Barthélemy, André Carion and Jean Balcou (eds) (Rennes, 2001), pp. 227–61, esp. pp. 232–3.

47 The expansion of the series beyond Mme Geoffrin's immediate circle is clearly marked in the 1760s by the inclusion of foreign notables, many of them visitors to, but none residents of, Paris, starting with Horace Walpole, and including David Hume and David Garrick. See Jombert, *Catalogue de l'œuvre de... Cochin*, p. 178, cat. nos 78, 80, 81.

48 Jean-Baptiste Le Blanc, *Observations sur les ouvrages de MM. de l'Académie de peinture et de sculpture* (n.p., 1753), pp. 45–6; comte de Caylus, 'Exposition des ouvrages de l'Académie royale de peinture et de sculpture', *MdF* (Oct. 1753), 158–65.

49 Étienne La Font de Saint-Yenne, *Sentiments sur quelques ouvrages de peinture, sculpture et gravure, écrits à un particulier en province* (Leyden, 1754), p. 176.

50 *MdF* (June 1755), vol. 1, 197 (Chardin); (Apr. 1774), vol. 1, 181 (La Condamine); (Oct. 1774), vol. 1, 188 (Raynal).

51 Harry Berger, Jr, 'Fictions of the Pose: Facing the Gaze of Early Modern Portraiture', *Representations*, 46 (1994), 87–120.

52 According to Jacques Savary des Bruslons, the quality of Benoît's waxes arose from the 'secret' of casting from life, without loss of health or beauty; see *Dictionnaire universel de commerce*, 2 vols (Geneva, 1744), vol. 1, p. 903. On wax sculpture see Julius von Schlosser, *Histoire du portrait en cire* (1911), trans. Édouard Pommier (Paris, 1997); David Freedberg, *The Power of Images: Studies in the History and Theory of Response* (Chicago and London, 1989), pp. 212–31; Jacques Thuillier, 'Plaidoyer pour les "chiens perdus sans collier": La "Tête de cire" du Musée des beaux-arts de Lille', in *Curiosité: Études*

d'histoire de l'art en honneur d'Antoine Schnapper, Olivier Bonfait, Véronique Gerard-Powell and Philippe Sénéchal (eds) (Paris, 1998), pp. 1–6. See also *Theorizing Wax: On the Meaning of a Disappearing Medium*, *OAJ*, 36/1 (2013) [special issue], esp. Hanneke Grootenboer, 'On the Substance of Wax', 1–12; and Allison Goudie, 'The Wax Portrait Bust as *Trompe l'œil*? A Case Study of Queen Maria Carolina of Naples', 55–74. On the profile bust of Louis XIV see Pierre de Nolhac, 'Un Nouveau Portrait de Louis XIV au musée de Versailles', *Revue de l'art*, 34 (1913), 321–32; Milovan Stanić and Alexandre Maral, 'Portraits en cire de Louis XIV', in *Louis XIV: L'Homme et le roi*, exh. cat., Musée nationale des châteaux de Versailles et de Trianon, Nicolas Milanovic and Alexandre Maral (eds) (Paris, 2009), pp. 225–7.

53 See the descriptions in Germain Brice, *Description nouvelle de ce qu'il y a de plus remarquable dans la ville de Paris* (1684), 2nd edn (Paris, 1687), vol. 2, p. 221, and Louis-François Dubois de Saint-Gelais, *Histoire journalière de Paris, 1716–1717*, ed. Maurice Tournieux, 2 vols (Paris, 1885), vol. 2, pp. 222–3. For accounts of the reactions of foreign embassies see *Mercure galant* (Apr. 1699), 61–2 (Moroccan embassy); (July, 1704), 143 (Libyan embassy).

54 'Does the circle live? It seems to be breathing. / By some new secret, Benoît, your ingenious art seems to have given life to the wax.' Baraton, *Poésies diverses* (Paris, 1705), pp. 281–2, quoted in Dutilleux, 'Antoine Benoist', p. 87.

55 François-Timoléon de Choisy, *Mélanges historiques*, quoted in Spire Blondel, 'Les Modeleurs en cire', pt 3, *GBA*, 26 (1882), 431.

56 André Félibien, *Entretiens sur les vies et sur les ouvrages des plus excellents peintres anciens et modernes: Entretiens I et II*, ed. René Démoris (Paris, 1987), p. 123.

57 Ibid., p. 122.

58 Ibid., p. 123.

59 Ibid., p. 124.

60 *Lettres patentes*, 23 Sept. 1668, repr. in *BSHAF* (1874), 167.

61 Ibid.

62 See Benoît's disclosure to Bernini in Oct. 1665, recorded in Paul Fréart de Chantelou, *Diary of the Cavaliere Bernini's Visit to France*, ed. Anthony Blunt, trans. Margery Corbett (Princeton, 1985), p. 301.

63 Pierre-Jean Mariette, 'Pitau (les)', *Abecedario de P. J. Mariette*, ed. Philippe de Chennevières and Anatole de Montaiglon, 6 vols (Paris, 1853–62), vol. 8, pp. 179–80, cited in Meyer, 'Le Portrait gravé sous... Louis XIV', p. 171.

64 On the emergence of these categories in law see Bernard Edelman, 'The Law's Eye: Nature and Copyright', in *Of Authors and Origins: Essays on Copyright Law*, Brad Sherman and Alain Strowel (eds) (Oxford, 1994), pp. 79–91.

65 I have not been able to trace this privilege. However, the engraver Pierre-Adrien Le Beau, who worked regularly for Esnault and Rapilly, did obtain a privilege for a 'suite' of portraits of great men and women on 1 July 1774; BnF, Mss. f.f. 21966.

66 *Mémoire à consulter*, p. 11.

67 'Cire [Histoire ancienne / Histoire moderne]', in Diderot and d'Alembert, *Encyclopédie*, vol. 3, p. 472. Benoît's son was given an extension of the privilege for a further 20 years in 1717; see Stein, 'Nouveaux Documents sur... Antoine Benoist', pp. 803–4. The son's enterprise is mentioned in guidebooks up to the mid-18th century. See Dézallier d'Argenville, *Voyage pittoresque de Paris*, p. 355; Piganiol de La Force, *Description de Paris*, p. 291.

68 Louis de Jaucourt, 'Portrait, Image, Figure, Effigie', in Diderot and d'Alembert, *Encyclopédie*, vol. 13, p. 153.

69 Ibid.

70 Roger de Piles, *Cours de peinture par principes* (1708) (Paris, 1989), p. 25.

71 Ibid., p. 21.

72 Denis Diderot, *Diderot Salons*, ed. Jean Seznec and Jean Adhémar, 4 vols (Oxford, 1957–67), vol. 3, Salon 1767, p. 168. On the trope of the perfect portrait as one in which the sitter allows his head to be put through rather than simply on the canvas, see Antoine Houdard de La Motte, *Fables nouvelles*, illustrated by Claude Gillot (Paris, 1719), pp. 220–23; and other examples cited in Jean Chastelus, *Peindre à Paris au XVIIIe siècle* (Nîmes, 1991), p. 178.

73 *Diderot Salons*, vol. 3, Salon 1767, p. 168.

74 Famous examples of rhetorical paradox include Synesius' praise of baldness, Lucian's praise of a fly and Ovid's praise of a nut. See Rosalie Littell Colie, *Paradoxia epidemica: The Renaissance Tradition of Paradox* (Princeton, 1966). The ancient form of epideixis was intended to demonstrate the brilliance of the orator. For an 18th-century example in painting see Diderot's discussion of Chardin's *La Raie dépouillée* at the Salon of 1763 and his advice to Jean-Baptiste Marie Pierre: 'Monsieur Pierre, regardez bien ce morceau, quand vous irez à l'Académie, et apprenez, si vous pouvez, le secret de sauver par le talent le dégoût de certaines natures.' *Diderot Salons*, vol. 1, p. 223.

75 On the *embourgeoisement* of 18th-century portraiture see Jean Locquin, 'La Lutte des critiques d'art contre les portraitistes au XVIIIe siècle', *AAF*, 7 (1913), 309–20.

76 *Diderot Salons*, vol. 4, Salon 1769, p. 86. On the mask and the face in the European portrait, though not with reference to Diderot, see Belting, *Face and Mask*, esp. pp. 91–106.

77 Denis Diderot, *Essai sur la peinture* (1765), in *Œuvres esthétiques*, ed. Paul Vernière (Paris, 1965), p. 680. Note the comparison with his account of his own experience of sitting for Louis-Michel Vanloo in *Diderot Salons*, vol. 3, Salon 1767, pp. 166–8. See also Daniel Brewer, 'Portraying Diderot', in *Diderot: Digression and Dispersion*, Jack Undank and Herbert Josephs (eds) (Lexington, KY, 1984), pp. 44–59.

78 Diderot's argument is supported by Roger de Piles's account of the work of Giovanni Francesco Gonnelli, the so-called 'blind sculptor of Gambassi', whose waxes, de Piles claimed, achieved remarkable likeness by the lines of touch, but not life-likeness, for lack of colour, the province of sight. See de Piles, *Cours de peinture par principes*, pp. 161–3.

79 *Diderot Salons*, vol. 3, Salon 1767, pp. 169–70.

80 If Jean Le Rond d'Alembert defined 'caricature' in the *Encyclopédie* as an art that amuses, Diderot's definition of the French word 'charge' put the accent on caricature's objective to expose vice through ridicule – to make it, he implied, abhorrent. See 'Caricature', in Diderot and d'Alembert, *Encyclopédie*, vol. 2, p. 684; 'Charge', ibid., vol. 3, p. 202.

81 *Diderot Salons*, vol. 3, Salon 1767, p. 168.

82 Ibid.

83 Ibid.: 'J'ai vu peindre La Tour; il est tranquille et froid; il ne se tourmente point; il ne souffre point; il ne halète point; il ne fait aucune de ces contorsions du modeleur enthousiaste, sur le visage duquel on voit se succéder les ouvrages qu'il se propose de rendre, et qui semblent passer de son âme sur son front, et de son front sur sa terre ou sur sa toile. Il n'imite pas les gestes du furieux; il n'a point le sourcil relevé de l'homme qui dédaigne le regard de sa femme qui s'attendrit; il ne s'extasie point; il ne sourit point à son travail; il reste froid, et cependant son imitation est chaude.'

84 François de Salignac de La Mothe Fénelon, *De l'éducation des filles* (Paris, 1687), quoted in René Démoris, 'Original absent et création de valeur: Du Bos et quelques autres', *Revue des sciences humaines de l'Université de Lille III*, 1 (1975), 67.

85 *Diderot Salons*, vol. 1, p. 246. For an extended commentary, see Mary Sheriff, *Moved by Love: Inspired Artists and Deviant Women in Eighteenth-Century France* (Chicago and London, 2004), pp. 159–200.

86 *Diderot Salons*, vol. 3, Salon 1767, p. 169 (my emphasis).

87 On Vaucanson see especially André Doyon and Lucien

Liaigre, *Jacques Vaucanson: Mécanicien de Génie* (Paris, 1966). For automata in the Enlightenment see Daniel Cottom, 'The Work of Art in the Age of Mechanical Digestion', *Representations*, 66 (1999), 52–74; Simon Schaffer, 'Enlightened Automata', in *The Sciences in Enlightened Europe*, William Clark, Jan Golinski and Simon Schaffer (eds) (Chicago and London, 1999), pp. 126–65; Jessica Riskin, 'Eighteenth-Century Wetware', *Representations*, 83 (2003), 97–125.

88 Jean de La Bruyère, 'Des jugements', *Les Caractères*, preface by Robert Pignarre (Paris, 1965), p. 305, no. 21.

89 Roger de Piles, *Conversations sur la connoissance de la peinture* (Paris, 1677), p. 297. See also Annie Becq, 'La Métaphore de la machine dans le discourse esthétique de l'âge classique', *Revue des sciences humaines*, 108 (1982), 269–78.

90 On La Tour's training, see François Marandet, 'The Apprenticeship of Maurice-Quentin de La Tour (1704–88)', *Burlington Magazine*, 144 (2002), 502–5.

91 Mme de Sévigné closed a letter to her daughter on 8 Apr. 1671 as follows: 'Adieu, ma très-aimable enfant; je ne pense qu'à vous. Si, par un miracle que je n'espère ni ne veux, vous étiez hors de ma pensée, il me semble que je serois vide de tout, comme une figure de Benoist.' *Recueil des lettres de Madame la marquise de Sévigné à Madame la comtesse de Grignan, sa fille* (Paris, 1785), p. 135, cited in Blondel, 'Les Modeleurs en cire', p. 432.

92 Sarah Kofman, 'La Rassemblance des portraits (à propos du *Salon de 1767* consacré à La Tour)', *L'Esprit créateur*, 24/1 (1984), 13–32, esp. 19.

93 Diderot, *Pensées détachées sur la peinture*, in *Œuvres esthétiques*, pp. 335–8.

94 *Diderot Salons*, vol. 3, Salon 1767, p. 168.

95 On Jaquet-Droz's draughtsman see esp. Alfred Chapuis and Édouard Gelis, *Le Monde des automates: Étude historique et technique*, 2 vols (Paris, 1928), vol. 2, pp. 227–60.

96 Marcia Pointon, *Brilliant Effects: A Cultural History of Gem Stones and Jewellery* (New Haven and London, 2009), pp. 223–43.

97 Colie, *Paradoxia epidemica*, *passim*.

98 For an analogous discussion of grammar as the 'machine' of literature see Paul de Man, *Allegories of Reading: Figural Language in Rousseau, Nietzsche, Rilke, and Proust* (New Haven, CT, and London, 1979), pp. 293–4. De Man is concerned with the structure and the effect of the lie in Rousseau's *Confessions* (1782); paradox is perhaps more self-evidently machine-like in its repetition of a prescribed pattern or structure of contradiction. Diderot's use of paradox articulated formally a problem identified in discourse.

99 On waxes of the 1770s and later 18th century see Helen E. Hinman, 'Jacques-Louis David and Madame Tussaud', *GBA*, 66 (1965), 331–8; Jean Adhémar, 'Les Musées de cire en France, Curtius, le "Banquet royal", les têtes coupées', *GBA*, 92 (1978), 203–14.

100 Christian Michel, *Charles-Nicolas Cochin et le livre illustré au XVIIIe siècle* (Geneva, 1987), pp. 327–30; Antony Griffiths, *Prints for Books: Book Illustration in France, 1760–1800* (London, 2004), pp. 72–5.

101 On Cochin's friendships with both Diderot and Fréron see Michel, *Charles-Nicolas Cochin et l'art des Lumières*, pp. 123–7.

102 Charles-Nicolas Cochin, *De la diversité des jugements sur la rassemblance des portraits*, in *Œuvres diverses de M. Cochin*, 2 vols (Paris, 1771), vol. 2, p. 70.

103 Ibid., p. 85.

104 See, notably, de Piles, *Cours de peinture par principes*, pp. 131–3. This is not to say that portraits of women were not the object of illegal copies; on the piracies of Nicolas Lancret's portrait of Mlle de Carmargo and the court case that ensued see Émile Dacier, 'Les Portraits gravés de la Camargo au XVIIIe siècle', *Revue de l'art ancien et moderne*, 30 (1911), 143–8; Jules-Joseph Guiffrey, *Nicolas Lancret: Sa Vie et son œuvre, 1690–1743* (Paris, n.d.), pp. 66–76.

105 Cochin, *De la diversité des jugements*, p. 81: 'il est à supposer qu'ils [male portraits] n'exigent que l'exacte vérité'. For an earlier and more emphatic expression of this view see de Piles, *Cours de peinture par principes*, pp. 132–3.

106 Cochin, *De la diversité des jugements*, p. 86. For a contemporary consideration of the relations between coats of arms and portraits see Hans Belting, *An Anthropology of Images: Picture, Medium, Body*, trans. Thomas Dulap (Princeton, 2001), pp. 62–83.

107 Georges Didi-Huberman, 'The Moulding Image: Genealogy and the Truth of Resemblance in Pliny's *Natural History*, Book 35, 1–7', in *Law and the Image: The Authority of Art and the Aesthetics of Law*, Costas Douzinas and Lynda Nead (eds) (Chicago and London, 1999), pp. 71–88, esp. p. 84.

108 Schlosser, *Histoire du portrait en cire*, pp. 95–117.

109 It is, perhaps, worth noting that the example used to illustrate differentiation in the *Encyclopédie*'s entry on 'Portrait [peinture]' (vol. 13, p. 154) was distinguishing blacks one from another. In the case of a white subject, whiteness was a given; the black served, arguably, to enlighten understanding of the individuation demanded by modern, Western subjectivity.

110 William Pietz, 'The Problem of the Fetish', pt 1, *Res: Anthropology and Aesthetics*, 9 (1985), 5–17.

111 Ibid., p. 7.

112 Jean-Jacques Rousseau, *Julie, ou La Nouvelle Héloïse* (1761), ed. Michel Launay (Paris, 1967), pp. 188–9.

113 Bernard Vouilloux, Christine Cano and Peter Hallward, 'Drawing between the Eye and the Hand: (On Rousseau)', *YFS*, 84 (1994), 175–97. See also Rémy G. Saisselin, 'Rousseau and Portraiture: From Representation to Fiction', *SVEC*, 60 (1968), 201–24.

114 On Rousseau's use of imitation as duplicated presence see Jacques Derrida, *De la grammatologie* (Paris, 1967), pp. 289–90.

115 Compare Saint-Preux's first response in Rousseau, *Julie, ou La Nouvelle Héloïse*, pt II, Letter XXII, pp. 199–201, with his later reflection in pt II, Letter XXV, pp. 209–11. Ambivalence is, of course, a signature of fetishism in Freud's theory of fetishism. See Sigmund Freud, 'Fetishism', in *The Penguin Freud Library*, vol. 7: *On Sexuality: Three Essays on the Theory of Sexuality and Other Essays*, trans. James Strachey, ed. Angela Richards (Harmondsworth, 1991), pp. 351–7.

116 Rousseau, *Julie, ou La Nouvelle Héloïse*, pt II, Letter XXV, p. 210.

117 Ibid., p. 208.

118 Ibid., p. 209.

119 See the discussion of this point in Vouilloux, Cano and Hallward, 'Drawing between the Eye and the Hand,' pp. 184–5.

120 Rousseau, *Julie, ou La Nouvelle Héloïse*, pt II, Letter XXV, pp. 210–11.

121 Jean-Jacques Rousseau, *Essai sur l'origine des langues*, in *Œuvres complètes*, ed. Bernard Gagnebin and Marcel Raymond, vol. 5: *Écrits sur la musique, la langue et le théâtre* (Paris, 1995), pp. 175–83, on the myths of artistic origination and the play of the senses.

122 Ibid., pp. 412–13. Rousseau is, of course, recycling a judgment made by Aristotle in the *Poetics*, Book 6, 1450b.

123 Rousseau, *Julie, ou La Nouvelle Héloïse*, p. 209.

124 Cochin, *De la diversité des jugements*, p. 72.

125 Ibid., p. 76.

126 Ibid., pp. 76–7.

127 Ibid., pp. 75–6.

128 Clearly Rousseau's narrative of the portrait also invites an interpretation of it as a fetish in the Freudian sense. Such a reading is not, however, obviously pertinent here, though, as will shortly become apparent, the possibility exists of

thinking about copyright law as a kind of screen for the disavowal of the threat to 'genius' represented by the market.

129 Charles-Nicolas Cochin, 'Mémoire sur les portraits', in *Recueil de quelques pièces concernant les arts* (Paris, 1757), pp. 144–65.

130 The scandal of the real is discussed, classically, by Roland Barthes in relation to Mme Aubain's barometer in Flaubert's *Un Cœur simple*; see Roland Barthes, 'L'Effet du réel', *Communications*, 11 (1968), 84–9.

131 Cochin, 'Mémoire sur les portraits', p. 149.

132 Ibid., p. 163.

133 Pietz, 'The Problem of the Fetish', pt 1, p. 7.

134 Ibid.; see also Wiliiam Pietz 'The Problem of the Fetish', pt 3a: 'Bosman's Guinea and the Enlightenment Theory of Fetishism', *Res: Anthropology and Aesthetics*, 16 (1988), 105–24.

135 Mary Douglas and Baron Isherwood describe consumption as an area of behaviour governed by rules, rules that may include cultural prohibitions of the buying and selling of certain things. Portraiture, in the early modern period, was such a thing. See Mary Douglas and Baron Isherwood, *The World of Goods: Towards an Anthropology of Consumption* (Harmondsworth, 1980), p. 58.

136 In relation to British art see Louise Lippincott's provocative essay reversing the connections traditionally made between history painting and public virtue and between portraiture and private interest. Louise Lippincott, 'Expanding on Portraiture: The Market, the Public, and the Hierarchy of Genres in Eighteenth-Century Britain', in *The Consumption of Culture, 1600–1800: Image, Object, Text*, Ann Bermingham and John Brewer (eds) (London and New York, 1995), pp. 75–88.

137 Rousseau, *Julie, ou La Nouvelle Héloïse*, p. 208.

138 The exchange between the portraitist and the sitter as an exchange of gifts, in the making as well as in the product, is clearly expressed in the conversation between Louis XIV and Bernini while the latter was sculpting the king's portrait bust, reported by Chantelou on 28 June 1665; Fréart de Chantelou, *Diary of... Bernini's Visit to France*, pp. 43–4.

139 See, for example, the probate inventories published in Rambaud, *Documents du Minutier central concernant l'histoire de l'art*.

140 See Hendrik van Hulst's claims, in his catalogue of Hyacinthe Rigaud's engraved works, that the portrait of Jean de La Fontaine had been produced for nothing, such was Rigaud's esteem for the sitter. See Hendrik van Hulst, 'Catalogue de l'œuvre gravé de Hyacinthe Rigaud', in *Mémoires inédits sur la vie et les ouvrages des membres de l'Académie royale de peinture et de sculpture*, ed. Louis-Étienne Dussieux et al., 2 vols (Paris, 1854), vol. 2, p. 172. See also Pierre-Jean Mariette, 'Les Drevets: Liste des portraits de Mr Drevet', Fondation Jacques Doucet, Paris, Ms. Drevet. Mariette notes that in the case of the portrait of Mechtilde du Saint Sacrement, after Jacques-François Courtin, Drevet not only surrendered the copper plate to the sitter, as was customary with commissions, but was forbidden to keep back a single impression for commercial sale; likewise with the full-length portrait of Louis XIV after Rigaud, of which Mariette noted that the king had borne the costs of the plate 'pour donner aux ministres étrangers & à d'autres seigneurs'.

141 La Bruyère, *Les Caractères*, p. 305.

142 Cochin, *De la diversité des jugements*, p. 85.

143 Ibid., p. 84.

144 For a recent collection of essays on the portrait print in the Renaissance see the excellent special issue of *Word and Image*, 19/1–2 (2003), ed. Adrian W. B. Randolph. Of particular relevance here are Peter Parshall, 'Portrait Prints and Codes of Identity in the Renaissance: Hendrik Goltzius, Justus Lipsius, and Michel de Montaigne', 22–37; and Larry Silver, 'The Face is Familiar: German Renaissance Portrait Multiples in Prints and Medals', 6–21.

145 Karl Marx, 'The Commodity', in *Capital: A Critique of Political Economy*, trans. Ben Fowkes, vol. 1 (Harmonsworth, 1976), pp. 125–77. See also William Pietz, 'Fetishism and Materialism: The Limits of Theory in Marx', in *Fetishism as Cultural Discourse*, Emily Apter and William Pietz (eds) (Ithaca, NY, and London, 1993), pp. 119–51.

146 Cochin., *De la diversité des jugements*, p. 73.

147 'Paradoxe [Philosophie]', in Diderot and d'Alembert, *Encyclopédie*, vol. 11, pp. 894–5. See also Françoise Douay-Soublin, 'Le Paradoxe et son cortège: De l'*Encyclopédie* à l'*Encyclopédie méthodique*', in *Le Paradoxe en linguistique et en littérature*, Ronald Landheer and Paul J. Smith (eds) (Geneva, 1996), pp. 221–37.

148 *Jugement rendu par Monsieur Le Noir, conseiller d'état, lieutenant-général de police, commissaire du conseil en cette partie* (Paris, 1777), AN, O1 1914/36. The fine was set by Gaucher's privilege at 3,000 *livres*. The figure actually paid is given in the memorandum of another court case; see *Réponse pour le sieur Basset, graveur et marchand mercier; contre les sieurs Esnault et Rapilly, marchands étaleurs d'estampes* (Paris, 1779), p. 16.

149 For contemporary complaints about the *étaleurs* see Charles-François Joullain, *Réflexions sur la peinture et la gravure* (Paris, 1786), pp. 128–9.

150 Gaucher, letter of thanks to comte d'Angiviller, 15 Jan. 1777; d'Angiviller, letter of thanks to Le Noir, 17 Jan. 1717, for the outcome of the case; AN, O1 1914/33.

151 *Précis pour le sieur Gaucher*, p. 2.

152 *P-V*, vol. 9, p. 379, 8 Nov. 1788; letter from Jean-Baptiste Marie Pierre to comte d'Angiviller, 11 Nov. 1788, BnF, Mss. n.a.f. 2773; François Courboin, *L'Estampe française: Graveurs et marchands* (Brussels and Paris, 1914), p. 128. On the prints, see Vincent Lieber, *Les Portraits gravés de Jacques Necker conservés à la Bibliothèque de Genève* (Geneva, 1989), pp. 9–22, 76, cat. nos 47a, 47b, 86 (69a).

153 Jacques Necker was Contrôleur général des finances between 1776 and 1781. During his ministry the tax system was reformed in an effort to manage France's significant debt from the Amercian War of Independence. In 1781 Necker resigned; he was banished from Paris in 1787 for his attacks on his successor, Charles-Alexandre Calonne. He was reinstated as Contrôleur in 1788 as France's financial problems worsened.

154 *Journal de Paris* (26 Sept. 1788). For a similar warning, see *MdF* (Oct. 1788), pp. 191–2.

155 *Journal de Paris* (19 Sept. 1788). Saint-Aubin's print was advertised at 4 *livres*, de Launay's at 2 *livres*, 8 *sous*.

156 *Messieurs, amis de tout le monde* (n.d.), p. 15; *MdF* (Sept. 1783), 129. Cited in Jules Belleudy, *J. S. Duplessis: Peintre du roi, 1725–1802* (Chartres, 1913), pp. 111–12.

157 *Journal de Paris* (9 Jan. 1789): 'Cette Gravure en couleur est celle que nous ayons vu imitant davantage le Tableau; elle fait honneur à l'Artiste qui l'a executé & à M. de Saint-Aubin qui a dirigé son travail; nous croyons, sous tous les rapports, que ce Portrait fera grand plaisir au Public'. It was sold for 4 *livres*.

158 On these prints, see Raymond Gaudriault, *Répertoire de la gravure de mode française des origines à 1815* (Paris, 1988), pp. 146–70.

159 *Réponse pour le sieur Basset*, p. 16 n. The assertion was, as far as I can tell, unfounded.

160 BnF, Mss. f.f. 21967, 14 Aug. 1778. The privilege was granted for ten years.

161 *Réponse pour le sieur Basset*, p. 2.

162 Ibid., pp. 17–19.

163 Ibid., p. 2. Basset supported this view by mentioning that he had copied heads from the printer and publisher Valade's *Manuel de toilette dédié aux dames* (1777), and that Valade had been perfectly happy to let him do so, because, Basset implied, it had never occurred to Valade that fashion plates

fell potentially under the law of privilege. See *Réponse pour le sieur Basset*, pp. 5–6. It is worth noting that Valade also printed Basset's memorandum.

164 The question of quality is not addressed in Basset's printed memorandum, but he did raise it in court. It is summarised in Esnault and Rapilly's brief, *Mémoire pour les sieurs Esnauts et Rapilly, marchands d'estampes et propriétaires du privilège de la Galerie des modes françaises, demandeurs; contre le sieur Basset, graveur et marchand mercier, défendeur* (Paris, 1779), pp. 14–15.

165 *Réponse pour le sieur Basset*, p. 3.

166 *Gallerie des modes et costumes français dessinés d'après nature, gravés par les plus célèbres artistes en ce genre et colorés avec le plus grand soin par Madame Le Beau* (Paris, 1778–87), p. i.

167 *Mémoire pour les sieurs Esnauts et Rapilly*, p. 9. Their situation is contrasted with that where authors and publishers publish by subscription, when there is a duty to deliver what was promised in the prospectus.

168 Émile Campardon, 'Saisie et destruction de gravures représentant *Les Modes et coiffures françoises* (1779)', *NAAF*, 9 (1882), 300–09.

169 *Réponse pour le sieur Basset*, p. 6. A copy of this factum in the National Art Library at the Victoria and Albert Museum, London, is bound in with examples of the more erotic plates from the *Gallerie*, in addition to those in contention.

170 Pierre-François Basan, *Adresse à l'Assemblée nationale par les graveurs et propriétaires de planches gravées* (Paris, 1791).

171 *PSC*, France, 1793.

172 Édouard Pommier describes Watelet and Levesque's *Dictionnaire* as one of three 'monuments' of art theory, along with A. C. Quatremère de Quincy's *Dictionnaire historique d'architecture* (1788) and J.-J. Barthélemy, *Voyage du jeune Anacharsis en Grèce* (1788). See Édouard Pommier, 'La Théorie des arts', in *Aux armes et aux arts: Les Arts de la Révolution, 1789–99* (Paris, 1988), pp. 168–9.

173 Charles-Henri Watelet and Pierre-Charles Levesque, *Dictionnaire des arts de peinture, sculpture et gravure*, 5 vols (Paris, 1788–91), vol. 2, pp. 396, 399.

174 *Réponse pour le sieur Basset*, p. 15.

175 See, for example, Jacques Lacombe's definition of 'talent' in *Dictionnaire portatif des beaux-arts* (Paris, 1752), p. 661.

176 On portraiture during and immediately after the Revolution see esp. Tony Halliday, *Facing the Public: Portraiture in the Aftermath of the French Revolution* (Manchester, 2000).

177 Watelet and Levesque, *Dictionnaire*, vol. 5, p. 145.

178 Ibid., p. 159.

179 Ibid.

180 Ibid., pp. 149–51.

181 Halliday, *Facing the Public*, p. 547.

182 Tony Halliday, 'Academic Outsiders at the Paris Salons of the Revolution: The Case of Drawings "à la manière noire"', *OAJ*, 21 (1998), 71–86.

183 Lynn Hunt, *Politics, Culture, and Class in the French Revolution* (Berkeley, CA, 1984), pp. 74–86; Jean-Marc Devocelle, 'D'un costume politique à une politique du costume', in *Modes et révolutions, 1780–1804*, exh. cat., Musée de la mode et du costume, Palais Galliera, Paris (Paris, 1989), pp. 83–103; Richard Wrigley, *The Politics of Appearances: Representations of Dress in Revolutionary France* (Oxford and New York, 2002), pp. 77–87.

184 *L'Art de l'estampe et la Révolution française*, exh. cat., Musée Carnavalet, Paris (Paris 1977), pp. 21–2; Stéphane Roy, 'Un Panthéon des "personages qui ont éminemment marqué dans la Révolution, soit en bien, soit en mal": Les Portraits des *Tableaux historiques de la Révolution française*', in *La Révolution par la gravure... Les "Tableaux historiques de la Révolution française", une entreprise éditoriale d'information et sa diffusion en Europe (1791–1817)*, exh. cat. Musée de la Révolution française, Vizille (Paris and Vizille, 2002), pp. 50–75; Amy Freund, 'The Legislative Body: Print Portraits of the National Assembly, 1789–1791', *Eighteenth-Century Studies*, 41 (2008), 337–58.

185 *Moniteur universel* (15 Sept. 1798), 1440; see also *Collection des tableaux historiques de la Révolution française*, prospectus, 1797, reproduced in *La Révolution par la gravure*, p. 301. On Auber see also chapter 5, pp. 290–93.

186 Antoine de Baecque, *The Body Politic: Corporeal Metaphor in Revolutionary France, 1770–1800*, trans. Charlotte Mandell (Stanford, CA, 1997), pp. 209–46.

187 See Freund, 'The Legislative Body', p. 340.

188 Daniel Arasse, *The Guillotine and the Terror*, trans. Christopher Miller (Harmondsworth, 1991), pp. 133–43.

189 Berger, 'Fictions of the Pose'.

190 Arasse makes this argument first, but on the mistaken assumptions that the *portraits guillotinés* were engraved (the instances he cites were not) and that in the 18th century engraving was both actually and discursively mechanical. On the *physionotrace*, arguably the most mechanical form of reproduction before photography, see René Hennequin, *Edme Quenedey des Riceys (Aube): Portraitiste au physionotrace*, 2 vols (Troyes, 1926–7); Baecque, *The Body Politic*, p. 234; Halliday, *Facing the Public*, pp. 43–7.

191 On the early history of aquatint, see Antony Griffiths, 'Notes on Early Aquatint in England and France', *PQ*, 4 (1987), 255–62; Griffiths, *The Print before Photography: An Introduction to European Printmaking, 1550–1820* (London, 2016).

192 On the silhouette see Pommier, *Théories du portrait*, pp. 371–2.

193 On the impact of physiognomy on theories of imitation see Graeme Tytler, *Physiognomy in the European Novel: Faces and Fortunes* (Princeton, 1982), pp. 35–81.

194 This not to say that the reproductive illustrations in Lavater's *Physiognomische Fragmente* were treated as actually transparent. On the contrary, Lavater was aware of their reliance on the conventions of artistic artifice and, according to John Lyon, embraced the mediated construction of truth they afforded. *Physiognomische Fragmente* (Leipzig and Winterthur, 1775–8); French trans. as *Essai sur la physiognomie* (The Hague, 1781); see John B. Lyon, '"The Science of Sciences": Replication and Reproduction in Lavater's Physiognomics', *Eighteenth-Century Studies*, 40 (2007), 257–77.

195 Ewa Lajer-Burcharth, *Necklines: The Art of Jacques-Louis David after the Terror* (New Haven, CT, and London, 1999)

196 *Gazette des tribunaux: Journal de jurisprudence et des débats judiciaires* (1 Jan. 1829). The previous year the same journal reported summarily on an earlier case of copyright fraud involving the piracy of a portrait of Lamoignon de Malesherbes by Truby, see *Gazette des tribunaux* (22 Aug. 1828). On Saint-Elme, see Henri Lachize, *Une Amazone sous le Premier Empire: Vie d'Ida Saint-Elme* (Paris, 1902); it contains an account of the iconography of the subject, pp. xvii–xviii.

197 Camille Ladvocat, whose shop was in the Galerie des bois at the Palais royal, was in the vanguard of literary Romanticism, publishing Victor Hugo, Alfred de Vigny, translations of Byron, Shakespeare and Schiller, and among many memoirs those of Lamartine, Sainte-Beuve and Chateaubriand. Although Grévedon's portrait was said to have been commissioned by Sainte-Elme, it may always have been intended to illustrate her memoirs. On Ladvocat see Pascal Durand and Anthony Glinoer, *Naissance de l'éditeur: L'Édition à l'âge romantique* (Paris, 2005).

198 Moret said of Saint-Elme's *Mémoires* (1827–8; see n. 205) that 'les aventures sont à elle', but 'le style est, dit-on, emprunté à la plume ingénieuse de M. Malitourne'. In fact, the first two volumes were written by Le Sourd and only the last six by Malitourne.

199 It is not clear whether Malo bought the stone from Ida Saint-Elme, or whether he acquired it along with other stock from Camille Ladvocat, for whom he was initially acting. In 1829, on the verge of bankruptcy, Ladvocat was forced to sell the best of his stock to Malo and leave his shop at the Palais

royal. This case appears to coincide with Malo's takeover. The publicity may have been a benefit.

200 *Gazette des tribunaux* (3 Dec. 1828).

201 *Gazette des tribunaux* (16 Jan. 1829).

202 The examples of history paintings cited were David's *Les Sabines* and *Léonidas aux Thermopyles*, Anne-Louis Girodet's *Atala au tombeau* and François Gérard's *Bélisaire*; caricaturists mentioned by name were Nicola-Toussaint Charlet, Edme-Jean Pigal and Henry Monnier.

203 *Gazette des tribunaux* (16 Jan. 1829).

204 Ibid.

205 [Ida Saint-Elme], *Mémoires d'une contemporaine: Souvenirs d'une femme sur les principaux personnages de la République, du Consulat et de l'Empire*, 8 vols (Paris, 1827–8).

206 *Gazette des tribunaux* (16 Jan. 1829).

207 See above, p. 214, for discussion of the frame in the case of Gaucher's print. For an instance where the accessories were judged not to make a composition see the case of François de Saint-Eloy's *Plan figuratif de la Chambre des députés*, 1831, reported in *Gazette des tribunaux* (23 Dec. 1834).

208 Watelet and Levesque, *Dictionnaire*, vol. 5, pp. 149–51.

209 Ibid., vol. 5, p. 152. Of Rigaud's portraits Levesque commented, in an elaboration of Cochin's critique in 'Mémoire sur les portraits': 'Les portraits de Rigaud me semblent représenter des gens infatués de leurs richesses, & qui n'étant rien que par elles, cherchent à en faire un pompeux étalage.'

210 Jacques Derrida, *The Truth in Painting*, trans. Geoff Bennington and Ian McLeod (Chicago and London, 1987), pp. 17–147, esp. p. 54.

211 *Gazette des tribunaux* (16 Jan. 1829)

212 Ibid.

213 *Gazette des tribunaux* (11 Jan. 1834)

214 Ibid.

215 Ibid.

216 Francesco Antommarchi, *Mémoires du docteur F. Antommarchi, ou Les Derniers Momens de Napoléon*, 2 vols (Paris, 1825).

217 Eugène de Veauce, *Les Masques mortuaires de Napoléon* (Paris, 1971), p. 29.

218 Jérémie Benoît, Agnès Delannoy and Alain Pougetoux, *Napoléon: Le Retour des cendres, 1840–1990*, exh. cat. Musée national des châteaux de Malmaison et de Bois-Préau (Paris, 1990), p. 89.

219 Examples of both are to be found at the château de Malmaison. Having lost his case, Antommarchi sold the prototype to the bronze-casters Susse. For the reproduction of the mask throughout the nineteenth century, see Pierre Cadet, *Susse frères: 150 ans de sculpture, 1837–1987* (Paris, 1992).

220 See the framed impression of Géricault's death mask at the Musée des beaux-arts, Rouen, and the mounted impression of Napoleon's death mask at Malmaison, illustrated in Benoît, Delannoy and Pougetoux, *Napoléon: Le Retour des cendres*, fig. 67.

221 Ibid., fig. 68.

222 For an instance of comparison see the account given by a phrenologist in *Gazette de médecine* (July 1834).

223 Jacques Derrida, 'Economimesis', *Diacritics*, 11 (1981), 3–25.

224 *Gazette des tribunaux* (11 Dec. 1834). It is worth noting that plaster workers were unsuccessful in obtaining an extension of the 1793 Act to plaster-casting in 1794. See chapter 5, p. 289.

225 *Gazette des tribunaux* (11 Dec. 1834).

226 Ibid.

227 Halliday, *Facing the Public*, pp. 176–88.

228 On the relationship between fetishism and aesthetic see William Pietz, 'Fetishism', in *Critical Terms for Art History*, Robert S. Nelson and Richard Shiff (eds) (Chicago and London, 1996), pp. 197–201.

229 See *Gazette des tribunaux* (18 May 1834) for the case between the printsellers Delpech and Genty, Hautecœur-Martinet, Blaizot and Fatout over a reproduction of Charles Marie Émile Seurre's statue of Napoleon on top of the column in the place Vendôme, and the related issue of whether it belonged to the public domain. See also, but in the context of current legislation, Bernard Edelman, 'La Rue et le droit d'auteur', *Chronique*, 18 (1992), 91–7.

230 Quentin Bajac, 'Les "Procédés compromettants": Moulage sur nature et photographie face à la loi, 1830–1900', in Marie-Dominique de Teneuille, *À fleur de peau: Le Moulage sur nature au XIXe siècle*, exh. cat. Musée d'Orsay, Paris, and other venues (Paris, 2001), pp. 78–85; Meredith Shedd, 'A Mania for Statuettes: Achille Collas and other Pioneers in the Mechanical Reproduction of Sculpture', *GBA*, 120 (1992), 36–48.

231 *Gazette des tribunaux*, (11 Dec. 1834).

232 Watelet and Levesque, *Dictionnaire*, vol. 2, pp. 393, 405–6.

CHAPTER 4
INVENTION: The secrets of colour

1 Charles-Nicolas Cochin, *De la diversité des jugements sur la rassemblance des portraits*, in *Œuvres diverses de M. Cochin*, 2 vols (Paris, 1771), vol. 2, p. 72; see also chapter 3, pp. 225–6. Cochin here reiterates the position, first articulated by Roger de Piles, that colour is painting's 'difference'; de Piles, *Dialogue sur le coloris* (Paris, 1699), p. 23.

2 Roger de Piles, *Cours de peinture par principes* (1708) (Paris, 1989), p. 35.

3 Ibid, pp. 29–41. De Piles calls 'invention' a dimension of composition. That view was influenced by Charles-Alphonse Du Fresnoy's *De arte graphica* (1668), which de Piles translated into French, and to which he added an extensive gloss; *L'Art de la peinture de C. A. Dufresnoy*, ed. and trans. Roger de Piles (Paris, 1684), pp. 15–17. It remained the orthodox view at the Académie in the 18th century; see, for instance, Michel-François Dandré-Bardon, *Traité de peinture, suivi d'un essai sur la sculpture* (Paris, 1757), pp. 79–88.

4 Michel Foucault, 'What is an Author?' (1969), in *Language, Counter-Memory, Practice: Selected Essays and Interviews*, trans. Donald F. Bouchard and Sherry Simon, ed. Donald F. Bouchard (Oxford, 1977), pp. 113–38.

5 'Avertissement', in Denis Diderot and Jean Le Rond d'Alembert, *Encyclopédie, ou Dictionnaire raisonné des sciences, des arts et des métiers* (Paris and Neuchâtel, 1751–72), vol. 1, p. 3.

6 Ibid., vol. 8, pp. 848–9. For a discussion of 18th-century definitions of invention see also Liliane Hilaire-Pérez, *L'Invention technique au siècle des Lumières* (Paris, 2000), pp. 145–7. On the notion of discovery in science and its relation to the discourse on authorship see Simon Schaffer, 'Scientific Discoveries and the End of Natural Philosophy', *Social Studies in Science*, 16 (1986), 387–420.

7 Della Spina invented spectacles, Gutenberg the printing press, Gioja the marine compass and Leroy a mechanism for adjusting pendulums to temperature change. Appropriately, 'Gutenberg' is today the name of a resource of freely available electronic books (<www.gutenberg.org>).

8 On the *éloge* in the history of science see C. B. Paul, *Science and Immortality: The éloges of the Paris Academy of Sciences, 1699–1791* (Berkeley, CA, 1981).

9 In 1649, Pascal obtained a 20-year *privilège exclusif* for a calculating machine, the so-called Pascaline. For a social and professional profile of those applying for privilege see Hilaire-Pérez, *L'Invention technique*, pp. 145–88.

10 On the system of cross-referencing in the *Encyclopédie* see Gilles Blanchard and Mark Olsen, 'Le Système de renvois dans l'*Encyclopédie*: Une Cartographe des structures de connaissances au XVIIIe siècle', *RDE*, 31–2 (2002), 45.

11 On hyperbole as a rhetorical trope see Pierre Fontanier, *Les Figures du discours* (1830), with introduction by Gérard

Genette (Paris, 1977), pp. 123–5; Laurent Perrin, *L'Ironie mise en trope* (Paris, 1996), pp. 51–85.

12 Antony Griffiths, *The Print before Photography: An Introduction to European Printmaking, 1550–1820* (London, 2016), pp. 144–63.

13 *Gallerie des modes et costumes français dessinés d'après nature, gravés par les plus célèbres artistes en ce genre et colorés avec le plus grand soin par Madame Le Beau* (Paris, 1778–87)

14 AN, E 2159, fols 169r–v.

15 *Lettres patentes qui permettent aux sieurs Abraham Bosse graveur en taille douce et Charles de La Font d'imprimer sur toutes estoffes de soie, papier, velin, parchemin, cuir*, 6 Jan. 1637, BnF, Mss. f.f. 21732. fols 138–40. Bosse later described his technique in *Traicté des manières de graver en taille douce sur l'airin* (Paris, 1645), pp. 72–3. One of the 'persons of wit and invention' was probably François Perrier, the first intaglio printmaker in France to have experimented with colour printing; see Maxime Préaud's account of the origins of colour printing in *Anatomie de la couleur: L'Invention de l'estampe en couleurs*, exh. cat., Bibliothèque nationale de France, Paris, and Musée Olympique, Lausanne, Florian Rodari (ed.) (Paris, 1996), pp. 41–4, esp. n. 5. Almost exactly 40 years later, in January 1676, the bookseller Jean Tainturier and the printmaker Nicolas Verien similarly requested and were granted a privilege for 'a manner of engraving on copper plates in all kinds of colour'; *Lettres royales portant privilège à Jean Tainturier et Nicolas Verien*, 30 Jan. 1676, BnF, Mss. f.f. 22071, fol. 139; see Katie Scott, 'Invention and Privilege in Early Modern France: The Case of Colour', in *Les Chemins de la nouveauté: Innover, inventer au regard de l'histoire*, Liliane Hilaire-Pérez and Anne-Françoise Garçon (eds) (Paris, 2003), pp. 167–86.

16 The 1670s saw the rise of interest in replicating imported Indian printed cottons and, although French calicoes used relief printing until the end of the 18th century, it is worth stressing that Bosse (whose background was tailoring and the rag trade) gained a privilege that covered printed fabrics. On European *indiennage* see Olivier Raveux, '"À la façon du Levant et de Perse": Marseille et la naissance de l'indiennage européen (1648–1689)', *Rives nord-méditerranée*, 29 (2008), 37–51; Giorgio Riello, 'Asian Knowledge and the Development of Calico Printing in Europe in the Seventeenth and Eighteenth Centuries', *Journal of Global History*, 5 (2010), 1–28; *Interwoven Globe: The Worldwide Textile Trade, 1500–1800*, exh. cat., Metropolitan Museum of Art, New York, Amelia Peck (ed.) (New York, 2013), cat. nos 46, 49–50, 51a, 51b, 52, 54–8. As will become clear, the privileges in question were issued by different authorities; 20 years was average in the 18th century for a patent-privilege, just as six to ten years was standard for a copy-privilege. The point is still, however, relevant.

17 On Le Blon and tapestry see Cromwell Mortimer, *Le Blon's Principles of Printing and Weaving, in the Manner of Brocades* (London, 1731). The other expert members of Le Blon's 'jury' were the scientists Henri-Louis Duhamel du Monceau and Charles Du Fay and the miniature-painter at the Jardin royal des plantes, Madeleine Françoise Basseporte. See below, nn. 21, 140.

18 Joel Mokyr, *The Gifts of Athena: Historical Origins of the Knowledge Economy* (Princeton and Oxford, 2002), pp. 27–77. On craft secrecy and open science see H. Floris Cohen, *The Scientific Revolution: A Historiographical Inquiry* (Chicago, 1994), pp. 200–04; Anne-Françoise Garçon, 'Les Dessous des métiers: Secrets, rites et sous-traitance dans la France du XVIIIe siècle', *Early Science and Medicine*, 10 (2005), 378–91 [special issue *Openness and Secrecy in Early Modern Science*].

19 Jacques-Fabien Gautier d'Agoty started out in life simply as Gautier, signing his works 'Jacques Gautier'. I have preferred this form of his name to 'Gautier d'Agoty', to which it was changed in the later 1730s.

20 On French patents see Jacques Isoré, 'De l'existence des brevêts d'invention en droit français avant 1791', *Revue historique de droit français et étranger*, 4 (1937), 94–103; Hilaire-Pérez, *L'Invention technique*, *passim*, esp. pp. 52–9, on the administrative bodies involved in granting privileges; see also p. 338, n. 7, for a detailed list of archival and published sources. For the Bureau du commerce see Harold Talbot Parker, *The Bureau of Commerce in 1781 and its Policies with Respect to French Industry* (Durham, NC, 1979); Thomas J. Schaeper, *The French Council of Commerce, 1700–1715: A Study of Mercantilism under Colbert* (Columbus, OH, 1983), pp. 149–90. For the Académie royale des sciences see Roger Hahn, *The Anatomy of a Scientific Institution: The Paris Academy of Sciences, 1666–1803* (Los Angeles, 1971), pp. 65–83. For the Maison du roi see Alfred Hachette, 'La Maison du roi et les inventeurs', *Revue de l'histoire de Versailles et de Seine-et-Oise*, 34 (1932), 20–36. Only the Bureau du commerce and the Académie royale des sciences were specifically concerned with colour technology, and only the first with the patenting of colour. Sarah Lowengard, 'Colours and Colour Making in the Eighteenth Century', in *Consumers and Luxury: Consumer Culture in Europe, 1650–1850*, Maxine Berg and Helen Clifford (eds) (Manchester, 1999), pp. 103–17; and Lowengard, 'Prussian Blue: Transfers and Trials', in *The Materiality of Color: The Production, Circulation, and Application of Dyes and Pigments, 1400–1800*, Andrea Feeser, Maureen Daly Goggin and Beth Fowkes (eds) (Farnham, 2012), pp. 167–81.

21 On colour in botany and botanical illustration see David Freedberg, 'The Failure of Colour', in *Sight and Insight: Essays on Art and Culture in Honour of E. H. Gombrich at 85*, John Onians (ed.) (London, 1994), pp. 245–62. An impression of a colour print of the *Great American Aloe* by Elisha Kirkall (1729) in the Département des estampes et de la photographie at the Bibliothèque nationale de France is inscribed on the back in an 18th-century hand: 'Cette plante a été gravée en Angleterre dans le genre de la manière noire et imprimée en couleur; c'est un Essai qui fait voir où l'on peut, par cette gravure, imiter le Recueil des Plantes du Roi, peinte en miniature. Il a été envoyé à M. l'abbé Bignon, Bibliothécaire du Roi'; Bignon was an honorary member of the Académie royale des sciences, charged with furthering the printed dissemination of the Académie's research. It is worth noting that the miniaturist at the Jardin royal des plantes, Madeleine Françoise Basseporte, was appointed to the committee to review Le Blon's application for privilege. On colour in anatomical publication see K. B. Roberts and J. D. W. Tomlinson, *The Fabric of the Body: European Traditions of Anatomical Illustration* (Oxford, 1992), pp. 521–81. In another context, Michel Pastoureau has discussed the conventions developed by printmakers to compensate for lack of colour in publications on heraldry; Pastoureau, 'La Couleur en noir et blanc (XVe–XVIIIe siècles)', in *Le Livre et l'historien: Études offertes en l'honneur du professeur Henri-Jean Martin* (Geneva, 1997), pp. 197–213.

22 BnF, Mss. f.f. 21732, fol. 138v.

23 BnF, Mss. f.f. 21732, fol. 139v. Tainturier and Verien's 1676 privilege (BnF, Mss. f.f. 22071) made specific and additional reference to typesetters, printers and cardmakers, which suggests that playing cards and wallpapers were probably further applications of the new technology.

24 Philippe de Champaigne, *De l'éducation de la jeunesse suivant son génie naturel (Contre les copistes des manières), conférence*, 11 June 1672, in LM*Con*, vol. 1, pp. 461–3. For a discussion of the rhetoric of manner in 18th-century art discourse see Christian Michel, 'Manière, goût, faire, style: Les Mutations du vocabulaire de la critique d'art en France au XVIIIe siècle', in *Rhétorique et discours critiques: Échanges entre langue et métalangues* (Paris, 1989), pp. 153–9.

25 The same point could be made about realist fiction as compared with poetry: it is space-less on the page. For a full discussion see Brian McHale, *Postmodernist Fiction* (London, 1987), pp. 179–96, esp. pp. 181–2.

26 According to Gautier de Montdorge, when Le Blon wanted his colour prints to have the appearance of paintings he mounted them on canvas and varnished them. [Antoine Gautier de Montdorge], *L'Art d'imprimer les tableaux: Traité d'après les écrits, les opérations et les instructions verbales de J. C. Le Blon* (Paris, 1756), pp. 126–8.

27 For the history of the Académie's drive for artistic autonomy see Thomas E. Crow, *Painters and Public Life in Eighteenth-Century Paris* (London and New Haven, CT, 1985), pp. 23–36; Nathalie Heinich, *Du peintre à l'artiste: Artisans et académiciens à l'âge classique* (Paris, 1993); Christian Michel, *L'Académie royale de peinture et de sculpture (1648–1793): La Naissance de l'école française* (Geneva, 2012), esp. ch. 2. It did not, however, preclude the Académie from serving in an advisory capacity on technical inventions. See, for instance, a number of memoranda from the 1780s in the archives of the Académie royale de peinture et de sculpture, ENSBA, Ms. 237.6 (blue lapis); Ms. 237.10 (artificial ultramarine) and *P-V*, vol. 9, p. 299 (4 Nov. 1786), pp. 321–2 (2 June 1987), p. 336 (24 Dec. 1787); Ms. 237.11 (yellow) and *P-V*, vol. 9, p. 299 (4 Nov. 1786), p. 308 (27 Jan. 1787); Ms. 237.12 (Prussian blue); Ms. 237.15 (red lake) and *P-V*, vol. 9, p. 300.

28 The lawyer and diarist Mathieu Marais in fact compared the search for colour printing to that for the philosopher's stone. Mathieu Marais, *Journal de Paris*, ed. Henri Duranton and Robert Granderoute (Saint-Étienne, 2004), 18 May 1721. The work of William R. Newman on the continuing currency of alchemy in the early modern period and its relation to the new science of chemistry is fundamental to any study of the question. See, most recently, his edited collection of essays, *Chemical Knowledge in the Early Modern World* in *Osiris*, 29/1 (2014) [special issue], esp., as regards France, Lawrence M. Principe, 'The End of Alchemy? The Repudiation and Persistence of Chrysopoeia at the Académie royale des sciences in the Eighteenth Century', pp. 96–116; Bernard Joly, 'Étienne-François Godefroy (1672–1731): A Chemist on the Frontiers', pp. 117–31.

29 Joseph Koerner, 'Factura', *Res* 36 (Autumn 1996), 5–19. For a discussion of the rare instances when manner and matter in painting were discussed in 17th- and early 18th-century art theory see Jérôme Delaplanche, 'La Touche et la tache', in *Rubens contre Poussin: La Querelle du coloris dans la peinture françiase à la fin du XVIIe siècle*, exh. cat. Musée des beaux-arts, Arras, Emmanuelle Delapierre, Matthieu Gilles and Hélène Portiglia (eds) (Ghent, 2004), pp.61–9. See also the excellent article by René Démoris, 'Les Enjeux de la main en peinture au siècle classique', in *La Main* (Orléans, 1996), pp. 243–58.

30 Diderot to Sophie Volland, 20 Oct. 1760, in Denis Diderot, *Œuvres*, ed Laurent Versini, 5 vols (Paris, 1995–7), vol. 5, p. 271. The example he gives is yellow: 'l'or est jaune, la soie est jaune, le souci est jaune, la bile est jaune, la paille est jaune; à combien d'autres fils ce fil ne répond-t'il pas? La folie, le rêve, le décousu de la conversation consistent à passer d'un objet à un autre par l'entremise d'une qualité commune.'

31 On Le Blon see Georges Wildenstein, 'Jakob Christoffel Le Blon, ou Le "secret de peindre en gravant"', *GBA* 56 (1960), 91–100; Otto M. Lilien, *Jacob Christoph Le Blon, 1667–1741: Inventor of Three- and Four-Colour Printing* (Stuttgart, 1985); Florian Rodari, 'Jacob Christoph Le Blon: L'Œil trichrome', in *Anatomie de la couleur: L'Invention de l'estampe en couleurs*, exh. cat., Bibliothèque nationale de France, Paris, and Musée Olympique, Lausanne, Florian Rodari (ed.) (Paris, 1996), pp. 52–90; Dániel Margócsy, *Commercial Visions: Science, Trade and Visual Culture in the Dutch Golden Age* (Chicago and London, 2014), pp. 167–99; Mechthild Fend, *Fleshing Out Surfaces: Skin in French Art and Medicine, 1650–1850* (Manchester, 2017), pp. 35–9.

32 Lilien, *Jacob Christoph Le Blon*, p. 20; Rodari, 'Jacob Christoph Le Blon', pp. 53–4; and Hessel Miedema, 'Lambert ten Kate in the Correspondence with Hendrik van Limborch: Color Harmony and Chiaroscuro', *Simiolus: Netherlands Quarterly for the History of Art*, 35 (2011), 174–87. Miedema argues that Le Blon was only peripherally involved in the ten Kate and van Limborch experiments, which focused on colour mixing, not colour printing.

33 Martin Kemp, 'Yellow, Red and Blue: The Limits of Colour Science in Painting, 1400–1730', in *Natural Sciences and the Arts: Aspects of Interaction from the Renaissance to Abstraction*, James S. Ackerman (ed.) (Stuttgart, 1985), pp. 98–105; John Gage, *Colour and Culture: Practice and Meaning from Antiquity to Abstraction* (London, 1993), pp. 29–38; Alan E. Shapiro, 'Artists' Colors and Newton's Colors', *Isis*, 85 (1994), 600–30. John Gage notes the important connection between Le Blon's training as a miniature-painter and the elaboration of the idea of the three primaries in the literature on miniature painting; John Gage, 'Jacob Christoph Le Blon', *PQ*, 3 (1986), 65–7.

34 On mezzotint see Charles-Nicolas Cochin's additions to the 1745 edition of Abraham Bosse's treatise on printmaking, *De la manière de graver à l'eau forte et au burin. Et de la gravure en manière noire* (Paris, 1745), pp. 117–28. See also Carol Wax, *The Mezzotint: History and Technique* (London, 1990); Michel Roncerel, 'La Manière noire: Une Façon de graver facile et propre pour les peintres et autres gens de goût', in *Ars nigra: La Gravure en manière noire au XVIIe et XVIIIe siècles*, exh. cat., Musée des beaux-arts, Caen, Caroline Joubert (ed.) (Caen, 2002), pp. 27–36; Griffiths, *The Print before Photography*, p. 484.

35 Rocking plates was a tedious labour; by the end of the century, printmakers could buy pre-rocked plates from dealers. 'Lettre sur la gravure en manière noire', *MdF* (Sept. 1775), 186.

36 On the order of printing see Cochin in Bosse, *De la manière de graver*, p. 124: 'À l'égard de l'ordre que l'on doit suivre pour l'impression de ces trois couleurs, il varie suivant que l'exigent des sujets que l'on veut représenter. On sçaurra seulement en général qu'il faut commencer par la couleur qui est la moins apparente dans ce Tableau, & réserver la couleur dominante pour être imprimée la dernière.' However, according to Gautier de Montdorge's accounts of the process, the order of printing usually followed the order of execution in a sequence blue–yellow–red, irrespective, apparently, of subject. [Gautier de Montdorge], *L'Art d'imprimer les tableaux*, pp. 111–13; [Gautier de Montdorge], 'Gravure en couleurs à l'imitation de la peinture', in Diderot and d'Alembert, *Encyclopédie*, vol. 7, pp. 899–902.

37 Wax, *The Mezzotint*, pp. 87–8; Joubert (ed.), *Ars nigra*; Antony Griffiths, 'Early Mezzotint Publishing in England, I: John Smith, 1652–1743', *PQ*, 6 (1989), 242–57; Griffiths, 'Early Mezzotint Publishing in England, II: Peter Lely, Tompson and Browne', *PQ*, 7 (1990), 130–45. According to Antony Griffiths mezzotint was described as 'manière anglaise' as early as 1699 when it was so mentioned in the sale catalogue of the collector Claude Boucot. This was disputed by Cochin, who argued in an article in the *Journal de Paris* (6 Apr. 1787) that 'manière noire' was 'aussi françoise qu'angloise' (p. 419). On the multiple plates and printing inks used in Renaissance chiaroscuro woodcuts see Susan Dackerman, *Painted Prints: The Revelation of Color in Northern Renaissance and Baroque Engravings, Etchings, and Woodcuts*, exh. cat., Baltimore Museum of Art (University Park, PA, 2002); Achim Gnann, with David Ekserdjian and Michael Foster, *Chiaroscuro: Renaissance Woodcuts from the Collection of Georg Baselitz and the Albertina, Vienna*, exh. cat., Royal Academy of Arts, London (London, 2014).

38 Cochin talked of mezzotint in notably painterly terms: he described its effects as 'soft' and remarked upon its propensity 'to paint' in a broader and more unctuous manner than etching and to 'colour' its depictions; Cochin in Bosse, *De la manière de graver*, p. 122.

39 Lilien, *Jacob Christoph Le Blon*, p. 24; Rodari, 'Jacob Christoph Le Blon', pp. 56–9.

40 Lilien, *Jacob Christoph Le Blon*, pp. 24–5; Rodari, 'Jacob Christoph Le Blon', p. 58.

41 On patenting in early modern Europe see *Patents and Inventions* in *Technology and Culture*, 32/4 (1991) [special issue], esp. Christine Macleod, 'The Paradoxes of Patenting: Invention and its Diffusion in Eighteenth- and Nineteenth-Century Britain, France and North America', pp. 885–910; Liliane Hilaire-Pérez, 'Invention and the State in Eighteenth-Century France', pp. 911–31. See also Liliane Hilaire-Pérez, *L'Invention technique*.

42 Christine Macleod, 'The 1690s Patents Boom: Invention or Stock-Jobbing?', *Economic History Review*, 39 (1986), 549–71.

43 See Le Blon's inventory after death, in which are listed copper plates, tools and some pigments (including Prussian blue and red lake), 31 May 1741, ANMC, LIII/298 IAD; published in part in Wildenstein, 'Jakob Christoffel Le Blon', pp. 98–9.

44 Lilien, *Jacob Christoph Le Blon*, pp. 24–5.

45 The patent system in Britain required registration not examination. Novelty was therefore not fundamental. For a comparison of the two regimes see Hilaire-Pérez, *L'Invention technique*, pp. 83–142, esp. pp. 102–9 on specification.

46 *London Gazette* (6 June 1721); *Daily Courant* (10 June 1721); ibid. (26 June 1721). See also Lilien, *Jacob Christoph Le Blon*, pp. 42–3, 138–9.

47 *Journal des sçavans* (28 Apr. 1721), 256; (18 May 1722), 316–18; *MdF* (June–July, 1721), 115–16; (Dec. 1727), vol. 1, 2677–9; *P-V*, vol. 4, p. 402, 6 Oct. 1725.

48 John R. Harris, *Industrial Espionage and Technological Transfer: Britain and France in the Eighteenth Century* (Aldershot, 1998), p. 14.

49 Ibid., pp. 7–39. In a wider historical context see Liliane Hilaire-Pérez, 'Transfers technologiques, droits et territoire: Le Cas Franco-Anglais au XVIIIe siècle', *RHMC*, 44 (1997), 547–79. Le Blon, we can speculate, may have encouraged his habitual identification as 'Anglois' for the prestige it brought him.

50 The letter of privilege records that Le Blon 'est dans le dessein de donner son secret pour que l'on puisse en faire usage, lorsqu'il sera hors d'état de travailler', AN, E 2159, fol. 169. Infringement would be punished by a fine of 500 *livres*, of which Le Blon would have half and half would go to the poor of the Hôpital général.

51 One of the earliest patent-privileges in France was granted in 1551 for the manufacture of glass in the Venetian manner; Isoré, 'De l'existence des brevêts d'invention', p. 103. See also Hilaire-Pérez, *L'Invention technique*, pp. 47–50.

52 On the *arrêt* of 1692 and further information on the copper-plate printers see Marianne Grivel, *Le Commerce d l'estampe à Paris au XVIIe siècle* (Geneva, 1986), pp. 116–22.

53 Wax, *The Mezzotint*, p. 87; see also Bosse, *De la manière de graver*, pp. 123–5.

54 In a letter of 18 Aug. 1727 to the *Mercure de France*, Le Blon admitted the difficulty he had in introducing mezzotint to his workshop, before even attempting colour printing; *MdF* (Aug. 1727), 1802–3. On his difficulties with copper-plate printers, who rightly believed that he was using his own printers and not those of the guild, see *Lettres patentes de Louis XV portant privilège en faveur du sr Le Blon pour l'impression des tableaux coloriés avec trois planches; et arrêt du Parlement qui n'ordonne l'enregistrement desd. lettres qu'à la charge que ces impressions seroient faites par les imprimeurs en taille-douce*, 24 July 1739, 16 Dec. 1741, BnF, Mss. f.f. 22072.

55 Hilaire-Pérez, *L'Invention technique*, pp. 126–30.

56 AN, E* 2687. See the documents related to partnerships listed among his papers in his inventory after death, 31 May 1741, ANMC,/LIII/298, IAD. See also Lilien, *Jacob Christoph Le Blon*, pp. 65–6; Hilaire-Pérez, 'Transfers technologiques', p. 557; Hilaire-Pérez, *L'Invention technique*, pp. 120–121.

57 Charles Du Fay, in concluding his initial report, recommended that Le Blon be given lodgings and a studio in the Gobelins, and a pension of 1,000 *livres*, which on his death would pass to his wife and child. In a letter dated 8 Nov. 1737 Du Fay registered the lack of availability of studios at the Gobelins and the allocation of an alternative at the Marbrerie, AN, F12/993.

58 Pamela O. Long has insisted on the contingent meanings of 'invention' and 'authorship' in early modern Europe. Pamela O. Long, 'Invention, Authorship, "Intellectual Property," and the Origin of Patents: Notes towards a Conceptual History', *Technology and Culture*, 32 (1991), 846–84 [special issue *Patents and Inventions*].

59 Le Blon's workshop was located on rue Percée, in the parish of Saint-Séverin, near the printsellers on the rue Saint-Jacques.

60 Christine Macleod, *Inventing the Industrial Revolution; The English Patent System, 1660–1800* (Cambridge, 1988); Hilaire-Perez, *L'Invention technique*.

61 Abraham Bosse, *Traicté des manières de graver en taille douce sur l'airin* (Paris, 1645); Bosse, *Sentimens sur la distinction des diverses manières de peinture, dessein et graveure, et des originaux d'avec leurs copies* (Paris, 1649), ch. 6; André Félibien, *Des principes de l'architecture, de la sculpture, de la peinture et des autres arts qui en dépendent* (Paris, 1676).

62 De Piles, *Cours de peinture par principes*, pp. 29–41. See also Rensselaer W. Lee, *Ut pictura poesis: The Humanistic Theory of Painting* (New York and London, 1967), pp. 16–23, who, in discussing the interrelated issues of invention and genre, notes de Piles's 'liberal' conception of invention as a faculty definitively active in history painting but also in the lesser genres of landscape and still life. See, more recently, Thomas Puttfarken, *The Discovery of Pictorial Composition: Theories of Visual Order in Painting, 1400–1800* (New Haven, CT, and London, 2000), esp. pp. 263–77.

63 Lee, *Ut pictura poesis*, pp. 16–17, for the following account of Poussin's own view of invention as recounted by Bellori: 'The novelty of painting does not consist principally in a new subject, but in good and new disposition and expression, and thus the subject from being common and old becomes singular and new.' De Piles attributed this power of invention to 'enthousiasme'; De Piles, *Cours de peinture par principes*, pp. 70–73. See also Thomas Puttfarken, *Roger de Piles's Theory of Art* (New Haven, CT, and London, 1985), p. 120.

64 'Execudit' usually denotes the publisher of a print, but in this case the word underlines by repetition the attribution of the print's execution.

65 Rodari (ed.), *Anatomie de la couleur*, cat. no. 62. Robert's print reproduced not a cadaver but a painting of one, a painting listed in Le Blon's inventory of 31 May 1741 as 'le tableau sur toile représentant ledit sujet [d'anatomie] peint d'après nature pour servir de modèle', ANMC, LIII/298, IAD; Wildenstein, 'Jakob Christoffel Le Blon', p. 98. The announcement of the *Livre d'anatomie* in the *Mercure de France* (May 1741), 969, made a point of specifying that all the prints 'seront toutes faites sur des Tableaux nouveaux peints d'après nature', and not, by implication, after other prints. The manuscript copy of the *Plan d'un Livre d'anatomie* is at INHA, Mss. Carton 34, graveurs, J. C. Le Blon.

66 Jacques Derrida, *Psyche: Inventions de l'autre* (Paris, 1987), p. 42. See also Michel de Certeau, *L'Invention du quotidien* (Paris, 1980).

67 This is to oversimplify. On the differences and tensions in French art theory between those, like Fréart de Chambray and Félibien, who conceived of a picture's 'idea' primarily in literary terms, and those, mainly artists, for whom 'idea' was

already a picture in the head, see Puttfarken, *The Discovery of Pictorial Composition*, pp. 201–77.

68 For a discussion of the possible marks made by burin or etching needle and their representational values see Cochin's remarks on the treatment of human flesh in Bosse, *De la manière de graver*, pp. 70–72, 76–7.

69 Bosse, *Sentimens sur la distinction des diverses manières de peinture*, pp. 73–86; see also chapter 3, pp. 213–5.

70 Pierre Richelet, 'Ligne', in *Dictionnaire de la langue françoise ancienne et moderne*, 4 vols (Lyon, 1759), vol. 2, p. 527. For the development of this line of argument I am indebted to Joseph Hillis Miller, 'Ariadne's Thread: Repetition and the Narrative Line', *Critical Inquiry*, 3 (1976), 57–77.

71 Charles Le Brun, *La Manne dans le désert de Poussin, conférence*, 5 Nov. 1667, in *LMCon*, vol. 1, pp. 156–71. It was re-read to the assembled Académie in 1710 and again in 1735–6.

72 Ibid.

73 Charles Le Brun, *Sentiments sur le discours du mérite de la couleur, conférence*, 9 Jan. 1672, in *LMCon*, vol. 1, pp. 449–56. See also de Piles, *Dialogue sur le coloris*, pp. 26–7.

74 Lowengard, 'Colours and Colour Making'; Lowengard, 'Prussian Blue: Transfers and Trials'. On the materials and techniques of colour in the 18th century more generally see Sarah Lowengard, 'Sources, Materials, Techniques', in *The Creation of Color in Eighteenth-Century Europe*, <www.gutenberg-e.org/lowengard/> (accessed 23 Nov. 2017).

75 Michel Pastoureau, 'Mensonges et vérités de la couleur à l'aube des Lumières', in *Anatomie de la couleur: L'Invention de l'estampe en couleurs*, exh. cat., Bibliothèque nationale de France, Paris, and Musée Olympique, Lausanne, Florian Rodari (ed.) (Paris, 1996), pp. 91–3; Sarah Lowengard, 'Colour Quality and Production: Testing Colour in Eighteenth-Century France', *Journal of the History of Design*, 14 (2001), 91–103.

76 Wax, *The Mezzotint*, p. 261.

77 [Gautier de Montdorge], *L'Art d'imprimer les tableaux*, pp. 86, 113–14. See also Pietro Sarto, 'Les Rayons et les ombres', in *Anatomie de la couleur: L'Invention de l'estampe en couleurs*, exh. cat., Bibliothèque nationale de France, Paris, and Musée Olympique, Lausanne, Florian Rodari (ed.) (Paris, 1996), pp. 94–7, esp. pp. 95–6; more generally on the dirty business of ink production see Adrian Johns, 'Ink', in *Materials and Expertise in Early Modern Europe: Between Market and Laboratory*, Ursula Klein and Emma Spary (eds) (Chicago, 2009), pp. 101–24.

78 [Gautier de Montdorge], *L'Art d'imprimer les tableaux*, pp. 116–24. Indigo was used for trials because Prussian blue so stained the plates that it made revisions difficult. Michel Pastoureau associated Le Blon's trichromacy with blue; see also below, pp. 263, 272.

79 [Gautier de Montdorge], *L'Art d'imprimer les tableaux*, p. 99.

80 Cochin in Bosse, *De la manière de graver*, p. 122.

81 This was the case with his anatomical plates; his earlier reproductions of paintings were sold not only varnished but mounted on canvas to maximise the appearance that they were paintings. *MdF* (Dec. 1741), vol. 2, 2927–8; *MdF* (Oct. 1745), 99. On the practice of hand-colouring see Thomas Primeau, 'The Materials and Technology of Renaissance and Baroque Hand-Coloured Prints', in Susan Dackerman, *Painted Prints: The Revelation of Color in Northern Renaissance and Baroque Engravings, Etchings, and Woodcuts*, exh. cat., Baltimore Museum of Art (University Park, PA, 2002), pp. 49–78.

82 *MdF* (Aug. 1742), 1843.

83 On Loriot's fixative for pastel see *MdF* (Dec. 1753), 162–3, and *MdF* (Jan. 1754), 156–7, esp. 157, where verification by touch is mentioned. On concerns about the fragility of pastel see Thea Burns, 'The Political Construction of Fragility and French Arts Policy around 1750', *Studies in Conservation*, 43 (1998), 190–98. In 1779, with the encouragement of the Directeur des bâtiments du roi, the comte d'Angiviller, Loriot decided to make public his 'secret', for which he had a privilege for life. He first demonstrated and explained his fixatives and technique, for which he had gained approval in 1753 (*P-V*, vol. 6, pp. 367, 372–3, 6 Oct. 1753) to the Académie in January 1780 (*P-V*, vol. 9, p. 2). Loriot's written memorandum on the fixative was transcribed into the *Procès-verbaux* (*P-V*, vol. 9, pp. 5–11) and d'Angiviller ordered its publication by the Académie at its expense (*P-V*, vol. 9, pp. 15–16, 21). An edition of 600 copies was printed, of which a copy is currently to be found in the library of ENSBA. See also Loriot to d'Angiviller, 5 Feb. 1780, AN, O1 1915/49; *Détails du secret de M. Loriot pour fixer la peinture au pastel*, AN, O1 1915/50.

84 *Mémoire sur la peinture à l'encaustique et sur la peinture à la cire par M. le comte de Caylus de l'Académie des belles-lettres et M. Majault, docteur de la Faculté de médecine en l'Université de Paris* (Geneva, 1755), p. 66.

85 As an aside in his memorandum on the encaustic affair, Diderot advised the use of a perfumed frame to veil the reek of such a canvas. Denis Diderot, *L'Histoire et le secret de la peinture en cire* (Paris, 1755), p. 33. On Diderot and encaustic see also Liliane Hilaire-Pérez, 'Diderot's Views on Artists' and Inventors' Rights: Invention, Imitation and Reputation', *British Journal for the History of Science*, 35 (2002), 129–50.

86 Denis Diderot, *Diderot Salons*, ed. Jean Seznec and Jean Adhémar, 4 vols (Oxford, 1957–67), vol. 3, p. 128. The quotation is from Genesis 3:19.

87 On the early history of painting conservation see Noémie Étienne, *La Restauration des peintures à Paris (1750–1815)* (Rennes, 2012).

88 On the mnemonic function of prints see Roger de Piles, 'De l'utilité des estampes et leurs usage', *L'Idée du peintre parfait* (n.p., 1699), ch. 28.

89 Long, 'Invention, Authorship, "Intellectual Property," and the Origin of Patents'.

90 Foucault, 'What is an Author?'

91 Hilaire-Pérez, *L'Invention technique*, pp. 145–85.

92 'Lettre écrite de Londres par M. Desmaiseaux, membre de la Société royale à M. l'abbé de Veissiere, censeur royale des livres à Paris, touchant l'art d'imprimer des tableaux et portraits en couleurs. À Londres 28 février, 1722', *Journal des sçavants* (18 May 1722), pp. 316–18.

93 See, for example, Rodari, 'Jacob Christoph Le Blon', p. 62.

94 Ibid. This is not an unreasonable assumption; Jacques Gautier's later partnership agreement stipulated that subjects had to be agreed by all partners. See pp. 265–6.

95 Le Blon's print was not, in fact, used for William Cockburn's *The Symptoms, Nature, Cause, and Cure of a Gonorrhoea* (London, 1728); the author preferred a simple and less alarming engraving.

96 On the use of preparatory drawings and paintings for prints see Griffiths, *The Print before Photography*, pp. 255–9.

97 Its process bears comparison, of course, with wax, as discussed in chapter 3, pp. 217–8. On the legend of Veronica and the origin of painting see André Chastel, 'La Véronique', *Revue de l'art*, 40–41 (1978), 71–82; Gerhard Wolf, 'The Origins of Painting', *Res: Anthropology and Aesthetics*, 36 (1999), 60–78.

98 [Gautier de Montdorge], 'Gravure en couleurs', in Diderot and d'Alembert, *Encyclopédie*, vol. 8, p. 900: '[Un] cadre de carton est... preparé pour recevoir un *voile* qui sera cousu à points serrés sur les bords intérieurs; c'est ce *voile* qui sert à porter avec précision les contours. On le présentera donc sur l'original qu'on va graver; & après avoir tracé au pinceau avec du blanc à l'huile sur le *voile*, on attendra que l'huile soit sèche pour repasser les mêmes traits avec du blanc beaucoup plus liquide que celui qui a seché; on enfermera la première planche dans le cadre à carton; & le blanc encore frais marquera sur la grainure tous les contours dont le *voile* est

chargé. On repassera du blanc liquide sur les traits du *voile*, pour calquer les autres planches.'

99 Martin Kemp, 'Coming into Line: Graphic Demonstrations of Skill in Renaissance and Baroque Engravings', in *Sight and Insight: Essays on Art and Culture in Honour of E. H. Gombrich at 85*, John Onians (ed.) (London, 1994), pp. 221–44, esp. pp. 241–2.

100 There is an impression at the Yale Center for British Art. It is reproduced in Wax, *The Mezzotint*, p. 162.

101 For a discussion of Poussin's much more sophisticated deployment of Narcissus in defence of painting as imitation, not copy, see Richard Nerr, 'Poussin, Titian and Tradition: *The Birth of Bacchus* and the Genealogy of Images', *Word and Image*, 18 (2002), 267–81. My thanks to Matthew Hunter for this reference.

102 According to the review of the book by abbé Louis-Bertrand Castel, only 20–30 illustrated copies were ever published. *Mémoires pour l'histoire des sciences et des beaux-arts*, the so-called *Mémoires de Trévoux* (Aug. 1737), 1435–44, at 1439. On the history of the book, published without indication as to publisher or place or date of publication, see Lilien, *Jacob Christoph Le Blon*, pp. 88–111. Le Blon did, however, send a copy to the Académie royale de peinture et de sculpture in 1725. The text was reprinted in Gautier de Montdorge's *L'Art d'imprimer les tableaux* (1756), which enjoyed a second edition in 1758.

103 In the text, Le Blon remarked that the highest achievement of the painter is the representation of human flesh, and he offered a verbal account of the sequence of steps in learning to paint: first, 'un Objet blanc' such as a plaster head, progressing to 'une Tête de Platre teinte ou coloriée' and finally simply to a head. Le Blon, *L'Harmonie du coloris dans la peinture; réduite en pratique mécanique et à des règles sures et faciles: avec des figures en couleur* (n.p., n.d. [1725]), pp. 9–10.

104 In the text, Le Blon acknowledged that the bodies of men, women and children are different and was attentive to the skin colour appropriate to each; ibid., p. 21. For a stimulating discussion of the theme of Pygmalion and colour in printmaking in the 16th century see Walter S. Melion, '*Vivae dixisses virginis ora*: The Discourse of Color in Hendrick Goltzius's *Pygmalion and the Ivory Statue*', *Word and Image*, 17 (2001), 153–76. For an excellent discussion of Le Blon and the representation of skin see Fend, *Fleshing Out Surfaces*, pp. 35–9.

105 Rodari (ed.), *Anatomie de la couleur*, cat. no. 60. Rodari notes, importantly, that Le Blon's objective was to demonstrate that colour, both local and reflected colour, is everywhere. William Hogarth recycled Le Blon's demonstration of colour mixing in the transformation of a bust into a head in *The Analysis of Beauty* (London, 1753), ch. 14, esp. p. 115. He noted that even the fairest complexion ought not to be white like ivory, marble or wax, as the poets say of their mistresses, 'for either these in living flesh, would in truth be hideous' (p. 119). My warm thanks to Matthew Hunter for pointing out the connection between Le Blon's and Hogarth's texts.

106 Here Le Blon followed the arguments of de Piles, illustrated, in his case, by the creations of a blind sculptor; de Piles, *Dialogue sur le coloris*, pp. 17–23; de Piles, *Cours de peinture par principes*, pp. 161–3. See Fend, *Fleshing Out Surfaces*, pp. 37–8, for the development of this point.

107 Le Blon, *L'Harmonie du coloris*, pp. iv–v.

108 This is not, of course, to say that Le Blon did not actually employ mezzotinters but rather to note that their role, and thus the print's status as reproduction, is unacknowledged. The term 'peintre-graveur' is perhaps anachronistic. Today it is associated with the early 19th-century printmaker and curator Adam Bartsch, but already in 1745 Charles-Nicolas Cochin had said of mezzotint that it was 'facile' and therefore 'propre pour les Peintres et autres gens de goût qui sçavent dessiner'; Cochin in Bosse, *De la manière de graver*, p. 117.

109 For a recent discussion of allegory and secrecy in the context of science see Koen Vermeir, 'Openness versus Secrecy? Historical and Historiographical Remarks', *British Journal for the History of Science*, 45 (2012), 165–88. See also, in the context of painting, Jennifer Montagu's now classic essay 'The Painted Enigma and French Seventeenth-Century Art', *Journal of the Warburg and Courtauld Institutes*, 31 (1968), 307–35.

110 *Mémoires de Trévoux* (Aug. 1737), 1435.

111 *MdF* (Aug. 1738), 1803.

112 Ibid.

113 On Gautier see *IFF, XVIIIe siècle*, vol. 10, pp. 44–78; see also Corinne Le Bitouzé, 'Une Entreprise familiale', in *Anatomie de la couleur: L'Invention de l'estampe en couleurs*, exh. cat., Bibliothèque nationale de France, Paris, and Musée Olympique, Lausanne, Florian Rodari (ed.) (Paris, 1996), pp. 100–05.

114 Olivier Raveux, 'Spaces and Technologies in the Cotton Industry in the Seventeenth and Eighteenth Centuries: The Example of Printed Calicoes in Marseilles', *Textile History*, 36 (2005), 131–45; *Sublime Indigo*, exh. cat. Musées de Marseille (Marseille, 1987).

115 Marseille was one of the few cities in France with the right to produce printed cottons. The quality of industry was, however, low and the rewards modest. Raveux, 'Spaces and Technologies'.

116 AN, E 1184A, 5 Sept. 1741.

117 *Extrait des registres du Conseil d'état*, 5 Sept. 1741, AN, F12 993; *MdF* (Dec. 1741), vol. 2, 2924–8.

118 AN, F12 993.

119 Petition on behalf of Gautier, AN, F12 993. An *ordonnance* had been obtained from the *lieutenant de police* on 3 Feb. 1742 to proceed with the seizing of Gautier's tools and plates. According to the petition submitted by Gautier in protest at the action, the *saisie* was carried out with the maximum publicity, and the scandal (as was intended) severely damaged his reputation with the public.

120 *Compte, vente de privilège et déclaration*, 12 May 1742, ANMC, LIII/301. It is from this document that we learn that Antoine Gautier de Montdorge was the proprietor of one half of Le Blon's privilege, to whom Descatillon 'n'a fait que prêter son nom'.

121 *Extrait des registres du Conseil d'état*, 12 Nov. 1737, 1 Apr. 1738, AN, F12 993.

122 'Sur la requeste présenté au Roy en son Conseil par Marguerite Le Blond fille et unique héritière', *Mémoire pour Marguerite Le Blond fille unique héritière de Christophe Le Blond*, AN, F12 993.

123 Jean de La Clef, *Mémoire pour Jacques Gautier, privilegié du Roy; contre Marguerite Le Blond, fille et qualifiée d'unique héritière de Christophe Le Blond; et François Claude le Marchand des Castillons, se disant associé dudit sieur Le Blond*, (Paris, 1742), AN, F12 993; Jean de La Clef, *Au roy*, n.d., AN, F12 993.

124 On the difference between discovery and invention see Michael Polanyi, *Personal Knowledge: Towards a Post-Critical Philosophy* (London, 1958), pp. 174–84; Mokyr, *The Gifts of Athena*, pp. 29–56. It is worth noting that Gautier wilfully obscured the difference between operational principle and productivity to his own advantage.

125 De La Clef, *Mémoire pour Jacques Gautier*, p. 5, AN, F12 993. On the print see Rodari (ed.), *Anatomie de la couleur*, cat. no. 86; Rodari doubts that the design was Gautier's, though the execution was.

126 De La Clef, *Mémoire*, p. 5. On Le Blon's oeuvre see the nine works listed in *MdF* (July 1721), vol. 1, 115.

127 De La Clef, *Mémoire*, p. 5. On the *Cours d'anatomie* see *Plan d'un livre d'anatomie*, INHA, Mss. Carton 34, graveurs, J. C. Le Blon. See also *MdF* (May 1740), 969.

128 On the policy of the Bureau du commerce see David Kammerling Smith, 'Structuring Politics in Early Eighteenth-Century France: The Political Innovations of the French Council of Commerce', *JMH*, 74 (2002), 490–537.

129 *Compte, vente de privilège et déclaration*, 12 May 1742, ANMC, LIII/301.

130 For an introduction to the secret in relation to the arts see *Traverses*, 30–31 (1984), an important special issue entitled *Le Secret*; esp. Louis Marin, 'Logiques du secret', pp. 60–69.

131 On these fundamental differences see Pamela O. Long, 'Invention, Secrecy, and Theft: Meaning and Context in the Study of Late Medieval Technical Transmission', *History and Technology*, 16 (2000), 223–41.

132 Jean-Baptiste Oudry, *Sur la manière d'étudier la couleur, conférence*, 7 June 1749, in LMCon, vol. 5, pp. 319–39, at pp. 320–21. Oudry uses the word *corps*, which brooks no division.

133 Ibid., p. 323.

134 See, for the early 18th century, Antoine Coypel's *Commentaire sur l'épître à mon fils: Le Coloris et le pinceau*, in LMCon, vol. 4, pp. 87–8. There is a large secondary literature on 'la touche'; on the early 18th century see Delaplanche, 'La Touche et la tache'; Fend, *Fleshing Out Surfaces*, pp. 25–35, 40–42. For Jean-Honoré Fragonard and the later 18th century see Mary Sheriff, 'Invention, Resemblance, and Fragonard's *Portraits de fantaisie*', *Art Bulletin*, 69 (1987), 77–87.

135 Louis-Guillaume Baillet de Saint-Julien, 'Caractères des peintres français actuellement vivans', in *La Peinture* (Amsterdam, 1755), p. 5.

136 On Chardin's painting practice see Marianne Roland Michel, *Chardin*, trans. Eithne McCarthy (London, 1996), pp. 130–43; Juliet Carey, *Taking Time: Chardin's Boy Building a House of Cards and Other Paintings*, exh. cat., Waddesdon Manor, Buckinghamshire (London, 2012).

137 Antoine Furetière's definition of 'Secret' in volume 4 of his *Dictionnaire universelle* (The Hague, 1727) relates secrecy and novelty: 'On trouve tous les jours de nouveaux secrets.'

138 Le Blon, *L'Harmonie du coloris*, p. iv.

139 Mario Biagioli, 'From Print to Patents: Living on Instruments in Early Modern Europe', *History of Science*, 44 (2006), 139–86. Biagioli does not use the term 'mercantilism', but his account of the way patent was used by the early modern state as a powerful tool to import technology constitutes an apt description of its ideology. See also Hilaire-Pérez, 'Invention and the State', p. 915; Hilaire-Pérez, *L'Invention technique*, p. 52.

140 Le Blon feared, no doubt, that Basseporte, a painter of animal and botanical specimens at the Jardin royale des plantes, would see the possibilities in colour printing for the reproduction of her own vellums if the Imprimerie royale did not, and that the Academicians Duhamel du Monceau and Du Fay, would recognise profitable applications of trichromacy in dyeing and weaving.

141 Hahn, *The Anatomy of a Scientific Institution*, pp. 25–6, 68–9. On science as a collective endeavour see also William Eamon, 'From the Secrets of Nature to Public Knowledge: The Origins of the Concept of Openness in Science', *Minerva*, 23 (1985), 321–47.

142 On the Académie royale des sciences' periodical publication see Éric Brian and Christiane Demeulenaere-Douyère (eds), *Histoire et mémoires de l'Académie des sciences: Guide de recherches* (London, 1996); James E. McClellan III, *Specialist Control: The Publications Committee of the Académie royale des sciences (Paris), 1700–1793* (Philadelphia, 2003). It was on this basis that the Académie royale des sciences began its history and description of the trades. In a review of a typical 'book of secrets' published by Claude Jombert in 1723, the *Mémoires de Trévoux* made a point of insisting that, given the continuing existence of 'de véritables Secrets' concerning the arts and trades, 'on ne sçauroit trop s'empresser de rendre publics pour la perfection des Arts et des Sciences, & pour l'utilité des États & des Particuliers', *Mémoires de Trévoux* (Mar. 1723), 413.

143 See above, note 28. See also Pamela O. Long, 'The Openness of Knowledge: An Ideal and its Contexts in Sixteenth-Century Writings on Mining and Metallurgy', *Technology and Culture*, 32 (1991), 318–55, esp. 341–5.

144 See clause 9 of the *Statuts et règlemens*, 1648, appended to the *Arrest du Conseil d'estat*, 27 Jan. 1648, in Louis Vitet, *L'Académie royale de peinture et de sculpture: Étude historique* (Paris, 1861), pp. 213–14.

145 Jacques Derrida, 'Passions: "An Oblique Offering"', in *Derrida: A Critical Reader*, ed. David Wood (Oxford, 1992), pp. 5–35, at p. 21.

146 This was the role played by the Académie royale des sciences. *Extrait des registres de l'Académie royale des sciences*, 18 Jan. 1741, AN, F12 993. The chemist Charles-François de Cisternay Du Fay also wrote to the Contrôleur général des finances, Philibert Orry, on 15 Oct. 1737 to confirm the importance of the invention and to solicit further support for Le Blon, specifically accommodation at the Gobelins and a pension of 1,000 *livres*. From a second letter, 8 Nov. 1737, we learn that Le Blon was granted lodgings at the Marbrerie, there having been no vacancies at the Gobelins; AN, F12 993.

147 See Jean de La Clef's second (manuscript) memorandum, *Au roy*, AN, F12 993.

148 See pp. 269–78.

149 Cromwell Mortimer, 'An Account of Mr. James-Christopher Le Blon's Principles of Printing in Imitation of Painting, and of Weaving Tapestry, in the Same Manner as Brocades', *Philosophical Transactions of the Royal Society*, 37 (June–July 1731), 101–7.

150 Louis-Bertrand Castel, 'Compte rendu' of Jacob Christoph Le Blon, *L'Harmonie du coloris dans la peinture* (n.d. [1725]; also known as *Coloritto*) in *Mémoires pour l'histoire des sciences et des beaux-arts*, known commonly as *Mémoires de Trévoux* (Aug. 1737), 1435–44, at 1442–3.

151 De Piles strongly advised against inventing new allegorical figures and thereby risking confusion; see his *Cours de peintre par principes*, pp. 39–40. See also abbé Jean-Baptiste Du Bos's more thorough and developed critique of allegory and history in *Réflexions critiques sur la poésie et la peinture* (1719), ed. Dominique Désirat (Paris, 1993), pp. 72–77.

152 Roger de Piles, *Abrégé de la vie des peintres*, 2nd edn (Paris, 1725), pp. 405–8. In his *Cours de peinture par principes*, de Piles advised those who wanted to imitate Van Dyck's life-like manner to copy his portraits while imagining that they were nature; de Piles, *Cours de peinture par principes*, p. 144. On the taste for Van Dyck in the circle of Pierre Crozat see Martin Eidelberg, 'The Comte de Caylus tête à tête with Van Dyck', *GBA*, 131 (1998), 1–20.

153 Hendrik van Hulst, 'Vie de Hyacinthe Rigaud', in *Mémoires inédits sur la vie et les ouvrages des membres de l'Académie royale de peinture et de sculpture*, ed. Louis-Étienne Dussieux et al., 2 vols (Paris, 1854), vol. 2, pp. 126–41, at p. 131. Hulst records a case of alleged misattribution, in which Rigaud was shown his own work as that of Van Dyck; ibid. p. 132.

154 Georg Simmel, 'Secrecy', in *The Sociology of Georg Simmel*, trans. and ed. Kurt H. Wolff (London, 1950), pp. 330–40, at p. 333. See also Sissela Bok, *Secrets: On the Ethics of Concealment and Revelation* (Oxford, 1984), esp. 3–14, 29–44.

155 Polanyi argues that, in contrast to science, the novelty of technology is always directed at some (commercial) purpose; Polanyi, *Personal Knowledge*, pp. 174–84.

156 Carlo Ginzburg, 'High and Low: The Theme of Forbidden Knowledge in the Sixteenth and Seventeenth Centuries', *Past and Present*, 73 (1976), 2–41.

157 *Historical Memoirs of the Duc de Saint Simon*, trans. and ed. Lucy Norton, 3 vols (London, 1972), vol. 3, p. 480.

158 Gilles Deleuze and Félix Guattari, *A Thousand Plateaus: Capitalism and Schizophrenia*, trans. Brian Massumi (Minneapolis, 1987), pp. 286–7.
159 Michel Pastoureau, *The Devil's Cloth: A History of Stripes and Striped Fabric*, trans. Jody Gladding (New York, 1991).
160 Rodari (ed.), *Anatomie de la couleur*, cat. no. 53; but the entry invokes explanation rather than revelation in its account of the stripes.
161 Le Blon, *L'Harmonie du coloris*, p. 7.
162 On Pierre Coste's translation in the context of the reception of Newton in France see Henry Guerlac, *Newton on the Continent* (Ithaca, NY, 1981). See also A. Rupert Hall, 'Newton in France: A New View', *History of Science*, 1 (1975), 233–50; John Gage, 'Newton and Painting', in *Common Denominators in Science*, Martin Pollock (ed.) (Aberdeen, 1983), pp.16–25; J. B. Shank, *The Newton Wars and the Beginning of the French Enlightenment* (Chicago, 2008), ch. 3.
163 Isaac Newton *Traité d'optique sur les réflexions, réfractions, inflexions et couleurs de la lumière*, trans. Pierre Coste, 2nd edn (Paris, 1722). In the translator's preface (pp. 1–10) Coste relates that John Desaguliers, Newton's experimental assistant, helped him to verify his translation by repeating the experiments in 1715 in London.
164 Simon Schaffer, 'Glass Works: Newton's Prisms and Uses of Experiments', in *The Uses of Experiments: Studies in the Natural Sciences* (Cambridge, 1989), pp. 67–104. See also Alan E. Shapiro, 'The Gradual Acceptance of Newton's Theory of Light and Colour, 1672–1727', *Perspectives in Science*, 4 (1996), 59–140.
165 Louis-Bertrand Castel, 'Compte rendu' of Isaac Newton, *Traité d'optique* (1722) in *Mémoires de Trévoux* (Aug. 1723), 1428–50.
166 'New Theory of Light and Colour', was the title of the Newton's first letter on optics written to the Royal Society and published in the *Philosophical Transactions* in 1671 <doi: 10.1098/rstl.1671.0072Phil. Trans. 1671 vol. 6no. 80 3075-3087>. On tightness of knowledge see Mokyr, *The Gifts of Athena*, pp. 6, 18–20.
167 Edme Mariotte had been unable to replicate Newton's experiments in 1679, but by 1707 Nicolas Malebranche had done this so successfully that he dropped his own theory of colour for Newton's. See Nicolas Malebranche, *Traité de la vérité* (Paris, 1712). On experiments repeated in Paris and Béziers see Newton, *Traité d'optique*, p.10. See also Guerlac, *Newton on the Continent*, ch. 5; A. Rupert Hall, *All Was Light: An Introduction to Newton's Opticks* (Oxford, 1993), pp. 201–10; Shapiro, 'The Gradual Acceptance', 96–100.
168 On the role of beauty in the formulation of scientific knowledge see Polanyi, *Personal Knowledge*, pp. 134, 145–50.
169 Castel, 'Compte rendu' of Le Blon, *L'Harmonie du coloris*, (1737), 1439–40.
170 Mario Biagioli, 'From Ciphers to Confidentiality: Secrecy, Openness and Priority in Science', *British Journal for the History of Science*, 45 (2012), 213–33, esp. 222–4 on the problems with ciphers and Kepler's misreading of Galileo's anagram on the phases of Venus.
171 For a discussion of 'under-reading' see Frank Kermode, 'Secrets and Narrative Sequence', *Critical Inquiry*, 7 (1980–81), 83–101.
172 *MdF* (Aug. 1738), 1802–4.
173 *MdF* (Dec. 1727), vol. 1, 2677–9; *Philosophical Transactions of the Royal Society*, 37 (June–July, 1731), 101–7.
174 Rodari (ed.), *Anatomie de la couleur*, cat. no. 88.
175 *MdF* (Aug. 1742), 1839–43, esp. 1839–41. Assigning a history to printmaking was a way to dignify it. Bosse, 'Avant propos', in *Traicté des manières de graver*, esp. pp. 2–3.
176 *MdF* (March 1745), vol. 2, 143–6.
177 Ibid., p. 143.
178 Ibid., p. 144.
179 Le Blon, Gautier alleges, had been obliged, in any case, to cheat: he retouched the prints with a brush (ibid., p.145). In his account, Gautier aimed to convince by reproducing on a large scale the three stages of production, from the laying in of shadow to the final touches of finish that constituted conventional studio practice on a small scale. See Roger de Piles, *Les Premiers Éléments de la peinture pratique* (Paris, 1684) on the mixing of colours on a palette to paint a head. Moreover, given the importance attached to finish by academic theory, the story of the progress of printmaking served to secure for Gautier a pre-eminent position by virtue, precisely, of his later arrival in the evolution of colour technology. Such narratives contrast sharply with the accounts of development and progress in, for instance, dyeing. See Charles-François de Cisternay Du Fay's 'Observations physiques sur le meslange de quelques couleurs dans la teinture', *Mémoires de l'Académie royale des sciences* (1737), 253–68; Du Fay, 'Sur le mélange de quelques couleurs dans la teinture', *Histoire de l'Académie royale des sciences* (1740), 58–62.
180 For a model by which to understand the dynamics of the relationship between 'propositional' knowledge and 'prescriptive' knowledge, in order that invention may occur successfully, see Mokyr, *The Gifts of Athena*, pp. 15–25.
181 Louis-Bertrand Castel, 'Nouvelles Expériences d'optique et d'acoustique', *Mémoires de Trévoux* (July, 1735), 2048–9.
182 On blue as the first colour perceived by the human eye see Julia Kristeva, 'Giotto's Joy', in *Desire in Language: A Semiotic Approach to Literature and Art* (New York, 1980), pp. 210–36. Élisabeth Lavezzi calls it the 'mother' of all colours in Castel's system because it engenders others; Lavezzi, 'Le Clavecin irisé', *Revue d'histoire littéraire de la France*, 10 (2001), 327–39.
183 Griffiths, *The Print before Photography*, p. 38.
184 For an account of portrait print production in the 17th century see Véronique Meyer, 'Le Portrait gravé sous le règne de Louis XIV', in *Visages du Grand Siècle: Le Portrait français sous le règne de Louis XIV, 1660–1715*, exh. cat., Musée des beaux-arts, Nantes (Paris 1997), pp. 163–75; Maxime Préaud, 'Le Nez du maréchal de Turenne', in ibid., pp. 191–5.
185 McHale, *Postmodernist Fiction*, p. 90.
186 See Robert's advertisement in *MdF* (Nov. 1748), 163, for his colour reproduction of a Crucifixion after Nicolas Delobel.
187 See *MdF* (Dec. 1748), 178–80, for Gautier's last self-presentaion as the restorer and perfector of Le Blon's art.
188 On the tension between the Baconian vision of a scientific enterprise based on cooperation and the personal and competitive claims of discovery in the case of the Royal Society see Alan G. Gross's analysis of the controversy between Newton and Leibniz over priority in the invention of calculus, in 'The Rhetorical Invention of Scientific Invention: The Emergence and Transformation of a Social Norm', in *Rhetoric in the Human Sciences*, Herbert W. Simons (ed.) (London, 1989), pp. 89–107.
189 *MdF* (Nov. 1748), 163.
190 *MdF* (Dec. 1748), vol. 2, 179.
191 Ibid. Gautier pointed out, in support of his contention, that Robert had been able to study his copper plates, shares in the stock of which had passed to Maurice Viguier and Pierre Villars at the dissolution of the partnership with Gautier in May 1747. *Extrait de mémoire du sieur Gautier sur le 1er et le 2e chefs de demandes de ses parties, concernant le privilège d'imprimer les tableaux, dont les nouvelles contestations ont été évoquées au Conseil d'état pour arrest du 11 décembre 1751*, 8 Jan. 1752, BnF, Mss. f.f. 22136/5, fol. 13v.
192 *MdF* (April, 1749), 80.
193 *MdF* (Dec. 1748), vol. 2, 180. On micro-, or incremental, change versus macro-breakthroughs see Joel Mokyr, *The Lever of Riches: Technological Creativity and Economic Progress* (Oxford, 1990), pp. 12–13, 273–99.
194 ANMC, LIII/312, 29 Jan. 1745, Société.

195 *Mémoire de l'affaire d'entre Jacques Gautier, Maurice Vignier, son associé, et le sr Pierre Villars, intéressé dans les fonds et dans les dettes de la société*, BnF, Mss. F.F. 22136/6, fols 14–15.
196 ANMC, LXVIII/260, 6 Aug. 1746, Transport.
197 *Mémoire de l'affaire*, BnF, Mss. f.f. 22136/6, fol. 15.
198 Le Bitouzé describes him as 'homme de main des deux commanditaires de Gautier', and gives his name as La Bory. See 'Une Entreprise familiale', p. 102. The name could also be read as La Boizy.
199 Ibid.; *Extrait du procès entre les srs Gautier, Maurice Vignier, et Pierre Villars'*, BnF, Mss. f.f. 22136/24, fol. 8.
200 *Mémoire de l'affaire*, BnF, Mss. f.f. 22136/6.
201 Ibid., fols 17, 20–22.
202 Ibid., fol. 19 (point 3). Listed among the documents inventoried for the case of Gautier *c.* Viguier and Villars was a copy of a contract between the joiner Berthereau and Gautier, dated 5 Apr. 1745, for a press. It was countersigned by Viguier and Villars, 'preuve que Gautier n'avoit pas fait faire cette presse clandestinement, comme ses Associez l'accusent dans leurs mémoires', BnF, Mss. f.f. 22136/24, fol. 7.
203 Ibid., fol. 19 (point 5). This was not an unreasonable fear, given Gautier's past actions: he left Paris for London in 1743–4 in the middle of his disagreements with his first partners.
204 ANMC, LIII/312, 29 Jan. 1745, Société, Gautier, Vignier, Villars, arts. 5, 12; ANMC, CXIII/357, 13 Apr. 1746, Transport, arts. 1, 4.
205 BnF, Mss. f.f. 22136/6, fols 15–16. The situation between Gautier and Viguier deteriorated rapidly; Viguier's agent, La Bory, threatened Gautier. See also *Copie de la plainte formée par M. Gautier chez le commissaire Lavergné*, 24 Aug. 1746, BnF, Mss. f.f. 22136/22; *Mémoire contenant les abus qui résulteroient de la demande de l'associé du sr Gautier, les raisons qui s'y opposent et les présentations des auteurs; pour M. Duverney contre le sieur Viguier*, BnF, Mss. f.f. 22136/23, fols 56r–57r. See also Le Bitouzé, 'Une Entreprise familiale', p. 102; the author cites additional evidence from the papers of the Châtelet at the Archives nationales but without a reference. I have failed to locate these.
206 BnF, Mss. f.f. 22136/6, fol. 23.
207 BnF, Mss. f.f. 22136/6.
208 BnF, Mss. f.f. 22136/5, fol. 12v. See also the two memoranda written by Gautier in the name of the anatomist Jacques-François Duverney *fils*, whose influence, it was hoped, would lead Malesherbes to intervene: *Mémoire du sieur Duverney Me chirurgien, démonstrateur en anatomie et chirurgie au Jardin du roy et membre de l'Académie royale de chirurgie*, BnF, Mss. f.f. 22136/14; *Mémoire contenant les abus*, BnF, Mss. f.f. 22136/23.
209 See Viguier's attempts to get Malesherbes to intervene on his behalf in the division of plates and presses during the winding up of the company: Viguier to Malesherbes, 24 Apr. 1747, Viguier to Malesherbes, 18 May 1747, BnF, Mss. f.f. 22136/8, fol. 11.
210 BnF, Mss. f.f. 22136/5, fol. 13v.
211 *MdF* (Nov. 1748), 163. Gautier de Montdorge noted this in his 'Réponse de M. de Montdorge, aux informations de M. Rémond de Sainte-Albine, au sujet de la contestation entre deux élèves de feu Le Blond, dans l'art d'imprimer les tableaux', *MdF* (July 1749), 173–9, at 178.
212 At the Jardin royal des plantes, two brothers, Joseph-Guichard (1648–1730) and Jacques-François-Marie Duverney (1661–1748), were appointed as *démonstrateurs d'anatomie*. Of the two, the elder was the more celebrated. Bernard Le Bovier de Fontenelle's *éloge* for the elder provides a vivid account of the anatomist's oratorical style, which apparently attracted audiences that filled the 500-seat lecture theatre when he spoke at the Jardin royal, and which led also to a court appointment. Joseph-Guichard Duverney published little during his lifetime, but his anatomical preparations were justly famous and were on display at the Jardin royal and later at the Louvre. Gautier is (in my view, wilfully) ambiguous about which of the two brothers he collaborated with. The death of Joseph-Guichard make it highly unlikely that it was he. Jacques-François, who had collaborated with his brother, is the more likely candidate, but it is probable that they used Duverney the elder's anatomical preparations. Efforts were made after Joseph-Guichard's death to publish his works: his son Emmanuel-Maurice brought out his father's *Œuvres anatomiques* with Charles-Antoine Jombert in 1761. See Fontnelle's *éloge* reprinted in his *Œuvres*, 8 vols (Paris, 1790–92), vol. 7, pp. 363, 364. See also Anita Guerrini, 'Theatrical Anatomy: Duverney in Paris, 1670–1720', *Endeavour*, 33 (2009), 7–11. For the legal dispute between the Jardin royal des plantes and the Académie royale des sciences over Duverney's anatomical preparations and specimens after his death see Anita Guerrini, 'Duverney's Skeletons', *Isis*, 94 (2003), 577–603. The dispute raised questions about the intellectual property in such tools. The memoranda cite Duverney as Gautier's collaborator, possibly father followed by son. The *Mercure de France* notices claim that Duverney was replaced by Tarin, *démonstrateur d'anatomie* at the Charité; *MdF* (Jan. 1749), 159–61.
213 *Mémoire contenant les abus*, BnF, Mss. f.f. 22136/23, fol. 56v. Gautier claimed to have furnished capital of 1,551 *livres* from sales to keep the enterprise running until alternative sources could be found. For the terms of the subscription see *Essai d'anatomie en tableaux imprimés qui représentent au naturel tous les muscles de la face, du col, de la tête, de la langue et du larynx*, 1745, BnF, Mss. f.f. 2136/20; *MdF* (June 1749), 144–50, at 148, where Gautier stated that subscription had raised 4,000 *livres*.
214 On subscription in scientific publications in the early modern period see Dániel Margócsy, 'Advertising Cadavers in the Republic of Letters: Anatomical Publications in the Early Modern Netherlands', *British Journal for the History of Science*, 42 (2009), 187–210. On the attempts by the Bureau de la librairie to regulate subscription funding see Pierre-Jacques Blondel, *Mémoire sur les vexations qu'exercent les libraires et imprimeurs de Paris* (n.d. [1725]), in *PSC*, France, 1725–6; *Arrêt du conseil portant réglement sur le fait de la librairie et imprimerie*, 10 Apr. 1725, in *PSC*, France, 1725.
215 *MdF* (Oct. 1745), 99–102, at 99. On the anatomies as 'vrais originaux' because copied from cadavers and not after others' engravings see *Mémoire du sieur Duverney*, BnF, Mss. f.f. 22136/14, fol. 39.
216 *MdF* (Oct. 1745), 100–01.
217 For the role of imagination in hyperbole see César Dumarsais, *Des tropes, ou Des différents sens*, ed. Françoise Douay-Soublin (Paris, 1988), p. 133. On the commercialisation of inventions more generally in the 18th century see Liliane Hilaire-Pérez and Marie Thébaud-Soeger, 'Les Techniques dans l'espace public: Publicité des inventions et littérature d'usage au XVIIIe siècle (France, Angleterre)', *Revue de synthèse* (2006), 393–428.
218 'Lettre de M. Robert, graveur en couleur naturelle à M. Rémond de Sainte-Albine', *MdF* (June 1749), 150–54.
219 'Lettre à M. de Boze, de l'Académie françoise, et honoraire de l'Académie de peinture et de sculpture, garde des médailles et pierrerie du Cabinet du roi', *MdF* (July 1749), 158–72, at 168.
220 Ibid., pp. 169–72.
221 Shapiro, 'The Gradual Acceptance'.
222 *MdF* (July 1749), 166–72. See also Rodari, 'Jacob Christoph Le Blon'.
223 *MdF* (July 1749), 169.
224 'Réponse de M. de Montdorge', *MdF* (July 1749), 178.
225 Ibid., 174.
226 'Projet général des planches anatomiques de M. Gautier, pensionnaire du roi', *MdF* (July 1751), 162–72.

227 Ibid., 169–70.

228 *Observations sur l'histoire naturelle, sur la physique et sur la peinture*, 3 (1755), 41–5; *MdF* (Nov. 1755), 187–9. Gautier received his privilege for the *Observations* in October 1751 and the first articles in the journal are dated 1751, though they were not in fact published until 1752. Under Jacques Gautier's editorship, the journal was issued until 1757. From 1753 a campaign had been under way to engrave the Vence collection and thereby encourage the art of engraving. The two works mentioned by Gautier, night scenes both, had been engraved by Nicolas Dupuis and Pierre Basan respectively. William McAllister Johnson, 'From Verrue to Vence: Systematic Engraving of Private Painting Collections in France to 1760', *GBA*, 117 (1991), 77–92.

229 'Lettre à l'auteur du *Mercure*', *MdF* (Dec. 1755), 206–9.

230 'Lettre à l'auteur du *Mercure*, et réponse à la lettre anonyme insérée dans le premier volume de décembre, sur l'invention d'imprimer les tableaux', *MdF* (Jan. 1756), 189–203, at 196–7.

231 *MdF* (Dec. 1756), 208.

232 On the opening of a distinction between art and science see René Démoris, 'Peinture et science au siècle des Lumières: L'Invention d'un clivage', *Fabula: La Recherche en littérature* (2007) <www.fabula.org/colloques/documents628.php> (accessed 6 Dec. 2016).

233 On encaustic painting in the 18th century see Danielle Rice, *The Fire of the Ancients: The Encaustic Painting Revival, 1775–1812*, (Ann Arbor, MI, 1979); Rice, 'Jean-Jacques Bachelier et la redécouverte de la peinture à l'encaustique', in Hélène Mouradian et al., *Jean-Jacques Bachelier (1724–1806): Peintre du roi et de Madame de Pompadour*, exh. cat., Musée Lambinet, Versailles (Paris and Versailles, 1999), pp. 67–74. On the portrait of the Virgin painted by Joseph-Marie Vien for the comte de Caylus as a kind of *experimentum crucis* and shown at the Salon of 1755 see William McAllister Johnson, 'La Gravure des "peintures en cire", dites encore à l'encaustique ou inustion', *NE*, 78 (2001), 29–36.

234 Diderot, *L'Histoire et le secret de la peinture en cire*.

235 Ibid., p. 1.

236 Ibid., pp. 64–5.

237 Hilaire-Pérez, 'Diderot's Views'.

238 *Déclaration du roy concernant les privilèges en fait de commerce*, 24 Dec. 1762, in *PSC*, France, 1762; Frédéric Rideau, 'Commentary on the *Déclaration royale* on privileges granted to inventors', in *PSC*, France, 1762.

239 Hilaire-Pérez, 'Diderot's Views'.

240 'Lettre à l'auteur du *Mercure*', *MdF* (Apr. 1756), 209–12.

241 *Prospectus des vingt planches anatomiques du supplément* (1760); *Lettre circulaire à Messieurs les souscripteurs des planches anatomiques de Mr Gautier*, 1760, INHA, Mss. Carton 34, graveurs, Gautier. According to the prospectus, the prints were sold at Marseille via Antoine Favet, *libraire du port*; in Paris by Le Roy, *marchand bijoutier*; and in Amsterdam by Jean-Jacques Rousseau's editor, Marc-Michel Rey.

242 For the rhetorical definition of hyperbole as a trope by which falsehood aims to reveal a truth see Louis de Jaucourt, 'Hyperbole', in Diderot and d'Alembert, *Encyclopédie*, vol. 8, p. 404.

243 BnF, Mss. f.f. 21958, 31 Aug. 1745.

244 Longinus was translated into French by Nicolas Boileau-Despréaux in 1674; Jules Brody, *Boileau et Longinus* (Geneva, 1958); Ann T. Delehanty, *Literary Knowing in Neoclassical France: From Poetics to Aesthetics* (Plymouth, 2013), pp. 79–98.

245 'Lettre à M. Gautier', *MdF* (Mar. 1756), 198–213, at 205, 206.

246 Ibid., 198–9.

247 Significantly, in the 'Lettre à M. de Boze', Gautier had earlier dismissed in very similar terms Le Blon's claims to invention. He described them as an exaggeration; not so much a secret as an 'art de plaire', one, moreover, of a specifically commercial kind: a speculation. *MdF* (July 1749), 162–3.

248 Ibid., p. 163.

249 Ibid., p. 165.

250 Ibid., p. 163.

251 Ibid., p. 169.

252 *MdF* (Dec. 1755), vol. 2, 207.

253 Barbara Stafford, *Body Criticism: Imagining the Unseen in Enlightenment Art and Medicine* (Cambridge, MA, 1991), p. 47.

254 Stafford, *Body Criticism*, pp. 64–9.

255 Nicolas Boileau-Despréaux, *Œuvres de M. Boileau-Despréaux*, ed. Charles-Hughes Lefebvre de Saint-Marc, 5 vols (Paris, 1747), vol. 4, p. 78. Castel drew the parallels between the Sublime and invention in the context of a discussion of the nature of truth in poetic and scientific knowledge and rhetoric.

256 Castel in ibid., p. 78. Virgil's phrase is to be found in *The Aeneid*, ed. and trans. Robert Fitzgerald, Penguin Classics (London, 1985), Book VI, line 375, p. 169. Fitzgerald gives as the translation 'black night blots the colours of the world'; the translation in my text is derived from Castel's.

257 Castel in Boileau-Despréaux, *Œuvres*, vol. 4, pp. 78–9.

258 Antoine Furetière, 'Rouge', in *Dictionnaire universel contenant généralement tous les mots françois* (1690), 2nd edn, 3 vols (The Hague, 1701), vol. 3.

259 *MdF* (July 1751), 162–72. Gautier described how, for the anatomy of the head, he prepared the plates from dissections that were cast in plaster, from the moulds of which he made wax models to copy. He made no mention of the tradition of wax anatomies but it is possible, even likely, that he had seen those of Zumbo at the Jardin du roi or in private collections such as that of Joseph Bonnier de La Mosson; see Bonnier de La Mosson's sale catalogue, *Catalogue raisonné d'une collection considérable de diverses curiosités en tous genres, contenuës dans les cabinets de feu Monsieur Bonnier de La Mosson* (Paris, 1744), p. 3, lot 16. On Zumbo's anatomical waxes in France see Elena Taddia, '"Une Teste de cire anatomique". Un Sculpteur à la cour: Gaetano Giulio Zumbo, céroplaste, de la Sicile à Paris (1701)', *Bulletin du Centre de recherche du château de Versailles* (2016), <crcv.revues.org/13864> (accessed 23 Nov. 2017).

260 Boileau-Despréaux, *Œuvres*, vol. 4, pp. 82–3.

261 The scholarly literature on Castel's 'invention' is extensive. For the colour question specifically see Lavezzi, 'Le Clavecin irisé'.

262 'Suite de la lettre sur le système des quatres couleurs primitives du sr Gautier', *MdF* (Oct. 1749), 102–19, esp. 104–7.

263 Ibid., p. 105.

264 [Roger de Piles], 'Au lecteur', in *Abrégé d'anatomie accommodé aux arts de peinture et de sculpture* (Paris, 1667), unpaginated. De Piles says that the study of anatomy via the *Abrégé* will lead the artist to develop 'une manière ferme, grande et terrible, comme il est arrivé à tous ceux qui ont possédé cette partie'.

265 De Piles's six-step study to the learning of anatomy at no point necessitated attention to colour. Knowledge of the location, attachment and offices of each muscle was all that was required.

266 *Mémoires de Trévoux* (Aug. 1735), 1830.

267 *Myologie complette en couleur et grandeur naturelle* (Paris, 1746), pl. 14.

268 [De Piles], 'Au lecteur', in *Abrégé d'anatomie*, unpaginated.

269 This is to emphasise the conventionality of technologies of dissection and the innovation of those of reproduction. Duverney, in his 'observations' to Malesherbes did not see it quite this way. He identified himself and Gautier as authors with their names on the prints and noted that the *Myologie complette* was an 'ouvrage unique, immense, et dont on a tiré aucunes figures des autheurs tant anciens que modernes, estant de vrais originaux', *Mémoire du sieur Duverney*, BnF, Mss. f.f. 22136/14, fol. 39.

270 On rubrification see Martin-Dominique Fertel, *La Science pratique de l'imprimerie* (Saint-Omer, 1723), 291–2. Fertel

provided a recipe for red ink; he did not discuss the use of red letters, which had been in steep decline since the beginning of the 17th century. Gautier's use of red on his title-pages is highly idiosyncratic; his was not the only name in red.

271 Jean Le Rond d'Alembert, 'Couleur', in Diderot and d'Alembert, *Encyclopédie*, vol. 4, p. 328.

272 On red and blue dyeworks see Ernest Homburg, 'From Colour Maker to Chemist: Episodes from the Rise of the Colourist, 1670–1800', in *Natural Dyestuffs and Industrial Culture in Europe, 1750–1880*, Robert Fox and Agustí Nieto-Galan (eds) (Canton, MA, 1999), pp. 219–57.

273 For a definiton of 'contes jaunes' see Furetière, 'Jaune', in *Dictionnaire universelle*, vol. 2.

274 *MdF* (July 1749), 173.

275 When asked why he had not sought to exploit the possibilities of colour printing for anatomy, Gautier de Montdorge replied: 'Je vous avouerai franchement que j'ai trouvé qu'il se présentoit dans la vie cent occupations plus séduisantes que celle de tourner les entrailles ou le cœur d'un pendu.' *MdF* (July 1749), 178.

276 *MdF* (Mar. 1756), 199.

277 For a discussion of Gautier's manipulation of mezzotint for his anatomy prints see Rodari (ed.) *Anatomie de la couleur*, p. 112, and cat. nos 97–9.

278 [Julien Offray de La Mettrie], *L'Homme machine* (Leyden, 1748).

279 *MdF* (Mar. 1756), 205–6.

280 As cited by Gautier de Montdorge in 'Réponse de M. de Montdorge', *MdF* (July 1749), 177.

281 Sigmund Freud, 'The "Uncanny"' (1919), trans. James Strachey, *Penguin Freud Library*, vol. 14: *Art and Literature* (Harmondsworth, 1990), pp. 339–76, esp. pp. 341–7.

282 *MdF* (July 1751), 164.

283 Freud, 'The "Uncanny"', pp. 354–5.

284 Terry Castle, *The Female Thermometer: Eighteenth-Century Culture and the Invention of the Uncanny* (Oxford, 1995), p. 10.

285 See the description in *MdF* (Apr. 1738), 738–9; *Le Pour et le contre* (1739), 212–13; see also chapter 3, pp. 221–2.

286 Cochin in Bosse, *De la manière de graver*, pp. 123–8, esp. p. 124.

287 The phrase is Castle's; see *The Female Thermometer*, p. 9.

288 Furetière, 'Noir', in *Dictionnaire universel*, vol. 2.

289 Arnaud Levy, 'Évaluations étymologiques et sémantiques du mot "secret"', *Nouvelle revue de psychanalyse*, 14 (1976), 117–29; see also Marin, 'Logique du secret'.

290 *MdF* (June 1749), 152.

291 Gautier de Montdorge, 'Réponse de M. de Montdorge', pp. 176–7.

292 Nicolas Abraham and Mária Török, *The Shell and the Kernel*, ed. and trans. Nicholas T. Rand (Chicago, 1994), pp. 79–98.

293 Nicolas Abraham, 'The Phantom of Hamlet, or The Sixth Act: Preceded by the Intermission of "Truth"', *Diacritics*, 18 (1988), 2–19.

294 Esther Rashkin, *Family Secrets and the Psychoanalysis of Narrative* (Princeton, 1992), pp. 30–32.

295 *MdF* (Dec. 1755), 207–8.

296 Freud, 'The "Uncanny"', pp. 372–6.

297 Ibid. For a discussion of storytelling as a craft very possibly informed by Freud see Walter Benjamin, 'The Storyteller: Reflections on the Works of Nikolai Leskov' (1936), in *Illuminations*, ed. Hannah Arendt, trans. Henry Zohn (London, 1973), pp. 83–109.

298 On the critical role of guilds in technical transfer see Stephan R. Epstein, 'Craft Guilds, Apprenticeship and Technological Change in Pre-Industrial Europe', *Journal of Economic History*, 53 (1998), 684–713.

299 The great exception is Abraham Bosse's *De la manière de graver à l'eau forte et au burin* (1645), expanded by Charles-Nicolas Cochin *fils* and published by Charles-Antoine Jombert in 1745.

300 Stephan R. Epstein, 'Transferring Technical Knowledge and Innovating in Europe, *c*.1200–1800', Working Paper on *The Nature of Evidence: How Well do 'Facts' Travel?*, Working Paper no. 01/05 (2005), pp. 25–6 <eprints.lse.ac.uk/22547/1/0105Epstein.pdf> (accessed 24 Nov. 2017).

301 Barbara Whitney Keyser, 'Between Science and Craft: The Case of Berthollet and Dyeing', *Annals of Science*, 47 (1990), 213–60. Claude-Louis Berthollet was a member of the Académie royale des sciences and was appointed an expert to the Gobelins. He was co-author of the *Méthode de nomenclature chimique* (Paris, 1787), which made the connection of the name of a substance to its composition a cornerstone of chemistry.

302 *MdF* (July 1749), 169–72.

303 On unconscious learning see Kenneth S. Bowers, 'On Being Unconsciously Influenced and Informed', in *The Unconscious Revisited*, Kenneth S. Bowers and Donald Meichenbaum (eds) (New York, 1984), pp. 227–72; Arthur S. Reber, *Implicit Learning and Tacit Knowledge: An Essay on the Cognitive Unconscious* (Oxford, 1993).

304 On the limits of visual imagery in the sciences see Wolfgang Le Fèvre, 'The Limits of Pictures: Cognitive Functions in Practical Mechanics, 1400–1600', in *The Power of Images in Early Modern Science*, Wolfgang Le Fèvre, Jürgen Renn and Urs Schoepflin (eds) (Berlin, 2003), 69–87.

305 Le Bitouzé, 'Une Entreprise familiale', p. 103.

306 Jacques Gautier, 'Observations III sur les tableaux exposés dans le Salon du Louvre au mois d'août, 1751', *Observations sur l'histoire naturelle* (1752), 43–7. See also *J.-B. Oudry, 1686–1755*, exh. cat., Grand Palais, Paris (Paris, 1982), cat. no. 151; Élisabeth Lavezzi, 'Peinture et savoirs scientifiques: Le Cas des *Observations sur la peinture* (1753) de Jacques Gautier d'Agoty', *Dix-huitième siècle*, 31 (1991), 233–47.

307 Jacques Gautier, 'Observations IV sur l'organe de la vuë par rapport au sentiment de Monsieur Bouffon et réflexions à ce sujet sur les tableaux exposés cette année 1753 dans le Salon du Louvre', *Observations sur l'histoire naturelle* (1753), 77–91.

308 *PSC*, France, 1762, and Rideau, 'Commentary on the *Déclaration royale* on privileges granted to inventors'.

309 Hilaire-Pérez, 'Invention and the State', p. 923.

CHAPTER 5
ART AND INDUSTRY: Intellectual property and the French Revolution

1 *PSC*, France, 1793, art. 1.

2 Ibid., art. 4. Failure to deposit did not undermine the author's natural right but it did deprive him or her of the standing to bring legal proceedings against *contrefacteurs*.

3 James Guillaume (ed.), *Procès-verbaux du Comité d'instruction publique de la Convention nationale*, 7 vols (Paris, 1891–1957), vol. 2, p. 82.

4 *PSC*, France, 1790.

5 Gastambide, *Traité théorique*, p. 5.

6 The guilds were finally abolished in February 1791 as a secondary measure to the suppression of customs duties (*aides*) introduced by Pierre-Gilbert Leroy, baron d'Allarde, on behalf of the Comité des impositions. See Liana Vardi, 'The Abolition of the Guilds during the French Revolution', *French Historical Studies*, 15 (1988), 704–17; Michael P. Fitzsimmons, *From Artisan to Worker: Guilds, the French State and the Organization of Labour, 1776–1821* (Cambridge, 2010), ch. 1, esp. pp. 40–44.

7 On interests see Albert O. Hirschman, *The Passions and the Interests: The Political Arguments for Capitalism before its Triumph* (Princeton, 1977); William Scott, 'The Pursuit of "Interests" in the French Revolution: A Preliminary Survey', *French Historical Studies*, 19 (1996), 811–51.

8 Jane C. Ginsburg, 'A Tale of Two Copyrights: Literary Property in Revolutionary France and America', in *Of Authors*

and Origins: Essays on Copyright Law, Brad Sherman and Alain Strowel (eds) (Oxford, 1994), pp. 131–58, esp. pp. 143–51.

9 On the suppression of the guilds see Vardi, 'The Abolition of the Guilds'; Fitzsimmons, *From Artisan to Worker*; Steven Kaplan, *La Fin des corporations* (Paris, 2001). On the Bureau du commerce see Sébastien Vosgiev, 'Le Bureau du commerce et la Révolution (1788–1791)', *Revue historique de droit français et étranger*, 90 (2012), 549–70.

10 *Décret portant suppression de tous les droits d'aides, de toutes les maîtrises et jurances, et établissement des patentes*, 2–17 Mar. 1791, in Jean B. Duvergier, *Collection des lois, décrets, ordonnances, réglemens, avis du Conseil d'état*, 2nd edn (Paris, 1834–), vol. 1, pp. 229–32. See also Fitzsimmons, *From Artisan to Worker*, pp. 59–63.

11 *Rapport de M. de Boufflers au nom du Comité d'agriculture et de commerce, relatif aux encouragements et aux privilèges à accorder aux inventeurs de machines et de découvertes industrielles*, in *PSC*, France, 1790; report of Isaac Le Chapelier on behalf of playwrights, in *PSC*, France, 1791; report of François Hell on behalf of writers, in *PSC*, France, 1791.

12 *Rapport de M. l'abbé Sieyès sur la liberté de la presse, et projet de loi contre les délits qui peuvent se commettre par la voie de l'impression, et par la publication des écrits et des gravures*, in *PSC*, France, 1790. See also Carla Hesse, *Publishing and Cultural Politics in Revolutionary Paris, 1789–1810* (Berkeley, 1991), pp. 105–10.

13 Pierre-François Basan et al., *Adresse à l'Assemblée nationale, par les graveurs et propriétaires de planches gravées*, in *PSC*, France, 1790–91.

14 On Basan's activity in the 1750s see William McAllister Johnson, 'Documents publiés, I: Les Estampes de privilèges', *NE* (1979), 10–13; see also chapter 1. For Gaucher see chapter 3; see also Christian Michel, 'La Contrefaçon devant la jurisprudence de l'ancien régime', *NE*, 173–4 (2000–01), 44–51. On Ponce as an illustrator before the Revolution see Hetty Joyce, 'Nicolas Ponce's *Arabesques antiques*: A Problem in Eighteenth-Century Archaeology', *GBA*, 114 (1989), 183–201. See also the life of the artist in Duchesne *l'aîné*, *Catalogue des tableaux, dessins, estampes du cabinet de M. Ponce* (Paris, 1831); the author, in addition to noting Ponce's close relationship with Gaucher (p. vi), also describes his activities, political and artistic, during the Revolution, notably his hardships (p. vii). Basan, Gaucher and Ponce were closely tied by professional and social bonds. Gaucher had been one of Basan's pupils, and he was closely acquainted with the Ponce household, thus linking three generations of engravers.

15 Basan et al., *Adresse*. See also Joëlle Raineau, 'Une Question de statut? L'Organisation des graveurs sous la Révolution et l'Empire', *NE*, 248 (2015), 34–42. We know that the so-called artist-inventors regrouped informally after the Revolution to petition collectively for a patent law; reference in the *Adresse* to an assembly of the Paris printmakers and publishers, from whose deliberations the petition was by implication the outcome, suggests that these artists did the same. For the inventors' petition see *Respectueuse pétition des artistes-inventeurs à l'Assemblée nationale*, in *Recueil des lois et des règlements en vigueur sur les brevets d'invention chez les différents peuples, précédés des rapports qui ont déterminés la législation française*, ed. J. B. C. Dujeux (Brussels, 1846), pp. 28–37. On the inventors' petitions see Christiane Demeulenaere-Douyère, 'Les Pétitions et leur rôle dans le vote des lois de l'invention en 1791', *Revue administrative* (2008), 61–9 [special issue *L'individu face au pouvoir*].

16 See Préaud, *DEE*; Roger Portalis and Henri Draibel, *Charles-Étienne Gaucher, graveur: Notice et catalogue* (Paris, 1879), pp. 53–4.

17 Over 30 pages long and with a decorative headpiece, it must have been some time in preparation. Addressed to the Assemblée nationale, it was presumably partly written in 1789 since the Assemblée existed under that title and in that form only until the end of that year. However, the draft regulations are alleged to have been agreed at an 'assemblée générale' in March 1791. The title-page of the copy at the Bibliothèque nationale de France is annotated '31 May 1791' which can, I think, confidently be taken as the precise moment of its publication. The *Journal de Paris* (2 June 1791) reported that: 'une députation des Graveurs de Paris s'est présenté... pour demander, non des faveurs que les Puissances ont si souvent accordées aux Arts pour les asservir autant que pour les encourager, mais une protection suffisante pour les assurer le prix que le goût de la France et de l'Europe met à leurs productions, pour empêcher le brigandage que les contrefaçons exercent dans l'art de la Gravure comme dans l'art de l'imprimerie'.

18 On law and memory see Jean Charbonnier, 'The French Civil Code', in *Rethinking France*, vol. 1: *State*, Pierre Nora (ed.), trans. Mary Trouille (Chicago, 2001), 335–60.

19 Basan et al., *Adresse*, p. 3.

20 See 'Mémoire sur la Chambre syndicale de Paris, relativement à la gravure et au commerce d'estampes', and 'Pièce justificative', in Basan et al., *Adresse*, pp. 21–6, 27–32.

21 Henry Lapauze (ed.), *Procès-verbaux de la Commune générale des arts de peinture, sculpture, architecture et gravure, et de la Société populaire et républicaine des arts* (Paris, 1903), 4 Oct. 1793, pp.145–6. François-Anne David had been among the most energetic and consistent petitioners for *privilèges en librairie* in the late 1770s and 1780s; see chapter 1. In surrendering them he played his part in the broader movement of symbolic destruction by the burning of documents related to aristocratic titles, especially feudal titles. Such was the value of paper that a letter to the Comité d'instruction publique in 1794 proposed, instead, its pulping and recycling. See AN, F17 1307A.

22 The *Déclaration* is alluded to, but not cited, in Basan et al., *Adresse*, p. 7.

23 Basan et al., *Adresse*, pp. 3–6; *Déclaration des droits de l'homme et du citoyen*, arts. 6, 17. See also *Adresse*, p. 7, on the citizen's right to participate in law-making. The metaphors of reading and writing are justified by the definition of printmaking as 'un language muet'.

24 Alexis de Tocqueville, *The Old Régime and the French Revolution*, trans. Stuart Gilbert (New York, 1955), p. 202.

25 Basan et al., *Adresse*, p. 5.

26 See, for the playwrights, Isaac Le Chapelier, *Rapport fait par M. Le Chapelier au nom de la Comité de constitution sur la pétition des auteurs dramatiques*, 13 Jan. 1791, p. 16, in *PSC*, France, 1791. According to Le Chapelier, those rights were 'the most sacred, the most legitimate, the most unassailable... and the most personal of all properties'.

27 Ibid., p. 9: 'La propriété seroit une chimère dans l'état de la nature, mais dans l'état civil, la propriété est un droit positif, qui assure à chaque individu la jouissance et le produit de ses facultées naturelles ou acquises.'

28 Basan et al., *Adresse*, pp. 9, 12.

29 Ibid., p. 9.

30 Ibid., p. 12. On the subsequent deployment of copyright in relation to the reproduction of the Louvre's collections see the important work of George D. McKee, notably 'Collection publique et droit de reproduction: Les Origines de la Chalcographie du Louvre, 1794–1797', *Revue de l'art*, 98 (1992), 54–65. See also *Mémoires du visible: Cuivres et estampes de la Chalcographie du Louvre*, exh. cat., Musée du Louvre, Paris (Paris, 2003). On copyists at the Louvre from the 1790s see George D. McKee, 'L'Art de dessiner l'art: Ingres, Bouillon, Dutertre et autres copistes au service de la gravure vers 1800', *Revue du Louvre*, 44 (1995), 73–90.

31 Basan et al., *Adresse*, pp. 12. On the 1667 privilege see Marianne Grivel, *Le Commerce de l'estampe à Paris au XVIIe siècle* (Geneva, 1986), p. 100; Antony Griffiths, *The Print before Photography: An Introduction to European Printmaking, 1550–1820* (London, 2016). On Marigny's efforts to enforce the 1667 act see Marigny to Sartine, 27 Apr. 1763, BnF, Mss. f.f. 22071/116; and two letters by printmakers on the same subject, BnF, Mss. f.f. 22071/117 (Gallica).

32 On *biens nationaux*, though primarily concerned with land not movable property, see Bernard Bodinier and Éric Teyssier, *L'Événement le plus important de la Révolution: La Vente des biens nationaux (1789–1867) en France et dans les territoires annexés* (Paris, 2000).

33 Basan et al., *Adresse*, pp. 11–12.

34 Ibid., p.10. On the bust, worked up from a death mask by Jean-Baptiste-Fernand Mulnier, a miniaturist and friend of the hero, and presented by the painter Jean-Jacques-François Le Barbier to the Assemblée nationale on 26 January 1791, see Pierre Le Bastart de Villeneuve, *André Désilles: Un Officier dans la tourmente révolutionnaire* (Paris, 1977). Among the artists eager to reproduce it were Julien, Tilly, François Godefroy and Pierre Laurent.

35 Basan et al., *Adresse*, p.11. An entry 'Personalité' appeared for the first time in the 1762 edition of *Le Dictionnaire de l'Académie françoise*, defined as 'caractère, qualité de ce qui est personnel. *L'auteur de cet ouvrage ne s'est pas nommé, mais la personalité l'a fait reconnoître*' (my emphasis); *Le Dictionnaire de l'Académie françoise*, 2 vols (Paris, 1762), vol. 2, p. 355.

36 *Mémoire pour les sieurs Esnauts et Rapilly, marchands d'estampes et propriétaires du privilège de la Galerie des modes françaises, demandeurs; contre le sieur Basset, graveur et marchand mercier, défendeur* (Paris, 1779), p. 11. See also chapter 3, pp. 229–30.

37 Basan et al., *Adresse*, p. 12. In so many words: 'sa composition particulière, ou le mode d'expression de sa pensée... est le signe de sa propriété'.

38 The medalist Nicolas-Marie Gatteaux was among many to discuss how to design *assignats* 'inimitables', and argued that simplicity and design quality (not materiality and technology) were the key, because they rendered the notes memorable and thus enabled all to identify forgeries. See Nicolas-Marie Gatteaux, *Aperçu sur la fabrication des assignats* (Paris, 1793). See also *Vües sur la fabrication d'un papier de banque envisagé sur le rapport de l'art*, c.1793, BnF, Mss. n.a.f. 21657/84. On the relation between design and authenticity in banknotes in Britain and the USA in the early 19th century see Frances Robertson, 'The Aesthetics of Authenticity: Printed Banknotes and Industrial Currency', *Technology and Culture*, 46 (2005), 31–50; Jennifer Roberts, 'The Currency of Ornament: Machine-Lathed Anticounterfeiting Patterns and the Portability of Value', in *Histories of Ornament: From Global to Local*, Gülru Necipoglu and Alina Payne (eds) (Princeton, 2016), pp. 308–19. The equation of design value and exchange value rendered the *assignat* a perfect analogy for artistic property. See Gatteaux, *Aperçu sur la fabrication des assignats*, pp. 3–4. During the Terror, the *assignat* would bear on its face the warning 'The Law Punishes the Counterfeiter with Death'. For some cases of the application of the death penalty for forgery, see *Extraits des minutes du greffe du Tribunal criminel du Département de Paris*, BnF, Mss. n.a.f. 3660: Jean Durand, peintre, 21 Jan. 1793; Pierre-François Montalaut, peintre en paysage, 15 Apr. 1793, etc. For the fines proposed by Basan, Gaucher and Ponce, see the 'Projet de décret' at the end of the *Adresse*, p. 20: fines were, it proposed, never to be less than 3,000 *livres* or more than 12,000, and were to be calculated on the basis of 1,000 copies at the sale price of the original. If found guilty, the defendant would also bear the costs of the trial.

39 On the *assignat* and the visual satires to which it gave rise see Richard Taws, 'L'Usage politique du trompe-l'œil à l'époque révolutionnaire et post-révolutionnaire', in *Le Trompe-l'œil: Plus vrai que nature?*, exh. cat., Musée de Brou, Bourg-en-Bresse (Bourg-en-Bresse, 2005), pp. 32–40, esp. 36–9 (on this print see cat. no. 58); Taws, *The Politics of the Provisional: Art and Ephemera in Revolutionary France* (University Park, PA, 2013), ch. 1. On this particular print, see *Le Trompe-l'œil*, cat. no. 58.

40 Hesse, *Publishing and Cultural Politics*, pp. 83–124.

41 Ibid., p. 115.

42 Basan et al., *Adresse*, p. 13.

43 *PSC*, France, 1793.

44 Lapauze (ed.), *Procès-verbaux*, 19 July 1793, p. 8.

45 See chapter 1, pp. 87–90, and the exchange of letters between Cochin and Descamps.

46 On the relation with copper-plate printers and especially binders see the Basan brothers to Joseph de Busscher, 27 floréal, an III [16 May 1795]; 13 thermidor, an III [31 July 1795]. On payment by *assignat* see Basan brothers to Joseph de Busscher, 13 vendémiaire, an IV [5 Oct. 1795], and 7 nivôse, an IV [28 Dec. 1795]. 25 Lettres, Basan frères au citoyen Busscher, libraire, Bruges, INHA, Ms. 106.

47 *Décret de la Convention nationale du dix-neuf juillet 1793 relatif aux droits de propriété des auteurs d'écrits en tout genre, des compositeurs de musique, des peintres et des dessinateurs*, in *PSC*, France, 1793, arts. 7 and 1.

48 *Pétition des citoyens mouleurs à la Convention nationale, le 13 ventôse de l'an II* [3 Mar. 1794], AN, F17 1304.

49 On the case see Frédéric Rideau 'Commentaire sur la décision de la Cour de cassation du 17 novembre 1814 sur les sculptures', in *PSC*, France, 1814.

50 Basan et al., *Adresse*, p. 18, art. 8.

51 On the *patente* see Édouard Pommier, 'De l'art libéral à l'art de la liberté: Le Débat sur la patente des artistes sous la Révolution et ses antécédents dans l'ancienne théorie de l'art', *BSHAF* (1992), 147–67.

52 Georges Chabaud, *La Protection légale des dessins et modèles* (Paris, 1913), p. 47.

53 *Journal du palais*, 75 (10 germinal, an X [31 Mar. 1802]), 17–20.

54 *Mémoire pour le citoyen Jean, marchand d'estampes, défendeur; contre le citoyen Auber, se disant propriétaire des 'Tableaux historiques des campagnes d'Italie', demandeur; et contre le citoyen Desrais, dessinateur, appelé en garantie* (Paris, Sept. 1801) [hereafter *Mémoire* A]; *Mémoire pour le citoyen Jean, marchand d'estampes; contre le citoyen Auber, éditeur d'estampes; réponse à l'Analyse du citoyen Auber* (Paris, Mar. 1802) [hereafter *Mémoire* B]; *Supplément au Mémoire pour le citoyen Jean, contre le citoyen Auber* (Paris, n.d.) [hereafter *Mémoire* C].

55 *Tableaux historiques des campagnes d'Italie, depuis l'an IV jusqu'à la bataille de Marengo* (Paris, 1806). On the *Tableaux* see Stephen Bann, *Parallel Lines: Printmakers, Painters and Photographers in Nineteenth-Century France* (London, 2001), pp. 43–57.

56 Desrais and Le Beau were, of course, both involved in Esnault and Rapilly's *Gallerie de modes* (Paris, 1777–87). See figs **71**, **72**.

57 *Mémoire* A, pp. 2–18.

58 Ibid., p. 5; *Mémoire* B, pp. 14–15; *Mémoire* C, pp. 1–6.

59 Bagetti subsequently worked in an official capacity for Napoleon, via the office of the Dépôt de la guerre and under the direction of Jean-François Martinel. On this later phase of his career see Anne Godlewska, 'Resisting the Cartographic Imperative: Giuseppe Bagetti's Landscapes of War', *Journal of Historical Geography*, 29 (2003), 22–50; Godlewska, Marcus R. Létourneau and Paul Schauerte, 'Maps, Painting and Lies: Portraying Napoleon's Battlefields in Northern Italy', *Imago mundi*, 57 (2005), 149–63. The corpus of works from Bagetti's studio, now at the Galleria civica d'arte moderna e contemporanea in Turin, does not include sketches that correspond to Jean's earlier initiative.

60 *La Bataille de Mondovi* on 23 May 1799; *Le Passage du Pô* and *Le Pont de Lodi* on 24 Aug. 1799.
61 Jean paid Desrais 90 *francs* for each of the drawings on 12 Dec. 1800 (*Passage du Pô*), 15 Jan. 1801 (*Bataille de Mondovi*) and 22 Mar. 1801 (*Pont de Lodi*). See 'Pièces justificatives', *Mémoire* A, p. 56.
62 The drawing of *Le Passage du Pô* was delivered on 12 Nov. 1800 and the print was published six weeks later, on 20 Jan. 1801; *La Bataille de Mondovi* was delivered on 5 Jan. 1801 and the print published on 20 Apr. 1801; *Le Pont de Lodi* was delivered on 22 Mar. 1801 and the print published on 24 July 1801. See *Mémoire* A, p. 4.
63 An *officier de la paix*, Chabanetti, seized 54 impressions of *La Bataille de Mondovi*, 42 of *Le Passage du Pô*, and 36 of *Le Pont de Lodi*. The copper plates had to be retrieved from the copperplate printer Richomme. See *Mémoire* A, p. 13.
64 Bacler d'Albe's *Pont de Lodi* was deposited at the Bibliothèque nationale de France for copyright on 23 Aug. 1800; see ibid., p. 3.
65 Auber deposited his prints for copyright on 27 July 1801.
66 The case was between François Bonneville and Auber over Bonneville's portrait of Armand Gensonné, engraved by François Guibert, possibly for Bonneville's *Portraits des personnages célèbres de la Révolution* (1796–1802). See *Mémoire* A, p.33; *Mémoire* C, pp. 7–15.
67 That is, by tracing; *Mémoire* A, p. 34.
68 *Mémoire* B, p. 22.
69 *Mémoire* A, pp. 8–9, 40–48.
70 Ibid, p. 10.
71 *Mémoire* B, pp. 10–11. See the account of Le Brun's emulation of Raphael in *La Défaite de Maxence* at the request of Cardinal Richelieu, Claude Nivelon, *Vie de Le Brun*, ed. Lorenzo Pericolo (Geneva, 2004), pp. 269–74. See also *Mémoire* A, pp. 46–7.
72 *Mémoire* B, pp. 8–9.
73 Ibid., p. 8. The same point was also made by the witness François-Étienne Joubert, in ibid., p. 9.
74 In the first half of the 18th century, only one application was made for landscape: in 1747 by Nicolas-Henri Tardieu for *Vue de la ville de Beauvais* after Jean-Baptiste Oudry. Later in the century, Charles-Louis Clérisseau and Jean-Pierre Houël were granted privileges, respectively in 1778 and 1782–3, for their topographical publications, the *Antiquités de la France* and the *Voyage pittoresque des isles de Sicile, de Malte et de Lipari*.
75 See *Mémoire* B, pp. 14–16; *Mémoire* C, pp. 2–6.
76 *Mémoire* B, p. 12 (David), p. 6 (Prud'hon), p. 13 (Guérin).
77 *Mémoire* A, p. 28.
78 Ibid., pp. 28–9.
79 Ibid., pp. 27, 31.
80 Ibid., pp. 51–2 n. 1. Vernet claimed that the effect of such 'copies' was 'mettre son talent dans la boue'.
81 Ibid., pp. 23–4. Delavigne, Jean's lawyer, compared literary property not with land but with mortgages and substituted securities.
82 Ibid., p. 15.
83 Ibid., pp. 7–8, 51. Jean noted that the speed and carelessness with which the drawings had been roughed out precluded signature.
84 That he did, however, do so in the aftermath of this affair is implied by the full title of the 1806 book *Tableaux historiques*: 'The views have been for the most part taken on the spot, and the prints are engraved after the original drawings of Carle Vernet'. But it is not, I think certain; see Bann, *Parallel Lines*, p. 47.
85 The map in the 1806 book was of Mondovi and its environs, executed in pen and ink; the three sketches were in pencil (*mine de plomb*). Delavigne thought the importance of the sketches overrated by Auber. More important was the talent that developed them. *Mémoire A*, pp. 5–6.
86 Ibid., p. 10 n.
87 Ibid., p. 16.
88 Ibid. In a footnote, pp. 9–10, Delavigne records that Desrais had explained to the court 'le secret de ceux qui, dans leurs cabinets à Paris, composent des batailles en Italie et ailleurs'. Desrais acknowledged as sources prints of the battles of Alexander and Constantine after Charles Le Brun's paintings, and prints after unspecified battle paintings by Adam Frans van der Meulen and Joseph Parrocel. 'On fait contribuer les études de son porte-feuille. On tache de mettre du feu et de l'action dans l'emploi des matériaux découpés... La réunion de tout cela fait une bataille.'
89 The first plate signed 'composé & dessiné par Carle Vernet' is *Entrée des Français à Turin, 20 frimaire, an VII*, facing p. 81 of *Tableaux historiques des campagnes d'Italie* (1806).
90 Bernard Edelman, *Le Sacre de l'auteur* (Paris, 2004), pp. 357–62.
91 *Journal du palais*, 75 (10 germinal, an X [31 Mar. 1802]), 20. The fine was calculated on the basis of the retail price of Auber's prints at 3 *francs* 10 *sous*, and not Jean's which sold for 18 *sous*.
92 Auber was, in Jean's words, a serial abuser of the copyrights of others, and his just indictment for piracy would lay waste his stock.
93 See Claudette Hould, 'Les Tableaux historiques de la Révolution française: Mémoire et révision de l'histoire', in *La Révolution par la gravure*, exh. cat., Musée de la Révolution française, Vizille (Paris and Vizille, 2002), pp. 14–49, esp. p. 20; and Stéphane Loire, 'Un Panthéon des "personnages qui ont éminemment marqué dans la Révolution, soit en bien, soi en mal": Les Portraits des *Tableaux historiques de la Révolution française*', in ibid., pp. 50–75.
94 Susan Siegfried, 'Naked History: The Rhetoric of Military Painting in Post-Revolutionary France', *Art Bulletin*, 75 (1993), 7–28.
95 On Pierre Jean during the *ancien régime* and as partner of Mondhare, see Préaud, *DEE*.
96 *Mémoire* A, pp. 41–2.
97 According to the catalogue of Jean's business stock in 1810, he sold *vues d'optiques* in three formats: the largest, hand-coloured, at 12 *sous*, medium-sized at 4 *sous*, small at 1 *sou* 6 *deniers*. See *Catalogue par ordre alphabétique des planches gravées par les meilleurs maîtres anciens et modernes... qui se trouvent chez Jean, marchand d'estampes, rue Saint-Jean-de-Beauvais* (Paris, 1810), nos 1859–61.
98 *Mémoire* A, p. 8.
99 See *IFF, après 1800*, vol. 11, pp. 310–11.
100 *Mémoire* A, p. 8.
101 Ibid., p. 11.
102 Ibid., p. 17.
103 Edelman, *Le Sacre de l'auteur*, pp. 262–78.
104 On the Isabey portrait see Susan Siegfried, *The Art of Louis-Léopold Boilly: Modern Life in Napoleonic France* (New Haven, CT, 1995), pp. 96–107.
105 François-Étienne Joubert, *Définition des mots 'copie' et 'contrefaçon' en gravure* (Paris, 1801); see also Joubert, *Réflexions sur la propriété des arts et du génie* (Paris, n.d.).
106 *Catalogue des productions industrielles qui seront exposées dans la grande cour du Louvre pendant les cinq jours complémentaires de l'an 9* (Paris, an IX [1800–01]). Among the exhibitors were wallpaper manufacturers from Paris.
107 On Bance, who in later life moved into book publishing, becoming one of the most important Paris publishers of architectural books, see Béatrice Bouvier, 'Les Bance, marchands d'estampes et libraires à Paris (1793–1862): Portrait de famille', *NE*, 163 (1999), 23–33.
108 The first reference to this case in the secondary literature is in Sally Wells-Robertson, 'Marguerite Gérard et les Fragonard', *BSHAF* (1977), 179–89. Since then the wallpaper

scholar Véronique de Bruignac-La Hougue has devoted considerable attention to it in her recent monograph on Joseph Dufour, jointly authored with Denys Prache and published in 2016. See Denys Prache and Véronique de Bruignac-La Hougue, *Joseph Dufour: Génie des papiers peints* (Paris, 2016), pp. 73–9, 82–5, 408–12.

109 *Mémoire et consultation pour le citoyen Bance aîné, graveur, marchand d'estampes; contre le citoyen Simon, fabricant de papiers peints à Paris*', in Ambroise Falconnet, *Le Barreau français, partie moderne, contenant les plaidoyers, mémoires et consultations des plus célèbres avocats*, 2 vols (Paris, 1806–7), vol. 1, p. 421.

110 Also witnesses were the printmakers Coigny, Massard, Baltard, André Gérard, Moreau *le jeune*, Mallapeau and Duplessi-Bertaux and the wallpaper manufacturers Jacquemart et Bénard and Arthur et Robert.

111 The fine was calculated on the basis of an indemnity of 6 *francs* for each print of Bance's first edition, a print run of 500 impressions of each pendant. See Falconnet, *Le Barreau*, p. 483.

112 On the importance of these memoranda see Falconnet's preface to *Le Barreau*. On the moment of their publication at strategic points in the case see Simon on Bance in ibid., p. 454; and Bance on Simon in ibid., p. 477.

113 The prints themselves acknowledge only Gérard, as the executant, but in a breakdown of the costs included in a footnote of Bance's appeal it was revealed that others received payment for unspecified work on the project. Alexandre Chaponnier was paid 2,000 *francs*, Victor Pillement 1,000 *francs*, and a certain Perret 400 *francs*. Bance claimed that when the cost of the paintings (2,700 *francs*), the price of the copper plates, and the cost of paper, ink and printing were added, 'on verra que cette spéculation a exigé de moi une avance de près de 15,000 fr.' (Ibid., p. 478 n. 1.)

114 On Joseph Dufour see H. Clouzot and C. Folliot, *Histoire du papier peint en France* (Paris, 1935), p. 199; Henri Clouzot, *Chefs-d'œuvre du papier peint: Tableaux-tentures de Dufour et Leroy* (Paris, n.d.), introduction (unpaginated).

115 Bance and Henry Gérard offered slightly different accounts of the circumstances of Bance's purchase of Marguerite Gérard's paintings. In the first memorandum Bance merely reported having bought them (Falconnet, *Le Barreau*, p. 423). Henry Gérard in his witness statement elaborated further: according to him, Bance 'a fait faire ces tableaux-là exprès pour me les faire graver' (ibid., p. 442). However, when pressed for more detail, Gérard was led to say, in apparent contradiction to the above: 'Le citoyen Bance ayant vu dans le Salon ces tableaux, il a cru que cela pourroit plaire au public; il a prié Mademoiselle Gérard de lui en faire... destinés pour les faire imprimer.' (Ibid.) In his appeal, Bance added further explanation: 'En l'an 4, je la pria (on ne commande pas à un génie) d'imaginer quelques sujets qui puissent servir de pendans à ses premières compositions, et former avec celles-ci une collection véritablement intéressante. Ce fut dans cet esprit qu'elle executa pour moi les deux tableaux que j'ai fait graver sous les titres de *L'Élan de la Nature* et du *Baiser de l'Innocence*'. (Ibid., p. 477.) The other pictures in the series were *Le Premier Pas de l'enfance* and *L'Enfant chéri*.

116 For proof that the prints were still not published, one need only note that they had not been announced in the papers; as Bance remarked, 'ce préliminaire seul en constate la mise en vente', ibid., p. 422.

117 Bance's account of events was slightly different on appeal. There he claimed that he had started to sell his prints before being made aware by his correspondents in the provinces of the *contrefaçons* in circulation. He had offered them copies of the prints, which his correspondent in Bordeaux had declined on the grounds that the market was already saturated with Dufour's wallpapers. See *Mémoire en cassation pour le citoyen Bance, graveur et marchand d'estampes, cessionnaire de tous les droits d'auteur de Mademoiselle Gérard, peintre, sur deux tableaux qui ont été gravés sous les titres de l'Élan de la nature et du Baiser de l'innocence; contre le cit. Simon, manufacturier et marchand de papiers peints*, in Falconnet, *Le Barreau*, vol. 1, pp. 480, 488–9. The inflated trade in print proofs was a matter of considerable anxiety for both producers and consumers; see, for example, the letter published in the *Mercure de France* in response to publication of Flipart's print after Jean-Baptiste Greuze's *Gâteau des rois* (Dec. 1777), 177–8. See also the methods used by one print publisher, David, to stem the tide of proofs in the case of his etching of the *Marchand d'orviétan* after Karel Dujardin; *MdF* (Apr. 1777), 186.

118 See Falconnet, *Le Barreau*, vol. 1, p. 480.

119 Ibid., p. 422.

120 See *Plaidoyer prononcé au Tribunal criminel du département de la Seine, pour le citoyen Simon, marchand de papiers peints, appellant; contre le citoyen Bance, marchand d'estampes, intimé*, in Falconnet, *Le Barreau*, p. 451.

121 Ibid., p. 452.

122 Bance may be referring here to Boizot's bas-reliefs for the monument to général Hoche, which were exhibited at his studio, Cour du palais des sciences et des arts, on 30 January 1800 and following days; he charged an entrance fee in the manner 'authorised' by citoyen David, according to one reviewer, and justified it by 'l'accueil favourable que le public vient de faire à une innovation si favourable au progrès des arts'. Boizot also opened a subscription for a set of five prints reproducing the monument and the four bas-reliefs of the sarcophagus. See *Notice descriptive des quatres bas-reliefs de marbre statuaire, executés par le citoyen Boizot sculpteur et destinés à décorer le monument à la mémoire de Hoche* (Paris, 1797); *L'Ami des lois* (29 nivôse, an VIII [19 Jan. 1800]), 4.

123 Falconnet, *Le Barreau*, vol. 1, pp. 424–5.

124 For the witness statements of the printmakers Masquelier, Ponce, Coigny and Massard see ibid., pp. 440–41.

125 Ibid., p. 464.

126 See Christian Michel, 'Les Débats sur la notion de graveur-traducteur en France au XVIIIe siècle', in *Delineavit et sculpsit: Dix-neuf Contributions sur les rapports dessin-gravure du XVIe au XXe siècle*, François Fossier (ed.) (Lyon, 2003), pp. 151–61.

127 Lépidor's use of the metaphor of translation can only be inferred from Bance's printed memorandum. At the appeal and in Lépidor's *Plaidoyer* for it, the defence had abandoned the analogy, to focus, rather, on the material differences between prints and wallpapers.

128 Falconnet, *Le Barreau*, vol. 1, pp. 432–44.

129 Ibid., p. 428.

130 Ibid., p. 425 n. 1. In the debates about the *patente*, or occupational licence, payment by honorarium was the deciding factor in determining whether an occupation was an art or a commercial enterprise; see Fitzsimmons, *From Artisan to Worker*, p. 59. It remained a distinction in law throughout the 19th century. See Mikhaïl Xifaras, 'Science sociale, science morale? Note sur la pénétration de l'économie dans la pensée juridique française au XIXe siècle', in *Wirtschaft und Wirtschaftstheorien in Rechtsgeschichte und Philosophie*, Jean-Francois Kervégan and Heinz Mohnhaupt (eds) (Frankfurt, 2004), pp. 185–225. Warm thanks to Michael Sonenscher for introducing me to Xifaras's work, though unfortunately my work was too far advanced to allow me to take full advantage of it.

131 Falconnet, *Le Barreau*, vol. 1, p. 495.

132 Bance argued that the law of 1793 lent artistic property 'une existence purement viagière, au lieu d'une existence perpétuelle qu'elle auroit eu sans elle, et qui lui appartenoit plus justement peut-être qu'à toute autre espèce de propriété',

ibid. He also noted that for literature this change constituted a radical break with the perpetual copyright measure of the *ancien régime*.

133 Ibid., p. 461.

134 Ibid., p. 462. On Gérard and Fragonard's collaborations see Perrin Stein 'Sous les yeux de Fragonard: The Prints of Marguerite Gérard', *PQ*, 29 (2012), 142–62, esp. 158–62 on the questions of authorship and attribution.

135 Falconnet, *Le Barreau*, vol. 1, p. 462.

136 Ibid., p. 464.

137 Ibid. It was an argument supported in the judge's summing up and judgment; see ibid., p. 482.

138 Ibid., pp. 456–57.

139 Ibid., p. 467.

140 Ibid., p. 468.

141 Ibid., p. 486. Bance replied, 'La gravure en taille-douce n'est pas simplement destinée à reproduire les chefs-d'œuvre de la peinture, pour les transmettre à la postérité. Elle a une autre destination plus populaire, s'il est permis de le dire; elle s'applique à la décoration intérieure des appartements', ibid., p. 487.

142 Ibid., p. 474.

143 Ibid., pp. 473, 474–55.

144 Ibid., p. 488.

145 Ibid., p. 499.

146 Indeed, one of Simon's repeated complaints about copyright was that it assumed knowledge of which works of art had been reproduced – information that was not easily to hand outside the art world; see ibid., pp. 453–4.

147 The relevant passage from the 1778 edition of the *Encyclopédie* was reprinted at the end of the memorandum by the Avocat général Charles-François Quequet in defence of Bance for the Cour de cassation; see Falconnet, *Le Barreau*, vol. 1, pp. 505–7. On the techniques and history of woodcut see ibid., pp. 484–5; on wood engraving and the artistic advances of the English wood engraver Thomas Bewick see ibid., p. 487.

148 BnF, Mss. f.f. 21957, 10 Nov. 1739 (Aubert); BnF, Mss. f.f. 21968, 10 Nov. 1779 (Réveillon).

149 On 11 brumaire, an VIII, for example, Simon deposited a sample arabesque paper; BnF, Département des estampes et de la photographie, Li 19.

150 *Règlement concernant la contrefaçon des papiers peints et tontisses, dans la Communauté des maîtres relieurs* [et] *papetiers-colleurs en meubles*, 11 Sept. 1778, p. 1, BnF, F-21198/56 (Gallica). The syndics claimed that 'il leur est fait *journellement* des plaintes sur les infidélités qui se commettent dans les contrefactions qui se font des desseins des papiers peints et tontisses' (my emphasis).

151 Ibid., pp. 2–3, arts. 1–3.

152 Ibid., p. 4, art. 7.

153 Molly Nesbit, 'What was an Author?', *YFS*, 73 (1987), 229–57, at 239.

154 *Règlement concernant la contrefaçon des papiers peints et tontisses*, p. 3, art. 4. The privileges were renewable. Réveillon's decision in 1779 to apply for a privilege from the Chancellerie rather than the Communauté des maîtres relieurs et papetiers-colleurs en meubles was probably because it allowed him to obtain one for 10 years.

155 Jacquemart et Bénard regularly deposited its wallpaper designs for copyright; see BnF, Département des estampes et de la photographie, Li 14 (papiers de tenture Jacquemart et Bénard, an VII & VIII), Li 21 (papiers de tenture, Jacquemart et Bénard, an IX).

156 Jacquemart et Bénard to Antoine Chaptal, 13 pluviôse, an X [2 February 1802], AN, F12 2285.

157 By contrast, art. 8 of the 1778 regulation of the Communauté des maîtres relieurs et papetiers-colleurs en meubles stated that, 'Les desseins seront censés copiés, non seulement quant ils seront calqués ou copiés en entier, mais encore quand les principaux sujets ou la principale composition aura été imitée, et lesdits desseins ne diffèrent que par les accessoires.' *Règlement concernant la contrefaçon*, p. 4.

158 See Falconnet, *Le Barreau*, vol. 1, pp. 501–2 for the argument that wallpaper makers are allowed to copy Old Masters but not works under copyright, and for an example of good practice in the relations between the wallpaper- and printseller André Basset and the painter Pierre-Paul Prud'hon with respect to *L'Amour réduit à la raison*, *Le Cruel rit des pleurs qu'il fait verser*, *Cérès* and *L'Amour vengé*.

159 Request for the establishment of a Conseil de prudhommes, addressed to Jean-Antoine Chaptal, Mar. 1808, AN, F12 4647.

160 Report to the Ministre de l'intérieur, Jean-Antoine Chaptal, 2 ventôse, an X [21 Feb. 1802], AN, F12 2285.

161 Ibid., fol. 8.

162 *Projet de loi*, probably by Claude-Anthelme Costaz, AN, F12 2285.

163 See Albert Vaunois, *Les Dessins et modèles de fabrique: Doctrine, législation, jurisprudence* (Paris, 1898), p. 14.

164 See *Journal de Paris* (22 Mar. 1802), 1091; (21 June 1802), 1689; (5 Jan. 1803), 659.

165 BnF, Collection Deloynes 28: no. 778, 730 (*Journal des débats*, 1802) (Gallica).

166 BnF, Collection Deloynes 27: no. 1039, 573–8 (*Journal de l'Empire*, 1806) (Gallica).

167 Cf. Antoine Renou, *L'Art de peindre: Traduction en vers français du poème latin de C. A. Dufresnoy avec remarques* (Paris, 1789), pp. 35–8.

SELECT BIBLIOGRAPHY
Primary sources

Works were published *sine loco* unless a place of publication is cited.

Amerval, Eloy d', *Le Livre de la déablerie* (1508)

Bachaumont, Louis Petit de, *Essai sur la peinture, la sculpture et l'architecture* (1751), 2nd edn (1752)

Blondel, Pierre-Jacques, *Mémoire sur les vexations qu'exercent les libraires et imprimeurs de Paris* (Paris, n.d. [1725])

Bonafous, Louis Abel, abbé de Fontenay, *Dictionnaire des artistes*, 2 vols (Paris, 1776)

Bosse, Abraham, *De la manière de graver à l'eau forte et au burin. Et de la gravure en manière noire* (1645), with additions by Charles-Nicolas Cochin *fils* (Paris, 1745)

——, *Sentimens sur la distinction des diverses manières de peinture, dessein et graveure, et des originaux d'avec leurs copies* (Paris, 1649)

——, *Traicté des manières de graver en taille douce sur l'airin* (Paris, 1645)

Campardon, Émile, 'Saisie et destruction de gravures représentant *Les Modes et coiffures françoises* (1779)', *NAAF* (1882), 300–09

Caylus, comte de, and Michel-Joseph Majault, *Mémoire sur la peinture à l'encaustique et sur la peinture à la cire par M. le comte de Caylus de l'Académie des belles-lettres et M. Majault, docteur de la Faculté de médecine en l'Université de Paris* (Geneva, 1755)

Chevalier, André, *L'Origine de l'imprimerie de Paris: Dissertation historique et critique* (Paris, 1694)

Clicquot-Blervache, Simon, *Considérations sur le commerce, et en particulier sur les compagnies, sociétés et maîtrises* (Amsterdam, 1758)

Cochin, Charles-Nicolas, *Œuvres diverses de M. Cochin*, 2 vols (Paris, 1771)

——, *Recueil de quelques pièces concernant les arts* (Paris, 1757)

Conférences de l'Académie royale de peinture et de sculpture, ed. Henry Jouin (Paris, 1883)

Corneille, Pierre, *Les Quatres Livres de l'Imitation de Jésus Christ* (Rouen, 1656)

Correspondance de M. de Marigny avec Coypel, Lépicié et Cochin, ed. Marc Furcy-Raynaud, 2 vols, *AAF*, 19–20 (1903–4)

Correspondance des directeurs de l'Académie de France à Rome avec les surintendants des bâtiments, ed. Anatole de Montaiglon, 18 vols (Paris, 1887–1912)

Coypel, Antoine, *Discours prononcez dans les conférences de l'Académie royale de peinture et de sculpture* (Paris, 1721)

Dandré-Bardon, Michel-François, *Traité de peinture, suivi d'un essai sur la sculpture* (1757), 2nd edn, 2 vols (Paris, 1765)

Dézallier d'Argenville, Antoine-Joseph, *Abrégé de la vie des plus fameux peintres*, 3 vols (Paris, 1745) [and later edns]

Dézallier d'Argenville, Antoine-Nicolas, *Voyage pittoresque de Paris* (Paris, 1752)

Dialogue sur la peinture (1773)

Diderot, Denis, *Diderot Salons*, ed. Jean Seznec and Jean Adhémar, 4 vols (Oxford, 1957–67)

——, *Essai sur la peinture* (1765), in *Œuvres esthétiques*, ed. Paul Vernière (Paris, 1965)

——, *Lettre sur le commerce de la librairie* (1763), ed. Michel Parfenov (Paris, 2001)

——, *L'Histoire et le secret de la peinture en cire* (Paris, 1755)

Diderot, Denis, and Jean Le Rond d'Alembert, *Encyclopédie, ou Dictionnaire raisonné des sciences, des arts et des métiers*, 17 vols (text), 9 vols in 11 (plates) (Paris and Neuchâtel, 1751–72)

Du Bos, Jean-Baptiste, *Réflexions critiques sur la poésie et la peinture* (1719), ed. Dominique Désirat (Paris, 1993)

Du Sault, *Nouveau Stile des lettres des chancelleries de France, comme elles sont à présent en usage* (Paris, 1666)

[Estève, Pierre], *Lettre à un partisan du bon goût sur l'exposition des tableaux dans le grand Salon du Louvre* (1755)

Estienne, Charles, *De dissectione partium corporis humani* (Paris, 1545); Fr. trans. *De la dissection des parties du corps humain* (Paris, 1546)

Estienne, Robert, *Dictionarium latinogallicum*, 3rd edn (Paris, 1552)

Falconet, Étienne-Maurice, *Réflexions sur la sculpture* (Paris, 1761)

Félibien, André, *Des principes de l'architecture, de la sculpture, de la peinture et des autres arts qui en dépendent* (Paris, 1676)

Ferrand, Jacques-Philippe, *L'Art du feu ou de peindre en émail* (Paris, 1721)

Fertel, Martin-Dominique, *La Science pratique de l'imprimerie* (Saint-Omer, 1723)

Furetière, Antoine, *Dictionnaire universel contenant généralement tous les mots françois* (1690), 2nd edn, 3 vols (The Hague, 1701) [and later edns]

Gastambide, Adrien, *Traité théorique et pratique des contrefaçons en tous genres, ou de la propriété en matière de littérature, théatre, musique, peinture, dessin, gravure. . . sculpture* (Paris, 1837)

Gaucher, Charles-Étienne, *Précis pour le sieur Gaucher, graveur en taille-douce, de l'Académie des arts d'Angleterre; contre les sieurs Esnauts et Rapilly, marchands d'estampes et le sieur Hubert; et encore par les sieurs Née et Masquelier, graveurs en taille-douce; contre lesdits sieurs Esnauts et Rapilly, le sieur Dupin et le sieur André* (Paris, 1776)

Gaultier de Biauzat, Jean-François, *Mémoire à consulter pour les libraires et imprimeurs de Lyon, Rouen, Toulouse, Marseille et Nîmes* (1776)

Gautier, Jacques, 'Observation IV sur l'organe de la vuë par rapport au sentiment de Monsieur Bouffon et réflexions à ce sujet sur les tableaux exposés cette année 1753 dans le Salon du Louvre', *Observations sur l'histoire naturelle, sur la physique et sur la peinture avec des planches imprimés en couleur* (1753), pp. 77–91

[Gautier de Montdorge, Antoine], *L'Art d'imprimer les tableaux: Traité d'après les écrits, les opérations et les instructions verbales de J. C. Le Blon* (Paris, 1756)

Guiffrey, Jules-Joseph, *Collection des livrets des anciennes expositions depuis 1673 jusqu'en 1800*, 5 vols (Paris, 1869–71)

Guyot, Joseph-Nicolas, *Répertoire universel et raisonné de jurisprudence civile, criminelle, canonique et bénéficiale*, 64 vols (Paris, 1775–83)

Héricourt, Louis d', *Mémoire de Louis d'Héricourt à Monseigneur le Garde des sceaux* (Paris, n.d. [1725]), *PSC*, France, 1725–6

——, *Mémoire en forme de requête à M. le Garde des sceaux*, in Édouard Laboulaye and Georges Guiffrey, *La Propriété littéraire au XVIIIe siècle: Recueil de pièces et de documents* (Paris, 1859), pp. 13–40

——, *Œuvres posthumes de maistre Louis d'Héricourt*, 4 vols (Paris, 1759)

Houdard de La Motte, Antoine, *Fables nouvelles*, illustrated by Claude Gillot (Paris, 1719)

Hozier, Pierre d', *Les Noms, surnoms, qualitez, armes, et blasons des chevaliers et officiers de l'Ordre du S. Esprit* (Paris, 1634)

Jean, Pierre, *Mémoire pour le citoyen Jean, marchand d'estampes, défendeur; contre le citoyen Auber, se disant propriétaire des 'Tableaux historiques des campagnes d'Italie', demandeur; et contre le citoyen Desrais, dessinateur, appelé en garantie* (Paris, 1801)

——, *Mémoire pour le citoyen Jean, marchand d'estampes; contre le citoyen Auber, éditeur d'estampes; réponse à l'Analyse du citoyen Auber* (Paris, 1802)

——, *Supplément au Mémoire pour le citoyen Jean, contre le citoyen Auber* (n.d. [1802])

Jombert, Charles-Antoine, *Catalogue de l'œuvre de Charles-Nicolas Cochin fils* (Paris, 1770)

Joubert, François-Étienne, *Définition des mots 'copie' et 'contrefaçon' en gravure* (Paris, 1801)

Joullain, Charles-François, *Réflexions sur la peinture et la gravure* (Paris, 1786)

Labbé, *Labbé plaidant pardevant nos seigneurs tenans la Cour de parlement, en la Chambre de l'édict à Paris, pour Melchior Tavernier maistre graveur, imprimeur en taille-douce, deffendeur, opposant et demandeur à la fin de la main levée de la saisie sur lui faicte le premier décembre dernier passé à la requeste de Laurent Sonius, Gabriel Clopjot, Jean Daumale, et François Julliot, se disans scindics et gardes des marchands libraires, imprimeurs, et relieurs de cette ville de Paris* (n.d. [1621])

Lacombe, Jacques, *Dictionnaire portatif des beaux-arts* (Paris, 1752)

La Font de Saint-Yenne, Étienne, *Réflexions sur quelques causes de l'état présent de la peinture en France* (The Hague, 1747)

——, *Sentiments sur quelques ouvrages de peinture, sculpture et gravure, écrits à un particulier en province* (Leyden, 1754)

[La Porte, Joseph de], *Sentimens sur plusieurs des tableaux exposés cette année dans le grand Salon du Louvre* (1755)

Le Blanc, Jean-Baptiste, *Observations sur les ouvrages de MM. de l'Académie de peinture et de sculpture* (1753)

Le Blon, Jacob Christoph, *L'Harmonie du coloris dans la peinture; réduite en pratique mécanique et à des règles sures et faciles: avec des figures en couleur* (n.d. [1725]) [also known as *Coloritto*]

Le Brun, Abbé, *Almanach historique et raisonné des architectes, peintres, sculpteurs, graveurs et cizeleurs*, 2 vols (Paris, 1776–7)

Le Dictionnaire de l'Académie françoise, 2 vols (Paris, 1694) [and later edns]

Lépicié, François-Bernard, *Vies des premiers-peintres du roi, depuis M. Le Brun jusqu'à présent*, 2 vols (Paris, 1752)

Les Conférences de l'Académie royale de peinture et de sculpture, 1648–1792, ed. Jacqueline Lichtenstein and Christian Michel, 6 vols (Paris, 2007–15)

Les Images ou tableaux de platte peinture des deux Philostrates sophistes Grecs, trans. Blaise de Vigenère (Paris, 1614)

Lettre sur le Salon de 1755, adressée à ceux qui la liront (Amsterdam, 1755)

Malesherbes, Guillaume-Chrétien de Lamoignon, *Mémoires sur la librairie, Mémoire sur la liberté de la presse*, ed. Roger Chartier (Paris, 1994)

Mariette, Pierre-Jean, *Abecedario de P. J. Mariette*, ed. Philippe de Chennevières and Anatole de Montaiglon, 6 vols (Paris, 1853–62)

Marion, Simon, *Plaidoyez second sur l'impression des Œuvres de Sénèque, reveuës et annotées par feu Marc Antoine de Muret* (1586)

Marsy, François-Marie de, *Dictionnaire abrégé de peinture et de sculpture*, 2 vols (Paris, 1746)

Mémoire à consulter et consultation pour le sieur Gaucher, graveur en taille-douce, de l'Académie des arts d'Angleterre; contre les sieurs Esnauts et Rapilly, marchands d'estampes (Paris, 1776)

Mémoires inédits sur la vie et les ouvrages des membres de l'Académie royale de peinture et de sculpture, ed. Louis-Étienne Dussieux et al., 2 vols (Paris, 1854)

Mémoire sur la contestation qui est entre les libraires de Paris et ceux de Lyon au sujet des privilèges et des continuations que le roy accorde pour l'impression des livres (n.d. [1690s])

Montaiglon, Anatole de, 'Charles-Étienne Gaucher, 1788', *NAAF* (1874–5), 360–63

Mormoro, Antoine-François, *Traité élémentaire de l'imprimerie, ou Le Manuel de l'imprimeur* (Paris, 1793)

Mortimer, Cromwell, 'An Account of Mr. James-Christopher Le Blon's Principles of Printing in Imitation of Painting, and of Weaving Tapestry, in the Same Manner as Brocades', *Philosophical Transactions of the Royal Society*, 37 (June–July 1731), 101–7.

Newton, Isaac, *Traité d'optique sur les réflexions, réfractions, inflexions et couleurs de la lumière*, trans. Pierre Coste, 2nd edn (Paris, 1722)

[Offray de La Mettrie, Julien], *L'Homme machine* (Leyden, 1748)

Pernety, Antoine-Joseph, *Dictionnaire portatif de peinture, sculpture et gravure* (Paris, 1757)

Picart, Bernard, *Impostures innocentes, ou Recueil d'estampes d'après divers peintres illustres* (Amsterdam, 1734)

Piganiol de La Force, Jean-Aymar, *Description de Paris, de Versailles, de Marly* (Paris, 1765)

Piles, Roger de, *Conversations sur la connoissance de la peinture* (Paris, 1677)

——, *Cours de peinture par principes* (1708) (Paris, 1989)

——, *Dialogue sur le coloris* (Paris, 1699)

——, *Les Premiers Éléments de la peinture pratique* (Paris, 1684)

——, *L'Idée du peintre parfait* (1699), ed. Xavier Carrière (Paris, 1993)

Pluquet, François-André-Adrien, *Lettre à un ami sur les arrêts du Conseil du 30 août 1777* (Paris, 1778)

Primary Sources on Copyright (1450–1900), ed. L. Bently and M. Kretschmer, <www.copyrighthistory.org>

Procès-verbaux de l'Académie royale de peinture et de sculpture, 1648–1792, ed. Anatole de Montaiglon, 10 vols (Paris, 1875–92)

Recueil général des anciennes lois françaises depuis l'an 420 jusqu'à la révolution de 1789, ed. Athanase-Jean-Léger Jourdan et al., 29 vols (Paris, 1821–33)

Renouard, Augustin-Charles, *Traité des droits d'auteurs, dans la littérature, les sciences et les beaux-arts*, 2 vols (Paris, 1838)

Réponse pour le sieur Basset, graveur et marchand mercier; contre les sieurs Esnault et Rapilly, marchands étaleurs d'estampes (Paris, 1779)

Représentations et observations en forme de mémoire sur l'état ancien et actuel de la librairie, ses règlements, ses privilèges et autres objets relatifs à son commerce et aux gens de lettres, présentées à M. de Sartine, Maître des requêtes, Directeur général de la librairie et imprimerie, par les syndics et adjoints en charge au mois de mars 1764 (1764)

Richelet, Pierre, *Dictionnaire de la langue françoise ancienne et moderne*, 2 vols (Amsterdam, 1706); rev. edn, 4 vols (Lyon, 1759)

Rousseau, Jean-Jacques, *Julie, ou La nouvelle Héloïse* (1761), ed. Michel Launay (Paris, 1967)

——, *Œuvres complètes*, ed. Bernard Gagnebin and Marcel Raymond, 5 vols (1959–95)

[Saint-Yves, Charles Léoffroy de], *Observations sur les arts, et sur quelques morceaux de peinture et de sculpture exposés au Louvre en 1748* (Leyden, 1748)

Saugrain, Claude-Marin, *Code de la librairie et imprimerie de Paris* (Paris, 1744)

Savary des Bruslons, Jacques, *Dictionnaire universel de commerce* (1723), 2nd edn, 3 vols (Paris, 1741) [and later edns]

Servin, Louis, *Actions notables et plaidoyez de Messire Louys Servin* (Paris, 1639)

——, *Arrest de la Cour de parlement donné en l'audience de la Chambre de l'édict le sixième iour de mars mil six cent vingt; entre les syndics et gardes des marchands livraires, imprimeurs, relieurs de cette ville de Paris, appelants de l'entherinement de lettres par le prévost de Paris le vingtième novembre mil six cent dix huit, et sentence du dixhuitième janvier ensuivant d'une part; et Melchior Tavernier, imprimeur en taille douce d'autre, maître* [Louis] *Servin* (n.d. [1620])

Statuts et règlemens des imprimeurs et libraires de Paris, 21 Aug. 1686 (1687)

Thevet, André, *Les Vrais Pourtraits et vies des hommes illustres grecz, latins et payens* (Paris, 1584)

Tory, Geoffroy, *Champfleury* (Paris, 1529)

——, *Horæ in laudem beatiss. semper virginis Mariæ, secundum consuetudinem curiæ Romanæ* (Paris, 1525)

Valdor, Jean, *Les Triomphes de Louis le juste, XIII* (Paris, 1649)

Watelet, Charles-Henri, and Pierre-Charles Levesque, *Dictionnaire des arts de peinture, sculpture et gravure*, 5 vols (Paris, 1788–91)

Secondary sources

Armstrong, Elizabeth, *Before Copyright: The French Book-Privilege System, 1498–1526* (Cambridge, 1990)

——, *Robert Estienne: Royal Printer* (Cambridge, 1954)

Arquié-Bruley, Françoise, 'Documents notaires sur Greuze', *BSHAF* (1981), 125–54

Baldwin, Peter, *The Copyright Wars: Three Centuries of Trans-Atlantic Battle* (Princeton, 2014)

Barber, Giles, 'French Royal Decrees Concerning the Book Trade, 1700–1789', *Australian Journal of French Studies*, 3 (1966), 316–17

Barron, Anne, 'Copyright, Art and Objecthood', in *Dear Images: Art, Copyright and Culture*, Daniel McClean and Karsten Schubert (eds) (London, 2002), pp. 277–311

Benjamin, Walter, 'The Work of Art in the Age of Mechanical Reproduction', rev. edn (1939), repr. in *Illuminations*, ed. Hannah Arendt, trans. Harry Zohn (London, 1973), pp. 217–51

Biagioli , Mario, and Peter Galison, *Scientific Authorship: Credit and Intellectual Property in Science* (New York and London, 2003)

Birn, Raymond, 'The Profit of Ideas: *Privilèges en librairie* in Eighteenth-Century France', *Eighteenth-Century Studies*, 4 (1970–71), 131–68

Bloom, Harold, *The Anxiety of Influence: A Theory of Poetry* (1973), 2nd edn (New York and Oxford, 1997)

Bourdieu, Pierre, *Outline of a Theory of Practice*, trans. Richard Nice (Cambridge, 1977)

——, 'Rethinking the State: Genesis and Structure of the Bureaucratic Field', *Sociological Theory*, 12 (1994), 1–18

Bousquet-Bressolier, Catherine, 'Charles-Antoine Jombert (1712–1784): Un Libraire entre sciences et arts', *Bulletin du bibliophile*, 2 (1997), 299–333

Broc, Numa, 'Une Affaire de plagiat cartographique sous Louis XIV: Le Procès Delisle-Nolin', *Revue d'histoire des sciences et de leurs applications*, 23 (1970), 141–53

Brown, Cynthia Jane, *Poets, Patrons and Printers: Crisis of Authority in Late Medieval France* (Ithaca, NY, and London, 1995)

Buskirk, Martha, 'Authorship and Authority', in *The Contingent Object in Contemporary Art* (Cambridge, 2005), pp. 21–56

Casselle, Pierre, 'Le Commerce des estampes à Paris dans la seconde moitié du XVIIIe siècle', PhD diss., École nationale des chartes, Paris, 1976

Chartier, Roger, 'Figures of the Author', in *The Order of Books*, trans. Lydia G. Cochrane (Stanford, CA, 1992), pp. 25–59

——, *The Cultural Origins of the French Revolution*, trans. Lydia G. Cochrane (London, 1991)

Chartier, Roger, and Henri-Jean Martin (eds), *L'Histoire de l'édition française*, 4 vols (Paris, 1983–7)

Clark, Alvin L., Jr, 'Vouet and his Printmakers', in *French Prints from the Age of the Musketeers*, exh. cat., Boston Museum of Fine Arts (Boston, 1998), pp. 28–42

Coombe, Rosemary J., 'Embodied Trademarks: Mimesis and Alterity on American Commercial Frontiers', *Cultural Anthropology*, 11 (1996), 202–24

Courboin, François, *L'Estampe française: Graveurs et marchands* (Brussels and Paris, 1914)

Coyecque, Ernest, *Inventaire de la Collection Anisson sur l'histoire de l'imprimerie et de la librairie*, 2 vols (Paris, 1900)

Cropper, Elizabeth, *The Domenichino Affair: Novelty, Imitation and Theft in Seventeenth-Century Rome* (New Haven, CT, 2005)

Crow, Thomas, *Painters and Public Life in Eighteenth-Century Paris* (London and New Haven, CT, 1985)

Dahlberg, Leif, 'Achilles' Foot and the Law: Legal Space(s), Striated and Smooth', in *Practising Equity, Addressing Law: Equity in Law and Literature*, Daniela Carpi (ed.) (Heidelberg, 2008), pp. 119–39

Darnton, Robert, *The Business of the Enlightenment: A Publishing History of the Encyclopédie, 1775–1800* (Boston, 1979)

Demarte, Isabelle C., 'Détournements d'auteur: Les Surprises de l'épistolarité dans la *Lettre sur le commerce de la librairie* de Denis Diderot', in *Architecture, Cultural History, Autobiography*, Jonathan Mallinson (ed.), Studies on Voltaire and the Eighteenth Century (Oxford, 2008), pp. 127–66

Dulac, Georges, 'Louis-Jacques Goussier, Encyclopédiste et "original sans principes"', *Recherches nouvelles sur quelques écrivains des Lumières*, Jacques Proust (ed.) (Geneva, 1972), pp. 63–110

Edelman, Bernard, *La Propriété littéraire et artistique* (Paris, 1989)

——, *Le Droit saisi par la photographie: Éléments pour une théorie marxiste du droit* (Paris, 1973)

——, *Le Sacre de l'auteur* (Paris, 2004)

——, *Quand les juristes inventent le réel: La Fabulation juridique* (Paris, 2007)

Falk, Henri, *Les Privilèges de librairie sous l'ancien régime: Étude historique du conflit des droits sur l'œuvre littéraire* (1906) (Geneva, 1970)

Foucault, Michel, 'Leçon du 17 janvier 1979', in *Naissance de la biopolitique: Cours au Collège de France (1978–1979)*, François Ewald, Alessandro Fontana and Michel Senellart (eds) (Paris, 2006), pp. 29–51

——, 'What is an Author?' (1969), in *Language, Counter-Memory, Practice: Selected Essays and Interviews*, trans. Donald F. Bouchard and Sherry Simon, ed. Donald F. Bouchard (Oxford, 1977), pp. 113–38 [lecture given to the Société française de philosophie, Paris, 1968]

Frow, John, 'Gifts and Commodities', in *Time and Commodity Culture: Essays in Cultural Theory and Postmodernity* (Oxford, 1997), pp. 102–217

Fuhring, Peter, 'The Market for Prints under Louis XIV: Charles Le Brun', *PQ*, 19 (2002), 3–11

——, 'The Print Privilege in Eighteenth-Century France, I', *PQ*, 2 (1985), 174–93

——, 'The Print Privilege in Eighteenth-Century France, II', *PQ*, 3 (1986), 19–33

Gaskell, Roger, 'Printing House and Engraving Shop: A Mysterious Collaboration', *Book Collector*, 53 (2004), 213–51

Gaucheron, Roger, 'La Préparation et le lancement d'un livre de luxe au XVIIIe siècle: L'Édition des Fables de La Fontaine, dite d'Oudry', *Arts et metiers graphiques*, 2 (1927), 77–82

Ginsburg, Jane C., 'A Tale of Two Copyrights: Literary Property in Revolutionary France and America', in *Of Authors and Origins: Essays on Copyright Law*, Brad Sherman and Alain Strowel (eds) (Oxford, 1994), pp. 131–58

——, '"Une Chose publique"? The Author's Domain and the Public Domain in Early British, French and US Copyright Law', *Cambridge Law Journal*, 65 (2006), 636–70

Gregory, Christopher, *Gifts and Commodities*, 2nd edn (Chicago, 2015)

Griffiths, Antony, *Prints for Books: Book Illustration in France, 1760–1800* (London, 2004)

——, 'Proofs in Eighteenth-Century French Printmaking', *PQ*, 21 (2004), 3–17

——, *The Print before Photography: An Introduction to European Printmaking, 1550–1820* (London, 2016)

Grivel, Marianne, '*Executit* et privilège: Les Éditeurs de Simon Vouet', in *Simon Vouet: Actes du colloque internationale*, Stéphane Loire (ed.) (Paris, 1992), pp. 307–29

——, *Le Commerce de l'estampe à Paris au XVIIe siècle* (Geneva, 1986)

Guichard, Charlotte, *Graffitis: Inscrire son nom à Rome, XVIe–XIXe siècles* (Paris, 2014)

——, *La Griffe du peintre: Essai sur la valeur de l'art* (Paris, 2018)

——, 'La signature dans le tableau aux XVIIe et XVIIIe siècles: Identité, réputation et marché de l'art', *Société et representation*, 25 (2008), 47–77

Halliday, Anthony, *Facing the Public: Portraiture in the Aftermath of the French Revolution* (Manchester, 1999)

Hesse, Carla, 'Enlightenment Epistemology and the Laws of Authorship in Revolutionary France, 1777–1795', *Representations*, 30 (1990), 109–37

Hilaire-Pérez, Liliane, 'Diderot's Views on Artists' and Inventors' Rights: Invention, Imitation and Reputation', *British Journal for the History of Science*, 35 (2002), 129–50

——, 'Invention and the State in Eighteenth-Century France', *Technology and Culture*, 32 (1991), 911–31 [special issue *Patents and Inventions*]

——, *L'Invention technique au siècle des Lumières* (Paris, 2000)

——, 'Transfers technologiques, droits et territoire: Le Cas Franco-Anglais au XVIIIe siècle', *RHMC*, 44 (1997), 547–79

Hoffmann, Georges, *Montaigne's Career* (Oxford, 1998)

Huard, Georges, 'Les Planches de l'*Encyclopédie* et celles de la *Description des arts et métiers* de l'Académie des sciences', in *L'Encyclopédie et le progrès des sciences et des techniques* (Paris, 1952), pp. 35–46

Hunt, Lynn, *Inventing Human Rights: A History* (New York, 2007)

Jaffe, Kineret S., 'The Concept of Genius: Its Changing Role in Eighteenth-Century French Aesthetics', *Journal of the History of Ideas*, 41 (1980), 579–99

Jaszi, Peter, 'Towards a Theory of Copyright: The Metamorphoses of Authorship', *Duke Law Journal*, 2 (1991), 455–502

Johns, Adrian, 'The Property Police', in *Making and Unmaking Intellectual Property: Creative Production in Legal and Cultural Perspective*, Mario Biagioli, Peter Jaszi and Martha Woodmansee (eds) (Chicago, 2011), pp. 199–213

Kafker, Frank A., and Madeleine Pinault Sørensen, 'Notices sur les collaborateurs du Recueil de planches de l'*Encyclopédie*', *RDE*, 18–19 (1995), 201–30

Kaucher, Greta, *Les Jombert: Une Famille de libraires parisiens dans l'Europe des Lumières, 1680–1824* (Geneva, 2015)

Laran, Jean, *Inventaire du fond français après 1800*, 15 vols (Paris, 1930–)

Lefranc, David, 'Historical Perspective on Criminal Enforcement', in *Criminal Enforcement of Intellectual Property: A Handbook of Contemporary Research*, Christopher Geiger (ed.) (Cheltenham, 2012), pp. 101–27

Lévy-Lelouch, Claire, 'Quand le privilège de librairie publie le roi', in *De la publication: Entre Renaissance et Lumières*, Christian Jouhaud and Alain Viala (eds) (Paris, 2002), pp. 139–59

Liang, Lawrence, 'Beyond Representation: The Figure of the Pirate', in *Making and Unmaking Intellectual Property: Creative Production in Legal and Cultural Perspective*, Mario Biagioli, Peter Jaszi and Martha Woodmansee (eds) (Chicago, 2011), pp. 167–80

Lilien, Otto M., *Jacob Christoph Le Blon, 1667–1741: Inventor of Three- and Four-Colour Printing* (Stuttgart, 1985)

Long, Pamela O., 'Invention, Authorship, "Intellectual Property" and the Origin of Patents: Notes towards a Conceptual History', *Technology and Culture*, 32 (1991), 846–84 [special issue *Patents and Inventions*]

McAllister Johnson, William, *French Royal Academy of Painting and Sculpture Engraved Reception Pieces, 1672–1789*, exh. cat., Agnes Etherington Art Centre, Kingston, Ontario, and other venues (Kingston, 1982)

McClean, Daniel, and Karsten Schubert (eds), *Dear Images: Art, Copyright and Culture* (London, 2002)

McKee, George D. 'Collection publique et droit de reproduction: Les Origines de la Chalcographie du Louvre, 1794–1797', *Revue de l'art*, 98 (1992), 54–65

Maclean, Ian, *Scholarship, Commerce, Religion: The Learned Book in the Age of Confessions, 1560–1630* (Cambridge, MA, 2012)

McLeod, Jane, *Licensing Loyalty: Printers, Patrons and the State in Early Modern France* (Philadelphia, 2011)

Madero, Marta, '*Tabula picta*: L'Écriture, la peinture et leur support dans le droit médiéval', *Annales: Histoire, sciences sociales*, 56 (2001), 831–47

Martin, Henri-Jean , 'La Librairie française en 1777–1778', *Dix-huitième siècle*, 11 (1979), 87–112

——, *Print, Power and People in Seventeenth-Century France*, trans. David Gerard (Metuchen, NJ, 1993)

Maza, Sarah, *Private Lives and Public Affairs: The causes célèbres of Pre-Revolutionary France* (Berkeley, 1993)

Meyer, Véronique, 'Le Brun éditeur: Étude d'après les inventaires du peintre et de sa veuve', in *Curiosité: Études d'histoire de l'art en honneur d'Antoine Schnapper*, Olivier Bonfait, Véronique Gerard-Powell and Philippe Sénéchal (eds) (Paris, 1998), pp. 103–14

Michel, Christian, *Charles-Nicolas Cochin et l'art des Lumières* (Rome, 1993)

——, *Charles-Nicolas Cochin et le livre illustré au XVIIIe siècle* (Geneva, 1987)

——, *L'Académie royale de peinture et de sculpture (1648–1793): La Naissance de l'école française* (Geneva, 2012)

——, 'La Contrefaçon devant la jurisprudence de l'ancien régime', *NE*, 173–4 (2000–01), 44–51

——, 'Réflexion sur la comparaison entre gravure et traduction au XVIIIe siècle', in *Delineavit et sculpsit: Dix-neuf Contributions sur les rapports dessin-gravure du XVIe au XXe siècle. Mélanges offerts à Marie Félicie Perez-Pivot*, François Fossier (ed.) (Lyon, 2003), pp. 151–61

Mitchell, W. J. T., *Picture Theory: Essays on Verbal and Visual Representation* (Chicago, 1995)

——, *What do Pictures Want? The Lives and Loves of Images* (Chicago, 2005)

Nesbit, Molly, 'What was an Author?', *YFS*, 73 (1987), 229–57

Parshall, Peter, '*Imago contrafacta*: Images and Facts in the Northern Renaissance', *Art History*, 16, (1993), 554–79

Parshall, Peter (ed.), *The Woodcut in Fifteenth-Century Europe*, exh. cat., National Gallery, Washington, DC (New Haven, CT, 2009)

Parshall, Peter, and Ramer Schoch (eds), *Origins of European Printmaking: Fifteenth-Century Woodcuts and their Public*, exh. cat., National Gallery, Washington, DC (New Haven, CT, 2005)

Pastoureau, Mireille, 'Contrefaçon et plagiat des cartes de géographie et des atlas français de la fin du XVIe siècle au début du XVIIIe siècle', in *Les Presses grises: La Contrefaçon du livre (XVIe–XIXe siècles)*, François Moureau (ed.) (Paris, 1988), pp. 275–302

Patry, William, *Moral Panics and Copyright Laws* (Oxford, 2009)

Pepperkorn, David, 'Malesherbes on the Rights and Duties of Authors', in *Intellectual Property and Information Law: Essays in Honour of Herman Cohen Jehoram*, Jan J. C. Kabel and Gerard J. H. M. Mom (eds) (The Hague and London, 1998), pp. 223–39

Pfister, Laurent, 'Author and Work in the French Print Privileges System: Some Milestones', in *Privilege and Property: Essays in the History of Copyright*, Ronan Deazley, Martin Kretschmer and Lionel Bently (eds) (Cambridge, 2010), pp. 115–36

——, 'L'Usage illicite du signe d'autruit: Quelques observations sur les enseignes et marques de l'ancien droit', *Mémoires de la Société pour l'histoire du droit et des institutions des anciens pays bourguignons, contois et normands*, 65 (2008), 171–93

Pinault, Madeleine, 'À propos des planches de l'*Encyclopédie*', *SVEC*, 254 (1988), 351–61

——, 'Diderot et les illustrateurs de l'*Encyclopédie*', *Revue de l'art*, 66 (1984), 17–38

Pinault Sørensen, Madeleine, 'À propos des planches de l'*Encyclopédie*', *RDE*, 15 (1993), 143–52

——, 'Les Dessinateurs de l'Académie royale des sciences', in *Règlement, usages et sciences dans la France de l'absolutisme*, Christiane Demeulenaere-Douyère and Eric Brian (eds) (Paris, 2002), pp. 147–67

Pommier, Édouard, *Théories du portrait: De la Renaissance aux Lumières* (Paris, 1998)

Pottinger, David T., *The French Book Trade in the ancien régime, 1500–1791* (Boston, 1958)

Préaud, Maxime, 'L'Inventaire après décès de François Chauveau, 20–28 février, 1676', *AAF*, 26 (1984), 91–104

Préaud, Maxime, Pierre Casselle, Marianne Grivel and Corinne Le Bitouzé, *Dictionnaire des éditeurs d'estampes à Paris sous l'ancien régime* (Paris, 1987)

Proust, Jacques, *Diderot et l'Encyclopédie* (1962) (Paris, 1965)

——, 'La Documentation technique de Diderot dans l'*Encyclopédie*', *Revue d'histoire littéraire de la France*, 57 (1957), 335–52

——, 'Pour servir à une edition de la *Lettre sur le commerce de la librairie*', *Diderot Studies*, 3 (1961), 321–45

Puttfarken, Thomas, *The Discovery of Pictorial Composition: Theories of Visual Order in Painting, 1400–1800* (New Haven, CT, and London, 2000)

Randall, Marilyn, *Pragmatic Plagiarism: Authorship, Profit and Power* (Toronto and London, 2001)

Rigogne, Thierry, *Between State and the Market: Printing and Bookselling in Eighteenth-Century France*, Studies on Voltaire and the Eighteenth Century (Oxford, 2007)

Rodari, Florian (ed.), *Anatomie de la couleur: L'Invention de l'estampe en couleurs*, exh. cat., Bibliothèque nationale de France, Paris, and Musée Olympique, Lausanne (Paris, 1996)

Rose, Carol, *Property and Persuasion: Essays on the History, Theory, and Rhetoric of Ownership* (Boulder, CO, and Oxford, 1994)

Rose, Mark, *Authors and Owners: The Invention of Copyright* (Boston, 1993)

Rosenberg, Daniel, 'An Eighteenth-Century Time Machine: The Encyclopedia of Denis Diderot', in *Postmodernism and the Enlightenment: New Perspectives in Eighteenth-Century French Intellectual History*, Daniel Gordon (ed.) (New York and London, 2001), pp. 45–66

Roy, Stéphane, 'The Art of Trade and the Economies of Trade: The English Print Market in Paris, 1770–1800', in *Architecture, Cultural History, Autobiography*, Jonathan Mallinson (ed.), Studies on Voltaire and the Eighteenth Century (Oxford, 2008), pp. 167–92

Schapira, Nicolas, 'Quand le privilège de librairie publie l'auteur', in *De la publication: Entre Renaissance et Lumières*, Christian Jouhaud and Alain Viala (eds) (Paris, 2002), pp. 121–37

Schmidgen, Wolfram, 'The Politics and Philosophy of Mixture: John Locke Recomposed', *Eighteenth Century*, 48 (2007), 205–23

Schnapper, Antoine, 'La Fortune de Charles Le Brun', *Revue de l'art*, 114/4 (1996), 17–22

Schneider, *Voleurs de mots: Essai sur le plagiat, la psychanalyse et la pensée* (Paris, 1985)

Schroder, Anne L., 'Reversals of Power: Artistic Property, Counterfeiture, and the 1793 Copyright Act', *Visual Resources*, 16 (2000), 143–54

Scott, Katie, 'Maps, Views and Ornament: Visualising Property in Art and Law', in *Privilege and Property: Essays on the History of Copyright*, Ronan Deazley, Martin Kretschmer and Lionel Bently (eds) (Cambridge, 2010), pp. 254–88

Shapiro, Alan E., 'The Gradual Acceptance of Newton's Theory of Light and Color, 1672–1727', *Perspectives in Science*, 4 (1996), 59–140

Sherman, Brad, and Lionel Bently, *The Making of Modern Intellectual Property: The British Experience, 1760–1911* (Cambridge, 1999)

Simonds, Roger T., 'John Locke's Use of Classical Legal Theory', *International Journal of the Classical Tradition*, 3 (1997), 424–32

Smentek, Kristel, '"An exact imitation acquired at little expense": Marketing Color Prints in Eighteenth-Century Paris', in *Colorful Impressions: The Printmaking Revolution in Eighteenth-Century France*, Margaret Morgan Grasselli (ed.) (Washington, DC, 2003), pp. 9–21

——, 'Sex, Sentiment, and Speculation: The Market for Genre Prints on the Eve of the French Revolution', in *French Genre Painting in the Eighteenth Century*, Philip Conisbee and Elizabeth Cropper (eds) (Washington, DC, 2007), pp. 221–43

Stafford, Barbara, *Body Criticism: Imagining the Unseen in Enlightenment Art and Medicine* (Cambridge, MA, 1991)

Talbot, Charles, 'Prints and the Definitive Image', in *Print and Culture in the Renaissance: Essays on the Advent of Printing in Europe*, Gerald P. Tyson and Sylvia S. Wagonheim (eds) (Newark, NJ, and London, 1986), pp. 189–207

Taws, Richard, *The Politics of the Provisional: Art and Ephemera in Revolutionary France* (University Park, PA, 2013)

Turnovsky, Geoffrey, 'Conceptualising the Literary Market: Diderot and the *Lettre sur le commerce de la librairie*', in *Voltaire, Diderot, Demography, Women's Studies, Poètes et versificateurs, the Influence of the Enlightenment*, Studies on Voltaire and the Eighteenth Century (Oxford, 2003), pp. 135–70

Van Gompel, Stef, '*Les formalités sont morts, vive les formalités!* Copyright Formalities and the Reasons for their Decline in Nineteenth-Century Europe', in *Privilege and Property: Essays on the History of Copyright*, Ronan Deazley, Martin Kretschmer and Lionel Bently (eds) (Cambridge, 2010), pp. 157–206

Van Hout, Nico, 'Copyright Rubens: Cum privilegiis', in *Rubens et l'art de la gravure*, exh. cat., Koninklijk Museum voor schone kunsten, Antwerp, and Musée nationale des beaux-arts, Quebec (Ghent, 2004), pp. 30–39

Viala, Alain, 'La Triple Économie du littéraire', in *Art et argent en France au temps des premiers modernes (XVIIe–XVIIIe siècles)*, Martial Poirson (ed.), Studies on Voltaire and the Eighteenth Century (Oxford, 2004), pp. 19–34

Walravens, Nadia, 'The Concept of Originality in Contemporary Art', in *Dear Images: Art, Copyright and Culture*, Daniel McClean and Karsten Schubert (eds) (London, 2002), pp. 170–95

Wax, Carol, *The Mezzotint: History and Technique* (London, 1990)

Woodmansee, Martha, *The Author, Art, and the Market: Rereading the History of Aesthetics* (New York, 1994)

INDEX

Page numbers in *italic* refer to the illustrations.

PICTURE CREDITS

© 2016 The Art Institute of Chicago / Art Resource, NY / Scala Florence: figs 74, 77
© 2016 The Frick Collection: fig. 34
© 2017 Museum of Fine Arts, Boston: figs 71, 72
© ACTIVE MUSEUM / Alamy Stock Photo: fig. 66
© Artepics / Alamy Stock Photo: fig. 109
© BNF: figs 3–11, 13, 16, 17, 19–22, 28–30, 33, 38, 55–57, 68, 70, 75–6, 85–90, 96, 102–106, 108, 110, 112
© The British Library Board. Ref. C. 70 i 9 (2): fig. 83
© The British Library Board. 8715.f.26: fig. 91
© The British Library Board. 1832.e.17: figs 98, 100, 101
By permission of the Governing Body of Christ Church, Oxford: fig. 84
© Canadian Centre for Architecture: figs 1, 2
Cliché Conseil départemental des Yvelines, Daniel Balloud: fig. 51
© The College of Physicians of Philadelphia: fig. 81
© Conway Library, Courtauld Institute of Art, London: fig. 44
Courtesy National Gallery of Art, Washington: fig. 54
© Fitzwilliam Museum, Cambridge: fig. 35
Image Conway Library, Courtauld Institute of Art, London. Photo © Victoria and Albert Museum, London: fig. 46
Image courtesy the Witt Library, Courtauld Institute of Art, London: fig. 63
Image courtesy the Witt Library, Courtauld Institute of Art © Sotheby's, London: fig. 60
Image Rijksmuseum, Amsterdam: fig. 14
Imaging Department © President and Fellows of Harvard College: fig. 50, 78
Katie Scott: fig. 27
© MNHN-AC / B. Faye: fig. 99
© MuCEM, Dist. RMN-Grand Palais / image MuCEM: figs 23, 24
Musée d'art et d'histoire, Neuchâtel: figs 64, 65
© Musée Jean de La Fontaine – Château-Thierry: fig. 15
© Muséum national d>Histoire naturelle, Dist. RMN-Grand Palais / image du MNHN, bibliothèque centrale: fig. 59
© National Gallery, London, UK / Bridgeman Images: fig. 52
© The National Trust, Waddesdon Manor: fig. 69
Photo: Centre de documentation Joseph Dufour: fig. 111
Photograph Courtesy of Sotheby's, Inc. © 2017: fig. 61
Private collection: fig. 80
© Reims, Bibliothèque Municipale. Fic, XVI-III-b-13: fig. 79
© RMN-Grand Palais (Château de Versailles) / Christophe Fouin: fig. 62
© RMN-Grand Palais (Institut de France) / Michel Urtado: figs 18, 25, 31, 32
© RMN-Grand Palais (musée du Louvre) / Michel Urtado: figs 26, 42, 43
© RMN-Grand Palais (musée du Louvre) / Philippe Fuzeau: fig. 47
© RMN-Grand Palais (musée du Louvre) / Pierre Philibert: fig. 45
© RMN-Grand Palais (musée du Louvre) / Michèle Bellot: fig. 41
© RMN-Grand Palais (musée du Louvre) / Thierry Le Mage: figs 39, 40
© Samuel Courtauld Trust, Courtauld Gallery, London: fig. 107
© The State Hermitage Museum /photo by Pavel Demidov: figs 48, 49
© Trustees of the British Museum: figs 36, 37, 53, 58, 67, 73, 82, 92–95, 97
© Victoria and Albert Museum, London 2017: fig. 12